Understanding Complex Systems

Springer Complexity is an interdisciplinary program publishing the best research and academic-level teaching on both fundamental and applied aspects of complex systems—cutting across all traditional disciplines of the natural and life sciences, engineering, economics, medicine, neuroscience, social and computer science.

Complex Systems are systems that comprise many interacting parts with the ability to generate a new quality of macroscopic collective behavior the manifestations of which are the spontaneous formation of distinctive temporal, spatial or functional structures. Models of such systems can be successfully mapped onto quite diverse "real-life" situations like the climate, the coherent emission of light from lasers, chemical reaction-diffusion systems, biological cellular networks, the dynamics of stock markets and of the internet, earthquake statistics and prediction, freeway traffic, the human brain, or the formation of opinions in social systems, to name just some of the popular applications.

Although their scope and methodologies overlap somewhat, one can distinguish the following main concepts and tools: self-organization, nonlinear dynamics, synergetics, turbulence, dynamical systems, catastrophes, instabilities, stochastic processes, chaos, graphs and networks, cellular automata, adaptive systems, genetic algorithms and computational intelligence.

The three major book publication platforms of the Springer Complexity program are the monograph series "Understanding Complex Systems" focusing on the various applications of complexity, the "Springer Series in Synergetics", which is devoted to the quantitative theoretical and methodological foundations, and the "Springer Briefs in Complexity" which are concise and topical working reports, case studies, surveys, essays and lecture notes of relevance to the field. In addition to the books in these two core series, the program also incorporates individual titles ranging from textbooks to major reference works.

Indexed by SCOPUS, INSPEC, zbMATH, SCImago.

John F. Haldon • Ricardo Fernandes
Editors

Bridging History and Policy

Essays on Resilience, Sustainability and Systems Modelling

Springer

Editors
John F. Haldon
History Department
Princeton University
Princeton, NJ, USA

Ricardo Fernandes
Max Planck Institute of Geoanthropology
Jena, Thüringen, Germany

Faculty of Archaeology
University of Warsaw, Warsaw, Poland

ISSN 1860-0832 ISSN 1860-0840 (electronic)
Understanding Complex Systems
ISBN 978-3-032-24378-2 ISBN 978-3-032-24379-9 (eBook)
https://doi.org/10.1007/978-3-032-24379-9

This work was supported by Princeton University (Climate Change & History Research Initiative).

This Springer imprint is published by the registered company Springer Nature Switzerland AG
The registered company address is: Gewerbestrasse 11, 6330 Cham, Switzerland

Foreword and Acknowledgements

The papers in this volume are the revised and expanded versions of a series of papers delivered at a colloquium held at Princeton University in May 2024 under the aegis of the Climate Change and History Research Initiative, with the addition of papers delivered at the "Bridging the Gap: Integrating Historical Knowledge and Complex Human-Environmental Systems Modeling" workshop held at the Max Planck Institute of Geoanthropology (MPI GEA), Jena, in December 2023. They address questions of scale, complexity, systems modelling, information-sharing, and challenges of policy relevance with the aim of moving our fields forward in better mobilizing our results for actionable use. Given the overlap in theme as well as a longstanding collaboration between the CCHRI and the MPI-GEA at Jena, this seemed an appropriate way to integrate two sets of papers dealing with similar issues and challenges.

The past five years have seen many breakthroughs in establishing the past as a key dimension for global change researchers and highlighting the need to bring environmental history, archaeology, complexity studies, environmental humanities, and environmental science disciplines together with policymakers and nonacademic holders of local and traditional knowledge and practitioners attempting to address policy challenges and manage resources for sustainability. In multiple fields we are seeing acceptance of the importance of stories of long-term human ecodynamics for current and future sustainability efforts. Heritage and community engagement are now recognized as key elements in shaping more successful responses to global change impacts and in rallying support for action on climate change.

But many challenges remain for teams to move from isolated and often superficially understood "lessons of history" to deliver actionable advice to managers and decision-makers. Problems of disciplinary structure (single-author books vs. multi-authored articles), survival of early career scholars in multidisciplinary projects, and effective use of scientific data by humanists (and historical data by scientists) are all widely recognized problems. International, interdisciplinary programmes such as IHOPE (Integrated History and Future of People on Earth), Princeton CCHRI (Climate Change and History Research Initiative), and NABO Cooperative (North Atlantic Biocultural Organization) have worked to cross disciplinary boundaries and are increasingly working to integrate local and traditional knowledge and communities. Cross-regional comparisons are working to identify recurring patterns in human reaction to past ecodynamic processes in an attempt to identify patterns that cross-cut very different world regions and local cultures. These developments suggest that we have an opportunity to share lessons of success (and failure) and good practice ideas and tools for using diverse datasets in effective and creative ways.

The present collection bridges the domains of history and archaeology, systems modelling, and policymaking. By integrating the insights of historians, archaeologists, complex systems modellers, and sustainability experts, our aim is to generate actionable knowledge to inform policies targeting pressing modern-day problems such as climate change, regional and global conflicts, mass migrations, and resource scarcity. Given that experimenting with large social-environmental systems is impractical and ethically contentious, historical records provide important observational data to study the dynamics of complex systems over time. History reveals patterns of resilience and collapse in response to past challenges and offers lessons that can inform contemporary strategies. One of the key themes of this book is the use of complex systems theory and historical data to understand better the intricate interplay between climatic, social, political, economic, and technological systems. The contributors explore theoretical and methodological aspects essential for formulating effective policies to promote sustainable development, reduce socio-economic inequalities, and prevent systemic collapses, as well as presenting examples of both successes and failures.

This interdisciplinary exploration includes cutting-edge techniques in systems modelling, highlighting the burgeoning role of machine learning and artificial intelligence. By facilitating collaborative efforts among diverse experts, the book aims to create a foundation for more robust, evidence-based policies to address better the multifaceted challenges facing today's society. Collectively, we hope that this volume will serve as a resource for policymakers, modellers, and researchers involved in the study of the past who are interested in leveraging interdisciplinary approaches to tackle modern-day challenges.

The editors and CCHRI core group (Lee Mordechai, Tim Newfield, and Adam Izdebski) are grateful to the Princeton Institute for International and Regional Studies for technical and financial support, the High Meadows Environmental Institute, the Seeger Center for Hellenic Studies, and the Center for Collaborative History, and at Jena to the Max Planck Institute of Geoanthropology for providing funding and support for the 2023 workshop "Bridging the Gap: Integrating Historical Knowledge and Complex Human-Environmental Systems Modeling" organized by Ricardo Fernandes and Adam Izdebski.

Princeton, NJ, USA
Jena, Thüringen, Germany
September 2025

John F. Haldon
Ricardo Fernandes

Contents

About the Editor and Contributors

About the Editors

John F. Haldon is a fellow of the British Academy and Director of the *Climate Change and History Research Initiative* at Princeton University. His research focuses on the history of the medieval eastern Roman (Byzantine) empire, on premodern state systems and structures in western Eurasia, on the impact of environmental stress on societal resilience in premodern social systems, and on the challenges of making historical research relevant to contemporary environmental policy.

Ricardo Fernandes heads the Systems Archaeology research group at the Max Planck Institute of Geoanthropology in Jena, Germany. He is also an adjunct professor at the University of Warsaw, Poland, and an associate professor at Masaryk University in Brno, Czech Republic. Ricardo employs complex systems theory to better understand patterns of historical causation so that acquired knowledge can make a useful contribution to modern-day policymaking and risk analysis. Among others, he is investigating the impact of human agency in shaping historical trajectories, human–environment interactions, the interplay between socio-economic inequality and societal stability, and the emergence and spread of new technologies.

About the Contributors

Andrew Agha is an historical archaeologist and CEO of Aghatech Industries LLC. His research focuses on the seventeenth-century origins of agriculture in South Carolina.

Felicia O. Akinyemi works in the Department of Environmental and Life Sciences at Karlstad University.

Luci Attala is Associate Professor of Anthropology at the University of Wales Trinity Saint David (UWTSD), Senior Fellow of the Higher Education Academy, and an award-winning educator and researcher. She currently serves as Deputy Executive Director of the UNESCO-MOST BRIDGES Coalition and leads the UK BRIDGES Hub at UWTSD, driving transdisciplinary collaboration for a more sustainable future. Her anthropological research focuses on the materiality of water and the entanglements between humans and the environment, using a New Materialities framework. She has conducted fieldwork in Spain, Wales, and among the Giriama horticulturalists in coastal Kenya, where her work earned a United Nations Gold Star Award for its social and environmental impact. She is currently collaborating with the Kogui in Colombia on a conservation water project titled Munekán Masha ("Let it be reborn") and is co-investigator on an AHRC-funded mission award in Swansea, *Retrofitting for the Future: Nature-Based Solutions for Climate Adaptation*. She is also engaged in Coastal TALES, a project focused on adaptation and resilience in coastal communities in Ireland, S. Wales, and Alaska. Luci is a recognized leader in education for sustainable development, receiving the Green Gown Award in 2015. She is a series editor for *Materialities in Anthropology and Archaeology* with the University of Wales Press, Director of the Educere Alliance (Oxford), and Fellow of the World Academy of Art and Science (WAAS), reflecting her global and transdisciplinary commitments.

Robert Baldwin is an endowed chair of conservation ecology at Clemson University and Executive Director of the Clemson University Forest. His interests lie in the intersection of human uses and relationships to the natural world and biodiversity conservation.

Martin Bauch is Junior Research Group Leader and Senior Researcher at the Leibniz Institute for the History and Culture of Eastern Europe (GWZO) in Leipzig. He earned his doctorate from TU Darmstadt in 2012 and has held positions at the German Historical Institute in Rome as well as several German universities. Since 2017, he has led a Volkswagen Freigeist Fellowship, i.e. a Junior Research Group. He specializes in medieval environmental and climate history, with a focus on East Central Europe and the Mediterranean—but also from a global perspective. His research spans climate reconstruction from archival sources, medieval epidemics, premodern infrastructures, responses to extreme weather events, and devotional practices. Currently, he leads two major initiatives: www.epimeddat.net, a collaborative database for late medieval epidemic data, and the "Dantean Anomaly" project, which examines rapid climate change and its societal impacts. He is also Corresponding Fellow at the Czech Academy of Sciences' Center for Medieval Studies and serves on the editorial board of *Climates and Cultures in History*. Dr. Bauch co-edited a volume *The Crisis of the 14th Century. Teleconnections between Environmental and Societal Change?* (2019) and published major articles on late Medieval Flood events like the St. Mary Magdalene's Flood in 1342.

Andrew Bridges is President and CEO of the Nemours Wildlife Foundation, whose mission is to facilitate conservation and human well-being in the ACE Basin and beyond through collaborative scientific research, leadership development, management demonstration, and experiential education.

Viktor J. Bruckman works at the IIASA-Rat of the Österreichische Akademie der Wissenschaften.

Jane E. Buikstra is a Regents' Professor of Bioarchaeology in the School of Human Evolution and Social Change at Arizona State University in Tempe, Arizona, USA. She received her B.A. from DePauw University, her M.A. (1969) and PhD (1972) in anthropology from the University of Chicago, and a DSc (hon) from Durham University (UK) in 2014. Considered the founder of (human) bioarchaeology, Buikstra has published over 200 articles and chapters and more than 20 books. Her research interests include paleopathology, mummy science, forensic anthropology, paleodiet, and paleomobility. Regional contributions to bioarchaeology focus on the Americas and the Mediterranean.

A. Rita Carrasco works at the Centre for Marine and Environmental Research (CIMA) of the University of Algarve.

Gina E. C. Charnley is Recognized Researcher in the Global Health Resilience Group at the Barcelona Supercomputing Center and Honorary Research Fellow in University College London's Institute for Global Health and Imperial College London's School of Public Health. Her educational background is in veterinary medicine and climate science, and she earned her PhD from Imperial College London in 2023 in Epidemiology. Her research interests include climate-sensitive infectious diseases, climate and global change, armed conflicts, and population vulnerabilities. Her work focuses on using statistical modelling and machine learning to explore transmission dynamics and infectious disease outbreak hotspots in Europe, Africa, South Asia, and Latin America and the Caribbean. She uses data-driven approaches to investigate the complex relationships between risk factors and cascading risks, and how these link to emerging infectious diseases, especially those related to climate and extreme weather

Joanne Clarke is an archaeologist and heritage specialist of the Middle East and Africa based in the Department of Archaeology at Durham University. Her interdisciplinary expertise is in climate change losses and damages, resilience, and adaptation. She has published individually and co-authored many research articles and policy reports, including a white paper in 2022 co-sponsored by the IPCC, UNESCO, and ICOMOS. She was a contributing author to the Africa chapter of the IPCC's 6th Assessment Report, Working Group II on Impacts, Adaptation and Vulnerability, and she is currently a Lead Author of the States and Trends chapter of the United Nations Environment Programme's Global Environment Outlook 7. She is a co-lead of a heritage and climate change literacy award funded by the British Academy and a CLARE-funded project exploring the role of heritage in catalysing climate change resilience for local communities in Bénin.

Pedro Conceição is Director of the Human Development Report Office, United Nations Development Programme (UNDP), since January 2019. Prior to that he held other roles at the UNDP, including Director for Strategic Policy, Chief-Economist for Africa, and Director of the Office of Development Studies. He has published on financing for development inequality, global public goods, the economics of innovation and technological change, and development in several journals and books. He is the lead author of the 2019, 2020, 2021/22, 2023/24, and 2025 Human Development Reports. In preparation for the 2026 Human Development Report, he co-authored a perspective published in June 2025 in *Nature* titled "An aspirational approach to planetary futures" (642: 889–899). Prior to coming to the UNDP, he taught at the Instituto Superior Técnico, University of Lisbon, Portugal. He has degrees in physics from Instituto Superior Técnico and economics from ISEG (Lisbon School of Economics and Management) and a PhD from the University of Texas at Austin, where he studied with a Fulbright scholarship.

Stefani A. Crabtree is Associate Professor of Social-Environmental Modeling at Utah State University and External Professor at the Santa Fe Institute. She blends the fields of archaeology and ecology to have a deep understanding of past human–environment interactions. Her recent paper "Towards a Science of Archaeoecology" in *Trends in Ecology and Evolution* argues for stronger ties between ecology and archaeology to understand our trajectory as a species. She holds two PhDs, one from Washington State University in Anthropology and one from the Université de Franche-Comté from the Maison des Sciences de l'Homme et l'Environnement. Her work leverages computational tools and deep time data to better understand the trajectory of human–environment interactions to lead to a better and more just present and future.

Alison Damick is the Associate Curator of Environmental Archaeology and the Manager of the Laboratory of Environmental Archaeology in the McClung Museum of Natural History and Culture at the University of Tennessee Knoxville. She is an environmental archaeologist who uses geoarchaeological and microbotanical methods to explore changing relationships between humans, land, plants, and water in the Holocene, particularly across periods of acute climatic and social change. Whilst her own research is focused on Southwest Asia and the American Southwest, specifically in Lebanon and New Mexico, she is also involved in collaborative projects in North Africa, the American Southeast, and the eastern Mediterranean.

Dagomar Degroot is an associate professor of environmental history at Georgetown University. He is the author of *The Frigid Golden Age: Climate Change, the Little Ice Age, and the Dutch Republic, 1560–1720* (Cambridge University Press, 2018) and *Ripples on the Cosmic Ocean: An Environmental History of Our Place in the*

Solar System (Belknap Press/Viking, 2025) and the co-editor of volumes such as *The Oxford Handbook of Resilience in the History of Climate Change* (Oxford University Press, 2026) and numerous articles in scientific and historical journals. He is the producer and host of the Climate Chronicles podcast.

Andrew J. Dugmore teaches across degree programmes in Geography at the University of Edinburgh, where he is Professor of Geosciences, a post he has held since 2007. Following doctoral studies at the University of Aberdeen, he joined the University of Edinburgh in 1987 as Research Fellow and pioneered the development of cryptotephrochronology. A founding member of the North Atlantic Biocultural Organization (NABO: https://www.nabohome.org/) he has developed and applied Icelandic tephrochronology in glacial geomorphology, to refine environmental studies and in understanding of social ecological systems. Whilst the principal geographical focus of his research is the North Atlantic region from Scandinavia to Greenland, his studies of environmental change and human–environment interactions have also taken him from Scotland to the Pacific NW of America, and collaborations include comparative study of the pre-Hispanic American southwest. Andrew has a long-term affiliation with the City University of New York and is Fellow of the Royal Scottish Geographical Society.

Bikem Ekberzade works in Earth System Sciences at the Avrasya Yer Bilimleri Enstitüsü.

Edda Fields-Black teaches history at Carnegie Mellon University in Pittsburgh PA and serves as Director of the Dietrich College Humanities Center. She is a specialist in the transnational history of West Africa rice, peasant farmers in the pre-colonial Upper Guinea coast, and enslaved labourers on antebellum Lowcountry South Carolina and Georgia rice plantations. She is the author of *Deep Roots: Rice Farmers in West Africa and the African Diaspora* and co-editor of *Rice: Global Networks and New Histories*. She is executive producer and librettist of *Unburied, Unmourned, Unmarked: Requiem for Rice* (with three-time EMMY™ Award-winning classical music composer, John Wineglass), and has worked as a consultant at the Smithsonian National Museum of African American History and Culture, the International African American Museum, and the Senator John Heinz History Center.

Travis H. Folk is a wildlife biologist in the Lowcountry of South Carolina. He manages and restores historic rice fields across coastal South Carolina and was a lead investigator (along with Dr. Ernie Wiggers formerly of Nemours Wildlife Foundation and Dr. Rob Baldwin of Clemson University) for the Rice Field Mapping Project.

Nicolas Gauthier is Assistant Curator of Artificial Intelligence for Cultural and Biological Diversity at the Florida Museum of Natural History at the University of Florida. He is an anthropologist, geographer, and Earth system scientist who uses methods and tools from the geosciences to study past and present human societies over the past 10,000 years.

George Hambrecht is Associate Professor in the Department of Anthropology at the University of Maryland, College Park. He is an active member of the NABO (North Atlantic Biocultural Organization, nabohome.org), and his research concentrates on the zooarchaeology of the North Atlantic. His temporal range starts with the Norse Period and ends in the Early Modern. Recently, his work has been focused on marine historical ecology, especially through the NSF, Navigating the New Arctic Program, funded project, the Central North Atlantic Marine Historical Ecology Project (CAMHEP, NSF # 2022656). CAMHEP is generating a paleoecological record of the North Atlantic over the last 1100 years focusing on Atlantic Cod (Gadus morhua). The most recent CAMHEP article is Campana et al. 2025, *Science Advances*.

Daniel Hanks is a research aquatic ecologist for Weyerhaeuser's Southern Environmental Research Team. His research interests aim to identify opportunities for improved conservation outcomes at the landscape scale, primarily through operational efficiencies within the forest industry.

Dean Harrigal is Certified Wildlife Biologist working with Folk Land Management and has over 40 years of experience as a wildlife biologist and wildlife habitat manager. He has spent nearly his entire career working in the Lowcountry of South Carolina, principally the ACE Basin region between Charleston and Beaufort. His areas of expertise include upland and wetland habitat development and management for a wide range of wildlife species, especially managed wetland enhancement for waterfowl, wading birds, and shorebirds.

Chloe Hill is originally from Tasmania, Australia, but has lived, worked, and studied in Europe since 2012. Chloe has been working as the EGU's Policy Officer in Munich since May 2017. In this position, Chloe undertakes activities to enhance the EGU's connection with policymakers and organizations who work at the science–policy interface. She has a Master's in Environmental Governance from the University of Freiburg and a Bachelor's in Environmental Science from the University of Tasmania. Prior to starting with the EGU, Chloe worked in the renewable energy sector for the African EU Energy Partnership, and as a research assistant for the Indo-German Centre for Sustainability, the Institute of Climate and Sustainable Cities, and Forestry Tasmania.

Adam Izdebski works at the Institute of Advanced Studies at Nicolaus Copernicus University.

Rowan C. Jackson is a lecturer in the Global Academy of Agriculture and Food Systems at the University of Edinburgh. His expertise is in environmental history, archaeology, and cultural heritage spanning the North Atlantic (Greenland, Iceland, and Scotland), South Africa and Kenya, Sri Lanka, and Indonesia. Rowan has experience researching the impacts of climate change in the North Atlantic over the last 1200 years and the implications of contemporary climate change on archaeological heritage in the Arctic and Sub-Arctic. In the last 5 years, his research has focused on international cultural heritage research and policy, including a project on climate change and natural hazard impacts on cultural heritage of the community of Elandskloof in South Africa, rural water management practices in Sri Lanka, and volcanic impacts on the Code River in Yogyakarta, Indonesia.

Aleksandra Kaye is a postdoctoral researcher at the Max Planck Institute of Geoanthropology in Jena, Germany. A historian by training, she is enthusiastic about the potential of transdisciplinary practice for enriching historical scholarship. Her current work focuses on understanding the long-term effects of environmental decisions made in the nineteenth century, especially in relation to forest management and petroleum extraction. She also studies the impact of intercontinental migration on the production, circulation, transfer, and acceptance of scientific knowledge across regions. She co-convenes the Mining Conversations | The Futurepasts of … series, hosted by the Max Planck Institute of Geoanthropology and Anthropocene Commons. A couple of her recent, co-authored publications are "Sandalwood and the Entanglement of the Juan Fernández Islands in Eco-Cultural Networks", *The Journal of Pacific History*, 2025 https://doi.org/10.1080/00223344.2025.2513412, and "Socio-Epistemic Networks: A Framework for History of Knowledge", *History of Intellectual Culture* 3 (2024) https://doi.org/10.1515/9783111291383-012

Sarah Klassen is an archaeologist whose work bridges urbanism, resilience, and water management, providing empirical insights into the long-term adaptability of ancient cities. She specializes in the use of remotely sensed data, particularly lidar, to investigate large-scale settlement systems. She currently directs the Koh Ker Archaeological Project (kkap.org) and serves as Associate Director of the Center for Collaborative Synthesis in Archaeology at the University of Colorado Boulder. Her research has been supported by major funding bodies, including the U.S. National Science Foundation, the Social Sciences and Humanities Research Council of Canada, the European Research Council, and the Australian Department of Education and Training. Since earning her PhD, Dr. Klassen has led and contributed to major international collaborations, including leadership roles in European Research Council and NSF-funded projects, and partnerships with institutions in Australia, Canada, France, Germany, the Netherlands, and Cambodia. Her achievements have been recognized with the Institute for Southeast Asian Archaeology Early Career Award (2022) and the Shanghai Archaeological Forum Research Award (2023) for her outstanding contributions to the advancement of our knowledge of the human past. Her work has attracted significant public and scholarly attention, featuring in outlets such as *The Guardian* ("Revealed: Cambodia's vast medieval cities hidden beneath the jungle") and *The Atlantic* ("Unearthing an Origin Story for Gentrification"). She has appeared as an expert contributor and presenter for numerous media productions, most notably the Discovery Channel's two-hour special Lost Cities of the Jungle, which highlighted the groundbreaking results of the Cambodian Archaeological Lidar Initiative, which she co-directed.

Luke Kemp researches the end of the world. He is Senior Research Associate at the Centre for the Study of Existential Risk (CSER) at the University of Cambridge and Visiting Fellow with the Cascade Institute. He has advised and led foresight studies for multiple international organizations, including the WHO and Convention on Biological Diversity. His work has been covered by media outlets such as the BBC, the *New York Times*, and the *New Yorker*. His first book, *Goliath's Curse: The History and Future of Societal Collapse*, was published with Penguin in July 2025.

Samantha (Sam) Krause is Assistant Professor at Texas State University in the Department of Geography and Environmental Studies. She specializes in geomorphology, soil geochemistry, and geoarchaeology, focusing on the American Southwest and Mesoamerica.

Annegret Larsen works in the Soil Geography and Landscape Group at Wageningen University & Research.

Lee Mordechai is a senior lecturer at the History Department in the Hebrew University of Jerusalem. His research examines interactions between environment and society in the premodern Eastern Mediterranean, focusing on disasters such as diseases and earthquakes. He has published papers in journals such as *the American Historical Review* and the *Proceedings of the National Academy of Sciences*. Lee is currently finalizing his second book, an investigation of the 536 CE "Dust Veil" event.

Kathleen D. Morrison is the Sally and Alvin V. Shoemaker Professor of Anthropology, Curator in Charge in the Asian Section at the University of Pennsylvania Museum of Archaeology and Anthropology, Director of the Penn Paleoecology Lab, and faculty director of the Environmental Innovations Initiative. Her research focuses on anthropogenic changes in land use and land cover at local, regional, and global scales. Current projects include LandCover6k, a global database of Holocene land use and land cover, and South Indian Landscape Trajectories, an analysis of the last 5000 years of farming, food, and power, and their connections to environmental change in the semi-arid regions of peninsular India. She is the author of *Forests, Foragers, and Empires: Socionatural Histories of Southern India* (2024), *Fields of Victory: Vijayanagara and the Course of Intensification* (1995, 2000), and *Daroji Valley: Landscape, Place, and the Making of a Dryland Reservoir System* (2009), co-author of *The Vijayanagara Metropolitan Survey* (2007), and co-editor of *The Social Lives of Forests: Past, Present, and Future of Woodland Resurgence* (2014), *Forager-Traders in South and Southeast Asia* (2001), and *Empires: Perspectives from Archaeology and History* (2000).

John T. Murphy is an independent researcher in anthropology, archaeology, and computational social science. He is Volunteer Affiliate with Northern Illinois University, where he worked previously as Faculty Research Associate in the Department of Anthropology and was Honors Faculty Fellow (2021–2022). His experience includes 13 years as Computational Engineer at Argonne National

Laboratory and related work with appointments at the University of Illinois Chicago and the University of Chicago. During this time he applied computational approaches and simulation modelling, especially agent-based modelling, to an array of projects addressing international conflict, disease spread, dialogue and disinformation on social media, infrastructure robustness and resilience, circular economies, and non-market management of natural resources, inter alia. His focus in anthropology and archaeology is on challenges for reconciling computational and modelling approaches with social theory and on long-term adaptation to climate change, rural–urban dynamics, and societal resilience. His book (as co-editor with Carole L. Crumley) *If the Past Teaches, What Does the Future Learn?* explores how past urban forms are related to alternative power structures, and considers the implications of drawing on a vast and varied archaeological record for the design of a more resilient, just, and equitable future.

Takeshi Nakatsuka (PhD at Nagoya University in 1995) is Professor in the Graduate School of Environmental Studies, Nagoya University. His research topics cover a wide range of environmental studies using natural abundance of stable isotopes, including oceanography, ecology, carbon cycle, paleoceanography, and paleoclimatology. During the last two decades, he has focused on high-temporal-resolution climate reconstruction during the last several millennia using tree-ring cellulose isotope ratios in Asia, especially in Japan, and its applications to understand past climate–society relationships. From 2014 to 2019, he conducted an interdisciplinary research project *Societal Adaptation to Climate Change: Integrating Palaeoclimatological Data with Historical and Archaeological Evidences* in the Research Institute of Humanity and Nature, Kyoto. The research results are now contributing not only to the development of innovative methods in paleoclimatology (e.g. Nakatsuka et al. 2020. “A 2600-year summer climate reconstruction in central Japan by integrating tree-ring stable oxygen and hydrogen isotopes”, *Climate of the Past* 16: 2153–2172), but also to the promotion of interdisciplinary studies by many historians and archaeologists in Japan (e.g. Nakatsuka et al. (eds). 2020–21. *Reconsidering Japanese history from the viewpoint of climate variations*, vols. 1–6. Rinsen-Shoten, Kyoto).

Jeffrey S. Reznick, PhD, is senior historian on the federal staff of the National Library of Medicine (NLM) at the National Institutes of Health (NIH) where he maintains a diverse, interdisciplinary, and highly collaborative historical research portfolio supported by the NLM and serves as a senior advisor to staff and leadership on partnerships, scholarly activities, and engagement with the library’s world-renowned collection, as well as its growth and preservation for future generations. He also serves as the NLM’s ex officio representative to several organizations, including the College of Physicians of Philadelphia, Friends of the National Library of Medicine, Medical Center Archives at NewYork-Presbyterian/Weill Cornell Medicine, Office of NIH History and Stetten Museum, Osler Library of the History of Medicine at McGill University in Montreal, Canada, and Science History Institute. Prior to his current position, he was chief of the NLM’s History of

Medicine Division, and before his federal service he held executive leadership positions in the national nonprofit sector. Author of four books and an elected member of the Royal Historical Society, he earned his PhD degree in history from Emory University. He contributed to this book and its associated colloquium as part of his official duties and with support of the NLM/NIH.

Daniel D. Richter is T.S. Coile Distinguished Professor of Soil and Earth Sciences at Duke University.

Felix Riede is Professor of Archaeology at Aarhus University in Denmark. He heads the Laboratory for Past Disaster Science, and his research focuses on the Palaeolithic and Mesolithic of Europe.

Gwen Robbins Schug is Professor of Biology at UNC Greensboro, where her research integrates bioarchaeology, climate change, and social inequality to explore human resilience in the face of environmental crises. Her work examines how past societies—from South Asia to the Mediterranean—adapted (or failed to adapt) to challenges like urbanization, agricultural shifts, and climatic instability, with a focus on the consequences of structural inequities. She is particularly interested in how lessons from the past can inform contemporary policy on sustainability and crisis response. She has authored *Bioarchaeology and Climate Change* (2011) and edited the *Routledge Handbook of the Bioarchaeology of Climate and Environmental Change* (2020), seminal works bridging archaeology, history, and environmental science. She has published over 45 articles and chapters on these themes. For a critical perspective on resilience and climate adaptation in premodern societies, see her recent (2023) *PNAS* paper, "Climate Change, Human Health, and Resilience in the Holocene". A former co-Editor-in-Chief of *Bioarchaeology International*, she serves on several editorial boards and advisory boards for the Triangle Center for Evolutionary Medicine and Oxford's Climate Adaptation in Society and Culture. Her current fieldwork spans India, Oman, and Italy, investigating long-term human–environment dynamics.

Arlene Miller Rosen received her PhD in Anthropology at the University of Chicago. Currently, she is Professor of Anthropology and Environmental Archaeology in the Department of Anthropology, University of Texas at Austin, and Fellow of the American Association for the Advancement of Science. She specializes in Geoarchaeology and Phytolith analysis to understand human–environment relations during later prehistory and in early complex societies in the Mediterranean Levant, China, Mongolia, and New Mexico. She is the author of *Civilizing Climate: Social Responses to Climate Change in the Ancient Near East* (2007: Altamira Press) and numerous journal articles dealing with issues of human adaptations to climate change and human impact on the environment

Rachel Singer is a PhD candidate at Georgetown University. She approaches infectious disease, climate change, and gender in early medieval Britain and Gaul with an interdisciplinary methodology combining rigorous textual criticism with data from archaeology and the natural sciences. Her work has appeared in *Early Medieval Europe*, *The English Historical Review*, and *Speculum.*

Michael E. Smith is Professor of Archaeology in the School of Human Evolution and Social Change at Arizona State University. He is an archaeologist who has excavated houses at Aztec provincial sites to reconstruct household and community organization and the political economic context of Aztec provincial society. He has published 15 books and more than 100 articles on his field research. His book, *At Home With the Aztecs: An Archaeologist Uncovers Their Daily Life* (2016), won the Best Popular Book award from the Society for American Archaeology. He now works primarily on comparative urbanism, focusing on premodern cities. He has participated in several transdisciplinary research projects addressing key urban topics in past and present cities, including inequality, neighbourhoods, scaling properties, and the long-term persistence and resilience of cities and settlements. He uses research and concepts on contemporary urbanism to inform analyses of past cities whilst using findings on past urbanism to inform contemporary debates in the realm of urban adaptations to climate change and other environmental shocks. He is Fellow of the American Association for the Advancement of Science.

Katherine C. Snow is an environmental philosopher and research associate at Princeton University whose work examines links between past and current Western philosophies of nature and our contemporary environmental crisis. Snow's recent monograph *Our Inevitable Third Spinoza Controversy: Ontologies of Necessity and Environmental Nihilism* critiques the long-lasting influence in the West of early German romantic ideas of nature and presents Spinoza Controversy-linked arguments for a turn to environmental realism; a follow-up book, *Rural Philosophy*, is now in progress. As a former US government official and the founder of a new nonprofit consultancy (Gaia Morgan Group) aimed at helping governments think strategically about the environment, Snow is also always working on identifying and developing new policy and national security sub-frameworks and tools, under the environmental realist umbrella, which are able to accommodate and be useful to both policymakers and theorists.

Adriano Sofo works in the Department of Agricultural, Forestry, Food and Environmental Sciences (DAFE) at the Università degli Studi della Basilicata.

Gesine A. Steudle is a postdoctoral researcher at the Max Planck Institute of Geoanthropology in Jena, Germany. Her main research focus is how to account for human agency in mathematical models to better understand the dynamics of complex social-technical, socio-economic, or socio-ecological system, and how a better analytical understanding of the co-evolution of such coupled systems can be used to think about possible intervention points to foster change or enhance stability. Gesine studied physics in Berlin and Granada (Spain) and obtained her PhD from Humboldt University of Berlin in the field of experimental quantum optics. She worked at a private consulting company in the area of energy efficiency and renewable energies before she returned to academia and did mathematical modelling of economic systems, such as models for green growth or sustainable mobility, with a focus on agent-based models of complex socio-economic systems at the Global Climate Forum and the Zuse Institute Berlin.

Malte Vogl studied Physics at the TU Berlin and the University of Nairobi, Kenya, and obtained his PhD in 2013. In 2016, he joined the Max Planck Institute for the History of Science in Berlin to work as a PostDoc in collaboration with the cluster of excellence TOPOI at Humboldt University of Berlin. In 2021, he became first PostDoc and then PI of the BMBF-funded ModelSEN project. Since 2023, he is a senior research fellow at the Max Planck Institute of Geoanthropology.

Ernie Wiggers is a Certified Wildlife Biologist with 40 years of experience teaching and conducting research on wildlife conservation topics. Formerly CEO of the Nemours Wildlife Foundation located in the Lowcountry of South Carolina, he now works part-time with Folk Land Management assisting landowners develop and implement conservation practices on their property.

Sarah Wolf recently joined Technische Universität Berlin as a professor for Sustainable Transport Systems and Data Science. Before, she was the head of a junior research group on Mathematics for Sustainability Transitions at Freie Universität Berlin as part of the Berlin Mathematics Research Center MATH+. With a background in mathematics, she has worked in interdisciplinary research teams since her PhD studies at the Potsdam Institute for Climate Impact Research. Her research focus is on agent-based modelling of complex social systems, in particular, in the context of sustainable mobility, and on embedding such models and their simulations in stakeholder dialogues—with practice experts, citizens, and students—in a Decision Theatre format.

Making History Relevant

Introduction: Can We Translate History into Policy? Problems and Perspectives

John F. Haldon and Michael E. Smith

Abstract How relevant can history be to policy? History can have enormous persuasive power and offer a long-term cultural-historical context through which policymakers and other stakeholders can make sense of emerging phenomena. Historical analysis can also serve as a quantitative or qualitative tool for benchmarking and evaluation, indicating best (or worst) practices that can emerge under a given set of circumstances. But reaching a situation where historical and archaeological evidence has a positive influence on policy decisions is a particularly difficult task. In this introductory chapter we address questions of quality of data, timescale, types of historical analysis, the kinds of effect research can have in the policy domain, the range and types of audience for historical research, as well as issues of knowledge transfer. We conclude by emphasizing that greater precision is needed in what we can offer, to whom, and with what aims; that we need to identify those policy areas in which our research results have some relevance; and that greater attention should be paid to the important role of mediators, who can provide links to policy but whose role is at present largely ignored in discussions in the historical literature. Historians and archaeologists need to interact and collaborate with policy specialists to achieve acceptance for our research findings beyond our own disciplines.

Keywords Relevance · Data quality · Policy · Resilience · Sustainability · Knowledge transfer · Mediators

The degree to which researchers working in fields that entail study of past environment and climate can make their work "relevant" has been a contentious issue but one that is increasingly prominent (Degroot and Singer, this volume). History (in the broadest sense) can have enormous persuasive power, and narrative and

J. F. Haldon (✉)
Princeton University, Princeton, NJ, USA
e-mail: jhaldon@princeton.edu

M. E. Smith
Arizona State University, Tempe, AZ, USA
e-mail: mesmith9@asu.edu

J. F. Haldon, R. Fernandes (eds.), *Bridging History and Policy*, Understanding Complex Systems, https://doi.org/10.1007/978-3-032-24379-9_1

story-telling are important and well-tried tools of communication, with policy makers and politicians as much as with the wider public (Cronon 1992). The question of the extent to which a better understanding of how past societies dealt with environmental and climatic challenges should indeed, one would think, inform our response to contemporary problems of a similar nature and magnitude (e.g. Hotchkiss et al. 2022; Rockman and Hritz 2020; Lane 2015). But then one would also think that the goal of basing policy on empirical evidence should be universal, yet in fact scientific or scholarly evidence plays a rather minor role in most policy domains (Black 2001; Reimer and Brett 2013). The implication is that reaching a situation where historical and archaeological evidence has a positive influence on policy decisions is a particularly difficult task. This is one of the reasons for the present volume and was the motivating force behind the original colloquium.

As governments grapple with increasingly complex challenges, two roles have emerged in which historical knowledge and analysis plays a role: first, to provide a long-term cultural-historical context through which policymakers and other stakeholders can make sense of emerging phenomena, and secondly, as quantitative or qualitative tools for benchmarking and evaluation, indicating best (or worst) practices that can emerge under a given set of circumstances. The application of historical analysis brings different benefits to different fields of policymaking, including defence, urban planning, energy, the environment, and others. Historians and archaeologists have expressed concerns about the absence of a historical perspective at the environmental policy table and have proposed a range of strategic initiatives through which to redress this imbalance (e.g. Jackson et al. 2017; Riede et al. 2016; Riede 2014; Van de Noort 2013; Costanza et al. 2007). But with some exceptions they still represent marginal players in the discussion, whether locally or in major policy foci such as the IPCC. The papers in this volume explore the reasons for the limited role of historical evidence in the policy realm, and they provide empirical, conceptual, and logistical advances to help remedy this situation.

In this brief introductory essay we will comment on four key aspects of the problem as revealed in the chapters that follow. We look at this from four perspectives: the quality of data, time scales, relevance, and intellectual context.

1 The Quality of Data

Historical and archaeological data are, by their very nature, difficult to relate directly to the social and environmental worlds today. First, the incompleteness and variable quality of our data presents a problem that cannot be overcome simply by assuming connections between disparate sets of evidence that may not in fact be valid—not only because of the likely incommensurability of datasets, but also the risk of confirmation bias, the tendency to search for, recall and interpret data in a way that confirms preexisting assumptions. Evidence needs to be good enough to support the outcomes it is being used for; it needs to be selected and codified on the basis of agreed and consistent criteria in ways that render it useful in reconstructing and interpreting a cultural context. Selection reflects—usually—the question(s) that inform the research as a whole; but selection is itself part of the problem of subjectivity that historians confront. Archaeologists face the same problem—it is rarely possible to excavate all of a site or survey all of a particular area, nor to analyze in detail all the material collected (e.g. ceramic sherds, soil samples, etc.), so a sampling process is essential in most cases (Shafer 2016). Theoretical and methodological tools through which sampling and selection can be managed have been developed, but the issue of selection nevertheless remains a basic challenge for all historical analysis. It is important to make these issues both transparent and easily understood by those involved in policy planning if the contribution that historical/archaeological knowledge can make can be properly evaluated.

A second issue concerns interpretation, which depends on both subjective assessment and evaluation of different types of evidence as well as different and sometimes competing theoretical and epistemological frameworks. At the heart of this is frequently the relationship between proximate and ultimate causal factors (Mayr 1961), since consensus on this among specialists is often difficult to achieve. The situation varies from case to case according to the chronological timeframe, the nature of the evidence, the quality of the associated historiographical tradition and a range of other cultural factors. But this means that all conclusions are by definition provisional, and we are more often than not working with the currently best-available hypothesis on any given issue. This is especially true of the big questions about historical structures and social processes, for which alternative hypotheses can rarely be rejected with certainty. Historians are aware that unknowns and uncertainties compound as data are aggregated and as interpretation moves towards larger scales of analysis (Cronon 1992; Lucas 2018). But while a broad consensus about key issues can generally be reached (Hulme 2011; White et al. 2023), this does not help policy strategists, who require clear answers to specific questions, or at the least, clear guidelines about what the historical data is telling us.

These features of historical and archaeological data make it especially difficult to relate our research to concerns in the policy world. What is needed for research results to become useful and relevant? Sustainability scientists (leaving aside for the present the problematic nature of the term "sustainability" itself—see Morrison, this volume) and policy analysts have devoted much attention to this general issue. A key concept is "usable knowledge," or "actionable knowledge" (Clark et al. 2016): scientific findings that can be used in the policy domain. Useable knowledge is evaluated in terms of three criteria: credibility (is the knowledge true or accurate?), saliency (is it relevant to the policy concern), and legitimacy (is it fair and unbiased?); see Cash et al. (2003), Matson et al. (2016: chapter 5), and Tuinstra et al. (2019).

The concern for usable knowledge starts with the basic empirical methods of the historical sciences. Roosen and Curtis (2018) show the problems that arise for studies of past infectious disease when proper historiographical methods are not followed. "When scholars fail to apply source criticism or do not reflect on the content of the data they use, the reliability of their results becomes highly questionable" (Roosen and Curtis 2018: 103). Too often, scholars who pursue relevance do so at the expense of methodological and empirical rigor. This was one component of economic historian Mark Koyama's critique of *The History Manifesto* (Guldi and Armitage 2014), a call for relevance published a decade ago (Koyama 2015); his other critique was the failure of historians promoting relevance to integrate their findings with the social science literature.

Although they do not use the concept of usable knowledge, Degroot et al. (2021) discuss these issues for historical research on past episodes of climate change. They identify a series of empirical and conceptual problems that plague past research in this area and insist on the importance of basic historiographical rigor. A similar argument is made by archaeologists Kohler and Rockman (2020), who suggest that without making improvements in methods and data quality, archaeology will not be able to contribute to the work of the Intergovernmental Panel on Climate Change (IPCC).

Smith (2023a) takes this line of thought further, emphasizing that rigorous methods of data collection alone are insufficient to create usable knowledge. Rather, scholars need to make use of adequate methods of argumentation to create meaning out of our empirical findings. We cannot simply line up case studies and claim that they are important, relevant or exemplary. Models and hypotheses need to be tested, and principles of comparative analysis and case study research need to be followed (Gerring 2017; Ragin 2014). Smith critiques Degroot et al. (2021) for limiting their methodological guidelines to data assembly but then failing to employ adequate argumentation to establish the implications of the findings (Smith 2023a); see also Smith (2023b).

One of the goals of this volume is to promote high-quality historical and archaeological research that has the potential to become usable knowledge in the policy realm. Many of the chapters contribute to this goal. For example, Hambrecht's chapter presents an important recent case study illustrating how archaeological and historical data can be used to create much deeper records of important natural resources (in this case Atlantic Cod) than have previously existed. Such data is crucial in developing long-term records necessary to navigating Shifting Baseline Syndrome. This concept describes the ways in which successive generations accept the environmental conditions they first observe as their baseline, not recognizing that their baseline has already shifted from earlier baselines. The result can be a progressive erosion of standards for ecosystem health. Schug and Buikstra, and Charnley, discuss the ways in which historical perspectives are providing crucial insights for addressing contemporary health challenges in the context of climate change, permitting better understanding of long-term human adaptations to environmental change and more effective, equitable responses to current health crises. Bauch's contribution notes how historic floods in Germany that predate instrumental measurements have nevertheless bequeathed a robust source base that, in the context of anthropogenic climate change in combination with higher drought risks, can offer valuable data that can contribute to the development of strategies for risk prevention.

2 Time Scales

While many topics that historians and archaeologists study can potentially contribute to policy research, one of the overlying strengths of our research—in comparison with other disciplines—is the access to change over long periods of time. Braudel (1972) first articulated a three-part scheme of the varying temporal scales accessible to the historian. Events are the short-term changes that range from individual decisions to battles and other political changes. Conjunctures are decades-scale transformations such as the rise and fall of empires, or the development of cities or social structures. The longue durée is the centuries-long backdrop of the environment and climate within which shorter processes play out. There are literatures within both history (Armitage 2012) and archaeology (Knapp 1992) exploring the implications of Braudel's temporal insights for a variety of themes.

The notion that different temporal processes operate at different scales has also been important in other historical fields such as geomorphology and geoarchaeology (Butzer 1982, 2011). More recently sustainability science has rediscovered this insight, although rarely citing the earlier work in history, archaeology, or geomorphology (Chhetri et al. 2019; Kates et al. 2012). Table 1, based on (Smith 2023a), summarizes some of these schemes.

The medium- and long-term social processes and transformations documented by history and archaeology provide background frameworks within which broader trends can be identified (e.g. Hegmon et al. 2018; Riede 2014; Vésteinsson et al. 2019). One approach that has helped communicate the value of knowledge of the past effectively is that of viewing the historical record as one of "completed experiments", a perspective that permits us to understand diachronic changes to socio-ecological systems in sufficient chronological depth to identify longer-term characteristics of cultural limits to adaptation, path dependency, cycles of resilience, and the social impacts of vulnerability. We are not referring to "experiments" in a technical scientific sense (that is, they are not repeatable under a specific and determinate set of control conditions).

Table 1 Time scales in different disciplines (after Smith 2023a)

Discipline	Author	Time scale		
		Short	Medium	Long
History and social archaeology	Braudel (1972)	Event	Conjuncture	Longue durée
Geomorphology	Butzer (2011)	Seasonal stress	Medium-term pulse	Long-term environmental shift
Environmental archaeology	Butzer (1982)	Adaptive adjustment	Adaptive modification	Adaptive transformation
Sustainability science	Kates et al. (2012) and Chhetri et al. (2019)	Coping adaptation	Incremental adaptation	Transformational adaptation
		(Shorter)	→	(Longer)

The notion of the past as a series of completed experiments appears in ecology and archaeology and in the early twenty-first century has been deployed with the aim of achieving a better understanding of the longer-term evolutionary track of a socio-ecological system (Jackson et al. 2018; Nelson et al. 2010; Smith 2012). Since many processes operate over extremely long timescales, the integration of instrumental, palaeoenvironmental, archaeological and documentary data contributes to building up "socio-ecological profiles" (Dearing 2011; Dearing et al. 2010; Turner and Spalding 2013). These help to identify path-dependencies and the processes through which the competitive selection of social practices (Runciman 1989) might lead to socio-cultural success as well as to maladaptations (Dugmore et al. 2012). The idea is to build causal complexity into our understanding of transformations in practice and to deepen our socio-ecological and holistic understanding of cause-and-effect relationships. Such profiles can help in developing policies and strategies where successful management of key environmental processes, ecological services and their interaction is critical (Spielmann et al. 2016).

3 Types of Potentially Relevant Historical Analysis

Haldon et al. (2024) identify three broad types of historical analysis that may be relevant to policy concerns. *Type 1 research* consists of broad-brush quantitative analyses based on mathematical modelling. This kind of research can identify broad patterns of change through time. Peter Turchin's SESHAT project is a prominent example of this kind of research (Turchin et al. 2015, 2018, 2023); other published examples include Riris and de Souza (2021) and Riris et al. (2024). Large-scale quantitative analyses can suggest potential future trends and problems based on past structural and systemic evolutionary tracks. They can highlight issues of settlement persistence, demographic resilience, responses to risk and strategies for dealing with hazards, and such general socio-ecological properties can be of relevance today. The discussion in this volume in the chapters by Kemp and Steudle et al. exemplify different facets of Type 1 research, both in terms of concepts of transformation and collapse over both the long and short term, as well as in respect of the potential advantages of systems-modelling in managing complex and extensive historical datasets. While the chapter by Fernandes remains at a relative high level of theoretical abstraction it likewise sets out a framework which can facilitate the integration of historical analysis into policymaking via systems thinking, in order to address the complexities of human-environmental systems.

Type 2 research is "big-picture" comparative discussion of one or more major societal transformations, including those which look in greater detail at the role of agency, beliefs and social praxis. There is a literature on comparative analysis in the historical disciplines, much of which is useful for this kind of research (Gordon 2020; Hoyer and Manning 2018; Kocka 2003; Smith 2012). Examples of studies pursuing this kind of research on human-environmental interactions include Izdebski et al. (2024), Haldon et al. (2020), and Izdebski et al. (2018), as well as

Travis et al. (2023), Rick and Sandweiss (2020) and Jackson et al. (2017), with comments on some aspects of this sort of research in Mordechai's chapter, below (see also Tubi et al. 2022). The papers in the present collection by Klassen, Morrison, Nakatsuka and Rosen et al. exemplify some aspects of this approach.

Type 3 research consists of single historical case-studies of specific regional or local social-ecological systems. This is highly localized research that can be exploited to identify structures, beliefs and behaviors in a specific region under particular conditions in the past which led to vulnerability or resilience. Such studies can suggest lessons on the impacts of societal responses for a given society as well as indicate where contemporary or future alternative or mitigating strategies may be appropriate. The vast majority of historical and archaeological publications promoting relevance to environmental factors fits in Type 3, including many of the chapters in this volume—see, for example, the contributions to this volume by Bauch and by Clarke, as well as some of the locally-focused projects mentioned in Dugmore and Jackson. Folk et al. show how collaboration between public and private stakeholders has facilitated continued conservation of a historic landscape and management of wetlands in the US southeast.

How "relevance" is understood is a point for debate. Whatever the likely relevance of these types for the historian or archaeologist, we cannot expect those concerned with policy to be either aware of or interested in them. Just as importantly, and in particular when working with or addressing members of traditional or indigenous communities and cultures, relevance is in the eye of the beholder in respect of cultural identities and recognized needs as much as in the evaluation of scientific specialists or representatives of the state. Additionally, "relevance" for the policy world generally means "actionable" or "usable", as discussed above.

In a paper on archaeology's relevance to global challenges, Smith (2021) describes a typology of kinds of relevance for archaeological knowledge that is similar to the three types identified by Haldon et al. His scheme has four types (see Table 2):

1. Heritage or descendant concerns focus on archaeological sites as places of history and heritage, and on the needs of local descendant communities. While this kind of relevance is important for many archaeological sites, that is a different kind of concept from the relevance of knowledge of past societies to contemporary environmental concerns.
2. Local practical topics. These are studies of small-scale agricultural methods or water supply systems for which past successes may hold insights for practices today.
3. Middle-range empirical and conceptual issues. This category describes most of the chapters in this book. Research deals with economic systems such as land use and food supply, settlement patterns and urbanism, social inequality, and other similar topics.
4. Abstract conceptual topics describe research that claims past-to-present continuities in highly abstract phenomena, such as sustainability in general, fairness, or agency and practice.

Table 2 Types of Relevance for archaeological findings (after Smith 2021)

1 *Heritage or descendant concerns*
Sacred places or shrines
Identity, history and human remains
Land claims and resource rights
Symbolically important relics
2 *Local practical topics*
Small-scale agricultural method
Small-scale water supply system
3 *Middle-range empirical and conceptual topics*
Economic systems and institutions
Urban neighborhoods or city size
Social inequality
4 *Abstract conceptual topics*
Sustainability
Fairness and justice
Agency and practice

These two typologies converge in several ways. One notable convergence is on the value of good empirical research on local conditions and processes. In contrast to academic historical research, historical and archaeological work on the ground often can and does engage directly with local community or stakeholder interests. Such work often begins with no intentional focus on a practical application from learning from the past, but nevertheless turns out to be relevant or applicable in a very particular context. Archaeological understanding of topics like historic water-management systems, or premodern cropping and land-use strategies, for example, has been applied in both Old as well as New World contexts to help local farming communities or district authorities better manage their resources in times of stress (Da Luna et al. 2022; Fields-Black et al. 2022; England et al. 2022). This material tends to relate to specific highly-localized settings and is rarely known beyond the area of its immediate practical deployment. Nevertheless, it serves as a significant indication of where historical and archaeological research might have a purchase in certain types of policy thinking, and thus potentially a broader impact. The task in creating knowledge for policy lies in the combination and synthesis of local studies to allow general patterns and trends to be identified.

The most useful, it appears, because readily applicable and of value to local stakeholder concerns, are studies that focus on a specific place and on specific aspects of social organisation, and these come from many parts of the world. There is a substantial number of such projects and they have had or are having a significant beneficial impact in a variety of ways. Archaeological-historical projects on Roman and medieval water-management and land-use in various regions of Turkey, for example, have generated significant local interest and in several cases a restructuring of rural land-use practices today (Peker et al. 2023–24; Wainright et al.

2021–2023; Koparal et al. 2022). Similar involvement of local stakeholders as well as governments in respect of North Atlantic fisheries and ocean management, as well as Greenlandic foodways and resource management, originated in archaeo-historical projects on the societies and economies of both indigenous and incoming populations to Iceland and Greenland during the medieval period (Hambrecht, this volume; Hartman et al. 2017; Hicks et al. 2016). The historical and archaeological analysis of the rice agriculture of the Carolina and Florida wetlands has fed directly and deliberately into local land-management and conservation policy and involved local communities and NGOs working in partnership (Fields-Black et al. 2022; Folk et al. this volume). This kind of project—engaging stakeholders, government, archaeologists and historians—has addressed topics as diverse as the history of flood control in the Taipei Basin in Taiwan, or water management in the Andes, cases that represent both new research and the potential for significant practical application to a contemporary problem.

In his chapter below, Smith argues for narrowing the focus of past-present comparisons for archaeological data. Instead of examining resilience or adaptation on a society-wide basis, Smith focuses specifically on cities. This narrowing of focus allows comparisons to be more precise and specific, and it has the advantage of exploiting a topic of increasing prominence in the field of adaptation and sustainability science: cities and urban populations. Thus instead of trying to determine whether society today will collapse or suffer unspecified harms, the past can be used to address specific hypotheses derived from the analysis of urban adaptations to climate change today. As an approach, this appears to us both less subject to the tendency to exaggerate for effect ("warnings from the past") and more constructive in terms of attempting to identify particular configurations of past relationships between urbanism, society and environment that may have promoted or facilitated, or hindered and negated specific historical instances of sustainable pathways.

4 Relevance and Policy

Much has been published on the ways that scientific research influences policy at various levels. Studies focusing on social science and environmental topics have considerable insight for our topic of the relevance of historical and archaeological findings. We review this literature in relation to four questions: What kinds of effect can research have in the policy domain? Who is the audience? Who decides what is relevant? And, How can knowledge be transferred from archaeology and history into the policy realm? This discussion is predicated on the requirement for rigorous data and empirical quality, discussed above.

4.1 Question One: What Kinds of Effect Can Research Have in the Policy Domain?

Luk van Langenhove (2011: 107) suggests that—for policy use—"Any social scientific activity should aim at having three kinds of effects." The first is *generating new knowledge*. His emphasis is on raising the level of knowledge and understanding among policy-makers and other involved in public discourse. Clearly, historians and archaeologists generate new knowledge within their disciplines, but such knowledge rarely penetrates into the realm of policy. Van Langenhove's second effect is *forming attitudes and opinions*. It is not enough to simply offer data or findings to practitioners in the policy world; that knowledge has to contribute to their base of understanding so that they can put it to work. The third effect is *initializing actions*. Those in the policy realm need to use the findings and knowledge to take action, talking with colleagues, writing drafts of bills or policy statements, and the like.

For most historians and archaeologists, the knowledge we produce in our disciplinary contexts rarely gets far enough into the policy domain to activate van Langenhove's three kinds of effects. To explore this situation further, we can consider the second question on research and policy:

4.2 Question Two: Who Is the Audience?

The question of the audience for research and scholarship can be complex. Indeed, Smith (2000) identified no fewer than 16 different audiences or publics that were relevant to his archaeological excavation project in the Mexican town of Yautepec. For present purposes, we list some of the potential audiences for historical and archaeological research in Table 3.

Local residents and descendants are important—particularly for research on archaeological sites and local history projects. Good examples are provided in the work of the Campaign for the Protection of Rural England which, together with other major NGOs in the UK, has worked together with historians and archaeologists to substantially influence government environment, sustainability and land use strategies since the 1970s (Burton 2022). Similarly effective has been the work of the international NABO (North Atlantic Biocultural Organization) project, which integrates work on local histories, identities and assumptions with both educational and economic initiatives within local communities as well as centrally-managed environmental, heritage and policy agencies (see Hambrecht, and Jackson and Dugmore, this volume; and for a case where these issues are not properly taken into account, the chapter by Clarke). Similar examples can be found elsewhere in both northern and southern hemispheres, where academic researchers, including historians, worked hand-in-hand with a range of other environmental pressure groups to effectively influence public policy.

Table 3 Who is the Audience?

Local setting
Local residents
Descendants
Public discourse
The general public
Science and scholarship
Other historians and archaeologists
Scholars in other disciplines
Policy realm
Federal policymakers
United Nations and international organizations
Frontline practitioners
State and local agencies
Mid-level administrators
Advocacy groups and think tanks
Intermediaries

The second category in Table 3—public discourse—is the realm of outreach and the communication of science and scholarship. While this category lies outside of the policy realm proper, this can provide an avenue for the communication of historical and archaeological findings into the policy realm. Smith (2021: 1066) argues that, for addressing relevance,

> a potentially productive approach is to focus on the scientists in the target domains, rather than the policy-makers. This makes sense for both policy and science. Policymakers on social issues are not going to pay attention to archaeologists. A local politician looking to design policy on, for example, urban neighbourhoods will look at work by sociologists and economists. If archaeologists can convince scholars in these fields that our data are relevant and useful, we can play a small, indirect role in policy-making.

One reason for this suggestion is the difficulty of the policy process, a point underlined from a range of perspectives in some of the contributions to this volume. Embedding historical and archaeological understanding and knowledge in any sort of policy-orientated administrative body can be extremely time-consuming, as the experience of colleagues working with policy fora in the European Commission and in the UK have discovered (Hill et al., this volume) as well as within the USA (Murphy's contribution, this volume; see also Crabtree, this volume). The fourth category in Table 3 lists various audiences in the policy realm. This list is taken from policy scholar Vivian Tseng (2012), with the addition of the United Nations domain (see Conceiçao, this volume).

The lesson may be, in consequence, that while those who have the opportunity should continue to directly engage with policy and planning fora at all levels, engagement through community activism, NGOs and a range of other pressure-groups may be just as, and possibly more effective for those historians and archaeologists who are directly engaged with the present-day inhabitants of the regions in which they work (Crowley et al. 2022; Kaufman et al. 2018).

4.3 Question Three: Who Decides What Is Relevant?

General pleas for the relevance of our research (Barker et al. 2016; Guldi and Armitage 2014; Logan 2023) have accomplished little in the policy area. One reason is a faulty understanding of what relevance is and where it comes from. When knowledge moves from one field (such as history or archaeology) to another (such as the policy domain), only members of the second domain can determine whether the knowledge is relevant to their concerns (Fischhoff 2013; Kieser and Leiner 2011). "Only practitioners are in a position to authentically attribute relevance to knowledge" (Kieser and Leiner 2011: 897). If one were to claim, in an archaeology journal to an audience of peers, that a research finding is relevant to understanding the effects of climate change today, it will have little actionable impact. But if scholars or experts in the realm of climate change mitigation and adaptations—such as writers of reports by the Intergovernmental Panel on Climate Change (IPCC)—were to see our results and consider them useful, they can establish the relevance of our findings. This is one reason Kohler and Rockman (2020) urge archaeologists (and historians) to collaborate with the IPCC process.

A more extreme view is that unless a claim is accepted in the receiving domain and acted upon, it is not—and cannot be—relevant. Our findings need to be more than potentially relevant in some hypothetical sense; they need to be actionable and accepted in the target domain. This is why the participation of policy experts and practitioners is so important in projects such as this one; without the participation of such experts, our claims of relevance are empty (see Conceição, this volume).

4.4 Question Four: How Can Knowledge Be Transferred from Archaeology and History Into the Policy Realm?

The process of knowledge transfer for policy is known as translation: findings have to be translated for the users identified above. This normally requires specialized individuals or institutions—mediators—who carry out the translation; these are the "intermediaries" identified by Tseng, listed in Table 3 above. Intermediaries (mediators) are:

> organizations and individuals who translate and package research for use by legislators, agency staff, and nonprofit and private service providers. They also broker relationships between researchers and practitioners/policymakers. The number of intermediaries has proliferated in recent decades. Advocacy groups and think tanks play an important role in determining which policy ideas gain ground, which reform efforts fail, and how money gets appropriated (Tseng 2012: 5).

A big problem for archaeology and history is that we have few established intermediaries who can translate our research in this way. A case in point is that of Chloe Hill (see Hill et al., below), the European Geosciences Union Policy Officer, whose role is specifically to enhance the EGU's connection with policymakers and organisations who work at the science-policy interface. But professional societies, such as the American Historical Association or the Society for American Archaeology, have little to offer in this respect. University press offices may serve this role in a superficial way, but with a focus on the general public, not the policy realm.

Further compounding the difficulties of translating our research into policy is that many scholars evidently accept what van Langenhove (2011) calls the "limestone model" of knowledge transfer. This model holds that the results of our research will slowly penetrate society, like water seeping through, and slowly shaping, limestone. Researchers just need to present their findings in a readable format, and someone in the policy realm will eventually find them. Akin and Schaufele (2017) call this the "knowledge deficit model": the public needs good knowledge, so scientists create it and the public finds it. Although these and other scholars of policy and science communication have demonstrated the inadequacy of this approach to knowledge transfer, it remains popular in history and archaeology. An obvious corrective to this, and one that is now generally seen as the best approach through which to engage interest, is to start from the present and work back, to begin by identifying and targeting the specific policy-related issues for which we believe our historical case studies can offer useful information and to show how that information bears on the contemporary challenges. This must, of course, be done sensitively, with an eye to the cultural and political contexts in question (Opitz et al. 2021; Kaufman et al. 2018), but it has the key advantage of focusing in on what policy-advisers and policy-makers themselves would consider relevant transferable knowledge. Smith's contribution to this volume offers a helpful exemplification of this template in respect of historical and contemporary urban sustainability.

5 The Scholarly Context

5.1 Archaeology vs. History

Archaeologists have had a great deal more success in transmitting the relevance of their work to policy-makers and stakeholders, in general, than historians, perhaps in part because they are often dealing with on-the-ground and clearly "visible" aspects of the human past and the impacts of human action in and on the landscape (see the contributions in Sect. 3 of this volume). It is also evident in the growth of the historical ecology movement in particular, where archaeology has been able to have direct input and participation—in the USA, for example, in NSF programs such as *Coupled Natural and Human Systems*, and the *Arctic Social Sciences Program*. Yet much of the world is not drawn into such initiatives or is at best marginal to their funding and operational reach.

5.2 Other Projects Linking Past and Present

One issue is the fact that, unlike in the case of those concerned with environmental protection, for example, there exists no over-arching strategy among historians for achieving the sort of impact that has been achieved in the more locally- or regionally-focused Type 3 studies. This is because Type 3 studies have largely been the result of highly localized situations, opportunities, practices and politics. Some initiatives do exist that provide an overarching institutional framework through which historians, among others, can become aware of, or address, relevant policy fora or become directly involved and institutionally integrated into such structures.

Perhaps the most prominent project in this respect to date has been IHOPE—the *Integrated History and Future of People on Earth*, part of the Future Earth initiative within the remit of the IPCC. IHOPE is focused on very long-term societal and biophysical systemic transformation and does place emphasis on communicating knowledge of past change, with the aim of informing about present and potential future socio-ecological and environmental challenges (https://ihopenet.org/). While some publications by the IHOPE team have devoted effort to establish quality of data and argumentation (Hartman et al. 2017), it remains the case that many of the IHOPE contributions put more emphasis on calls for relevance than on ensuring the rigor of their data and argumentation (Chase and Scarborough 2014; Costanza et al. 2007; Murphy and Crumley 2022).

Also under the Future Earth umbrella is the PAGES (*Past Global Changes*) network, providing a framework that brings researchers and projects together in order to support information collection and synthesis, reconstructions and the modeling of past climate, ecosystem, environmental and societal dynamics (https://www.pastglobalchanges.org/). Both of these bodies incorporate a large number of inter- and transdisciplinary projects relating to historical socio-ecological systems and their evolution at both macro- and micro-scales, and provide access to resources relevant to policy discourse. Other fora, such as the EU-funded MedCliVar (*Mediterranean Climate Variability and Predictability*) similarly include a historical dimension, although here it is less prominent, and again provide access to a substantial interdisciplinary network and to policy issues (https://www.medclivar.eu/). Additionally, historians are engaged with aspects of policy formation through individual membership of informal advisory groups, such as the UN Human Development Report office, in the preparation of material for the compilation of its annual reports, to name but one example (Conceiçao, this volume). The situation is, therefore, by no means without hope (Cooper 2012).

6 Into the Future with the Past

It is clear that if we want to influence policy and engage with the communities impacted by policy-makers' decisions, then we need to know precisely what it is that we think we can offer, to whom, and with what aim in mind (Murphy, this volume). We also need to identify those policy areas in which our research results have some relevance, preferably through the support, guidance and input of mediators who can provide links to policy fora. The role of mediators seems to us to be especially important and, as far as we can see at present, largely ignored in discussions in the historical literature. Mediators understand both the language through which policy fora can be addressed and the terms in which we need to present our argument for involvement, terms that the policy-makers themselves can recognize.

Initiating contact through the appropriate channels, presenting findings in an accessible and usable format (Rockman and Hritz 2020; Harrison et al. 2016), and publishing in appropriate policy-focused media are thus prerequisites that we need to prioritize. None of this is to suggest that "from the ground up" Type 3 local historical/archaeological initiatives should conform to a single pattern—each project or initiative will (and does) develop its own particular, locally-tailored approach. But in general historians and archaeologists need to begin the process of outreach rather than bemoan the fact that policy-makers as a rule do not reach out to historians (Jackson et al. 2017). Policy specialists must know from the beginning what potential applications within their own concerns historical research may have.

Much of what we have written in this Introduction is already part of the discipline-specific internal discourses of history, archaeology and, by extension, heritage management. But the contributors to this volume believe that while there has been plenty of debate about how to achieve a more effective integration—or at least awareness—of historical knowledge into policy, there is a pressing need for a more proactive approach, at least for those who believe that their work and insights have something to offer. At the outset of this Introduction we noted that reaching a situation where historical and archaeological evidence has a positive influence on policy decisions is a particularly difficult task. This volume illustrates many of these difficulties in detail, while also offering ways forward. We hope that this will prove helpful in formulating future strategic thinking in respect of practical actions to insert historical knowledge and insight more effectively into the processes informing environmental and sustainability policy planning.

References

Akin, H., and D. A. Schaufele. 2017. Overview of the science of science communication. In *The Oxford handbook of the science of science communication*, ed. K. H. Jamieson, D. M. Kahan, and D. A. Schaufele, 25–33. New York: Oxford University Press.

Armitage, D. 2012. What's the big idea? Intellectual history and the longue durée. *History of European Ideas* 38 (4): 493–507.

Barker, G., C. Roberts, C. Gosden, A. Horning, and K. Welham. 2016. *Reflections on archaeology*. London: The British Academy.

Black, N. 2001. Evidence based policy: Proceed with care. *British Medical Journal* 323:275–278.

Braudel, F. 1972. *The Mediterranean and the Mediterranean world in the age of Philip II*. Trans. S. Reynolds. New York: Harper and Row.

Burton, A. 2022. The role of civil society in policymaking: A CPRE case study. In *Lessons from the history of UK environmental policy*, ed. S. Owens, 26–32. London: British Academy.

Butzer, K. W. 1982. *Archaeology as human ecology: Method and theory for a contextual approach*. New York: Cambridge University Press.

Butzer, K. W. 2011. Geoarchaeology, climate change, sustainability: A Mediterranean perspective. In *Geoarchaeology, climate change, and sustainability*, ed. A. B. Brown, L. S. Basell, and K. W. Butzer, vol. 476, 1–14. New York: Geological Society of America.

Cash, D. W., W. C. Clark, F. Alcock, N. M. Dickson, N. Eckley, D. H. Guston, et al. 2003. Knowledge systems for sustainable development. *Proceedings of the National Academy of Sciences* 100 (14): 8086–8091.

Chase, A. F., and V. L. Scarborough, eds. 2014. *The resilience and vulnerability of ancient landscapes: Transforming Maya archaeology through iHOPE*. Vol. 24. Washington, DC: American Anthropological Association.

Chhetri, N., M. Stuhlmacher, and A. Ishtiaque. 2019. Nested pathways to adaptation. *Environmental Research Communications* 1 (1): 015001.

Clark, W. C., L. Van Kerkhoff, L. Lebel, and G. C. Gallopin. 2016. Crafting usable knowledge for sustainable development. *Proceedings of the National Academy of Sciences* 113:4570–4578.

Cooper, J. 2012. Weathering climate change. The value of social memory and ecological knowledge. *Archaeological Dialogues* 19 (1): 46–51. https://doi.org/10.1017/S1380203812000062.

Costanza, R., L. J. Graumlich, and W. Steffen, eds. 2007. *Sustainability or collapse? An integrated history and future of people on earth*. Cambridge, MA: MIT Press.

Cronon, W. 1992. A place for stories: Nature, history, and narrative. *Journal of American History* 78 (4): 1347–1376.

Crowley, K., R. Jackson, S. O'connell, D. Karunarthna, E. Anantasari, A. Retnowati, and D. Niemand. 2022. Cultural heritage and risk assessments: Gaps, challenges and future research directions for the inclusion of heritage within climate change adaptation and disaster management. *Journal of Climate Resilience and Sustainability* 1 (3): e45.

Da Luna, K., T. Kinnaird, E. Koparal, and J. Fleisger. 2022. Lessons for modern environmental and climate policy from iron age south Central Africa. In *Perspectives on public policy in societal-environmental crises: What the future needs from history*, ed. A. Izdebski, P. Filipkowski, and J. Haldon, 191–204. Cham: Springer Nature.

Dearing, J. A. 2011. Learning from the past. *Global Change* 77:16–19.

Dearing, J. A., A. K. Braimoh, A. Reenberg, B. L. Turner, and S. van der Leeuw. 2010. Complex land systems: The need for long time perspectives to assess their future. *Ecology and Society* 15 (4): 21. http://www.ecologyandsociety.org/vol15/iss4/art21/.

Degroot, D., K. Anchukaitis, M. Bauch, J. Burnham, F. Carnegy, J. Cui, et al. 2021. Towards a rigorous understanding of societal responses to climate change. *Nature* 591:539–550. https://doi.org/10.1038/s41586-021-03190-2.

Dugmore, A. J., T. H. McGovern, O. Vésteinsson, J. Arneborg, R. Streeter, and C. Keller. 2012. Cultural adaptation, compounding vulnerabilities and conjunctures in Norse Greenland. *Proceedings of the National Academy of Sciences* 109 (10): 3658–3663.

England, J., H. Elton, A. Hadland, Ç. Şenkul, P. Free, and W. J. Eastwood. 2022. Olive cultivation at high altitudes in Anatolia: Exploiting micro-localities in ancient Asia minor. In *Değişim Rüzgarları/Winds of Change*, ed. C. Roosevelt and J. Haldon, 219–227. Istanbul: RCAC.

Fields-Black, E., R. D. Hanks, T. F. Folk, R. Baldwin, E. P. Wiggers, A. Agha, D. D. Richter, and R. H. Coen. 2022. Resilience of coupled socio-ecological systems: Historic rice fields of the U.S. south. In *Perspectives on public policy in societal-environmental crises: What the future needs from history*, ed. A. Izdebski, P. Filipkowski, and J. Haldon, 273–289. Cham: Springer Nature.

Fischhoff, B. 2013. The sciences of science communication. *Proceedings of the National Academy of Sciences* 110:14033–14039.

Gerring, J. 2017. *Case study research: Principles and practices*. 2nd ed. New York: Cambridge University Press.

Gordon, P.E. 2020. Why historical analogy matters. *New York Review of Books* (NYR Daily, Jan 7, 2020). https://www.nybooks.com/daily/2020/01/07/why-historical-analogy-matters/

Guldi, J., and D. Armitage. 2014. *The history manifesto*. New York: Cambridge University Press.

Haldon, J., M. Eisenberg, L. Mordechai, A. Izdebski, and S. White. 2020. Lessons from the past, policies for the future: Resilience and sustainability in past crises. *Environment Systems and Decisions* 40:287–297.

Haldon, J., L. Mordechai, A. Dugmore, M. Eisenberg, G. Endfield, A. Izdebski, et al. 2024. Past answers to present concerns. The relevance of the premodern past for 21st century policy planners: Comments on the state of the field. *Wiley Interdisciplinary Reviews: Climate Change* 16 (1): e923.

Harrison, P., R. Dunford, I. Holman, and M. Rounsevell. 2016. Climate change impact modelling needs to include cross-sectoral interactions. *Nature Climate Change* 6:885–890. https://doi.org/10.1038/nclimate3039.

Hartman, S., A. E. J. Ogilvie, J. H. Ingimundarson, A. Dugmore, G. Hambrecht, and T. H. McGovern. 2017. Medieval Iceland, Greenland, and the new human condition: A case study in integrated environmental humanities. *Global and Planetary Change* 156:123–139. https://doi.org/10.1016/j.gloplacha.2017.04.007.

Hegmon, M., M. A. Peeples, and on behalf of the LTVTP-NABO Collaboration. 2018. The human experience of social transformation: Insights from comparative archaeology. *PLoS One* 13 (11): e0208060. https://doi.org/10.1371/journal.pone.0208060.

Hicks, M., Á. Einarsson, K. Anamthawat-Jónsson, Á. Edwald, Æ. T. Thórsson, and T. H. McGovern. 2016. Community and conservation: Documenting millennial scale sustainable resource use at Lake Mývatn, Iceland. In *The Oxford handbook of historical ecology and applied archaeology*, ed. C. Isendahl and D. Stump. Oxford University Press. https://doi.org/10.1093/oxfordhb/9780199672691.013.36.

Hotchkiss, C., E. Seekamp, and A. McGill. 2022. Strategies for meaningful engagement: A commentary on collaboration in archaeological climate adaptation planning. Parks stewardship forum 38(3): 412–427. George Wright Society. doi:https://doi.org/10.5070/P538358980.

Hoyer, D., and J. G. Manning. 2018. Empirical regularities across time, space, and culture: A critical review of comparative methods in ancient historical research. *Historia* 67 (2): 160–190.

Hulme, M. 2011. Reducing the future to climate: A story of climate determinism and reductionism. *Osiris* 26 (1): 245–266.

Izdebski, A., L. Mordechai, and S. White. 2018. The social burden of resilience: A historical perspective. *Human Ecology* 46 (3): 291–303.

Izdebski, A., K. Bloomfield, W. J. Eastwood, R. Fernandes, D. Fleitmann, P. Guzowski, et al. 2024. The emergence of interdisciplinary environmental history: Collaborative approaches to the late Holocene. *Annales. Histoire, Sciences Sociales*1–43. https://doi.org/10.1017/ahsse.2022.21.

Jackson, R., A. Dugmore, and F. Riede. 2017. Towards a new social contract for archaeology and climate change adaptation. *Archaeological Review from Cambridge, 211* 32 (2): 197.

Jackson, R., A. Dugmore, and F. Riede. 2018. Rediscovering lessons of adaptation from the past. *Global Environmental Change* 52:58–65. https://doi.org/10.1016/j.gloenvcha.2018.05.006.

Kates, R. W., W. R. Travis, and T. J. Wilbanks. 2012. Transformational adaptation when incremental adaptations to climate change are insufficient. *Proceedings of the National Academy of Sciences* 109:7156–7161.

Kaufman, B., C. Kelly, and R. S. Vachula. 2018. Paleoenvironment and archaeology provide cautionary tales for climate policymakers. *The Geographical Bulletin* 59 (1): 5–24.

Kieser, A., and L. Leiner. 2011. On the social construction of relevance: A rejoinder. *Journal of Management Studies* 48 (4): 891–898.

Knapp, A. B., ed. 1992. *Annales, archaeology, and ethnohistory*. New York: Cambridge University Press.

Kocka, J. 2003. Comparison and beyond. *History and Theory* 42:39–44.

Kohler, T. A., and M. Rockman. 2020. The IPCC: A primer for archaeologists. *American Antiquity* 85 (4): 627–651.

Koparal, E., V. Demirciler, and S. Turner. 2022. Archaeology for landscape management and planning: Historic landscape characterization of Urla (İzmir). *Arkeoloji Bilimleri Dergisi/Turkish Journal of Archaeological Sciences*140–154.

Koyama, M. 2015. Review of the history manifesto. By Jo Guldi and David Armitage. *The Journal of Economic History* 75 (2): 584–587.

Lane, P. J. 2015. Archaeology in the age of the Anthropocene: A critical assessment of its scope and societal contributions. *Journal of Field Archaeology* 40 (5): 485–498.

van Langenhove, L. 2011. Social sciences and policy impact: The case for a participatory approach. In *Social science and policy challenges—democracy, values and capacities*, ed. G. Papanagnou, 95–111. Paris: UNESCO.

Logan, A. L. 2023. We need social archaeology to understand resilience and build usable pasts. *African Archaeological Review* 40 (4): 819–822. https://doi.org/10.1007/s10437-023-09562-5.

Lucas, G. 2018. Periodization in archaeology. Starting in the ground. In *Time and history in prehistory*, ed. S. Souvatzi, A. Baysal, and E. Baysal. London: Routledge.chapt. 5

Matson, P., W. C. Clark, and K. Andersson. 2016. *Pursuing sustainability: A guide to the science and practice*. Princeton, NJ: Princeton University Press.

Mayr, E. 1961. Cause and effect in biology. *Science* 134:1501–1506.

Murphy, J. T., and C. L. Crumley, eds. 2022. *If the past teaches, what does the future learn? Ancient urban regions and the durable future*. Delft: TU Delft and IHOPE.

Nelson, M. C., K. W. Kintigh, D. R. Abbott, and J. M. Anderies. 2010. The cross-scale interplay between social and biophysical context and the vulnerability of irrigation-dependent societies: Archaeology's long-term perspective. *Ecology and Society* 15 (3): 31. http://www.ecologyandsociety.org/vol15/iss3/art31/.

van de Noort, R. 2013. *Climate change archaeology: Building resilience from research in the world's coastal wetlands*. Oxford: Oxford University Press.

Opitz, R., C. Strawhacker, P. Buckland, J. Cothren, T. Dawson, A. Dugmore, G. Hambrecht, et al. 2021. A lockpick's guide to dataARC: Designing infrastructures and building communities to enable transdisciplinary research. *Internet Archaeology* 56. https://doi.org/10.11141/ia.56.15.

Peker, E. et al. 2023–24. Rainwater harvesting for climate change adaptation: Training programme for municipalities. London: British Institute at Ankara. https://biaa.ac.uk/research/rainwater_harvesting_for_climate_change_adaptation

Ragin, C. C. 2014. *The comparative method: Moving beyond qualitative and quantitative strategies*. 2nd ed. Berkeley: University of California Press.

Reimer, B., and M. Brett. 2013. Scientific knowledge and rural policy: A long-distant relationship. *Sociologia Ruralis* 53 (3): 272–290.

Rick, T. C., and D. H. Sandweiss. 2020. Archaeology, climate, and global change in the age of humans. *Proceedings of the National Academy of Sciences* 117 (15): 8250–8253. www.pnas.org/cgi/doi/10.1073/pnas.2003612117.

Riede, F. 2014. Towards a science of past disasters. *Natural Hazards* 71 (1): 335–362.

Riede, F., P. Andersen, and N. Price. 2016. Does archaeology need an ethical promise? *World Archaeology* 48 (4): 466–481.

Riris, P., and J. G. de Souza. 2021. Formal tests for resistance-resilience in archaeological time series. *Frontiers in Ecology and Evolution* 9. https://doi.org/10.3389/fevo.2021.740629.

Riris, P., F. Silva, E. Crema, A. Palmisano, E. Robinson, P. Siegel, and X. Ren. 2024. Frequent disturbances enhanced the resilience of past human populations. *Nature* 629:837–842.

Rockman, R., and C. Hritz. 2020. Expanding use of archaeology in climate change response by changing its social environment. *Proceedings of the National Academy of Sciences* 117 (15): 8295–8302.

Roosen, J., and D. R. Curtis. 2018. Dangers of noncritical use of historical plague data. *Emerging Infectious Disease journal* 24 (1): 103–110. https://doi.org/10.3201/eid2401.170477.

Runciman, W. G. 1989. *A treatise on social theory, 1: The methodology of social theory*. Cambridge: Cambridge University Press.

Shafer, H. J. 2016. Research design and sampling techniques. In *Field methods in archaeology*, ed. T. R. Hester, H. J. Shafer, and K. L. Feder, 7th ed. New York: Routledge.chapt. 3

Smith, M. E. 2000. Archaeology in the middle of political conflict in Yautepec, Mexico. In *Working together: Native Americans and archaeologists*, ed. K. E. Dongoski, M. Aldenderfer, and K. Doehner, 191–197. Washington, DC: Society for American Archaeology.

Smith, M. E., ed. 2012. *The comparative archaeology of complex societies*. New York: Cambridge University Press.

Smith, M. E. 2021. Why archaeology's relevance to global challenges has not been recognized. *Antiquity* 95:1061–1069. https://doi.org/10.15184/aqy.2021.42.

Smith, M. E. 2023a. How can research on past urban adaptations be made useful for sustainability science? *Global Sustainability* 6:e4. https://doi.org/10.1017/sus.2023.2.

Smith, M. E. 2023b. Making good arguments in archaeology. In *Discourse and argumentation in archaeology: Conceptual and computational approaches*, ed. C. González-Pérez, P. Martin-Rodilla, and M. Pereira-Fariña, 37–54. New York: Springer.

Spielmann, K., M. A. Peeples, D. M. Glowacki, and A. Dugmore. 2016. Early warning signals of social transformation: A case study from the US southwest. *PLoS One* 11 (10): 1–18.

Travis, C., P. Holm, F. Ludlow, C. Kostick, R. McGovern, and J. Nicholls. 2023. Cowboys, cod, climate, and conflict: Navigations in the digital environmental humanities. In *Routledge handbook of the digital environmental humanities*, ed. C. Travis, D. Dixon, L. Bergmann, R. Legg, and A. Crampsie, 17–39. London-New York: Routledge.

Tseng, V. 2012. The uses of research in policy and practice. *Social Policy Report* 26 (1): 1–22.

Tubi, A., L. Mordechai, E. Feitelson, P. Kay, and D. Tamir. 2022. Can we learn from the past? Towards better analogies and historical inference in society-environmental change research. *Global Environmental Change* 76:102570.

Tuinstra, W., E. Turnhout, and W. Halffman. 2019. Usable knowledge. In *Environmental expertise: Connecting science, policy and society*, ed. E. Turnhout, W. Halffman, and W. Tuinstra, 126–140. New York: Cambridge University Press.

Turchin, P., R. Brennan, T. Currie, K. Feeney, P. Francois, D. Hoyer, et al. 2015. Seshat: The global history databank. *Cliodynamics. The Journal of Quantitative History and Cultural Evolution* 6 (1): 77–107.

Turchin, P., T. E. Currie, H. Whitehouse, P. François, K. Feeney, D. Mullins, et al. 2018. Quantitative historical analysis uncovers a single dimension of complexity that structures global variation in human social organization. *Proceedings of the National Academy of Sciences* 115:e144–E151. https://doi.org/10.1073/pnas.1708800115.

Turchin, P., H. Whitehouse, J. Larson, E. Cioni, J. Reddish, D. Hoyer, et al. 2023. Big gods and big science: Further reflections on theory, data, and analysis. *Religion, Brain and Behavior* 13 (2): 218–231. https://doi.org/10.1080/2153599X.2022.2065354.

Turner, N., and P. R. Spalding. 2013. "We might go back to this"; drawing on the past to meet the future in northwestern North American indigenous communities. *Ecology and Society* 18 (4): e29.

Vésteinsson, O., M. Hegmon, J. Arneborg, G. Rice, and W. G. Russell. 2019. Dimensions of inequality. Comparing the North Atlantic and the US southwest. *Journal of Anthropological Archaeology* 54:172–191. https://doi.org/10.1016/j.jaa.2019.04.004.

Wainright, J. et al. 2021–2023. Fragile landscapes: Past, present and future of sustainable water management on the Konya Plain, Turkey. London: British Institute at Ankara. https://biaa.ac.uk/research/fragile-landscapes/

White, S., Q. Pei, K. Kleemann, L. Dolák, H. Huhtamaa, and C. Camenisch. 2023. New perspectives on historical climatology. *WIREs Climate Change* 14 (1): e808.

Why and How Can Insights from History Help to Advance Human Development?

Pedro Conceição

Abstract Is advancing human development feasible as we confront narratives of limits to growth, planetary boundaries, ecosystem collapse? In framing, and addressing, this question, the natural sciences dominate, as we can see from the influence of the IPCC on climate policy and debate. But it is clear that the natural sciences are not enough because people are the protagonists in shaping how we address the question. To fully account for the possibilities to advance human development at a time of dangerous planetary change also needs a deeper engagement with the humanities. This chapter reviews the potential held by history, and environmental history in particular, to contribute. History helps to bring human agency to the fore, and not describe humans as passive recipients of environmental change, which results in environmental determinism. History also brings to the fore contingency, including intended and unintended consequences of actions taken to respond to specific threats or shocks. In short, by engaging with history, we bring the human back in, recognizing people as informed agents.

Keywords Human development · Humanities · Planetary change · Agency

1 Atoms in Motion

In the first of his celebrated lectures on physics, physicist Richard Feynman asks: "If, in some cataclysm, all of scientific knowledge were to be destroyed, and only one sentence passed on to the next generations of creatures, what statement would contain the most information in the fewest words?" Feynman's answer was "atoms

P. Conceição (✉)
Human Development Report Office, United Nations Development Program, New York City, USA
e-mail: pedro.conceicao@undp.org

J. F. Haldon, R. Fernandes (eds.), *Bridging History and Policy*, Understanding Complex Systems, https://doi.org/10.1007/978-3-032-24379-9_2

in motion." These three words convey the atomic hypothesis that all matter is composed of little particles in constant motion.[1]

The theory is only an approximation of "the truth" (atoms are composed of even tinier particles) but it is powerful because it not only explains many attributes of matter but it is also the foundation for other branches of science, from chemistry to biology. It shows how science takes us beyond our immediate perceptions (even with the most powerful microscopes, atoms are virtually impossible to see) and what may seem like many disparate things with a multitude of shapes and colors (rocks, buildings, organisms, water, air) towards a simple theory, reached through reasoning and experiments. Science often makes us see the world afresh, identifying risks unseen by the naked eye and novel ways to improve lives.

This is exactly what is happening with climate change. Science is the basis of our understanding of climate risks and of what we need to do to mitigate climate change. Beyond the glare of the climate emergency, science is telling us that this is but one of a set of processes of dangerous planetary change that poses risks to people and all life on our planet. The increase in the frequency of new and reemerging zoonotic diseases, the loss of biodiversity and of ecosystem integrity are other examples. This is happening not locally or regionally, as has been the case for millennia, but globally and at an unprecedented pace.[2]

The term "Anthropocene," even though it has not been formally adopted by geologists as an epoch in the geological time scale, has been used to capture this new planetary reality.[3] Much like the atomic hypothesis takes us beyond our immediate perceptions to a more fundamental understanding of all matter, the reality described as the Anthropocene points to human choices as the drivers of a wide range of dangerous planetary change that may seem disparate and distinct. Life and geological processes have been mutually constitutive over billions of years, since life first emerged on our planet, but for the first time ever one species—ourselves—is consciously driving planetary transformations (Lenton 2019). Resulting catastrophic

[1] The videos of the lectures are available here: https://www.feynmanlectures.caltech.edu/flptapes.html. The first lesson is titled "Atoms in motion."

[2] The so-called "great acceleration" in human-driven changes to planetary processes is often described to have started in the middle of the twentieth century (Steffen et al. 2015).

[3] Head et al. (2022a, 2022b) presented evidence supporting the case for a new epoch, with Crawford Lake, in Canada, proposed by the Anthropocene Working Group as a "golden spike" (formally, a global boundary stratotype section and point) candidate site of the Anthropocene (McCarthy et al. 2023). Geologists decided not to adopt the recommendation of the working group (Witze 2024) but the debate on the implications of this decision continues (Zalasiewicz et al. 2024). This decision does not detract from the widely accepted notion that humans are transforming our planet in unprecedented ways, with the concept of the Anthropocene having gone beyond geology: Malhi (2017) providing perspectives ranging from ecology to evolutionary biology. Even beyond the natural sciences, many other disciplines look at the Anthropocene as a "emergent, unfolding, intensifying event" (Edgeworth et al. 2023: 1; see also Gibbard et al. 2022a, 2022b; Bauer et al. 2021; Waters et al. 2023, offer a contrasting view). Many historians have engaged with the concept, see, for example Butzer 2015; Thomas 2014, 2019; Frankopan 2023.

risks potentially threatening human existence depend for the first time ever more on human choices than natural hazards (Ord 2020).

In sum, the widely accepted notion that humans are transforming our planet in unprecedented ways has fundamental implications for current and future prospects for human development.[4] And the fact that we are both the protagonists and those affected implies that we have to have some mental model—either explicitly stated or, as happens most frequently, implicit—about how people make choices, why, and what it would take to make different choices.

2 People as Atoms in Motion

Much of economics, political science, international relations and other social sciences often draws from a model of human behaviour where people are understood to be selfishly making choices to fulfil what they like while assuming that everyone else is doing the same. There are many variations of this model, but at their core they all see people more or less like atoms in motion, engaging in social, economic, and political interactions that advance each individual's self-interest. And while atoms are constrained in their movement by the laws of physics, people need to abide by some set of rules of the game that shape their interaction (including those codified in formal institutions or implicit in social norms) (North 1990).

A bare-bones version of this model assumes that people's behaviour is determined by what they like (their preferences) and their beliefs (which they form by seeking and processing information about the world). The two are independent. That is, if someone does not like to walk around the street drenched, the choice about whether to leave home with an umbrella depends on the belief on whether it is going to rain. With a bit more structure on preferences (things like if one prefers apples to oranges, and oranges to pears, then one also prefers apples to pears) this—not at all implausible—model of human behaviour goes a long way in helping to understand a range of social and economic processes. And to provide much policy guidance on a wide range of subjects, from the very consequential decision about what to tax and how much, to the more banal question of determining the fairest and most efficient way of dealing with an overbooked flight.[5]

Under this model, one perennial recommendation to address challenges like climate change is to make people incorporate in their behaviour the negative impact of choices that result in greenhouse gases emissions. The negative impact is widely dispersed through society, but it is possible to estimate a social cost of carbon emissions (the culprits driving climate change) by integrating biophysical with economic

[4] United Nations Development Programme (UNDP) 2020.

[5] Description and examples draw from Elster (2015, 2020) and Hoff and Stiglitz (2016). The overbooked flight is an example of how the field of mechanism design helps decision making. One of the founders of mechanism design, economist Eric Maskin, called it the engineering side of economics (Maskin 2008).

simulations.[6] With these estimates, it is also possible to get a sense of how practices like subsidizing fossil fuels cost society (burning fossil fuels to produce energy is one of the activities that contributes the most to climate change). The International Monetary Fund (IMF) regularly publishes estimates of these costs, which run globally into the \$6–7 trillion range, equivalent to the size of the Japanese economy or 6–7% of global Gross Domestic Product (GDP) (Black et al. 2023). Moreover, the benefits of these subsidies accrue more (in relative terms) to well-off people, which do not need them as much as those living on low incomes. It therefore seems like a no-brainer to remove these subsidies: it would curb climate change because it would price something people today think of as free, it would generate much potential revenue, and it would be progressive, benefiting the most those that have the least.

Putting a price on carbon would be the way to go to mitigate climate change. Economic incentives would be aligned, and this would certainly be important, as has been demonstrated many times, particularly for firms and business investment and technological adoption decisions. But people do not simply respond to economic incentives. A recent study found that household gas consumption during an energy crisis in Europe during the 2022/23 winter did not respond to economic incentives (Dertwinkel-Kalt et al. 2024). Moreover, it has proven exceedingly difficult in practice to implement measures that price carbon according to its social cost, let alone taking the partial step of reducing fossil fuel subsidies. This is not due to hostility to, for example, taxation, because there are multiple ways of implementing such carbon pricing (through regulation or cap and trade schemes for emissions, which have been successfully deployed in many contexts).[7] There are many reasons that make phasing out fossil fuel subsidies difficult (Rentschler and Bazilian 2017). But one lurking in the background is rarely mentioned: could the model of human behaviour have limitations that blind us to some of the reasons that make it difficult to implement what looks like rational and fair interventions?

One of the seemingly innocuous and reasonable assumptions of the bare-bones model of human behaviour is that people deal with gains and losses as perfectly equivalent. Preferences are assumed to be such that a loss of \$100 dollars is disliked in exactly the same way a gain of \$100 is liked. Yet, much evidence suggests that people deviate from this assumption: they care more about losing \$100 than gaining

[6] More rigorously, this social cost corresponds to the damages associated with an additional unit of greenhouse houses emissions. It is possible to have emissions converted to carbon (because CO_2 is one of the greatest contributors and for other greenhouse gases it is possible to find an equivalence between their climate forcing and that produced by these other gases). Thus, usual estimates refer to the social cost of carbon, expressed as a value in dollars per ton of CO_2 emissions). See Nordhaus 2017; Barrage and Nordhaus 2024, for one approach and set of estimates of the social cost of carbon. This same approach can be used for other planetary challenges, like biodiversity loss, Frank and Sudarshan 2024.

[7] Cap and trade schemes put an overall cap on emissions of damaging substances and distribute permits to emit those gases across emitting firms, which are then free to trade them with each other, leading to the emergence of a market and a price for the emissions. For instance, in the United States, the acid rains were curbed through the implementation of cap-and-trade scheme https://www.epa.gov/acidrain/acid-rain-program

the same amount.[8] This is called loss aversion. With this insight, it may not be that surprising, or seem that "irrational," for people to react against the prospect of a reduction in a fuel subsidy they currently benefit from.[9] Even if they are promised that they will receive back a money transfer equal to the subsidy that was lost, loss aversion may imply that they would still resist. Even people living on low incomes that are promised a transfer larger than the amount they currently benefit from through the subsidy could resist if the increment is not large enough to compensate for loss aversion.[10]

Loss aversion is only one of the "anomalies" that economists and other social scientists have recently been "discovering" in the booming fields of behavioural economics and behavioural science. A leading review of these findings identified three types of "anomalies," describing them as non-standard preferences, beliefs, and cognition (DellaVigna 2009). Loss aversion is an example of non-standard preferences. We have already seen how accounting for loss aversion could help explain why people may react against the implementation of seemingly rational and beneficial policies framed under assumptions that ignore it. Another example of non-standard preferences is so-called "social preferences:" the idea that people can care not only about their own self-interest, but also give some weight to other people's welfare (Fehr and Charness 2025). Social preferences have implications for how people view things like income redistribution which, in turn, is shaped in part by how much economic inequality people accept and what is considered to be fair. Inequalities in both driving the planetary pressures of the Anthropocene and being exposed to their harms are rampant, both within and across countries.[11]

So how to redress inequalities? Normative theories premised on the bare bones model of human behaviour often hold a meritocratic view: inequalities due to differences in effort or skill are fair, those due to luck are unfair (Fleurbaey 1995). But the reality is that social preferences are very heterogenous across countries. In many countries, the majority of people do hold meritocratic views, but in others the majority of the population is libertarian—meaning that they consider that any inequality is acceptable (Fig. 1). And a varying but substantial share of the population holds an egalitarian view—no inequalities are acceptable. It turns out that in some cases it is the difference between the share of egalitarians and libertarians that matters the most as to how countries are perceived, not the share of meritocratic people. For example, the US and Norway have vastly different policies when it comes to social safety nets and income redistribution more broadly but they have a roughly similar

[8] More rigorously, choices reflecting a larger aversion to potential losses than the appeal of an equal-size gain relative to some point of reference (Tversky and Kahneman 1992; Kahneman and Tversky 1979).

[9] Efforts to measure economic rationality have proven consistently difficult (Nitsch et al. 2022). Assigning the label "rational" to the assumptions about preferences and beliefs of the standard selfish choice model discussed here is a matter of nomenclature.

[10] This example draws from United Nations Development Programme (UNDP) 2022, where it was developed in more detail.

[11] United Nations Development Programme (UNDP) 2020.

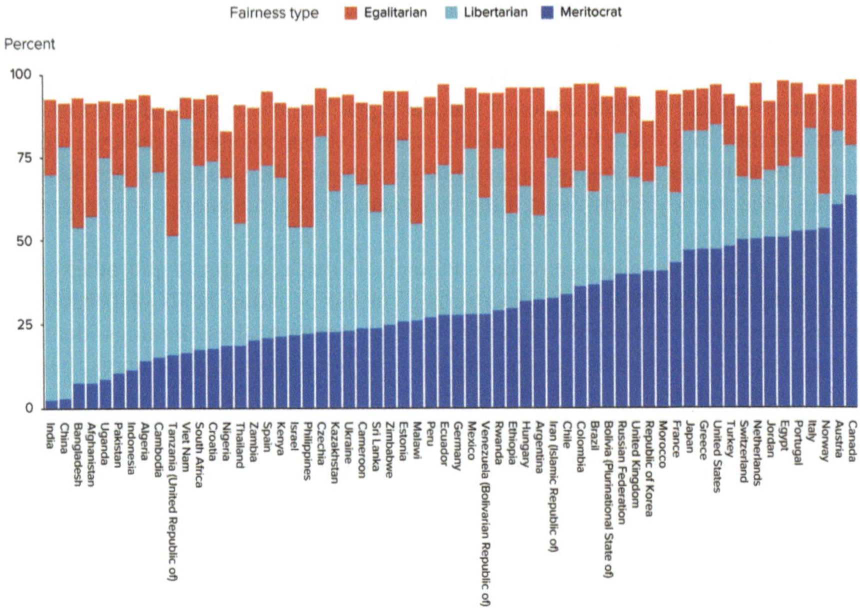

Fig. 1 Social preferences. Note: Egalitarians find all inequalities unfair, meritocratic individuals accept inequalities due to differences in performance as fair but those due to luck as unfair and libertarians accept all inequalities as fair. Source: Almås et al. 2024

share of the population (which is the majority) holding the meritocratic view. However, the share of libertarians is much higher in the US than Norway (Almås et al. 2020).

Non-standard beliefs include aspects like motivated reasoning, where preferences and goals have a direct bearing on belief formation (Zimmermann 2020). Going back to the decision on whether to take an umbrella, wishful thinking may lead someone to decide to leave the umbrella at home, even if it the skies are grey (Bénabou and Tirole 2016; Engelmann et al. 2024). More consequentially, unless you really don't like to be drenched, someone may not update political beliefs after being given new information that goes against those beliefs, dismissing that information as unimportant or even fake (Barron et al. 2025; Stagnaro et al. 2023). The assumption of the bare bones model of human behaviour that people update their beliefs based on new information drives much of the effort of international collaborative scientific initiatives like the IPCC or IPBES that synthesize the scientific consensus on, respectively, climate change and biodiversity. Warnings from science about what may come to pass if we don't act on the challenges of the Anthropocene should lead people to update their beliefs.[12]

[12] Scientists have been making vocal warnings to humanity (Ripple et al. 2017; Merz et al. 2023), as well as to the United Nations and the public at large (Hansen et al. 2025).

There is no question that science has been central in shaping beliefs about climate change (Cointe and Guillemot 2023). Today, most people believe that human actions are the cause for climate change (Steg 2023). Focusing on the climate denialists at the margins is not helpful and may even be counterproductive (Bretter and Schulz 2023; Gounaridis and Newell 2024). But a very different thing are the beliefs about whether we are doing too little or too much to address climate change. In that respect, beliefs are often polarized along cleavages that are associated with identity conflicts and longstanding political rifts (McCoy and Somer 2019; Bradley and Chauchard 2022).[13] These differences are exacerbated and leveraged for political gain with strategies of identifying someone over something to blame for grievances (McCoy et al. 2018). Issuing another report or warning by scientist with scientific information about the dangers of climate change addresses none of these challenges. Yet, reports and warnings keeping coming out, perhaps driven by the unstated assumptions of the bare bones model that people update their beliefs on the basis of new information, when belief formation is driven by much more.[14]

As the "discovery" of non-standard preferences and non-standard beliefs illustrates, the bare bones model of human behaviour is obviously wrong.[15] But the point here is not to challenge that model, or list the modifications needed to incorporate "anomalies," on epistemic grounds. The point here is a bit less demanding, and more pragmatic: to assess if the bare bones model is being helpful to make decisions that advance human development while easing planetary pressures and, if not or not sufficiently, what else might be required.

In science, we can rely on models known to be wrong if they do a good enough job at giving us what we need to achieve our goals. For example, if I am driving from London and need to get to Birmingham to make a meeting on time, Newtonian classical mechanics is enough. We now know fully well that this theory is "wrong," in the sense that it does not incorporate the insights from Einstein's theories of restricted and general relativity. Still, with a set time for when I need to be in Birmingham, the distance between the two cities and an estimate of the average driving speed, classical mechanics suffices to help me determine when I need to leave London. But the GPS I will be relying on to guide me through the streets and highways better not use Newtonian classical physics. If it did, I wouldn't make it to my destination, because classical mechanics needs to be adjusted for both restricted and general relativity effects (classical relativity tells us that GPS satellites moving very fast—in fact, accelerating as they remain on their orbit—relative to my car exhibit time dilation, and because satellites are very far from the earth they have

[13] These rifts are sometimes used by political actors and leaders to leverage group-based grievances and us versus them competition to mobilize supporters. Competing political beliefs, opinions and worldview are often also basis of social identity (Hobolt et al. 2021).

[14] A good account as to how good people come to hold bad beliefs is Levy (2022).

[15] Just for completeness, when it comes to non-standard cognition, close to 200 so-called cognitive bias have been documented (Davis 2023; Stango and Zinman 2022; Goeree and Louis 2021). For a compelling visualization of the multitude of cognitive biases, see: https://commons.wikimedia.org/wiki/File:Cognitive_bias_codex_en.svg

exerted on them less gravitational pull than my car, which general relativity tells us makes clocks in the satellites run slower) (Ashby 2003).

Much of the current policy debate is framed under a fairly narrow set of assumptions about human motivations and behaviours that frustrates policymakers, because often we know what needs to be done but we somehow struggle to do it—like acting decisively and collectively to mitigate climate change. So what to do?

It often seems that an unstated assumption is that humans are seen as "Malthusian," bound to exploit resources with no end until their backs are against the wall. This draws from economist and philosopher Amartya Sen contrast between how Condorcet and Malthus saw people acting to balance population growth with the means available to sustain them (Sen 1994). Malthus argued that only when people surpassed their means of subsistence would population growth start to decline, while Condorcet held the view that people could exercise reasoned agency to confront problems. Many of the narratives and messaging around the Anthropocene appear to have a distinct goal to scare people into acting. Or else, we are told, limits or boundaries will be trespassed that risk societal collapse. Science has been mobilized to justify, sustain and support this account, but so has history, sometimes with explicit links between narratives of societal collapse of the past and the need to learn the lesson now as we confront climate change so that we don't collapse as well (Diamond 2005).

It is important to make an important distinction here. It is one thing to disseminate findings from science that show the risks of reaching tipping points in biophysical systems as a result of climate change that can lead to catastrophic outcomes like the collapse of the Atlantic meridional overturning circulation (roughly, the Gulf stream) that will have devastating consequences (Armstrong McKay et al. 2022; Lenton et al. 2008; Ditlevsen and Ditlevsen 2023; Steffen et al. 2018). This is crucial information to inform the public and decision makers on the stakes and the importance of acting quickly and forcefully. It is quite another thing to assume that this information can be deployed strategically to get people to act out of fear of catastrophic collapse (Kemp et al. 2022). One of the reasons why people fail to act together even when they face the prospect of catastrophe is associated with the uncertainty not so much about potential effects, but about the timing of when the bad effects will happen (Barrett and Dannenberg 2012, 2014; Barrett 2013; Dannenberg and Barrett 2018). Just providing more and more scarier information about the catastrophe won't necessarily conduce people to act together, unless uncertainty about the timing is also reduced, but there is an overwhelming emphasis in the mobilization of scientific findings to characterize the boundaries and the consequences again, perhaps, because of the implicit model of people as Malthusian.[16]

Moreover, fear often paralyzes and polarizes, as people tend to react to fear by rallying around their ingroup with which they strongly identify with (Buchanan 2020; Wildavsky et al. 2001; Lerner and Keltner 2001; van Prooijen et al. 2015;

[16] The argument on the relative lack of effort in reducing and resolving timing uncertainty is elaborated in United Nations Development Programme (UNDP) (2024).

Campante et al. 2024; Halevy 2023; Jost et al. 2017; Satici et al. 2020). Fear can drive within group cooperation, but tends to harm cooperation across groups, and it is that kind of cooperation that is required to address global challenges like climate change (Obaidi et al. 2023; Chinn et al. 2020; Egan and Mullin 2017; Bretter and Schulz 2023; Hornung 2022; Barfuss et al. 2020; Barfuss and Mann 2022). Frames based on boundaries or limits in which science is invoked to present these as fixed and deterministic downplay the fact that boundaries or limits and peoples' choices are endogenous, that is, mutually determined.[17] Making people feel trapped in that they don't have a choice or say, curtails the scope for the broader discussions and processes of individual and public reasoning necessary to consider scientific facts (Biermann and Kim 2020). It deprives people of agency, and engenders instead distress and anxiety, with many young people overrepresented in expressing these emotions (Adger et al. 2022).

Science can be mobilized to help people reason and act to face the challenges of the Anthropocene in a very different way. It can be used to shape processes in which individual actions are meaningfully part of broader processes of cooperation so that people have agency (Toivonen 2022). People support actions on climate change when they see them as effective and fair, so science can be mobilized to show how this kind of policies work (Bergquist et al. 2022; Dechezleprêtre et al. 2022). Addressing climate change involves a portfolio of economic and other policies where science plays a crucial role in illuminating trade-offs between different options (Blanchard et al. 2023). Processes that are pluralistic and open, integrating different voices and valuations of what matters to people, including perspectives from Indigenous Peoples, can draw on science to design and implement action-oriented dialogues (Pascual et al. 2023; Zafra-Calvo et al. 2020). People often agree on concrete actions, which science has a critical role to inform—for example, people may hold very different beliefs on how much action one should take to address climate change and still agree that advancing renewable energy is a good thing (Hamilton et al. 2018). All of this points much more in the direction of seeing people as Condorcet did, as reasoning beings capable of using science to make choices that advance human development while easing planetary pressures, as opposed to seeing them as Malthusian agents.

The new interdisciplinary field of sustainable science dates only from around the turn from the twentieth to the twenty-first century (Bettencourt and Kaur 2011). But it has clearly shown that urgent action to address the challenges of the Anthropocene is a human problem (Clark and Harley 2020). For example, in mobilizing insights from the social sciences that show that hope does tend to support cooperation (Halevy 2017, 2023; Lerner and Keltner 2001). Hope-based framings of the Anthropocene could enhance action on these challenges (Bretter and Schulz 2023; Lehman et al. 2021). Hope, an emotion, is different from being optimistic or pessimistic about something (which is a belief) (Snyder 1995, 2000). Science can inform

[17] A compelling argument for this endogeneity is expressed in Cohen (1995), discussion of our planet's "carrying capacity" for human population.

our beliefs, and there are certainly many reasons to be pessimistic at the time of writing given slow action on climate change amongst others challenges of the Anthropocene. But science can also inspire hope even amongst the pessimists (Pereira et al. 2019; Raudsepp-Hearne et al. 2020).

Hope, and emotions more generally, is something absent in the bare bones model of human behaviour. We can try to run a catalogue of shortcomings of the bare bones model and try to supplement it with insights from behavioural economics and the broader social sciences. But something deeper is needed. Broadening the understanding of human motivations and behaviour. This calls for a much deeper engagement with the humanities to help us to confront the challenges of the Anthropocene. That is why history is needed, so that we see people not as atoms in motion, but as people.

3 People as People

Human development was inspired in part by Amartya Sen's critique of some of the assumptions of the selfish bare bones model of human behaviour described earlier (Sen 1973, 1977, 1997). Human development is about enabling people everywhere to live their lives to their full potential. To assess progress and evaluate policies the focus shifts from means, such as income, to ends: wellbeing (comprised of aspects like standards of living as well as achievements in health and education, as captured by the Human Development Index).[18] The human development approach provided a stark departure from the notion that progress meant simply holding ever more material resources. Instead, it focused on the ability of people to be and do what they value and have reason to value. Human development is not only about wellbeing, but also the ability of people to make different choices. As people reason about what they value and why, the new reality of the Anthropocene is becoming ever more present. It can no longer be left in the background of human choices but needs to be brought to the fore. And so, the next frontier in human development implies expanding freedoms while easing planetary pressures.

Science has shown that in the Anthropocene humans have the power to alter planetary processes. But humans also have the power to cooperate and make choices that ease planetary pressures. While avoiding a cataclysm of the type that Richard Feynman invoked is by no means certain, mobilizing history is crucial to not only avoid the worst, but enable people to continue to pursue and meet expanded aspirations. So, how could history help? Perhaps it could in at least three ways.

First, it can help instrumentally. That is, insights from history can be drawn by decisionmakers to inspire, guide, or justify discourse or actions (Haldon et al. 2025). Policymakers are often anxious for solutions, and "learning from the past" is a long-standing strategy to find them, particularly drawing from specific case studies that

[18] For a review of the concept of human development and its relationship with metrics, see Conceição et al. 2021.

they can relate to their challenges and opportunities.[19] Another instrumental contribution is by providing long term information about, for example, environmental variability and societal responses that can be helpful in applications in today's world such as improving index insurance programs (Bell et al. 2013).[20] Instrumental insights can also be mobilized in the other direction, for instance using contemporary frameworks to assess wellbeing and agency to interpret the past, encompassing also archaeology. For example, the popular notion of resilience in sustainability science and policy making aimed at sustainability has been deployed for historical analysis in several important and illuminating studies (Xoplaki et al. 2018; Haldon et al. 2020b; Haldon 2021; Mordechai and Haldon 2024). Amartya Sen's capabilities approach and even its quantification through the Human Development Index have been explored in ancient contexts (Smith 2019; Arponen et al. 2024; Munson and Scholnick 2022).[21] Another concept close to human development, human security, has also been used in an archeological context (Ingram and Patrick 2021). This casting of contemporary notions and concerns onto the past can help decisionmakers today to see the past not as something alien or irrelevant for today's complex societies, but instead as something that helps to "bring the human back in" to the fore of the policy debate. Often, however, the mobilization of insights from the past instrumentally appears more discursive than substantive (Mordechai and Tubi 2024).

A second contribution of history is more constitutive with the human development approach. It draws in part from the limitations of the purely instrumental "use" of history when decisionmakers seek to establish neat causal links. This is particularly harmful when the presumed causal links are either non-existent or more nuanced than some discourse in policymaking circles purports them to be. One example, already alluded to earlier, is around narratives of societal collapse due to either environmental hazards or people destroying the environmental foundations of their livelihoods. As noted, these narratives are deploying strategically in policymaking as a sort of warning about what might happen if we don't get our act together. Yet, the emerging field of history of climate and society has shown that narratives of societal collapse linked to environmental change are over-represented in popular and policy accounts (Haldon et al. 2018; Linkov et al. 2024; Butzer 2012; Butzer and Endfield 2012). They often ignore or downplay human capacities to adapt, transform, and change societies (Degroot et al. 2021, 2022).[22]

[19] What Haldon et al. (2025) classify as type 3 in their taxonomy of approaches to historical analysis that can be used by policymakers.

[20] The use of quantitative approaches to historical analysis also has the potential to advance insights on what drives social complexity and how it changes (Turchin et al. 2018b, 2018a, 2022; Scheffer et al. 2023).

[21] Smith (2023) uses another contemporary index, UN Habitat's City Prosperity Index to investigate patterns of urban adaptation over the long run.

[22] For the specific case how the Rapanui (Easter Island) case, that is often invoked as a case of self-imposed environmental harm leading to societal collapse, is not consistent with the evidence see, for example, Moreno-Mayar et al. 2024; Garlinghouse 2020.

This type of insights from history helps to bring human agency to the fore, rather than describing humans as passive recipients of environmental change, which results in environmental determinism. This is constitutive with human development because it reinforces the idea that enhancing human development is not only about improving wellbeing but also agency (Haldon et al. 2020a). This shows the importance of seeing people as agents, not patients, to use a phrase often invoked by Amartya Sen. It also shows the importance of beliefs and the cultural context in enabling people to respond to shocks (Haldon et al. 2022). Beliefs and culture are deep rooted and path dependent, and it is hard to understand how to make sense of them and how they change without history (Muthukrishna et al. 2021). One example are efforts and recommendations to change food diets to make them healthier and to contribute less to climate change (Springmann et al. 2016; Willett et al. 2019; Romanello et al. 2023). Given that dietary habits are deeply cultural and relational, implementing such recommendations could benefit from insights from history in recognizing people's agency to reason about what they value and why (Biesbroek et al. 2023).

Third, history is explicit about contingency, including intended and unintended consequences of actions taken to respond to specific threats or shocks. Much more important than linking climate events with collapse, it is crucial to learn from history about the contingent pathways that help establish what allows for societies to transform (Robbins Schug et al. 2023; Ellis 2024; Larsen 2023). This implies having as an integrated a perspective as possible in recognizing how deeply intertwined social, economic, and planetary processes. Despite the policymaker anxiety in finding solutions to solve problems, history can show how seeing challenges as isolated problems can have unintended consequences. For instance, a focus on electrification to mitigate climate change may ignore demand for minerals that destroy ecosystems and lead to the violation of human rights. Such narrow framings of separate problems to be solved are broadened when we mobilize insights from history, presenting the challenge of transforming our world as a "predicament to be navigated" (Sen 2014).

It is not easy to mobilize insights from history to inform policy debates and decisions. Objections range from lack of relevancy of the past to today's technologically advanced societies, to the need to focus on the future rather than the past. But it is hard to see how we can get unstuck from the lack of forceful action at the national level and internationally without history. Without it, we risk looking at the Anthropocene as something disempowering and fatalistic. But with history, we can see how people hold in themselves the potential to continue to expand human aspirations.

References

Adger, W. N., J. Barnett, S. Heath, and S. Jarillo. 2022. Climate change affects multiple dimensions of Well-being through impacts, information and policy responses. *Nature Human Behaviour* 6 (11): 1465–1473.

Almås, I., A. W. Cappelen, and B. Tungodden. 2020. Cutthroat capitalism versus cuddly socialism: Are Americans more meritocratic and efficiency-seeking than Scandinavians? *Journal of Political Economy* 128 (5): 1753–1788.

Almås, I., A. W. Cappelen, E. Sorensen, and B. Tungodden. 2024. Attitudes to inequality: Preferences and beliefs. *IFS Deaton Review of Inequalities. Oxford Open Economics* 3 (Supplement 1): i64–i79. https://doi.org/10.1093/ooec/odae001.

Armstrong McKay, D. I., A. Staal, J. F. Abrams, R. Winkelmann, B. Sakschewski, S. Loriani, I. Fetzer, et al. 2022. Exceeding 1.5°C global warming could trigger multiple climate tipping points. *Science* 377 (6611): eabn7950.

Arponen, V. P. J., R. Ohlrau, and T. Kerig. 2024. The capability approach and archaeological interpretation of transformations: On the role of philosophy for archaeology. *Open Archaeology* 10 (1): 20240013. https://doi.org/10.1515/opar-2024-0013.

Ashby, N. 2003. Relativity in the global positioning system. *Living Reviews in Relativity* 6 (1): 1–42.

Barfuss, W., and R. P. Mann. 2022. Modeling the effects of environmental and perceptual uncertainty using deterministic reinforcement learning dynamics with partial observability. *Physical Review E* 105 (3): 034409.

Barfuss, W., J. F. Donges, V. V. Vasconcelos, J. Kurths, and S. A. Levin. 2020. Caring for the future can turn tragedy into comedy for long-term collective action under risk of collapse. *Proceedings of the National Academy of Sciences* 117 (23): 12915–12922.

Barrage, L., and W. D. Nordhaus. 2024. Policies, projections, and the social cost of carbon: Results from the Dice-2023 model. *Proceedings of the National Academy of Sciences* 121 (13): e2312030121.

Barrett, S. 2013. Climate treaties and approaching catastrophes. *Journal of Environmental Economics and Management* 66 (2): 235–250.

Barrett, S., and A. Dannenberg. 2012. Climate negotiations under scientific uncertainty. *Proceedings of the National Academy of Sciences* 109 (43): 17372–17376.

Barrett, S., and A. Dannenberg. 2014. Sensitivity of collective action to uncertainty about climate tipping points. *Nature Climate Change* 4 (1): 36–39.

Barron, K., A. Becker, and S. Huck. 2025. Motivated political reasoning: On the emergence of belief-value constellations. *European Economic Review* 172:104929.

Bauer, A. M., M. Edgeworth, L. E. Edwards, E. C. Ellis, P. Gibbard, and D. J. Merritts. 2021. Anthropocene: Event or epoch? *Nature* 597 (7876): 332–332.

Bell, A. R., D. E. Osgood, B. I. Cook, K. J. Anchukaitis, G. R. McCarney, A. M. Greene, B. M. Buckley, and E. R. Cook. 2013. Paleoclimate histories improve access and sustainability in index insurance programs. *Global Environmental Change* 23 (4): 774–781.

Bénabou, R., and J. Tirole. 2016. Mindful economics: The production, consumption, and value of beliefs. *Journal of Economic Perspectives* 30 (3): 141–164.

Bergquist, M., A. Nilsson, N. Harring, and S. C. Jagers. 2022. Meta-analyses of fifteen determinants of public opinion about climate change taxes and laws. *Nature Climate Change* 12 (3): 235–240.

Bettencourt, L. M. A., and J. Kaur. 2011. Evolution and structure of sustainability science. *Proceedings of the National Academy of Sciences* 108 (49): 19540–19545.

Biermann, F., and R. E. Kim. 2020. The boundaries of the planetary boundaryframework: A critical appraisal of approaches to define a "safe operating space" for humanity. *Annual Review of Environment and Resources* 45 (1): 497–521.

Biesbroek, S., F. J. Kok, A. R. Tufford, M. W. Bloem, N. Darmon, A. Drewnowski, S. Fan, et al. 2023. Toward healthy and sustainable diets for the 21st century: Importance of sociocultural and economic considerations. *Proceedings of the National Academy of Sciences* 120 (26): e2219272120.

Black, M. S., A. A. Liu, I. W. Parry, and N. Vernon. 2023. *IMF Fossil Fuel Subsidies Data: 2023 Update*. Washington D.C.: International Monetary Fund. (Working Paper No. 2023/169).

Blanchard, O., C. Gollier, and J. Tirole. 2023. The portfolio of economic policies needed to fight climate change. *Annual Review of Economics* 15 (1): 689–722.
Bradley, M., and S. Chauchard. 2022. The ethnic origins of affective polarization: Statistical evidence from cross-national data. *Frontiers in Political Science* 4:920615.
Bretter, C., and F. Schulz. 2023. Why focusing on "climate change denial" is counterproductive. *Proceedings of the National Academy of Sciences* 120 (10): e2217716120.
Buchanan, A. 2020. *Our moral fate: Evolution and the escape from tribalism*. Cambridge, MA: MIT Press.
Butzer, K. W. 2012. Collapse, environment, and society. *Proceedings of the National Academy of Sciences* 109 (10): 3632–3639.
Butzer, K. 2015. Anthropocene as an evolving paradigm. *The Holocene* 25 (10): 1539–1541.
Butzer, K. W., and G. H. Endfield. 2012. Critical perspectives on historical collapse. *Proceedings of the National Academy of Sciences* 109 (10): 3628–3631.
Campante, F., E. Depetris-Chauvin, and R. Durante. 2024. The virus of fear: The political impact of Ebola in the United States. *American Economic Journal: Applied Economics* 16 (1): 480–509.
Chinn, S., P. S. Hart, and S. Soroka. 2020. Politicization and polarization in climate change news content, 1985-2017. *Science Communication* 42 (1): 112–129.
Clark, W. C., and A. G. Harley. 2020. Sustainability science: Toward a synthesis. *Annual Review of Environment and Resources* 45 (1): 331–386.
Cohen, J. E. 1995. Population growth and earth's human carrying capacity. *Science* 269 (5222): 341–346.
Cointe, B., and H. Guillemot. 2023. A history of the 1.5°C target. *WIREs Climate Change* 14 (3): e824.
Conceição, P., M. Kovacevic, and T. Mukhopadhyay. 2021. Chapter 4 - human development: A perspective on metrics. In *Measuring Human Capital*, ed. B. Fraumeni, 83–115. London: Academic.
Dannenberg, A., and S. Barrett. 2018. Cooperating to avoid catastrophe. *Nature Human Behaviour* 2 (7): 435–437.
Davis, J. W. 2023. Better than a bet: Good reasons for behavioral and tational choice assumptions in Ir theory. *European Journal of International Relations* 29 (2): 476–500.
Dechezleprêtre, A., A. Fabre, T. Kruse, B. Planterose, A. S. Chico, and S. Stantcheva. 2022. *Fighting climate change: International attitudes toward climate policies*. Cambridge, MA: National Bureau of Economic Research.
Degroot, D., K. Anchukaitis, M. Bauch, J. Burnham, F. Carnegy, J. Cui, K. de Luna, et al. 2021. Towards a rigorous understanding of societal responses to climate change. *Nature* 591 (7851): 539–550.
Degroot, D., K. J. Anchukaitis, J. E. Tierney, F. Riede, A. Manica, E. Moesswilde, and N. Gauthier. 2022. The history of climate and society: A review of the influence of climate change on the human past. *Environmental Research Letters* 17 (10): 103001.
DellaVigna, S. 2009. Psychology and economics: Evidence from the field. *Journal of Economic Literature* 47 (2): 315–372.
Dertwinkel-Kalt, M., C. Feldhaus, A. Ockenfels, and M. Sutter. 2024. Household reduction of gas consumption in the energy crisis is not explained by individual economic incentives. *Proceedings of the National Academy of Sciences* 121 (48): e2411740121.
Diamond, J. 2005. *Collapse: How societies choose to fail or succeed*. New York, NY: Penguin.
Ditlevsen, P., and S. Ditlevsen. 2023. Warning of a forthcoming collapse of the Atlantic meridional overturning circulation. *Nature Communications* 14 (1): 4254.
Edgeworth, M., P. Gibbard, M. Walker, D. Merritts, S. Finney, and M. Maslin. 2023. The stratigraphic basis of the Anthropocene event. *Quaternary Science Advances* 11:100088.
Egan, P. J., and M. Mullin. 2017. Climate change: US public opinion. *Annual Review of Political Science* 20 (1): 209–227.

Ellis, E. C. 2024. The Anthropocene condition: Evolving through social–ecological transformations. *Philosophical Transactions of the Royal Society B: Biological Sciences* 379 (1893): 20220255.

Elster, J. 2015. *Explaining social behavior: More nuts and bolts for the social sciences*. New York: Cambridge University Press.

Elster, J. 2020. *France before 1789: The unraveling of an absolutist regime*. Princeton, NJ: Princeton University Press.

Engelmann, J. B., M. Lebreton, N. A. Salem-Garcia, P. Schwardmann, and J. J. van der Weele. 2024. Anticipatory anxiety and wishful thinking. *American Economic Review* 114 (4): 926–960.

Fehr, E., and G. Charness. 2025. Social preferences: fundamental characteristics and economic consequences. *Journal of Economic Literature* 63 (2): 440–514.

Fleurbaey, M. 1995. Equality and responsibility. *European Economic Review* 39 (3): 683–689.

Frank, E., and A. Sudarshan. 2024. The social costs of keystone species collapse: Evidence from the decline of vultures in India. *American Economic Review* 114 (10): 3007–3040.

Frankopan, P. 2023. *The earth transformed: An untold history*. New York: Alfred A. Knopf.

Garlinghouse, T. 2020. Rethinking Easter Island's historic 'collapse'.

Gibbard, P., M. Walker, A. Bauer, M. Edgeworth, L. Edwards, E. Ellis, S. Finney, et al. 2022a. The Anthropocene as an event, not an epoch. *Journal of Quaternary Science* 37 (3): 395–399.

Gibbard, P. L., A. M. Bauer, M. Edgeworth, W. F. Ruddiman, J. L. Gill, D. J. Merritts, S. C. Finney, et al. 2022b. A practical solution: The Anthropocene is a geological event, not a formal epoch. *Episodes Journal of International Geoscience* 45 (4): 349–357.

Goeree, J. K., and P. Louis. 2021. M equilibrium: A theory of beliefs and choices in games. *American Economic Review* 111 (12): 4002–4045.

Gounaridis, D., and J. P. Newell. 2024. The social anatomy of climate change denial in the United States. *Scientific Reports* 14 (1): 2097.

Haldon, J. 2021. Historicizing resilience: The paradox of the medieval East Roman state—Collapse, adaptation, and survival. In *Empires and communities in the post-Roman and Islamic world, C. 400–1000 CE*, ed. R. Kramer and W. Pohl, 89–120. Oxford: Oxford University Press.

Haldon, J., L. Mordechai, T. P. Newfield, A. F. Chase, A. Izdebski, P. Guzowski, I. Labuhn, and N. Roberts. 2018. History meets palaeoscience: Consilience and collaboration in studying past societal responses to environmental change. *Proceedings of the National Academy of Sciences* 115 (13): 3210–3218.

Haldon, J., A. F. Chase, W. Eastwood, M. Medina-Elizalde, A. Izdebski, F. Ludlow, G. Middleton, et al. 2020a. Demystifying collapse: Climate, environment, and social agency in pre-modern societies. *Millennium* 17 (1): 1–33.

Haldon, J., M. Eisenberg, L. Mordechai, A. Izdebski, and S. White. 2020b. Lessons from the past, policies for the future: Resilience and sustainability in past crises. *Environment Systems and Decisions* 40 (2): 287–297.

Haldon, J., A. Izdebski, L. Kemp, L. Mordechai, and B. Trump. 2022. SDG 13: Climate action. How societies succeeded or failed to respond to environmental disruption. In *Before the UN sustainable development goals: A historical companion*, ed. M. Gutmann and D. Gorman, 385–424. Oxford: Oxford University Press.

Haldon, J., L. Mordechai, A. Dugmore, M. Eisenberg, G. Endfield, A. Izdebski, R. Jackson, et al. 2025. Past answers to present concerns. The relevance of the premodern past for 21st century policy planners: Comments on the state of the field. *WIREs Climate Change* 16 (1): e923.

Halevy, N. 2017. Preemptive strikes: Fear, hope, and defensive aggression. *Journal of Personality and Social Psychology* 112 (2): 224.

Halevy, N. 2023. Fear can promote competition, defensive aggression, and dominance complementarity. *Behavioral and Brain Sciences* 46:e63.

Hamilton, L. C., E. Bell, J. Hartter, and J. D. Salerno. 2018. A change in the wind? US public views on renewable energy and climate compared. *Energy, Sustainability and Society* 8 (1): 11.

Hansen, J. E., P. Kharecha, M. Sato, G. Tselioudis, J. Kelly, S. E. Bauer, R. Ruedy, et al. 2025. Global warming has accelerated: Are the United Nations and the public well-informed? *Environment: Science and Policy for Sustainable Development* 67 (1): 6–44.
Head, M. J., W. Steffen, D. Fagerlind, C. N. Waters, C. Poirier, J. Syvitski, J. A. Zalasiewicz, et al. 2022a. The great acceleration is real and provides a quantitative basis for the proposed Anthropocene series/epoch. *International Union of Geological Sciences* 45 (4): 359–376.
Head, M. J., J. A. Zalasiewicz, C. N. Waters, S. D. Turner, M. Williams, A. D. Barnosky, W. Steffen, et al. 2022b. The proposed Anthropocene epoch/series is underpinned by an extensive array of mid-20th century stratigraphic event signals. *Journal of Quaternary Science* 37 (7): 1181–1187.
Hobolt, S. B., T. J. Leeper, and J. Tilley. 2021. Divided by the vote: Affective polarization in the wake of the Brexit referendum. *British Journal of Political Science* 51 (4): 1476–1493.
Hoff, K., and J. E. Stiglitz. 2016. Striving for balance in economics: Towards a theory of the social determination of behavior. *Journal of Economic Behavior & Organization* 126:25–57.
Hornung, J. 2022. Social identities in climate action. *Climate Action* 1 (1): 4.
Ingram, S. E., and S. M. Patrick. 2021. Human securities, sustainability, and migration in the ancient U.S. southwest and Mexican northwest. *Ecology and Society* 26 (2):
Jost, J. T., C. Stern, N. O. Rule, and J. Sterling. 2017. The politics of fear: Is there an ideological asymmetry in existential motivation? *Social Cognition* 35 (4): 324–353.
Kahneman, D., and A. Tversky. 1979. Prospect theory: An analysis of decision under risk. *Econometrica* 47 (2): 263–291.
Kemp, L., C. Xu, J. Depledge, K. L. Ebi, G. Gibbins, T. A. Kohler, J. Rockström, et al. 2022. Climate endgame: Exploring catastrophic climate change scenarios. *Proceedings of the National Academy of Sciences* 119 (34): e2108146119.
Larsen, C. S. 2023. The past 12,000 years of behavior, adaptation, population, and evolution shaped who we are today. *Proceedings of the National Academy of Sciences* 120 (4): e2209613120.
Lehman, C., S. Loberg, M. Wilson, E. Gorham, and E. 2021. Ecology of the Anthropocene signals hope for consciously managing the planetary ecosystem. *Proceedings of the National Academy of Sciences* 118 (28): e2024150118.
Lenton, T. M. 2019. Biodiversity and global change: From creator to victim. In *Biological extinction: New perspectives*, ed. P. Dasgupta, P. H. Raven, and A. L. Mcivor, 34–79. Cambridge: Cambridge University Press.
Lenton, T. M., H. Held, E. Kriegler, J. W. Hall, W. Lucht, S. Rahmstorf, and H. J. Schellnhuber. 2008. Tipping elements in the earth's climate system. *Proceedings of the National Academy of Sciences* 105 (6): 1786–1793.
Lerner, J. S., and D. Keltner. 2001. Fear, anger, and risk. *Journal of Personality and Social Psychology* 81 (1): 146–159.
Levy, N. 2022. *Bad beliefs: Why they happen to good people*. Oxford: Oxford University Press.
Linkov, I., S. E. Galaitsi, B. D. Trump, E. Pinigina, K. Rand, E. H. Cline, and M. Kitsak. 2024. Are civilizations destined to collapse? Lessons from the Mediterranean bronze age. *Global Environmental Change* 84:102792.
Malhi, Y. 2017. The concept of the Anthropocene. *Annual Review of Environment and Resources* 42 (1): 77–104.
Maskin, E. S. 2008. Mechanism design: How to implement social goals. *American Economic Review* 98 (3): 567–576.
McCarthy, F. M., R. T. Patterson, M. J. Head, N. L. Riddick, B. F. Cumming, P. B. Hamilton, M. F. Pisaric, et al. 2023. The varved succession of Crawford Lake, Milton, Ontario, Canada as a candidate global boundary stratotype section and point for the Anthropocene series. *The Anthropocene Review* 10 (1): 146–176.
McCoy, J., and M. Somer. 2019. Toward a theory of pernicious polarization and how it harms democracies: Comparative evidence and possible remedies. *The Annals of the American Academy of Political and Social Science* 681 (1): 234–271.

McCoy, J., T. Rahman, and M. Somer. 2018. Polarization and the global crisis of democracy: Common patterns, dynamics, and pernicious consequences for democratic polities. *American Behavioral Scientist* 62 (1): 16–42.
Merz, J. J., P. Barnard, W. E. Rees, D. Smith, M. Maroni, C. J. Rhodes, J. H. Dederer, et al. 2023. World scientists' warning: The behavioural crisis driving ecological overshoot. *Science Progress* 106 (3): 00368504231201372.
Mordechai, L., and J. Haldon. 2024. Resilience in environmental history discourse: Past, present, and future? *The American Historical Review* 129 (4): 1420–1451.
Mordechai, L., and A. Tubi. 2024. Learning from past society-environment interactions is discursive rather than substantive. *Environmental Research Letters* 19 (12): 124068.
Moreno-Mayar, J. V., B. Sousa da Mota, T. Higham, S. Klemm, M. Gorman Edmunds, J. Stenderup, M. Iraeta-Orbegozo, et al. 2024. Ancient Rapanui genomes reveal resilience and pre-European contact with the Americas. *Nature* 633:389–397.
Munson, J., and J. Scholnick. 2022. Wealth and Well-being in an ancient Maya community. *Journal of Archaeological Method and Theory* 29 (1): 1–30.
Muthukrishna, M., J. Henrich, and J., and E. Slingerland. 2021. Psychology as a historical science. *Annual Review of Psychology* 72 (1): 717–749.
Nitsch, F. J., L. M. Lüpken, N. Lüschow, and T. Kalenscher. 2022. On the reliability of individual economic rationality measurements. *Proceedings of the National Academy of Sciences* 119 (31): e2202070119.
Nordhaus, W. D. 2017. Revisiting the social cost of carbon. *Proceedings of the National Academy of Sciences* 114 (7): 1518–1523.
North, D. C. 1990. *Institutions, institutional change and economic performance*. Cambridge: Cambridge University Press.
Obaidi, M., G. Anjum, K. Bierwiaczonek, J. F. Dovidio, S. Ozer, and J. R. Kunst. 2023. Cultural threat perceptions predict violent extremism via need for cognitive closure. *Proceedings of the National Academy of Sciences* 120 (20): e2213874120.
Ord, T. 2020. *The precipice: Existential risk and the future of humanity*. New York: Hachette Books.
Pascual, U., P. Balvanera, C. B. Anderson, R. Chaplin-Kramer, M. Christie, D. González-Jiménez, A. Martin, et al. 2023. Diverse values of nature for sustainability. *Nature* 620 (7975): 813–823.
Pereira, L., E. Bennett, R. Biggs, A. Mangnus, A. V. Norstrom, G. Peterson, C. Raudsepp-Hearne, M. Sellberg, and J. Vervoort. 2019. Seeding change by visioning good Anthropocenes. *Solutions Journal* 10 (3):
van Prooijen, J.-W., A. P. M. Krouwel, M. Boiten, and L. Eendebak. 2015. Fear among the extremes: How political ideology predicts negative emotions and outgroup derogation. *Personality and Social Psychology Bulletin* 41 (4): 485–497.
Raudsepp-Hearne, C., G. D. Peterson, E. M. Bennett, R. Biggs, A. V. Norström, L. Pereira, J. Vervoort, et al. 2020. Seeds of good Anthropocenes: Developing sustainability scenarios for northern Europe. *Sustainability Science* 15 (2): 605–617.
Rentschler, J., and M. Bazilian. 2017. Policy monitor—Principles for designing effective fossil fuel subsidy reforms. *Review of Environmental Economics and Policy* 11 (1): 138–155.
Ripple, W. J., C. Wolf, T. M. Newsome, M. Galetti, M. Alamgir, E. Crist, M. I. Mahmoud, and W. F. Laurance. 2017. World scientists' warning to humanity: A second notice. *Bioscience* 67 (12): 1026–1028.
Robbins Schug, G., J. E. Buikstra, S. N. DeWitte, B. J. Baker, E. Berger, M. R. Buzon, A. Davies-Barrett, et al. 2023. Climate change, human health, and resilience in the Holocene. *Proceedings of the National Academy of Sciences* 120 (4): e2209472120.
Romanello, M., C. d. Napoli, C. Green, H. Kennard, P. Lampard, D. Scamman, M. Walawender, et al. 2023. The 2023 report of the "lancet" countdown on health and climate change: The imperative for a health-centred response in a world facing irreversible harms. *The Lancet* 402 (10419): 2346–2394.

Satici, B., M. Saricali, S. A. Satici, and M. D. Griffiths. 2020. Intolerance of uncertainty and mental wellbeing: Serial mediation by rumination and fear of Covid-19. *International Journal of Mental Health and Addiction* 20 (5): 2731–2742.

Scheffer, M., E. H. van Nes, L. Kemp, T. A. Kohler, T. M. Lenton, C. Xu, and C. 2023. The vulnerability of aging states: A survival analysis across premodern societies. *Proceedings of the National Academy of Sciences* 120 (48): e2218834120.

Sen, A. 1973. Behaviour and the concept of preference. *Economica* 40 (159): 241–259.

Sen, A. 1977. Rational fools: A critique of the behavioral foundations of economic theory. *Philosophy & Public Affairs* 6 (4): 317–344.

Sen, A. 1994. Population and reasoned agency: Food, fertility, and economic development. In *Population, economic development, and the environment*, ed. K. Lindahl-Kiessling and H. Landberg, 4–27. Oxford: Oxford University Press.

Sen, A. 1997. Maximization and the act of choice. *Econometrica* 65 (4): 745–779.

Sen, A. 2014. Global Warming Is Just One of Many Environmental Threats That Demand Our Attention. *The New Republic* August 22. https://newrepublic.com/article/118969/environmentalists-obsess-about-global-warming-ignore-poor-countries

Smith, M. E. 2019. Quality of life and prosperity in ancient households and communities. In *The Oxford handbook of historical ecology and applied archaeology*, ed. C. Isendahl and D. Stump, 486–505. Oxford: Oxford University Press.

Smith, M. E. 2023. Urban success and urban adaptation over the long run. *Open Archaeology* 9 (1): 20220285.

Snyder, C. R. 1995. Conceptualizing, measuring, and nurturing hope. *Journal of Counseling & Development* 73 (3): 355–360.

Snyder, C. R. 2000. *Handbook of Hope: Theory, measures, and applications*. San Diego, CA: Academic.

Springmann, M., H. C. J. Godfray, M. Rayner, and P. Scarborough. 2016. Analysis and valuation of the health and climate change cobenefits of dietary change. *Proceedings of the National Academy of Sciences* 113 (15): 4146–4151.

Stagnaro, M. N., B. M. Tappin, and D. G. Rand. 2023. No association between numerical ability and politically motivated reasoning in a large US probability sample. *Proceedings of the National Academy of Sciences* 120 (32): e2301491120.

Stango, V., and J. Zinman. 2022. We are all behavioural, ore, or less: a taxonomy of consumer decision-making. *The Review of Economic Studies 90(3): 1470–1498.*

Steffen, W., W. Broadgate, L. Deutsch, O. Gaffney, and C. Ludwig. 2015. The trajectory of the Anthropocene: The great acceleration. *The Anthropocene Review* 2 (1): 81–98.

Steffen, W., J. Rockström, K. Richardson, T. M. Lenton, C. Folke, D. Liverman, C. P. Summerhayes, et al. 2018. Trajectories of the earth system in the Anthropocene. *Proceedings of the National Academy of Sciences* 115 (33): 8252–8259.

Steg, L. 2023. Psychology of climate change. *Annual Review of Psychology* 74 (1): 391–421.

Thomas, J. A. 2014. History and biology in the Anthropocene: Problems of scale, problems of valuehistory and biology in the Anthropocene. *The American Historical Review* 119 (5): 1587–1607.

Thomas, J. A. 2019. Why the "Anthropocene" is not "Climate Change" and why it matters. *Asia Global Online*, January 10, 2019. https://www.asiaglobalonline.hku.hk/anthropocene-climate-change.

Toivonen, H. 2022. Themes of climate change agency: A qualitative study on how people construct agency in relation to climate change. *Humanities and Social Sciences Communications* 9 (1): 102.

Turchin, P., T. E. Currie, H. Whitehouse, P. François, K. Feeney, D. Mullins, D. Hoyer, et al. 2018a. Quantitative historical analysis uncovers a single dimension of complexity that structures global variation in human social organization. *Proceedings of the National Academy of Sciences* 115 (2): E144–E151.

Turchin, P., H. Whitehouse, A. Korotayev, P. Francois, D. Hoyer, O. Peregrine, G. Feinman, et al. 2018b. Evolutionary pathways to statehood: old theories and new data. *SocArXiv* Prepr. https://doi.org/10.31235/osf.io/h7tr6

Turchin, P., H. Whitehouse, S. Gavrilets, D. Hoyer, P. François, J. S. Bennett, K. C. Feeney, et al. 2022. Disentangling the evolutionary drivers of social complexity: A comprehensive test of hypotheses. *Science Advances* 8 (25): eabn3517.

Tversky, A., and D. Kahneman. 1992. Advances in prospect theory: Cumulative representation of uncertainty. *Journal of Risk and Uncertainty* 5 (4): 297–323.

United Nations Development Programme (UNDP). 2020. *Human development report 2020. The next frontier: Human development and the Anthropocene*. New York: United Nations Development Programme.

United Nations Development Programme (UNDP). 2022. Human development report 2021-22. In *Uncertain times, unsettled lives: Shapting our future in a transforming world.* New York: United Nations Development Programme.

United Nations Development Programme (UNDP). 2024. *Human development report 2023–24. Breaking the gridlock: Reimagining cooperation in a polarizing world.* New York, NY: United Nations Development Programme.

Waters, C. N., M.J. Head, J. Zalasiewicz, F.M.G. McCarthy, S.L. Wing, P.K. Haff, M. Williams, et al. 2023. Response to Merritts et al. (2023): The Anthropocene is complex. Defining it is not. *Earth-Science Reviews* 238: 104335.

Wildavsky, A., K. Dake, and C. Darwin. 2001. Theories of risk perception: Who fears what and why. *Daedalus* 119(4): 41-60; repr. In *Environmental risk planning and management*, ed. S. Gerard, R. Kerry Turner, and I. J. Bateman, 231–250. Northhampton, MA: Edward Elgar Publishing.

Willett, W., J. Rockström, B. Loken, M. Springmann, T. Lang, S. Vermeulen, T. Garnett, et al. 2019. Food in the Anthropocene: The eat-*lancet* commission on healthy diets from sustainable food systems. *The Lancet* 393 (10170): 447–492.

Witze, A. 2024. Geologists reject the Anthropocene as earth's new epoch—After 15 years of debate. *Nature* 627 (8003): 249–250.

Xoplaki, E., J. Luterbacher, S. Wagner, E. Zorita, D. Fleitmann, J. Preiser-Kapeller, A. M. Sargent, et al. 2018. Modelling climate and societal resilience in the eastern Mediterranean in the last millennium. *Human Ecology* 46 (3): 363–379.

Zafra-Calvo, N., P. Balvanera, U. Pascual, J. Merçon, B. Martín-López, M. van Noordwijk, T. H. Mwampamba, et al. 2020. Plural valuation of nature for equity and sustainability: Insights from the global south. *Global Environmental Change* 63:102115.

Zalasiewicz, J., J. Adeney Thomas, C. N. Waters, S. Turner, and M. J. Head. 2024. The meaning of the Anthropocene: Why it matters even without a formal geological definition. *Nature* 632 (8027): 980–984.

Zimmermann, F. 2020. The dynamics of motivated beliefs. *American Economic Review* 110 (2): 337–361.

What Archaeologists Talk About When They Talk About Climate Change

Stefani A. Crabtree and Felix Riede

Abstract Humanity faces unprecedented challenges such as pandemics, climate change, and mass migrations that demand innovative, global responses. However, history and archaeology reveal that similar crises have been navigated before, offering invaluable insights into human adaptability and resilience. Archaeological and historical records can extend our temporal perspective, providing data on past human-environment interactions that illuminate how societies have responded to climatic fluctuations and local anthropogenic changes. These time-depth analyses allow for retrospective assessments of causality and consequence, enabling modern forecasting and strategic planning. Yet there can be challenges in imprecise analogies between the past and the present, and dangers in linking natural climate fluctuations in the past with human agency. This paper highlights the dual roles of archaeology in studying historical climatic responses and anthropogenic impacts, demonstrating its relevance to contemporary issues while also discussing the caution needed to properly link archaeological data with the present.

Keywords Analogies · Climate fluctuations · Agency · Causality · Anthropogenic change

1 Unprecedented Problems, Familiar Patterns

The challenges confronting humanity today often appear insurmountable. From the cascading crises of pandemics and mass migrations to the accelerating impacts of global climate change, these issues demand unprecedented coordination among citizens, scientists, and nations. Yet, despite their daunting scale, such challenges are

---

S. A. Crabtree (✉)
Utah State University, Logan, UT, USA

The Santa Fe Institute, Santa Fe, NM, USA

F. Riede
Department of Archaeology and Heritage Studies, Aarhus University, Højbjerg, Denmark

J. F. Haldon, R. Fernandes (eds.), *Bridging History and Policy*, Understanding Complex Systems, https://doi.org/10.1007/978-3-032-24379-9_3

not unprecedented. An examination of historical and archaeological records reveals that past societies also grappled with diasporas, widespread disease, and even anthropogenic environmental change. The scale of the problem may be different, but the scope of the problem is comparable.

Because of this, archaeology and history offer a time-depth to study contemporary challenges that would otherwise only be calibrated with data reaching back across the past few decades, limiting the reach and scope of our understanding of the present (e.g., Metzger et al. 2007). Moreover, these data offer the advantage of retrospectivity: causes and consequences, actions and reactions can be studied. For example, studies of modern ecological composition would be incomplete without understanding the ecosystems as they existed in the deep past (Allen et al. 2025; Burge et al. 2023; Soga and Gaston 2018)—forecasting future ecosystem states would be impossible without data from the past (Burke et al. 2018; Haywood et al. 2011; Ordonez et al. 2024). In the American Southwest, for instance, recent droughts have seemed unique, but studies of droughts as they existed in the 1200s based on archaeological research have helped situate what the likely challenges will be facing farmers in the next decade (Kohler et al. 2012; Scheffer et al. 2021; Thompson 2021). The application of archaeology can be concretely helpful for those living in the Four Corners to know what they may expect.

Indeed, many recent studies in archaeology have called on the idea that a study of the past can be useful for understanding the vexing challenges we face today (Allen et al. 2025; D'Alpoim Guedes et al. 2016; Jackson et al. 2018b; Kintigh et al. 2014a, 2014b). From discussions of paleopathology and their relevance to the COVID-19 pandemic (Gamble et al. 2021) to discussions of the twin challenges of food security with climate change (Nelson et al. 2016), the past indeed has many aspects that parallel modern issues. The time-depth of the archaeological record makes it a natural partner in studying modern challenges as we can leverage archaeology as a calibration dataset for understanding the state of modern environments. Indeed, the European Commission identified the relevance of archaeology in Regulation (EU) No. 1291/2013 specifying that disciplines that study history need to have "leading roles" in the study of the present and future (Kerr 2020: 2). By examining modern challenges within the frame of the past, archaeological research has the ability to "demonstrate the relevance of our discipline" (Scarre 2016: 285), something that can help ensure the survival of the discipline in a political climate where humanities research is often disparaged (Anderson 2023).

1.1 The Danger of Imprecise Analogies

The past is, however, a proverbial 'foreign country' (cf. Lowenthal 1985) and the farther removed from today the more 'foreign' it becomes. While many archaeological studies do precisely link data from the past to challenges of the present (e.g., Crabtree et al. 2023; Gamble et al. 2021; Nelson et al. 2016) there are an equal number that do not provide direct links between archaeological data and studies of modern challenges beyond merely stating that there is 'relevance' (Smith 2021), or by loosely deploying terms such as resilience without, however, defining or operationalizing these. Although archaeology can, in principle, provide valuable insights into contemporary issues, its relevance depends on establishing a robust and principled connection between past and present—often achieved with reference to behavioral ecological and cultural evolutionary theory (Brewer and Riede 2018; Jones et al. 2021; Kaaronen et al. 2023) and through statistical analysis or model building (D'Alpoim Guedes et al. 2016; Wren et al. 2025). Without such methods, the analogy between historical data and modern challenges remains speculative, leaving the burden on other disciplines to draw meaningful conclusions from archaeological evidence. Furthermore, the canonical language of climate change adaptation in the present is quantitative (cf. Kohler and Rockman 2020) making it harder for more traditional qualitative and particularistic archaeological studies to gain traction, and for policymakers to dismiss any past cases as irrelevant.

There is also a threefold danger in drawing imprecise analogies between the archaeological past and contemporary issues. On the less harmful end of the spectrum, the frequent assertion of archaeology's relevance risks diluting its impact. If archaeology is presented as essential to addressing every pressing issue, its message can lose focus, undermining its credibility even in areas where it is genuinely significant. From the perspective of other disciplines, archaeology's insistence on its applicability to modern problems—often without rigorous statistical comparisons between past and present—may inadvertently appear as an argument for its irrelevance. To effectively demonstrate the value of archaeology in addressing contemporary and future challenges, it is crucial to critically assess which aspects of the past hold true relevance and establish clear, evidence-based linkages to present-day issues such as were done by (Crabtree et al. 2023; Gamble et al. 2021; Nelson et al. 2016). Relevance needs to be demonstrated not claimed (see Smith 2021).

Seemingly innocuous, yet subtly problematic, are claims of past societal resilience that stem from researchers' understandable empathy for the ancient communities they study. Too often, however, such claims lack a strong empirical foundation. Without robust estimates of past health, inequality, or genetic legacies, how can we determine whether settlement persistence truly signals resilience in a meaningful sense, for instance? The coarse chronological resolution of the archaeological record rarely allows us to distinguish between Ostrom-esque adaptive foresight and Malthusian selection. Moreover, many studies are not designed to do so. Yet, romantic assertions of ancient resilience remain pervasive in archaeological literature, often implying—without sufficient evidence—that a lack of resilience is chiefly a problem of somehow less enlightened modern societies.

On the more harmful side, when analogies are imprecise this leaves open the opportunity for others to misinterpret the results. For example, in 2019 this statement appeared in the Department of the Interior's Bureau of Land Management (BLM) environmental impact statement regarding drilling in the Arctic (Columbia Law School 2019):

> The BLM does not agree that the proposed development is inconsistent with maintaining a livable planet (i.e., there is not a climate crisis). The planet was much warmer within the past 1000 years prior to the Little Ice Age, based on extensive archaeological evidence (such as farming in Greenland and vineyards in England). This warmth did not make the planet unlivable; rather, it was a time when societies prospered.

This statement selectively misinterprets archaeological evidence to support the claim that modern climate change is a natural continuation of the Earth's emergence from the Little Ice Age rather than an anthropogenic event. By invoking an archaeological analogy, it suggests that societies historically thrived during warmer periods, implying that contemporary societies are also likely to benefit from rising temperatures. The message from the BLM conveys two key points: first, because mean global temperatures were warmer before the Little Ice Age they suggest modern warming is merely a return to pre-Little Ice Age conditions, and two, in the time before the onset of the Little Ice Age people took advantage of the warmer temperatures and 'prospered,' framing current warming as potentially advantageous. The dangers inherent in projected future changes in key climatic parameters such as temperature and precipitation are clear and present, however (see: Kemp et al. 2022; Lenton et al. 2023; Scheffer et al. 2024; Xu et al. 2020).

A closer examination of the evidence cited by the BLM reveals two flawed analogies drawn from the archaeological record. Research on the Norse colonization of Greenland indicates that while Norse farmers lived there for approximately 500 years, their society faced significant challenges—and eventually disappeared. These included obstinate inertia in farming strategies amidst a changing climate, the impacts of glacial isostatic adjustment, rising sea levels, advancing ice, as well as their inability to adapt to uncertain future conditions (Borreggine et al. 2023; Dugmore et al. 2012; Jackson et al. 2018a; Kuijpers et al. 2005). Unlike the local Thule Indigenous peoples who foraged locally predominately relying on sea mammals, the Norse reliance on farming ultimately proved unsustainable. Furthermore, evidence suggests that life for the Norse in Greenland was likely arduous and precarious, undermining the notion that their society 'prospered' in these conditions.

Similarly, while it is true that vineyards existed in England during the Medieval Warm Period, the history of winemaking in England began much earlier, during Roman occupation, and has continued intermittently into the modern day. This long continuity undermines the BLM's implication that Medieval vineyards were solely a product of warmer temperatures (Hall 2014).

We can argue that this statement by the BLM from 2019 was an intentional misuse of the archaeological record to promote a political purpose. While this appears to have been a deliberate effort to frame climate change as benign or even beneficial, it highlights the critical need for the responsible and accurate use of historical and archaeological data in discussions of contemporary relevance. Archaeology offers powerful tools for understanding past human-environment interactions, but its findings must be presented with care to avoid misuse or politicization. This is particularly vital in the context of modern climate change, where the stakes are high, and the potential for distortion is significant. Clear, evidence-based arguments are essential to ensure archaeology contributes meaningfully and responsibly to these urgent global conversations (Kohler and Rockman 2020), not least because the culturally contingent inertia in, for instance, the US agricultural sector is creating an evident lag between the pressures exerted by rapid anthropogenic climate change and cropping strategies (Kling et al. 2024; Waring et al. 2023).

2 What Do Archaeologists Talk About When They Talk About Climate Change?

There are two main aspects to the archaeology of climate change. The first is studying peoples' reactions to naturally occurring climatic fluctuations, and using the probable reactions of people in the past to understand likely outcomes of humans being impacted by similar anthropogenic climate changes today.

The second is studying local anthropogenic change in the past, such as deforestation, salinification of soils, erosion, and other ecosystem modifications. Each of these can be useful for understanding aspects of modern climate change. We here address each in turn.

2.1 Natural Climate Fluctuations

Natural climatic fluctuations are driven by complex and interconnected phenomena, including variations in Earth's orbital cycles, solar activity, volcanic eruptions, et cetera. These fluctuations have profound effects on all life forms, including humans, shaping ecosystems and influencing societal development across the globe. Throughout history, human communities have exhibited a remarkable diversity of responses to climatic shifts, adapting to environmental challenges in ways that reveal their resilience as well as vulnerability (Degroot et al. 2022).

To understand how humans navigated these natural climate fluctuations, scientists must first reconstruct accurate climate records for the periods under study. Given the limitations of direct instrumental data which extend back only a few decades, researchers rely on proxy records to infer past climatic conditions. These proxies include ice cores, speleothems, coral reefs, lake and ocean sediments, tree rings, packrat middens, and more. Each dataset provides critical insights into historical patterns of temperature, precipitation as well as other climate parameters, forming the foundation of paleoclimatology.

Once compiled, proxy records allow scientists to infer the broad contours of past climates. However, these reconstructions are often constrained by the resolution of the proxies themselves, limiting the granularity with which we can observe ancient climatic events. By integrating these climatic datasets with historical and archaeological records, researchers seek to correlate environmental changes with societal shifts, uncovering potential causal links. Yet, without primary sources—written accounts from the past—direct attribution of observed events to specific climate fluctuations remains challenging. Good theory grounded in behavioral ecology and social transmission thinking allows us to go from correlations between paleoclimatic and 'paleosocietal' timeseries to robust causal arguments.

A defining characteristic of natural climatic fluctuations in the preindustrial past is that humans were rarely the drivers of these changes. While some localized activities, such as ancient metallurgy (Martínez Cortizas et al. 2016), may have had minor environmental impacts, the broader forces driving climate variation were largely independent of human action. In these contexts, human agency is best understood through the lens of adaptation and response to changing climates rather than as a source of climatic shifts. In essence, while human activities shaped societal structures and local environments, they did not alter the global climatic systems in the ways we observe today. This distinction underscores the fundamentally different nature of past and present human-environment interactions, offering critical lessons for navigating our current era of anthropogenic climate change (Ordonez et al. 2024; Svenning et al. 2024).

2.2 Local Anthropogenic Change

People in the past, however, did significantly influence their local environments and ecosystems, often with profound consequences for their societies. These human-driven changes—whether through deforestation, soil degradation, or overhunting etc.—frequently changed the underlying ecosystem. In some cases, the impacts of these activities were observable within a single generation, pressing societies to respond. However, such responses often required drastic measures, ranging from large-scale shifts in resource management to migrations or societal restructuring. While these historical and archaeological instances of environmental impact were generally confined to local or regional scales, they bear notable parallels to modern climate change. The cascading effects of localized anthropogenic changes, when considered collectively, offer striking similarities to the complex, interconnected challenges posed by climate change today. By examining these parallels, we gain a nuanced understanding of how societies have historically navigated environmental tipping points, providing valuable insights for addressing the escalating pressures of our time. Notably and worryingly, these societal responses more often than not appear to have been associated with considerable costs in lives and livelihoods (see Brovkin et al. 2021).

2.3 *The Combination of Local Anthropogenic Change and Natural Climate Fluctuations*

One of the most powerful insights offered by archaeology lies in examining the interplay between local anthropogenic changes and natural climatic fluctuations. Societies have faced challenges shaped by the compound forces of environmental pressures and human activities. Together, these forces often created feedback loops that magnified the consequences of each, pushing societies to adapt in variable and often unsustainable ways.

For example, during periods of natural climatic stress such as prolonged droughts or temperature shifts, human-driven changes in land use or resource exploitation could exacerbate vulnerabilities. The depletion of soil fertility or the loss of forest cover in regions already strained by fluctuating precipitation patterns might have accelerated ecological collapse. In Iceland, for example, large-scale erosion has been estimated to impact up to 30% of the landmass of the island, brought about by a society founded upon animal husbandry, and a problem that began during Norse occupation of the island and that was exacerbated by local adaptations to global climate conditions (Dugmore et al. 2020). Slowing or stopping erosion would require completely changing land use practices, something that would require massive coordination of citizens and society at large. The necessary knowledge was lacking, and Norse society appears to have been locked in an unduly normative framework, within which such transformative change was impossible. These intertwined processes highlight the delicate balance between natural forces and human agency, underscoring the importance of understanding how past societies navigated these challenges.

By studying the overlap of local anthropogenic change and natural climatic fluctuations, researchers can identify patterns of resilience and vulnerability that hold relevance for today's global climate crisis. In the preindustrial past humans were not the primary drivers of global climate changes, yet their localized actions often determined how societies experienced and responded to broader environmental shifts. This historical lens emphasizes the necessity of addressing human impacts on ecosystems in tandem with mitigating larger-scale climate dynamics, offering critical lessons for forging sustainable pathways in an era increasingly shaped by human-induced climate change.

3 How Can Archaeology Be Linked to Policy?

The archaeological record is a database of human responses to climatic and environmental change, and a record of human impacts on climate locally, regionally and—eventually—globally (Meneganzin et al. 2020). It may be fragmented but it is also extensive. It is a truly massive database containing rich information on how communities practicing different forms of socio-economic—or in other words functional ecological—strategies have coped or failed to cope with climatic challenges. We contend that the full relevance of archaeology for climate change adaptation remains to be realized and highlight that claims of perceived relevance are not sufficient. Instead, relevance needs to be empirically demonstrated and translated into actionable, policy-relevant guidance that is recognized as such by those making policies. Demonstrating this relevance scientifically and politically is hard work, and work often not immediately rewarded. With reference to selected works, we here want to highlight archaeological research that has been used to guide policy within the realm of understanding climate change, and how so.

Recently, work examining the human place in food webs in deep-time in Australia (Crabtree et al. 2019) has been cited in Final Report No. 368 of the Sustainable Indigenous housing in regional and remote Australia (Lea et al. 2021) and the Australia State of the Environment (2021), two key documents addressing environmental sustainability and Indigenous housing. This paper reconstructs the role of humans in the Western Australian food web during historic times using archaeological data, observational studies, and interviews with descendant communities. The paper then compares the historic food web to the modern food web which has been altered by species extinctions and invasions, and develops counterfactual scenarios to model food webs without human involvement. The findings reveal that the removal of Martu Aboriginal people from their traditional ecological roles in the Western Desert led to the unraveling of the food web and a marked simplification of the ecosystem. The study underscores Martu Aboriginal peoples' critical role as key nodes in the network, whose absence caused the food web to fragment into disconnected components.

The paper's influence on policy likely stems from its specificity and rigor in illustrating the integral relationship between humans and their ecosystems. By explicitly demonstrating the ecological consequences of human displacement, it highlights the ecosystem services provided by the Martu within their traditional environment. Additionally, the use of computer simulations to model food web dynamics bridges the gap between historical data and modern ecological forecasting, offering a nuanced and actionable framework for policymakers.

Working in the rather different context of north-western Europe, historical and archaeological data have been leveraged to better connect past hydrological shifts and their societal impacts to future projections, directly aligning with the UN's Sustainable Development Goals. In the context of a major, EU-funded project that included administrators, policymakers, environmental consultants, as well as water managers and engineers (https://www.c2ccc.eu/), historical maps, instrumental and climate proxies and archaeological data were used to craft place-based narratives that served as platforms for debating and catalyzing citizen-driven climate action (Kerr et al. 2022). Strictly data-driven approaches coupled instrumental rainfall data across scales to global climate change (Allen et al. 2022), while locally anchored heritage locales provided the vital links between policymaking and on-the-ground action (Kerr and Riede 2022; Riede and Krogh 2019).

Breaching the research-policy divide and demonstrating the value of archaeological data in the context of such a managerially dominated project was difficult and likely we are only beginning to see the impacts of such work. Yet, the papers, reports, and video footage—placed strategically such as to reach the right audiences—has not only had a clear impact on the shape of the project in its totality but also an afterlife in which they may serve as inspiration or even actionable template for similar projects elsewhere.

Each of these studies demonstrates ways that data from the past can be used to understand the present. By using specific cases that show the ways that humans live in ecosystems, the ways that humans adapt to changing environments, and how specifically humans embed themselves in their ecosystems and environments we can better understand the way that the past led to positive adaptations or poor resilience. Further, using real data combined with simulations as counterfactuals is an impactful way to link to modern policy, where counterfactuals are used to understand things like public health outcomes (O'Gara et al. 2023). This method of linking empirical data with predictive simulations ensures the study's findings are both precise and applicable, avoiding the pitfalls of oversimplified narratives and reinforcing its utility for guiding sustainable environmental management.

4 What Can Archaeology Tell Us?

With appropriate and humble caution, archaeology holds significant potential to contribute to contemporary discussions about pressing challenges, but its application demands precision, rigor, and clarity. Effective integration requires statistical or computational modeling and a well-defined articulation of how archaeological insights are relevant to modern issues. Archaeology provides invaluable perspectives on how humans have historically responded to natural climate fluctuations, the ways they have modified local ecosystems to create anthropogenic change, and the critical role humans play within ecosystems over time and space. Such insights are instrumental in improving our understanding of current ecosystems and the human dimensions within them. Of particular importance is the study of local anthropogenic change, which mirrors contemporary challenges because these past disruptions were also human-driven and often required large-scale, coordinated efforts to address—paralleling the complexity of today's global climate crisis.

The recent debates surrounding the identification of a 'golden spike' to mark the Anthropocene as a formal geological epoch underscore the importance of archaeology's role in studying human-environment interactions. After considerable deliberation, scientists appeared to converge on Crawford Lake, a small lake west of Toronto, as the potential marker for the Anthropocene, dating its onset to 1950 CE—a period characterized by dramatic, global-scale human impacts on Earth's systems, specifically the invention of nuclear technology and its subsequent global fallout. However, the Subcommission on Quaternary Stratigraphy ultimately decided against designating the Anthropocene as a formal epoch (Mitchell 2024).

Had Crawford Lake been chosen, it would have symbolized 1950 CE as the starting point of a new epoch shaped by human actions. Yet many archaeologists argue that this date is late in the timeline of human influence, as humans have been altering ecosystems at least since the advent of domestication and agriculture in the Holocene, and likely much earlier than that during their dispersal out of Africa to populate the globe. The rejection of the Anthropocene as a formal epoch is a missed opportunity for cementing the scientific as well as societal relevance of climate change research conducted across disciplines. By the same token, it opens the door for archaeology to play an even more impactful role in understanding the origins and trajectory of human-driven environmental changes (Svenning et al. 2024; but see also Boivin et al. 2024).

The Anthropocene may not have been formalized as an epoch, but it remains an unfolding event—one that archaeology is uniquely positioned to illuminate. By tracing the long and step-wise buildup of human influence on ecosystems, archaeology reveals how antecedent behaviors have culminated in the planetary-scale challenges we face today, and precisely which aspects of human behavior have led to this particular quandary. To fully realize this potential, archaeologists must strive for precision in linking the past to the present, employing principled data collection, computational modeling, simulated counterfactuals, and interdisciplinary collaborations. By forging strong connections with the natural and social sciences focused on contemporary challenges, archaeology can reaffirm its relevance and contribute meaningful insights to addressing humanity's most urgent environmental and societal issues.

References

Allen, K. J., F. Riede, C. Gouramanis, B. Keenan, M. Stoffel, A. Hu, and M. Ionita. 2022. Coupled insights from the palaeoenvironmental, historical and archaeological archives to support social-ecological resilience and the sustainable development goals. *Environmental Research Letters* 17 (5): 055011. https://doi.org/10.1088/1748-9326/ac6967.

Allen, K. J., C. Gouramanis, and D. Sauchyn. 2025. Paleo-data is policy relevant: How do we better incorporate it in policy and decision making? *Global Planetary Change* 246:104707. https://doi.org/10.1016/j.gloplacha.2025.104707.

Anderson, N. 2023. College is remade as tech majors surge and humanities dwindle. *Washington Post*: May 5 2023. https://www.washingtonpost.com/education/2023/05/19/college-majors-computer-science-humanities/

Boivin, N., T. Braje, and T. Rick. 2024. New opportunities emerge as the Anthropocene epoch vote falls short. *Nature Ecology & Evolution* 8:844–845. https://doi.org/10.1038/s41559-024-02392-x.

Borreggine, M., K. Latychev, S. Coulson, E. M. Powell, J. X. Mitrovica, G. A. Milne, and R. B. Alley. 2023. Sea-level rise in Southwest Greenland as a contributor to Viking abandonment. *Proceedings of the National Academy of Sciences* 120 (17): e2209615120. https://doi.org/10.1073/pnas.2209615120.

Brewer, J., and F. Riede. 2018. Cultural heritage and climate adaptation: A cultural evolutionary perspective for the Anthropocene. *World Archaeology* 50:554–569. https://doi.org/10.1080/00438243.2018.1527246.

Brovkin, V., E. Brook, J. W. Williams, S. Bathiany, T. M. Lenton, M. Barton, et al. 2021. Past abrupt changes, tipping points and cascading impacts in the earth system. *Nature Geoscience* 14:550–558. https://doi.org/10.1038/s41561-021-00790-5.

Burge, O. R., S. J. Richardson, J. R. Wood, and J. M. Wilmshurst. 2023. A guide to assess distance from ecological baselines and change over time in palaeoecological records. *Holocene* 33:905–917. https://doi.org/10.1177/09596836231169986.

Burke, K. D., J. W. Williams, M. A. Chandler, A. M. Haywood, D. J. Lunt, and B. L. Otto-Bliesner. 2018. Pliocene and Eocene provide best analogs for near-future climates. *Proceedings of the National Academy of Sciences* 115 (2): 13288–13293. https://doi.org/10.1073/pnas.1809600115.

Columbia Law School. 2019. Interior Department Arctic drilling study concludes there is not a climate crisis. In *Sabin center for climate change law*. Columbia University. https://climate.law.columbia.edu/content/interior-department-arctic-drilling-study-concludes-there-not-climate-crisis.

Commonwealth of Australia. 2021. *Australia state of the environment 2021: Overview*. Commonwealth of Australia. https://doi.org/10.26194/f1rh-7r05.

Crabtree, S. A., D. W. Bird, and R. B. Bird. 2019. Subsistence transitions and the simplification of ecological networks in the Western Desert of Australia. *Human Ecology* 47:165–177. https://doi.org/10.1007/s10745-019-0053-z.

Crabtree, S. A., J. G. Kahn, R. Jackson, S. A. Wood, et al. 2023. Why are sustainable practices often elusive? The role of information flow in the management of networked human-environment interactions. *Global Environmental Change* 78:102597. https://doi.org/10.1016/j.gloenvcha.2022.102597.

D'Alpoim Guedes, J. A., S. A. Crabtree, R. K. Bocinsky, and T. A. Kohler. 2016. Twenty-first century approaches to ancient problems: Climate and society. *Proceedings of the National Academy of Sciences* 113 (51): 14483–14491. https://doi.org/10.1073/pnas.1616188113.

Degroot, D., K. J. Anchukaitis, J. E. Tierney, F. Riede, et al. 2022. The history of climate and society: A review of the influence of climate change on the human past. *Environmental Research Letters* 17:103001. https://doi.org/10.1088/1748-9326/ac8faa.

Dugmore, A. J., T. H. McGovern, O. Vésteinsson, J. Arneborg, R. Streeter, and C. Keller. 2012. Cultural adaptation, compounding vulnerabilities and conjunctures in Norse Greenland. *Proceedings of the National Academy of Sciences* 109 (10): 3658–3663. https://doi.org/10.1073/pnas.1115292109.

Dugmore, A., R. Jackson, D. Cooper, A. Newton, Á. D. Júlíusson, and T. H. McGovern. 2020. Chapter 6. Continuity in the face of a slowly unfolding catastrophe: The persistence of Icelandic settlement despite large-scale soil erosion. In *Archaeological perspectives on socio-ecological crisis, response, and collapse*, ed. F. Riede and P. Sheets, 162–199. New York-Oxford: Berghahn Books. https://doi.org/10.1515/9781789208658-009.

Gamble, L. H., C. Claassen, J. W. Eerkens, D. J. Kennett, P. M. Lambert, et al. 2021. Finding archaeological relevance during a pandemic and what comes after. *American Antiquity* 86:2–22. https://doi.org/10.1017/aaq.2020.94.

Hall, C. M. 2014. The changing self-identity of English wine. In *Wine and identity*, ed. M. Harvey, L. White, and W. Frost. London: Routledge.

Haywood, A. M., A. Ridgwell, D. J. Lunt, D. J. Hill, M. J. Pound, et al. 2011. Are there pre-quaternary geological analogues for a future greenhouse warming? *Philosophical Transactions of the Royal Society A: Mathematical, Physical and Engineering Sciences* 369:933–956. https://doi.org/10.1098/rsta.2010.0317.

Jackson, R., J. Arneborg, A. Dugmore, C. Madsen, et al. 2018a. Disequilibrium, adaptation, and the Norse settlement of Greenland. *Human Ecology* 46:665–684. https://doi.org/10.1007/s10745-018-0020-0.

Jackson, R. C., A. J. Dugmore, and F. Riede. 2018b. Rediscovering lessons of adaptation from the past. *Global Environmental Change* 52:58–65. https://doi.org/10.1016/j.gloenvcha.2018.05.006.

Jones, J. H., E. Ready, and A. C. Pisor. 2021. Want climate-change adaptation? Evolutionary theory can help. *American Journal of Human Biology* 33:e23539. https://doi.org/10.1002/ajhb.23539.

Kaaronen, R. O., T. M. Waring, and M. Borgerhoff Mulder. 2023. Applying cultural evolution to address climate and environmental challenges. In *The Oxford handbook of cultural evolution*, ed. J. J. Tehrani, J. R. Kendal, and Rachel L. Kendal. Oxford: Oxford University Press. https://doi.org/10.1093/oxfordhb/9780198869252.013.73.

Kemp, L., C. Xu, J. Depledge, K. L. Ebi, G. Gibbins, T. A. Kohler, et al. 2022. Climate endgame: Exploring catastrophic climate change scenarios. *Proceedings of the National Academy of Sciences* 119 (34): e2108146119. https://doi.org/10.1073/pnas.2108146119.

Kerr, S. 2020. The future of archaeology, interdisciplinarity and global challenges. *Antiquity* 94:1337–1348. https://doi.org/10.15184/aqy.2020.138.

Kerr, S., and F. Riede. 2022. Upscaling local adaptive heritage practices to internationally designated heritage sites. *Climate* 10 (7): 102. https://doi.org/10.3390/cli10070102.

Kerr, S., U. Krogh, and F. Riede. 2022. Experimental participatory methodology brings local pasts to contemporary climate action. *Climate Action* 1 (5): https://doi.org/10.1007/s44168-022-00006-5.

Kintigh, K. W., J. H. Altschul, M. C. Beaudry, R. D. Drennan, A. P. Kinzig, et al. 2014a. Grand challenges for archaeology. *Proceedings of the National Academy of Sciences* 111 (3): 879–880. https://doi.org/10.1073/pnas.1324000111.

Kintigh, K. W., J. H. Altschul, M. C. Beaudry, R. D. Drennan, A. P. Kinzig, et al. 2014b. Grand challenges for archaeology. *American Antiquity* 79:5–24. https://doi.org/10.7183/0002-7316.79.1.5.

Kling, M. M., C. T. Brittain, G. L. Galford, T. M. Waring, et al. 2024. Innovations through crop switching happen on the diverse margins of US agriculture. *Proceedings of the National Academy of Sciences* 121 (42): e2402195121. https://doi.org/10.1073/pnas.2402195121.

Kohler, T. A., and M. Rockman. 2020. The IPCC: A primer for archaeologists. *American Antiquity* 85:627–651. https://doi.org/10.1017/aaq.2020.68.

Kohler, T. A., R. K. Bocinsky, D. Cockburn, S. A. Crabtree, M. D. Varien, et al. 2012. Modelling prehispanic Pueblo societies in their ecosystems. *Ecological Modelling* 241:30–41. https://doi.org/10.1016/j.ecolmodel.2012.01.002.

Kuijpers, A., N. Mikkelsen, S. Ribeiro, and M.-S. Seidenkrantz. 2005. Impact of medieval fjord hydrography and climate on the western and eastern settlements in Norse Greenland. *Journal of the North Atlantic* 6:1–13. https://www.eaglehill.us/JONAonline/articles/JONA-Sp-6/10-Kuijpers.shtml.

Lea, T., L. Grealy, M. Moskos, A. Brambilla, et al. 2021. *Sustainable indigenous housing in regional and remote Australia. AHURI Final Report*,, 1–107. Melbourne: Australian Housing and Urban Research Institute Limited. https://doi.org/10.18408/AHURI7323701.

Lenton, T. M., C. Xu, J. F. Abrams, A. Ghadiali, S. Loriani, et al. 2023. Quantifying the human cost of global warming. *Nature Sustainability* 6:1237–1247. https://doi.org/10.1038/s41893-023-01132-6.

Lowenthal, D. 1985. *The past is a foreign country*. Cambridge: Cambridge University Press.

Martínez Cortizas, A., L. López-Merino, R. Bindler, T. Mighall, and M. E. Kylander. 2016. Early atmospheric metal pollution provides evidence for chalcolithic/bronze age mining and metallurgy in southwestern Europe. *Science of the Total Environment* 545–546:398–406. https://doi.org/10.1016/j.scitotenv.2015.12.078.

Meneganzin, A., T. Pievani, and S. Caserini. 2020. Anthropogenic climate change as a monumental niche construction process: Background and philosophical aspects. *Biology and Philosophy* 35:38. https://doi.org/10.1007/s10539-020-09754-2.

Metzger, K. L., A. R. E. Sinclair, K. L. I. Campbell, R. Hilborn, et al. 2007. Using historical data to establish baselines for conservation: The black rhinoceros (Diceros bicornis) of the Serengeti as a case study. *Biological Conservation* 139:358–374. https://doi.org/10.1016/j.biocon.2007.06.026.

Mitchell, A., 2024. The Anthropocene is here—and tiny Crawford Lake has been chosen as the global ground zero. *Canadian Geographic*: 11 July 2023. https://canadiangeographic.ca/articles/the-anthropocene-is-here-and-tiny-crawford-lake-has-been-chosen-as-the-global-ground-zero/#:~:text=Crawford%20Lake%2C%20a%20tiny%20body%20of%20water%20barely,shaping%20the%20planet%E2%80%99s%20fate.%20%28Photo%3A%20Colin%20Boyd%20Shafer%29

Nelson, M. C., S. E. Ingram, A. J. Dugmore, R. Streeter, M. A. Peeples, et al. 2016. Climate challenges, vulnerabilities, and food security. *Proceedings of the National Academy of Sciences* 113 (2): 298–303. https://doi.org/10.1073/pnas.1506494113.

O'Gara, D., S. F. Rosenblatt, L. Hébert-Dufresne, R. Purcell, M. Kasman, and R. A. Hammond. 2023. TRACE-omicron: Policy counterfactuals to inform mitigation of COVID-19 spread in the United States. *Advanced Theory and Simulations* 6:2300147. https://doi.org/10.1002/adts.202300147.

Ordonez, A., F. Riede, S. Normand, and J.-C. Svenning. 2024. Towards a novel biosphere in 2300: Rapid and extensive global and biome-wide climatic novelty in the Anthropocene. *Philosophical Transactions of the Royal Society B: Biological Sciences* 379:20230022. https://doi.org/10.1098/rstb.2023.0022.

Riede, F., and U. Krogh. 2019. *Combatting Climat change culturally: How cultural and natural heritage can strengthen climate change adaptation*. Århus: Århus Universitet.

Scarre, C. 2016. Editorial. *Antiquity* 90:283–289. https://doi.org/10.15184/aqy.2016.61.

Scheffer, M., E. H. van Nes, D. Bird, R. K. Bocinsky, and T. A. Kohler. 2021. Loss of resilience preceded transformations of pre-Hispanic Pueblo societies. *Proceedings of the National Academy of Sciences* 118 (18): e2024397118. https://doi.org/10.1073/pnas.2024397118.

Scheffer, M., W. N. Adger, S. R. Carpenter, C. Folke, et al. 2024. Anticipating the global redistribution of people and property. *One Earth* 7:1151–1154. https://doi.org/10.1016/j.oneear.2024.06.008.

Smith, M. E. 2021. Archaeology, relevance and science. *Antiquity* 95:1085–1087. https://doi.org/10.15184/aqy.2021.91.

Soga, M., and K. J. Gaston. 2018. Shifting baseline syndrome: Causes, consequences, and implications. *Frontiers in Ecology and the Environment* 16:222–230. https://doi.org/10.1002/fee.1794.

Svenning, J.-C., M. R. Kerr, N. A. Mungi, A. Ordonez, and F. Riede. 2024. Defining the Anthropocene as a geological epoch captures human impacts' triphasic nature to empower science and action. *One Earth* 7:1678–1681. https://doi.org/10.1016/j.oneear.2024.08.004.

Thompson, J., 2021. A megadrought is hurting Colorado farmers. *5280: Denver's Mile High Magazine*. October 2021. https://www.5280.com/a-megadrought-is-hurting-colorado-farmers/

Waring, T. M., M. T. Niles, M. M. Kling, S. N. Miller, et al. 2023. Operationalizing cultural adaptation to climate change: Contemporary examples from United States agriculture. *Philosophical Transactions of the Royal Society B: Biological Sciences* 378:20220397. https://doi.org/10.1098/rstb.2022.0397.

Wren, C. D., I. Romanowska, and F. Riede. 2025. Bad year econometrics: Agent-based modeling of risk management strategies under varying regimes of environmental change. *Science Advances* 11:eadr0314. https://doi.org/10.1126/sciadv.adr0314.

Xu, C., T. A. Kohler, T. M. Lenton, J.-C. Svenning, and M. Scheffer. 2020. Future of the human climate niche. *Proceedings of the National Academy of Sciences* 117 (21): 11350–11355. https://doi.org/10.1073/pnas.1910114117.

Using Climate's Past: An Analysis of History of Climate and Society Studies in the Fight Against Global Warming

Dagomar Degroot, Rachel Singer, Nicolas Gauthier, and Sarah Klassen

Abstract Can the study of human responses to past climatic changes inform the fight against present-day global warming? Scholars in History of Climate and Society Studies (HCSS) often make that claim. They argue, for example, that the purported collapse of ancient empires, dynasties, city-states, and settlements can provide lessons to strengthen climate adaptation policies today. By examining 1191 publications published between 2017 and 2021, we evaluate how HCS scholars extract these lessons from the past. We reveal that although most publications in the field claim to have relevance for present-day activism and policymaking, only a tiny minority include takeaways that are actionable for policymakers. We show how these takeaways are influenced by the region, period, discipline, and method of each study. Quantitative studies are more likely to include lessons, for example; so are publications that focus on Europe or Asia in the modern or early modern periods. Ultimately, we argue that there is a disconnect between what HCSS publications claim to contribute to the fight against global warming, and what they actually do. It is a disconnect that scholars must now work to resolve.

Keywords Climate change · History · Archaeology · Climatology · Policy

---

D. Degroot (✉) · R. Singer
Georgetown University, Washington, DC, USA
e-mail: dagomar.degroot@georgetown.edu; rbs73@georgetown.edu

N. Gauthier
Florida Museum of Natural History, Gainesville, FL, USA

S. Klassen
Florida Museum of Natural History, Gainesville, FL, USA

University of Colorado, Boulder, CO, USA

J. F. Haldon, R. Fernandes (eds.), *Bridging History and Policy*, Understanding Complex Systems, https://doi.org/10.1007/978-3-032-24379-9_4

1 Introduction

Scholars have long attempted to determine how trends, variability, and anomalies in climate have influenced human history. Over the past two decades, this field of study—recently synthesized as the *History of Climate and Society* (HCS), or *History of Climate and Society Studies* (HCSS)—has rapidly expanded, diversified, and grown in sophistication. The number of HCSS publications published every year seems to be rising rapidly; more academic disciplines are now incorporated within HCSS; and many distinct forms of evidence and methods of interpreting evidence are increasingly brought to bear in HCSS studies. HCSS is increasingly influential both in other fields of study and, seemingly, in discourse around the development of climate change policy, especially policy that aims to enhance social or societal resilience to global warming (Degroot et al. 2022, 2021).

In this chapter, we provide a broad assessment of the popularity, characteristics, and policy utility of HCSS as it is practiced today. First, we attempt to measure aspects of the recent growth of HCSS. Then, we identify three broad reasons for this expansion of the field. Next, we assess how HCSS scholars frame the relevance of their work in ongoing efforts to better understand and address the crisis of anthropogenic global warming (AGW). Finally, we evaluate why, how, and with what effectiveness HCSS researchers are attempting to influence the development of policies that aim to confront today's climate crisis.

To assess HCSS, we introduce a new database of 1191 HCSS publications, written primarily in English, that appeared in the 5 years between 2017 and 2021. We consulted a bibliographical project maintained by the Climate History Network (CHN), an organization uniting hundreds of HCSS scholars, to identify many of the publications in our database (Climate History Network Zotero Bibliographical Project).[1] Although the CHN bibliography was intended to be comprehensive, we expanded it with additional publications, many of which were written by environmental archaeologists. After reading every publication, we used 17 distinct categories to interpret their evidence, methods, and recommendations for policy development or implementation. Our database has 20,247 data points, making it a unique resource for evaluating the development of HCSS.

Our dataset reveals three major findings. First, HCSS is today a growing, dynamic, and multidisciplinary field. Second, it is a deeply unbalanced field, with major inequalities among the disciplines, analytical methods, periods, and places that can be associated with its scholarship. Third, it is a field that may be less useful than it could be in today's efforts to limit global warming and adapt to its consequences. In the following chapter, we break down each of these findings and suggest possible explanations for them.

[1] Climate History Network Zotero Bibliographical Project. Climate History Network. Available at: https://www.climatehistory.net/bibliography

2 The Growth of HCSS: Evidence and Causes

There is little doubt that HCSS is now a much more popular and diverse field than it was several decades ago. It is, however, harder to establish exactly how much it has grown and exactly how large and influential it is today. A search for publications in climate history (HCSS as undertaken by historians), historical climatology (a term that can be synonymous with climate history, but can also refer to reconstructions of climate change developed using societal archives), and past climate more broadly, undertaken in Web of Science and PubMed, provides only a rough indication of the number of publications in HCSS. Even this incomplete assessment of publication counts, however, reveals a dramatic rise, especially in the last decade (Fig. 1).

Part of the rise, however, may be due to the increasing use of the terms "climate history" and "historical climatology" to refer to the study of climate change by historians, rather than the growth of HCSS as a discipline. Another part may be due to the growing popularity of climate reconstruction, as opposed to the study of human responses to past climate change. More rigorous approaches to identifying trends in HCSS can target narrower sub-fields, such as the study, by historians, of the Little Ice Age (LIA) in Europe. Owing in part to the sheer quantity of textual sources written by early modern Europeans and preserved in accessible archives, no topic has garnered greater attention from climate historians than the European experience of

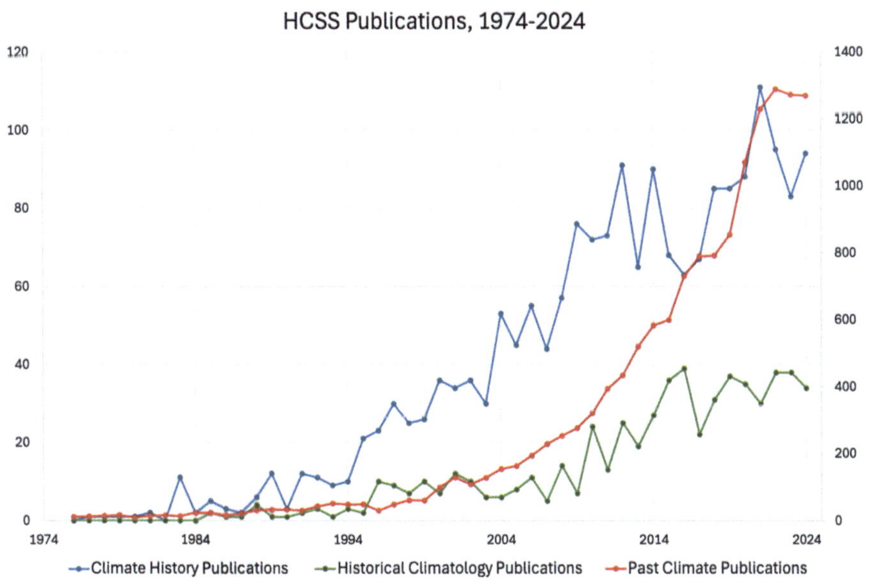

Fig. 1 Manuscripts published between 1974 and 2024, identified using the search terms "Climate+History" and "Historical Climatology" in Web of Science (plotted on the left y axis), and "past climate" in PubMed (right y axis)

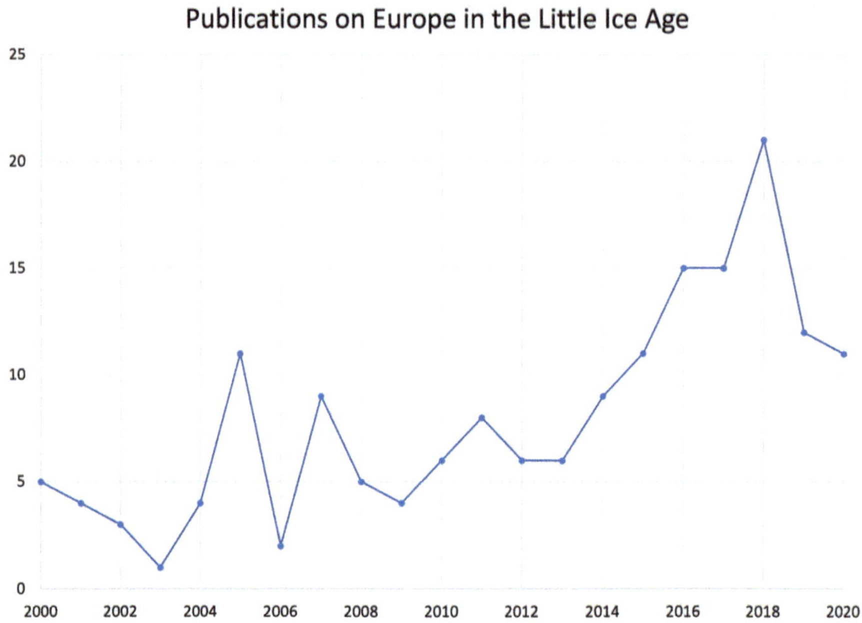

Fig. 2 Publications on the Little Ice Age in Europe, published between 2000 and 2020. From Dagomar Degroot et al., "Towards a rigorous understanding of societal responses to climate change"

the LIA. An analysis of publications in that relatively niche field again reveals a steady increase in quantity (Fig. 2) (Ljungqvist et al. 2021).

Because our database covers a 5-year sample that coincides with the COVID-19 pandemic, it cannot illustrate trends in the quantity of HCSS publications. Unlike other datasets, however, it can provide a nearly comprehensive and more-or-less current snapshot of the overall number of HCSS publications in major European scholarly languages, and in turn the size of the field. It reveals, first and foremost, that the annual number of HCSS publications in those languages is now very high, at around 250. It also indicates that, if the COVID-19 pandemic reduced the number of publications in the field, the effect was modest and fleeting (Fig. 3).

There are many reasons for the recent, explosive growth of HCSS. One undoubtedly includes the sheer determination and energy of a small group of HCSS scholars who have, among other things, established new organizations and research efforts that connect academics across disciplinary boundaries; mentored young scholars and contributed to established conferences; and engaged in sustained public outreach in diverse media.[2]

[2] It is interesting to consider the role of contingency, and the actions of individuals, in spurring the development of a field of study (perhaps especially for HCSS scholars, who often think in terms of structures). In HCSS, scholars who established and managed organizations that include Past Global Changes (PAGES), the Climate History Network (CHN), and the Climate Change and History Research Initiative (CCHRI), have played important roles.

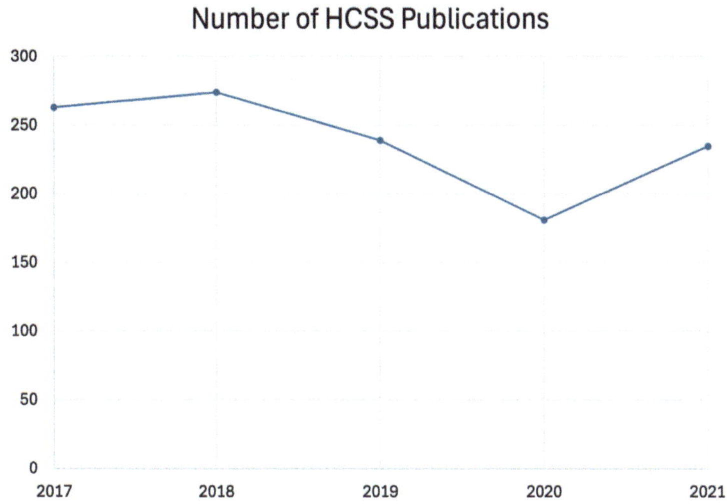

Fig. 3 The number of HCSS publications in our database, between 2017 and 2021

However, there seem to be three paramount reasons for the recent boom in HCSS. First, evidence for past climate change, especially evidence derived by paleoclimatologists from proxy sources in natural archives, is much more abundant, diverse, accurate, and precise (or in other words, "high-resolution") than it was even two decades ago. Climate reconstructions—ways of visualizing and identifying past climate change—are accordingly available for more times and places than ever before. Many reconstructions now show climate changes or anomalies on spatio-temporal scales that are small enough to allow archaeologists, geographers, or historians to identify compelling connections between those changes or anomalies and distinct human actions or decisions. These reconstructions are moreover much more accessible than they once were. Online tools, such as the Paleoclimatology Data map provided by the National Oceanic and Atmospheric Administration, allow researchers to easily identify both climate reconstructions and the raw data in reconstructions that are derived from different proxies, or are relevant to different times and places.[3] Other tools, such as the Monsoon Asia, North American, and Old World Drought Atlases or, more recently, ClimeApp, allow researchers to easily create their own visualizations based on high resolution proxy data. Large language models are also enabling scholars of the past to statistically interpret climate reconstructions in ways that once required specialized knowledge (Cook et al. 2010a, b, 2015; Warren et al. 2024).

A second reason for the growth of HCSS is the environmental turn in different disciplines that examine the human past. This environmental turn unfolded at different times and in different ways in distinct disciplines, and it occurred for intwined

[3] Paleoclimatology Data. *National Centers for Environmental Information*, NOAA. https://www.ncei.noaa.gov/maps/paleo/

but also contradictory reasons. Environmental archaeology, for example, partly emerged out of the early twentieth century imperial fascination in imperial metropoles with the 'exotic' people and environments on the periphery of empire, but also from a rise in collaboration between archaeologists and natural scientists. Environmental history can identify its origins in growing concerns over the sustainability of modern life that matured with the mid-twentieth century growth of the environmental movement. Environmental turns in scholarship of the human past came and went, but they have now entrenched themselves as awareness grows in many fields of study that humanity cannot be extricated from its non-human contexts (Beinart and Hughes 2007; Murphy and Fuller 2017; McNeill 2010).

A final reason for the recent expansion of HCSS is mounting concern over the entangled environmental crises of the late-twentieth and twenty-first centuries. For HCSS, the most important of these crises has been global warming. Broad concern about global warming among scholars, many policymakers, and the public has strengthened the first two reasons for the growth of HCSS by, first, motivating and financially supporting efforts to reconstruct climate change and thereby find a baseline against which to compare modern warming, and second, discrediting the idea once prevalent among many scholars of the past that the environment was not a meaningful force in human history (Howard 2019; Degroot et al. 2022).

Fears of global warming have also spurred HCSS in other ways. They have helped spark broad public interest in scholarship about past climate change, which has enhanced and been enhanced by a growing number of high-profile interviews, newspaper columns, magazine articles, podcasts, and websites that all target a broad audience (of many examples: Chaplin 2025; Demuth 2024; Degroot 2019). Concerns over global warming have also motivated both established and aspiring scholars of the past to consider how their work might tangibly contribute to perceived solutions to the climate crisis. For some, the answer has been to identify the influence of climate change on human history, and thereby to pursue HCSS. Global warming concerns have moreover led governmental and non-governmental organizations, including the IPCC, the US Department of Defense, and the UN Development Programme, to welcome fresh perspectives on climate change in their reports, conferences, and internal deliberations (Morgan et al. 2022; Degroot 2022). That has created openings for HCSS scholars to influence policy development, and thereby expand the reach of their field of study.

3 Characteristics of HCSS Today

To assess the characteristics of HCSS as it is practiced today, we carefully evaluated the geographic and temporal focus; primary academic discipline; analytical method; and publication format of the 1191 publications in our dataset. This evaluation required us to sort publications into categories, and both the process of sorting and the creation of the categories inevitably involved a degree of arbitrariness and simplification. For example, when we categorized publications by their region of focus, we selected regions of unequal size, and used terms to refer to these regions that do not always align with how the terms are typically used. For us the Middle East did not include Egypt; Oceania included Australia, New Guinea, and New Zealand; and the Americas included the Caribbean and sub-Arctic Greenland. Similarly, we selected time periods that are of radically uneven length. One time period—the Pleistocene—covers nearly two and a half million years, while another—the twenty-first century—covers just 26!

It is important to note that we created these unequal spatial and temporal categories in order to include a meaningful sample of our publications within each category. The consequence is that our analysis can understate inequalities in, for example, the geographic or temporal focus of the publications in our dataset. It is therefore particularly striking that we nevertheless identified severe imbalances within the contemporary practice of HCSS.

We found, for example, that Europe (29%) and Asia (23%) account for the most common geographic foci in our database of HCSS publications (Fig. 4). Indeed, Europe (especially western and central Europe) and Asia (especially China) have long attracted disproportionate attention from HCSS scholars. Pioneers in the modern development of the field, such as Zhu Kezhen, Christian Pfister, Emmanuel le Roy Ladurie, and Hubert Lamb, were after all based in Europe and China, partly because textual evidence for weather and human responses is especially old and dense in both places. In the case of Europe, and more recently China, abundant funding for climate research may also account for the quantity of HCSS publications concentrating on the region. Research funding and institutional support for both HCSS and paleoclimate reconstruction may also partly account for the quantity of publications on the Americas (15%).

What is salient in our sample is the very small share of publications that focus on the Middle East (5.1%), Africa (3.8%, or 45 publications), the Polar Regions (Antarctica and the Arctic, 3.4%, or 40 publications), and Oceania (2.1%). The paucity of publications from these regions is clear evidence for a major geographical imbalance in HCSS. Indeed, some 72% of publications in our sample concentrate on the northern hemisphere, if Africa is grouped within the southern hemisphere (otherwise, fully 75% of publications focus on the northern hemisphere).

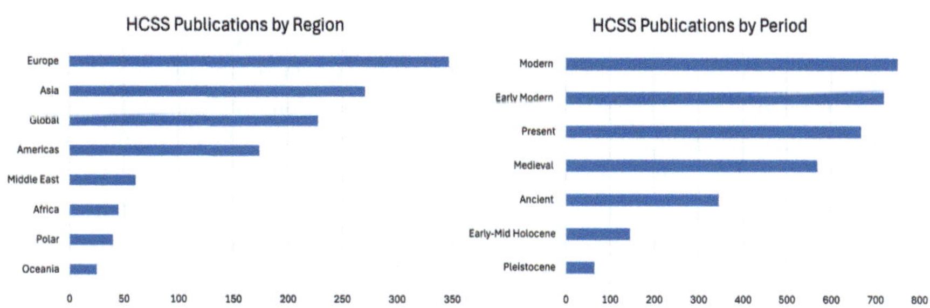

Fig. 4 The number of HCSS publications in our database that focus on different world regions (left) and cover different periods (right)

We also categorized the time period considered by publications in our database, assigning multiple periods to publications that transgressed the temporal boundaries we assigned (Fig. 4). Here, too, we found that HCSS gives surprisingly disproportionate attention to some subjects at the expense of others. Only a tiny fraction (2%) of the publications in our sample consider the Pleistocene (2.58 million to 11,700 years ago), even though the epoch encompasses some 96% of *Homo sapien* history and is defined by global climatic shifts of staggering speed and scale. Similarly, only 4.4% of the publications in our sample investigate the early to middle Holocene (for us, 11,700 years ago to 3000 BCE), when climatic trends continued to so profoundly alter regional environments—most importantly the Sahara—that they, in all likelihood, influenced the subsequent trajectory of human history (Brookfield 2011; Williams 2021; Degroot et al. 2022).

A larger but still small share (11%) of the publications in our sample consider the ancient world (from 3000 BCE to 500 CE) and the medieval period (500 CE to 1500 CE). The overwhelming majority of our publications examine the early modern (1500 CE to 1800 CE, 22%) and modern periods (1800 to 2000 CE, 23%). Another 667 publications—20% of our sample—consider the twenty-first century (from 2000 CE to the present).

To gain greater insight into the contemporary practice of HCSS, we categorized publications in our database by discipline. We associated publications with particular disciplines by assessing the disciplinary background of the (lead or corresponding) author, the journal (for articles) or publisher (for books) where the publication appeared, and the methods and sources used in the publication. We found that, in our large sample, a strong plurality (46%) of publications that identify human responses to past climate change can be associated primarily with climatology (a category which, for us, included both paleoclimatology, which reconstructs past climate from natural archives, and historical climatology, which does so using historical documents). Perhaps this should not have been surprising. Paleoclimatologists wrote most of the publications we associated with climatology. Natural science disciplines typically have a higher pace of publication than their counterparts in the humanities and social sciences, and there may be more paleoclimatologists than there are historians or archaeologists whose work focuses on the history of climate change.

History (17%) and archaeology (13%) are the disciplines primarily associated with the second- and third-most publications in our sample. All other disciplines—literature (2.9%), geography (2.1%), economics (0.4%), and epidemiology (0.2%)—account for a very small share. Of course, some publications are so interdisciplinary that they cannot be associated with a single discipline; we included publications in this category if they employed methods from multiple disciplines, rather than simply having authors from diverse disciplinary backgrounds. These publications take up some 18% of our sample. A small number of publications in other disciplines (1.1%) take up the rest (Fig. 4). Given the influence (as measured by citation counts) of HCSS publications written by geographers and economists, who have used statistical, econometric methods to identify human responses to climate change, it is

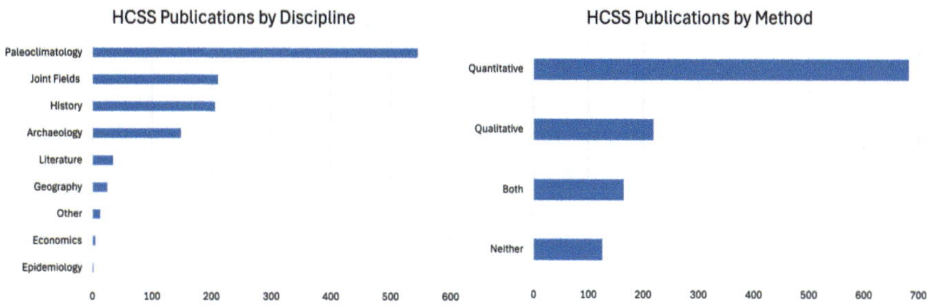

Fig. 5 The number of HCSS publications in our database that can be primarily associated with different disciplines (left), and that use different analytical methods (right)

surprising how few publications in our sample can be primarily associated with these disciplines (Fig. 5).

The dominance of paleoclimatology and paleoclimatologists in HCSS publications suggests that the field is dominated by a relatively narrow selection of methods, models, and sources. To investigate, we divided our sample between publications that used quantitative methods, those that used qualitative methods, those that used both, and those that used neither (for instance, a literature review would fall into this category). We found that indeed, quantitative methods primarily used by paleoclimatologists—and by the far fewer geographers and economists in our sample—dominate HCSS, accounting for some 57% of the publications in our database.

By contrast, only 18% of our publications used qualitative methods, 14% used both quantitative and qualitative methods, and 11% used neither. Most of the publications in our sample (86%) did undertake original research, and the majority (74%) were published as articles, with far smaller numbers published as book chapters (21%) and books (4.6%), which are more common publishing formats in the humanities. The methods and publishing models of the natural sciences therefore dominate HCSS.

In short, even though our categorization scheme understates some of the inequalities in our dataset, it is obvious that severe disparities exist within the 1191 publications we examined. The unprecedented size and comprehensiveness of our sample of HCSS publications allow us to conclude that its inequalities are representative of the field as a whole.

Minor imbalances in the characteristics of a field of study are not necessarily problematic, and indeed some may be inevitable. However, inequalities in the practice of HCSS seem to be so severe that the overwhelming majority of human history, which played out across the vast timespans of the Pleistocene and early Holocene, and in the world beyond Europe and China, is simply neglected by the field. Meanwhile, the primacy of natural scientific publications and methods in HCSS may mean that the field as a whole is better at robust and rigorous analyses of environmental than social changes. That may in turn hinder how effectively the field identifies historical responses to climatic trends or anomalies.

4 HCSS Contributions to Policy Development

It is worrisome enough that inequalities in HCSS may distort how scholars understand the past. What is even more concerning, however, is that these inequalities may undermine how the past can be leveraged in today's efforts to confront global warming.

The purpose of some of the earliest work in HCSS was explicitly to help governments prepare for extreme weather that could otherwise destabilize societies. For centuries, some scholars have believed that the study of past environmental changes, and human responses to those changes, benefits society primarily by improving forecasts of future environmental risks, and informing efforts to resist, adapt to, and even exploit those risks. At the turn of the nineteenth century, the astronomer William Herschel, for instance, sought to use grain price records to identify downturns in solar radiation and in turn periods of climatic cooling, which he believed could trigger famine if they happened again. Later in the nineteenth century, the economist William Stanley Jevons used Herschel's methods to seek correlations between lows in solar output, climatic trends, and fluctuations in proxies for societal wellbeing, such as commodity prices or plague deaths, all to safeguard the stability of the British Empire (Maas 2005; Clark 2007; Degroot 2025).

Yet such work was inconclusive and controversial in its day. As HCSS matured in different disciplines in the late twentieth century, most of its practitioners contented themselves with establishing that climate change had influenced history. When public concern over global warming mounted in the late twentieth and early twenty-first centuries, however, many HCSS scholars adopted at least one of four approaches to establishing the present-day relevance of their work. Our dataset allows us not only to evaluate how many scholars follow these approaches, but also to identify differences in how scholars in different disciplines, using different methods and focusing on distinct times and places, use each approach (White et al. 2023).

The first approach has simply been to assert that scholarship in HCSS is fundamentally, indeed inherently connected to serious issues and concerns surrounding anthropogenic global warming. Our database reveals that this is a common approach. Fully 55% of the HCSS publications in our sample explicitly connect their work to modern global warming (Fig. 6). Most do so in order to establish the significance of some element of their analyses. Some, for example, use global warming to justify the spatial parameters of their research, claiming, for example, that because warming is having a severe impact on a region, this impact should be contextualized by analyzing the history of that region. Others justify their topics by arguing, for example, that global warming has forced scholars in a particular discipline to reappraise the forces that shaped the human past.

These claims of present-day relevance vary across the disciplines, regions, methods, and publication formats in our dataset. Of all publications in our sample which use global warming to justify their analyses or claim relevance, some 55.5% can be primarily associated with climatology. This is only partly a consequence of this field accounting for the largest number of publications in our database. Fully 67% of

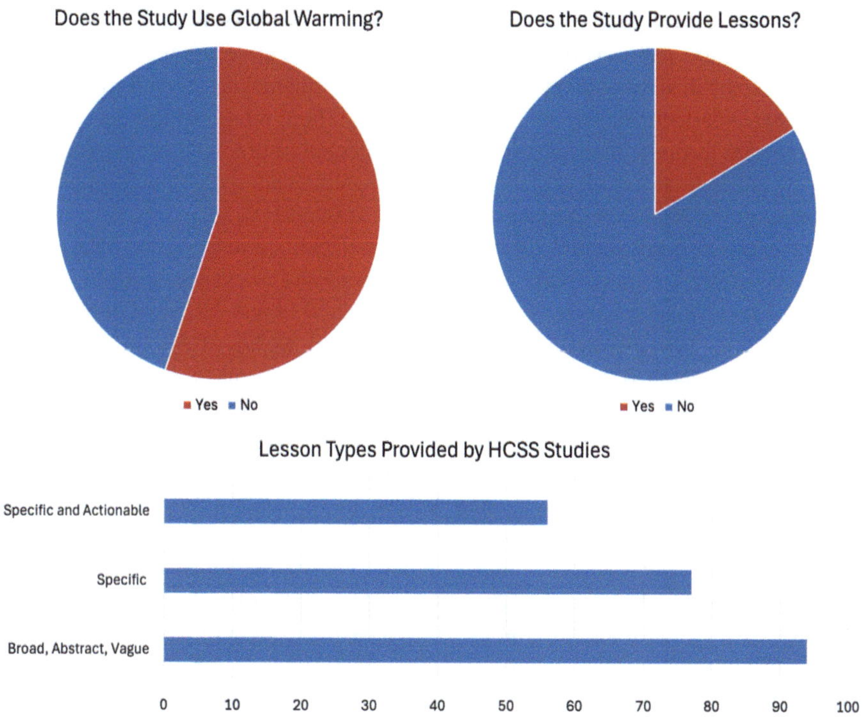

Fig. 6 The number of publications in our dataset the use global warming to establish their relevance (top left), and that provide lessons for the present and future, based on the past (top right). Bottom: a breakdown of the different lesson types in the publications that offer lessons

publications written primarily by climatologists claim significance for modern warming, compared to only 45.8% of publications that we associate with other disciplines. A possible reason is that work in climatology requires costly fieldwork and data analysis, requiring grant applications that emphasize the present-day significance of historical research. The most prestigious publishing venues in climatology are also major scientific journals that accept publications partly on the basis of perceived contemporary relevance.[4]

Because publications in climatology overwhelmingly use quantitative methods to establish causation between human and climatic histories, it is unsurprising that 61.6% of the publications in our sample that use exclusively quantitative methods contend that they are relevant to modern warming, whereas only 46.8% of publications using other analytical methods make the same claim. Beyond the incentives for referring to global warming in climatology that we outline above, there may be

[4]See, for example: NSF 22–612: Paleo Perspectives on Present and Projected Climate (P4CLIMATE). National Science Foundation. Available at: https://www.nsf.gov/funding/opportunities/p4climate-paleo-perspectives-present-projected-climate/nsf22-612/solicitation?utm_source=chatgpt.com

another reason that quantitative methods encourage references to modern warming. The econometric methods often associated with quantitative scholarship in HCSS seem to establish statistical relationships between climatic and societal trends, such as economic performance or the frequency of war. These relationships can appear to be consistent through time, including in the projected future, so it is easy for quantitative studies to at least imply that their findings indicate the potential impacts of global warming (classic examples: Burke et al. 2009, 2015).

There are also substantial differences in how publications in our dataset that focus on different regions make claims of present-day relevance. Fully 67.2% of publications about Asia make these claims, compared to just 39.2% of publications about Europe. This difference arises partly because 33.4% of studies using only quantitative methods focus on Asia, whereas just 23.3% focus on Europe. That disparity may partly originate from the longer and more continuous textual record that documents the history of China, versus the history of Europe, which provides a larger sample for econometric methods that have been pioneered by Chinese geographers (Fan 2015 for a slightly dated review; more recent publications: Lee and Qiang 2023; Lee 2022; Zhang et al. 2022).

There are also significant differences among the smaller subsets of publications in our dataset that focus on other regions. Some 85% of publications on polar regions, 64% on Oceania, 58% on the Americas, and 51.1% on Africa make these claims of present relevance, compared to just 37.7% of publications on the Middle East. It is possible that the number of publications in our dataset that focus on each region is small enough to create a small sample bias that provides extreme results. It is also possible, however, that HCSS scholarship on the polar regions and Oceania is more likely to mention global warming because these regions are most directly influenced by past and present climate change, owing to shifts in sea ice and sea level.

In HCSS, claims of present-day relevance also seem to vary by publication format. Some 60% of articles and 71% of books in our dataset refer to global warming to emphasize their relevance, but only 34% of edited volume chapters do. This difference may stem from the reality that claims of broad, existential relevance tend to be concentrated in the introduction or conclusion of edited volumes (which we categorized under "book") and not repeated in each individual chapter.

5 From Claims of Relevance to Lessons from the Past

One problem with this first approach to establishing the contemporary relevance of HCSS scholarship is that it is too vague to be meaningful. It is, in fact, not self-evident that research on the past has any tangible significance for present-day efforts to confront global warming, given the radical differences between the modern world and that of the pre-industrial or indeed pre-digital period, not to mention between today's climate and environmental changes and those of the past. A second approach HCSS scholars have taken has therefore been to draw explicit parallels between the past, present, and future human responses to climate change. In other words, scholars may identify "lessons" for the present in how communities of the past experienced climate change (Kageyama et al. 2024).

Only a small minority (16%) of the publications in our dataset include these lessons (Fig. 6). In fact, of the 55% of publications that used anthropogenic warming to establish their relevance, only 25% attempt to demonstrate that relevance by providing lessons. Once again, there are significant differences in the quantity of HCSS publications from different disciplines, focusing on different regions and periods, in distinct publication formats, that provide lessons (Fig. 7). However, assessing some of these differences is complicated by small sample bias.

Publications considering the Pleistocene, for example, were most likely to provide lessons (31%), yet represented only a small fraction (10.2%) of the total publications providing lessons (Fig. 7). The reason is probably the very small percentage of publications covering the Pleistocene in the database (2%). Conversely, publications in our dataset that focus on Asia were among the least likely to include lessons (8.9%), but they nevertheless account for a substantial share (12.3%) of all publications that include lessons, probably because they amount to such a large proportion of our overall database (22.8%).

The most striking differences in the use of lessons in our dataset involves divisions among disciplines and methods. Climatology publications are the most likely to argue that their findings are relevant to present-day global warming (67% made this claim), but they are the least likely to provide lessons (only 8.3% of climatology articles provide them). By contrast, 31% of publications in literature, 27% in archaeology, and 22% in history provide lessons.

As a result, even though our sample includes far more publications in climatology than in history or archaeology, and even though a far larger proportion of paleoclimatology publications make claims of present-day relevance than literature (57% of publications in that discipline claim relevance), archaeology (50%), or history (37%), the overall percentage of publications in our dataset that provided lessons and originated from paleoclimatology (23%) was actually slightly lower than the percentage that came from history (24%) and only marginally higher than the percentage that came from archaeology (21%). In fact, only 11% of publications that used only quantitative analytical methods provided lessons, compared to 21% of publications that used both quantitative and qualitative methods, and 29% of those that used only qualitative methods.

It is striking that the discipline (paleoclimatology) and method (quantitative analysis) most likely to be associated with publications that use global warming to highlight their relevance are also least likely to be associated with publications that provide clear explanations for what the past can tell us about the present or future. In theory, such lessons can influence present-day efforts to confront global warming by strengthening public support for policies that mitigate climate change and adapt to its effects.

However, lessons in HCSS studies can be so broad, abstract, or vague that the second approach to establishing relevance in the field can resemble the first one. Studies may conclude, for example, that it is useful to think more seriously about

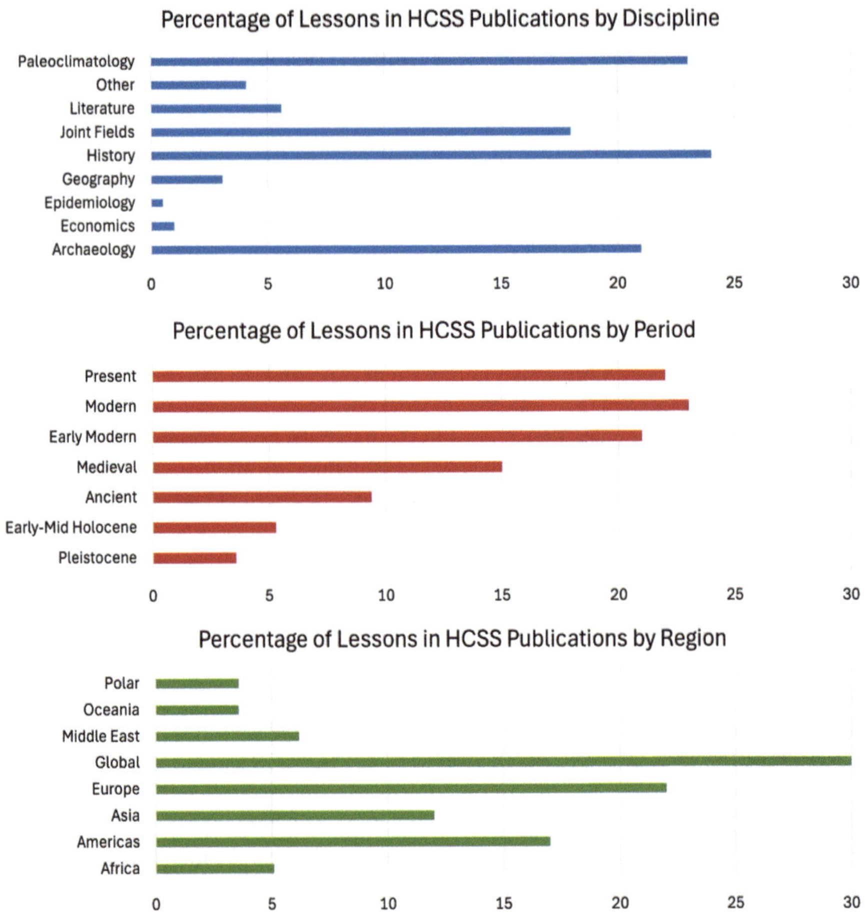

Fig. 7 Lessons provided by the HCSS publications in our database, broken down by Discipline (top), period (middle), and region (bottom)

previously understudied relationships between climate change and humanity, but what that actually means for climate change policymaking and activism is far from clear. Alternatively, broad lessons in HCSS publications can merely confirm truisms in climate change activism and policymaking, such as the idea that greenhouse gas emissions need to be mitigated, or that inequality might undermine resilience in the face of climate change (Tubi et al. 2022).

In some political contexts, there is value in providing yet more support for such truisms. Broad lessons derived from climate's past could, in theory, help motivate activists and policymakers. Yet it seems unlikely that a study about the distant past could provide a truly meaningful increase in motivation when the effects of climate change are obvious in today's world. Nor does it seem likely that lessons pertaining to the whole world, or all of history, can tangibly inform the development or implementation of climate change policies pursued by a particular government with a specific target timeframe (Adamson et al. 2018).

Some HCSS researchers have therefore taken a third approach to establishing relevance by analyzing the past to unearth lessons that are specific to particular times and places. A study might conclude, for example, that transparent communication of climate hazards is essential to avoiding a detrimental outcome *for a distinct community*, or that economic inequality must be reduced to build resilience *in a particular coastal region*.

Of the 16% of HCSS publications in our database that provide lessons, only 34% offer lessons that are specific to a time or place (by comparison, 41% give lessons that are vague and abstract) (Fig. 6). Although the sample is small, it seems that publications in archaeology (13% of all publications in that discipline) and history (9% of all publications) are most likely to provide specific lessons. That may be because most publications in these fields concentrate on a particular time and place, whereas publications in climatology (3.4% of all publications offer specific lessons) can cover larger spatial or temporal scales. It should be noted, however, that of the relatively small number of publications in these three disciplines that provide lessons, a roughly similar fraction provide specific lessons. The sample size for the other disciplines was too small to provide meaningful results.

When publications providing specific lessons are sorted by their geographical and temporal focus, there are some surprising results. In our dataset, more publications with a global focus provide specific lessons (38.9% of the globally focused publications that provide lessons) than publications that focus on distinct regions. One cause is that publications with a wider spatial scope are more likely to constrain their analyses by concentrating on narrow timeframes or a particular kind of community.

A similar dynamic may explain why publications that focus on early time periods seem to provide at least as many specific lessons as those that concentrate on more recent periods. Some 46.5% of publications that consider the early to middle Holocene, for example, provide specific lessons, compared to 35.3% that cover the modern period, and 36.8% of those that examine the present. Again, publications that are broader in one dimension—in this case, spatial—tend to narrow their analyses in others, which in turn makes them likelier to provide specific lessons.

Specific lessons are nevertheless not necessarily translatable into specific actions by policymakers or activists. They are, in other words, not intrinsically *actionable.* A small subset of HCSS scholars have accordingly taken a final, fourth approach to establishing their present-day relevance by formulating lessons that are both specific and theoretically actionable to policymakers or activists.

For example, a study taking the first approach to demonstrating relevance in HCSS may claim that a historical analysis of drought and human responses to drought along the Colorado River is valuable in the fight against global warming. A study taking the second approach could argue that this analysis contributes to the fight by revealing how populations that prepare for drought can survive its effects. A study taking the third approach might pinpoint how a particular form of irrigation farming had proven resilient in the face of historical droughts along the Colorado

River. Finally, a study taking the fourth approach could provide guidance on how water from the Colorado should be allocated to specific communities on the basis of historical variance in year-to-year and decade-to-decade precipitation. A characteristic of this last approach is that it provides lessons that are unique to HCSS, meaning they can only be derived by studying the past (Fig. 8).

Until recently, few if any scholars pursued the fourth approach to HCSS, perhaps because it requires detailed knowledge of policy landscapes, possibly at the local level, and in some cases direct engagement with policymakers. It requires HCSS scholars to, in essence, fulfil the role of policy advisors by translating the findings of scholarship into the language of policy. It may even involve working with policy professionals to develop research projects tailored to the needs of policymakers or activists. There are, in other words, daunting barriers that may prevent many HCSS scholars from taking the fourth approach to establishing the relevance of their work.

Scholars associated with some disciplines are much more likely to include specific, actionable lessons. Out of all the publications in our database that offer lessons, some 37.3% in climatology include actionable lessons, compared to 13.2% of publications in history, and 27.1% in archaeology. As a result, some 33.3% of

Approach	Example	Theory of Change
Mention Global Warming, No Lesson	Dutch history in the Little Ice Age (LIA) matters today	Influence public opinion, increase support for further research
Broad, Abstract, Vague Lesson	Dutch resilience to the LIA shows the value of being flexible when climate changes	Influence the public as well as policymakers and activists
Specific Lesson	LIA floods in Zeeland reveal that dams offer imperfect protection when climate changes	Indirectly contribute to policy development and activism
Specific, Actionable Lesson	LIA floods in Zeeland show that local *wisselpolders* must be created to elevate land	Directly contribute to policy development or implementation, and activism

Fig. 8 Different approaches to establishing relevance in HCSS, including examples and theoretical contributions to current efforts in mitigating greenhouse gas emissions and adapting to anthropogenic global warming

publications that use quantitative analytical methods and use lessons provide actionable lessons, while just 16.9% of publications that use qualitative methods do so. Even though the climatology publications in our dataset are least likely to include lessons, they are therefore most likely to include lessons that are valuable in the formulation of policy. Again, econometric methods can lend themselves to modelling the future, in ways that may encourage HCSS scholars to provide actionable lessons (Holm and Winiwarter 2017).

Our dataset also reveals significant differences in the likelihood that publications examining various regions provide specific, actionable lessons. Out of all publications in our database that provide lessons, 38.5% that focus on Asia, 39.5% that consider the Americas, and 50% that concentrate on Africa offer specific, actionable lessons (though we should note that our sample of publications on Africa is small). By contrast, just 12.8% of publications focusing on Europe provide such lessons, and 6.3% of publications that consider the Middle East (though again, our sample of publications on the Middle East is small). Part of the reason is that studies by historians, using qualitative methods, have tended to focus on Europe.

There is, however, a remarkable similarity in the tendency of publications exploring different time periods to provide specific, actionable lessons. The percentage ranges from 30.1% for publications that concentrate on the present, to 23.5% for those that focus on the ancient world (again, out of all publications that provide lessons). It may seem that it is easier to extract actionable lessons from analyses of recent periods, which can be studied with high resolution data and involve populations that are more similar to those of today. In fact, if there is any connection between time period and the tendency to provide actionable lessons, it is very modest.

It is important to note that although the fourth approach to establishing relevance in HCSS may be more directly applicable to the development of policy, it is not necessarily superior to other approaches. Applied research can easily seem more valuable in addressing present-day concerns than basic research. Yet, of course, applied research builds on basic research, and it is not always clear in advance what basic research will be most useful when applied. Moreover, the value of HCSS in ongoing efforts to address global warming lies partly in its capacity to reveal relationships between climatic and human changes that research in other fields cannot detect. This capacity can be limited when HCSS is pursued in order to address the specific requirements of policymakers.

HCSS publications that pursue the fourth approach to establishing relevance can also be less accessible to the public. Although their direct implications for policy development can be more obvious, their indirect contributions—in shaping public opinion—can be weaker. This is an important shortcoming, because the key challenge in climate change policymaking is less the formulation of effective policy and more the creation of public and political support for policy, especially policy that reduces greenhouse gas emissions.

Nevertheless, it is impossible to pin down how important HCSS has been in influencing public opinion, and thereby shaping policy development. Far more tangible are the contributions to policy documents that become possible when HCSS scholars take the fourth approach to establishing present-day relevance. It is these contributions that seem to unlock the possibility for HCSS to meaningfully influence the development, creation or implementation of climate change policies, and thereby to directly contribute to the present-day fight against global warming.

6 HCSS Today: Evaluating Strengths, Weaknesses, and Ways Forward

Our database confirms that HCSS has become a thriving field, with numerous studies published annually across many disciplines. However, we also find that the field has significant shortcomings that undermine its potential contributions to both the study of historical change, and the ongoing effort to confront the crisis of anthropogenic climate change.

Perhaps the gravest shortcoming of the field is that it is imbalanced. Our large dataset indicates that climatologists publish nearly half of all HCSS publications, and accordingly the field is dominated by their quantitative methods of establishing causation between climatic and historical changes. More than half of all publications in the field seem to consider Europe and Asia, while some two-thirds concentrate on the last five centuries.

Owing to these inequalities in HCSS, historical topics that resist quantitative analysis have not been thoroughly explored by HCSS scholars—the role of gender in shaping the social impacts of climate change, for instance—while vast regions and timescales have been largely ignored. For example, by some metrics human history has overwhelmingly unfolded in Africa amid the spectacular climatic fluctuations of the Pleistocene, yet in our dataset there are fewer publications on that sweeping history than there are on the Little Ice Age in corners of Europe.

As a result of these imbalances, HCSS does not come close to comprehensively revealing how climate change influenced human history. It also cannot contribute meaningfully to the development of climate change solutions across much of the world, or involving every aspect of human identity.

A second major shortcoming of HCSS is that scholars have either overstated their contribution to climate change policymaking or missed opportunities to engage directly with policy development. It is certainly not the case that all HCSS studies should include specific, actionable recommendations for policy development. Yet it is surely not helpful for HCSS scholars to argue that their findings help solve the climate crisis unless they clearly explain how those findings actually contribute to global warming solutions. It does not reflect well on the field that although many HCSS publications claim relevance in the fight against global warming, only a small minority actually seek to substantiate that claim. Worse, publications associated with the discipline that dominates the field (climatology) are least likely to substantiate their claims to relevance.

To fully realize its potential for illuminating the past and safeguarding the future, HCSS must therefore evolve in two ways. First, it must grow more diverse. It must involve greater contributions from more disciplines, with more kinds of evidence interpreted using more analytical methods, and it must, to a greater extent, examine more periods and places.

Second, HCSS publications can no longer provide misleading claims to present-day relevance. Such claims must either be supported with clear explanations of how and why the past should matter today, or they must be omitted altogether. Not all publications should provide specific and actionable lessons. Yet it is surely a problem for the field that only 6.3% of all publications in our 1191-entry dataset provide specific lessons for the present that are derived from the past, and only 4.6% give specific and actionable lessons. We believe that, for HCSS to be truly useful in the urgent effort to confront global warming, these percentages must increase.

Until very recently, no society that ever confronted an existential threat could study the 300,000-year-record of human history to learn how other societies had coped with similar challenges. HCSS scholars have forged that tool for our civilization. Yet to make it truly useful, we have more work ahead of us. We hope that this chapter has provided a roadmap for that work.

References

Adamson, G., M. Hannaford, and Eleonora Rohland. 2018. Re-thinking the present: The role of a historical focus in climate change adaptation research. *Global Environmental Change* 48:195–205.

Beinart, W., and Lotte Hughes. 2007. *Environment and empire*. Oxford: Oxford University Press.

Brookfield, M. 2011. The desertification of the Egyptian Sahara during the Holocene (the last 10,000 years) and its influence on the rise of Egyptian civilization. In *Landscapes and societies: Selected cases*, ed. I. P. Martini and W. Chesworth, 91–108. Dordrecht: Springer.

Burke, M. B., E. Miguel, S. Satyanath, J. A. Dykema, and D. B. Lobell. 2009. Warming increases the risk of civil war in Africa. *Proceedings of the National Academy of Sciences* 106 (49): 20670–20674.

Burke, M., S. M. Hsiang, and E. Miguel. 2015. Global non-linear effect of temperature on economic production. *Nature* 527:235–239.

Chaplin, Joyce. 2025. What Ben Franklin knew about climate change—in 1740. *Washington Post*, March 3, 2025.

Clark, S. 2007. *The Sun kings*. Princeton: Princeton University Press.

Cook, E. R., K. J. Anchukaitis, B. M. Buckley, R. D. D'Arrigo, G. C. Jacoby, and W. E. Wright. 2010a. Asian monsoon failure and megadrought during the last millennium. *Science* 328:486–489.

Cook, E. R., R. Seager, R. R. Heim Jr., R. S. Vose, C. Herweijer, and C. Woodhouse. 2010b. Megadroughts in North America: Placing IPCC projections of hydroclimatic change in a long-term palaeoclimate context. *Journal of Quaternary Science* 25:48–61.

Cook, E. R., R. Seager, Y. Kushnir, K. R. Briffa, U. Büntgen, D. Frank, et al. 2015. Old world megadroughts and pluvials during the common era. *Science Advances* 1 (10): e1500561.

Degroot, D. 2019. Little ice age lessons. *Aeon Magazine*, 11 November 2019.

Degroot, D. 2022. Spotlight 1.1, beyond crisis and collapse: Climate change in human history. In *Human development report 2021/22: Uncertain times, unsettled lives—Shaping our future in a transforming world*. New York: United Nations Development Programme.

Degroot, Dagomar. 2025. *Ripples on the cosmic ocean: An environmental history of our place in the solar system*. Cambridge, MA: Harvard University Press.
Degroot, D., K. Anchukaitis, M. Bauch, J. Burnham, F. Carnegy, J. Cui, et al. 2021. Towards a rigorous understanding of societal responses to climate change. *Nature* 591:539–550.
Degroot, D., et al. 2022. The history of climate and society: A review of the influence of climate change on the human past. *Environmental Research Letters* 17 (10): 103001.
Demuth, Bathsheba. 2024. Major climate force has been ignored for decades. *The Atlantic*. January 4, 2024.
Fan, K. 2015. Climate change and Chinese history: A review of trends, topics, and methods. *Wiley Interdisciplinary Reviews: Climate Change* 6 (2): 225–238.
Holm, P., and Verena Winiwarter. 2017. Climate change studies and the human sciences. *Global and Planetary Change* 156:115–122.
Howard, A. J. 2019. Environmental archaeology, progress and challenges. *Internet Archaeology* 53. https://doi.org/10.11141/ia.53.1.
Kageyama, M., P. Braconnot, C. M. Chiessi, K. Rehfeld, Y. Ait Brahim, M. Dütsch, et al. 2024. Lessons from paleoclimates for recent and future climate change: Opportunities and insights. *Frontiers in Climate* 6:1511997.
Lee, H. F. 2022. Historical climate-war nexus in the eyes of geographers. *Asian Geographer* 39 (1): 93–112.
Lee, H. F., and Wei Qiang. 2023. Climatic extremes, violent conflicts, and population change in China in 1741–1910: An investigation using spatial econometrics. *Anthropocene* 41:100372.
Ljungqvist, F. C., Andrea Seim, and Heli Huhtamaa. 2021. Climate and society in European history. *Wiley Interdisciplinary Reviews: Climate Change* 12 (2): e691.
Maas, H. 2005. *William Stanley Jevons and the making of modern economics*. Cambridge: Cambridge University Press.
McNeill, J. R. 2010. The state of the field of environmental history. *Annual Review of Environment and Resources* 35 (1): 345–374.
Morgan, Ruth, et al. 2022. Water. In *Climate change 2022: Impacts, adaptation and vulnerability. Contribution of working group II to the sixth assessment report of the intergovernmental panel on climate change*, ed. Hans-Otto Pörtner, Debra C. Roberts, Helen Adams, Carlo Adler, Carolina Alder, David Ali, Sherilee Harper, et al., 551–712. Cambridge: Cambridge University Press.
Murphy, Charlene, and D. Q. Fuller. 2017. The future is long-term: Past and current directions in environmental archaeology. *General Anthropology* 24 (1): 1–10.
Tubi, A., L. Mordechai, E. Feitelson, P. Kay, and D. Tamir. 2022. Can we learn from the past? Towards better analogies and historical inference in society-environmental change research. *Global Environmental Change* 76:102570.
Warren, R., N. E. Bartlome, N. Wellinger, J. Franke, R. Hand, S. Brönnimann, and H. Huhtamaa. 2024. ClimeApp: Data processing tool for monthly, global climate data from the ModE-RA palaeo-reanalysis, 1422 to 2008 CE. *Climate of the Past* 20 (12): 2645–2662.
White, S., Q. Pei, K. Kleemann, L. Dolák, H. Huhtamaa, and C. Camenisch. 2023. New perspectives on historical climatology. *Wiley Interdisciplinary Reviews: Climate Change* 14 (1): e808.
Williams, M. 2021. *When the Sahara was green: How our greatest desert came to be*. Princeton: Princeton University Press.
Zhang, S., Qing Pei, and D. D. Zhang. 2022. A quantitative analysis of the relationship between climate change and war along the silk road regions during the little ice age. *Quaternary Sciences* 42 (1): 250–260.

Bridging History and Policymaking via Systems Thinking

Ricardo Fernandes

Abstract This article examines the integration of historical analysis into policymaking via systems thinking to address the complexities of human-environmental systems. It discusses practical, epistemological, and ontological uncertainties in applying historical insights to policy. The article advocates for interdisciplinary collaboration, transparent workflows, and formal modelling to align policies with historical insights and enhance decision-making processes.

Keywords System · Complexity · Human-environment relationship · Chaos · Ontology · Epistemology · Modelling

1 Introduction

The past is studied for various reasons. Among these, perhaps one purpose stands out with long-lasting appeal, advocated by many historians across generations, yet also critiqued as challenging to achieve: the application of history to policymaking. My perspective on the topic emerged from my work within archaeological sciences, where I spent years developing and improving methods to reconstruct the past under the various theoretical perspectives proposed by colleague archaeologists and historians, enlarging the range of informative material remains, modelling uncertainties, and producing results aiming at the best possible precision and accuracy. This pursuit has driven my career, seeking to ensure the robustness of the workflow linking material remains, historical sources, models, and theory so that answering historical questions and testing alternative hypotheses becomes a reliable endeavour. I saw this as the platform on which the understanding of the past and its potential application to policymaking should rest. Yet, as my interest in the role of the past in

R. Fernandes (✉)
Max Planck Institute of Geoanthropology, Jena, Thüringen, Germany

Faculty of Archaeology, University of Warsaw, Warsaw, Poland
e-mail: fernandes@gea.mpg.de

J. F. Haldon, R. Fernandes (eds.), *Bridging History and Policy*, Understanding Complex Systems, https://doi.org/10.1007/978-3-032-24379-9_5

policymaking grew, I encountered broader and sometimes more fundamental types of uncertainty which extended beyond such a narrow workflow: deeper epistemological and ontological issues, core uncertainties imposed by the nature of complex systems, and communication uncertainties among researchers, policymakers, and the public. This article offers a personal overview of the bridging process and associated uncertainties linking history, which is understood here as the inter- and multidisciplinary study of the past and policymaking via systems thinking. Previous in-depth discussions across these topics can be found elsewhere (e.g., Turchin 2008, 2011; Geyer and Cairney 2015; Haldon et al. 2018; Daems 2021; Davis 2024).

2 Systems Thinking for Human-Environmental Systems

Systems thinking is the general framework for the discussion that follows. Within this, complexity, characterised by various features (e.g., emergence, nonlinearity, critical transitions), is increasingly recognised as a topic of research across research disciplines, including history, economics, and environmental sciences. Big History, for instance, describes complexification processes across time, starting with the Big Bang and continuing to modern societies (Christian 2004). There is no universally accepted system definition, but I will describe it here as a set of interconnected components that exchange signals, energy, or matter following some rules. This definition can characterise diverse ontologies of economic, social, cultural, environmental, and technological systems collectively termed human-environmental systems. A simple example of an isolated two-component system is that of a human group with access to constrained food resources: population growth, assuming no population control, increases food demands, leading to scarcity, which reduces population size in a feedback loop, often manifesting as boom-and-bust cycles. Such nonlinear dynamics are mathematically described using relatively simple interaction rules grounded on historical (e.g., Malthusian model) and ecological (prey-predator) studies. Similar models describe human relationships with other types of resources (e.g., fossil fuels, wages). Understanding such dynamics directly impacts policies directed towards scarcity problems (e.g., population control, productivity increases, innovation into alternative resources).

A chaotic system is deterministic but exhibits high sensitivity to initial conditions, where slight variations can lead to vastly different outcomes, rendering long-term predictions difficult. A chaotic system is more predictable at short time scales, but as stochasticity increases over time, predictive power is reduced. Nonetheless, chaotic systems may reveal patterns or attractors (a range of preferred states visited across time) towards which they will gravitate. For instance, the historical examples compiled by Scheidel in "The Great Leveler" revealed that economic inequality is almost exclusively reduced by major catastrophic events (wars, political revolutions, pandemics, or state collapses) that disrupt historically established social, political, and economic relationships (Scheidel 2017). In contrast to fully chaotic systems, complex systems show lower dependence on initial conditions and exhibit self-organisation and higher-level emergent properties that cannot be predicted from the behaviour of individual components (Mitchell 2009). Emergence is opposed to reductionist approaches, as properties of human-environmental systems like cultural phenomena or forms of social and political organisation cannot be analytically deduced solely from isolated individual behaviours. Although the concept of emergence is debated and contested, there are clear computational limitations when it comes to predicting the behaviour of higher-level properties of a system from its components (e.g., predicting consciousness from cell properties, or crowd behaviours from individual characteristics) (Kim 1999; Mitchell 2009). In this respect, Stephen Wolfram introduced the concept of computational irreducibility, according to which complex systems' behaviour must be simulated since it cannot be analytically predicted (Wolfram 2002).

Complex adaptive systems (CAS) are a subset of complex systems where system components can learn and have the ability to adapt their properties and behaviours. Classified as such are humans, the associations they form, and their interactions with their surrounding environment. Human agents process signals to generate information and can imagine alternative future scenarios to inform decisions and actions involving the exchange of energy and matter with other human agents and their environment. However, these actions are not only the result of deliberate and careful thought but often of fast, non-immediately conscious mental processes that are essential for daily survival but that may also result in errors and biases that are potentially counterproductive towards set goals (Kahneman 2011). Human learning and mental model development result from loop-feedbacks taking place at different time scales among individual and cultural learning histories and of a genetic legacy (Gopnik and Wellman 2012; Heyes 2018). Research into neuroplasticity has revealed that the human brain can reorganise itself in response to individual experiences (Maguire et al. 2000). The exchange of information and models among humans relies on different coding systems, but verbal language in oral and written formats predominates. So much so that natural language is often equated to thought, although non-verbal forms of learning suggest that thinking processes are likely positioned at a deeper level (Chomsky 2000; Pinker 2003). This catalogue of human characteristics, and their immutability or mutability, is certainly selective and subject to dispute. Still, it illustrates some of the considerations that must be made in modelling and simulation exercises aimed at anticipating future scenarios and reproducing emergent behaviours. Selections of human characteristics and relationships have been structured across a theoretical spectrum (e.g., game theory, social exchange theory, rational choice theory, prospect theory) that can be constrained and evaluated using historical data (Levy 2003; Greif 2006; Voigtländer and Voth 2012; Cederman and Weidmann 2017).

Emerging from individual human interactions are organisations classified into different ontological units (e.g., communities, institutions, states) which can be described as agents with goals and learning and adaptation abilities. Complexification continues into higher ontological levels (e.g., civilisations, international organisations), stretching across local, national, and global politics. Although such taxonomy is familiar, there are alternatives, and similarly, there are a variety of proposals for system delimitation and ontological units across social, economic, technological, and environmental systems. For instance, models of technological systems may include connections among artefacts, research institutions, knowledge, and social organisations with agency in some proposals given to artefacts (Latour 2005). Broader systems of systems may include transversal links or links within nested systems. The concept of downward causation has been employed to describe the impact of higher-level system components on lower-level components (Campbell 1974). While niche construction, an idea initially developed within evolutionary biology and ecology, describes the loop-feedback interactions between organisms and their environments, leading to evolutionary pressures and evolutionary responses (Odling-Smee et al. 2003). Niche construction has been extended to encompass cultural, technological, and social feedback loops (Stotz 2010). However, a wide, holistic perspective of human-environmental systems, although often associated with systems thinking, can result in computationally intractable modelling problems and uninterpretable simulations. A potential way forward is to focus on key actors, as exemplified by realism theory in international relations. This simplifies international political dynamics by setting great powers as the primary drivers of political outcomes (Waltz 1979; Mearsheimer 2001). This approach finds empirical support in historical network analyses revealing that a small fraction of nodes have disproportionate influence over time (Pareto rule or Matthew effect via preferential attachment). Historical comparisons may also indicate that diverse complexity features show strong correlations, allowing for simplified models (Turchin et al. 2018).

Historical analysis oscillates between idiographic views, which treat historical moments as unique and nomothetic perspectives, which propose common patterns. These may have separate policymaking implications, with the former cautioning against overgeneralising context-specific examples, while the latter may enable probabilistic forecasting of systemic behaviours. To aid in navigating this divide, I introduce here a classification of human-environmental systems, based on the system classification introduced by Stephen Wolfram for cellular automata (Wolfram 2002), which classifies human-environmental systems according to the historical behaviour of selected system properties:

- Type 1 systems: stable patterns over time with inputs having predictable outputs. Examples: isolated and centralised authoritarian regimes and persistent social and cultural norms (e.g. caste system).
- Type 2 systems: periodic patterns. Examples: demographic and economic cycles (Kondratieff 1935; Turchin and Nefedov 2009).
- Type 3 systems: chaotic (aperiodic), showing high sensitivity to slight variations in system conditions. Examples: phases of political or economic turbulence with potential cascading effects.
- Type 4 systems: complex systems with emergent structures, adaptation, and non-repeating but coherent patterns. Examples: cities, market economies, and democratic societies.

Adaptive human-environmental systems are assigned by default to Type 4. Such systems are described as being at the "edge of chaos", where complex systems are most likely to exhibit self-organisation, spontaneously developing order and structure without external control (Kauffman 1993). Nonetheless, assuming a Lindy effect (the longer something non-biological has existed, the more probable it is that it will continue to exist in the future) (Taleb 2014), the classification can aid in modelling choices when human-environmental systems approach Types 1–3 behaviours. The classification is tied to ontological and spatiotemporal scales of analysis, which are relevant to policymaking. In this respect, complex systems may exhibit a deep history of path dependencies, often arising from accidental events (Gell-Mann 1995). There is currently an intense debate on the origins of human environmental impacts at a planetary scale with alternative proposals setting its onset with development of farming, capitalism, human cognitive features and the Enlightenment, the industrial revolution, and the post WWII economic system (McGilchrist 2009; Steffen et al. 2015; Moore 2016; Rosen 2023). Answering such questions requires time-extended and high-resolution datasets to detect change points and undertake counterfactual modelling. For datasets extending until the present, tipping point detection methods can be employed to identify critical thresholds and anticipate system transitions (Scheffer 2009; Dakos et al. 2024).

Policymaking insights offered by historical perspectives and systems thinking can be found across temporal scales. Political and societal systems that undergo slow growth can undergo a sudden collapse (Seneca effect) (Bardi 2017). In "The Collapse of Complex Societies" Tainter described how, as societies increase in complexity and demand more energy to solve problems, they may reach a point of diminishing returns on that complexity, leading to collapse (Tainter 1988). Preceding this work, the 1972 "The Limits to Growth" report by the Club of Rome argued that continued exponential growth in population and resource use would inevitably lead to a collapse of human-environmental systems (Meadows et al. 1972).

The 2007 financial crisis revealed feedback loops linking economic, political, and social systems, with austerity measures destabilising social order and leading to major political unrest, not unlike previous economic crises (Reinhart and Rogoff 2009). The COVID-19 pandemic exposed vulnerabilities in optimised global trade networks, suggesting that redundant, albeit less efficient trade systems, promote robustness with historical research linking societal resilience to access to decentralised trade networks (Diamond 2005; Bang 2009). Anti-fragile systems, which thrive under stress, have been associated with higher resilience of decentralised systems, including governance systems (Taleb 2014). Historical cyclical patterns of political violence in the USA were linked to immiseration and elite overproduction and accurately predicted the 2020s instability (Turchin 2010, 2023). The interplay between innovation and path dependencies is illustrated by the rise of internal combustion vehicles that were less numerous than electric vehicles around the late 19th and early 20th centuries and whose rise shaped current global economy, transportation infrastructures, and culture (Kirsch 1997). Chesterton's Fence principle warns against dismantling existing systems without understanding their purpose. An example was the negative consequences of dismantling Bali's traditional rice fields during the well-intentioned Green Revolution (Lansing et al. 2017; Lansing and Cox 2019). Conversely, negative path dependencies, such as systemic inequality, demand policy interventions to break historical patterns (Acemoglu and Robinson 2012).

Policymaking is an iterative process through which governing bodies and other formal or informal organisations set agendas, design and implement selected policies, and evaluate outcomes to control, promote, and hinder change (Lindblom 1959; Kingdon 1995; Weimer and Vining 2005). Policymakers faced with decision-making must consider primary policy goals, multi-order consequences, resource allocation, tempo of measure implementation, and whether to pursue bottom-up or top-down approaches (Baumgartner and Jones 2010; Elmore 1979; Hood 1983; North 1990; Pierson 2000). Furthermore, political stability is a critical feedback loop, and voting cycles in democratic societies impact policy design. A substantial body of literature promotes systems thinking for policy design and implementation (e.g., Rittel and Webber 1973; Cohen and Axelrod 1999; Room 2011; Geyer and Cairney 2015). Policymaking recommendations under complexity may include raising awareness for loop-feedback mechanisms, mapping interconnected risks, the planning of infrastructure with redundant features, multi-scenario planning, the use of models such as agent-based modelling for policy simulation, undertaking small scale trials across alternative policy options, creating multidisciplinary teams, and dynamic policy evaluation. The study of the past can make multiple contributions to policymaking. At the forefront it aids in the conceptualisation of systems and can offer scenarios relevant to policy goals. It is a source of observational data relevant, when policy experimentation is impractical or unethical, and can thus contribute to identifying past policy failures and successes and in enabling counterfactual analysis. The study of the past can identify path dependencies and lasting legacies that must be assessed prior to pursuing policy goals. Finally, by assessing historical trends, that carry until the present, it may offer insights to anticipate emerging shifts and threats.

3 Ontological and Epistemological Aspects

Navigating the ontological possibilities of human-environmental systems can pose a formidable challenge for historians and policymakers. The act of orienting attention to demarcate systems and define their components and interactions reflects policy decisions and historical contexts that shape conceptual frameworks (Ingold 2000; Latour 2005). Historians and others engaged with the study of the past must construct ontologies and analyse dynamic human-environmental scenarios across time (Smail and Shryock 2013; White 2014). Such scenarios include the development and evolution of concepts, shaped by cultural, technological, economic, and social factors (Cronon 1992; McNeill and Engelke 2016). In policymaking, where concepts are employed across specific time scales, historians' ability to identify the possibilities and limitations of both time-specific and transversal, abstract concepts, such as "resilience" or "sustainability", can contribute to making policy models align with actionable timeframes (Folke 2006). Historical analysis can offer a critical lens for balancing continuity and adaptability in proposing the ontological models supporting policy design (Scott 1998; Jasanoff 2004).

Our understanding of the past is neither static nor universally agreed upon; it is contested and continually reshaped by access to new data, evolving methodologies across the various historical disciplines and sub-disciplines, and conceptual innovations (Carr 1961; Ginzburg 1980; Iggers 2013). This fluidity complicates the establishment of shared ontologies which is compounded by fundamental differences in epistemological and theoretical views. Postmodern perspectives generally argue that modern and historical narratives are socially constructed, imbued with subjective interpretations (Jenkins 2003; White 2014). A claim to subjective knowledge is itself an absolute claim, and broad causal models are not absent from postmodern perspectives. Michel Foucault focused on power dynamics and how, from such dynamic concepts like "madness" or "punishment", emerge and serve to legitimise social orders (Foucault 1989, 2013, 2019). Language constructs, such as those linked to national or religious identity, profoundly influence human behaviour (Ranger and Hobsbawm 1983; Said 1978; Anderson 2006). Power dynamics can dictate historical narratives, as seen in revisionist accounts serving ideological ends (Bhaskar 1975; Nora 1989; Appleby et al. 2011). However, a purely constructivist view, denying the past's independent existence, ignores the bidirectional nature of knowledge creation, where historical evidence constrains present interpretations (Bunzl 1997; Evans 1997).

While social construction undeniably shapes proposals for human-environmental systems (Berger and Luckmann 1966), realist arguments impose constraints on the range of possible models. Non-naïve realistic views hold that objective reality exists independently of human perception but that our knowledge of it is mediated by conceptual systems, social constructs, and fallible methods, requiring iterative processes to approximate truth (Bhaskar 1975; Castree 2004). Structural realism posits that while postulated unobservable entities may change across iterative knowledge processes, relational structures describing relationships are preserved (Worrall 1989; Ladyman 1998). Here, I will invoke the non-contradiction principle and the need for internal coherence for proposals of human-environmental systems. This position does not impose the proposal of wide-scale unifying models and their ontological entities. Separate system definitions and hierarchies of systems can be proposed, however, internal coherence within each system must be preserved, as well as coherence for the relationships that link separate systems. Contradictions are handled by updating model definitions.

Another realist argument concerns the alignment of proposals for human-environmental models with fundamental physical realities, particularly biological realities, such as human death and biological finitude (Jonas 1966; Rose 1990). While natural sciences are not immune to social construction, which is evident in debates over medical definitions of human death, there are physical universal constraints that are difficult to dispute (Searle 1995; Hacking 2000). Historically, death has been both a policy instrument, as in armed conflicts or capital punishment, and a problem to address, as in public health initiatives or speculative pursuits of technological immortality (Hayles 1999; Foucault 2003; Esposito 2008). Within contemporary policymaking multiple global challenges underscore the urgency of models grounded in physical and biological realities: armed conflicts and an underlying new global cold war, pandemics, climate crises, and potential AI-driven disruptions (Bostrom 2016; Correia and Willis 2022; Anderson and May 2023; Global conflict tracker 2025). Climate policies, for instance, must account for the finite resilience of Earth systems to temperature changes and tipping points, just as pandemic responses must address mortality rates (Steffen et al. 2018; Brovkin et al. 2021; Rockström et al. 2023). In a globalised world, where interconnected systems amplify the consequences of policy failures, models that ignore physical boundary conditions risk catastrophic misalignment (Armstrong McKay et al. 2025).

The coherence argument applies to the fit between model and data. Data is itself the result of a conceptualisation and selection process where a theory (often an explanatory narrative) is translated into formal models and their variables (e.g., Gini coefficient), which are linked to the phenomena of interest (e.g., inequality). Immediate model variables may themselves result from a process involving lower-level variables, with the process being itself described via sub-models (e.g., calculating the Gini coefficient from archaeological data) (Crema et al. 2025). Constraining the set of possible models becomes a task for historical research (Turchin et al. 2018). However, multiple competing models may equally fit the data, and the data itself is prone to errors and biases. This is particularly important for historical data, which is inherently observational, not experimental, though sometimes characterised as the latter (Diamond and Robinson 2011). Thus, evaluating and improving model-data fit is necessarily an iterative and recursive process. Such a process should follow three interlocked principles (3 T principles): 1) triage where the rationale for model and data selection, including theory-model translation, is described; 2) traceability where the entire workflow (and workflow phylogenies) from data to results, including links within models and sub-models, are clearly presented; 3) transparency that ensures that triage criteria and traceable processes are long-term shared in open formats and easily accessible and readable by other researchers. These principles align with academic norms for data (Open Access, Open Linked Data formats, FAIR principles), software (Open Source), and Open workflow sharing (Wilkinson et al. 2016). These are critical to mitigate the widely recognised replication and reproducibility crisis in academic research (Ioannidis 2005).

4 Systems Modelling

Models are simplified representations of realities (Frigg and Hartmann 2020). They have limitations, but they should present some utility in distilling target systems into actionable frameworks for policymaking. Within the social sciences, theories typically consist of explanatory narratives. Translating theory to formal models involves higher degrees of abstraction, which risks oversimplification and loss of contextual depth, historical nuance, and interpretive richness (Abbott 2004). While formal models, encompassing mathematical, statistical, logical, and algorithm models, reduce ambiguity and improve clarity, allow for reproducible hypothesis testing, can be employed to explore counterfactuals, produce actionable results, and overcome cognitive limitations in assessing large volumes of diverse data (Epstein 2008). The translation process between theory and a formal model benefits from understanding data formation processes linking data to observable phenomena. It is at this stage that biases should be recognised. For instance, an inverse survivorship bias, a selection bias, arises when only collapsed societies are subject to modelling, skewing the interpretation of the results. However, this constitutes a known bias and can be incorporated into the modelling process, although it may contribute to producing imprecise outputs. Unknown biases, on the other hand, are not incorporated into the modelling process and lead to inaccurate outputs, although these may present desirable levels of precision (Winship and Morgan 1999). This type of uncertainty is classified as epistemic, reflecting incomplete system knowledge.

Modelling uncertainty arises from the tension between simplification and fidelity (Walker et al. 2003). These gaps manifest in distinct epistemic forms. Some uncertainties are quantifiable, emerging from measurable stochasticity or known data limitations, while others are structural, rooted in the impossibility of fully capturing nonlinear interactions or contextual nuance. A further layer arises from ontological indeterminacy, including the translation process between theory and model implementation. Uncertainties in modelling results may allow clear decisions among alternative hypotheses, while no such choice is possible in others, and decisions are made under uncertainty. From a modelling triage perspective, the following four categories describe the fundamental types of uncertainty that influence a model's reliability and applicability:

- Known knowns: human mortality, physical properties of materials.
- Known unknowns: measurement errors, stochastic processes, computational error propagation.
- Unknown unknowns: unrecognised biases, black swan events, emergent phenomena (cannot be predicted but may sometimes be simulated).
- Unknown knowns: known components of a system feature that are not included within a model, for instance, due to the impossibility of translating theoretical aspects into variables. Conversely, variables included in a model that are known not to belong.

Various formal modelling methods are employed to study systems' behaviours. Below, I briefly describe a list of selected methods.

Differential equations (DEs) describe dynamic interactions within systems via relationships that relate system variables and their derivatives. DEs require data on initial conditions (e.g., population size, resource amounts) and parameters (e.g., growth rates, strength of interactions) that can be derived from historical records or proxies. Modelling outputs, obtained analytically or numerically, predict system trajectories, enabling interpretation of stability, oscillations, or bifurcations. Uncertainties arise from parameter estimation errors, incomplete data, and model simplifications, with DE systems potentially exhibiting sensitivity to minor parameter variations. Differential equations are commonly used in econometrics to assess system dynamics and chaotic behaviours (Zhang 1989). DEs have also been used to study ancient demographic and state dynamics (Turchin 2003; Turchin and Nefedov 2009).

Network analysis, static and dynamic, requires relational data to represent system components as nodes and interactions as edges in a graph (Faust and Wasserman 1994). Analysis involves assessing metrics like degree centrality (indicating influence) or modularity (revealing community structures), which can highlight key nodes or actors. Uncertainties arise from incomplete or noisy data, such as missing interactions or biased sampling.

Agent-based modelling (ABM) simulates interactions among agents (individuals, groups, or entities) within a defined environment following specified rules (Romanowska et al. 2021). It can identify emergent system-level behaviours and capture nonlinear dynamics and feedback loops. Results are interpreted through aggregate patterns, such as population dynamics or resource depletion, often visualised via time series or spatial maps. Uncertainties in ABM include parameter uncertainty (e.g., inadequate rules), structural uncertainty (e.g., oversimplified interactions), and stochasticity in agent decisions. This can lead to sensitivity to minor parameter variations, requiring robust sensitivity analyses to assess outcome stability.

Scaling analysis reveals how system properties change with scale, often showing underlying patterns through power-law relationships (West 2017). Invariant scaling exponents describe how variables such as size, frequency, or intensity correlate across scales, offering insights into system behaviour. The method requires data (e.g., population sizes, event frequencies) across multiple scales, often from historical or empirical records. Results are interpreted by fitting data to power-law distributions. Uncertainties arise from data quality, sample size, and model assumptions, such as whether a power law is appropriate or if alternative distributions (e.g., log-normal) fit better. Scaling analyses of ancient and modern cities revealed that urban metrics like innovation and infrastructure scaled differently with population size, offering recommendations for urban policies (Bettencourt et al. 2007).

System analysis using time series data includes change point analysis, counterfactual inference, and tipping point detection. Change point analysis may allow for the detection of path dependencies by identifying critical junctures in temporal datasets where data properties abruptly changed (e.g., slope, variance) (Horváth and Rice 2024). Conversely, counterfactual inference evaluates the impact of an event (versus its non-occurrence) on a target time series through comparisons with other time series (Liu et al. 2024). Tipping point detection, finally, identifies thresholds where systems undergo rapid and often irreversible transitions. It relies on indicators like critical slowing down (increased variance, or autocorrelation) (Scheffer 2009; Scheffer et al. 2012). These longitudinal methods require sufficient data resolution and the absence of data artefacts and lag times between events and data impact.

5 Interdisciplinarity

Systems thinking is an inherently interdisciplinary endeavour. The complexification of academic research, coupled with the rapid expansion of data availability, demands closer collaboration across disciplines and the implementation of translational mechanisms to integrate diverse contributions effectively for policymaking. Interdisciplinary integration should occur at multiple stages, from theoretical discussions and model development to data harmonisation, interpretation and communication of results. Both historians and policy stakeholders are increasingly interdisciplinary, and further integration can be naturally achieved, for instance, through the inclusion of historians in policy panels (Bryson et al. 2015; Haldon et al. 2018; Izdebski et al. 2022). Research findings must be communicated to the public at an appropriate resolution to promote collaborative efforts and the impact of gained knowledge, conveying policy goals and implications clearly while ensuring transparency and traceability in the knowledge generation workflow.

Sustaining interdisciplinary efforts requires dedicated funding from academic institutions and government bodies. Financial support should prioritise initiatives that foster research collaborations with policymaking objectives, rather than reinforcing narrow specialisation. This includes funding for institutions and groups devoted to systems research (e.g., Santa Fe Institute, Vienna Complexity Hub), policy-oriented research projects, and complementary activities such as training workshops. Additionally, systems thinking should be increasingly integrated into university curricula, providing students with theoretical foundations and practical applications. Technology can leverage interdisciplinarity by promoting easier access to knowledge resources, facilitating communication, and decomplexifying the research process. User-friendly modelling software, supported by guided modelling assistance, can streamline access to advanced modelling. Critically informed AI methods, including large language models, can support various tasks from theory to model translation, data harvesting and structuring, workflow documentation, and results summarisation (Dwivedi et al. 2023). Interactive visualisation systems where stakeholders can simultaneously engage, such as the University of Arizona's Decision Theatre, enable policymakers to directly engage with real-time modelling options, fostering an intuitive grasp of policy modelling implications (Miller et al. 2019). The general public would also benefit from similar platforms where complex policy insights are presented in accessible, multimedia, interactive formats.

6 Conclusions

Systems thinking provides a framework for integrating historical insights into policymaking by addressing the complexities of human-environmental systems through formal modelling and interdisciplinary collaboration. Historical analysis reveals path dependencies, cyclical patterns, and systemic vulnerabilities, offering policymakers empirical data for scenario testing and risk mitigation. However, from model simplifications to contested historical interpretations, epistemic uncertainties demand transparency, iterative refinement, and alignment with physical realities. By combining historical knowledge, computational tools, and adaptive governance, policymakers can better navigate nonlinear dynamics, anticipate tipping points, and design robust interventions while avoiding the pitfalls of reductionist approaches. The path forward lies in open workflows, interdisciplinary cooperation, and public engagement to translate systems-aware historical research into actionable policy.

References

Abbott, A. 2004. *Methods of discovery: Heuristics for the social sciences*. New York: W. W. Norton.

Acemoglu, D., and J. A. Robinson. 2012. *Why nations fail: The origins of power, prosperity, and poverty*. New York: Crown Business.

Anderson, B. 2006. *Imagined communities: Reflections on the origin and spread of nationalism*. London: Verso.

Anderson, R. M., and R. M. May. 2023. *Infectious diseases of humans: Dynamics and control*. Oxford: Oxford University Press.

Appleby, J., L. Hunt, and M. Jacob. 2011. *Telling the truth about history*. New York: W. W. Norton.

Armstrong McKay, D. I., et al. 2025. Exceeding 1.5°C global warming could trigger multiple climate tipping points. *Science* 377 (6611): eabn7950. https://doi.org/10.1126/science.abn7950.

Bang, P. F. 2009. *The Roman bazaar: A comparative study of trade and markets in a tributary empire*. Cambridge: Cambridge University Press.

Bardi, U. 2017. *The Seneca effect: Why growth is slow but collapse is rapid*. Cham: Springer.

Baumgartner, F. R., and B. D. Jones. 2010. *Agendas and instability in American politics*. Chicago: University of Chicago Press.

Berger, P. L., and T. Luckmann. 1966. *The social construction of reality: A treatise in the sociology of knowledge*. New York: Doubleday.

Bettencourt, L. M. A., et al. 2007. Growth, innovation, scaling, and the pace of life in cities. *Proceedings of the National Academy of Sciences* 104 (17): 7301–7306. https://doi.org/10.1073/pnas.0610172104.

Bhaskar, R. 1975. *A realist theory of science*. York: Routledge.

Bostrom, N. 2016. *Superintelligence: Paths, dangers, strategies*. Oxford: Oxford University Press.

Brovkin, V., E. Brook, J. W. Williams, S. Bathiany, T. M. Lenton, M. Barton, et al. 2021. Past abrupt changes, tipping points and cascading impacts in the earth system. *Nature Geoscience* 14 (8): 550–558. https://doi.org/10.1038/s41561-021-00790-5.

Bryson, J. M., B. C. Crosby, and M. M. Stone. 2015. Designing and implementing cross-sector collaborations: Needed and challenging. *Public Administration Review* 75 (5): 647–663. https://doi.org/10.1111/puar.12432.

Bunzl, M. 1997. *Real history: Reflections on historical practice*. London-New York: Routledge.

Campbell, D. T. 1974. "Downward causation" in hierarchically organised biological systems. In *Studies in the philosophy of biology*, ed. F. J. Ayala and T. Dobzhansky. London: Palgrave. https://doi.org/10.1007/978-1-349-01892-5_11.

Carr, E. H. 1961. *What is history?* New York: Knopf.

Castree, N. 2004. Nature is dead! Long live nature. *Environment and Planning A: Economy and Space* 36 (2): 191–194. https://doi.org/10.1068/a36209.

Cederman, L.-E., and N. B. Weidmann. 2017. Predicting armed conflict: Time to adjust our expectations? *Science* 355 (6324): 474–476. https://doi.org/10.1126/science.aal4483.

Chomsky, N. 2000. *New horizons in the study of language and mind.* Cambridge-New York: Cambrdge University Press.
Christian, D. 2004. *Maps of time: An introduction to big history*. Berkeley-London: California University Press.
Cohen, M. D., and R. M. Axelrod. 1999. *Harnessing complexity: Organizational implications of a scientific frontier*. New York: The Free Press.
Correia, T., and K. Willis. 2022. Applying critical realism to the COVID-19 pandemic to improve management of future public health crises. *The International Journal of Health Planning and Management* 37 (2): 599–603. https://doi.org/10.1002/hpm.3376.
Crema, E. R., M. Fochesato, A. G. Mejía Ramón, J. Munson, and S. G. Ortman. 2025. Toward multiscalar measures of inequality in archaeology. *Proceedings of the National Academy of Sciences* 122 (16): e2400700121. https://doi.org/10.1073/pnas.2400700121.
Cronon, W. 1992. A place for stories: Nature, history, and narrative. *The Journal of American History* 78 (4): 1347–1376.
Daems, D. 2021. *Social complexity and complex systems in archaeology*. London: Routledge.
Dakos, V., C. A. Boulton, J. E. Buxton, J. F. Abrams, B. Arellano-Nava, D. I. Armstrong McKay, et al. 2024. Tipping point detection and early warnings in climate, ecological, and human systems. *Earth System Dynamics* 15 (4): 1117–1135. https://doi.org/10.5194/esd-15-1117-2024.
Davis, D. S. 2024. Past, present, and future of complex systems theory in archaeology. *Journal of Archaeological Research* 32 (4): 549–596. https://doi.org/10.1007/s10814-023-09193-z.
Diamond, J. 2005. *Collapse: How societies choose to fail or succeed*. New York: Viking.
Diamond, J., and J. A. Robinson. 2011. *Natural experiments of history*. Cambridge MA: Belknap Press.
Dwivedi, Y. K., N. Kshetri, L. Hughes, E. L. Slade, A. Jeyaraj, A. K. Kar, et al. 2023. Opinion paper: "So what if ChatGPT wrote it?" multidisciplinary perspectives on opportunities, challenges and implications of generative conversational AI for research, practice and policy. *International Journal of Information Management* 71:102642. https://doi.org/10.1016/j.ijinfomgt.2023.102642.
Elmore, R. F. 1979. Backward mapping: Implementation research and policy decisions. *Political Science Quarterly* 94 (4): 601–616.
Epstein, J. M. 2008. Why model? *Journal of Artificial Societies and Social Simulation* 11 (14):
Esposito, R. 2008. *Bíos: Biopolitics and philosophy*. Minneapolis: University of Minnesota Press.
Evans, R. J. 1997. *In defence of history*. Cambridge: Granta.
Faust, K., and S. Wasserman. 1994. *Social network analysis: Methods and applications*. Cambridge: Cambridge University Press.
Folke, C. 2006. Resilience: The emergence of a perspective for social–ecological systems analyses. *Global Environmental Change* 16 (3): 253–267. https://doi.org/10.1016/j.gloenvcha.2006.04.002.
Foucault, M. 1989. *Madness and civilization*. London-New York: Routledge.
Foucault, M. 2003. *Society must be defended*. New York: Picador.
Foucault, M. 2013. *Archaeology of knowledge*. London: Taylor & Francis.
Foucault, M. 2019. *Discipline and punish*. London: Penguin Books.
Frigg, R., and S. Hartmann. 2020. Models in science. In *The Stanford encyclopedia of philosophy (summer 2025 edition)*, ed. Edward N. Zalta and Uri Nodelman. https://plato.stanford.edu/archives/sum2025/entries/models-science/.
Gell-Mann, M. 1995. What is complexity? *Complexity* 1 (1): 16–19. https://doi.org/10.1002/cplx.6130010105.
Geyer, R., and P. Cairney, eds. 2015. *Handbook on complexity and public policy*. Cheltenham UK-Northampton MA: Edward Elgar Publishing.
Ginzburg, C. 1980. *The cheese and the worms: The cosmos of a sixteenth-century Miller*. Baltimore: Johns Hopkins University Press.
Global conflict tracker. 2025. https://www.cfr.org/global-conflict-tracker.

Gopnik, A., and H. M. Wellman. 2012. Reconstructing constructivism: Causal models, Bayesian learning mechanisms, and the theory theory. *Psychological Bulletin* 138 (6): 1085–1108. https://doi.org/10.1037/a0028044.

Greif, A. 2006. *Institutions and the path to the modern economy*. Cambridge: Cambridge University Press.

Hacking, I. 2000. *The social construction of what?* Cambride, MA: Harvard University Press.

Haldon, J., L. Mordechai, T. P. Newfield, A. F. Chase, A. Izdebski, P. Guzowski, et al. 2018. History meets palaeoscience: Consilience and collaboration in studying past societal responses to environmental change. *Proceedings of the National Academy of Sciences* 115 (13): 3210–3218. https://doi.org/10.1073/pnas.1716912115.

Hayles, N. K. 1999. *How we became posthuman*. Chicago: Chicago University Press.

Heyes, C. 2018. *Cognitive gadgets: The cultural evolution of thinking*. Cambridge, MA: Harvard University Press.

Hood, C. 1983. *The tools of government*. London: Macmillan.

Horváth, L., and G. Rice. 2024. *Change point analysis for time series*. Cham: Springer.

Iggers, G. G. 2013. *Historiography in the twentieth century: From scientific objectivity to the post-modern challenge*. Hanover, NH: Wesleyan University Press.

Ingold, T. 2000. *The perception of the environment: Essays on livelihood, dwelling and skill*. London-New York: Routledge.

Ioannidis, J. P. A. 2005. Why most published research findings are false. *PLoS Medicine* 2 (8): e124. https://doi.org/10.1371/journal.pmed.0020124.

Izdebski, A., K. Bloomfield, W. J. Eastwood, R. Fernandes, D. Fleitmann, P. Guzowski, et al. 2022. L'émergence d'une histoire environnementale interdisciplinaire: une approche conjointe de l'Holocène tardif. *Annales. Histoire, Sciences Sociales* 77 (1): 11–58. https://doi.org/10.1017/ahss.2022.114.

Jasanoff, S. 2004. The idiom of co-production. In *States of knowledge. The co-production of science and the social order*, ed. S. Jasonoff. London: Routledge.

Jenkins, K. 2003. *Rethinking history*. London-New York: Routledge.

Jonas, H. 1966. *The phenomenon of life: Toward a philosophical biology*. New York: Harper and Row.

Kahneman, D. 2011. *Thinking, fast and slow*. New York: Farrar, Straus and Giroux.

Kauffman, S. 1993. *The origins of order: Self-organization and selection in evolution*. Oxford: Oxford University Press.

Kim, J. 1999. Making sense of emergence. *Philosophical Studies* 95:3–36.

Kingdon, J. W. 1995. *Agendas, alternatives, and public policies*. 2nd ed. Boston: Longman.

Kirsch, D. A. 1997. The electric car and the burden of history: Studies in automotive systems rivalry in America, 1890-1996. *Business and Economic History* 26 (2): 304–310.

Kondratieff, N. D. 1935. The long waves in economic life. *The Review of Economic Statistics* 17 (6): 105–115.

Ladyman, J. 1998. What is structural realism? *Studies in History and Philosophy of Science Part A* 29 (3): 409–424. https://doi.org/10.1016/S0039-3681(98)80129-5.

Lansing, J. S., and M. P. Cox. 2019. *Islands of order: A guide to complexity modeling for the social sciences*. Princeton: Princeton University Press.

Lansing, J. S., S. Thurner, N. N. Chung, A. Coudurier-Curveur, Ç. Karakaş, K. A. Fesenmyer, and L. Y. Chew. 2017. Adaptive self-organization of Bali's ancient rice terraces. *Proceedings of the National Academy of Sciences* 114 (25): 6504–6509. https://doi.org/10.1073/pnas.1605369114.

Latour, B. 2005. *Reassembling the social: An introduction to actor-network-theory*. Oxford: Oxford University Press.

Levy, J. S. 2003. Applications of prospect theory to political science. *Synthese* 135 (2): 215–241. https://doi.org/10.1023/A:1023413007698.

Lindblom, C. E. 1959. The science of 'muddling through'. *Public Administration Review* 19 (2): 79–88.

Liu, L., Y. Wang, and Y. Xu. 2024. A practical guide to counterfactual estimators for causal inference with time-series cross-sectional data. *American Journal of Political Science* 68 (1): 160–176. https://doi.org/10.1111/ajps.12723.
Maguire, E. A., D. G. Gadian, I. S. Johnsrude, C. D. Good, J. Ashburner, R. S. Frackowiak, and C. D. Frith. 2000. Navigation-related structural change in the hippocampi of taxi drivers. *Proceedings of the National Academy of Sciences* 97 (8): 4398–4403. https://doi.org/10.1073/pnas.070039597.
McGilchrist, I. 2009. *The master and his emissary*. New Haven: Yale University Press.
McNeill, J. R., and P. Engelke. 2016. *The great acceleration: An environmental history of the Anthropocene since 1945*. Cambridge, MA: Harvard University Press.
Meadows, D. H., D. L. Meadows, J. Randers, and W. W. Behrens III. 1972. *The limits to growth; a report for the club of Rome's project on the predicament of mankind*. New York: Universe Books.
Mearsheimer, J. J. 2001. *The tragedy of great power politics*. New York: W.W. Norton.
Miller, J., Salla, R., Amresh, A., Smith, H., Kandala, S., Hinrichs, M., et al. 2019. *The decision theater: collaborative research methodology*. https://dt.asu.edu/sites/default/files/2020-07/CollaborativeResearchMethodology.pdf.
Mitchell, M. 2009. *Complexity: A guided tour*. Oxford: Oxford University Press.
Moore, J. W. 2016. *Anthropocene or capitalocene? Nature, history, and the crisis of capitalism*. Oakland, CA: PM Press.
Nora, P. 1989. Between memory and history: Les lieux de mémoire. *Representations* 26:7–24.
North, D. C. 1990. *Institutions, institutional change and economic performance*. Cambridge: Cambridge University Press.
Odling-Smee, F. J., K. N. Laland, and M. W. Feldman. 2003. *Niche construction: The neglected process in evolution*. Princeton: Princeton University Press.
Pierson, P. 2000. Increasing returns, path dependence, and the study of politics. *American Political Science Review* 94 (2): 251–267. https://doi.org/10.2307/2586011.
Pinker, S. 2003. *The language instinct: How the mind creates language*. London: Penguin Books.
Ranger, T., and E. Hobsbawm. 1983. *The invention of tradition*. Cambridge: Cambridge University Press.
Reinhart, C. M., and K. S. Rogoff. 2009. *This time is different: Eight centuries of financial folly*. Princeton: Princeton University Press.
Rittel, H. W., and M. M. Webber. 1973. Dilemmas in a general theory of planning. *Policy Sciences* 4 (2): 155–169.
Rockström, J., J. Gupta, D. Qin, S. J. Lade, J. F. Abrams, L. S. Andersen, et al. 2023. Safe and just Earth system boundaries. *Nature* 619 (7968): 102–111. https://doi.org/10.1038/s41586-023-06083-8.
Romanowska, I., C. D. Wren, and S. A. Crabtree. 2021. *Agent-based modeling for archaeology: Simulating the complexity of societies*. Santa Fe: Santa Fe Institute Press.
Room, G. 2011. *Complexity, institutions and public policy: Agile decision-making in a turbulent world*. Cheltenham/UK-Northanpton MA: Edward Elgar Publishing.
Rose, M. R. 1990. *Evolutionary biology of aging*. Oxford: Oxford University Press.
Rosen, A. M. 2023. The arc of the Anthropocene. In *Anthropology and climate change*, ed. S. A. Crate and M. Nuttall, 25–46. New York: Routledge.
Said, E. W. 1978. *Orientalism*. London: Routledge and Kegan Paul.
Scheffer, M. 2009. *Critical transitions in nature and society*. Princeton: Princeton University Press.
Scheffer, M., S. R. Carpenter, T. M. Lenton, J. Bascompte, W. Brock, V. Dakos, et al. 2012. Anticipating critical transitions. *Science* 338 (6105): 344–348. https://doi.org/10.1126/science.1225244.
Scheidel, W. 2017. *The great leveller: Violence and the global history of inequality from the stone age to the present*. Oxford: Oxford University Press.
Scott, J. C. 1998. *Seeing like a state: How certain schemes to improve the human condition have failed*. New Haven: Yale University Press.
Searle, J. 1995. *The construction of social reality*. New York: Free Press.

Smail, D., and A. Shryock. 2013. History and the "pre". *The American Historical Review* 118 (3): 709–737.

Steffen, Will, W. Broadgate, L. Deutsch, O. Gaffney, and C. Ludwig. 2015. The trajectory of the Anthropocene: The great acceleration. *The Anthropocene Review* 2 (1): 81–98. https://doi.org/10.1177/2053019614564785.

Steffen, W., J. Rockström, K. Richardson, T. M. Lenton, C. Folke, D. Liverman, et al. 2018. Trajectories of the earth system in the Anthropocene. *Proceedings of the National Academy of Sciences* 115 (33): 8252–8259. https://doi.org/10.1073/pnas.1810141115.

Stotz, K. 2010. Human nature and cognitive–developmental niche construction. *Phenomenology and the Cognitive Sciences* 9 (4): 483–501. https://doi.org/10.1007/s11097-010-9178-7.

Tainter, J. 1988. *The collapse of complex societies*. Princeton: Princeton University Press.

Taleb, N. N. 2014. *Antifragile: Things that gain from disorder*. New York: Random House.

Turchin, P. 2003. *Historical dynamics: Why states rise and fall*. Princeton: Princeton University Press.

Turchin, P. 2008. Arise "cliodynamics". *Nature* 454 (7200): 34–35. https://doi.org/10.1038/454034a.

Turchin, P. 2010. Political instability may be a contributor in the coming decade. *Nature* 463 (7281): 608. https://doi.org/10.1038/463608a.

Turchin, P. 2011. Toward cliodynamics—An analytical, predictive science of history. *Cliodynamics: The Journal of Quantitative History and Cultural Evolution* 2:167–186.

Turchin, P. 2023. *End times: Elites, counter-elites, and the path of political disintegration*. New York: Penguin Press.

Turchin, P., and S. A. Nefedov. 2009. *Secular cycles*. Princeton: Princeton University Press.

Turchin, P., T. E. Currie, H. Whitehouse, P. François, K. Feeney, D. Mullins, et al. 2018. Quantitative historical analysis uncovers a single dimension of complexity that structures global variation in human social organization. *Proceedings of the National Academy of Sciences* 115 (2): E144–E151. https://doi.org/10.1073/pnas.1708800115.

Voigtländer, N., and H.-J. Voth. 2012. Persecution perpetuated: The medieval origins of anti-semitic violence in Nazi Germany. *The Quarterly Journal of Economics* 127 (3): 1339–1392. https://doi.org/10.1093/qje/qjs019.

Walker, W. E., P. Harremoës, J. Rotmans, J. P. Van Der Sluijs, M. B. Van Asselt, P. Janssen, and M. P. Krayer von Krauss. 2003. Defining uncertainty: A conceptual basis for uncertainty management in model-based decision support. *Integrated Assessment* 4 (1): 5–17. https://doi.org/10.1076/iaij.4.1.5.16466.

Waltz, K. N. 1979. *Theory of international politics*. Reading, MA: Addison-Wesley Publishing Company.

Weimer, D. L., and A. R. Vining. 2005. *Policy analysis: Concepts and practice*. 4th ed. Englewood Cliffs, NJ: Prentice Hall.

West, G. 2017. *Scale*. New York: Penguin Books.

White, H. 2014. *Metahistory: The historical imagination in nineteenth-century Europe*. 40th ed. Baltimore: Johns Hopkins University Press.

Wilkinson, M. D., M. Dumontier, I. J. Aalbersberg, G. Appleton, M. Axton, A. Baak, et al. 2016. The FAIR guiding principles for scientific data management and stewardship. *Scientific Data* 3 (1): 160018. https://doi.org/10.1038/sdata.2016.18.

Winship, C., and S. L. Morgan. 1999. The estimation of causal effects from observational data. *Annual Review of Sociology* 25:659–706. https://doi.org/10.1146/annurev.soc.25.1.659.

Wolfram, S. 2002. *A new kind of science*. Champaign, Ill: Wolfram Media, Inc.

Worrall, J. 1989. Structural realism: The best of both worlds? *Dialectic* 43 (1–2): 99–124. https://doi.org/10.1111/j.1746-8361.1989.tb00933.x.

Zhang, W. 1989. *Differential equations, bifurcations and chaos in economics*. Singapore-Hackensack NJ-London: World Scientific Publishing Company.

Pitfalls in Learning from the Past: Analogies, Presentism and Ethics

Lee Mordechai

Abstract In recent decades the idea of "learning from the past" has become increasingly popular among historians and others. This paper critically examines this discourse and its underlying assumption—that the past offers meaningful lessons for the present. It distinguishes between non-reflective approaches, in which the past is used to justify present-day positions, and reflective approaches, which engage with the methodological and theoretical challenges of drawing such lessons. The first section analyzes examples of non-reflective uses of the past in which presentism influences research. A subsequent section explores how these issues manifest in policymaking, with attention to the pitfalls of analogy and oversimplification. The next section investigates a particular case study that has drawn much public attention—the different attempts to remove Gazans from Gaza since the early twentieth century—and reflects on how this history is relevant for the present. Ultimately, the paper argues that although the past can inform our understanding of the present, its relevance is contingent and shaped by the ethical frameworks through which observers interpret the past.

Keywords Learning from the past · Interdisciplinary history · Historical analogies · Presentism

1 Introduction

"Those who cannot remember the past are condemned to repeat it". George Santayana's 1905 quote—or a paraphrase of it—has gained much popularity in public discourse, as the many online memes about it attest. As an aphorism, it seems like something most interlocutors can agree upon, and it is well suited to early

L. Mordechai (✉)
The Hebrew University of Jerusalem, Jerusalem, Israel
e-mail: lee.mordechai@mail.huji.ac.il

J. F. Haldon, R. Fernandes (eds.), *Bridging History and Policy*, Understanding Complex Systems, https://doi.org/10.1007/978-3-032-24379-9_6

twenty-first century discourse replete with talking points and soundbites. If the past is a massive repository of human experience, it is only natural to employ it in service of the present. Being on the right side of history, so to speak, should be attractive to members of the general public as well as scholars of the past, who supposedly gain some additional public legitimacy as custodians of the said past. And yet the many people who repeat these words overlook their context. Santayana did not produce a grand reflection on humans and their history. Rather, he was thinking about human progress, which he connected to memory and learning from experience (Santayana 1905: 284):

> Progress, far from consisting in change, depends on retentiveness. When change is absolute there remains no being to improve and no direction is set for possible improvement: and when experience is not retained, as among savages, infancy is perpetual. Those who cannot remember the past are condemned to repeat it. In the first stage of life the mind is frivolous and easily distracted; it misses progress by failing in consecutiveness and persistence. This is the condition of children and barbarians, in whom instinct has learned nothing from experience.

Only adults ("men") can make true progress since "old age is as forgetful as youth, and more incorrigible" (Santayana 1905: 285). In this light, the twenty-first-century discursive uses of the quote decontextualize it in service of the present by making an argument about the importance of history, which is used in present-day discussions. The repeated use of the quote also implicitly legitimizes the use of historical analogies—it implies that historical patterns repeat themselves so that progress requires a correct identification of these patterns as a prerequisite to avoid the ones with undesirable results. Both the interpretation of the past through contemporary values and assumptions, and the use of analogies, are problematic methodologically.

This paper explores some of the discourse surrounding the common assumption that the past is relevant for the present. It distinguishes between reflective and non-reflective approaches. Non-reflective approaches include cases in which the idea of learning from the past is used for present-day justifications—whether of a present course of action, or of the study of the past as relevant to the present. Reflective approaches, on the other hand, are aware of the methodological and theoretical issues surrounding the idea of learning from the past. Scholars working within such an approach would re-examine the idea itself, for example by casting doubt on its central assumption or part of it. Reflective approaches do not have to be deconstructive as they can also produce more systematic and robust attempts to learn from the past—for example by providing context to present-day developments or by suggesting a potential course of action and scenario. After outlining both approaches through a few case studies, the paper will present a case in which the past can inform the present by examining a specific question—the history of attempts to remove Palestinians from Gaza, a reality that is roughly analogous to the present-day option circulating in public discourse and on the ground. It will then use this case study to reflect on the ethical dimension of history.

The set of problems this paper focuses on belongs to a much broader debate about objectivity, narrative and the role of the observer in the construction of historical knowledge. On one side are those who assert that an objective account of the past is possible through careful attention to documentary evidence and verifiable facts. This "positivist" approach draws upon the work of early historians such as Leopold von Ranke who pointed out that the task of the historian is "simply to show how it really was" (debate and other examples in Carr 1961: 3–5). In the present, this approach to history is dominant in K-12 education and public discourse. This approach is also particularly conducive to arguments about learning from history. If a single, objective history is possible, one could more easily identify patterns and more general rules within the past.

On the other side are historians who emphasize the interpretative nature of writing history. Objectivity, according to this side, is unattainable as both the sources from the past and the historian who evaluates them in the present are shaped by their respective contexts, biases and limitations, only some of which are known. For example, our understanding of fifth-century BCE Athens is disproportionately shaped by the voices of elite male citizens while other groups such as women, children, slaves and lower classes are largely invisible. A different set of biases operates on contemporary observers. Historians have long noticed that present-day norms and values shape present-day writing about the past. Over the first half of the twentieth century, for example, German conceptions of ancient Sparta changed fundamentally. If Germans rediscovered Sparta after the trauma of World War I, during the Nazi era (1933–1945) Sparta became an explicit model for German society—only to be marginalized in both academic research and public discourse after World War II (Rebenich 2018). Both examples reveal that historical interpretation is hardly straightforward. This paper adopts the view that historical knowledge is contingent and constructed by the historian's contemporary context.

In 1961, Edward Carr gave a series of lectures which were soon published as the influential book *What is History?*. Although his book remained a cornerstone of courses about the theory and philosophy of history as a discipline for decades, many of his insights were forgotten. One of Carr's most important arguments was that historical facts—then, as today, popular—are neither neutral nor objective nor do they simply "speak for themselves". Rather, they undergo a double selection process. First, only a small part of the past is recorded in a process that is pre-selected and predetermined for us. Then in the present we choose which parts of that corpus to use and which not, a process that is constrained by the present and the questions we choose to ask based on our personal inclinations and the discourses around us. This double selection process shapes our understanding of the past. As Carr (1961:26) explained,

> The facts are really not at all like fish on the fishmonger's slab. They are like fish swimming about in a vast and sometimes inaccessible ocean; and what the historian catches will depend partly on chance, but mainly on what part of the ocean he chooses to fish in and what tackle he chooses to use—these two factors being, of course, determined by the kind of fish he wants to catch. By and large, the historian will get the kind of facts he wants.

While nineteenth century scholars had hoped to establish a comprehensive body of knowledge that would finally settle all disputed issues, by the mid-twentieth century hopes became more modest—to advance progressively from one fragmentary hypothesis to another. History became less a fixed factual conclusion and more a set of interpretations that reflect what experts publicly accept at a given point in time. These interpretations are shaped by value-laden judgements (Carr 1961: 70–112), which are themselves based on present-day social norms as well as the individual inclinations of the observer of the past. The norms of the present thus constrain and inform how the past is narrated. This implies that historical writing is more rigorous analytically when it explicitly acknowledges the normative frameworks and interpretative assumptions on which it depends (also Collingwood 1946: 7–10).

2 Non-reflective Approaches: Scholars Arguing for Their Relevance to the Present

Unfortunately, most discourse is not reflective, and as will be discussed below, there are several incentives to avoid such reflection. For example, some scholars employ the present in their discussions of the past as a rhetorical tool to highlight the relevance of their study to the present. This dynamic can lead to sharp increases in attention to certain topics at particular moments in time. One such example is bioterrorism—i.e. the intentional use of micro-organisms to harm humans, animals or crops. Interest in bioterrorism drew upon earlier interest in infectious diseases, a topic that saw a sharp and consistent increase in scholarly attention between the mid-1990s and the early 2020s (Washer 2010: 1–19). A Web of Science search reveals that 1110 scholarly papers concerning infectious diseases were published in 1995. The number increased 25-fold in a quarter century, reaching 27,895 in 2021 (before a sharp change in the trend, decreasing to 19,871 in 2024).[1] Within this large movement—which is also reflected in the study of premodern infectious diseases—there was a shorter wave of attention to bioterrorism. Web of Science records a single paper with "bioterrorism" as its topic in 1996, but that number quickly increases, reaching a high of 1603 in 2005 before declining in subsequent years, dropping to only 143 in 2024.[2] The reasons for the shifts in the popularity of bioterrorism—a modern concept that was first used in 1987—have much to do with their present.[3] References to bioterrorism originated alongside a modest increase in US federal funding for improved responses to bioterrorism in the late 1990s, influenced in part by a fictional novel on the topic that President Bill Clinton had read at the time. The Anthrax envelope attacks and the 9/11 attacks in 2001 led to massive increases in both funding and public concerns of bioterrorism. Attention continued

[1] https://www.webofscience.com/wos/alldb/summary/2d106d6c-c279-47db-bcc7-ebbc28d51895-016115201a/relevance/1

[2] https://www.webofscience.com/wos/alldb/summary/77510262-fb02-4598-b713-eeb4190c87ad-d551a895/relevance/1

[3] https://www.oed.com/dictionary/bioterrorism_n?tl=true

to increase against the backdrop of the preparations for and the beginning of the Iraq war, primarily since the United States alleged that Iraq was developing biological weapons. Memorably, in 2003 US Secretary of State Colin Powell appeared before the UN to argue for the necessity of a war with Iraq, presenting a model vial of anthrax that Iraq was planning to weaponize as a "weapon of mass destruction". No evidence for an Iraqi biological weapons program was presented before the war or found during it, leading to the decline of bioterrorism as a perceived threat and as a topic of study (Washer 2010: 127–147).

All this percolated into academic research of premodern diseases, where any discussion of bioterrorism—as opposed to biological warfare—was irrelevant. One of the premodern disease events that drew much attention in the early twenty-first century was the Justinianic Plague/first plague pandemic (c. 541–c. 750). An edited volume based on papers from a 2001 conference reveals that bioterrorism was present in discussions. One contributor attempted to reject anthrax as the identity of the disease underlying the pandemic, pointing out the weakness of this idea "as clearly shown by the acts of bioterrorism in 2001 in the United States involving anthrax". Anthrax was "not an ideal biological weapon, and it is extremely unlikely that it played a significant role in the Justinianic Plague" (Sallares 2007: 238). A different contributor in the same volume attempted to highlight the importance of plague as a disease by looking at World Health Organization data "even leaving aside the problem of bioterrorism" (McCormick 2007: 291). A 2004 monograph on famine and disease between the third and eighth centuries pointed out the dangers of infectious diseases in the twenty-first century, stating that "the most serious threat derives from bioterrorism" (Stathakopoulos 2004: 3). Bioterrorism featured in other premodern diseases as well in the first half of the 2000s. A 2004 paper on the second century CE Antonine Plague—an epidemic often associated with smallpox—stated that it might be "similar to the current threats of anthrax outbreaks and bioterrorism" even though there was little to suggest that the Antonine Plague was anthrax. The description of this disease in a third century source was similarly "reminiscent of modern fears of bioterrorism" (Fears 2004: 73–74). In all these cases, the references to bioterrorism were brief and included almost no discussion. Rather than a helpful part of the analysis, the references to bioterrorism served as a tool to highlight the relevance of these studies of ancient diseases to the present. This discourse had both financial incentives and implications. For example, scientific studies about late antique plague received funding from the US Department of Homeland Security at least until 2014 (Harbeck et al. 2013; Wagner et al. 2014). The basis for this funding was probably related to US government attempts to investigate potential threats of bioterrorism.

In a more systematic attempt to examine how researchers talk about the relevance of their studies for the present, scholars conducted a meta-analysis of the discourse of learning from the past in the context of the premodern Maya in Mesoamerica and their interactions with the local environment. The fate of the Maya has been a common case study in discussions of societal collapse. The demise of the Mayan urban centers, especially in the Yucatan Peninsula, has drawn much public and popular attention, and some of the factors that have been used to explain this demise were socio-environmental, such as drought (i.e. a reduction in precipitation) or land use management. The meta-analysis identified 71 articles on Mayan interactions with the local environment that purported to learn from the past in some manner.

These papers began appearing as part of a trend in the early 2000s, growing more common over the next couple of decades. The increasing prevalence of the studies over this time frame may have been influenced by common discourses around topics such as the Anthropocene, societal collapse, and planetary boundaries, all of which developed over the same time and drew both public and scholarly attention (Mordechai and Tubi 2024).

The meta-analysis found that almost all the examined papers were discursive rather than substantive. In other words, these papers commonly made statements about lessons that can be learned or the importance of learning from the past. These statements frequently appeared in the more prominent parts of the papers: their introductions and conclusions, but tended to be very brief—often only a sentence or two long. Only a handful of papers attempted to reach more robust conclusions about learning from the past—as reflected in a more robust research design that would develop the analogy between past and present, or by employing an approach that would acknowledge the challenges in extracting lessons from the past. Some four fifths of the papers framed their results in a general manner, implying that their conclusions—the lessons they taught—were widely applicable to present-day societies. A similar number of papers included either vague lessons ("more resilience is necessary") or refrained from including any clear lesson, leaving few papers that included specific lessons relevant to present-day policy (for example, that potentially sustainable resource-use practices became less sustainable under certain circumstances).

These findings align with those observed in the bioterrorism case study above. Within an early twenty-first century discourse scholars face increasing pressure to frame their work as relevant to present-day concerns. The two cases above reflect common responses to this pressure. In the bioterrorism case, scholars introduced present-day concerns into their work to highlight the relevance of their work for those concerns. In the Maya case, scholars included generalized claims about the "lessons" of the past which often remain unsubstantiated. In both cases the studies at question were rarely cited, appear to have received negligible public attention, and remained confined to specialist readerships. This raises a critical question: if these relevance claims are typically brief, underdeveloped, and largely ineffective beyond their respective scholarly fields, why are they included in the first place?

One explanation is that these statements function primarily as symbolic gestures within the scholarly community. Rather than true outreach, they act as markers of academic legitimacy by signalling to peers that the research speaks to contemporary issues at least nominally. As the humanities are regularly called upon to justify their existence and demonstrate their relevance to the present, employing such rhetorical tools to assert present-day significance serves as a low-cost means of reinforcing the legitimacy and value of both the study and the broader field to peers. The function of these statements is often performative rather than substantive and in general they are not useful for actual learning from the past.

3 Non-reflective Presentism Influences Research

In the cases of bioterrorism and the Maya the inclusion of present-day markers and statements of relevance had little impact on the research itself or its design. Yet present-day concerns can also shape scholars' perception of the past. In non-reflective types of presentism,[4] observers of the past analyze and interpret it in a manner that is predicated upon present-day discourse. The case study of the 536 CE event highlights such presentism (Mordechai forthcoming). In 536 CE, five historical sources report an unusual atmospheric event that dimmed the sunlight in a noticeable manner for a prolonged period. Most of the historical sources use the event in their literary narratives as a portent, an ominous sign that heralds bad things to come. In all cases the description of the atmospheric event is brief and includes few direct impacts. Apart from some discussion during the late eighteenth century, historians have largely overlooked this event until the late twentieth century. Beginning in the 1980s, however, the 536 event began to attract more attention in three distinct waves: the mid-1980s, the mid-1990s to 2000, and c. 2010 until the present. In all cases research was interdisciplinary, involving history and archaeology but also natural scientists and distinct methodologies such as tree ring studies or ice core studies. Each of these waves drew more scholarly and public attention and involved scholars from more diverse disciplines than the former one. At present, at least six books and hundreds of articles have discussed the 536 event or aspects of it. In 2018 the prestigious journal *Science* portrayed 536 CE as "the worst year to be alive" in an award-winning science news article (Gibbons 2018), leading some scholars to adopt this title and use it in their research or outreach efforts. The combination of scholarship and public attention has led to the proliferation of content related to the 536 event on social media, where on YouTube alone there are some 40 million views on documentaries and commentaries on this event.

Yet despite the obvious attention to the 536 event, a closer examination of its modern construction reveals that in all three waves present-day concerns had a significant influence on how scholars and the general public understood it. In the 1980s observers interpreted the event as the result of a past volcanic eruption, echoing the increased attention to contemporary volcanic eruptions in their present. The event was further important, 1980s observers thought, since it highlighted some of the potential results of a nuclear war in their present or near future—an event that seemed imminent to many because of increased tensions between the United States and the Soviet Union. Once the interest in contemporary volcanic eruptions and the political tensions with the Soviet Union declined, attention to the 536 event dissipated. A different, larger group of scholars noticed the 536 event in the 1990s, but interpreted it through their contemporary concerns of a collision between Earth and a comet or meteor, drawing on events such an observed collision between the Shoemaker-Levy 9 comet and Jupiter in 1994. Although there was no positive evidence for a sixth-century collision or near-collision of such a celestial body with

[4] For presentism, see Armitage (2023).

Earth, the hypothesis that the 536 event was the result of such a collision took over scholarly discourse and retained its popularity for almost a decade. After the 9/11 attacks, as more worldly concerns regarding global terrorism took precedence over space rocks, attention to the 536 event dissipated again.

Scholarly interest in the 536 event re-emerged only in the years around 2010, this time reflecting concerns about anthropogenic climate change. If earlier interpretations of the 536 event saw it as a brief event that lasted for a year, or at most a decade, an influential 2016 study soon recast it as the beginning of a whole new period in history, the so-called "Late Antique Little Ice Age" (LALIA) which lasted for over a century (Büntgen et al. 2016). The assumption—sometimes explicit—was that a closer examination of this premodern case of climate change would allow us to better prepare for the anthropogenic climate change of our near future. As one key paper in the development of this discourse put it in its abstract, "Such historical data [as discussed in the paper] may provide a basis for counteracting the recent political and fiscal reluctance to mitigate projected climate change" (Büntgen et al. 2011). The important book *The Fate of Rome: Climate, Disease, and the End of an Empire* linked the LALIA to the narrative of the fall of the Roman Empire, drawing parallels between the Roman Empire and its present-day American counterpart (Harper 2017). The book received much scholarly and public attention, receiving reviews in media outlets ranging from The New York Times and The Guardian to Foreign Affairs and the sports news website Deadspin. Many of these media outlets, as well as the Press' marketing strategy, explicitly highlighted the analogy with the present. This wave of publications peaked with the aforementioned 2018 *Science* article, amplifying the message about the 536 event to reach tens of millions (Mordechai forthcoming).

The 536 event case study highlights some of the risks in presentism that emerge even when discussing a seemingly negligible event 1500 years ago. The repeated implicit and explicit connections to contemporary concerns in present-day scholarly analyses of the event have shifted its scholarly interpretations, sometimes drastically. While such shifts might be tolerated if one uses the past only for inspiration or edifying narratives, the dependencies between past narratives and present concerns make it far more problematic (and risky) to base any kind of decision-making or policy on these lessons as they would likely continue to change.

4 Analogies with Past Precedents and Policy

The presence of the historical past in public discourse or lived experience can provide analogues for the present for planners and decision makers. A book that examined analogies in policy decision making concluded that they "matter most during the evaluation and selection of policy options, and they exert their impact by influencing the assessments and evaluations that policymakers must make in order to choose between alternative options" (Khong 1992: 253). A major source of the power of analogies is their heuristic versatility as they can perform several diagnostic functions at once—for instance providing a comprehensive picture as well as supplying an implied solution.

The question is whether planners and decision-makers employ a robust and substantive interpretation of the analogy they draw between the past and their present. As the 536 event case demonstrates, such a robust interpretation is difficult even for academics on seemingly apolitical questions about past events. The norm appears to be a more superficial and discursive interpretation of the precedents of a given event. The 1965 American decisions to launch an air war and subsequently a ground war in Vietnam are an unusual case study in this regard. In this particular moment many educated officials—some of whom even taught these subjects in academia—served in key roles in the American administration, to the extent that these policymakers have been described as "the best and the brightest" (Khong 1992: 13). In both private discussions and public messaging these officials repeatedly and frequently drew parallels to past events, highlighting a few that seemed particularly relevant for their times. These analogies served to diagnose the uncertain reality they faced within a familiar framework, advocate for the policy they supported, and justify it to their surroundings.

One such event was the 1938 Munich Agreement, in which the United Kingdom, France, Italy and Germany agreed to allow the German annexation of the Sudetenland in Czechoslovakia. Although many Europeans celebrated the agreement at the time as they believed it was the way to prevent another large-scale war in Europe, the outbreak of World War II less than a year later proved them wrong. The Munich Agreement has since been used as a shorthand analogy against appeasement of authoritarian or totalitarian states. A more robust (and popular) analogy for the 1965 present was North Korea's earlier invasion of South Korea in 1950, which itself was seen as analogous to the actions of Mussolini, Hitler and Japan during the 1930s. Back then, the US was able to disrupt the expansionist plans of North Korea and its supporters the Soviet Union and China by militarily intervening in the Korean Peninsula. In 1965, American planners and decision makers utilized both these analogies to argue for American intervention in Vietnam which soon materialized, launching the US into a disastrous decade-long war. On the other hand, the minority view among planners and decision makers employed a different historical analogy—that of France's experience in Vietnam during the 1950s. Since this analogy indicated that Vietnam would be an unwinnable war, a policy based on it suggested that the US should cut its losses and withdraw from Vietnam.

These and other analogies featured prominently in a key debate on strategy in July 1965. The debate involved the highest foreign policy elites in the United States: the President, high officials from the State and Defense Departments (including both Secretaries and two ambassadors to southeast Asia), the CIA, the White House, and the US Information Agency, further demonstrating both the power of analogies and the shared discourse around them.[5] A key book on the subject argued that the Korean analogy in particular explained why the US decided to intervene in Vietnam

[5] For an account of the debate, see Khong (1992: 123–133).

(Khong 1992: 97). Rather than merely justify a particular course of action, the Korean analogy framed the entire policy question. As such, it also shaped the administration's definition of the challenge in Vietnam, prescribed policy, set the stakes, predicted the chances of success, identified potential dangers, and assessed its morality, among others.

The case study is indicative since the American decision-makers operated under far more favorable key conditions than many subsequent attempts to draw lessons from the past. As discussed above, they represented a highly educated and well-informed group. They were serious in their efforts to draw conclusions from the historical analogies they invoked, as evidenced by their private use of these analogies that suggests that they did not use them merely as rhetorical devices for public consumption. Moreover, there was general agreement among the elites about what had happened in the past and how it should be understood. The fact that they nonetheless selected the wrong analogies, leading to a disastrous decade-long war, reveals the profound risks inherent in determining policy based on historical analogy.

Furthermore, despite their attractiveness the use of historical analogies quickly runs into several challenges that are theoretical and methodological in nature. As a general rule, if "the past is a foreign country; they do things differently there" (Hartley 1953: 7), the further back we go, the more foreign the past becomes. In the case of environmental questions and the pre-industrial past, for example, there are major differences—e.g. systemic, cultural, epistemological—that are rarely acknowledged among those present-day observers who employ analogies from this past within their discourse, leading to a more superficial discourse in comparison with the Vietnam case study.

One fundamental difference is that the past is largely unknown, especially compared to the present (Tubi et al. 2022). Even in the supposedly more empirical environmental history there are considerable gaps in our understanding of the causal chain underlying society-environment interactions in the past. These uncertainties have continued until surprisingly recent times. As an example, volcanologists have attributed an 1831 volcanic forcing event to the eruption of Babuyan Claro, a volcano in the Philippines. A recent study, however, examined all the evidence for this eruption—a few dozen texts—and determined that they are mostly dependent on each other and that the said eruption never happened (Garrison et al. 2018). If so much of the past is unknown, the lessons we claim to learn as we study it can hardly be robust. In fact, it appears that analogies were more popular in the case of the Vietnam decision making in 1965 precisely because there was general agreement between all discussants on what happened and how, while the events took place within living memory.[6] More distant historical analogies would not feature a similar shared experience.

[6] As some observers pointed out, the Vietnam debacle itself was more difficult to use in the future as an analogy since people did not agree on what exactly happened and why.

There are other issues with the use of historical analogies (Tubi et al. 2022). One such difference, for instance, is the shrinking of space: in the past, historical social processes often occurred in local to regional scales. Today, however, the present world is far more interconnected. This connectivity allows societies to mitigate local or regional conditions such as drought or geography-related constraints rapidly and with relative ease. Another major difference is the fact that present-day planners can predict challenges (e.g. climate change) and plan ahead. Their models offer an awareness that the baseline conditions are changing in a persistent manner, which was far more difficult to perceive in the past without instrumental measurements and statistical tools. These and other issues, which are rarely acknowledged in scholarly attempts to learn from the past, hinder any attempt to draw analogies with the past and learn from it.

5 Case Study: The Removal of Palestinians from the Gaza Strip

One might ask whether it is even possible to learn from the past given the pitfalls described above. This chapter would argue that the overall answer is yes, but only to a limited extent and within certain constraints. The past analogues to the present should be carefully selected, the lessons are neither obvious nor self-explanatory, and the robustness of the lessons is predicated on the strength of the links between the past analogue and the present scenario.

A case study relevant to the present-day is the issue of the complete or partial removal of Gaza's civilian population from parts or all of the Gaza Strip. Since very early in the Israel-Gaza war (Oct. 2023–present) certain institutions and individuals in the Israeli state worked towards this objective, for example planning to move the Palestinian population to other countries through negotiated settlements (e.g. Avraham 2023). The idea featured continuously in domestic Israeli discourse, which euphemized the issue as voluntary emigration even among nominally left-wing parties. Israel's role in making the Gaza Strip uninhabitable—by widespread destruction of buildings, built and social infrastructure, and the removal of elites such as medical staff, journalists and academics by killing them, detaining them or threatening them—was rarely acknowledged. As a result, when in early 2025 US President Donald Trump proposed a plan in which the local Palestinian population will not remain in Gaza after the war—it was widely approved by Israelis. Polls found that at most 10% of Jewish Israelis, who are more than three quarters of Israel's population, rejected the Trump plan or similar intentions on moral grounds (Spungin 2025; Jewish People Policy Institute 2025; see also Hazkani and Sorek 2025; Sorek and Hazkani 2025). Both Israel and Trump received some international criticism for these plans but as of writing there have been few direct obvious negative consequences. Interestingly, the discourse surrounding these plans featured no awareness of former attempts—by both the Ottoman Turks and the Israelis—to remove the civilian population of Gaza for political reasons since the early twentieth century. These earlier plans and attempts were diverse: they differed in their reasons for displacing the population, the permanence of the displacement, the nature and quality of the locations to which the population was to be displaced, the extent to which force was used, the secrecy of the process and the public legitimacy they enjoyed.

The earliest—and most successful attempt—was the temporary evacuation of Gaza in World War I. As British forces pushed towards Palestine from Egypt, the Ottoman rulers of Palestine decided to use Gaza's strategic position on the coastal route between Egypt and Palestine to attempt to stop the British advance. Although Gaza was the third-largest city in Palestine at the time, in 1917 the Ottomans ordered the evacuation of its population from the city, giving the Gazans 2 days to do so and forcibly removing those who did not comply. The Ottomans offered to move some of the displaced population to northern Syria which was then under their control. Some of the 40,000 residents decided to accept the offer, but many others preferred to move to lands they owned in nearby villages, or resettle in the large cities in the region, often based on their existing social networks. After the British captured Palestine, the displaced Gazans slowly began to return to their homes in the city. The city had largely been destroyed in British bombardments and took decades to rebuild and recover. In 1922 the city's population (17,480) was less than half its population before the war. The population remained at a similar level in 1933, and only eventually grew to its pre-World War I levels, reaching almost 38,000 in 1946 (Halevy 2014). A few years later the 1948 wars—a civil war in Palestine that turned into the first Arab-Israeli war—would result in the movement of tens of thousands of Palestinian refugees to Gaza and its surroundings, rapidly tripling the population in the area.

Israel has explored policies of removing Gazans more permanently on several occasions. In fact, already in the years after Israel's independence in 1948, it aimed to pressure Arab states to disperse those Palestinian refugees of 1948 who had been displaced to locations near the armistice lines—such as the newly created Gaza Strip—further away in the Arab world from Israel (Rokach 1980: 21–22). After the 1956 war with Egypt, when Israel briefly occupied the Gaza Strip, its leadership was dismayed when Gazans did not flee as they had done in 1948 (Masalha 1996: 57–58). Drawing on some of their own lessons from the 1948 war, the Palestinian civilian population may also have decided to avoid further displacement by staying put despite the increased risk. During Israel's short occupation—5 months in total—it had set up a secret committee to resettle Palestinian refugees elsewhere. Little is known about the plans of this committee, but some of the people involved in it were also involved in a scheme to resettle Palestinians in Libya (Masalha 1996: 60–61). The Israeli Foreign Ministry and its embassy in Jerusalem were involved in efforts to encourage the emigration of refugees to more distant countries—such as the United States or countries in Latin America (Masalha 1996: 63–67). Its use of force, however, was indirect.

Days after the second Israeli occupation of the Gaza Strip in June 1967, Israeli planners had already decided to work towards moving Palestinian refugees away from the Gaza Strip. Early plans attempted to encourage Palestinians to move to the newly occupied West Bank and from there to Jordan. To achieve the move Israel did not use physical force but deliberately manufactured poor economic conditions in the Gaza Strip, such as an unemployment rate of 50% and low living standards, to encourage Palestinians to move out voluntarily. Palestinians began leaving already in late 1967, reaching an average of about 2800 departures/month between November 1967 and August 1968 (the population of the Gaza Strip in 1967 was about 400,000). In parallel, Israeli Prime Minister Levi Eshkol created a secret unit that was tasked with encouraging emigration to other countries. The immediate destination was Jordan, where Gazans could either resettle or continue east towards the wealthy Gulf States. Over 6000 Gazans left between May and July 1968 until Jordan decided to close its borders. As armed Palestinian resistance to Israel increased in subsequent months, Israeli planners changed course and allowed tens of thousands of Gazans to work in Israel (Raviv 2023: 147–162).

In parallel, Israel attempted two other plans to move Palestinians out of Gaza. One plan was to encourage young, educated Palestinians to move to Egypt for their higher education, under the assumption that many of those students would remain there. Between 1970 and 1978 about 1500 Gazans left to study in Egypt every year until this plan was stopped by Egyptian President Anwar Sadat. In retrospect, some of Hamas' founding leaders studied in Egypt during this period and were influenced there by the Muslim Brotherhood, bringing those ideas back from Egypt and ultimately forming Hamas. In parallel, in 1969 the Israeli Mossad reached an agreement with Paraguay to resettle 60,000 Palestinians there. Israel agreed to pay Paraguay for each Palestinian worker who moved, cover their transportation expenses, and provide the workers with some funds to help them start their new lives. Only a few dozen Gazans appear to have accepted this offer, and two of them ended up killing the local Israeli ambassador's secretary after they felt that they did not receive the support from Israel they had expected. The program was stopped after the killing (Raviv 2023: 162–164).

After the wave of Palestinian popular resistance to Israeli rule known as the first intifada in the late 1980s certain far-right voices within Israel called for the expulsion of Palestinians en masse. These hopes did not materialize, and in 1992 Israel decided to deport a few hundred Palestinians to Lebanon which did not agree to accept them (B'Tselem 1993). This plan backfired as many of the deportees were Hamas officials, who used their shared experience to reinforce their organization's ethos and make new connections outside Israel. As a result, Hamas emerged stronger from its ordeal.[7]

Similar ideas continued to circulate in Israeli discourse. In 2014 against the backdrop of one of the rounds of hostilities between Israel and Gaza, the deputy-speaker of the Knesset proposed to pay Palestinians to emigrate to European countries (Ezra 2014; Times of Israel Staff 2014). In 2019, Israeli media reported that Israel had been negotiating agreements with other countries about moving

[7] The plan backfired since it brought Hamas to regional and international attention, and gave Hamas opportunities to expand its network of supporters as well as lay the foundations for their political and paramilitary organization (Ben-Dror 2020: 399).

Palestinians to them (Eichner 2019). The Israeli Minister of Justice stated openly that she supported a policy of encouraging Palestinians to emigrate overseas as this was the interest of both Israel and some Palestinians (N12 2019). In response to the poor economic conditions in the Gaza Strip—including an unemployment rate of some 70%—which increased armed resistance to Israel, the Israeli government again allowed tens of thousands of Palestinians to work within Israel between 2021 and 2023. As became clear, this temporary solution did not prevent the October 7 attack on Israel later in 2023.

A persistent theme in this chronicle of attempts to remove Palestinians over the past several decades is Israel's effort to calibrate and operate a complex apparatus of social control, adjusting its levers to manage the population while avoiding threats to Israel's security concerns. The continued "de-development" and economic strangulation of the Gaza Strip served as factors that pushed Gazans away from Israel. In this sense, the present-day destruction of the Gaza Strip and its infrastructure represents an extreme version of this policy. Since this approach tended also to increase armed resistance, Israel attempted at times to suppress that resistance with the use of military force, while sometimes also allowing some economic relief, for example in the form of allowing Palestinians to work in Israel (which also provided Israelis with cheap labor).

As an analogy, therefore, the issue of removing Palestinians from the Gaza Strip is quite robust as the historical examples share several key variables with the present situation. They all happen in the same place as the present-day problem, and mostly involve the same political entities and the same power relations. So what can we learn from examining this past?

6 Conclusion: History as Ethics

The Gaza case study demonstrates that even when we avoid the pitfall of analogy by selecting a group of relatively similar analogues to the present, and largely avoid the pitfall of presentism by focusing on a present-day event, the past—in the sense of the empirical facts described above—does not provide any clear lessons by itself (Historian On The Edge 2025). Different observers could analyze the events of the past century and reach very different conclusions. One observer could read the various proposals and plans and conclude that the removal of Palestinians from Gaza is not only immoral and against international laws and norms, but also impossible within the constraints of realpolitik, with various unintended but detrimental consequences. Israeli decisions to send the Gazan youth to Egypt and keep Gaza poor and undeveloped help explain the rise of Hamas, whose leaders were exposed to Muslim Brotherhood ideas in their formative years. Similarly, deporting some Palestinians to Lebanon only strengthened their resolve and their movement. Yet another observer could read the same material and conclude that the way to solve "the Gaza problem" from Israel's perspective based on the lessons from the past is to systematically destroy the urban and social infrastructure of the Gaza Strip and to remove

Palestinians permanently by force. This observer might regret the serious infraction of international law and norms, but would justify it by arguing that the issue of Gaza is an existential one for Israel. The same evidence can be used to justify both interpretations. Despite the favorable conditions, the discipline of history by itself cannot provide a single clear lesson from this case.

Historical facts derive their meaning from the ways in which present-day observers arrange, interpret and use them. As the Vietnam case study revealed, an observer's pre-existing views shape not only the lessons drawn from history but also how they construct the narrative that ties together the empirical facts. Since one's pre-existing views are subjective by definition, the lessons based on them are similarly subjective. From the perspective of the discipline of history, both observers of the history of Gaza expulsions above use the same source material and agree on what happened in the past. Although both are plausible within historical reasoning, they differ in their ethics—one attempts to conform to post-World War II norms while the other justifies an extreme policy that sets a dangerous precedent for the future by unapologetically eviscerating those norms. The plurality of valid and sometimes opposite interpretations is hardly new in history, and affects even the interactions between human societies and their environments in the field of environmental history—as discussed above in the 536 event case (Cronon 1992).

A potential robust solution to this problem requires both personal and explicit reflection on the process itself in multiple stages to avoid the flaws described in the Maya and bioterrorism case studies.

1. *Research design*: Researchers should design their work in ways that allow for historically-informed reflection. This includes articulating the rationale for comparison, clarifying why the analogy might be meaningful, and choosing meaningful and relevant variables for comparison.
2. *Limitations*: Researchers should also reflect in writing upon the limitations of the analogy and explain the value of the analogy despite these limitations. Subsequently, researchers should evaluate how the limitations affect the robustness of their findings and the process of learning from the past.
3. *Transparency*: Scholars should reflect on their own attitudes and assumptions about the present-day dilemma as well as the historical analogies. Transparency about the authors' ethical positions on the issue at hand is desirable in itself as well as necessary for an open discussion. It could be useful to highlight how a different a priori ethical position could result in a different lesson being learned from the same case study.

Given this outline of a process, for example, one could adopt an ethical position that evaluates the post-World War II international order as ultimately positive and mostly protective of marginalized communities. From this perspective, the Gaza case study demonstrates that Israel's plan to remove Palestinians is not a viable option. The historical analogues suggest that the political and ethical costs of attempting such a policy would be exceedingly high, and any such attempt would have unforeseeable but very likely negative consequences. Beyond these costs, the actual removal of Palestinians from the Gaza Strip would not only entail grave violations of the rights of Gaza's overwhelmingly civilian population, but also seriously damage the international order that helps protect vulnerable communities globally. These scenarios strongly indicate that the policy of removing Palestinians is not only undesirable, but it would also deeply destabilize existing systems, societies and institutions. As an alternative ethical perspective, a social Hobbesian position that holds a pessimistic view of human nature, values security over liberty, and looks down upon international norms could learn different lessons from the Gaza case. Such an observer could argue that history teaches that more force must be used to solve the problem and that consequences would be manageable, ultimately supporting the Trump plan. As this example demonstrates, an open reflection would clarify that differences are primarily ethical.

Taken together, the aforementioned case studies demonstrate that lessons from the past are neither obvious nor simple. The entire process of attempting to extract such lessons is replete with pitfalls. Scholars use the past to justify the present, they inadvertently shape the past with the present in mind, they use problematic analogies between past and present, and they overlook the key role of ethics in interpreting the past for any present-day purpose. In this context scholars should be wary of any attempt to extract simple lessons from the past, highlighting instead the contingency of history and the probability rather than certainty of any course of action. Past historical scenarios and counterfactual histories might be helpful to think with and map the variety of options, but they should not prescribe policy. Perhaps the only simple lesson history teaches us is to refrain from abusing it.

References

Armitage, D. 2023. In defense of presentism. In *History and Human Flourishing*, ed. D. McMahon, 44–69. Oxford: Oxford University Press.

Avraham, Y. 2023, October 28. המסמך המלא של משרד המודיעין: כיבוש עזה וטרנספר כולל לתושביו. *שיחה מקומית*. https://www.mekomit.co.il/המסמך-המלא-של-משרד-המודיעין-כיבוש-עזה-ו/

Ben-Dror, E. 2020. We were getting close to god, not deportees: The expulsion to Marj al-Zuhur in 1992 as a milestone in the Rise of Hamas. *The Middle East Journal 74 (3): 399–416.*

B'Tselem. 1993. *Deportation of Palestinians from the Occupied Territories: The Mass Deportation of December 1992*. https://www.btselem.org/publications/summaries/199306_deportation

Büntgen, U., V. S. Myglan, F. C. Ljungqvist, M. McCormick, N. Di Cosmo, M. Sigl, J. Jungclaus, S. Wagner, P. J. Krusic, J. Esper, J. O. Kaplan, M. A. C. de Vaan, J. Luterbacher, L. Wacker, W. Tegel, and A. V. Kirdyanov. 2016. Cooling and societal change during the Late Antique Little Ice Age from 536 to around 660 AD. *Nature Geoscience* 9 (3): 231–236.

Büntgen, U., W. Tegel, K. Nicolussi, M. McCormick, D. Frank, V. Trouet, J. O. Kaplan, F. Herzig, K.-U. Heussner, H. Wanner, J. Luterbacher, and J. Esper. 2011. 2500 Years of European Climate Variability and Human Susceptibility. *Science* 331 (6017): 578–582.

Carr, E. H. 1961. *What is History?* New York: Vintage.

Collingwood, R. G. 1946. *The Idea of History*. Oxford: Clarendon Press.

Cronon, W. 1992. A place for stories: nature, history, and narrative. *Journal of American History 78 (4): 1347–1376.* https://doi.org/10.2307/2079346

Eichner, I. 2019, August 19. *ישראל מעודדת הגירה מעזה: "נאפשר להם להמריא מהנגב אם יהיה מי שיקלוט אותם."* ynet. https://www.ynet.co.il/articles/0,7340,L-5571847,00.html

Ezra, G. 2014, July 29. *ןילגייפ: "סהל רוזעל רשפא םא םתוא גרהל המל?"* Srugim. https://www.srugim.co.il/85073-ןילגייפ-המל-גורהל-םתוא-םא-אפשר-לעזור-ל

Fears, J. R. 2004. The plague under Marcus Aurelius and the decline and fall of the Roman Empire. *Infectious Disease Clinics* 18 (1): 65–77.

Garrison, C., C. Kilburn, and S. Edwards. 2018. The 1831 eruption of Babuyan Claro that never happened: Has the source of the one of the largest volcanic climate forcing events of the nineteenth century been misattributed? *Journal of Applied Volcanology* 7:8.

Gibbons, A. 2018, November 15. *Why 536 was 'the worst year to be alive'. Science.* https://www.science.org/content/article/why-536-was-worst-year-be-alive

Halevy, D. 2014. Gaza and its people: exile and destruction (Heb.). *Zmanim* 126:40–51.

Harbeck, M., L. Seifert, S. Hänsch, D. M. Wagner, D. Birdsell, K. L. Parise, I. Wiechmann, G. Grupe, A. Thomas, P. Keim, L. Zöller, B. Bramanti, J. M. Riehm, and H. C. Scholz. 2013. Yersinia pestis DNA from skeletal remains from the 6th century AD reveals insights into Justinianic Plague. *PLoS Pathogens* 9 (5): e1003349. https://doi.org/10.1371/journal.ppat.1003349.

Harper, K. 2017. *The Fate of Rome: Climate, Disease, and the End of an Empire*. Princeton: Princeton University Press.

Hartley, L. P. 1953. *The Go-Between*. London: Hamish Hamilton.

Hazkani, S. and T. Sorek. 2025, May 28. Yes to Transfer: 82% of Jewish Israelis Back Expelling Gazans. *Haaretz*. https://www.haaretz.com/israel-news/2025-05-28/ty-article-magazine/.premium/yes-to-transfer-82-of-jewish-israelis-back-expelling-gazans/00000197-12a4-df22-a9d7-9ef6af930000

Historian On The Edge. 2025, February 25. What's history got to do with it? (1). *Historian on the Edge*. https://edgyhistorian.blogspot.com/2025/02/whats-history-got-to-do-with-it-1.html

Khong, Y. F. 1992. *Analogies at War: Korea, Munich, Dien Bien Phu, and the Vietnam Decisions of 1965*. Princeton: Princeton University Press.

Masalha, N. 1996. The 1956-57 occupation of the Gaza Strip: Israeli proposals to resettle the Palestinian refugees. *British Journal of Middle Eastern Studies* 23 (1): 55–68.

McCormick, M. 2007. Toward a molecular history of the Justinianic pandemic. In *Plague and the End of Antiquity: The Pandemic of 541-750*, ed. L. K. Little, 290–312. Cambridge: Cambridge University Press.

Mordechai, L. Forthcoming. *"The Worst Year to Be Alive": 536 CE, Presentism and the Premodern Environment*. Oxford: Oxford University Press.

Mordechai, L., and A. Tubi. 2024. Learning from past society-environment interactions is discursive rather than substantive. *Environmental Research Letters* 19 (12): 124068.

News 12. 2019, August 20. *שקד: "עידוד הגירה תושבי עזה—אינטרס ישראלי."* N12. https://www.mako.co.il/news-politics/2019_Q3/Article-9855879e0cdac61027.htm

Oxford English Dictionary. 2025. *Bioterrorism*. https://www.oed.com/dictionary/bioterrorism_n

Raviv, O. S. 2023. "עידוד הגירה: "פלסטינים מרצועת עזה" 1967-1969. In *עזה: מקום ומדיו במרחב הישראלי*, ed. O. Ben Yehuda and D. Halevy, 145–169. Gama.

Rebenich, S. 2018. Reception of Sparta in Germany and German-speaking Europe. In *A Companion to Sparta*, ed. A. Powell, 685–703. Wiley Blackwell.

Rokach, L. 1980. Israeli state terrorism: An analysis of the Sharett Diaries. *Journal of Palestine Studies* 9 (3): 3–28.

Sallares, R. 2007. Ecology, evolution, and epidemiology of lague. In *Plague and the End of Antiquity: The Pandemic of 541-750*, ed. L. K. Little, 231–289. Cambridge: Cambridge University Press.

Santayana, G. 1905. *The Life of Reason; or, The phases of Human Progress*. New York: Charles Scribner's Sons.

Sorek, T. and S. Hazkani. 2025, June 12. One cannot stay neutral when confronted with expulsion. *Local Call*. https://www.mekomit.co.il/אי-אפשר-להישאר-ניטרליים-מול-רכבת-הגירה/

Spungin, T. 2025, February 11. Majority of Israelis support Trump's Gaza plan, relocation of Palestinians in exclusive "Post" poll. *The Jerusalem Post*. https://www.jpost.com/israel-news/article-841693

Stathakopoulos, D. 2004. *Famine and Pestilence in the Late Roman and Early Byzantine Empire: A Systematic Survey of Subsistence Crises and Epidemics*. Aldershot: Ashgate.

The Jewish People Policy Institute. 2025, February 3. *Majority of Israelis support Trump's proposal to relocate Gaza's population to other countries*. https://jppi.org.il/en/סקר-החברה-הישראלית-לחודש-פברואר-רוב-גד/

Times of Israel Staff. 2014, August 5. Knesset member: Retake Gaza, put civilians in 'tent camps.' *The Times of Israel*. http://www.timesofisrael.com/knesset-member-retake-gaza-put-civilians-in-tent-camps/

Tubi, A., L. Mordechai, E. Feitelson, O. Kay, and D. Tamir. 2022. Can we learn from the past? Towards better analogies and historical inference in society-environmental change research. *Global Environmental Change* 76:102570.

Wagner, D. M., Klunk, J., Harbeck, M., Devault, A., Waglechner, N., Sahl, J. W., Enk, J., Birdsell, D. N., Kuch, M., Lumibao, C., Poinar, D., Pearson, T., Fourment, M., Golding, B., Riehm, J. M., Earn, D. J., Dewitte, S., Rouillard, J. M., Grupe, G., Wiechmann, I., … Poinar, H. (2014). Yersinia pestis and the plague of Justinian 541–543 AD: a genomic analysis. *The Lancet. Infectious diseases, 14(4), 319–326.* https://doi.org/10.1016/S1473-3099(13)70323-2

Washer, P. 2010. *Emerging Infectious Diseases and Society*. Cham: Springer.

Lee Mordechai is a Senior Lecturer at the History Department at the Hebrew University of Jerusalem. He works on premodern environmental history in the Eastern Mediterranean, covering topics such as the Justinianic Plague and earthquakes. His second book, '"The Worst Year to Be Alive": 536 CE, Presentism, and the Premodern Environment' is forthcoming with Oxford University Press.

Agent-Based Modelling of Possible Pasts and Futures: Possibilities and Limitations

Gesine A. Steudle, Malte Vogl, Aleksandra Kaye, and Sarah Wolf

Abstract Politics is the art of the possible. Policy-making needs to react to external demand but more importantly to decide between possible future pathways and shape them. This comprises recognising possibilities for future developments as well as the ability to implement the choices that were made. For both, insights from historically informed modelling can play a role. Firstly, patterns in historical data can give insights in cause-effect-relationships, understanding what is important for implementing policies to achieve agreed goals. These insights are often derived from analysing time series data. However, in the historic context, the data that is at the core of such an analysis might have been gathered in a way that is structured by the socio-technical context as e.g. decisions have been made in the past about which artefacts to archive, and those were influenced by the technical possibilities at the time. In these cases agent-based modelling can not only play a role in analysing the existing data but also for investigating the ways how data collections are formed and the resulting implications for an analysis. Secondly, history shapes the space of possible futures; models for assessing future developments have to take into account the memory of the system and how it influences the probabilities for future trajectories as e.g. through path dependencies. Similarly, collective decision making is influenced by such information about past developments. For complex systems, these relations are usually not fully transparent and accessible, such that the simulation of future developments has to rely on a wide range of assumptions. This necessitates innovative approaches for continuous collaboration between modellers and stakeholders, such as e.g. the Decision Theatre method.

Keywords Agent-based modelling · Epistemics of simulation · Modelling history · Possible futures · Path dependence · Socio-cultural evolution

---

G. A. Steudle (✉) · M. Vogl · A. Kaye
Max Planck Institute of Geoanthropology, Jena, Germany
e-mail: steudle@gea.mpg.de

S. Wolf
Chair Sustainable Transport Systems and Data Science, Technische Universität Berlin, Berlin, Germany

Institut für Mathematik, Freie Universität Berlin, Berlin, Germany

J. F. Haldon, R. Fernandes (eds.), *Bridging History and Policy*, Understanding Complex Systems, https://doi.org/10.1007/978-3-032-24379-9_7

1 Introduction

Policy-making is inherently concerned with shaping future developments in ways that are considered desirable in a given context. This involves, on the one hand, negotiating what is considered desirable, and on the other hand, it is often useful to know the past and to understand how present structures emerged from it. In fact, history can be important for policy-making in various ways. Many of them are related to using knowledge about the past in forecasting or making predictions. If one can identify patterns in history that repeat, these insights might lead to projections for similar situations in the future.

Maybe more importantly, there are path dependencies and inertias due to which not all possible states of a system are available in an arbitrarily short amount of time, as e.g. the beliefs or habits of people do not change instantaneously, or production facilities cannot be remodelled from one day to the other. Some kind of such "accumulated history" (e.g. infrastructures, institutions, mentalities, social norms) has hence to be taken into account when assessing future options.[1]

Here, mathematical modelling of history and of possible futures can be useful. Results of mathematical models are used widely in the natural sciences to make precise predictions about the behaviour of a particular system under study. For the creation of policies, such predictive power for socio-technical or -ecological systems would be desirable; models are being employed as one of many elements supporting decision processes, as was to be observed, for example, during the recent pandemic. Historians, on the other hand, have often been rather hesitant, even reluctant, to such approaches in their discipline. Arguments against them are usually built around the specificity of a given historical context and the assumption that two situations in the past always differ from each other in too many ways to extract abstract universal rules or even laws. Nonetheless, there have always also been attempts to find something similar to general laws in history (among others, but not limited to Hegelianism, historical materialism, L'École des Annales), and lately there are more and more efforts to subject historical data to statistical analysis to find general behaviours, also caused by the recent advances in data science (see e.g. Nunn 2020). Statistical methods applied to (big) historical data can give insights into correlations between various indicators, as e.g. between energy consumption and GDP growth (Bercegol and Benisty 2022; Chontanawat 2020). However, to explain how these correlations come about, theories are needed, e.g. for determining interactions between different actors and their individual decision making. The formulation of such theories in mathematical terms corresponds to the creation of models. These models, by having to be calibrated with potentially fuzzy data from past events, but being able to predict possible future trajectories, can thus link pasts and futures. For

[1] There are, of course, many more ways in which history has an influence on policy making, as e.g. historical narratives play an important role for political decisions. In this text however, we will focus on the aspects mentioned.

the case of individuals and their interactions, agent-based models are particularly useful, as shall be discussed below.

2 Agent-Based Modelling

Agent-based models (ABMs) define the system to be modelled by characterising its individual elements, in particular those that have agency, referred to as agents, but also other entities, their common environment and network structures in the system. The dynamics of the system derive from the decision and interaction rules of agents, i.e. algorithms defined to represent these rules. The overall, or macro-level structures resulting from them are given by the simulation. Modelling a system by micro-level interactions means identifying and making explicit mechanisms behind the system's overall behaviour.[2]

A (complex) system's overall behaviour may exhibit features that we would not expect to result from the rules for the behaviour of its individual entities. Such emergent phenomena are overall features of the system and they are sometimes seen as a process of self-organization.[3] Agent-based models often exhibit emergent behaviour, as e.g. in Schelling's model where strongly separated living areas emerge in a population of two kinds of agents even though the agents only have a mild preference for living close to their own kind (Schelling 1971). ABMs thus make a connection between micro-level (inter-)action rules in a population of agents embedded in a socio-technical or -ecological environment on the one hand and system-level dynamics compatible with these rules on the other hand. They may be employed considering either of these sides given, to investigate the other side: for understanding which mechanisms are responsible for the emerging overall dynamics and (resulting) structures of a system, or positing rules, for exploring their potential consequences in terms of the system's overall dynamics.

Agent-based models have been widely applied for both simulating the future and analysing the past.

Generally speaking, the main difference when building ABMs for the future or for the past is the following: For simulations of the future one can gather information about the agents' decision and interaction rules empirically, e.g. through surveys about preferences, collecting data on how agents are linked etc. The structures that will emerge from these rules in the future are unknown; possible future structures are the outcome of the simulations. Agent-based simulations of the past are made in very different circumstances: the emerging structures (archaeological

[2] Another advantage of ABMs is that they can more easily be explained to a non-technical audience than models for overall system dynamics, because the decision and interaction rules of the micro entities are usually easier to understand, especially for complex systems. This also often makes them a useful tool to facilitate interdisciplinary research.

[3] Examples for emergent phenomena are life or consciousness, but also certain data structures as e.g. archival data.

artefacts, historical archives etc.) have been—at least partly—found, but the decisions and interactions that led to these structures are often unknown. Agent-based modelling can then be used as a tool to test different assumptions about how these structures emerged.[4]

In both cases, agent-based modelling is used to construct different scenarios. This is a feature deriving from the rule-based nature of ABMs, which e.g., the analysis of time series cannot offer. For ABMs of the past, this means that by assuming different decision and/or interaction rules for the agents, different hypothetical pasts are created and can be sorted out by comparing their "predictions" of the past with the artefacts or data actually observed. Thus, certain hypotheses about the past can be evaluated and some may be discarded.

ABMs for the future are also used to create different scenarios. By assuming changes to empirically elicited rules that represent different policy settings, different future trajectories of the system are created, and can be used e.g. for decision support. Through simulations, possible effects of different policies, and in particular their combined effects can then be assessed. In the following subsections we give some examples to illustrate this.

3 Agent-Based Modelling of the Past

As Hammel succinctly put it in 1979, regarding experimental history and explaining the present in terms of the past: "To explain any result is to consider the possibility of variation in its causes, even if only implicitly by stressing the uniqueness of the cause and effect relationship" (Hammel 1979, p.274). This can be achieved in different ways. According to Rubio-Campillo "The discipline of History presents its ideas as descriptive models expressed in natural language." (Rubio-Campillo 2016, p.2). When ABMs are applied, these descriptive models are translated into a different format of formal language, that reduces ambiguity. Rubio-Campillo asserts that such a shift could help historians assess how well a working hypothesis explains a historical dynamic by measuring the gap between model predictions and observed evidence. (Rubio-Campillo 2016, p.15). Coming from the discipline of archaeology, Madella et al. present a similar idea, in an introduction to a special issue of the *Journal of Archaeological Method and Theory* on simulating the past, when they point out their discipline's reliance on abductive reasoning based on incomplete sets

[4] One might add a category of "ABM for (understanding) the present" with the aim of testing which mechanisms may be behind structures observed in the real-world at present. Epstein and Axtell's famous question of "can you grow it?" goes into this direction "Perhaps one day people will interpret the question, 'Can you explain it?' as asking 'Can you grow it?' Artificial society modeling allows us to 'grow' social structures in silico demonstrating that certain sets of micro specifications are sufficient to generate the macro phenomena of interest." (Epstein and Axtell 1996: 20). As these models are often of a more abstract kind than the ones we are interested in here, i.e., rather than a concrete system in a concrete situation that one has data about, they investigate which rules may lead to which outcomes in a more general setting, we skip these models here.

of observations (Madella et al. 2014). They continue by highlighting that in archaeology non-explicit models are used to study changes and processes without much thought given to the equifinality and uncertainty of such an approach as those are perceived as unlikely to be overcome. Madella and others, however, propose that model building and inferential reasoning could be used to tackle those issues.

In the context of the past, ABMs are thus principally employed for their explanatory or exploratory potential. The application of formal modelling and simulation in archaeology to investigate aspects of human behaviour is still relatively new. This is even more acutely the case in the discipline of history. Yet, the growing number and variety of recent studies of the past using ABMs, as well as books such as "Agent-based Modeling and Simulation in Archaeology" (Wurzer 2015), or the more recent "Agent-Based Modeling for Archaeology: Simulating the Complexity of Societies" (Romanowska 2021) attest to the growing interest and approval for the approach. For example, Rubio-Campillo, Valdés Matías, and Ble utilised agent-based models to examine the role of centurions in Roman legions during the transition period of the civil wars (first century BCE, Rubio-Campillo et al. 2015). Their model indicates that centurions with higher capabilities had a greater impact on troop charges, while even those who were less experienced or trained could significantly influence the cohesion of their units. In a different research, David Ortega and others used ABM simulations of an obsidian exchange network to better understand this long-distance trade during the Near Eastern Neolithic period in the Near East. They conclude that while their simulation confirmed that "a type of small-world network rather than a down-the-line model, was responsible for obsidian exchange", a more hierarchical and fine-tuned model would be needed to better explain the past exchange networks (Ortega et al. 2014). In the MayaSim, an ABM of the ancient Maya social-ecological systems, Scott Heckbert studied "the relationship between population growth, agricultural production, soil degradation, climate variability, primary productivity, hydrology, ecosystem services, forest succession, and the stability of trade networks." (Heckbert 2013). This ABM allows researchers to explore the conditions that shaped the densely populated and interconnected geography of the ancient Maya, highlighting the mutual influence between past societies and their environment. These are just three examples, of many historical and archaeological studies employing ABMs and covering subjects as varied as pottery production or wool-sheep domestication. Below we detail our attempt at harnessing ABM to better understand the historical archival process.

Example: Communication and archiving processes in the Republic of Letters Source criticism, that is, critically assessing and evaluating the validity of historical sources, is one, if not the most fundamental, tool of the discipline of history. Individual sources have their strengths and limitations, as do entire collections. While archives reflect the past, they also actively shape the present and future, especially when used for generating new knowledge. Given the importance of archives as repositories of human knowledge upon which new knowledge can be generated, it is precisely the archival process that we put under scrutiny in the Historical Letters ABM (Vogl et al. 2024a,b). The model is influenced by work on reconstruction of the Republic of Letters (Hotson & Wallnig 2019), a period between 1500 and 1800 in which the rise of postal communication allowed people across Europe to form a loose society of intellectuals. By the nature of the discourse via letters, sources of this period are distributed across Europe with quite different states of preservation. This renders a historical reevaluation of that period challenging.

In the model, the agents are letter senders and receivers that additionally are able to change their position. The agents are initialized with a random internal topic and a geographic position drawn from a distribution corresponding to population estimates of medieval European cities (Cesaretti et al. 2016). In each round, agents generate two distinct neighbourhoods with different reach, one for finding potential letter receivers and one for finding potential targets for changing the current geographic position. All agents additionally have personal social networks increasing the list of potential exchange partners. Finding a movement or communication partner are both self-reinforcing processes, modelled as Pólya urns, i.e. an agent with an already large number of received letters is more likely to receive even more letters. If an agent is able to send a letter, the topic of the letter is chosen from its own or the receivers previously held topics and the letter is sent. The receiver then adapts its current internal topic state to the topic of the letter by a randomly chosen amount, ranging from complete ignorance of the topic to its complete acceptance. Independent of this adoption, a new social network edge is created between sender and receiver agent. This process is repeated for all agents for the desired amount of rounds. Depending on the model settings, agents have a social network at initialization or grow their social network during the model run. Furthermore, the activation of an agent in each round can be random. For a detailed description of all the possible model configurations, see Vogl (2024).

With the application of simulations to this topic, we can address two aspects of biases in archives. We can try to create agent-based models that simulate the emergence of the archive by giving the agents rules to decide on the knowledge or sources to be preserved and compare the structure of the simulated archives with empirical data from existing archives. This could e.g. concern the distribution of preserved letters as a function of gender and time, or the number of books as a function of length and written language. Other works have e.g. used simulations based on birth-death processes to estimate the number of lost books (Kestemont et al. 2022). These approaches are faced with the challenge of a suitable calibration baseline. If the existing historical data encodes biases of librarians, archivists, as well as the creators of the archival material themselves, any reconstruction based on these will reproduce the embedded biases (Ortolja-Baird and Nyhan 2022). A historical interpretation of these reconstructions can, therefore, misrepresent the actual dynamics of, for example, communication processes or scientific productivity. Subsequent policy decisions based on such misinterpreted skewed representations of historical data will inherit and further reinforce the biases.

To address the issue of suitable, bias-aware baselines for historical data, we can add a second layer of simulations on the above approach of archival generation. At the end of the model run of the Historical Letters model, a letter ledger of all successful letter sending events is created, corresponding to an archive without any omissions or losses. Instead of a direct calibration on the empirical existing archives, we thus assume the generated virtual data to be complete in the limits of the simulation that generated it (Vogl et al. 2024b). From this ledger a baseline communication network between the senders and receivers is created. We can then formulate hypotheses on the processes that lead to forgetting or omitting specific documents or persons in the transition from living to archival data. Each hypothesis is formulated as a combination of first a ranking applied to the generated data, e.g. based on degrees[5] of agents in a network, age of publications, or based on geographical regions, and second a distribution of the likeliness of the ranked units to make it into the archived data. The simulation then creates pruned virtual archives from the simulated data by randomly deleting entries with weights based on the ranked likeliness. By repeating the process for all hypotheses and comparing the results with empirical archival data we can find likely processes that generated the biases embedded in the empirical archives (Avena-Koenigsberger et al. 2015) and reject other hypotheses.

4 Agent-Based Modelling of the Future

Agent-based modelling for policy applications is usually done if one wants to evaluate the implications of certain policy measures before (possibly) implementing them. This is especially helpful if it is unclear which interactions between different possible options are to be expected and the combined effect on the system is not assumed to result from just adding up the effects of individual measures (see e.g. Alonso-Betanzos et al. 2017; Bonabeau 2002; Heckbert et al. 2010). Main challenges of agent-based modelling for such applications are calibration and validation of models, that is, assuring that a model represents the real-world situation and phenomena under study sufficiently well so that one trusts the model to provide useful representations of potential futures. Here, calibration refers to setting model parameters in such a way that a model reproduces some given data or patterns[6]—usually from a recent past—well enough and is often obtained by minimising a pre-defined error between model output and these data. Validation in turn means to check the thus calibrated model against other data or patterns to ensure its more general validity than just for the calibrated situation.

An ABM gauged in this way can then be used for exploring effects of different policies or other alternative assumptions by defining how these policies influence the agent behaviour at the micro-level and observing effects of the respective influences at the macro-level. Given that the simulations compute each single agent,

[5] The degree of a node in a network is the number of connections it has with other nodes.

[6] See also the work by Grimm and colleagues on "pattern-oriented modelling" (Grimm and Railsback 2012).

such effects can be observed at different levels of detail, e.g., to compare policy-induced changes for different social groups etc.

As political decisions are often required in situations where there is no objective best solution but rather a trade-off between different points of view is required, ABMs can not only be useful for simulating possible futures but can also be employed in discussions of such trade-offs with different stakeholder groups. A format for doing so is the Decision Theatre (DT).[7] Such an event supports discussions of a societal challenge with visualisations of empirical data and model results on a few large screens. Participants can interact with a model, e.g., by composing scenarios from a list of available choices (policy measures or other influences on the system) and exploring their modelled results.

Example: Pandemics

ABMs were widely used to estimate effects of different policies in the recent Covid19-pandemic (Lorig et al. 2021), but have been employed in epidemiologic contexts much longer (Tracy et al. 2018). In particular at the beginning of an epidemic outbreak, when numbers of infected are low, the network structures in a given population can play an important role. It is hence useful to make these explicit in an ABM, which tracks the movement and resulting contacts between people in which infections may occur, together with the individual disease progressions, which in turn can determine whether a person is still able to infect others at each point in time. Also, differentiating vulnerable groups is rather straightforward in a micro-level model, where agents can be equipped with their age or previous conditions at the individual level. Given rules for interaction (contacts, infections, and disease progression), policy influences on these rules are also quite straightforward to define, e.g. decreasing numbers of contacts through a lock-down or infectivity to represent wearing of masks. Such ABMs have been employed in policy consultations, to cite just one example, the MATSim Episim model[8] was at the basis of discussions between policy makers and modellers as well as of regular reports such as (Nagel et al. 2023).

We have also used such an ABM for developing Decision Theatre events for high school students (Wiebe et al. 2024). These are built around the GERDA-model (Goldenbogen et al. 2022) which was developed for representing infection dynamics in smaller towns based on geographic and demographic data from open sources. In the events, students play the role of local politicians in a fictitious decision-making process after first getting information about the model. Then they may simulate a few scenarios in small groups, choosing these scenarios according to how they think they can best obtain information from the model. In a second step, they decide upon the policy measures they consider best—defining themselves what "best" means whereby they can take into account also policy implications that GERDA does not model, such as collateral effects from a lock-down for mental

[7] The Decision Theater is a registered trademark by the Arizona State University, see https://dt.asu.edu/

[8] See also https://covid-sim.info/

health or for the local economy. While in this case the DT was developed as a learning tool for students, it illustrates how modelled scenarios can support discussions about policies in that simulations show expected or unexpected effects of different policy combinations. At the same time, students discuss aspects of policies that are external to the model, showing that the discussion goes beyond using the model for finding an in any sense "optimal" solution.

The school setting also underlines that ABM are easy to explain to a general audience, as the elements modelled are familiar and the representation of the world within an ABM remains rather similar in structure. Also, repeated interactions computed in simulations are easier to communicate than e.g., compartmental models with differential equations.

One particular feature of the GERDA model is that under some policy configurations, different model runs—that have to be done to see and communicate stochasticity in outcomes—show a wide variability or bimodality, that is, for a certain percentage of simulation runs, the disease dies out while for the remainder, a strong outbreak is observed (Goldenbogen et al. 2022). This relates to viewing the future as a stochastic process, a topic we will come back to in the following section.

Example: Mobility

Another example for an ABM which we have used for engaging citizens in model-supported discussions about possible futures is the simulation of mobility demand in Germany with the agent-based Mobility Transition Model (MoTMo, Wolf et al. 2023). MoTMo simulates private mobility demand in Germany with a time horizon up to 2035. It can be used for exploring potential shifts to new technologies, such as electric vehicles, and new behaviours, such as car sharing. It is used to experiment with different options, such as the implementation of possible policy measures or alternative exogenous developments. The resulting different scenarios for the future can then be compared, for example, in terms of the dynamics and spatial distribution of the different means of transport and total greenhouse gas emissions from the private mobility sector. MoTMo has been used in Decision Theatres to support discussions about sustainable mobility.

In MoTMo, the available means of transport that persons can use are classified into five mobility types: combustion engine cars, electric cars, public transport, car sharing, and non-motorized mobility, that is, walking or biking. The model provides a temporal evolution for these mobility types. For some features, the temporal evolution is exogenously given, for example the trend to an increasing number of heavy cars (SUVs) is based on empirical data. In other cases, the temporal evolution is (partly) endogenous, that is, it depends on the number of persons that use a mobility type; the effect is known, for example for production price development through learning-by-doing.

MoTMo has three types of agents, connected through a multilayered network. Persons represent the individuals that chose a mobility type. Persons are connected to other persons that form their social network. Households represent collectives of agents that take coordinated mobility decisions, every person belongs to exactly one household. Cells build a regular 5 km by 5 km grid of locations on the map of

Germany. They collect spatial information, as the population density, and other developments like e.g. the changing charging infrastructure for electric vehicles. Every household is located in one cell. MoTMo uses a synthetic population of Germany for persons in households, and the households' location in cells, i.e. agents statistically match distributions of the German population in terms of age, income, household type, and population density.

Persons in MoTMo aim to maximize the utility gained from their mobility choice. The utility function is a Cobb-Douglas function with four factors, representing four types of consequences from the use of a mobility type: costs, ecology, innovation, and convenience. Different persons weight these consequences differently. However, persons do not know the true consequences of all mobility types; their choices of a certain type are not made by calculating utilities with their utility function, but rather by copying peers in their social network that experience a high utility and by learning about which copy choices have been useful in the past. The actual decision for a mobility type is then made at the household level, to take into account budget constraints based on the household's income.

To explore possible futures of private mobility demand in Germany, different policy measures, which were debated at the time the model was created, have been implemented in MoTMo as well as investment strategies, and alternative expectations on exogenous developments. With these options different scenarios can be composed.[9] In the business-as-usual (BAU) scenario (no option activated), current trends are projected into the future. Other scenarios can be composed by choosing among other options provided by the model. These options are implemented through parameter changes in the model, for example price parameters or those of the conveniences of the different mobility types. Users can explore the model's predictions until 2035 for their chosen set of options, including maybe unintended consequences as unexpected feedbacks between different policies. The simulation outcomes are the mobility types used per person over time, from which different measures can be calculated as overall usage or CO_2 emissions. Because outputs are given per agent, the results can easily be resolved spatially, or with respect to different agent types such as different income classes or different household types etc.

5 Past and Future as Stochastic Processes

Analysing possible futures and constructing history are two sides of the same coin in the sense that there is a continuous process of things happening in which only our position in time makes past and future two objects of different categories for us, where common sense seems to say that there is only one past but many possible futures. As seen above, agent-based modelling can be used for representing both, just with different inputs and outcomes, illustrating this view.

[9] A scenario is a specific combination of model options.

The example models for past and future discussed above have several things in common: There are algorithms defining the behaviours and interactions of the entities (agents) of the systems under study, and these algorithms have deterministic but also stochastic elements; mathematically speaking, it means to model past and future as stochastic processes (Izquierdo et al. 2009).[10]

The idea that stochastic processes can serve as an approximate representation of history has been formulated explicitly by Wolpert et al. (2024). If this is assumed, it should be the same for the future.

Stochastic processes can be of various types; when looking at the course of history and trying to extrapolate it into the future, Markov processes of different order are of particular interest. Roughly speaking, a Markov chain or first-order Markov process is a stochastic process in which the probabilities for future states of the system only depend on the present state of the system independently of the past, i.e. it does not matter how the system reached its present state. This is very rarely the case for the systems political decision making deals with. In many cases, however, one can define a Markov processes of higher order by extending the system's state space to include a number of previous states. This new definition of the process makes precise how far back into the past one has to look and which information from this past is needed to be able to calculate probabilities for the future evolution of the system. A thus extended state space of a system can be considered to contain the "accumulated history" that shapes the future (in a probabilistic way, still).[11]

A similar idea is expressed by the concept of path dependencies: what happens in the near future shapes the possibilities of what is going to happen further down the road. Path dependencies are one of the challenges of formal approaches in computational history (Jost et al. 2023), as well as for formal approaches to modelling possible futures. Modelling past and future as higher order Markov processes would make explicit how deep into the past or the future such dependencies reach.[12]

A further concept that can be related is *niche construction* from ecology (e.g. Laland et al. 1999; Odling-Smee et al. 2013), which describes how organisms shape their environment and thus create a second mode of heredity to their descendants. Niche construction combined with further elements from evolution theory, such as the stochastic processes of genetic mutation and selection as well as with the concept of *regulatory networks* (that determine the expression of genes) has been described as the framework of *extended evolution*, and has also been used to study

[10] In mathematics, a stochastic process (in discrete time, but we do not need to go into continuous time processes here) is a sequence of random variables, where the index of the sequence often represents time. The randomness involved does not mean that there are not any regularities to the process, in fact the mathematics of stochastic processes classifies different types of these processes by their characteristics and analyses such classes of processes.

[11] For a reduced version of the mobility model discussed above this mathematical analysis can be found in Steudle et al. (2024).

[12] The term path dependence is often used in the sense of "history matters", but a more refined concept of it denotes it "(...) a property of a stochastic process which obtains under two conditions (contingency and self-reinforcement) and causes lock-in in the absence of exogenous shock." (Vergne and Durand 2010).

cultural dynamics (Laubichler and Renn 2015). Like path dependency, the framework of extended evolution points to the importance of the "accumulated past" for present processes; however, the latter goes beyond the concept of path dependency insofar as it is a more complex description of different kinds of feed-backs at work at different time scales.

Looking at the past as well as to the future through the lens of such an evolutionary framework with stochastic elements and complex feed-backs is an interpretation of the world that has implications for the way in which policies are developed. Such a system does not usually have an optimal development path; this perspective differs from a rather technocratic or standard-economic point of view where usually objective functions are defined in the first place. Neither is the system usually in equilibrium (in the sense of a fixed point of a dynamic system).[13]

In the previous section it was discussed that agent-based simulations can show a wide variability or bi-modality in the outcomes, which is a common feature in stochastic processes, and that at best probability distribution for the different outcomes can be calculated. This can pose a challenge for making political decisions on the bases of these kind of simulations.

Contrary to biological evolution, considerations of socio-cultural evolution have to take into account the question of human agency, which is also the core of political decision making. Modelling the history using the kind of ABMs discussed above means to model it as a stochastic process with complex feed-backs which resembles frameworks of evolution. How to implement human agency into these is ongoing research.

6 Conclusions

ABMs are employed for modelling both, the past as well as the future, albeit with different purposes for the output. This is due to the fact that our position in time is different with respect to them. Policy making is usually concerned with the future,

[13] In many complex systems, as e.g. in physics, ecology, finance, or history, phases of relatively stable states often alternate with rapid shifts, as phase transitions, revolutions, the emergence or extinction of species etc. Physics, as well as e.g. classical economics (adopting concept from physics), tends to see these stable states as equilibria, i.e. as the result of some optimisation process. From the point of view of evolution theory, there are no equilibria in this sense, as the stochastic processes and feedbacks of evolution constitute continuous development all the time. However also in the fossil record, stable phases of populations with little evolutionary change alternate with phases of relatively rapid phases of branching of species; this has been described by Eldrege and Gould in the theory of punctuated equilibria (Eldredge and Gould 1972). Concepts very similar to the one of punctuated equilibria can be found in political theory and history, where the phases of fast change are often called critical junctures (e.g. Sewell 1996; Capoccia and Kelemen 2007). Whereas there are comprehensive mathematical descriptions for the dynamic behaviour of physical systems between equilibria in physics, a theory of critical junctures, to our knowledge, has not been represented in mathematical terms.

or more precisely with the effects of today's decisions on the further course of history. When it comes to agent-based modelling, we see the following "bridges" between modelling the future and modelling past developments:

1. How far the past can be used to calibrate or validate models for the future is debatable but for some events, as e.g. major transition of the socio-technical systems due to environmental conditions, history provides—although not in the exact same circumstances—at least some observation points, or patterns that can support simulations of possible futures.
2. Modelling historical circumstances can give a better understanding of the things (data, artefacts) handed down from the past that are influencing our assessment of the future. These circumstances have to be taken into account when using the information transmitted; similarly, models of the past might be helpful to restore information that has been lost.
3. The probabilities for different possible future developments depend on the past, as for example the built infrastructure, production facilities, habits, or opinions have been formed over time and cannot be changed drastically arbitrarily fast. Modelling can help to understand these dependencies. They can also give insights into how present day decisions influence not only the near future but also determine the set of choices that are available and their likeliness at much later points in time.

Using ABMs for simulations of future scenarios has the advantage that as agents can be defined heterogeneous the analysis of simulation results with respect to certain subgroups (for example different social groups) is straightforward. Furthermore, it is quite easy in an agent-based model to make the network of links between the agents explicit and to study effects of shocks to these networks, or the influence of different network topologies in general.

Modelling history using the kind of ABMs discussed above imposes a certain interpretation of it (as it would for other model choices as well). This includes the ideas that decisions which might not seem very big can be decisive even for the far future (as the idea of path dependence suggests), or a notion of how institutions (or other ways to build "environmental niches") emerge as a consequence of human action but not necessarily human design, but via their feed-backs have important influence on the possible future developments.

References

Alonso-Betanzos, A., N. Sánchez-Marono, O. Fontenla-Romero, J. G. Polhill, T. Craig, J. Bajo, and J. M. Corchado, eds. 2017. *Agent-Based Modeling of Sustainable Behaviors*. Cham: Springer.

Avena-Koenigsberger, A., J. Goñi, R. Solé, and J. Sporns. 2015. Network morphospace. *Journal of the Royal Society Interface* 12:20140881. https://doi.org/10.1098/rsif.2014.0881.

Bercegol, H., and H. Benisty. 2022. An energy-based macroeconomic model validated by global historical series since 1820. *Ecological Economics* 192:107253. https://doi.org/10.1016/j.ecolecon.2021.107253.

Bonabeau, E. 2002. Agent-based modeling: Methods and techniques for simulating human systems. *Proceedings of the National Academy of Sciences* 99:7280–7287. https://doi.org/10.1073/pnas.082080899.

Capoccia, G., and R. D. Kelemen. 2007. The study of critical junctures: Theory, narrative, and counterfactuals in historical institutionalism. *World Politics* 59 (3): 341–369. https://doi.org/10.1017/S0043887100020852.

Cesaretti, R., J. Lobo, L. M. A. Bettencourt, S. G. Ortman, and M. E. Smith. 2016. Population-area relationship for medieval European cities. *PLoS ONE* 11 (10): e0162678. https://doi.org/10.1371/journal.pone.0162678.

Chontanawat, J. 2020. Dynamic modelling of causal relationship between energy consumption, CO_2 emission, and economic growth in SE Asian countries. *Energies* 13 (24): 6664. https://doi.org/10.3390/en13246664.

Eldredge, N., and S. J. Gould. 1972. Punctuated equilibria: An alternative to phyletic gradualism. In *Models in Paleobiology*, ed. T. J. M. Schopf, 82–115. San Francisco: Cooper & Co.

Epstein, J. M., and R. L. Axtell. 1996. *Growing Artificial Societies: Social Science from the Bottom Up*. Cambridge MA: MIT Press. https://doi.org/10.7551/mitpress/3374.001.0001.

Goldenbogen, B., S. O. Adler, O. Bodeit, J. A. H. Wodke, X. Escalera-Fanjul, A. Korman, et al. 2022. Control of COVID-19 outbreaks under stochastic community dynamics, bimodality, or limited vaccination. *Advanced Science* 9 (23): 2200088. https://doi.org/10.1002/advs.202200088.

Grimm, V., and S. F. Railsback. 2012. Pattern-oriented modelling: A 'multi-scope' for predictive systems ecology. *Philosophical Transactions of the Royal Society B* 367 (1586): 298–310. https://doi.org/10.1098/rstb.2011.0180.

Hammel, E. A. 1979. The Harvey Lecture Series: Experimental history. *Journal of Anthropological Research* 35 (3): 274–291. https://doi.org/10.1086/jar.35.3.3629903.

Heckbert, S., T. Baynes, and A. Reeson. 2010. Agent-based modeling in ecological economics. *Annals of the New York Academy of Sciences* 1185 (1): 39–53. https://doi.org/10.1111/j.1749-6632.2009.05286.x.

Heckbert, S. 2013. MayaSim: An agent-based model of the ancient Maya social-ecological system. *Journal of Artificial Societies and Social Simulation* 16 (4): 11. https://doi.org/10.18564/jasss.2305.

Hotson, H., and T. Wallnig, eds. 2019. *Reassembling the Republic of Letters in the digital age: Standards, systems, scholarship*. Göttingen: Universitätsverlag Göttingen. https://doi.org/10.17875/gup2019-1146.

Izquierdo, L. R., S. S. Izquierdo, J. M. Galán, and J. I. Santos. 2009. Techniques to understand computer simulations: Markov chain analysis. *Journal of Artificial Societies and Social Simulation* 12 (1): 6. https://www.jasss.org/12/1/6.html.

Jost, J., R. Lalli, M. D. Laubichler, E. Olbrich, J. Renn, G. Restrepo, F. P. Stadler, and D. Wintergrün. 2023. Computational history: Challenges and opportunities of formal approaches. *Journal of Social Computing* 4 (3): 232–242. https://doi.org/10.23919/JSC.2023.0017.

Kestemont, M., F. Karsdorp, E. De Bruijn, M. Driscoll, K. A. Kapitan, P. Ó. Macháin, et al. 2022. Forgotten books: The application of unseen species models to the survival of culture. *Science* 375 (6582): 765–769. https://doi.org/10.1126/science.abl7655.

Laland, K. N., F. J. Odling-Smee, and M. W. Feldman. 1999. Evolutionary consequences of niche construction and their implications for ecology. *Proceedings of the National Academy of Sciences* 96:10242–10247.

Laubichler, M. D., and J. Renn. 2015. Extended evolution: A conceptual framework for integrating regulatory networks and niche construction. *Journal of Experimental Zoology Part B* 324 (7): 565–577. https://doi.org/10.1002/jez.b.22631.

Lorig, F., E. Johansson, and E., and P. Davidsson. 2021. Agent-based social simulation of the COVID-19 pandemic: A systematic review. *Journal of Artificial Societies and Social Simulation* 24 (3): 5. https://doi.org/10.18564/jasss.4601.

Madella, M., B. Rondelli, C. Lancelotti, A. Balbo, D. Zurro, X. Rubio Campillo, and S. Stride. 2014. Introduction to simulating the past. *Journal of Archaeological Method and Theory* 21 (2): 251–257. https://doi.org/10.1007/s10816-014-9209-8.

Nagel, K., I. Bostanci, K. Maier, S.A. Müller, S. Paltra, C. Rakow, J. Rehmann, T. Conrad, and C. Schütte (2023). *Analyse des zeitlichen Abstands zwischen COVID-19 Wellen und Szenarien für den Winter 2023/2024*. MODUS-COVID Bericht. https://depositonce.tu-berlin.de/items/50bb250e-463f-41d0-a47a-989aa0395ebf

Nunn, N. 2020. The historical roots of economic development. *Science* 367 (6485): eaaz9986. https://doi.org/10.1126/science.aaz9986.

Odling-Smee, F. J., D. H. Erwin, E. P. Palkovacs, M. W. Feldman, and K. N. Laland. 2013. Niche construction theory: A practical guide for ecologists. *The Quarterly Review of Biology* 88 (1): 4–28.

Ortega, D., J. J. Ibañez, L. Khalidi, V. Méndez, D. Campos, and L. Teira. 2014. Towards a multi-agent-based modelling of obsidian exchange in the Neolithic Near East. *Journal of Archaeological Method and Theory* 21 (2): 461–485. https://doi.org/10.1007/s10816-013-9196-1.

Ortolja-Baird, A., and J. Nyhan. 2022. Encoding the haunting of an object catalogue: on the potential of digital technologies to perpetuate or subvert the silence and bias of the early-modern archive. *Digital Scholarship in the Humanities* 37 (3): 844–867. https://doi.org/10.1093/llc/fqab065.

Romanowska, I. 2021. *Agent-based modeling for archaeology*. Santa Fe: SFI Press. https://doi.org/10.37911/9781947864382.

Rubio-Campillo, X. 2016. Model selection in historical research using approximate Bayesian computation. *PLoS ONE* 11 (1): e0146491. https://doi.org/10.1371/journal.pone.0146491.

Rubio-Campillo, X., P. Valdés Matías, and E. Ble. 2015. Centurions in the Roman Legion: Computer simulation and complex systems. *The Journal of Interdisciplinary History* 46 (2): 245–263. http://www.jstor.org/stable/43829751.

Schelling, T. C. 1971. Dynamic models of segregation. *The Journal of Mathematical Sociology* 1 (2): 143–186. https://doi.org/10.1080/0022250X.1971.9989794.

Sewell, W. H. 1996. Historical events as transformations of structures: Inventing revolution at the Bastille. *Theory and Society* 25 (6): 841–881. http://www.jstor.org/stable/657830.

Steudle, G. A., S. Winkelmann, S. Fürst, and S. Wolf. 2024. Understanding memory mechanisms in socio-technical systems: The case of an agent-based mobility model. *Advances in Complex Systems* 27 (3): 2440003. https://doi.org/10.1142/S0219525924400034.

Tracy, M., M. Cerdá, and K. M. Keyes. 2018. Agent-based modeling in public health: Current applications and future directions. *Annual Review of Public Health* 39:77–94. https://doi.org/10.1146/annurev-publhealth-040617-014317.

Vergne, J.-P., and R. Durand. 2010. The missing link between the theory and empirics of path dependence: Conceptual clarification, testability issue, and methodological implications. *Journal of Management Studies* 47 (4): 736–759. https://doi.org/10.1111/j.1467-6486.2009.00913.x.

Vogl, M., B. S. Buarque J. M. Schmitz, and A. Kaye. 2024a. *Historical Letters* (Version 1.1.1). CoMSES.https://www.comses.net/codebases/111fbcc0-77a0-4699-9913-4b5ddee95dda/releases/1.1.0/

Vogl, M., B. S. Buarque and A. Kaye. 2024b. *Growing and Pruning the Republic of Letters: An Agent-Based Model to Build Letter Correspondence Networks (forthcoming)*.

Vogl, M. 2024. *Historical letters – Objectives, design, details* (Version 1.0.1). Zenodo. https://doi.org/10.5281/zenodo.11277767

Wiebe, J., C. Lieben, and E. Gretenkord. 2024. A Decision Theatre Lab on infection disease spreading: Connecting school mathematics to societal challenges in a digital environment. In *Proceedings of the 17th ERME Topic Conference MEDA4, 3–6 September 2024, Bari*, 458–459.

Wolf, S., S. Fürst, A. Geiges, M. D. Laublichler, J. Mielke, G. A. Steudle, K. Winter, and C. Jaeger. 2023. The Decision Theatre Triangle for societal challenges—An example case and research needs. *Journal of Cleaner Production* 394:136299. https://doi.org/10.1016/j.jclepro.2023.136299.

Wolpert, D. H., M. H. Price, S. A. Crabtree, T. A. Kohler, J. Jost, J. Evans, P. F. Stadler, H. Shimao, and H., and M.D. Laubichler. 2024. The past as a stochastic process. *Journal of Computer Applications in Archaeology* 7 (1): 134–152. https://doi.org/10.5334/jcaa.113.

Wurzer, G. 2015. *Agent-based modeling and simulation in archaeology*. Cham: Springer.

Policy, Politics and the Past

The Creative Complications and Challenges of UNESCO-MOST BRIDGES Transdisciplinary Research Method: Experiencing Dreaming as an Approach—My Story

Luci Attala

Abstract This chapter explores the complex and creative dimensions of transdisciplinary research within the UNESCO-MOST BRIDGES programme. It begins by discussing the nature of transdisciplinary approaches, emphasising the value of integrating diverse perspectives and collaborating across disciplinary boundaries. The second part shifts focus to a personal narrative, using a dream as a case study to delve deeper into alternative research methodologies. Indigenous perspectives view dreams as a powerful form of knowledge, offering insights into personal, collective and ancestral wisdom. My dream illustrates how research assumptions can be challenged and promotes a novel and critical reflection on the role of societal partners in research. Through telling this story, I highlight the importance of reflexivity and equity in deconstructing academic hierarchies and truly embracing co-design methods that incorporate alternative, often marginalised, perspectives as legitimate knowledge. By working with Indigenous knowledge systems, particularly with regard to the spiritual and cultural significance of dreams, this chapter advocates for the recognition of alternative methodologies in transdisciplinary research, emphasising their potential to broaden the scope of enquiry and deepening research relationships. By embracing these alternatives, the chapter calls for a more inclusive and creative approach to research that transcends conventional disciplinary silos, offering a new way of thinking about the relationship between research, society, and the production of knowledge.

Keywords Transdisciplinary · Research methods · Dreaming as a method · Indigenous research methods · Humanities-informed sustainability science

Many thanks to Prof. Louise Steel and Dr. Amy Shawanda for their encouragement, additions and edits in writing this.

L. Attala (✉)
UNESCO-MOST BRIDGES, University of Wales Trinity Saint David, Swansea, UK
e-mail: l.attala@uwtsd.ac.uk

J. F. Haldon, R. Fernandes (eds.), *Bridging History and Policy*, Understanding Complex Systems, https://doi.org/10.1007/978-3-032-24379-9_8

1 What Is BRIDGES?

UNESCO-MOST BRIDGES is a programme that champions a transdisciplinary, humanities-informed sustainability science methodology, known informally as TH-iSS. TH-iSS was created to strengthen the sustainability science domain in the context of the SDGs and the global poly-crises. Discussions proposed to champion an inclusive methodology that embraced and adopted local and non-traditional expertise so that approaches out from the academy could play a central role in supporting a new branch of knowledge.

In association, BRIDGES makes a conscious effort to support context-specific or local wisdom and unexpected collaborations that draw in knowledges less heard to produce inclusive eco-social answers. Thus, BRIDGES aims to avoid the dominant Euro-American, colonial human exceptionalist approach and, in doing so, intends to open doors to creative thinking in support of hope-filled, inclusive eco-justice and genuine more-than-species flourishing for a better, fairer future for every entity.

BRIDGES was established in 2021 and is now an important component of UNESCO's Management of Social Transformations (MOST) programme, an initiative which actively contributes to UNESCO's Social and Human Sciences Sector's mandate of building inclusive and sustainable economies and societies. MOST's overarching purpose is to support strengthening the connection between research and action by collecting evidence in support of sustainable transformative social action. Within this framework, BRIDGES was devised to promote and nurture unexpected collaborative combinations between communities, disciplines and societal partners to bring knowledge and evidence to the Member States' table as policy recommendations for consideration. Thus, by pooling expertise with a range of organisations and institutions, BRIDGES works both to facilitate and champion research that combines methods and theories in pursuit of gathering evidence for the development of innovative, affordable, non-extractive, culturally sensitive solutions that resonate with local populations. BRIDGES, therefore, operates on the principle that local knowledge and expertise in combination with a range of specialisms working co-creatively has the power to generate astonishing solutions in context, which can then be scaled and adapted for wider benefit or impact, if appropriate.

This chapter examines these transdisciplinary goals of UNESCO-MOST BRIDGES, and, by introducing the concept of dreaming as a research methodology, highlights the potential of innovative thought regarding, and responses to, societal challenges.

1.1 Understanding the Ambitions of UNESCO-MOST BRIDGES

BRIDGES is the first transdisciplinary, humanities-informed sustainability science programme within the UN family of organisations. It was launched by three main founding partners: UNESCO, the Humanities for the Environment (HfE), and the

International Council for Philosophy and Human Sciences (CIPSH), in response to concerns about achieving global sustainability targets. After 2 years of discussions, in agreement of the need to strengthen the sustainability science domain, the partners created BRIDGES. Sustainability science focuses on the intersection between society and the environment and BRIDGES' role is to suture the gap between different approaches and knowledge systems—for example, the natural sciences and the humanities, but also wisdoms not typically taught in the academy—in pursuit of a new science that facilitates integration without losing the distinctiveness or richness of different, existing approaches. This method avoids siloed practice, creating contact that encourages cross-disciplinary knowledge transfer, fostering greater collaboration, mutual learning and has the potential to produce insights and solutions that transcend disciplinary boundaries.

The founding partners noted that despite numerous well-intentioned and robust research initiatives, humanity remains on track to exceed critical tipping points, leading to climate breakdown that disproportionately affects those who have contributed least to global emissions. The evidence is frankly overwhelming and simply compelling, seen in a range of changing environmental conditions, including, significantly, land degradation, failing harvests and ice melt. Simultaneously, there is a worrying persistent failure to engage effectively with the Sustainable Development Goals, which, in combination with the tendency to prioritise technological solutions—such as product innovation and industrial advancements—over more effective, community-centred approaches that facilitate interpersonal and intersectoral collaboration, suggests that humanity will not meet our own milestone targets of 2030, '40 or '50.

In light of these coalescing factors and the extra challenges they bring, the founding partners sought to establish a body able to spark changes. This aim grew from the realisation that solutions require overt 'humanising' only achievable through input from those that fundamentally understand humanity, and are able to comment on the cultural, historical, religious and political contexts from which situations emerge, amongst other dynamics. Thus, it was agreed, that by blending expertise and diverse perspectives and approaches, the deleterious tendency to reduce people to abstractions or quantities could be avoided in solution generation and by prioritising values beyond mere efficiency or cost effectiveness, the complexities and diversities of experience including the complicated 'messiness' of multiple realities could be embraced. BRIDGES (and its method (TH-iSS)) was born with a mandate to produce evidence and solutions to foster the kind of change that people can get behind.

1.2 Breaking Down 'TH-iSS'

T is for Transdisciplinary

Transdisciplinarity is not a one-size-fits-all approach; it varies based on context and discipline. In medical research, for instance, it might mean integrating patient testimonies into research processes, while in other contexts, it could involve something as simple as organising a focus group. This flexibility allows the term to be widely used but also leads to ambiguity, which means it is sometimes used in ways that overlap with terms like citizen science or participatory action research, but they aren't always synonymous. Citizen science involves non-expert participation in data collection or analysis, while participatory action research focuses on collaboration with marginalised or community groups for social change. Transdisciplinarity can, but does not always, involve these elements.

Many definitions emphasise that transdisciplinary research is 'science-driven' and 'solution-oriented', specifically aiming to address complex problems that require the involvement of non-expert actors. This aligns with the broader trend of public engagement, but the specifics of how that engagement is achieved can vary significantly.

For BRIDGES, the goal of transdisciplinarity goes beyond mere public involvement. In the first instance inclusivity and co-creation are central pillars of BRIDGES transdisciplinary collaborations, with emphasis on deeper, more meaningful collaborations that come together to integrate or weave knowledges and methods into new approaches. As a result, BRIDGES advocates the building of robust and equitable relationships between all partners, societal or otherwise. This approach contrasts with more superficial engagement strategies, such as sending out surveys or holding focus groups, which are increasingly criticised for lacking lasting impact or depth. Thus, the core distinction between the approach BRIDGES advocates and other approaches lies in a commitment to long-term collaborations and the creation of equitable partnerships that are co-transformative and not just consultative. In other words, it's not enough for non-experts or the public to be notionally involved—they must be embedded co-creators of knowledge and solutions, contributing equally and meaningfully to the process from the outset.

This form of transdisciplinarity highlights the importance of trust-building and shared ownership of the process and outcomes, something which can often be missing in more transactional forms of participation. By aiming for deeper, sustained collaboration, BRIDGES aligns with a radical reinterpretation of transdisciplinarity—one that prioritises systemic change over simple data collection or consultation.

The ethics of public engagement Transdisciplinarity, when implemented poorly, risks perpetuating existing inequalities instead of addressing them. Notional public engagement in transdisciplinary work comes with a series of important ethical concerns that need serious attention if one is to avoid exploitation, unequal power dynamics and the all too familiar commodification of relationships. Without awareness of, and attention to, these issues, transdisciplinary research, while well-intentioned, can find itself falling into the trap of being ineffective and even harmful, leaving itself open to criticisms of extraction or misuse—where the knowledge or resources from participants (often marginalised groups) are used without ensuring equitable power dynamic and benefits in return. This situation can lead to disillusionment, loss of trust and the reproduction of existing and unacceptable power imbalances.

Over 20 years ago, Banerjee (2003) applied the term tokenistic participation, where the involvement of societal partners or community members is merely symbolic, or worse, for show ('window dressing') rather than substantively integrated into the research or decision-making process. Today, this kind of superficial inclusion can be seen as a modern manifestation of colonialist attitudes, where the dominant group or institution extracts knowledge or resources from communities while maintaining control over the direction and conclusions of the research. Such practices reproduce the ubiquitous colonial power dynamics that the academy is founded upon, where the so-called expert continues to benefit potentially at the exclusion of those who provide the input. BRIDGES' approach can be seen as part of a broader call to reimagine research methodology eco-systems—not just to innovate but to place inclusivity, equity and justice at the heart of this environment. This highlights the need for methods that are both ethically sound and capable of fostering genuine empowerment for all involved.

In addition, the term 'stakeholder', with its origins in business and management, needs examination (see, Reed et al. 2024). Stakeholders are any individual or group with an interest in a company's activities, often in a transactional way. The problem with applying this corporate-derived concept to research or social science contexts is that it risks framing the relationship with communities or societal partners as transactional—focused on achieving specific, often short-term, goals rather than fostering a more relational, long-term partnership. Therefore, by framing people as 'stakeholders', there's a danger of reducing their roles to that of resource providers or interest groups whose primary function is to contribute to the success of a project. This overlooks the deeper, more nuanced relationships that collaborators—Indigenous peoples, local communities or other groups—might have with their lands, knowledge and culture. Such relationships are often holistic and rooted in ancestral ties or spiritual connections, and they cannot (and should not) be reduced to transactional, utilitarian terms. Consequently, when communities are treated solely as stakeholders, their deep, emotional and historical knowledge can be appropriated, trivialised or commodified. This deeply worrying approach requires a shift from transactional to relational engagement, where communities are viewed as active, equal partners in the knowledge creation process, not merely as contributors who offer something to the project and receive little in return. For example, Indigenous peoples' connections to their environment are often framed as a relationship of stewardship rather than ownership—a distinction that recognises an important alternative conception of human relationships with the wider world and if taken seriously, changes the focus of the way conclusions can be reached.

In alignment with the current burgeoning of decolonising frameworks, BRIDGES' approach notes that if transdisciplinarity is to overcome the critiques of being exploitative or extractive, it must go beyond tokenistic gestures. The methodology must embed participation in the structure of research itself and employ a long-term commitment to mutual benefits. Moreover, BRIDGES argues for transformations that recognise the complexity of relationships, challenge existing power structures and focus on genuine inclusion and respect for different knowledges and approaches. This fundamental transformation goes beyond a superficial attempt to include non-experts or marginalised groups; it requires shared decision-making, mutual respect and the recognition of all parties as co-creators of knowledge. Decolonisation of research and knowledge systems is crucial. It's not enough to simply involve different groups; we must rethink the very nature of knowledge itself, including how we define expertise, whose knowledge is valued and how we frame research goals. True epistemic justice means allowing communities to shape the research questions, define the problems, and determine the solutions in a way that respects multiple worldviews and practices.

The recent International Science Council's publication on the future of transdisciplinary research offers a succinct history of the method and echoes some of Banerjee's concerns (Kaiser and Gluckman 2023). It emphasises that transdisciplinarity is not solely about public engagement; rather, it aims to transcend disciplinary boundaries by incorporating voices that are typically side-lined, from the beginning or research question stage. This raises critical questions about resources and the feasibility of such pre-research collaborations, suggesting a dramatic shift in perspective and a call for a reconfiguration of what research entails, not just in terms of methodology, but also in redefining who qualifies as an expert, and challenging traditional notions of what knowledge is and how to create it.

According to Kaiser and Gluckman (2023), transdisciplinarity is able to find mutually accepted solutions by respecting and building-from local societal value landscapes with local knowledges. As a result, this form of working is unlike other collaborations in that it fundamentally reconfigures how partnerships are conceived. Following this, BRIDGES understands transdisciplinarity as an approach that transcends traditional academic boundaries by integrating local knowledge from communities with various fields to tackle real-world problems. Advocates of this form of transdisciplinarity claim its integration allows for a more holistic understanding of social phenomena as it provides a creative, sincere and open space where a diverse range of methodologies and theoretical frameworks can be drawn from and combined.

As a result, one could argue that transdisciplinarity's most significant distinction and facility is to challenge traditional assumptions concerning expertise. By collaborating closely with a multitude of diverse knowledge holders from the very beginning (including the design stage of a project), transdisciplinarity fosters genuine multi-actor participation, relying on and being receptive to a wide range of beliefs, knowledge systems and different values. These include perspectives from citizens, societal partners, counter-cultural groups and Indigenous knowledges as well as the social sciences, humanities, arts and natural sciences.

However, drawing in diverse voices comes with its own problems, including those associated with power dynamics. To ensure equity of voice in all dealings, open and concerted dialogue is central to these partnerships, which must pragmatically emerge within the cultural and socio-political contexts of the research space. In concert, developing a common language is the primary goal of these partnerships, which acknowledges a shared social responsibility and promotes democratic legitimacy. Mutual reflexivity is a crucial prerequisite for effective collaboration, requiring all participants to confront and acknowledge their identities, assumptions and biases. This process of self and group reflection allows individuals to question their beliefs and theoretical perspectives, revealing how these views influence their decisions and practices. By engaging in this process, reflexive actors can better understand the dynamics at play and work towards more informed and inclusive solutions. This process is not about the usual compromises expected and necessary in all collaborations but offers an opportunity to do things fundamentally differently.

In summary, transdisciplinarity offers a deeply different approach to tackling complex societal or so-called "wicked" problems within their specific contexts and provides an alternative route to creating a rich tapestry of insights to inform policy and practice. Therefore, at the heart of BRIDGES' transdisciplinary ambitions is the commitment to a form of community engagement that reflects local knowledges and realities. This 'immersed' and thoroughly engaged participatory approach ensures that research outcomes are relevant, context-specific and actionable, and, most importantly, by valuing local knowledge and perspectives, these collaborative endeavours aspire to empower communities and promote creative, sustainable social transformations.

'H-i is for Humanities-Inspired' BRIDGES uses the term 'humanities' as a reminder to include voices from beyond the sciences in discussions aimed at addressing contemporary problems. Therefore, 'humanities' is used to describe a diverse body of disciplines including the arts and social sciences and different forms of knowledge and methodologies. Noting that most of today's pressing problems are social and stem from human actions, BRIDGES maintains that the expertise that considers human culture, history and motivation can contribute valuable insights that the family of sciences or STEM subjects tend to overlook. Moreover, they provide a vital alternative to the numerical, data-driven approaches currently increasingly favoured in many fields.

At the same time, BRIDGES takes pains to distinguish itself from humanism, which emphasises human agency and often prioritises human flourishing over that of other species. Rather than reinforcing a human-centric worldview, BRIDGES is fundamentally focused on promoting *more-than-human* flourishing—recognising that all life forms are interconnected and interdependent. This ethos extends into how BRIDGES engages with data and technology and the growing dominance of data-driven thinking, which is seen as reductive, overshadowing the richness of human and ecological experience.

These days, the term 'data' is applied to all collected or analysed information but strictly speaking only refers to numbers, figures and statistics, rather than to lived experiences, storytelling, dialogue or the cultural narratives and meanings of practices that individuals use to make sense of their lives. Hand-in-hand with trust put in the scientific method comes a reliance on the notion of 'data' as objective and factual. However, this increasing emphasis on understanding humanity through numbers—rather like painting with numbers—provides a limited and restricted perspective that fundamentally fails to capture the wealth of eco-social experiences. Lived experiences, emotions, hopes, dreams and phenomenological understandings cannot be reduced satisfactorily to mere statistics, especially if one's aim is to create a future that recognises people as more than just economic units.

In addition, the subjects and methods of the humanities and arts bring culturally informed ethics into creative, enriching conversation and promote crucial critical thinking that many other disciplines have all but abandoned. These forms of knowledge and ways of knowing are deeply situated within historical, political, economic and geographical contexts, which understands and recognises the shaping forces of social relations, modes of production, power dynamics, norms, expectations and biases. Consequently, BRIDGES asserts that any attempt to address current issues would benefit from understanding these historic, contemporary and entrenched relations across various temporal and geographic scales. Most importantly, the humanities and arts teach us how to approach problems with moral courage and a fresh perspective. As Holm et al. (2015: 21) note in *The Value of Humanities:*

> It is only in the humanities and social sciences that … still produce 'critical discourse'. Science, technology and even economics have stopped performing that function. The curricula in these areas have no element of criticism per se, making it difficult for them to contribute to the formation of critical citizenship. It has been proved more than once in the course of the last century that pure science and economics have failed to produce an understanding of the symbolic life that makes us social and therefore human.

Additionally, Holm explains that only the humanities can guide us in using technologies and policies wisely. Therefore, the concept of being 'humanities-inspired' goes beyond simply integrating established disciplines or taking inspiration from them. It hopes to reconsider the type of 'industrial thinking' that Bateson (1972) criticised or the hierarchical neuro-intellectualism of the academic production line, that Taussig (1991) calls 'the Nervous System'—a method of anxious truth-seeking, a writing agri-business and colonising knowledge plantation, that knows by flattening experience into straight lines proved true by applying numbers. For BRIDGES knowledge production must extend into the realms of creativity, innovation and novelty by fostering associations between unexpected partners. In doing so, it acknowledges the power of relationships and thereby provides a space for unusual collaborations to combine and give birth to novel solutions. This approach encourages creativity and possibilities, ultimately enriching our understanding and response to complex challenges.

SS is for Sustainability Science Sustainability science emerged as a distinct and urgent field in the late twentieth century, spurred by growing concerns about environmental degradation, resource scarcity and the social inequities exacerbated by these global challenges. The Brundtland Report (1987), formally known as '*Our Common Future*', was a pivotal moment in this process, defining sustainable development as meeting the needs of the present without compromising the ability of future generations to meet their needs. From this foundation, sustainability science has evolved to address the intricate relationship between human societies and the environment, focusing on both the scientific understanding of these interactions and the development of practical solutions.

Central to sustainability science is its interdisciplinary nature. The field draws heavily from environmental science and ecology to understand the physical and biological processes that underpin ecological systems. It also incorporates insights from the social sciences—such as economics, political science, psychology and sociology—to address the human dimensions of sustainability, such as social equity, cultural values and governance structures. This broad and integrative approach enables sustainability scientists to examine the complex, interconnected systems that make up the planet's biosphere and human society.

One of the defining aspects of sustainability science is its emphasis on long-term, systemic thinking. Rather than focusing on isolated problems or short-term solutions, sustainability science aims to understand the dynamics of change and transformation across different time scales, from immediate issues like climate change or resource depletion to long-term trajectories of human development and ecological balance. The field recognises that human actions are deeply embedded within the natural environment and that sustainability requires a balance between the needs of both human and non-human systems. Moreover, sustainability science is often solution-oriented, with a focus on finding pathways for sustainable development that can be implemented in the real world. This typically involves collaboration with a wide range of societal partners—including governments, businesses, local communities, and civil society organisations—to ensure that solutions are grounded in the realities of the contexts in which they are applied.

However, while sustainability science is undeniably a vital and innovative field, it still tends to be constrained by some limitations. One such limitation is the field's tendency to rely heavily on quantitative and data-driven approaches—such as environmental modelling, resource assessments, and economic analyses—that, while powerful, can sometimes obscure the deeper cultural, historical, and ethical dimensions of sustainability. Sustainability science is undoubtedly interdisciplinary, but it has yet to fully bridge the knowledge gaps between the hard sciences, social sciences and the humanities in a way that acknowledges the richness of human experience, moral questions and the cultural dynamics that shape how people perceive and act on sustainability challenges.

The BRIDGES perspective challenges sustainability science to think beyond purely scientific and policy-driven approaches, encouraging a broader, more integrative view of human life that includes the ethical, emotional and cultural dimensions of sustainability. By incorporating a range of insights, BRIDGES advocates for a deeper, more imaginative engagement with sustainability, one that recognises the importance of narrative, human values and more-than-human relations that help us imagine new ways of living, new systems of governance or alternative economic models that prioritise not only the survival of ecosystems but also the flourishing of diverse life forms—human and non-human alike. Furthermore, the humanities encourage critical reflection on the very assumptions that underpin many of the solutions currently proposed in sustainability science, including assumptions about what constitutes progress, development and wellbeing.

In sum, while sustainability science is a crucial field for addressing the environmental and social crises facing our world, it stands to benefit from the broader, more critical, and more imaginative approach championed by BRIDGES. By integrating the insights of the humanities and emphasising the interconnectedness of all life forms, research could evolve into a truly holistic and transformative discipline—one that doesn't just address the symptoms of ecological and social crises but seeks to change the very systems and values that sustain them. In keeping with this aim, BRIDGES embraces alternative methodologies, including Indigenous techniques and methods which prioritise local context, community engagement and the lived experiences of individuals in shaping sustainable solutions.

2 Dreaming as a Research Methodology: My Story

Incorporating dreaming as a research methodology may seem unconventional, yet it aligns remarkably well with the BRIDGES transdisciplinary approach outlined above. Dreams encompasses both literal dreams and metaphorical aspirations and can offer a unique lens for exploring complex social issues by allowing researchers to tap into the imaginative capacities of the individuals and communities with whom they work.

However, the validity and value of dream experiences are also understandably questioned by those perspectives that judge dreams as purely subjective, rooted perhaps in personal psychology and little more. Notwithstanding any contentions associated with the value of interrogating the meaning of dreams and dreaming, in certain cultures, dreams are understood as opening a route into ancestral or cosmically stored knowledge that is otherwise unavailable to humanity. Consequently, using this perspective, the contents of dreams can deliver important information relevant for the receiver to know and use. Following BRIDGES' approach, this must be taken seriously in the context of transdisciplinarity, mutual reflexivity and meaningfully collaboration.

As a result, when I had a dream that was notably different from my other dreams, I was prompted to critically examine not only my assumptions and biases, but also how my research colleagues understood such experiences. As an anthropologist—who embraces the concepts of the ontological turn (Holbraad and Pedersen 2017), Kohn's anthropology of life (2013), multispecies ethnography (Kirksey and

Helmreich 2010) and the notion of plants as teachers (Attala 2017; Attala and Steel 2023; Gagliano 2018; Narby and Pitzuri 2021)—one might think I was prepared for what I am about to describe. But I wasn't.

A bit of back story: because of my work with BRIDGES and a small UK charity (the Tairona Heritage Trust), I have been developing a conservation project (called *Munekan Masha*) with the Indigenous Kogui people in Santa Marta, Colombia for several years now.

The Kogui worldview is a profound expression of their spiritual and cosmological understanding, where the Earth is not merely a physical space but a living, sentient entity that sustains and nurtures all forms of life. Thus, to imagine the Earth is an object is a shameful misunderstanding of her subjectivity, similar to the misogynistic objectification that women around the world still fight against. Their ancestral territories, the Sierra Nevada de Santa Marta Mountains in Colombia, are considered the beating heart of the world's body from which the Law of Origin flows. This law, a fundamental guiding principle for Kogui life, dictates that human behaviour must align with the original order to maintain harmony and balance in the universe.

For the Kogui, every element of existence—whether human, animal, plant or elemental—is interconnected, and human beings are seen as caretakers, rather than dominators, of the Earth, who is the mother of life. Their practices, beliefs and way of life are centred around ensuring the continued well-being of her and all inhabitants. This requires more than just passive coexistence; it demands active stewardship of the environment and a commitment to maintaining the original balance. Human actions, therefore, must be in tune with the rhythms and needs of the Earth, fostering sustainability and honouring the intricate relationships between all living beings. Thus, the Kogui way of life is imbued with a sense of duty to protect and nurture the planet, understanding that the survival of humanity depends on the survival of the mother that nurtures us.

The Kogui are one of four Indigenous groups in the Sierra Nevada de Santa Marta in northern Colombia, and their culture is based on an intensely hierarchical socio-cultural structure that upholds this spiritual law. The *mamos* (male spiritual leaders) and *sagas* (female spiritual leaders) are the most highly trained members of their society and play a pivotal role in guiding the community. These spiritual elites are trained to access *Aluna*—the Kogui term for 'spirit' or 'the spiritual realm'. To access *Aluna* and understand how to maintain and preserve the Earth's balance, requires the *mamos* and *sagas* undergo years of rigorous training. Their training is not merely intellectual; it is deeply experiential, based on meditative and contemplative practices that allow the trained the ability to communicate with the spiritual forces of the land. Restoring balance requires careful actions including thought, dance, prayer, introspective practices and focused attention to understand what the Earth needs. This approach to restoration integrates spirituality, culture and science in a way that challenges the conventional, often compartmentalised approaches to conservation and environmental management.

In practical terms, this means that the Kogui's restoration efforts and relationship with the landscape are not merely ecological in nature—they are also spiritual acts. Therefore, the collaborative efforts we have been developing are not simply about addressing land degradation or promoting environmental restoration in the conventional sense but are focused on finding ways to learn from each other's methods with the intention of locating or developing life-affirming and productive synergies. To get a clearer understanding of how the Kogui understand territory, the Cabildo of the Kogui people, from his offices in Santa Marta, summarised their perspective. He wrote:

> "For the Kogui people, all existence in nature has an Order, pre-existing before materialization; everything in nature has an invisible, intangible order that determines what each being is. "Mu" refers to this invisible Principle that exists in all of nature, containing the seed bank of thoughts for what is to be created—trees, water, breeze, animals, people—we all have an order before birth that determines our function or purpose in the territory.
>
> Everything is sown and born from an arrangement; when it materializes in the territory, we can see the diversity of nature—mountains, lands, water, stones, plants; we see life developing.
>
> With this brief explanation, we want to convey the principle of environmental and cultural restoration of the territory. It is the principle that underpins the strategy of the Kogui people to reclaim the lands of their ancestral territory, through the purchase of lands that may have degraded ecosystems or significant environmental disturbances and sociocultural damages, yet hold great environmental and cultural value due to the presence of sacred sites that are the parents and mothers of nature's diversity, thus serving to reclaim the ancestral territory of the Kogui People.
>
> Once the lands are purchased, the Mamos can work on the sacred sites of nature beings to reconnect damaged ecosystems with their Origin principle. For example, a forest that has been cleared, disturbed, can be reconnected with its seed bank in the Mother's thought to restore its energy, thought strength, and replant it in that place. Then the place must be left alone, with minimal interventions, to allow the Original order to be restored, solely through spiritual work to unite with the living beings of water, breeze, earth, and fire.
>
> For this purpose, there exists a self-governing space called "Ezuama de Mungueka", whose function is associated with this process. The Kogui people have decided that it is time to share this ancestral knowledge that we have maintained and used for millennia to care for nature and the territory. Nowadays, there are many impacts, damages to the territory, water, and social conflicts that deteriorate all species; these impacts are generated by various historical and current situations, and all must be repaired with ancestral knowledge, with the territory's norms, with the practices and techniques that the Mamos know, maintain, and live.
>
> "The Munekan Masha Project is based on a process of regeneration and care for nature based on these principles and ancestral knowledge; therefore, our word, 'Muzhigaba', also comes from this principle because our dialogue must always be United with the Mother."
>
> Author: Arregocés Conchacala—Governor's Council of the Kogui People
>
> Writer: Yanelia Mestre—Professional Support of Gonawindua

In 2019, finding it increasingly difficult to maintain planetary health (for all of us), the Kogui offered to teach academics their environmental management methods so that more people could understand their approach and, by finding points of contact between methodologies, help in developing inclusive strategies to restore balance and degraded territories. This was a huge step. Their warnings about ecological damage had been sent to the world since the 1990s but now, as the messages have not created the change they had hoped for, they resolved to go further and teach non-Kogui how to care properly in the form of a project, *Munekan Masha* (see above).

The discussions and co-design processes of the project began in earnest at the end of 2019 and therefore were achieved online during the pandemic. In 2022 the environmental science component of team visited the Sierra and in 2023, I secured philanthropic funding from a conservation foundation which would allow us to learn from each other for an initial period of 3 years. The work I was doing in the development of the project had no contact with the spiritual elite of the Kogui, focusing instead on the administrative office of the Kogui people.

Fast forward to a few days before my departure for Colombia in April 2024. I was flying to Santa Marta to meet with the administrative head of the official representative body of the Indigenous government of the Kogui, as well as, for the first time, one of the senior *mamos* (spiritual elders), a man called Shibulata. The purpose of the trip was to address a significant issue: the philanthropic funding had collapsed after a series of delays caused by tensions between various partners and when the Kogui decided to make some substantial changes, including requesting more financial support for their administrative office. The funders expressed their concerns, feeling that the Kogui's demands didn't represent 'value for their money'. This led to mistrust regarding motives and the funder's belief that their resources could be better utilised elsewhere. The Kogui were not concerned, even appeared sanguine, as if this was to be expected but I felt irritated by the shameless withdrawal after making promises and grand claims about their support for Indigenous People and worried that the opportunity was lost. My goal for this trip was to recover some of the lost position—if possible—to co-redesign the project to accommodate the new requests and understand how these changes would impact our shared aims and objectives. In short, it felt as if the project was hanging by a thread, potentially irreparably damaged.

Now, I should mention that, like most people, I tend to have incoherent dreams that I simply overlook or recount only because of their absurdity. However, just days before my trip, I experienced a startlingly vivid and coherent dream:

> I was arguing with some people who wanted to build a greenhouse high on an exposed area of a steep mountain. As we walked to the exposed area. I said this place was too far from anywhere and it would attract snakes.
>
> An unknown man walked with me, saying that he heard my worries. He put his hand on my back. Then, as I predicted, a huge prehistoric snake emerged from a crack that opened in the bare rock. It was enormous, marked with bright earthy colours and a diamond pattern. It moved across the mountain and towards a space where I knew children were.
>
> Everyone ran to kill the snake. I ran too and met the snake head on who transformed into a young woman holding a basket. She said, if you have come to this exposed high place, you must be hungry, and she gave me the basket full of what looked like bread. I was immediately transported down to the base of the mountain, and she was huge, above me as the top of a mountain. She reached both hands down. I reached up and we laced our fingers together, prompting us both to cry—her eyes forming into pools that filled and spilled over. I watched the tears pour down I felt them fall onto my upward-looking face. I woke feeling euphoric and overwhelmingly relieved, realising that she was there to help me.

Shaken, I communicated this dream to colleagues and, frankly, there is a paper simply in the variety of meanings people found in it. Regardless of what others think, the dream continued to affect me lingering in my thinking with a feeling that there was something I needed to understand.

Despite being a universal human experience, in Euro-American cultures dreams remain largely unexplained. Freud (2010) believed dreams reveal unrealised desires; Jung (1970) had other ideas about collective symbols. Some say dreams are a form of therapy able to ameliorate personal anxieties and many agree that it is possible to interpret dreams. Regardless of different approaches and schools of meanings, dreams, like pain or love, are fundamentally subjective experiences and realities that are difficult to validate or share reliably. Consequently, scholarship tends to focus on the biological or psychological functions of dreaming, but even despite that body of work, the academic community has not arrived at a consensus on what dreaming is or even if there is a function. This, of course, is countered by those who know the world of dreams is as real and important 'as that of the markets' (Obeyesekere 1990: 66).

In certain circles, dreaming as a route to knowledge is discounted, even ridiculed. In others, it assumes mystical relevance and spiritual significance—being much more than random, private mental experiences. Indigenous traditions and a growing body of Indigenous scholars' writings assert that dreams are sources of essential information and, more importantly for the purposes of this chapter, offer a useful research methodology and opportunity for the dreamer to dialogue with the universe (Shawanda 2020; Shawanda and Manitowabi 2023).

While the quality and content of dreams can vary—ranging from mundane to symbolically dramatic—they remain relevant and can be informative. Hallowell (1966) emphasised that dreaming is never random or without value for the Ojibwe. Nor is it thought merely a neurological process or a reflection of unconscious personal psychology. Instead, dreaming is a knowledge system that can be accessed at any time with the proper skills. Those who dream are able to distinguish between dreams that provide 'revealed knowledge' and those that do not. Dreams that 'reveal knowledge' are sacred, profound and spiritual in origin, enabling meaningful connections between humans and non-humans. Echoing this sentiment, Borrows (2010: 189) notes, that dreams can be one of the most important life experiences for the guidance and assistance they offer, which, simply, cannot be found elsewhere.

According to Montalvo and Andrés Baquero-Diaz (2024), dreaming is the first language of the world, and it allows people to communicate with nature or the 'protective beings' like 'trees or lagoons' that need to be heard. Dreams, using this approach, offer insight into the enormous, complicated, symbolically charged, living interconnections, and, as such, they also deliver a route to hear and sense how and what the non-humans or the intelligence often called 'nature', feels and knows. In *Braiding Sweetgrass*, Kimmerer (2013) emphasises the importance of bringing humans back into conversation with nature. Challenging traditional pedagogical concepts, she argues that it is the various processes of being—if we pay close, care-filled attention—that truly teach us. Intelligence, she suggests, manifests in many forms and is not limited to human cognition. While humans can communicate eloquently verbally, other 'persons' in the natural world possess their own alternative ways of communicating. Kimmerer urges us to listen—or sense—more carefully the intelligence that flows through the landscape. Dreams may allow us to hear the messages being broadcast by life.

Shawanda and Manitowabi (2023: 30) explain that by 'listening to our dreams, we have a gift to help people' but also state that it is our job to determine what the ancestors are trying to communicate. In this regard, I was mindful of, and felt cautioned by, the writings of Tuhiwai Smith who expresses sharp concerns about non-Indigenous people appropriating Indigenous beliefs and 'merely interpreting their 'own' (individualized) dreams as an indigenous *[sic]* spiritual experience' (2012: 105). In my defence, I was unable to interpret my dream—and, luckily, there was no need for me to try because I had an Indigenous spiritual leader to interpret mine.[1]

The day after I arrived in Santa Marta, I had a meeting with the octogenarian Kogui spiritual leader, Shibulata. He was waiting at the assigned meeting place near the small coastal town of Dibulla and after preliminary greetings, he almost skipped up the steep hill to our destination—the piece of land we were thinking of using for the project—while I laboured up the slope, apologising for slowing the group down. Once at our destination, the translator suggested I tell Shibulata the dream and so I did. Speaking in English, my words needed to be translated into Spanish and then Koggian. And so, we all waited patiently. The Spanish speaking Kogui present gasped audibly as they heard the account. However, Shibulata turned to me and said,

> With all due respect, I know your dream. That snake… that's *Jaba Nabobá* your spiritual mother. She's has been talking with my original father. She is reminding you of your mission.

Everyone present, except me, seemed to know her. Shibulata named her based on my description and said her appearance in the dream was reminding me of the work I had to do—work, he explained, she was supporting and sustaining. His comment made it sound like 'our parents' had been colluding, working behind the scenes for some shared purpose. He didn't explain further other than to state that the work *Jaba Nabobá* was communicating concerned "showing the world as it really is" and taking the two small stones I had brought from Wales as a gift or offering to him, he ritually received them, placed them on the soil to introduce them to the mountain we were standing on and told me to take them back to Wales. Their purpose—to form a mechanism by which the territories would connect. I was told I was "*saga*", a female with wisdom.

Other than pandering to my vanities, there is lots to unpack here. Certainly, the dream was palpably different to any other I have ever had, but now this exchange suggested I was communicating in a language the Kogui readily understood. Previous interchanges had illustrated the vast differences between conceptions of the environment and how to measure and attend to environmental ill health. The dream appeared to brush that aside, along with any doubt about whether the project

[1] But I did contact Prof. Amy Shawanda to ask if this should be included as a part of my research methodology or if I was overthinking it. She, very kindly, replied 'You are definitely overthinking it! This should be part of your methodology section in the research you're about to do.' (personal communication, 25/5/2024).

should go ahead. The ancestors had spoken. Now we just had to work out how the project would happen.

After the trip, I found reference to *Jaba Nabobá* in an unpublished manuscript pdf, co-written with Kogui leaders including Shibulata, that I had been given a year before but hadn't yet read. *Nabobá* is listed as one of the parents of "Contradictory Principles" (Mestre and Adams 2018: 70) a group of characters—the children of the Great Mother—who possess the knowledge of the order of the universe and the power to break that order to repair it. According to the text, the original Mother "sensed that conflicts in the future would arise with the materialization of the world and that these confrontations between the negative and the positive would always be present" (ibid. 70). The ability to abandon the rules, held by those of the contradictory principles, made it possible to repair and heal them when the order was damaged. In other words, 'they are necessary to rebuild the order and cure the illnesses of the territory' (ibid).

As well as being contradictory, *Jaba Nabobá* is described as the "mother of lagoons and negative rains" (Ibid. 79). She knows the rules of water and previously travelled in the spirit realm of *Aluna* able to instantly appear in places around the world. Now, she resides as a lagoon next to the snowy peaks of the Sierra Nevada de Santa Marta where she "teaches us how to repair the damage and harm done by people to water" (ibid.). She was brought to the Sierra by the mother of negative winds, lightning and thunder and placed snakes in certain water sources of the Sierra to stop negative forces. In the complicated family tree of ancestral parents, there is another mother who established the principles of sight, "the ability to see beyond what the eye sees… to light the path and walk in a positive way" (ibid. 53). This principle, called, *kunchawa*, refers specifically to the lower eyelid and water. Without any knowledge of the contents of the book, I found this imagery spoke curiously directly to my dream, seemingly referencing the eyes as pools brimming over. Reading on, I learnt that without the principle *kunchawa*, there would be "no eyes, no sleep, *no dreams that would leave positive messages*" (ibid., my emphasis).

According to Wilson (2008) research should be understood as a ceremony, the purpose of which is to build stronger relationships or bridge the distance between aspects of the cosmos and ourselves. For the Kogui, thoughts, created originally in the spirit world, precede physical manifestation and feed all aspects of nature (Mestre and Adams 2018: 52). Thoughts must be clear and clean to avoid mistakes; negative thoughts do damage to the world, which must be repaired so that the wisdom of thought can be rebuilt (ibid.). Following this thinking or approach, being a researcher should avoid extraction and focusing on answering questions—and should be reframed as a means by which you are answering to all your relations. This means you are not looking to answer questions of validity or reliability or making judgments of better or worse. You are fulfilling your relationships with the world around you. This fundamental refiguring of the purpose of research adds a new dimension and raises questions about methodology, including—what knowledge is and what knowledge is for. For Absolon (2011: 12) a key Indigenous methodological principle states that knowledges are found within—like thoughts arising or bubbling up—and should be used as guides to make the unknown known. As dreaming may be a type of thinking, it provides a connection to the cosmos and the knowledge it holds. Consequently, receiving a dream should be acknowledged for it offers insights and instructions (Shawanda 2020; Shawanda and Manitowabi 2023). Moreover, if you do dream and sense you have been communicated with, they suggest that there are questions you must answer to use the dream as a method, which includes determining its message, what specific instructions have been received, how it informs participants' relationships, and one should honour Indigenous protocols and conduct the research through an Indigenous spiritual paradigm (adapted from: Shawanda and Manitowabi 2023). Aspects that I am still hoping to fully understand and address.

These are markedly different methodological questions that introduce a temporality in addition to the relationality mentioned previously. Indigenous scholars maintain that they are fundamental to harnessing the knowledge received and validating it within the researcher's Indigenous community. But what if the researcher isn't part of an Indigenous community?

Circling back to the ISC definition of transdisciplinarity reminds us that transdisciplinary work requires dialogue that embraces knowledges of all kinds and the development of a common language in partnerships. The dream I received could be understood as an example of experiential learning and the teaching of a method of communication I had previously discounted. And, perhaps, still, in some quarters, it could be judged indulgent and trivial (Pratt 1986: 31)—even within an anthropological research context. As Rappaport (1979: 130) noted the "empirical and logical rationality that defines knowledge as objective fact" does not easily accommodate the insights of dreams. Yet, as many are aware, it is these insights that have the power to shape and change history—as James Watson's dream of a spiral staircase helped him understand the shape of the DNA chain effortlessly demonstrates.

It is clear, that to mobilise meaningful change, we need a new set of values that don't uphold the current dominant logics. If we don't interrogate the deeper values that form the foundations of everything we have built, it is unlikely the genuine innovation required will be produced. For me, this dream has shaken my ground and provides another cultural example of how to listen, open to difference for what it is, and is an experience that has shown me how to avoid translating what is fundamentally meaningful to others away. Moreover, it is demanding not only answers but new questions.

In addition, my experience and the dream's message(s) unexpected and greatly facilitated dialogue with the Kogui, yet it is difficult to find ways to articulate this experience within a conventional Euro-American academic framework. Transdisciplinarity, on the other hand, recognises the value of listening to and respecting Indigenous knowledges/expertise as one of many knowledge systems. While "no knowledge system should claim *a priori* superiority", Kaiser and Gluckman (2023: 16) tell us, the tendency of academia to privilege objectivity and empiricism stubbornly remains because it is "*impossible* to conflate knowledge systems—[as] they are based on different framings and principles" (Kaiser and Gluckman 2023: 17, my emphasis).

Similarly, Indigenous researchers have drawn attention to the problems of aligning academic and Indigenous knowledges in other contexts but, in contrast, emphasise that alternative methods are equally legitimate and offer alternative understandings of the world in which we live. A Euro-American perspective might seek and prioritise so-called 'correct' answers while Indigenous scholars encourage a more flexible approach that allows for multiple co-existing answers and methods as the famous coyote trickster stories told by the Syilx Okanagan and Secwepemc peoples and the following quotes from Indigenous authors, illustrate.

> Maintaining the knowledge did not mean finding a 'right' story but widening the possibilities of storys [*sic*]. Information of different variations is preferred, pooled and maintained as a bundle of possibilities, *without judgement*. Different storys which contradict each other, do not conflict, but simply co-exist (Hokari 2000: 8–9)

> Stories go in circles. They don't go in straight lines. It helps if you listen in circles because there are circles inside and between stories, and finding your way through them is as easy and as difficult as finding your way home. Part of finding is getting lost, and when you are lost, you start to open up and listen (Tafoya 1995: 12).

Nerida Blair (2015, 2019) uses "lilyology" to explain some differences between approaches to knowledge. For Blair, academic environments are characterised using brick—as consisting of rigid walls creating purposefully unbending structures with separate compartments (or disciplines), which protect and block ideas from growing together. On the other hand, Indigenous knowledge is more organic, plant-like—comprised of spreading roots, stems and petals which interconnect, feed each other and grow together, just as the rhizomes, stems and flowers of water lilies. While the brick walls of the academy can feel restrictive and unyielding, closed to alternative episto-ontologies, Blair sees an in-between space where the 'architecture' of practice can be nature-based, open plan and plant friendly—and where no single knowing or knowledge is more powerful or superior to the other producing a space where both co-exist; a challenging space, but also one of potential dynamic and transformative co-creation.

My experience brought the apparent incompatibility of research methods into sharp relief, but also knocked open a new methodological avenue and understanding of what meaningful transdisciplinary futures can look like. Personal discussion with Indigenous scholars has unlocked doors in previously closed rooms and the proliferation of calls to decolonise approaches demonstrates how different worldviews not only can co-exist but perhaps even should inform each other on the path to engendering powerful and transformative relationships.

Dreaming as a transdisciplinary research method is a fascinating and creative approach, one that transcends traditional disciplinary boundaries and engages with a deeper, perhaps unconscious level of understanding. While it may seem unconventional at first, dreams can serve as an important tool, particularly in fields that deal with complex, ambiguous or deeply human experiences. Dreams are also able to integrate diverse ways of knowing and can act as a form of non-rational or non-linear knowledge production that enriches the research process in profound ways. They cross discipline boundaries, not fitting into any one specific discipline, managing to pull from multiple sources, weaving together personal, cultural, historical and social elements.

The use of this dream has helped me tap into diverse forms of knowledge beyond the verbal or logical, opening the door to understanding the inner world of the research participants, which some conventional methods can ignore. Reflexivity is a core principle of transdisciplinary research, which requires critically examining one's own role in the process, including the biases, assumptions and emotions that influence how one conducts and interprets research (Marg and Theiler 2023; Nastar 2023). Dreams, it turns out, can be a powerful tool for this form of self-enquiry and self-awareness, having revealed unconscious prejudices that influenced my researcher perspective. For example, this dream brought to light unresolved conflicts and assumptions that were shaping the way the research team interacted. Consequently, the dreams not only offered a way of interrogating my own predispositions but also enriched my understanding of how one's inner world shapes research.

As transdisciplinary research often involves bridging different forms of knowledge—scientific, experiential, artistic, spiritual and more. Dreaming, as an intuitive and creative process, can help integrate these diverse ways of knowing, drawing from the symbolic, metaphorical and artistic realms. In fields like eco-psychology, arts-based research, or, indeed, Indigenous knowledge systems, dreaming captures more than purely analytical methods, having the potential to bring together fragmented pieces of knowledge and thereby allow for a more holistic understanding of complex issues. It is not only the Kogui, but many Indigenous cultures, that place great importance on dreams and the spiritual messages they convey. In this context, dreaming offers a valid form of wisdom that can decolonialise research, linking ideas across different domains or practices. In other contexts, particularly in community-based or participatory research, engaging with participants' dreams can provide deeper insights into the lived experiences of individuals or communities. This can be especially valuable in research that aims to understand cultural narratives, trauma or collective memory, where dreams provide access to layers of meaning that might not be articulated in everyday conversation. Collective dreams or shared symbols within a group can reveal common values, fears and aspirations that might otherwise be overlooked. This aligns with the co-creation of knowledge central to transdisciplinary methods.

In conclusion, dreaming as a transdisciplinary research method offers a way to access deep, sometimes hidden layers of knowledge, fosters reflexivity, integrates diverse ways of knowing and opens up new pathways for creative and collaborative problem-solving. It's a tool that challenges conventional boundaries and allows for more holistic, integrated approaches to addressing complex research questions. The imagination plays a crucial role in envisioning future possibilities and solutions, and, it could be argued, dreams and dreaming allows researchers and participants to step beyond the constraints of current realities and consider alternative futures. This process encourages creativity and innovation, fostering a space where new ideas can emerge. As highlighted by scholars like Bachelard (1994), engaging with dreams can lead to profound insights about human experiences and aspirations.

UNESCO-MOST BRIDGES exemplifies the transformative potential of transdisciplinary research in addressing complex social challenges. By integrating dreaming as a research methodology, BRIDGES fosters innovative thinking and empowers communities to envision and create their desired futures. As the initiative continues to evolve, its commitment to collaboration, engagement and imagination will be essential in driving meaningful social transformations.

References

Absolon, Kathy. 2011. *Kaandossiwin: How we come to know: Indigenous re-search methodologies*. Halifax and Winnipeg: Fernwood Publishing.

Attala, Luci. 2017. The 'Edibility Approach': Using edibility to explore relationships, plant agency and the porosity of species' boundaries. *Advances in Anthropology* 7 (3): 125–145. https://doi.org/10.4236/aa.2017.73009.

Attala, Luci, and Louise Steel. 2023. *Plants matter: Exploring the becomings of plants and people*. Cardiff: University of Wales Press.

Bachelard, Gaston. 1994. *The poetics of space: The classic look at how we experience intimate places*. Boston: Beacon Press.

Banerjee, Subhabrata Bobby. 2003. The practice of stakeholder colonialism: National interest and colonial discourses in the management of indigenous stakeholders. In *Postcolonial Theory and Organizational Analysis: A critical engagement*, ed. Anshuman Prasad, 255–279. New York: Palgrave Macmillan.

Bateson, Gregory. 1972. *Steps to an ecology of the mind: Collected essays in anthropology, psychiatry, evolution and epistemology*. New Jersey and London: Jason Aronson Inc.

Blair, Nerida. 2015. *Privileging Australian Indigenous Knowledge: Sweet potatoes, spiders, waterlilys and brick walls*. Champaign, IL: Common Ground Publishing.

Blair, Nerida. 2019. Lilyology as a transformative framework for decolonising ethical spaces within the Academy. In *Decolonising Research: Indigenous storywork as methodology*, ed. Jo-ann Archibald Q'um Q'um Xiiem, Jenny Bol Jun Lee-Morgan, and Jason De Santolo, 203–223. London: Zed Books.

Borrows, John. 2010. *Drawing out law: A spirit's guide*. Toronto: University of Toronto Press.

Brundtland, Gro Harlem. 1987. *Our common future*. https://sustainabledevelopment.un.org/content/documents/5987our-common-future.pdf. Accessed 28 Dec 2024.

Freud, Sigmund. 2010. *The interpretation of dreams: The complete definitive text*. New York: Basic Books.

Gagliano, Monica. 2018. *Thus spoke the plant: A remarkable journey of ground-breaking scientific discoveries and personal encounters with plants*. Berkeley, CA: North Atlantic Books.

Hallowell, Alfred Irving. 1966. The role of dreams in Ojibwa culture. In *The dream and human societies*, ed. Gustave von Grunebaum and Roger Caillois, 267–292. Oakland, CA: University of California Press.

Hokari, Minoru. 2000. History happening in/between body and place: Journey to the Aboriginal way of historical practice. In *Habitus 2000: A sense of place*, ed. John Stephens, 1–12. Perth, Australia: Curtin University of Technology.

Holbraad, Martin, and Morten Axel Pedersen. 2017. *The ontological turn: An anthropological exposition*. Cambridge: Cambridge University Press.

Holm, Poul, Arne Jarrick, and Dominic Scott. 2015. The value of the humanities. In *Humanities World Report 2015*. London: Palgrave Macmillan. https://doi.org/10.1057/9781137500281_2. Accessed 28 Dec 2024.

Jung, Carl. 1970. *Four archetypes: Mother, rebirth, spirit, trickster*. Bollingen Series, Princeton: Princeton University Press.

Kaiser, Matthais, and Peter Gluckman. 2023. *Looking at the future of transdisciplinary research: Discussion paper*. Centre for Science Futures https://council.science/wp-content/uploads/2024/06/2023-04-26Futureoftransdisciplinaryresearch.pdf. Accessed 28 Dec 2024.

Kimmerer, Robin Wall. 2013. *Braiding sweetgrass: Indigenous wisdom, scientific knowledge and the teachings of plants*. Minneapolis: Milkweed Editions.

Kirksey, Eben, and Stefan Helmreich. 2010. The emergence of multispecies ethnography. *Cultural Anthropology* 25 (4): 545–576. https://anthrosource.onlinelibrary.wiley.com/doi/10.1111/j.1548-1360.2010.01069.x. Accessed 28 Dec 2024.

Kohn, Eduardo. 2013. *How forests think: Towards an anthropology beyond the human*. Oakland, CA: University of California Press.

Marg, Oskar & Theiler, Lena. (2023). Effects of transdisciplinary research on scientific knowledge and reflexivity. *Research Evaluation. 32*. https://doi.org/10.1093/reseval/rvad033

Mestre, Yanelia Pacheco, and Peter Rawitscher Adams. 2018. *Shikwakala*. Santa Marta, Colombia: Resguardo Kogui-Malayo-Arhuaco.

Montalvo, José Gualinga, and Carlos Andrés Baquero-Diaz. 2024. The jungle is a living, intelligent and conscious being: A conversation. In *More than Human Rights: An Ecology of Law, Thought and Narrative of Human Flourishing*, ed. César Rodriguez-Garavito. New York: NYU Law.

Narby, Jeremy, and Rafel Chanchari Pitzuri. 2021. *Plant Teachers: Ayahuasca, tobacco and the pursuit of knowledge*. Novato, CA: New World Library.

Nastar, Maryam. 2023. A critical realist approach to reflexivity in sustainability research. *Sustainability* 15:2685.

Obeyesekere, Gananath. 1990. *The Work of Culture: Symbolic transformation in psychoanalysis and anthropology*. Chicago: The University of Chicago Press.

Pratt, Mary Louise. 1986. Fieldwork in common places. In *Writing Culture. The poetics and politics of ethnography*, ed. James Clifford and G. E. Marcus. Berkeley: University of California Press.

Rappaport, Roy. 1979. *Ecology, Meaning, and Religion*. Richmond: North Atlantic Books.

Reed, Mark, Bethan Garramon Merkle, J. Elizabeth, Caitlin Hafferty Cook, Adam Hejnowicz, Richard Holliman, Ian Marder, Ursula Pool, Christopher Raymond, et al. 2024. Reimagining the language of engagement in a post-stakeholder world. *Sustainability Science* 19:1481–1490. https://doi.org/10.1007/s11625-024-01496-4.

Shawanda, Amy. 2020. Baawaajige: Exploring dreams as academic references. *Turtle Island Journal of Indigenous Health* 1 (1): 37–47.

Shawanda, Amy, and Joshua Manitowabi. 2023. Anishinaabe dream methodology. *Turtle Island Journal of Indigenous Health* 1 (3): https://doi.org/10.33137/tijih.v1i3.38566.

Tafoya, Terry. 1995. Finding harmony: Balancing traditional values with western science in therapy. *Canadian Journal of Native Education* 21:7–27.

Taussig, Michael. 1991. *The Nervous System*. 1st ed. London: Routledge. https://doi.org/10.4324/9780203397244.

Tuhiwai Smith, Linda. 2012. *Decolonizing methodologies: Research and indigenous peoples*. 2nd ed. London: Zed books.

Wilson, Shawn. 2008. *Research is Ceremony: Indigenous research methods*. Halifax and Winnipeg: Fernwood Publishers.

Historical Landscapes, Conservation and Community: Lowcountry Wetlands and Rice Cultivation in South Carolina

Travis H. Folk, Ernie Wiggers, Dean Harrigal, Edda Fields-Black, Robert Baldwin, Daniel Hanks, Andrew Bridges, Daniel D. Richter, and Andrew Agha

Abstract Rice was a major commodity crop across the coasts of North Carolina, South Carolina, Georgia and Florida from the late seventeenth century until after the Civil War. Previous mapping efforts (by this team) documented hundreds of thousands of acres of rice fields, constructed and maintained by enslaved people, across the coast of South Carolina. To fully describe the landscape impact of rice as a commodity crop, we have now documented rice fields from Florida to North Carolina and totaling nearly 350,000 acres (141,600 ha). This final, multi-state mapping effort relied on several methodologies including digital elevation models, historical plats, historical references, older aerial photographs, and expert input. Rice fields in South Carolina became a major landscape feature for conservation of natural resources across the coast. Many of these rice fields (and the surrounding uplands) have voluntarily been placed under conservation easements and are managed by both state and federal entities but also private landowners. This chapter reflects on how rice culture transformed into conservation successes over many decades and how collaboration between public and private stakeholders has allowed continued conservation of a historic landscape and management of these wetlands for the benefit of all.

Keywords South Carolina · Rice fields · Waterbird habitat · Sea level rise · Conservation

T. H. Folk (✉)
Folk Land Management, Green Pond, SC, USA

E. Wiggers · D. Harrigal · A. Bridges
Nemours Wildlife Foundation, Yemassee, SC, USA

E. Fields-Black
Carnegie Mellon University, Pittsburgh, PA, USA

R. Baldwin
Clemson University, Clemson, SC, USA

J. F. Haldon, R. Fernandes (eds.), *Bridging History and Policy*, Understanding Complex Systems, https://doi.org/10.1007/978-3-032-24379-9_9

1 Introduction

Few landscapes bear the vestiges of an agricultural empire the way rice culture has influenced the Lowcountry of South Carolina (i.e., coastal counties along the Atlantic Coast of that southern US state). The wetland landscape of 300 years ago was substantially transformed by the production of this commodity. Dikes, quarter drains, and rice field trunks are some of the unique rice culture features found along this coast. When viewed from the air, rice fields appear as intricate geometric puzzles in a series of straight and parallel creeks and dikes that evoke the feelings of ancient Peruvian Nazca Lines. These features remind us that an entire landscape was transformed into a large "hydrological pump" designed for the planting and harvesting of one crop—rice. While rice culture in the Lowcountry is now relegated to history, these enslaved-created rice field systems from the seventeenth and eighteenth centuries are now playing an integral role in the conservation of the Lowcountry.

While all of these rice field features have their origins over 200 years prior, many have been built and maintained by enslaved people over generations and passed from one planter to another and, then, from one sportsman to another. The success of these planters led to vast fortunes which allowed the construction of plantation empires, built by enslaved Africans and their descendants. Rice was not to last though, and the story of rice fields after commercial rice production is one of evolution and persistence towards a conservation goal. South Carolina rice fields have evolved into a major conservation tool in addition to serving as visual reminders of the region's long, rich cultural and agricultural heritage, which started sadly through the hands of enslaved Africans that built this landscape for the planter's commodity crop.

2 History of Rice Culture Across the South Carolina Lowcountry

Despite its ultimate rise to an agricultural empire, little definitive information is known about the introduction of rice to South Carolina. As commercial rice production waned in the first decades of the twentieth century, many authors described the introduction and success of rice as inevitable, but also a history not without trial, failure, or experimentation (Porcher and Judd 2014). In fact, in the last 30 years a history of rice culture has emerged with academic researchers revealing several

D. Hanks
Weyerhaeuser, Clemson, SC, USA

D. D. Richter
Duke University, Durham, NC, USA

A. Agha
Aghatech Industries, Charleston, SC, USA

periods of rice culture and constant efforts by planters and enslaved people to experiment and improve husbandry techniques and increase crop yields (Smith 2020).

The year of rice introduction to the Carolinas is a topic that is fraught with myth and lore. Several accounts place the introduction of rice shortly after the 1670 establishment of Charles Towne on the banks of the Ashley River. John Drayton in *A View of South Carolina* (1802) suggests the first introduction was in 1688, but he says an enhanced variety was also introduced in 1696. An account given in David Ramsay's *History of South Carolina* (1858) mentions in 1693 Thomas Landgrave Smith received from a ship captain a bag of rice from Madagascar. Alexander Salley, secretary of the Historical Commission of South Carolina, suggested in a 1919 publication that the true introduction of rice to South Carolina was in 1685 when a Captain John Thurber gave Dr. Henry Woodward of Charles Towne "a peck of gold seed rice" (Salley 1919). The famed *Seed from Madagascar* (1937) by Duncan Clinch Heyward takes the later story as the true introduction of gold rice to the Lowcountry.

Whatever the true date and instance of introduction of rice to Carolina, it became a successful commodity in short time. For example, rice was valuable enough by the 1690s that the colonial legislature decided in 1691 to allow tax bills to be paid with rice (Coclanis 1989). Regardless of the timing of introduction, export records from Charles Towne indicate rice was shipped out of the province as early as 1698 (Coclanis 1989). This suggests that whatever the true date of introduction, early planters and enslaved people had developed the skills to grow and produce enough rice for economic gain.

The first type of economically successful rice was grown in non-tidal freshwater swamps. This form of rice culture, called *inland rice*, started in the late 1600s and began to decline in the mid- to late 1700s, although some inland fields were utilized until the early twentieth century. Inland rice fields were developed from linear wetlands dominated by bottomland hardwoods. These wetlands were cleared of trees, stumps removed, and rice field beds leveled. Dikes were also constructed across the newly leveled rice field bed perpendicular to the flow of water. These cross dikes allowed a planter to retain water in the area immediately upstream. When he needed to dewater (drain) the field water control structures in the downstream cross dike could be opened.

These fields also had a distinctive type of dike and canal that still exist today and can be used to identify former inland rice fields. These topographic features, called diversion dikes and diversion canals, were built on either side of the linear rice field and were placed immediately before the ground transitioned into upland. These diversion dikes and canals served several purposes, most importantly they prevented heavy rainfall runoff in spring and summer from flooding the planted rice. Runoff would first drain into a diversion canal and be prevented from further running into the field by the diversion dike. The diversion canal would allow this "freshet" water to run parallel to the field and down the diversion canal and ultimately to creeks and rivers. These diversion structures can still be seen in many Lowcountry inland rice fields (Fig. 1).

Fig. 1 Aerial photograph of inland rice field in Colleton County, South Carolina

Inland rice culture was a lucrative agricultural endeavor, but several factors contributed to its decline. This method of rice cultivation primarily relied on rainwater for irrigation. During drought years, crops suffered or would not materialize at all (Coclanis 1989). This made investment in new fields and infrastructure difficult because crop success was subject to the vagaries of weather. Also, by the late 1700s, per acre yields began to diminish and the American Revolution disrupted rice plantation activities (Smith 2020). After the war, many planters decided to adopt newer tidal rice cultivation methods rather than renovate inland fields.

Limited work with tidal rice culture began in the 1730s; but, by the 1750s Johnstone McKewn of Georgetown had developed a system of using tidal freshwater for flooding rice (Porcher and Judd 2014). Under this system, rice fields were constructed along portions of coastal rivers and creeks that possessed two traits: (1) they were close enough to the coast to be tidally influenced, yet (2) far enough inland to have fresh water. This form of rice culture greatly increased per-acre yields as compared to inland fields (Tuten 2010). Tidal water also allowed planters to more consistently flood growing rice as compared to inland fields that depended on rainfall and stored water in reserves. Tidal rice culture represents the culmination of generations of planters and enslaved people working with (and sometimes against) the forces of nature. These fields were intricate mazes of dikes, canals, and quarter drains with water control structures spread across miles of dikes. Tidal rice fields are perhaps the most commonly known type of rice field. Few visitors to the Lowcountry can pass through the region without chancing upon a beautiful vista across an historic tidal rice field. These impoundments can cover hundreds to thousands of acres (Fig. 2).

The planting of rice made many Lowcountry planters wealthy and the Civil War removed an essential ingredient to this scenario—enslaved labor capable of

Fig. 2 Aerial photograph of tidal rice fields in Colleton County, South Carolina. Photo by Dr. Ernie Wiggers, coauthor

performing the arduous and skilled tasks to bring crops to harvest and market. Rice culture was solely dependent on enslaved labor for the husbandry of the plant as well as the maintenance of the vast earthen infrastructure (e.g., dikes and canals) and large wooden, water control structures. The end of slavery-driven agriculture in these rice fields led to the slow decline of rice production in South Carolina and the maintenance of this constructed wetland landscape (Doar 1937).

3 From Rice to Ducks

The rice economy recovered to a limited degree. South Carolina's post-war rice production peaked in 1879, although that represented only a third of pre-war production (Coclanis 1989). Declining rice prices, increasing competition from other rice growing regions (e.g., Louisiana, Texas, California), and a series of hurricanes that destroyed rice field infrastructure all contributed to the decline of rice as a profitable venture for Lowcountry plantation owners.

Southern plantations have long been recognized for their sporting opportunities. One of the earliest and most interesting recollections is that of William Elliott. In his *Carolina Sports by Land and Water* (1846) he recounts tales of hunting and fishing, especially in the lands between the Ashepoo and Cheeha Rivers. His statement "...the rice-fatted wild-duck of Carolina...doubtless God never did create a better duck..." was likely appreciated by rice planters and enslaved people from the very first days of rice planting. As rice became less of a profitable endeavor, hunting began to be the predominant activity of former rice plantations (Lockhart 2015).

The convenience of east coast rail travel, mild winters, and abundant sporting opportunities made former rice plantations in the Lowcountry an attractive winter retreat for many northerners (Cuthbert and Hoffius 2009). The purchase of these properties in the late nineteenth and early twentieth centuries was timely as well. Many plantations had not been well maintained or managed. New ownership injected the capital necessary to maintain a rice plantation, especially when considering the infrastructure associated with former rice fields. The sale of these rice plantations in the early 1900s was a pivotal point for conservation in the Lowcountry. How would the next owner manage and care for these properties? Would they be willing to invest the money required to maintain rice field infrastructure if a commercial crop was not being grown? Would the properties be subdivided? All of these questions, in retrospect, had great influence on the landscape we see today. Luckily, many of these properties were bought by passionate sportsmen and were indeed, well managed to these ends.

For nearly a century and a half, rice farming had transformed the coastal regions from southeastern North Carolina to northeast Florida and migratory birds, especially waterfowl, discovered the tremendous food resources these fields provided. When mature, rice was hand cut, often stacked in the fields to dry, and when the mills were ready it was hand moved to barges which took the rice to the mill. This handling process resulted in a tremendous amount of waste rice being left in the fields. With the rice harvest occurring in September–November, the timing was ideal for the fall migration. Given the amounts of waste grain and the juxtaposition of this food resource to wetlands, it is easy to imagine the huge numbers of ducks which came to this region as part of their migratory cycle.

Because of their reputation for producing large flocks of waterfowl and many other game species such as bobwhite quail (Cuthbert and Hoffius 2015), and white-tailed deer, their location in the warmer southern environments, and the strong family and social traditions associated with sport hunting at this time, the historic rice plantation became very desired land holdings again. This was very fortuitous for these properties because it kept these lands in large parcels, maintaining landscape scale processes, and the owners and their families were very interested in conservation goals rather than commercial land development for most of the twentieth century (Fig. 3).

Fig. 3 Multiple species of waterbirds feeding in an historic rice field during a dewatering event. Photo by Dr Travis Folk, author

4 Development of a Conservation Community Around Lowcountry Rice Fields

By the 1980s, the coastal areas of South Carolina were experiencing significant population growth and development. This development was largely concentrated in areas like Myrtle Beach and Hilton Head, not areas where rice culture flourished; however, local conservationists realized this development would soon encroach upon transform rice field landscapes, especially rural areas like the rice growing region between the cities of Charleston and Beaufort, South Carolina. The increasing development of lands in this region again put the future of these historic rice plantations at a crossroads.

Fortunately, during this time, state and federal government agencies (e.g., US Fish and Wildlife Service and South Carolina Wildlife and Marine Resources Department) and nonprofit organizations (e.g., Ducks Unlimited, The Nature Conservancy and others) were beginning to focus on land conservation issues as well. In 1986, the U. S. Fish and Wildlife Service established the North American Waterfowl Management Plan (NAWMP). One goal of the NAWMP was to restore continental waterfowl populations through strategic protection of wetland and upland habitats by focusing on discreet identifiable geographic areas to concentrate protection efforts. This concept was called the Waterfowl Focus Area initiative. NAWMP and its Focus Area concept were widely adopted across the United States by state natural resources agencies, non-governmental organizations, and interested private land owners. In South Carolina, the South Carolina Wildlife and Marine Resources Department (now SC Department of Natural Resources, SCDNR) quickly embraced this concept and started working to identify focus areas within the state.

Nora Murdock, a USFWS biologist, produced a 1979 report identifying the Ashepoo, Combahee, and Edisto River systems between Charleston and Beaufort as a "significant wildlife resource area" worthy of a national wildlife refuge (Murdock 1981). To shorten its name and perhaps make it somewhat easier to remember, Murdock referred to this region as the "ACE Basin". Building on the attention this report brought, and with a growing grass roots effort by private landowners a partnership called the ACE Basin Task Force comprised of the USFWS, SCDNR, Ducks Unlimited (DU) and The Nature Conservancy (TNC) was created to oversee conservation programs within the recently approved ACE Basin Focus Area (SCDNR 1989).

The original ACE Basin Focus Area included portions of Beaufort, Charleston, Colleton, and Hampton counties and encompassed approximately 350,000 acres. The land protection tool most often used to protect private lands was conservation easements. The goal set in 1989 by the Task Force was to protect 90,000 acres with conservation easements by the year 2000. (Conservation easements are voluntary restrictions placed on a property by an owner and typically restrict subdivision of the land for development and the numbers of structures built on the property, thereby maintaining the land's conservation value into the future. Conservation easement are perpetual and do not expire with the sale of the land.) This goal was achieved by 1992, in part because a single signature by a plantation owner on a conservation easement might result in conservation of several thousands of acres. This is one of the unforeseen values these lands had by being held in large parcels and owned by a single private family.

In 2003, the USFWS through the Atlantic Coast Joint Venture offered the opportunity for Task Forces to increase their protection efforts by enlarging existing Waterfowl Focus Areas. The ACE Basin Task force enlarged the boundaries of the original Focus Area to include about 1 million acres. On its 35th anniversary celebration in 2024, the ACE Basin Task Force had protected over 350,000 acres. About 83% of the protected acres were in private ownership. The inclusion of publicly accessible lands such as the US Fish and Wildlife Service's Ernest F. Hollings National Wildlife Refuge and numerous SCDNR properties also contribute to the ACE Basin, a globally recognized model for landscape level conservation.

Over time, there have been numerous additional nonprofit organizations working in land conservation which have joined the ACE Basin Task Force. The Task Force continues to meet bi-monthly where all parties freely share information on property owners they are working with to secure a conservation easement. This helps prevent individual landowners from being bombarded by multiple conservation groups and allows the landowner to work with the organization of their choice. The one element which has remained constant for the Task Force is that it is guided by private landowners from the area and not by governmental agencies, state or federal. This partnership, which has no written bi-laws or formal organizational structure, is a testament to what can be accomplished when diverse groups with a common interest come together and work collaboratively for a common goal.

Over time the private landowners within the ACE Basin have embraced other management objectives such as providing habitats for migratory shorebirds and wading birds. Research efforts by federal and state agencies and local nonprofit organizations have provided these landowners with the necessary information needed to implement multi-species management activities while still achieving waterfowl management objectives (Bauer et al. 2024).

Further, the conservation ethic of private landowners in the ACE Basin has extended to include threatened and endangered species such as the Red-cockaded Woodpecker. Many properties in the Basin already managed their upland pine forests by thinning to a low basal area and frequent prescribed burns. These activities created excellent habitat for this threatened species and landowners have opened their property to receive translocated birds when available. The first release of the woodpecker in the ACE Basin occurred in early 2000s and the first successful nest occurred a year after this release. Nesting colonies of the Red-cockaded Woodpecker now occur on multiple properties across the ACE Basin.

Over time, the expanse of historic rice fields across the ACE Basin has become home to bird species expanding their range. Historically, Wood Storks (*Mycteria americana*) were infrequent visitors to the South Carolina coast prior to 1981 when the first successful nests in the state were documented (Murphy and Coker 2008). Today, nesting rookeries occur throughout the ACE Basin. In 2020, the first successful nest for the Roseate Spoonbill (*Platalea ajaja*) was observed in Charleston County (Hand and Bonafilia 2020). This colorful wading bird species is frequently seen foraging in historic rice fields, now managed for water bird species (Fig. 4).

The incredible avian habitat in historic rice fields (now referred to as managed tidal impoundments, MTI), especially by wading birds, has focused attention on these wetlands by researchers and wetland managers (Gordon et al. 1989; Bauer et al. 2020, 2023). A recent study of historic rice fields in South Carolina evaluated wetland selection by different waterbird guilds during fall and winter to determine habitat preferences (Masto et al. 2023). In this study, aerial surveys were used to record waterbird occurrence and relative abundance in the winters of 2017–2019. Waterbird–habitat relationships were modeled relative to managed and unmanaged coastal and inland wetlands, legally protected conservation lands (e.g. federal, state, and private easements), and habitat diversity. Waterbirds were observed in a variety of wetlands emphasizing the importance of wetland diversity within the landscapes. However, only managed tidal impoundments and protected conservation lands were selected across all waterbird guilds. These results suggest MTIs and protected conservation lands are contemporary 'keystone' habitats for wintering waterbird abundance and diversity in South Carolina and other South Atlantic coastal regions.

The authors of this study also brought additional focus on what might be the next crossroads threatening these critical wetland habitats in historic rice fields: sea level rise (Masto et al. 2023). Recent tropical storms and record-setting spring tides have impacted the ACE Basin region requiring private and governmental owners of MTIs to collectively invest millions of dollars to repair and rebuild dikes and other

Fig. 4 Wooden rice field trunk about to be installed in a dike. Structures like this one, whose design dates to the late 1700s, continues to enable management of water levels in historic rice fields for the enhancement of waterbird habitat. Photo by Dr Travis Folk, author

infrastructure. Further, water management within some MTIs has already been compromised, not by flooding from storms but by low tide levels which are now too high in elevation to allow for the release of water from within the MTIs. These higher, low tide pools are an unexpected consequence of sea level rise and without the ability to dewater MTIs, traditional management practices cannot be achieved.

Concerned federal and state agencies as well as other conservation groups are questioning the resiliency of some historic rice fields and recognize this resource and key conservation features may be lost due to sea level rise. Due to these realities, these groups are beginning the search for their replacements further inland. A key resource to identifying these new inland wetlands could be the recently completed multi-state regional map of all known historic rice fields which encompasses some 328,000 acres of the southeastern coastal plains (Folk 2024) (Fig. 5).

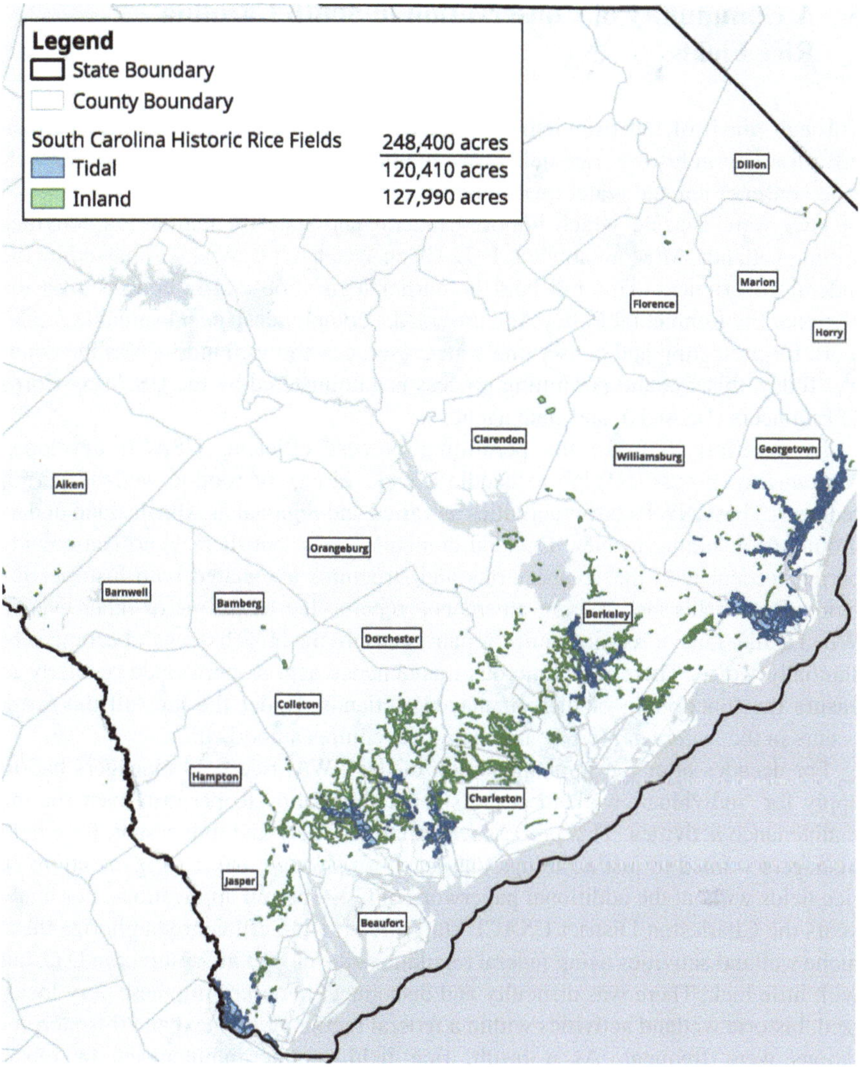

Fig. 5 Map of historic inland and tidal rice fields in South Carolina, as documented in Hanks et al. (2021) (Hanks, D. L., R. F. Baldwin, T. H. Folk, E. P. Wiggers, R. C. Coen, M. L. Gouin, A. Agha, D. D. Richter, E. L. Fields-Black. 2021. Mapping antebellum rice fields as a basis for understanding human and ecological consequences of the Era of Slavery. Land 10 (8): 831. https://doi.org/10.3390/land10080831)

5 A Community of Conservation in South Carolina Rice Fields

Through much of the twentieth century, the maintenance of the critical earthen infrastructure in historic rice fields was unregulated. However, as concern for wetland conservation and water quality began to increase in the United States a series of laws were enacted which imposed federal and state regulations on activities within wetlands. Most notably the 1972 Clean Water Act (CWA) was passed by the federal government. This bill built on earlier legislation and in concert with the National Environmental Policy Act, provided a comprehensive and valuable framework for protecting and conserving water resources and wetlands across the country. Today, this wetland permitting process is administered by the US Army Corps of Engineers (USACE), and state agencies.

In an effort to make the permitting process efficient, USACE developed *Nationwide Permits* (NWPs) to handle a wide variety of routine wetland permit requests. These NWPs cover activities as varied and regional as Appalachian underground coal mining to New England cranberry bogs, but there is no Nationwide permit to deal with the arcane terms and structures associated with historic rice fields. Rice fields also require emergency repairs due to storms or other events. When a dike fails, it requires quick repair to ensure the breach doesn't become substantially worse. There are numerous maintenance actions performed regularly to ensure the functioning of these managed wetlands. Under the law, all this work occurs in the *waters of the US*, and therefore requires authorization.

For decades after the implementation of the CWA, rice field managers had to apply for 'individual' wetland permits for authorization to perform even routine maintenance activities. This process was often untimely and unpleasant. Rice field managers wanted to just *do* things they have *traditionally* done for generations in rice fields without the additional paperwork of CWA permit applications. For many years the Charleston District USACE staff attempted to efficiently authorize these niche wetland activities using federal regulations developed in Washington D.C. but with little luck. There was difficulty and disconnect in describing these very localized, historic wetland activities within a federal regulatory context and misinterpretations were frequent. As a result, rice field routine maintenance or repair authorizations often required months of government processing.

The year 2010 marked a significant change in the wetland regulation of rice fields. Over a period of 2 years and several specific events, staff at the Charleston District HQ of USACE and individuals in the '*rice field community*' (e.g., plantation owners, managers, SCDNR and USFWS, conservation organizations) mutually realized neither party understood the other. To remedy this, the rice field community began conversations with the Charleston District of USACE about the history, ecology, and value of rice fields.

To overcome misunderstandings between the two parties, the Nemours Wildlife Foundation (a non-profit foundation located in the Lowcountry and focused on research and outreach related to natural resources), hosted a daylong conference in

September 2010 where USACE and other federal and state agencies presented to the rice field owners and managers their regulatory process and how it applied to rice fields directly. Attendance by private landowners and plantations managers *far* surpassed expectations and indicated to these federal agencies that the rice field community was sincerely interested in stronger collaborations. Also, it became abundantly clear to each side they were seeking a common goal which was high quality wetlands for wildlife.

One outcome of the meeting was the rice field community developed a document at the request of the regulators that, for the first time, described the traditional *regulatable* activities they routinely perform in rice fields. The importance of this document was that it described each action (such as *installing a rice field trunk*), how it was done and why it was performed in a particular fashion. This had never been done for rice fields, primarily because practitioners of these skills had learned them directly from the previous generations. Knowledge of how and why to perform these certain rice field maintenance activities has always been a skill set learned on a rice plantation and kept on a rice plantation. Another outcome was the USACE personnel began to appreciate why management of water levels in these impounded wetlands was so critical to providing habitat for waterfowl and a suite of other migratory species.

The Nemours meeting and the summary of rice field activities was the first communication between USACE and the rice field community. Meetings and phone calls followed, all of which were centered on trying to develop a better understanding on both sides. *It is important to underscore the significance of this moment: a federal agency said to their constituents "Let's work together to create a better regulatory process for what you need to do."* We should all take a moment to reflect on this statement and acknowledge those individuals from both the regulatory side and rice field community side who were willing to listen, learn, trust, and take the rather bold steps to make changes.

The Charleston District of the USACE, under the guidance of Lt. Col. Edward Chamberlayne, started the lengthy process to develop a *Regional General Permit (typically called the 'GP')*, for use *exclusively* in the Charleston District, that addressed the unique maintenance and repair activities in South Carolina's public and private rice fields.

Development of the GP was undertaken by designated Charleston District Project Managers Paul Hinchcliff, Tracy Sanders, and Mary Hope Green and a Citizens Advisory Team composed of plantation managers, members of conservation NGOs, private property owners, DNR, USFWS and others. The process was collaborative and productive. The USACE staff would develop tentative language for different components of the GP and would ask for the advisory team's input. Input was given, adjustments made, and incorporated into the next draft. Seeing their comments incorporated into the GP gave the advisory team and many in the rice field community hope that indeed useful regulations for rice fields would come out of the process. (It should be noted that the GP also applies to other types of impoundments that do not have their origin in rice agriculture; however, the vast majority—86%—of acreage of impoundments in coastal SC is historic rice fields.)

Fig. 6 The Managed Tidal Impoundment General Permit, as issued by the Charleston District of the Corps of Engineers, was successful. Conservation partners published this explanatory booklet that covers use of the General Permit and the history, ecology and management of historic rice fields and coastal impoundments

The final product was the issuance of the *Managed Tidal Impoundment General Permit* (MTI-GP) *SAC-2011-1157* on July 10, 2012. To perform work covered by the MTI-GP, properties need to be *qualified* by USACE. This involves submitting a document that shows the extent of the impoundments and location of the infrastructure components (e.g., trunk locations, dikes, etc.), descriptions of the various plant communities and the overall management plan for the impoundments. Once submitted, USACE responds to the owner and indicates which of their impoundments, typically all of them, are covered by the MTI-GP. Once deemed 'qualified', rice field maintenance and repair activities can commence as required (Fig. 6).

This communication and exchange of information continues today. For example, the USACE frequently brings new staff members to local properties to see first-hand the impacts of recent storms, how dikes are maintained, and trunks are built and installed. They are also able to interact with the people whose jobs are to maintain these wetlands and see first-hand their dedication and desire to be good stewards of the wetland resource. The value of these regular opportunities for both sides to interact cannot be overstated and much credit goes to those earlier individuals who had the foresight to change the status quo.

Development of the MTI-GP was seen by participants as an interesting, productive, and valuable exercise that ensured management activities that support this resource could be carried out legally and in a manner that met both parties' objectives. In the tradition of Lowcountry conservation, frank and sincere communication between the USACE Charleston District and South Carolina's rice field community led to a piece of federal regulation that today is critically valuable to the maintenance of this historically and ecologically significant resource. Many people participated in the original effort to get the GP developed and their efforts should not be forgotten. Further, it is critical for the current community of managers, landowners, conservation organizations, and regulators to remain committed to upholding the standards set in the GP and avoid repeating a part of history that was unproductive for all groups.

6 Historical Significance and Conservation Success in the Lowcountry of South Carolina

This case study of rice culture transforming into conservation successes has taken place over three centuries in the Lowcountry of South Carolina. It started with a landscape level transformation of wetlands by enslaved Africans and their descendants. While it created wealth for plantation owners, it was developed on the backs of enslaved people across the Lowcountry of South Carolina. This wetland landscape also had value for natural resources in the form of wintering waterfowl and numerous other species of waterbirds. Appreciation and connection to this history, landscape and sporting culture provided the impetus for conservation efforts in the late twentieth century.

These conservation successes have taken shape in several ways. The voluntary placement of conservation easements on rice field properties will ensure the historical and ecological values of the places will persist into the future. The commitment of private landowners (with private dollars) to conserve this landscape has and continues to be significant. Governmental agencies have recognized this effort by private landowners to manage and conserve these historic rice fields so much so that specifically tailored wetlands regulations enable private landowners to conduct maintenance and repair activities to the historic rice fields of coastal South Carolina. These successes have been the result of continued collaboration across the rice field community for one goal: conservation of this historically and ecologically valuable landscape.

References

Bauer, B. A., R. M. Kaminski, J. D. Lanham, P. D. Gerard, and E. P. Wiggers. 2020. Hydrological management for submersed aquatic vegetation in South Carolina coastal impoundments. *Wildlife Society Bulletin* 44 (3): 579–584. https://doi.org/10.1002/wsb.1116.

Bauer, B. A., R. M. Kaminski, P. D. Gerard, E. P. Wiggers, and J. D. Lanham. 2023. Aquatic invertebrate biomass in coastal South Carolina impoundments managed for waterfowl. *Journal of the Southeastern Association of Fish and Wildlife Agencies* 10:85–91.

Bauer, B., D. Harrigal, E. Wiggers, and A. Bridges. 2024. Managing tidal impoundments for wildlife. In *Historic Rice Fields & Coastal Impoundments for Wildlife*, ed. T. H. Folk, B. Bauer, E. Wiggers, D. Harrigal, A. Bridges, and J. Ayers, 2nd ed. Yemassee, SC: Nemours Wildlife Foundation.

Coclanis, P. A. 1989. *The Shadow of a Dream: Economic Life and Death in the South Carolina Lowcountry, 1670–1920*. New York: Oxford University Press.

Cuthberrt, R. B. and S. G. Hoffius. (editors) 2009. Northern money southern land: the Lowcountry plantation sketches of Chlotilde R. Martin. *University of South Carolina Press, Columbia,* South Carolina, USA.

Cuthbert, R. B., and S. G. Hoffius, eds. 2015. *Northern Money Southern Land*. Columbia, SC: University of South Carolina.

Doar, D. 1937. *Rice and Rice Planting in the South Carolina Low Country*. Charleston, SC: The Charleston Museum.

Drayton, J. 1802. *A View of South Carolina, as Respects Her Natural and Civil Concerns*. Charleston, SC: W. P. Young.

Elliott, W. 1846. *Carolina Sports by Land and Water*. New York: Derby & Jackson.

Folk, T. H. 2024. A 300-year history of South Carolina coastal impoundments and their conservation benefits. In *Historic Rice Fields & Coastal Impoundments for Wildlife*, ed. T. H. B. Folk, B. Bauer, E. Wiggers, D. Harrigal, A. Bridges, and J. Ayers, 2nd ed. Yemassee, SC: Nemours Wildlife Foundation.

Gordon, D. H., B. T. Gray, R. D. Perry, M. B. Prevost, T. S. Strange, and R. K. Williams. 1989. South Atlantic coastal wetlands. In *Habitat Management for Migrating and Wintering Waterfowl in North America*, ed. L. M. Smith, R. L. Pederson, and R. M. Kaminski, 57–92. Lubbock, TX: Texas Tech University Press.

Hand, C. E., and R. E. Bonafilia. 2020. First record of roseate spoonbills (*Platalea ajaja*) nesting in South Carolina. *Chat* 84:103–104.

Hanks, D. L., R. F. Baldwin, T. H. Folk, E. P. Wiggers, R. C. Coen, M. L. Gouin, A. Agha, D. D. Richter, and E. L. Fields-Black. 2021. Mapping antebellum rice fields as a basis for understanding human and ecological consequences of the Era of Slavery. *Land* 10 (8): 831. https://doi.org/10.3390/land10080831.

Heyward, D. C. 1937. *Seed from Madagascar*. Chapel Hill, NC: University of North Carolina Press.

Lockhart, M. A. 2015. "Rice Planters in their Own Right": Northern sportsmen and waterfowl management on the Santee River plantations during the baiting era, 1905-1935. In *Leisure Plantations, and the Making of a New South*, ed. J. Brock and D. Vivian. Lanham, MD: Lexington Book.

Masto, N. M., A. C. Hsiung, R. M. Kaminski, B. E. Ross, M. R. Kneece, et al. 2023. Waterbird-habitat relationships in South Carolina: implications for protection, restoration, and management of coastal and inland wetlands. *Restoration Ecology* 31 (7): e13956. https://doi.org/10.1111/rec.13956.

Murdock, N. A. 1981. *Significant Wildlife Resource Areas of South Carolina*. Ashville, NC: U.S. Fish and Wildlife Service.

Murphy, T. M., and J. W. Coker. 2008. A twenty-six year history of wood stork nesting in South Carolina. *Waterbirds* 31:3–7.

Porcher, R. D., and W. R. Judd. 2014. *The Market Preparation of Carolina Rice*. Columbia, SC: University of South Carolina Press.

Ramsay, D. 1858. *History of South Carolina*. Newberry, SC: W. J. Duffie.

Salley, A. S. 1919. The Introduction of Rice Culture into South Carolina. *Bulletins of the Historical Commission of South Carolina—No. 6*. Columbia, SC: The State Company.

Smith, H. R. 2020. *Carolina's Golden Fields*. Cambridge: Cambridge University Press.

South Carolina Wildlife and Marine Resources Department. 1989. *Project Plan: The ACE Basin, a Component of the Atlantic Coast Joint Venture of the North American Waterfowl Management Plan*. Columbia, SC.

Tuten, J. H. 2010. *Lowcountry Time and Tide: The Fall of the South Carolina Rice Kingdom*. Columbia, SC: University of South Carolina.

Shifting Baseline Syndrome: A Framework for Historical Data Integration in Marine Resource Management

George Hambrecht

Abstract This chapter examines shifting baseline syndrome (SBS) as a framework for integrating historical and archaeological data into contemporary marine resource management. First articulated by Daniel Pauly in 1995, SBS identifies how each generation accepts as baseline the environmental conditions they first observe, leading to progressive erosion of standards for ecosystem health. The chapter explores methodological challenges in historical data integration, discusses the development of Marine Historical Ecology as a response to SBS, and presents a case study of Atlantic cod in Iceland spanning 1100 years. This millennial-scale analysis revealed that pre-exploitation cod were 25% larger, three times older, and populations were 570% more abundant than modern specimens, with stable natural mortality rates throughout the period. These findings provide quantitative measures of pristine populations, establish concrete recovery targets, and demonstrate how archaeological and historical data can correct skewed perceptions by extending temporal perspectives beyond conventional scientific monitoring, with significant implications for setting more ambitious conservation goals in marine resource management.

Keywords Marine historical ecology · Archaeology · Shifting baseline syndrome · Fisheries

1 Introduction

The integration of historical data into contemporary marine resource management represents a significant challenge in marine conservation. This chapter proposes shifting baseline syndrome (SBS) as a productive framework for addressing this challenge. It will be argued that archaeological and historical data is an especially rich source for bridging the temporal gaps in observation that can lead to SBS. Foundational SBS literature as well as recent literature linking historical and archaeological data to contemporary marine resource exploitation will be discussed.

G. Hambrecht (✉)
University of Maryland, College Park, MD, USA

J. F. Haldon, R. Fernandes (eds.), *Bridging History and Policy*, Understanding Complex Systems, https://doi.org/10.1007/978-3-032-24379-9_10

Following this will be a more detailed analysis of a significant recent case study that illustrates how archaeological and historical data can be used to create much deeper records of important natural resources (in this case Atlantic Cod, *Gadus morhua*) than have previously existed. Such data is crucial for the generation of the long-term records that are needed in order to navigate SBS.

First articulated by Daniel Pauly in 1995, SBS is an issue that can be ameliorated through the use of archaeological and historical records (Pauly 1995). The concept identifies a fundamental challenge in environmental management: each generation accepts as baseline the environmental conditions they first observe, leading to a progressive erosion of standards for ecosystem health. This generational amnesia creates a situation where contemporary observers perceive resources or landscapes to be in pristine, or near-pristine, condition when often they have experienced centuries of human exploitation (Klein and Thurstan 2016; Soga and Gaston 2018).

Related to this issue of the idea of 'pristine nature' is the work of historical ecologists and environmental historians that has revealed the deep antiquity of human impacts on landscapes and environmental systems, and even on regional and possibly planetary climate levels (Ellis et al. 2021). Such work complicates the idea of the 'pristine' suggesting that 'baselines' might be a moving target, an idea with relevance to multiple generations and with a deep history.

The implications of SBS extend far beyond simple misperception, fundamentally affecting how we conceptualize and manage marine resources. If each successive generation accepts an already degraded ecosystem as natural, management targets become progressively less ambitious, creating a downward spiral of diminishing expectations (Sáenz-Arroyo et al. 2005; Plumeridge and Roberts 2017). Recovery goals often aim to restore populations to levels that represent only a fraction of their historical abundance, while the loss of knowledge about past ecosystem states leads to systematic underestimation of both ecosystem potential and the magnitude of human impacts (Jackson et al. 2001; Lotze and Worm 2009; McClenachan et al. 2015).

SBS affects perception and management across multiple ecological scales, from individual species to entire ecosystems. At the species level, it influences understanding of population size structures, growth rates, and behavioral patterns (Pinnegar and Engelhard 2008; Alleway and Connell 2015). At the community level, it shapes expectations about species composition, trophic relationships, and ecosystem function (McClenachan 2009). At the ecosystem level, it affects comprehension of habitat distribution, connectivity patterns, and system resilience (Knowlton and Jackson 2008; Bonebrake et al. 2018).

The economic implications of SBS are equally significant and often overlooked in traditional management frameworks. When historical abundance levels are forgotten or dismissed as unrealistic, the true economic losses from resource depletion may be severely underestimated (Roberts 2007; Thurstan et al. 2024). This underestimation can lead to inadequate compensation for resource degradation and insufficient investment in restoration efforts. Furthermore, the loss of knowledge about past resource abundance can result in reduced expectations for recovery potential, leading to acceptance of diminished economic returns as normal (O'Leary et al. 2016).

2 Theoretical Framework

SBS operates through several interconnected mechanisms that collectively shape our understanding of environmental change. While at its most basic level the syndrome describes a form of generational amnesia where knowledge of past conditions is lost as older generations are replaced by newer ones (Papworth et al. 2009), this simple description belies the complex ways in which shifting baselines influence environmental perception and management across temporal, spatial, and institutional scales.

The syndrome manifests through multiple pathways, from individual perception to institutional memory. As Klein and Thurstan (2016) demonstrate, it affects how scientific data is interpreted and how management targets are set. The gradual nature of environmental change, combined with limitations in human memory and institutional knowledge, creates conditions where significant degradation occurs without recognition of its true magnitude. This process is further complicated by the increasing rate of environmental change in the Anthropocene, which can outpace traditional mechanisms for maintaining ecological knowledge (Soga and Gaston 2018).

Research by Pinnegar and Engelhard (2008) reveals how SBS fundamentally affects scientific understanding of marine ecosystems. Their analyses demonstrate that even basic parameters such as maximum fish size and age can be misunderstood when historical data is ignored or improperly contextualized. This effect is particularly pronounced in systems with long histories of exploitation, where knowledge of pristine conditions has been lost through successive generations of resource users and managers. The implications of this knowledge loss extend beyond simple biological parameters to affect our understanding of ecosystem function and resilience (McClenachan et al. 2015).

The temporal aspects of SBS present challenges for ecosystem management that traditional monitoring approaches struggle to address. Long-term environmental changes often occur at rates too slow for individual observers to recognize, creating a temporal mismatch between human perception and ecological change (Bonebrake et al. 2018). This gradual change, combined with the human tendency to compare current conditions primarily with those experienced during one's own lifetime, creates systematic bias in perception of environmental change (Turvey et al. 2010). The challenge is further complicated by accelerating rates of environmental change that can render historical baselines seemingly irrelevant to contemporary management challenges.

Institutional factors compound these perceptual challenges through multiple mechanisms. Scientific monitoring programs rarely extend beyond a few decades, while significant environmental changes may occur over centuries or millennia (Lotze and Worm 2009; Armstrong et al. 2017). The resultant data gaps create artificial baselines that may already reflect significantly altered ecosystems. Additionally, the fragmentation of environmental knowledge across different institutions and stakeholder groups can impede recognition of long-term changes, creating silos of understanding that fail to capture the full temporal scope of ecosystem change (Stephenson et al. 2019).

Social and cultural factors exert significant influence on how baselines shift over time through complex interactions with knowledge transmission systems. Traditional ecological knowledge (TEK), once a crucial source of information about historical ecosystem states, has been progressively lost in many regions through disruption of cultural continuity and changing relationships with marine resources (Berkes et al. 2000). This loss removes important reference points for understanding long-term environmental change. Similarly, changes in cultural values and economic priorities can alter which environmental changes are noticed and recorded, creating selective pressures on knowledge retention (Cámara-Leret et al. 2019). The acceleration of environmental change in recent decades has further complicated this dynamic by potentially invalidating TEK when the 'normal' parameters of environmental and climate change move beyond experiences that construct the collective knowledge base of local communities.

The psychological dimensions of SBS add another layer of complexity to environmental management challenges. Humans tend to normalize the conditions they experience most frequently, making it difficult to maintain awareness of historical ecosystem states (Papworth et al. 2009). This normalization process can occur rapidly, particularly when direct experience with more pristine conditions is lacking, creating a psychological barrier to understanding the magnitude of environmental change (Soga and Gaston 2018; Jones et al. 2020). The process is further complicated by the role of social memory in shaping environmental perceptions and the increasing disconnection between human communities and marine ecosystems.

Recent research has identified several mechanisms that reinforce SBS in scientific and management contexts, creating institutional barriers to addressing the syndrome. The preference for readily available data can lead to overreliance on recent observations, while historical data may be overlooked due to perceived difficulties in interpretation or integration (McClenachan et al. 2012; Thurstan et al. 2015). Additionally, the emphasis on statistical significance in ecological studies may create bias against historical data that cannot meet modern standards for quantitative analysis, potentially excluding valuable long-term perspectives from consideration in management decisions (Schwerdtner Máñez et al. 2014).

At the core of all of these issues is the application of archaeological and historical analyses to contemporary resource management issues. In order to reveal more robust baselines and navigate the 'abnormal' masquerading as the 'normal' and all the negative decisions that can follow from SBS deeper temporal data is needed. Historical and archaeological data are among the only sources for such data (though genetic data will also be effective). The depth of the temporal range used in each SBS case is dependent on the available data. In some cases, and perhaps more so in the earlier days of SBS study the time depth might only be in the decadal scale. McClenachan (2009) is an example of using photography over the last century to measure the change in game fish size in Florida. More recently however many studies are pushing this temporal range into the century and millennial scale (i.e. Holm et al. 2022, Campana et al. 2025).

Marine Historical Ecology

Marine Historical Ecology (MHE) addresses many of the challenges posed by SBS in marine systems. This transdisciplinary approach to understanding long-term changes in marine ecosystems integrates historical, archaeological, and ecological data to construct more comprehensive and deeper temporal perspectives (Jackson et al. 2001; McClenachan et al. 2015; Engelhard et al. 2016; Thurstan 2022). The field developed in direct response to the growing recognition that modern ecological observations alone provide an insufficient temporal scale for understanding marine ecosystem dynamics and anthropogenic impacts.

By integrating archaeological remains, historical documents, early scientific surveys, and traditional ecological knowledge, MHE researchers can reconstruct historical baselines for marine populations, community structures, and ecosystem functions across centuries to millennia (Lotze and McClenachan 2013; Schwerdtner Máñez et al. 2014). This integration reveals dramatic changes in marine ecosystems that preceded systematic scientific observation, particularly regarding the abundance and size distribution of marine megafauna (Pandolfi et al. 2003; Thurstan et al. 2020, 2024; Frasier et al. 2022).

Archaeological data, particularly from coastal middens, provides the deepest temporal perspective in this framework, offering insights into marine resource use and ecosystem structure over millennia. These data sources have proven particularly valuable in documenting changes in species composition and size distributions of exploited marine populations, providing concrete evidence of long-term ecological change (Rick and Erlandson 2008; Barrett et al. 2020). The analysis of archaeological remains offers quantifiable data about past ecosystem states, though interpretation requires careful consideration of taphonomic processes and sampling biases.

Historical documents occupy a crucial intermediate position in the temporal framework, bridging the gap between archaeological and modern ecological data. These sources include fishing records, naturalist accounts, maritime documents, and early scientific surveys, each offering different perspectives on past ecosystem states (Engelhard et al. 2016; Thurstan et al. 2018). While the interpretation of historical documents requires careful consideration of historical context and potential biases, these sources provide invaluable quantitative and qualitative data about ecosystem conditions before the advent of systematic scientific monitoring.

MHE has played a pivotal role in identifying and documenting the effects of shifting baseline syndrome in marine conservation. By demonstrating that many marine ecosystems were dramatically altered by human activities before the onset of modern scientific monitoring, this field has fundamentally challenged existing assumptions about "natural" ecosystem states (Pauly 1995; Jackson et al. 2001). This understanding has significant implications for conservation and restoration goals, suggesting that many currently accepted baselines may represent significantly degraded states rather than historical norms (McClenachan et al. 2012).

The field continues to evolve methodologically, with increasing emphasis on quantitative approaches to data integration and growing recognition of the value of indigenous and local ecological knowledge in understanding long-term marine ecosystem change (Kittinger et al. 2015).

3 Data from the Past as a SBS Corrective

Shifting baseline syndrome (SBS) highlights problems of temporal scale in human perception of environmental systems. Correcting these skewed perceptions requires observations extending beyond conventional scientific monitoring, which rarely exceeds a century. Historical and archaeological data offer crucial opportunities for extending our temporal perspective (Thurstan et al. 2015).

Integrating historical and archaeological data however, presents significant methodological challenges. The heterogeneous nature of historical sources—from government surveys to merchant records—complicates comparative analysis (Schwerdtner Máñez et al. 2014; Klein and Thurstan 2016). Challenges also include temporal resolution, as different sources provide varying levels of detail. Customs records may provide annual data while traveler accounts offer only sporadic observations (McClenachan et al. 2012). Archaeological data can span long time-scales but rarely in a consistent and evenly distributed way. Spatial scale presents additional difficulties, with historical and archaeological records often reflecting local perspectives, at times biased toward economically important or marginal areas depending on the source (Rosenberg et al. 2005; Armstrong et al. 2017).

The qualitative nature of many historical sources complicates quantitative analysis. While some records provide numerical data, many observations are descriptive and require careful interpretation (Lotze and McClenachan 2013; Thurstan et al. 2018). The inconsistent distribution of archaeological data is also a complicating factor when trying to create quantitative data that is comparable to contemporary data. Recent methodological advances have improved our ability to generate quantifiable data from qualitative historical and archaeological records (Campana et al. 2025; O'Leary et al. 2016).

Observer bias requires particular attention. Historical records were often created for specific purposes, potentially overlooking valuable ecological aspects (Pauly 1995; Bonebrake et al. 2018). Robust methodological frameworks must account for these various forms of bias and uncertainty, with standardized approaches strengthening the utility of historical data in addressing SBS (Beller et al. 2017; Stephenson et al. 2019).

The discussion around the potential of SBS to highlight the value of historical data for contemporary issues is a mature and substantial one. As a quick and necessarily incomplete survey one might read Thurstan et al. 2024 for an excellent study that, using historical documents, maps the extent of European Flat Oyster reefs over the last 350 years in NW European coastal waters. They convincingly show that existing reef systems are a tiny remnant of what has existed over this period, and they discuss the profound implications for coastal marine biodiversity in NW Europe. Alleway et al. 2023 approach the issue in a broader more theoretical fashion, arguing that SBS is an effective bridge-builder between disciplines and that it is an excellent way to make historical data relevant and useful for the management of contemporary issues. The article goes on to discuss best practices for its use in the future. What follows is a discussion of a recent project that serves as an example of how historical and archaeological data can be used to address contemporary marine resource issues by addressing SBS.

4 Millennial-Scale Analysis: The Iceland Cod Study

Background and Context

Archaeological work in Iceland has been ongoing since the nineteenth century. One, more recent trend (among many) in Icelandic archaeology over the last 30 or so years has been a theoretical focus on environmental archaeology and a practical focus on the excavation of middens (garbage deposits, as opposed to structures). The connection between the two comes down to environmental archaeologies focus on organic remains and the fact that middens are often the best source for said organic remains. While many groups have been engaged in this trend the North Atlantic Biocultural Organization (NABO, nabohome.org) has been a leading participant in this sort of work for decades. As a result, collections of Icelandic midden material, recovered from sites spanning from the first colonization of Iceland by humans in the second half of the ninth century CE down to the twentieth century have been recovered by NABO and its main collaborators in Iceland, the University of Iceland (Haskoli Islands) and the Institute for Archaeology, Iceland (Fornleifastofnun Islands). These collections have all been excavated and analyzed in standardized ways and are thus easily comparable across regional and temporal contexts (nabohome.org for an explanation of excavation and analytical standards). The study discussed here is a product of the Central North Atlantic Marine Historical Ecology Project (CAMHEP), itself a NABO sponsored project. CAMHEP is funded by the US NSF Navigating the New Arctic Program (grant #2022656) and is attempting to build a record of the relationship between fishing, people, climate, marine ecology and Atlantic cod over the entirety of Icelandic history. CAMHEP has been sampling these existing collections in order to build a marine historical ecology of the waters around Iceland over the past 1100 years. The project explicitly addresses issues around SBS with the expectation that our results will shed light on the primary dynamics at play in SBS. What follows is a digest of one facet of this project (Campana et al. 2025).

Atlantic cod (*Gadus morhua*) has played a central role in North Atlantic fisheries for over a millennium, making it an ideal subject for long-term historical ecological analysis. The species' biological characteristics make it particularly suitable for such studies: cod are relatively long-lived, demonstrate strong site fidelity, and leave clear records of their life history in their otoliths. Otoliths are calcium carbonate structures, found in the inner ear, grow continuously throughout the fish's life, laying down annual growth rings similar to those found in trees. The chemical composition of these growth rings reflects environmental conditions at the time of formation, while their width indicates growth rates (Campana and Thorrold 2001). Otoliths can be used to determine both the age-at-death as well as the size (fork-length) of the fish. When preserved under appropriate taphonomic conditions, these otoliths provide a record of historical environmental and biological conditions that can be directly compared to contemporary data, creating an exceptional opportunity to test SBS concepts using empirical evidence. While CAMHEP is engaging in analysis of multiple bone elements of Atlantic cod, this digest discusses research that is solely focused on otoliths.

Iceland's cod fishery origins coincide with the island's settlement in the late ninth century, providing a clear starting point for analyzing human impacts on marine resources. Early fishing activities primarily served local consumption needs, but by the thirteenth century, dried cod had become a valuable export commodity. The development of the stockfish trade transformed both the intensity and organization of fishing effort, marking a crucial transition in human-marine resource relationships. Historical and archaeological records document the progression from small-scale local fishing to intensive commercial exploitation, particularly after the arrival of English fishing fleets in the fifteenth century (Hambrecht et al. 2022; Holm et al. 2022).

Methods

The Campana et al. (2025) study basically uses tools applied by contemporary fisheries scientists and managers and applies these to archaeological data to address SBS. The analysis of 651 cod otoliths recovered from twelve archaeological sites spanning the ninth through nineteenth centuries provides an unprecedented temporal perspective on marine population dynamics. These sites represent different periods of Iceland's fishing history, from early settlement through the development of commercial fishing to the beginnings of industrialized exploitation, offering a continuous record of human-marine resource interaction. The preservation conditions at the study sites proved exceptional for archaeological materials, particularly for organic remains such as otoliths. Rapid burial in pH neutral soils provided chemical stability that prevented dissolution of the calcium carbonate structures. Limited post-depositional disturbance preserved the spatial integrity of deposits, allowing relatively precise dating through a combination of stratigraphic analysis, radiocarbon dating, and tephrochronology. These favorable conditions enabled recovery of statistically robust sample sizes from each time period, facilitating robust quantitative analysis (i.e. Feeley et al. 2018).

A key point to note is that the fish remains being analyzed, such as the otoliths, were all fished, or selected, by humans. This makes them part of the historical record. Statistical analyses strongly suggest that the fisherfolk involved were not focusing on specific size segments, and that the selection represented by the midden material from each period is a good sample of the population as a whole.

Archaeological Context

The archaeological context of the samples provides insights into historical fishing practices and their evolution over time. Processing Atlantic cod into stockfish (the round-dried product that dominated the dried cod trade for much of the later medieval and early modern periods) or other dried fish products such as klipfisk (a flat-dried product often associated with earlier sites) involved standardized butchery practices that created predictable patterns in the archaeological record. The removal of the head and often the atlas and first thoracic vertebrae at processing sites, typically located at coastal landing areas, created distinctive depositional patterns that aid in site interpretation. These production sites contrast markedly with consumption sites in Iceland and Europe, where different elements of the fish skeleton, mainly precaudal and caudal vertebrae, predominate in the archaeological record (Perdikaris et al. 2007; Hambrecht et al. 2022).

The focus on otoliths, which are cranial elements, necessitated sampling from coastal drying/processing site bone assemblages (mostly midden deposits). These specialized locations proved particularly valuable for the study due to their dedicated function in preparing stockfish, resulting in large accumulations of fish remains from known seasons of capture. The standardized processing methods used at these sites created consistent patterns of bone and otolith deposition, facilitating comparison across time periods and providing a reliable source of data for population analysis (Krivogorskaya et al. 2005; Hambrecht et al. 2022).

Historical Data Integration

The study developed an approach to modeling fishing productivity for periods predating both documentary records and existing robust models. Historical and archaeological data on landscapes, particularly focusing on the number of farms in Iceland through time, were used to model population numbers across the study period. These population estimates then served as the basis for modeling potential domestic consumption of fish in Iceland, which in turn enabled the reconstruction of catches through time. This approach proved particularly valuable for understanding fishing pressure up to the fifteenth century, when foreign fishing became significant in Icelandic waters (Holm et al. 2022).

Results

The study's findings provide a demonstration of how shifting baseline syndrome can be addressed through systematic integration of archaeological and historical data. Analysis of Atlantic cod otoliths recovered from Viking-era through early modern archaeological sites in Iceland offers unprecedented insights into the population dynamics of a major marine resource prior to significant human exploitation. The temporal depth of the study, reconstructing population parameters across an 1100-year time series, allows for detailed examination of the transition from pristine conditions through progressive intensification of fishing pressure.

Several key findings emerge that fundamentally challenge our understanding of pre-exploitation marine ecosystems. Cod from the tenth to twelfth centuries were 25% larger and up to three times older than modern specimens, despite exhibiting slower density-dependent growth rates, roughly 22% lower than modern growth rates. Density dependence in fish biology refers to how population processes (like growth, mortality, or reproduction) change based on the population's density—essentially how crowded the fish are in their habitat, and how this impacts their access to resources and thus the variables listed before. This slower growth was attributed to a population abundance estimated to be 570% greater than modern levels. The study documented that the pristine population was characterized by abundant large and old animals, with individuals reaching ages almost three times that of modern cod. This age structure likely contributed to increased population stability and resilience, characteristics that were progressively eroded through fishing pressure (Campana et al. 2025).

The documentation of the transition from pristine to exploited state provides particularly valuable insights into the process of marine resource depletion. The research demonstrated that external fishing mortality progressively dominated natural mortality rates after the fourteenth century, coinciding with the expansion of commercial fishing.

The study provided insights into density-dependent processes in marine populations over an unprecedented temporal scale. The researchers documented a clear inverse relationship between population abundance and growth rates, with growth rates increasing by 20% as population abundance declined through the centuries. The persistence of this relationship provides insights into the fundamental biological processes governing marine populations over long time scales (Campana et al. 2025; Denechaud et al. 2020).

Of particular significance was the natural mortality rates in the earliest periods of the study. The study established that natural mortality remained at approximately 0.18–0.19 before the advent of human fishing pressures on these fish populations. These numbers are very close to the numbers used by contemporary fishing industries when estimating natural versus human caused mortality. This metric is a crucial aspect of fisheries management in that the natural mortality rate is the foundation upon which catch numbers are built. Estimating sustainable catch numbers is impossible without knowing natural mortality rates. This finding provides crucial empirical validation for key assumptions in modern fisheries models. This result was also of note in that it countered what many might assume was the case, that modern day fisheries managers had been using a mortality model that was fundamentally wrong and that this helped lead to overfishing and fisheries crashes. Instead, this data suggests that our assumptions about natural mortality were in fact correct and this, at the least, further complicates understandings of the underlying causes of collapsing fisheries.

The research makes several significant contributions to addressing shifting baseline syndrome by providing quantitative measures of a pristine population. These findings establish concrete reference points for population recovery targets and demonstrate the value of archaeological and historical data in reconstructing pre-exploitation baselines.

A final key finding emerged regarding the timing and impact of commercial fishing intensification. The study identified the fourteenth century as a transition period, when external fishing mortality began to significantly influence population dynamics. This timing coincides with historical records of expanding commercial fishing operations, particularly the arrival of English fishing fleets. Yet before this study, gauging the impact of this suggested increase in fishing was difficult to impossible. This data allows us to challenge the assumption that impacts on Atlantic cod populations would not be visible until the advent of modern industrial fishing in the nineteenth century. Though this study does reveal a major increase in this impact in the nineteenth century we can now see that pre-industrial fishing had a quantifiable impact as far back as the fifteenth century. The identification of this transition point provides valuable context for understanding the long-term impacts of commercial fishing on marine populations (Holm et al. 2022; Campana et al. 2025).

5 Management Implications

The integration of historical data through SBS has implications for contemporary marine resource management. The quantitative demonstration of historical population parameters provided by the Iceland cod study offers concrete benchmarks for recovery targets and helps define what constitutes a "healthy" ecosystem state (MacKenzie et al. 2011; Thurstan et al. 2020). This knowledge challenges current management assumptions and suggests the need for more ambitious conservation goals that better reflect historical ecosystem conditions.

Long-term perspectives from historical data help managers distinguish between anthropogenic impacts and natural fluctuations in marine ecosystems. This understanding becomes particularly crucial in the context of climate change, where historical data can help anticipate ecosystem responses to environmental change while accounting for natural variability (Engelhard et al. 2016; Smolinski et al. 2020).

The study's findings regarding density-dependent growth rates have relevance for contemporary management strategies. The documented relationship between population density and growth rates suggests that current management approaches may need to be adjusted to account for density-dependent effects when setting harvest targets and recovery goals. This understanding could lead to more effective management strategies that better account for the complex dynamics of marine populations (Denechaud et al. 2020).

The demonstration of substantially larger historical population sizes and individual fish dimensions challenges current assumptions about carrying capacity and optimal population levels. These findings suggest that many marine ecosystems may be capable of supporting much larger and more productive fish populations than previously assumed, with implications for setting harvest limits and conservation targets (Thurstan et al. 2018; O'Leary et al. 2016).

6 Future Research Directions

The application of SBS theory to contemporary management challenges continues to evolve. As environmental pressures increase and ecosystems continue to change, the value of historical perspectives grows increasingly important. Understanding past ecosystem states and human responses to environmental change provides crucial insights for modern management, particularly in the context of climate change and increasing anthropogenic pressures on marine systems (Bonebrake et al. 2018; Stephenson et al. 2019).

The direct empirical evidence for pre-exploitation marine ecosystems provided by studies like the Iceland cod analysis transforms our understanding of shifting baseline syndrome and its implications for marine resource management. This research demonstrates that the integration of archaeological and historical data can provide quantifiable metrics for understanding pristine population states, directly addressing key challenges in applying SBS theory to contemporary management challenges (Thurstan et al. 2020; McClenachan et al. 2015).

The synthesis of historical and archaeological approaches with modern marine science has revealed several crucial insights about marine ecosystem dynamics. First, pristine marine populations were characterized by significantly larger individual sizes, greater longevity, and substantially higher population densities than previously recognized. Second, fundamental biological parameters such as natural mortality rates can be used to determine when human pressure starts to become significant. Third, density-dependent processes play a crucial role in regulating population dynamics, with implications that extend from individual growth rates to ecosystem-level processes (Campana et al. 2025).

The future of marine resource management would benefit from increased integration of historical perspectives into contemporary decision-making frameworks. The successful application of SBS theory to practical management challenges depends on our ability to reconstruct and understand historical ecosystem states. The methodological advances demonstrated in recent research, particularly in the quantification of historical population parameters, provide a framework for this integration. As we face unprecedented environmental changes, the insights gained from historical ecology become increasingly valuable for predicting and managing marine ecosystem responses (Bonebrake et al. 2018; Stephenson et al. 2019).

This synthesis of historical ecology and contemporary marine science offers a path forward for addressing shifting baseline syndrome in marine resource management. By providing concrete evidence of historical ecosystem states, this approach enables more informed and ambitious conservation goals while also highlighting the complexity of marine ecosystem dynamics over long time scales. As we continue to develop our understanding of marine systems, the integration of historical perspectives will remain crucial for effective resource management and ecosystem conservation.

References

Alleway, H. K., and S. D. Connell. 2015. Loss of an ecological baseline through the eradication of oyster reefs from coastal ecosystems and human memory. *Conservation Biology* 29:795–804.

Alleway, Heidi K., Emily S. Klein, Liz Cameron, Kristina Douglass, Ishtar Govia, Cornelia Guell, Michelle Lim, Libby Robin, and Ruth H. Thurstan. 2023. The Shifting Baseline Syndrome as a connective concept for more informed and just responses to global environmental change. *People and Nature* 5 (3): 885–896. https://doi.org/10.1002/pan3.10473.

Armstrong, C. G., A. C. Shoemaker, I. McKechnie, A. Ekblom, P. Szabó, P. J. Lane, et al. 2017. Anthropological contributions to historical ecology: 50 questions, infinite prospects. *PLoS One* 12:e0171883.

Barrett, J. H., S. Boessenkool, C. J. Kneale, T. C. O'Connell, and B. Star. 2020. Ecological globalisation, serial depletion and the medieval trade of walrus rostra. *Quaternary Science Reviews* 229:106122.

Beller, E., L. McClenachan, A. Trant, E. W. Sanderson, J. Rhemtulla, A. Guerrini, et al. 2017. Toward principles of historical ecology. *American Journal of Botany* 104:645–648.

Berkes, F., J. Colding, and C. Folke. 2000. Rediscovery of traditional ecological knowledge as adaptive management. *Ecological Applications* 10:1251–1262.

Bonebrake, T. C., C. J. Brown, J. D. Bell, J. L. Blanchard, A. Chauvenet, C. Champion, et al. 2018. Managing consequences of climate-driven species redistribution requires integration of ecology, conservation and social science. *Biological Reviews* 93:284–305.

Cámara-Leret, R., M. A. Fortuna, and J. Bascompte. 2019. Indigenous knowledge networks in the face of global change. *Proceedings of the National Academy of Sciences* 116 (20): 9913–9918. https://doi-org.ezproxy.princeton.edu/10.1073/pnas.1821843116.

Campana, S. E., and S. R. Thorrold. 2001. Otoliths, increments, and elements: keys to a comprehensive understanding of fish populations? *Canadian Journal of Fisheries and Aquatic Sciences* 58:30–38.

Campana, S. E., G. Hambrecht, N. Misarti, et al. 2025. Mortality drives production dynamics of Atlantic cod through 1100 years of commercial fishing. *Science Advances* 11 (6): https://www.science.org/doi/10.1126/sciadv.adt4782.

2018, Carolyn J Lundquist, David Bowden, Katie Cartner, Fabrice Stephenson, Ian Tuck, Judi E Hewitt, Assessing benthic responses to fishing disturbance over broad spatial scales that incorporate high environmental variation, Frontiers in Marine Science, vol 5:405

Denechaud, C., S. Smoliński, A. J. Geffen, J. A. Godiksen, and S. E. Campana. 2020. A century of fish growth in relation to climate change, population dynamics and exploitation. *Global Change Biology* 26:5661–5678.

Engelhard, Georg H., Ruth H. Thurstan, Brian R. MacKenzie, Heidi K. Alleway, R. Colin, A. Bannister, Massimiliano Cardinale, Maurice W. Clarke, Jock C. Currie, Tomaso Fortibuoni, and Poul Holm. 2016. ICES meets marine historical ecology: placing the history of fish and fisheries in current policy context. *ICES Journal of Marine Science* 73 (5): 1386–1403.

2021, Erle C Ellis, Nicolas Gauthier, Kees Klein Goldewijk, Rebecca Bliege Bird, Nicole Boivin, Sandra Díaz, Dorian Q Fuller, Jacquelyn L Gill, Jed O Kaplan, Naomi Kingston, Harvey Locke, Crystal NH McMichael, Darren Ranco, Torben C Rick, M Rebecca Shaw, Lucas Stephens, Jens-Christian Svenning, James EM Watson, People have shaped most terrestrial nature for at least 12,000 years, PNAS, vol 118, issue 17

Frasier, Brenna A., Leah Springate, Timothy R. Frasier, Seth Brewington, Martin Carruthers, Ragnar Edvardsson, Ramona Harrison, Andrew C. Kitchener, Ingrid Mainland, and Vicki E. Szabo. 2022. Genetic examination of historical North Atlantic right whale (*Eubalaena glacialis*) bone specimens from the eastern North Atlantic: insights into species history, transoceanic population structure, and genetic diversity. *Marine Mammal Science* 38 (3): 1050–1069. https://doi.org/10.1111/mms.12916.

2018, Frank J. Feeley, Grace Cesario, Wendi Coleman, Kaitlin Crow, Alexander Huaylinos, Jason LeVasseur, Olha Lysa, Dorys Ojeda, Amber Rivers, Thomas Ryan, The Final Report on the Archaeofauna from Context 147 at the Medieval Fishing Station at Gufuskálar, Western Iceland., NORSEC Laboratory Report #65, Hunter College Zooarchaeology Laboratory.

2022, George Hambrecht, Frank Feeley, Konrad Smiarowski, Megan Hicks, Ramona Harrison, Seth Brewington, Grace Cesario, Kevin Gibbons, Quaternary Research, vol 108:64-80.

Holm, P., J. Nicholls, P. W. Hayes, J. Ivinson, and B. Allaire. 2022. Accelerated extractions of North Atlantic cod and herring, 1520-1790. *Fish and Fisheries* 23:54–72.

Jackson, J. B. C., M. X. Kirby, W. H. Berger, K. A. Bjorndal, L. W. Botsford, et al. 2001. Historical overfishing and the recent collapse of coastal ecosystems. *Science* 293:629–637.

2003, John M Pandolfi, Roger H Bradbury, Enric Sala, Terence P Hughes, Karen A Bjorndal, Richard G Cooke, Deborah McArdle, Loren McClenachan, Marah JH Newman, Gustavo Paredes, Robert R Warner, Jeremy BC Jackson, Global trajectories of the long-term decline of coral reef ecosystems, Science, vol 301, issue 5635:955-958

Jones, L. P., S. T. Turvey, D. Massimino, and S. K. Papworth. 2020. Investigating the implications of shifting baseline syndrome on conservation. *People and Nature* 2:1131–1144.

Kittinger, J. N., L. McClenachan, K. B. Gedan, and L. K. Blight. 2015. *Marine Historical Ecology in Conservation: Applying the Past to Manage for the Future*. Berkeley, CA: University of California Press.

Klein, E. S., and R. H. Thurstan. 2016. Acknowledging long-term ecological change: the problem of shifting baselines. In *Perspectives on Oceans Past*, ed. K. Schwerdtner Máñez and B. Poulsen, 11–29. Dordrecht: Springer.

Knowlton, N., and J. B. C. Jackson. 2008. Shifting baselines, local impacts, and global change on coral reefs. *PLoS Biology* 6:e54.

Krivogorskaya, Y., S. Perdikaris, and T. H. McGovern. 2005. Fish bones and fishermen: The potential of zooarchaeology in the Westfjords. *Archaeologia Islandica* 4:31–50.

Lotze, H. K., and L. McClenachan. 2013. Marine historical ecology: Informing the future by learning from the past. In *Marine Community Ecology and Conservation*, ed. M. D. Bertness, J. F. Bruno, B. R. Silliman, and J. J. Stachowicz, 165–200. Sunderland, MA: Sinauer.

Lotze, H. K., and B. Worm. 2009. Historical baselines for large marine animals. *Trends in Ecology & Evolution* 24:254–262.

MacKenzie, B. R., H. Ojaveer, and M. Eero. 2011. Historical ecology provides new insights for ecosystem management: Eastern Baltic cod case study. *Marine Policy* 35:266–270.

McClenachan, L. 2009. Documenting loss of large trophy fish from the Florida Keys with historical photographs. *Conservation Biology* 23:636–643.

McClenachan, L., F. Ferretti, and J. K. Baum. 2012. From archives to conservation: Why historical data are needed to set baselines for marine animals and ecosystems. *Conservation Letters* 5:349–359.

McClenachan, L., G. O'Connor, and T. Reynolds. 2015. Adaptive capacity of co-management systems in the face of environmental change: The soft-shell clam fishery and invasive green crabs in Maine. *Marine Policy* 104:216–224.

O'Leary, B. C., M. Winther-Janson, J. M. Bainbridge, J. Aitken, J. P. Hawkins, and C. M. Roberts. 2016. Effective coverage targets for ocean protection. *Conservation Letters* 13:e12711.

Papworth, S. K., J. Rist, L. Coad, and E. J. Milner-Gulland. 2009. Evidence for shifting baseline syndrome in conservation. *Conservation Letters* 2:93–100.

Pauly, D. 1995. Anecdotes and the shifting baseline syndrome of fisheries. *Trends in Ecology & Evolution* 10:430.

Pinnegar, J. K., and G. H. Engelhard. 2008. The 'shifting baseline' phenomenon: a global perspective. *Reviews in Fish Biology and Fisheries* 18:1–16.

Plumeridge, A. A., and C. M. Roberts. 2017. Conservation targets in marine protected area management suffer from shifting baseline syndrome: a case study on the Dogger Bank. *Marine Pollution Bulletin* 116:395–404.

Rick, T. C., and J. M. Erlandson. 2008. *Human Impacts on Ancient Marine Ecosystems: A Global Perspective*. Berkeley, CA: University of California Press.

Roberts, C. M. 2007. *The Unnatural History of the Sea*. Washington, DC: Island Press.

Rosenberg, A. A., W. J. Bolster, K. E. Alexander, W. B. Leavenworth, A. B. Cooper, and M. G. McKenzie. 2005. The history of ocean resources: modeling cod biomass using historical records. *Frontiers in Ecology and the Environment* 3:84–90.

2020, Ruth H Thurstan, Ben K Diggles, Chris L Gillies, Michael K Strong, Ray Kerkhove, Sarah M Buckley, Robert A King, Vince Smythe, Gideon Heller-Wagner, Rebecca Weeks, Fred Palin, Ian McLeod, Charting two centuries of transformation in a coastal social-ecological system: A mixed methods approach, Global Environmental Change, vol 61

Sáenz-Arroyo, A., C. M. Roberts, J. Torre, M. Cariño-Olvera, and R. R. Enríquez-Andrade. 2005. Rapidly shifting environmental baselines among fishers of the Gulf of California. *Proceedings of the Royal Society B* 272:1957–1962.

Schwerdtner Máñez, K., P. Holm, L. Blight, M. Coll, A. MacDiarmid, H. Ojaveer, et al. 2014. The future of the oceans past: towards a global marine historical research initiative. *PLoS One* 9:e101466.

2010, Samuel T Turvey, Leigh A Barrett, HAO Yujiang, Zhang Lei, Zhang Xinqiao, Wang Xianyan, Huang Yadong, Zhou Kaiya, TOM Hart, Wang Ding, Rapidly shifting baselines in Yangtze fishing communities and local memory of extinct species, Conservation Biology, vol 24, issue 3:778–787

Smoliński, S., J. Deplanque-Lasserre, E. Hjörleifsson, A. J. Geffen, J. A. Godiksen, and S. E. Campana. 2020. Century-long cod otolith biochronology reveals individual growth plasticity in response to temperature. *Scientific Reports* 10:16708.

Soga, M., and K. J. Gaston. 2018. Shifting baseline syndrome: causes, consequences, and implications. *Frontiers in Ecology and the Environment* 16:222–230.

2007, Sophia Perdikaris, George Hambrecht, Seth Brewington, Thomas H McGovern, Across the Fish Event Horizon: a comparative approach, in The Role of Fish in Ancient Times, editor Heidemarie Huster Plogmann, Verlag Marie Leidorf.

Stephenson, R. L., S. Paul, M. A. Pastoors, M. Kraan, P. Holm, M. Wiber, et al. 2019. Integrating fishers' knowledge research in science and management. *ICES Journal of Marine Science* 76:1459–1468.

Then, A. Y., J. M. Hoenig, N. G. Hall, and D. A. Hewitt. 2015. Evaluating the predictive performance of empirical estimators of natural mortality rate using information on over 200 fish species. *ICES Journal of Marine Science* 72:82–92.

Thurstan, R. H. 2022. The potential of Historical ecology to aid understanding of human–ocean interactions throughout the Anthropocene. *Journal of Fish Biology* 101 (2): 351–364. https://doi.org/10.1111/jfb.15000.

Thurstan, R. H., L. McClenachan, L. B. Crowder, J. A. Drew, J. N. Kittinger, et al. 2015. Filling historical data gaps to foster solutions in marine conservation. *Ocean & Coastal Management* 115:31–40.

Thurstan, R. H., A. B. Campbell, and J. M. Pandolfi. 2018. Nineteenth century narratives reveal historic catch rates for Australian snapper (*Pagrus auratus*). *Fish and Fisheries* 19:1–21.

Thurstan, R. H., Hannah McCormick, Joanne Preston, Elizabeth C. Ashton, Floris P. Bennema, et al. 2024. Records reveal the vast historical extent of European oyster reef ecosystems. *Nature Sustainability* 7 (12): 1719–1729.

Systems of a Down: A New Way to Define and Understand Societal Collapse

Luke Kemp

Abstract Societal collapse has always lacked a clear definition and is now often being replaced by critics with less-confronting alternatives such as 'resilience', fragility', and 'transformation', or shrouded in the idea of societal 'complexity'. None of these are convincing or reasonable alternatives to collapse. Resilience is even more vague than collapse, not a positive characteristic, and simply focuses on different aspects of historical case studies (such as the continuation of culture and local communities). Fragility has never been defined by those who use it and appears to be just a poor way of saying 'societies that are more predisposed to collapse'. Transformation is too broad to be either helpful or coherent. Complexity is ambiguous, nonsensical (hierarchies often simplify social relations), and smuggles in old, outdated notions of progress. If scholars don't like the apocalyptic depictions of collapse, then we just need better analysis and a better definition. Defining collapse as a rapid, severe, and lasting contraction and fragmentation of power structures is precise, reasonable, and reframes collapse as a process with costs and benefits, winners and losers, rather than as an ancient apocalypse. This new definition also helps us make better sense of the impacts of collapse and why they occur.

Keywords Collapse • Transformation • Resilience • Sustainability • Fragility

1 Introduction

Societal collapse is a commonly used term without a common definition. There has been a ferocious public debate over whether particular cases were collapses, whether collapse is the appropriate term, and whether historical collapses were a good or bad thing (Middleton 2017a, b; Robinson 2018; Haldon et al. 2020). One of the most common ways this scholarly conflict unfolds is by historians and archaeologists recasting a canonical collapse case study as an example of resilience, fragility, or

L. Kemp (✉)
Cambridge University, Cambridge, UK

J. F. Haldon, R. Fernandes (eds.), *Bridging History and Policy*, Understanding Complex Systems, https://doi.org/10.1007/978-3-032-24379-9_11

transformation (Middleton 2017a, b; Yoffee 2019; McAnany and Yoffee 2009). Collapse is in many ways, a passé term academically and a popular term publicly.

We are in dire need of a clearer definition and understanding of societal collapse. That is for a few reasons. First, collapse is now a legitimate sub-field of study. Second, it is an idea which is studied not just in archaeology but also in forward-looking and often more policy-influential disciplines, such as the study of systemic risk and existential risk. For instance, most definitions of existential risk usually incorporate some notion of global societal collapse (Rees 2004; Bostrom 2013; Ord 2020; MacAskill 2022; Kemp 2025).

In this article, I'll address why the alternative terms and framings for collapse—resilience, fragility, transformation, and complexity—are ultimately inadequate and why we still need the term collapse, put forward a new definition and framework, and demonstrate how this can help us to better understand collapse.

2 There Are No Innocent Terms

Several terms have been offered as alternatives to collapse. The most commonly used are 'resilience', 'fragility', and 'transformation'. Collapse is also often framed as a loss of 'complexity'. Unfortunately, none of these terms are useful or even logical as alternatives to collapse.

Resilience

One way to critique the idea of collapse is to instead reframe case studies as examples of resilience. For instance, the most prominent critique of Jared Diamond's bestselling '*Collapse: How Societies Choose to Succeed and Fail*' was an edited volume titled '*Questioning Collapse: Human Resilience, Ecological Vulnerability, and the Aftermath of Empire*' (McAnany and Yoffee 2009). In it, Diamond's key case studies—such as the collapse of the Lowland Classic Maya and the Rwandan Genocide—are depicted as cases of societal resilience, not collapse. There are, for example six million native Maya speakers living today, and when Spanish invaders arrived in the sixteenth century the Maya still lived in cities, still wrote in their glyphic script, and even traded in markets using currency.

While resilience may appear to be a more neutral and positive term than collapse, it carries its own problems. First, it's just as ambiguous as collapse, if not more so. Resilience has several different definitions including the ability for a system to maintain its essential functions, or identity, despite adverse perturbations (Grafton et al. 2019; Kemp and Cline 2021). These then bring up difficult questions of what constitutes the essential functions or (even trickier) the identity of a system.

Second, in most cases, scholars aren't using it as a replacement. They are simply using it to highlight a different aspect of a case study. The Maya people and much of their culture may have showed resilience, yet it's hard to say the social order or polities of the Lowland did. They were, by and large, destroyed. Most cases are examples of both resilience and collapse, depending on what we focus on. Simply using resilience rather than collapse doesn't help show this, it just provides a different analytical spin.

Third, resilience is not a positive term. It is often used as a rosier alternative, one that better meshes with concerns around sustainability and longevity, yet that is something of a misuse. It is morally neutral. It's a property of how systems can behave. Cancer is one of the most resilient entities in the universe, yet it is hard to label its resilience as a good thing. Similarly, the resilience of past empires and even cultures aren't necessarily for the better. The Neo-Assyrian approach of resilience through conquering others in the wake of the Late Bronze Age was not a benevolent policy (Kemp and Cline 2021). Similarly, we should be glad that the Third Reich didn't show greater societal resilience. Reframing past cases as examples of resilience can be useful, but it's not a replacement for the frame of collapse, nor even more accurate or illuminating.

Scholars of resilience are right that collapses rarely see the complete end of a people, culture, and social order. There are important continuities and elements which survive and even prosper (Yoffee and Cowgill 1991). That is no longer a point of debate. Yet, simply shifting entirely to what continued and why, obscures the important conversation to be had about what ended, what was damaged or destroyed, and why.

Fragility

One far less used, but seeming alternative to collapse is the idea of 'fragility', most notably in the edited volume '*The Evolution of Fragility: Setting the Terms*' (Yoffee 2019). Unfortunately, neither the editor nor any of the contributors to the volume ever define what fragility is. Fragility in its most common-sensical definition is simply how prone an object or entity is to being damaged or broken. In disaster-risk studies, it is essentially interchangeable with the idea of 'vulnerability'. Vulnerability or fragility are one determinant of what constitutes a risk (the likelihood of an adverse outcome), with the other factors being hazards (the force causing damage), exposure (to hazards or vulnerabilities), and response (reactions to the overall risk) (IPCC 2020; Simpson et al. 2021). In other words, fragility is just one factor which leads to collapse: it is a way of saying a society is more likely to collapse, not a substitute for the term collapse. Replacing collapse with fragility doesn't make any sense and just creates conceptual confusion.

Transformation

Another proposed alternative for collapse is the more neutral and anodyne term of 'transformation'. Through this lens, collapse is simply a large-scale transformation with long-term impacts on the environment, ideology, political structure, demographics and settlements, and other economic and social patterns (Middleton 2017a, b). Others see it as a shift in the political, social, and cultural boundaries of a group (Eisenstadt 1991). Such a definition is certainly broad enough to capture most case studies of collapse and avoid any strong moral or normative claims about collapse being bad or good.

The problem is that transformation is far too broad and ambiguous to be useful. Large-scale changes with lasting impacts on environment, society, and culture could encompass the creation of states, the intensification of agriculture, colonization, the industrial revolution, the post world-war II 'Great Acceleration' (Steffen et al. 2015), the advent of the internet, and the deregulation and globalization of finance and trade throughout the 1980s and 1990s. Lumping state failures and imperial falls with globalization and the internet doesn't seem intuitive or helpful, probably because it isn't. Similarly, a shift in the social, cultural, or political boundaries of a group could include any minor conquest, change in regime, or changes to religion. One could easily make the case that the Roman Empire was transforming every year from 509 BCE to 1453 CE. While technically true, it's a banal observation and not a remotely useful insight for understanding crisis and collapse.

Complexity (and Simplification)

Collapse is often defined as a sudden and enduring loss of societal complexity. This is the definition of collapse in the two most well-known canonical texts: Joseph Tainter's 1986 '*The Collapse of Complex Societies*' (Tainter 1990) and Jared Diamond's 1997 '*Collapse*' (Diamond 2011). It is perhaps the most enduring and commonly used definition in a highly contested field. The most popular collapse-focused podcast is titled '*The Great Simplification*' (Hagens 2020, 2025) and even skeptics of the term collapse, have highlighted complexity as the most useful and reasonable lens to understand collapse through (Middleton 2024).

There are a few problems with using complexity as the basis for a definition of collapse. The first is that it is ambiguous. Definitions of complexity have varied from "the size of a society, the number and distinctiveness of its parts, the variety of specialized social roles that it incorporates, the number of distinct social personalities present, and the variety of mechanisms for organizing these into a coherent, functioning whole" (Tainter 1990) to "the development of hierarchical (and/or heterarchical) social, economic, and political structures that manifest themselves materially in a number of ways stemming from control over labour and produce beyond the immediate family" (Hayden 2014). In other words, it ranges from occupational and organizational diversity through to social hierarchies which control labour.

Similarly, scholars trying to measure how complexity leads to collapse have used a wide array of proxies including the size of Roman armies (Roman and Palmer 2019), the coinage in the Roman economy (Tainter 2014), the yields of Roman fields (Homer-Dixon 2008), the population of the Rapa Nui and resources used by them (Roman et al. 2017), the number of monuments built by the Classic Lowland Maya (Roman et al. 2018), the public works of Cahokia (Tainter 2019) and the Puebloan communities (Tainter 1990), the number of patents per dollar spent on research and development (Tainter 2006), and even the energy return on investment for past resources and current fossil fuels (Bardi et al. 2019). Tainter himself has varied between referring to the size and extent of the Byzantine bureaucracy and government system through to modern global energy use (Tainter 1990, 2011). It's unclear why we expect all of these to be good, interchangeable indicators of complexity and collapse. Indeed, some of them don't even have a clear relationship to hierarchy or the variety of jobs a society has. At worst, such a broad definition encourages cherry-picking: choose whichever metric can be classified at a proxy for complexity and which best suits your conclusions.

The second is that it doesn't quite make sense. Archaeological definitions of complexity revolve around hierarchy and centralization, despite these two often simplifying social relations and decision-making. Few people would claim that a strict military chain-of-command in the Assyrian Empire is more complex than debates in an Athenian Assembly. On the contrary, the main reason that hierarchy is preferred is because it is supposed to be simpler and more efficient. Similarly, bureaucracies and administrations are by and large structures which simplify (Yoffee 2001), just as writing and scripts are simplistic abstractions of a far more complex and fluid language. It's a basic insight from James C. Scott: states attempt to simplify the world, for both aesthetic purposes and for control, whether that be for taxation or conscription (Scott 2008). This definition of the typical definition of societal complexity unjustifiably and implicitly sweeps away most of what makes up a society: the diversity and sophistication of the languages, norms, customs, diets, architecture, and environment. It is a little odd to ignore all of these aspects without explanation, especially when they are often being actively simplified during imperial formation, and often become more complex during periods of collapse (Kemp 2024, 2025).

Last, but not least, it's hard not to see old prejudices seeping into the language of complexity. Societal complexity is, in many ways, a continuation of the old stepladders of progress championed by evolutionary thinkers of the nineteenth century such as Henry Lewis Morgan (1818–1881), Herbert Spencer (1820–1903), and Sir John Lubbock (1834–1913). Spencer in his 1875 essay *Progress: Its Law and Cause* contends that all progress can be seen as an advance from sameness towards greater differentiation (Spencer 1875). To Spencer, complexity was inexorably growing in all areas of life whether it be customs, language, religion, or government. The divisions of labour and class that were growing during his time were just the latest manifestation of a longer trend of increasing complexity. Morgan put forward the idea that this wasn't just an increase in complexity, but it was a progression across distinct steps from savagery to barbarism to civilization (Morgan 2000). These thinkers were the pioneers of 'societal evolutionism'.

Eventually, the stepladders of progress fell out of favour. During the 1960s and 70s amid the peak of the civil rights movements scholars understandably wanted to avoid the racist connotations and unsavoury baggage associated with Spencer, Morgan, and Lubbock. They also came under the attack of anthropologists like Franz Boas who rejected the idea that societies moved smoothly between stages or could be ranked in terms of inferiority and superiority, or sometimes even compared at all. These debates led to a lasting division between archaeologists and anthropologists (Morris 2011).

Societal evolutionism slowly transformed into the far more nuanced 'neo-evolutionism'. The rungs of the stepladders of progress became instead a series of revolutions and a set of categories including bands, tribes, chiefdoms, and states (Yoffee 1993). The more innocuous idea of complexity was never dropped and stayed consistent from societal evolutionism through to neo-evolutionism. That is despite the fact that the stepladders of progress were always deeply intertwined with the idea of complexity. Groups moving up the stepladder were not just being more culturally advanced, but also more 'complex'. And the way complexity is used today is still largely the same. Societies that rely more on agriculture, have more hierarchy, and are more urban, are considered more 'complex'. And the world of modern, industralised, high-income countries is of course the pinnacle of complexity thus far. This is still essentially the same old idea of the stepladder of progress, just with more anodyne wording and a more flexible framework (a spectrum rather than a stepladder).

It still does carry old prejudices. Calling one group 'simpler' or 'less complex' than another has clear connotations of ignorance and 'backwardness'. It's difficult to escape the history and moral implications attached to the idea of societal complexity, and it is not worthwhile trying to salvage it given its vagueness and sheer lack of sense.

Each of these concepts—resilience, fragility, transformation, and complexity—have their uses, but none are either replacements for the term collapse or even particularly useful in clarifying its meaning.

To be frank, this new terminology was likely never offered because it is more precise or suitable. It is because many archaeologists and historians are annoyed by the apocalyptic connotations and depictions of collapse. Which is fine, but rather than trying to use analytically worse terms, a better approach is to simply create a more balanced and sensible definition of collapse. One which doesn't paint historical collapses as doomsday scenarios, but rather as a process with costs and benefits, and winners and losers.

3 Refining Collapse

Currently there are multiple competing definitions of collapse. Most can be grouped into a few key rough clusters:

- *Checklists*: several prominent definitions of collapse are essentially a checklist of indicators that characterise collapse. One of the earliest and most well-known is from the Cambridge archaeologist Colin Renfrew who saw collapse as the loss of the central administration, economy, state, and elite, and a population decline and settlement shift (Renfrew 1979). While useful, a checklist isn't quite the same thing as a definition per se, and some cases only meet some of the criteria.
- *Complexity*: as covered earlier, the canonical definitions of Joseph Tainter and Jared Diamond revolve around collapse being a significant and enduring reduction in pre-established levels of societal complexity. And as already mentioned, complexity is too ambiguous, non-sensical, and biased to be the basis for a decent definition.

- *Systems Identity*: Some definitions have tried to create a shared framework around collapse and resilience by focusing on systems identity. Two ecologists have suggested that collapse is a process that involves the loss of a systems identity and that loss of identity must be quick, involve a substantial loss of socio-ecological capital (such as population and settlements), and it must be enduring (Cumming and Peterson 2017). It's an admirable attempt to pair together collapse and resilience, however what constitutes 'systems identity' is deeply unclear and many cases of collapse actually see a growth and repair of ecological capital. The regrowth of forests across South and Central America after colonisation may have been so immense that it temporarily affected and cooled the climate (Koch et al. 2019).
- *Forward-Looking*: Several definitions of collapse focus on the future. In these views collapse is the sudden theft of any virtues that the modern, globalised world offers, such as a loss of writing, the rule of law, and the ability to create industrial or post-industrial technology (Ord 2020; MacAskill 2022). The fathers of the popular French collapsology movement (well, popular at least in France), Pablo Servigne and Raphaël Stevens, see it as a loss of the services provided by the state (Servigne and Stevens 2020). These are more reminiscent of post-apocalyptic films like '*The Road*' and '*Mad Max*' then historical examples, the definitions can't be applied to the past, and they are unnecessarily narrow by looking only at the good things provided by modern welfare states and global industrial infrastructure.
- *State Failure*: State failure is the closest modern phenomena we have to ancient societal collapses. Unfortunately, there is a similar lack of clear, shared definitions in the state failure literature (for an overview see Rotberg 2003). The best attempt to create a clear, operational definition looked at measurements of a state's ability to extract resources (a working taxation system), create laws (functioning courts and a working parliament), and maintain something resembling a monopoly on the legitimate use of force. The study found that over the period 1946–2014 only five cases met three of these criteria, five met two, and two fulfilled just one. Out of all these cases none lasted longer than 6 months (Lambach et al. 2015). It's an admirable step forward to craft and apply a precise, operational definition. However, it is unclear how well this definition can be applied to past case studies. Many early states had barely functioning resource extraction systems (many, such as the Akkadian Empire, relied on a loose system of conquest and tribute), had weak bureaucracies and little-to-no functioning judiciary, and maintained nothing close to a monopoly on violence. Just as importantly, the fall of the state is just one part of societal collapses, but it also often involves the breakdown of the economy, ideology, and large shifts in population.

None of the existing types of definitions—checklists, complexity, systems identity, forward-looking, or state failure—are fit for purpose and can flexibly cover both modern and ancient case studies. A more reasonable and effective definition would be one that concentrates on what each of these definitions ignore: power.

Societies are partly composed of different power networks. Mann originally referred to these key forms of power as economic, political, military, and ideological power (Mann 1986). Or, if we are to think more broadly we could say economic power (control over resources), political power (control of decision-making), violent power (control of violence and lethal force, including beyond the military), information power (control of information, whether it be ideology, administration, or modern digital data), and the great amplifier of power in demography (the size and health of the population) (Kemp 2025). Most societies that are studied in collapse have states or hierarchies (political power), bureaucracies and churches (information power), elites (economic power), and militaries (violent power). Societal collapse then is simply a rapid, severe, and lasting fragmentation and contraction of all or most of these power networks. When the state falls apart, we call it state failure or state collapse. When the economy breaks down, we call it a bust or economic collapse. When all or most power systems crumble together we call it a societal collapse (Kemp 2025).

Such a definition meshes with most of the pre-existing definitions of collapse. Renfrew's definition involves the loss of a centralized administration and state (political and information power), elite (economic power), and population decline and settlement shift (population). Complexity is mainly concerned with inequality, hierarchy, and centralization, all of which are reflections of power structures (as too are information and economic networks for coordinating or even controlling goods and people). The identity of the system can be boiled down to its power networks. Forward-looking definitions are worried about how the unravelling of global power structures—whether it be global financial networks, food systems, or geopolitical stability—could cause great damage. State failure is essentially just a precise and measurable way of assessing the collapse of the main political power structure: the state. Such a power-based definition is more precise than complexity or systems identity definitions, doesn't have the same normative connotations as resilience or complexity, and, like definitions of state failure, can be more precisely operationalized. Importantly, this power definition can also help us make better sense of how collapse unfolds.

4 The Impacts

While there is significant variation in the outcomes of collapse, there are some general commonalities across case studies. The most regular outcomes are depopulation (due to mortality or migration), increased violence, and the leveling of wealth inequality. When viewed through the lens of power, it becomes apparent why such impacts occur.

Mortality and Migration
The most catching and chilling indicator of collapse is a higher body count. People fear collapse because it presumably means death and destruction. Some of the

highest estimates do suggest that collapse can be catastrophic. Estimate for population loss during the Late Bronze Age, for example, range up to 30–75%, and for the invasion of the Americas up to 90% of the population may have been lost (Koch et al. 2019; Kemp 2025)

The numbers here are, of course, highly uncertain. Often, especially in more ancient case studies, the best estimates are based on Summed Probability Distributions (SPDs) of radiocarbon dates (Downey et al. 2016). In short, look at all of the dates we have for human occupation (such as pottery remains) in an area (using the amount of carbon-14 in organic matter to estimate the age of an artefact) and create a probability estimate of how many people were there. In cases with even less evidence archaeologists often must rely on other sources such as the level of food production or genetic data to reconstruct populations sizes and estimate if there is a population 'bottleneck': a sharp contraction of the human population inferred by a loss of genetic diversity. A combination of these approaches have been used to overturn the idea that there was a population collapse among the Rapa Nui prior to European contact (DiNapoli et al. 2021; Moreno-Mayar et al. 2024).

In more modern cases we can rely on other proxies, including coinage and written records (such as census documents). Often the most reliable approach is not to take any single measure, but to look across them. Recently, researchers have suggested that the Plague of Justinian may not have been a mass fatality event since there are few indicators in terms of buried coins, written accounts, or mass burials (Mordechai and Eisenberg 2019) (although this is contested).

Unfortunately, none of these methods are particularly reliable. A reduction in human settlements, pottery shards, and written records doesn't necessarily mean that everyone in the area died. They could have simply moved, often to areas which are less excavated by archaeologists (such as more remote, rural locations) and adopted less archaeologically visible lifestyles (living on farms rather than in cities replete with monuments).

Even where there are census records, such as for Imperial Rome and the Han Dynasty, estimating population is tricky. Our estimates of population data just for the peak of the Roman Empire can vary by around 17 million (from around 59 to 76 million). Then there is the problem that population drops in census data during a crisis may not indicate actual losses of life. People could have simply moved, or the state may simply lack the resources to survey as many people. Censuses are rarely a top priority during a period of civil war (Goldstone and Haldon 2009). This can lead to some enormous changes in population loss estimates. Stephen Pinker's estimate in the *Better Angels of our Nature* guessed that the death toll of the An Lushan Rebellion was 36 million, but this was later cut down to 13 million due to problems with census data.

There are good reasons to expect that most of the population loss we see during collapse is people moving rather than people dying. Even today during civil wars, twenty times as many people (or more) tend to move rather than die during states failures and civil strife. Around 186,901–210,296 people were killed during the Iraq war, while up to 3.4 million were displaced. Up to 620,000 people may have died in the Syrian Civil War, while around 14 million were displaced. Logically, people tend to move rather than face premature death, and we have no reason to believe that the past was dramatically different.

Why do people move? Economic opportunities is one key reason. A collapsing economy and insecure environment are not particularly good for reliable employment. That's why people leave rust-belt cities and similarly why many people left Rome after the provision of free-grain (the *Cura Annonae*) was eliminated. Another is simply safety. People often flee for safety as violence and conflict intensifies during a collapse. Both surging violence and an undermined economy are both outcomes of failing power structures.

Increased Violence

A recurring thread across collapses is that violence increases. Violence is intimately entwined with the idea of collapse, which is why future preppers tend to stockpile not just canned food, but also guns and ammo.

Violence is, undisputably, something which tends to rise during periods of crisis and collapse. For instance, around three-quarters of the cases of the crisis database involve civil war. Sometimes, like in the case of Teotihuacan, it is unclear whether this is due to an internal revolt, a coup or civil war between rival elite factions, or even outside invaders (Middleton 2017a, b). In some ways, it doesn't matter: all of these involve a rapid surge in lethal violence, and, in in the case of Teotihuacan, all of them meant a targeting of violence towards elites and their monuments. In some cases, such as the fall of the Wari, we have evidence of a significant and lasting rise in bloodshed. After the collapse, many skeletons begin to show signs of cannibalism, with indications that knives were cleaved close to the bone, to separate the meat cleanly from the skeleton (Arkush and Tung 2013).

There are several important reasons to be careful about the relationship between violence and collapse. First, there is enormous variation in how bloody different collapses were. The collapse of the Wari was ghastly, but the abandonment of Cahokia and Moundville seem to be relatively bloodless. Second, like population loss, our estimates of increased violence are often unreliable, particularly for more ancient case studies. We're often relying on an uncertain estimate of the population and then looking at the number of skeletons with signs of violent death, such as embedded projectiles, parry fractures, and cranial trauma, or the number of bodies found in sites that appear to have been razed. It's better than nothing, but not a precise art. Embedded arrowheads and broken skulls can be due to accidents, and we often have little indication as to whether they were caused in a coup, rebellion, or invasion. In other words, it can often be uncertain who was causing the violence and just how many people died.

That said, there are some general trends we can point to despite the uncertain data. One is that the violence of collapse is not usually caused by a broad cross-section of society. It is a Hobbesian assumption that collapse often means a panicked scramble for resources with much of the populace turning on each other. There's no evidence that this is the case. Instead, it is a small cross-section of society: usually fighting-aged men previously employed as mercenaries or soldiers. Whether it be in Rome during the Third Century Crisis, the 1994 Rwandan Genocide, or the Iraq War, violence is the profession of a small amount of the population. Rwanda court documents reveal that around 3% of the population was involved with violently enacting the genocide. They had a median age of 31 and 90% of them were male (Nyseth Nzitatira et al. 2023). Similarly, studies of natural disasters suggest that more constitutional emergency provisions for the executive, like martial law, results in higher fatalities (even when controlling for the size of the disaster) (Bjørnskov and Voigt 2020). The likely reason is that while people tend to respond to earthquakes and hurricanes well, elites are more likely to use it as an opportunity for a power grab (Bjørnskov and Voigt 2020), and soldiers and police are far more likely to unnecessarily resort to force, as occurred in the Great Earthquake of San Francisco (Solnit 2009).

Perhaps the best way of thinking about the violence of collapse is that it is the violence of state formation: a power vacuum opens, and a small group of armed men attempt to create a new state. It's a plausible hypothesis, especially given that the increases in violence seen during the creation of the first states, and later during the formation of iron age empires, is similar to the spike of violence which occurred during the late bronze age (based on a large-scale skeletal analysis from 12,000 to 400 BCE) (Baten et al. 2023). Again, the underlying factor here is that the fragmentation and contraction of power structures (in this case political and violent) creates an opportunity to create new hierarchies. The violence of collapse is a power struggle.

Wealth Levelling

Perhaps the most pervasive indicator of collapse is not a particularly nefarious one: the levelling of wealth disparities (Scheidel 2017). The fall of the Mycenae, the collapse of the Classical Lowland Maya (Strawinska-Zanko et al. 2018), and the collapse of Chinese Dynasties from the Qin to the Song (Wu et al. 2025), were all marked by wealth inequality growing beforehand, followed by that inequality dropping steeply during the collapse. Indeed, it may be one of the best ways to distinguish a genuine collapse from a crisis: was there a lasting contraction of wealth inequality. In the case of the Soviet Union there was not (and notably most elites maintained their place, despite the communist ideology thoroughly collapsing), in the case of Tiwanaku there was.

This is not to say that crisis or societal upheaval always levels wealth differentials. Civil wars, states crises, coups, and even severe pandemics such as the recurrent bouts of the Black Death in the fourteenth century CE all have the ability to worsen wealth inequality when extractive institutions capitalize on them (van Bavel and Scheffer 2021). Some have branded this trend of disasters worsening inequality and extractive institutions as 'the Shock Doctrine' (Klein 2008). Wealth levelling appears to only occur when there is a deep and lasting collapse of the state and other power hierarchies.

The reason for wealth levelling occurring during a deep collapse is intuitive: collapse destroys large amounts of capital and more importantly, the institutions of power which create and reinforce wealth inequalities. Economic elites rely on the coercive power of the state to operate, whether it be through courts and militaries upholding contracts, or the British navy directly intervening to protect the monopoly of the British East India Company. States in the case of autocracy are also often the site of huge accumulations of wealth and power. Unsurprisingly once the state collapses both public and private elites tend to lose capital, and the deeper the collapse, the deeper the leveling of inequality.

Collapse has positive and negative effects: increased mortality, displacement, and violence are all lamentable, while the levelling of wealth inequalities is usually a good thing. What unites them all is that they are obvious outcomes of power structures fragmenting and contracting.

5 Conclusion: It's About Power

Collapse is a growing sub-field but there is a lack of shared understanding of what collapse is and how the different impacts are related. That is a problem. Unfortunately, none of the offered alternative terminology is of much use. Resilience is ambiguous, not as positive as many seem to think it is, and simply re-focuses attention away from collapsing polities towards continuous culture and populations. Fragility is just another way of saying that a society is more vulnerable and likely to collapse. Transformation is impressively vague and not remotely helpful. 'Societal complexity' carries unsavoury baggage from the nineteenth century, is unclear, and ultimately non-sensical. We need to admit that scholars are ultimately just uncomfortable with the current apocalyptic depictions of collapse and instead try to craft better definitions.

Collapse as a rapid, severe, and enduring contraction and fragmentation of power structures (economic, political, violent, information, and population power) is a better more value-neutral way of conceiving of collapse. It is one that encompasses most of the previous definitions, doesn't have any unnecessary moral connotations or baggage, and rightfully recognises collapse as a process with costs and benefits, winners and losers. It is also a definition which helps us to better understand why people die, fight, move, and become more equal during times of collapse. It is a predictable outcome of power structures falling apart and the battle to rebuild them.

References

Arkush, E., and T. A. Tung. 2013. Patterns of war in the Andes from the Archaic to the Late Horizon: insights from settlement patterns and cranial trauma. *Journal of Archaeological Research* 21 (4): 307–369. https://doi.org/10.1007/s10814-013-9065-1.

Bardi, U., S. Falsini, and I. Perissi. 2019. Toward a general theory of societal collapse: a biophysical examination of Tainter's model of the diminishing returns of complexity. *BioPhysical Economics and Resource Quality* 4 (1): 3. https://doi.org/10.1007/s41247-018-0049-0.

Baten, J., G. Benati, and A. Sołtysiak. 2023. Violence trends in the ancient Middle East between 12,000 and 400 BCE. *Nature Human Behaviour* 7:2064–2073. https://doi.org/10.1038/s41562-023-01700-y.

Bjørnskov, C., and S. Voigt. 2020. You don't always get what you'd expect—on some unexpected effects of constitutional emergency provisions. *SSRN Electronic Journal [Preprint]*. https://doi.org/10.2139/ssrn.3189749.

Bostrom, N. 2013. Existential risk prevention as global priority. *Global Policy* 4 (1): 15–31. https://doi.org/10.1111/1758-5899.12002.

Cumming, G. S., and G. D. Peterson. 2017. Unifying research on social–ecological resilience and collapse. *Trends in Ecology & Evolution* 32 (9): 695–713. https://doi.org/10.1016/j.tree.2017.06.014.

Diamond, J. 2011. *Collapse: How Societies Choose to Succeed or Fail*. New York: Penguin Books.

DiNapoli, R. J., et al. 2021. Approximate Bayesian computation of radiocarbon and paleoenvironmental record shows population resilience on Rapa Nui (Easter Island). *Nature Communications* 12 (1): 3939. https://doi.org/10.1038/s41467-021-24252-z.

Downey, S. S., W. R. Haas, and S. J. Shennan. 2016. European Neolithic societies showed early warning signals of population collapse. *Proceedings of the National Academy of Sciences* 113 (35): 9751–9756. https://doi.org/10.1073/pnas.1602504113.

Eisenstadt, S. N. 1991. Beyond collapse. In *The Collapse of Ancient States and Civilizations*, ed. N. Yoffee and G. L. Cowgill, 236–243. Tucson: The University of Arizona press.

Goldstone, J. A., and J. F. Haldon. 2009. Ancient states, empires, and exploitation: Problems and perspectives. In *The Dynamics of Ancient Empires*, ed. I. Morris and W. Scheidel, 3–29. New York: Oxford University Press. https://doi.org/10.1093/oso/9780195371581.003.0001.

Grafton, R. Q., et al. 2019. Realizing resilience for decision-making. *Nature Sustainability* 2 (10): 907–913. https://doi.org/10.1038/s41893-019-0376-1.

Hagens, N. J. 2020. Economics for the future—beyond the superorganism. *Ecological Economics* 169:106520. https://doi.org/10.1016/j.ecolecon.2019.106520.

Hagens, N. 2025. *The Great Simplification*. https://www.thegreatsimplification.com/

Haldon, J., et al. 2020. Demystifying collapse: climate, environment, and social agency in pre-modern societies. *Millennium* 17 (1): 1–33. https://doi.org/10.1515/mill-2020-0002.

Hayden, B. 2014. *Social Complexity*. Oxford: Oxford University Press. https://doi.org/10.1093/oxfordhb/9780199551224.013.047.

Homer-Dixon, T. 2008. *The Upside of Down: Catastrophe, Creativity, and the Renewal of Civilization*. Washington, DC: Island Press.

IPCC, Reisinger, A., M. Howden, C. Vera, et al. 2020. *The Concept of Risk in the IPCC Sixth Assessment Report: A Summary of Cross-Working Group Discussions*, 1–15. Geneva: Intergovernmental Panel on Climate change. https://www.ipcc.ch/site/assets/uploads/2021/02/Risk-guidance-FINAL_15Feb2021.pdf

Kemp, L. 2024. Diminishing returns on extraction: how inequality and extractive hierarchy create fragility. In *How Worlds Collapse. What History, Systems, and Complexity Can Teach Us About Our Modern World and Fragile Future*, ed. M. Centeno, P. W. Callahan, P. A. Larcey, and T. S. Patterson, 37–60. New York: Routledge.

Kemp, L. 2025. *Goliath's Curse: The History and Future of Societal Collapse*. London: Penguin Random House.

Kemp, L., and E. Cline. 2021. Systemic risk and resilience: the Bronze Age collapse and recovery. In *Perspectives on Public Policy in Societal-Environmental Crises. Risk, Systems and Decisions*, ed. A. Izdebski, J. Haldon, and P. Filipkowski, 207–223. Cham: Springer. https://doi.org/10.1007/978-3-030-94137-6_14.

Klein, N. 2008. *The Shock Doctrine: The Rise of Disaster Capitalism*. New York: Picador.

Koch, A., et al. 2019. Earth System Impacts of the European Arrival and Great Dying in the Americas After 1492. *Quaternary Science Reviews* 207:13–36. https://doi.org/10.1016/j.quascirev.2018.12.004.

Lambach, D., E. Johais, and M. Bayer. 2015. Conceptualising state collapse: an institutionalist approach. *Third World Quarterly* 36 (7): 1299–1315. https://doi.org/10.1080/01436597.2015.1038338.

MacAskill, W. 2022. *What We Owe the Future*. London: Basic Books.

Mann, M. 1986. *The Sources of Social Power I: A History of Power from the Beginning to AD 1760*. Cambridge: Cambridge University Press.

McAnany, P., and N. Yoffee, eds. 2009. *Questioning Collapse: Human Resilience, Ecological Vulnerability, and the Aftermath of Empire*. Cambridge: Cambridge University Press.

Middleton, G. D. 2017a. *Understanding Collapse: Ancient History and Modern Myths*. Cambridge: Cambridge University Press.

Middleton, G. D. 2017b. The show must go on: collapse, resilience, and transformation in 21st-century archaeology. *Reviews in Anthropology* 46 (2–3): 78–105. https://doi.org/10.1080/00938157.2017.1343025.

Middleton, G. D. 2024. Collapse studies in archaeology from 2012 to 2023. *Journal of Archaeological Research* 33:57–115. https://doi.org/10.1007/s10814-024-09196-4.

Mordechai, L., and M. Eisenberg. 2019. The Justinianic Plague: an inconsequential pandemic? *Proceedings of the National Academy of Sciences* 116 (51): 25546–25554. https://doi.org/10.1073/pnas.1903797116.

Moreno-Mayar, J. V., et al. 2024. Ancient Rapanui genomes reveal resilience and pre-European contact with the Americas. *Nature* 633 (8029): 389–397. https://doi.org/10.1038/s41586-024-07881-4.

Morgan, L.H. 2000. *Ancient Societies*. 2nd edn., L.A. White. Cambridge MA: Belknap Press.

Morris, I. 2011. *Why the West Rules—For Now: The Patterns of History and What They Reveal About the Future*. London: Profile Books.

Nyseth Nzitatira, H., J. F. Edgerton, and L. C. Frizzell. 2023. Analyzing participation in the 1994 genocide in Rwanda. *Journal of Peace Research* 60 (2): 291–306. https://doi.org/10.1177/00223433221075211.

Ord, T. 2020. *The Precipice: Existential Risk and the Future of Humanity*. London: Hatchette Books.

Rees, M. J. 2004. *Our Final Century: Will Civilisation Survive the Twenty-First Century?* London: Arrow.

Renfrew, C. 1979. Systems collapse as social transformation: catastrophe and anastrophe in early state societies. In *Transformations. Mathematical Approaches to Culture Change*, ed. C. Renfrew and K. L. Cooke, 481–506. New York: Academic Press. https://doi.org/10.1016/B978-0-12-586050-5.50035-X.

Robinson, M. 2018. Geologists are feuding about the collapse of civilization. *The Atlantic*. https://www.theatlantic.com/science/archive/2018/09/the-geologist-mega-drama-about-an-ancient-mega-drought/570508/

Roman, S., and E. Palmer. 2019. The growth and decline of the Western Roman Empire: quantifying the dynamics of army size, territory, and coinage. *Cliodynamics: The Journal of Quantitative History and Cultural Evolution* 10 (2): 76–98. https://doi.org/10.21237/c7clio10243683.

Roman, S., S. Bullock, and M. Brede. 2017. Coupled societies are more robust against collapse: a hypothetical look at Easter Island. *Ecological Economics* 132:264–278. https://doi.org/10.1016/j.ecolecon.2016.11.003.

Roman, S., E. Palmer, and M. Brede. 2018. The dynamics of human–environment interactions in the collapse of the Classic Maya. *Ecological Economics* 146:312–324. https://doi.org/10.1016/j.ecolecon.2017.11.007.

Rotberg, R. I. 2003. Failed states, collapsed states, weak states: causes and indicators. In *State Failure and State Weakness in a Time of Terror*, ed. R. I. Rotberg, 1–25. Washington, DC: Brookings Institution Press.

Scheidel, W. 2017. *The Great Leveler: Violence and the History of Inequality from the Stone Age to the Twenty-First Century*. Princeton: Princeton University Press.

Scott, J. C. 2008. *Seeing Like a State: How Certain Schemes to Improve the Human Condition Have Failed*. New Haven: Yale University Press.

Servigne, P., and R. Stevens. 2020. *How Everything Can Collapse: A Manual for Our Times*, Translated by A. Brown. Medford: Polity.

Simpson, N. P., et al. 2021. A framework for complex climate change risk assessment. *One Earth* 4 (4): 489–501. https://doi.org/10.1016/j.oneear.2021.03.005.

Solnit, R. 2009. *A Paradise Built in Hell: The Extraordinary Communities That Arise in Disasters*. New York: Viking.
Spencer, H. 1875. Progress: its law and cause. In *Illustrations of Universal Progress: A Series of Discussions*, ed. H. Spencer, 1–60. New York: D. Appleton. https://doi.org/10.1037/12203-001.
Steffen, W., et al. 2015. The trajectory of the Anthropocene: the Great Acceleration. *The Anthropocene Review* 2 (1): 81–98. https://doi.org/10.1177/2053019614564785.
Strawinska-Zanko, U., et al. 2018. Capital in the first century: the evolution of inequality in ancient Maya society. In *Mathematical Modeling of Social Relationships*, ed. U. Strawinska-Zanko and L. S. Liebovitch, 161–192. Cham: Springer. https://doi.org/10.1007/978-3-319-76765-9_9.
Tainter, J. A. 1990. *The Collapse of Complex Societies*. Cambridge: Cambridge University Press.
Tainter, J. A. 2006. Social complexity and sustainability. *Ecological Complexity* 3 (2): 91–103. https://doi.org/10.1016/j.ecocom.2005.07.004.
Tainter, J. A. 2011. Energy, complexity, and sustainability: A historical perspective. *Environmental Innovation and Societal Transitions* 1 (1): 89–95. https://doi.org/10.1016/j.eist.2010.12.001.
Tainter, J. A. 2014. Collapse and sustainability: Rome, the Maya, and the modern world. *Archaeological Papers of the American Anthropological Association* 24 (1): 201–214. https://doi.org/10.1111/apaa.12038.
Tainter, J. A. 2019. Cahokia: urbanization, metabolism, and collapse. *Frontiers in Sustainable Cities* 1:6. https://doi.org/10.3389/frsc.2019.00006.
van Bavel, B., and M. Scheffer. 2021. Historical effects of shocks on inequality: the Great Leveler revisited. *Humanities and Social Sciences Communications* 8 (1): 76. https://doi.org/10.1057/s41599-021-00763-4.
Wu, Q., G. Tong, and P. Zhou. 2025. Long-term wage inequality in imperial China: From 202 BCE to 1912 CE. *PLoS One* 20 (1): e0315627. https://doi.org/10.1371/journal.pone.0315627.
Yoffee, N. 1993. Too many chiefs? (or, safe texts for the '90s). In *Archaeological Theory*, ed. N. Yoffee and A. Sherratt, 60–78. Cambridge: Cambridge University Press. https://doi.org/10.1017/CBO9780511720277.007.
Yoffee, N. 2001. *The Evolution of Simplicity*. Chicago: The University of Chicago Press.
Yoffee, N., ed. 2019. *The Evolution of Fragility: Setting the Terms*. Cambridge: Cambridge University Press.
Yoffee, N., and G. L. Cowgill, eds. 1991. *The Collapse of Ancient States and Civilizations*. Tucson: The University of Arizona press.

Institutional Resistance and Functional Failure: Challenges of Implementing Policy Change

John T. Murphy

Abstract How can researchers in the social sciences effectively engage with policymakers operating in large institutions? Decision makers in large institutions such as the U.S. federal government operate in the kinds of systems that have been considered by social theorists and archaeologists for some time. Considering these systems through the lens of social theory allows us to ask how contributions from the social sciences can be offered and, ideally, received. I present two contrasting example cases of the federal government in action and examine them through three theoretical lenses: standard theories of complex societies and states; a computational approach termed "variety" theory; and an approach that includes acephalous organizations and alternative formulations of power. This last approach, while having older roots, has recently received a resurgent interest in the archaeological community. The three approaches allow three different interpretations of how to understand the ways that the institutions in question operate and inform how members of those institutions may view social science and humanities research, how their institutions can and cannot operate, and how we as researchers might view our role as we engage with them outside our academic homes.

Keywords States · Complexity · Bureaucracy · Governance · Justice · Heterarchy

1 Introduction

The broad purpose of this volume is to discuss the obstacles that make it difficult for researchers in the humanities and social sciences to bring their insights out of the academic world and into implemented policy. This chapter's purpose is to consider the nature of the institutions within which policy is enacted, and the ways that these impact this effort. This chapter examines these through the lens of archaeology, and

J. T. Murphy (✉)
Northern Illinois University, DeKalb, IL, USA
e-mail: jmurphy7@niu.edu

J. F. Haldon, R. Fernandes (eds.), *Bridging History and Policy*, Understanding Complex Systems, https://doi.org/10.1007/978-3-032-24379-9_12

specifically theories that have been applied within archaeology to understand the rise and evolution of complex social systems.

This brief, exploratory chapter will necessarily be limited, and a significant limitation will be the need to paint "institutions of governance" with a very broad brush. The main reference point will be the systems in place in the United States. The U.S. system is highly stratified, with multiple levels of governance at local levels (town/city, township, county), state level (including some multi-state authoritative units), all falling below the U.S. federal government. Power is additionally shared and segmented vertically across executive, legislative, and judicial branches, and this is generally echoed at all levels. The federal government, while retaining sovereignty, participates in international policy and (some) governance through treaties and supra-national bodies such as the United Nations. This is far from universal in its details, but at the coarse level discussed here it should be a reasonable proxy for any modern, twenty-first-century nation-state and its associated bureaucracy.

The focus in this discussion will be at the federal level, and specifically the functions and processes of the federal government. This introduces a bias into the argument, which may not hold as effectively at local levels. But the scale, extent, and potential impact of the U.S. federal bureaucracy makes it an important case, and the idea that the processes are roughly replicated at state and lower levels is plausible enough that the question of how closely can be deferred for now.

2 Two Test Cases

I will approach this via two examples that might reasonably be considered in opposition: one that is very clearly "top-down", and the other that endeavored to be "bottom-up", insofar as a federally funded project can be. As a disclaimer, the two projects selected are two with which I have had personal experience. In the first, I worked on some extensions to the project beyond what is discussed here; in the second, I was deeply involved in several portions of the project and engaged with most of the other parts, and this included a large number of private and protected conversations among the extended project group, researchers and non-researchers alike. For both, I will limit my comments here to what appears in the published records.

As an additional disclaimer, I do not intend to critique the projects fully, nor by offering these partial critiques to imply that they have not been successes; I only want to use them to illustrate what I mean by internal and structural dynamics within projects that exist within federal agencies. I avoid discussion about the disciplinary repertoires of the people conducting these projects. There is much that could be said about the difficulties working across, for example, engineering and social science fields, both in terms of training and in the attitude of approach toward the problems. But I hope to avoid attributing challenges to the characteristics of individuals, and instead to look at the structural constraints within which individuals operate; this permits a better understanding of how to engage with these projects from a social science perspective agnostic of the personalities involved.

2.1 National Critical Functions

The first example is an effort by the U.S. federal government to inventory the collection of functions it considers critical to maintaining the operation of the country and the way of life of its citizens. Over the past several years, a study has been undertaken by the Cybersecurity and Infrastructure Security Agency (CISA), a subdivision of the Department of Homeland Security (DHS) within the executive branch of the U.S. government. The study's focus is on inventorying the "National Critical Functions" (NCFs) that are performed within the U.S. The initial outcome of this is a canonical list of NCFs (Cybersecurity and Infrastructure Security Agency 2019, 2021). The list is being compiled by the National Risk Management Center (NRMC), a division of CISA; the intent is to understand threats to these functions and interconnections among the functions that could cause disruptions to the operations providing one function directly to cause cascading disruptions in other domains.

The collection of 55 functions (grouped into four areas) is of some interest: it contains elements that have been concerns for all of human existence (water ["Supply Water"] and food ("Produce and Provide Human and Animal Food Products and Services"), for example), but also some newly modern additions that now rise to the level of "critical" ("Provide Positioning, Navigation, and Timing Services"—e.g., the GPS system). It is a useful exercise to ask what functions are missing here; the areas of focus and the lacunae give a sense about the ideas of governance and control that inhere in the U.S. system.

The 55 National Critical Functions (Cybersecurity and Infrastructure Security Agency 2019)

Connect: Operate Core Network ▪ Provide Cable Access Network Services ▪ Provide Internet Based Content, Information, and Communication Services ▪ Provide Internet Routing, Access, and Connection Services ▪ Provide Positioning, Navigation, and Timing Services ▪ Provide Radio Broadcast Access Network Services ▪ Provide Satellite Access Network Services ▪ Provide Wireless Access Network Services ▪ Provide Wireline Access Network Services

Distribute: Distribute Electricity ▪ Maintain Supply Chains ▪ Transmit Electricity ▪ Transport Cargo and Passengers by Air ▪ Transport Cargo and Passengers by Rail ▪ Transport Cargo and Passengers by Road ▪ Transport Cargo and Passengers by Vessel ▪ Transport Materials by Pipeline ▪ Transport Passengers by Mass Transit

Manage: Conduct Elections ■ Develop and Maintain Public Works and Services ■ Educate and Train ■ Enforce Law ■ Maintain Access to Medical Records ■ Manage Hazardous Materials ■ Manage Wastewater ■ Operate Government ■ Perform Cyber Incident Management Capabilities ■ Prepare for and Manage Emergencies ■ Preserve Constitutional Rights ■ Protect Sensitive Information ■ Provide and Maintain Infrastructure ■ Provide Capital Markets and Investment Activities ■ Provide Consumer and Commercial Banking Services ■ Provide Funding and Liquidity Services ■ Provide Identity Management and Associated Trust Support Services ■ Provide Insurance Services ■ Provide Medical Care ■ Provide Payment, Clearing, and Settlement Services ■ Provide Public Safety ■ Provide Wholesale Funding ■ Store Fuel and Maintain Reserves ■ Support Community Health
Supply: Exploration and Extraction Of Fuels ■ Fuel Refining and Processing Fuels ■ Generate Electricity ■ Manufacture Equipment ■ Produce and Provide Agricultural Products and Services ■ Produce and Provide Human and Animal Food Products and Services ■ Produce Chemicals ■ Provide Metals and Materials ■ Provide Housing ■ Provide Information Technology Products and Services ■ Provide Materiel and Operational Support to Defense ■ Research and Development ■ Supply Water

But for our purposes, the precise nature of the list is less important than its general nature, and of even greater concern is the process by which it is being created. This process is not incidental: it reflects the outcome of long-term trends within the U.S. government. The work is being done by a subdivision of the DHS. DHS was established in 2003 in the wake of the terror attacks in 2001. The explicit purpose of establishing DHS was to unite the various intelligence and security agencies that existed at the time and that were perceived to have been unable to prevent the attacks that had occurred (Bush 2002). CISA was established in 2018 (via a reorganization from an earlier division of DHS, the National Protection and Programs Directorate (Cybersecurity and Infrastructure Security Act of 2018. 2018)) to join this suite of other agencies and focus on infrastructure, including communications and the Internet. The NCF work itself is related to broader national security concerns, as spelled out in National Security Memo #22 (Biden 2024); this positions the work as part of a larger effort on the part of the federal government to centralize and integrate a variety of efforts to anticipate and respond to security challenges.

Additional work with the NCFs includes the establishment of a catalog of sub-functions through a process referred to as functional decomposition. By the end of 2021, the 55 NCFs had been decomposed to identify 294 “primary” sub-functions, and 3,319 “secondary” sub-functions (Cybersecurity and Infrastructure Security Agency 2021, 2023).

This general process of adding levels, agencies, and categorization schemes, and of explicitly inventorying, segmenting, and managing functions is a typical one, driven by conceptions of control specifically and, often, efficiency generally. In other words, it is the way these large institutions "get things done". As such it is business as usual, part of a march of "progress" as the institutions grow and evolve.

2.2 *PR100*

The second example is the effort of the U.S. Department of Energy (DOE) to contribute to the reconstruction and improvement of the electrical power grid in Puerto Rico, a project called the Puerto Rico Grid Resilience and Transitions to 100% Renewable Energy Study, or PR100. This project also sits in a historical context. In 2017, Puerto Rico was hit by Hurricane Maria. The electrical grid in Puerto Rico prior to Maria was unreliable and expensive. Maria devastated this already frail system, destroying or damaging large sections of it and leaving some people without power for months. The exact number of people this impacted, and the number of deaths that resulted, are disputed (Minet 2019).

After Maria Puerto Ricans saw an opportunity to not only repair but to improve their electrical system. The Commonwealth passed the Puerto Rico Energy Public Policy Act, Act 17 (Puerto Rico Legislative Assembly 2019), legislation that mandated that Puerto Rico would complete a move to 100% renewable energy by 2050.

PR100 was commissioned to allow the federal government to support this effort. It was funded from DOE directly; it was additionally to be done in concert with the Federal Emergency Management Agency (FEMA), which had funding available for reconstruction of the damage from Maria and was seeking technical input on how to proceed. The project was led by the National Renewable Energy Laboratory (NREL) and included a constellation of partners from other national laboratories and universities. The National Laboratory system is managed by the DOE Office of Science; the labs themselves are typically owned by the government but operated and staffed by contractors, often with university partnerships.

The PR100 project (Department of Energy 2024; Baggu and Burton 2024) included a collection of related and interconnected projects. Many of these were technical: these included simulation modeling of future climate conditions, simulation of the operation of a newly constructed power grid under different assumptions of that grid's structure, spatially explicit tools to understand the impact of this grid on the lives of the people in all parts the island, and economic analyses to understand how labor investment, supply chain issues, and other aspects of the transition to 100% renewable energy would play out over time.

But additionally, PR100 was explicitly grounded in principles of Energy Justice. This was linked to a larger effort within the administration termed "Justice 40"; the objective of Justice 40 (Tackling the Climate Crisis at Home and Abroad 2021) was to ensure that for every federally funded project, 40% of the funding (at least) was directed to communities that were traditionally underrepresented or otherwise challenged, such as poor and minority communities. A commitment to Energy Justice would parallel the intent behind Justice 40, but carry more specificity in the context of PR100. Of interest to our discussion are the various conceptions of "Energy Justice" that intersected in the project.

"Energy Justice" is itself a comparatively new term, arising in academic literature in the 2000s and early 2010s, and continuing to evolve today. It has a number of forebears, most significantly Environmental Justice, but focuses on distinctive aspects of energy systems. The discussions generally resolve around what have come to be called "pillars". The definitions of these have varied through time and among researchers, but the definitions used in PR100 were (quoted in full from Department of Energy 2024):

- **Distributive justice** refers to the way the costs and benefits of the energy system are distributed among the people connected to it. Costs and benefits range from basic elements such as the availability of energy and its price to any other outcome of the system, such as pollution.
- **Procedural justice** emphasizes that the processes for making decisions about the energy system must themselves be fair and inclusive in order to reach equitable outcomes. This means establishing decision-making processes that encourage input from all stakeholders and provide them with information about both the energy system and the decision-making process.
- **Recognition justice** focuses on the need to incorporate the views, concepts, and values of multiple stakeholders, and to do so in their own terms. Recognition can be broadly viewed as the incorporation of knowledge learned from sources across the collection of stakeholders, the full consideration of that knowledge, and the acknowledgement that this knowledge is valid.
- **Restorative justice** is the idea that an energy system moving forward should acknowledge past harms, attempt to remediate them when possible, and ensure they are not repeated.

It is significant that these definitions did not necessarily conform to other formulations of them across the Energy Justice literature. For example, restorative justice in the wider literature derives from criminal law, and focuses on restoring the social fabric that was rent by the act of the crime, so that both victim, perpetrator, and all others affected can return to the balance that existed in their previous social relationship (Menkel-Meadow 2007). Nevertheless, the framework provided by these "pillars" was valuable in the context of the PR100 study. Views on the nature of the new system varied widely; these principles were extremely useful in structuring discussions that attempted to cross these varying viewpoints, and in ensuring that spanning the viewpoints was kept as an explicit goal.

PR100 engaged in a collection of related activities to pursue the justice goals brought from the Secretary's office. These included the formation of an Advisory Group that at its peak included 100+ members of government, community representatives, and industry partners; the creation of a web site as a forum for discussion with the Advisory Group and a parallel site open to the public; meetings with the

Advisory Group as often as monthly, via videoconference and in-person; the publication of an "Energy Justice" bibliography; and coordination with the Secretary's office to tour several communities in Puerto Rico for in-person discussions with the Secretary and the PR 100 project leads. The data products from the work were also made available to any interested users via a publicly accessible data repository. The intent of all of this was to lay the groundwork for continued procedural justice and establish a framework for dialogue among all the energy system's participants that would outlive the 2-year remit of PR100 itself.

However, PR100 existed within constraints that shaped how and whether these principles could be addressed. U.S. National Laboratories are limited to scientific and technical analyses. PR100 could give technical insight into a range of possible solutions (and, in some ways more usefully, show that some were impossible), but could only facilitate the further discussion that would have to follow to use those technical insights. This differs from the role of the Secretary's office and of course differs from the desire of the different community partners and members of the Advisory Group, who were all seeking solutions. Additionally, there was a constellation of regulations and of financial obligations—including significant debt that the energy system had already incurred—that carried constraints that were necessarily incorporated into PR100's discussions and even into their modeling efforts. It should also be noted that, as explicitly noted in Act 17, previous interactions with the federal government were not viewed as either entirely beneficial or entirely benign (Klein 2018).

Consequently, PR100's role became that of an intermediary. All entities and individuals in the Advisory Group and in the further audience that PR100 reached desired a more reliable, resilient, and equitable energy system. How this might be operated in a technical sense could be modeled, and its wider interactions, for example, with a changing climate or with adjacent infrastructure systems like communications and water, or with emergency response systems and healthcare (critical functions), could be discussed and modeled objectively. But deciding what the system should look like, and even deciding who should decide this, were out of scope.

This restriction to objectivity remained true even though Energy Justice is explicitly framed to be subjective—that is, to incorporate a variety of views, accepting that these will vary.

The project additionally expanded beyond the four pillars to a more recent and radical addition: Transformative Justice. This framework embraced the possibility that the old power structure that had led to past problems be replaced with a new one, leading toward "Energy Democracy" (Baggu and Burton 2024). This is a profound shift: It involves the federal level of the government attempting to push for a downward redistribution of power, including the creation of new ways for people in the energy system (ultimately all of Puerto Rico's residents) to engage with that system and share control of it.

In a longer exposition it would perhaps be possible to map out all of the different institutions involved in this process, understand the unique constraints under which they operated and their different mandates and goals. The coarse view, however, is simply that the National Laboratories in PR100 acted as an intermediary to guide the discourse among these participants, a discourse informed and demanded by Energy Justice, and that this role was prompted by necessity: the labs filled a vacuum, because no other institution was positioned to do it. They were able to do it in part because of the official mandate of doing only objective, technical work, which allowed them to occupy a neutral position. But primarily they did it because the technical problems were more tractable than the social challenges. Building any of the possible grids is comparatively simple as a technical matter; understanding the social complexities is much more challenging.

As an example of this intermediary role, consider some work that was done creating metrics for understanding the costs of energy and of outages for consumers (Baggu and Burton 2024, Section 14). These were extensions and applications of generally applicable tools that had been developed by the national laboratories for use in multiple contexts (Wachtel et al. 2022). These were impressive and important tools; the "Social Burden" analysis described in the final report attempts to establish burden metrics that are specific to locations given geography and available infrastructure. Customization for the Puerto Rico context was done in a limited way: 15 categories of critical services were established via discussions with stakeholders, and thus represented the concerns of Puerto Ricans given their history of specific challenges. The models were then run (for floods, earthquakes, and landslides, individually and in combination) and used to generate a collection of reports. However, the proliferation of reports that could have been run using these variations and the 15 categories (singly or in combination) was very large, and instead of creating these, the raw data were made available for download, so that stakeholders could return to it and generate the reports that they saw as most relevant. This is an appropriate strategy, and represents a kind of compromise between the fully top-down analyses that the federal government can provide and the on-the-ground needs of a specific context, while simultaneously facilitating a further conversation beyond the technical analysis that PR100 was able to provide.

Together, then, our examples are, first, of a government doing the thing it does well: establishing agencies that then subdivide into further agencies, and then do the business of categorizing, inventorying, and analyzing, all to find ways to control; and, second, of a government attempting a thing it is not built to do: delegate power downward, and contribute to the design of a new structure to handle the management and control in a way that serves individuals better, with all the messiness that the many interpretations of "better" can bring.

These two examples provide a groundwork for exploring the question of how to interact with these institutions, but before we turn to it, we can look at them from the perspective of social sciences and archaeology.

3 Three Views of Complex Systems

The larger purpose of this chapter is to ask how social science and the humanities might be able to contribute to these efforts, or to guide or redirect them to help effect their purposes through different means. To reach that point, it is useful to consider how social science views these processes, and thus how we might critique them. A good starting point is to consider them as the operations of social complexity. Complex societies have received considerable theoretical attention, perhaps most specifically in archaeology, where their development, adaptation, transformation, and (not infrequently) collapse can be reviewed in the long-term record.

For this exercise, I consider three different views of these systems. They are not completely distinct, and many more connections among them might be traced. The first view represents what might be considered the standard approach; the second is an outlier that is offered here as intermediate; and the third is a novel, expanding theoretical front that may represent an impactful shift in archaeological thinking.

3.1 Organic Solidarity and Hierarchy: A Standard Theory of Complex Societies

The standard approach can be traced back at least to Durkheim's distinction between mechanical and organic solidarity (Durkheim 2013). Mechanical solidarity describes a society in which independent and largely similar autonomous units all perform all of the functions they need to survive (as in society comprised of households that grow their own food, generate their own textiles, make their own tools, etc.); organic solidarity is a society in which different societal functions are performed by specialized units (one household is the baker, another the cooper, another the smith, another the miller, etc.). Social complexity is viewed as increasing as specialization occurs and the number and variety of specialized functions increases. This is generally considered to be accompanied by the appearance of coordinative roles, and of stratification and the appearance of hierarchy.

For much of the time that the field has been a scientific profession, archaeologists expressed the process of increasing social differentiation as a hallmark of a "complex society". The acme of this process is "state-level" societies, often contrasted with other societies that fall under broader categorizations (going back to "bands, tribes, chiefdoms": Sahlins and Service 1960) or sub-categories ("archaic states": Feinman and Marcus 1998). In other words, archaeologists viewed highly stratified and functionally differentiated societies as "complex" and have relegated most others to another category—not "simple", usually, but not "complex".

Within this general framework there have been some attempts to understand the internal dynamics of complex societies in more formal terms. "General System Theory" was applied (notably by Flannery 1968), and this allowed the examination of how the societies may have had trajectories determined by systems processes including feedback loops and regulatory mechanisms. A rich array of mathematical approaches related to system theory have been assembled under the heading "complexity" (many reviews are available; see Murphy 2017) and have been applied to many archaeological examples; these have included discussions of the concepts of resilience, robustness, catastrophe theory, and "adaptive cycles", inter alia. Much of this in the last two decades has been undertaken, either explicitly or indirectly, in a wave of "model-based archaeology" that began its florescence with the publication by Kohler and van der Leeuw (Kohler and van der Leeuw 2007).

These approaches are excellent at some specific kinds of questions, especially those surrounding management of resources, population growth, and periods of ascendancy and collapse. For example, a model of land management and agricultural practices may clearly show that there is a difference in interest between the smallholder and the king, such that when central control is in place and large-scale concerns dominate decision-making, the smallholders' interests are overridden, leading to a suboptimal outcome on a fine scale but a preferable strategy across the wider region.

3.2 Computational Complexity and Variety

There is another discussion of complexity that offers some insights: "Variety" theory by Beer (Beer 2014; Thorn 2022) considers institutional complexity as a kind of computation. Building on the work of (Ashby 1991 [1958]), he posits, specifically, that an institution tasked with generating some set of outcomes—call them provisionally, "solutions"—in response to some set of inputs—or, "problems"—can be thought of as executing a kind of computation. An important component of Beer's approach is that the complexity of the institution must be adequate to deal with the complexity of the input-output operations needed. Beer conceived of this as quantifiable, with countable input and output states, akin to 1's and 0's in a computer. If the only output needed is one bit (a 1 or a 0), and the only input is also one bit, then the internal complexity need not be high; however, as the potential input states and output states (the "problems" being confronted and the "solutions" being generated; Beer's term for this is "variety") increased in number, the internal complexity needed to properly find solutions must also increase.

But, as Thorn points out (Thorn 2022), Beer's analysis also offers another perspective on how to deal with this increase in computational complexity: he posits that there are two ways: "to reduce the variety generated by the system … [or] … to amplify the variety of the regulatory part of the total system" (Beer 2014). That is, faced with a mismatch between the internal complexity of an institution and the richer complexity in the set of problems being faced, the institution can either increase its internal complexity or it can reduce the external complexity.

Reducing external complexity might seem impossible on its face. Beer acknowledges it as a strategy, but calls it "madness"; in his example of a department store, he equates it with only offering one size shoe. But some reflection shows that this is a core way that institutions function. A first level for this is requiring that input be standardized; most of us will at some point have been asked to fill out a form and discovered a set of alternatives in the form of checkboxes, and been frustrated that none of the options offered quite fits our situation. This reduces the complexity for the institution by filtering input. Beer's larger argument presupposes that computers will do this task, a kind of filtering. But more powerful institutions can force this on their subjects. They can also extend this further, and ensure that things that might be created, or occurrences that might happen, in the real world that don't fit the requisite boxes are forbidden.

This focus on computational complexity could be an important extension to understanding the operations of complex societies under the standard model. For example, consider the question above of a mismatch of scale that inheres between the interests of the central authority and the local landholder. Considering the possible inability to perform the computation required to manage resources and account for challenges offers a different perspective, separate from the mere consideration of competing interests.

The action of the central authority to regulate life under its control via the establishment and enforcement of categories is not without discussion in archaeological and broader social science literature. Eric Wolf discusses similar themes in his work on the Aztecs in Envisioning Power (Wolf 1999). James Scott visits similar themes in his works *Seeing Like a State* (Scott 2020) and *Against the Grain* (Scott 2017). Appadurai (2011) discusses a specific example of categorization, commodification. In these works, the establishment of categories and their enforcement are key to structuring relationships between humans and the natural world, and among members of social systems. It is the vehicle for, and expression of, power.

3.3 Alternative Views of Complex Social Systems

In addition to these two conceptions of complexity, there is a third that is increasingly being recognized. A book by Graeber and Wengrow, *The Dawn of Everything* (2021), proposes that archaeologists have missed large and important portions of humanity's past because of blinders that have compelled them to recognize societies and institutions in the past as either "states" or some small collection of "other" arrangements, and failed to understand that there can be a myriad of creative solutions to structuring power that are not easily incorporated into this framework. Their argument is grounded in the idea that, radically, we should listen to the indigenous voices that were coopted and then drowned out by Europeans during the various stages of colonialism (and continuing today), and that these should be considered political philosophers on a par with the European canon, even if radically different. From these different philosophical bases, a wide range of alternative societal structures can be built.

This line of thinking is not without other parallels and precedents. Latour (1996), for example, has critiqued the idea of organic "complexity" by noting that societies with high divisions of labor and "organic solidarity" actually reduce the complexity of the daily lives of their inhabitants: in an undifferentiated society, each individual must engage in a wide range of activities, interact with a larger number of other individuals, and manage all of these decisions independently, while in a highly differentiated society, individuals need only do some things for themselves and rely on others for the rest (replace a "complex" society with a "complicated" one). And it owes much to the work on heterarchy by Carole Crumley (1976, 1995, 2003), where heterarchy, in contrast with hierarchy, describes a condition in which multiple cross-cutting power structures coexist within a given society and can be deployed or exploited in multiple ways, permitting a fluidity that allows adaptation and, in some cases, belies notions of "collapse".

In these frameworks, people are able to be creative in how they construct new social arrangements (especially if not constrained by the idea that all of these should be financial, another modern idea). Archaeologists, now aware of and seeking them, are finding examples of societies where this creativity was expressed, and, critically, are now able to use this the expanded framework to recognize them. Non-state, acephalous societies are being found that exhibit "Power from Below" (to use the title from Thurston and Fernandez-Götz 2021). Scott's work recognizes this (Scott 2009), and as Thurston and Fernandez-Götz note, sometimes this dynamic is found in opposition to a state, by a group that is committed to "not being governed"; in other cases it is sui generis. Beyond archaeology, Graeber's work (and life) included work among non-hierarchical movements, including the Occupy Wall Street movement of the 2000s (Graeber 2015).

This is exciting work, and it presents a universe of possibilities. It suggests that the way we organize ourselves, the way we construct power, and the way we govern ourselves, is a much more open field, and that a wider array of solutions to today's problems are there for us to find and create.

But it carries an important implication that applies to both the social sciences and to the individuals and institutions that we hope to interact with and advise. The premise of the work is that we have misunderstood complexity because we are, ourselves, immersed in and products of one kind of complex system—modern states—from within which it is difficult to understand the other possibilities that can exist.

For example, it is not incidental to note that Archaeology, especially, is deeply familiar with the establishment of categories: Systematics and classification are at the heart of most archaeological efforts, and we establish and work with typologies, taxonomies, and hierarchical forms of classification in most of our efforts (see, for example, Dunnell 1971; Adams and Adams 1991; O'Brien et al. 1998). Ceramics, lithics, sites, decorative styles, and virtually every other element in the archaeological record are classified according to one or more of these systems, and although classification is a component of all sciences, the variety of elements in the archaeological record and the wide array of analyses to which they may be put makes systematics a special theoretical concern in that field. But when archaeologists classify their material, they are not just mimicking a state operation, they are part of it. This may be literal, if the research was funded by the state (e.g. the U.S. National Science

Foundation). But even if it is not literal, it is more than analogous, it is derivative from the same impulse. We see like states. Past societies walked past the ruins of their predecessors and did not feel a need to dig them up, classify them, sort them, count them, and "reconstruct" them; we do, and it serves us to recognize that there is nothing normal or natural about this impulse.

Categorization also affects our work by propping up boundaries around it. As Foucault has described (in multiple works, but we can cite the work whose title in English is appropriate for us, the *Archaeology of Knowledge*: Foucault 2012), there is a process of establishing the boundaries of a domain, and archaeology has fit under one set of boundaries that has shaped our research questions, and the range of answers that we explore. But boundaries around disciplines can be problematic. Consider, for example, Energy Justice. It is currently being promoted and practiced by individuals with a wide range of training, from engineering to law. Social sciences, writ large, should have much to contribute. But it is worth asking whether it is, strictly, compatible with "science"; if science is objective and intended to discover generalizable laws, and justice is subjective (which the recognition of multiple views implies), historically contingent, and contains a compass that points toward equity and toward ethical and moral outcomes, is "justice" within the domain of social science?

4 National Critical Functions and PR100 as Operations of Complex Institutions

When viewed through the lens of the "standard" model of a complex society, the NRMC process of establishing increasingly specialized agencies and deploying these to categorize the different critical functions performed throughout the country, and ultimately attempting to understand the way that the federal government can support and protect them, may be viewed as a highly bureaucratized extension of the general processes by which complexity increases. It is the march forward of organic solidarity and the establishment of hierarchy to manage, coordinate, and control. The PR100 project is an exercise in how established functional units can, or cannot, achieve a set of novel goals, and, perhaps, an attempt to establish new functional units as needed. Each could be supported by modeling, both in apprehending the processes that are their focus (as the PR100 project employs extensively and the NRMC goal of understanding interconnections among the functions implies) and in understanding the internal processes by which the projects themselves are operating.

From the view of Beer's variety theory and the operations of the federal institutions as a kind of computation, the exercises of the NRMC are a familiar attempt to "attenuate systemic variety" by categorizing and thereby simplifying it, expressed on a wide scale for the critical functions of the country, while also amplifying regulatory variety by expanding the responsive institutional apparatus. The purpose of this attempt is control—not, necessarily, control of all of the operations, but control to the degree that there can be an understanding of threats to the normal functioning of the system ("problems"), and responses to these challenges ("solutions").

In PR100, the process of categorization also plays an important role, but there is a tension between expanding and restricting the collection of categorizations. This is most saliently represented by the key position occupied by Recognition Justice. Recognition Justice is prerequisite to Distributive Justice, Restorative Justice, and Procedural Justice, in that the establishment of different needs of different groups (distributive), of past harms to specific groups (restorative), and of the ability of different groups to participate in decisions (procedural) rests on the establishment of the groups themselves. Recognition Justice also implies, however, that some institution or group has the authority or power to grant recognition, and therefore requesting recognition can carry an acknowledgement of the established power relationship. From that authority's point of view, the "problem" becomes more complicated as more groups are differentiated.

In PR100, a diligent attempt was made to inventory ways in which different groups (often self-identified) were affected by the energy system and by the potential changes that PR100 would eventually support. The PR100 Final Report, reflecting direct input from communities during tours with the Secretary of Energy, lists numerous examples of these based on region, proximity to hazards, previous historical impositions, disability status, income and wealth, and many other potential categories (see Baggu and Burton 2024, Appendix B.4). Modeling efforts and incorporated when possible, but the panoply of groups that could have been discussed, as might have been drawn from Baggu and Burton's full Appendix B, was generally outside the scope of the modeling efforts.

More generally, PR100 itself stayed in its intermediate role. It noted the various categories proposed by the array of stakeholders with whom it interacted, and documented these in the final report, but it explicitly did not presume to act as the authority that could grant "recognition". This left many categories contested and available for further discussion and decision, with acknowledgement that this was a role best left to the people of Puerto Rico themselves. Where the NCF project established a proliferation of categories and utilized these for their top-down analyses, PR100 facilitated the introduction of a wide range of possible categories, but stopped there, leaving the implementation for a different set of actors in a different process.

From the view of "new complexity" of Graeber and Wengrow and similar work, the two projects appear to be pursuing strategies that are an uncomfortable fit. With respect to the NCF work, the general directionality of the work—top-down—is clearly a reflection of a view of the state as central; the idea that the robustness of the map of functions would be left up to the lower-level actors is contra to the project's main thrust. Probably this would be difficult for the project managers to even envision, and not only because they are employed at the federal level. There is a sense in which the project makes the same mistake Graeber and Wengrow accuse archaeologists of making: that because they are immersed in states they have missed entirely the possibility of non-states. In this case, they have reached for a strategy of inventorying everything centrally and from the top down because that is the only way that they can see for states to "get things done". There is at least one piece of evidence on the record that suggests that the NCF work is a product of habit rather than defensible design: The Government Accountability Office reviewed the work in 2022, after it had been underway for 2 years, and noted that there was no document containing a "clear statement of the goals of the work"—that is, it was being done on the assumption that it would create an outcome that serves the institution's goals, but there was no clear plan to do so. This planning document remains pending, with a current expected date of April 2025 (U. S. Government Accountability Office 2022). [Note: In April 2025, during final edits but before this book went to press, this expected date was revised again to conform with an Executive Order issued in March 2025; the document is now expected March 2027.]

The PR100 project, in its acknowledgement that it is not the authority that can provide Recognition, is much more in keeping with a new complexity. Its difficulties are first that it is federally driven, and hence has a collection of tools and strategies that make sense only from a top-down perspective, and second that it is acting without a guidebook. What can a new structure for management of Puerto Rico's energy system look like? Here the available answers are drawn from the standard playbook: economic analyses, market-structures, and centralized systems make sense in the modern state; alternatives that recognize alternative models (e.g. decentralized control) do not exist off-the-shelf, and might need to be created in a bespoke way for the social context. This is a continual renegotiation of the kind that Graeber and Wengrow envision for non-state complexity, but it is difficult to see how this can work, or what is the process to achieve it, within a state framework.

5 Implications for Working with Policy Makers

To return to our original question of how to bring social sciences to policy makers, we must recognize that very little of this theory will be visible to those working in institutions like the U.S. federal government. Few members of these institutions have social science training, leading to immediate issues of vocabulary and shared knowledge base. But as an exercise, we can reverse the mirror and ask how the social sciences appear to the participants in the institutions that we have been examining. How are the social sciences themselves categorized and viewed?

The answer may be that they vary along a continuum. Economics offers quantifiable metrics and a claim to universality that is easily and widely incorporated into policy, and such approaches are always preferred. They are, defensible, manageable, and controllable—all good things—but are also expressions of the view that management and control are best implemented from the top, looking downward.

Anything outside of that paradigm faces a very difficult track, and in fact the far ends of the continuum can be very hazy. "Energy Justice" is certainly social, but is it social science? It is both theoretically driven and actually practiced by people with a wide array of training, from engineering to law. In its focus on human relations and in its holistic approach to understanding interactions between people, infrastructure, and the environment, it would seem to fall squarely within a social science, and its development as a body of theory, currently incomplete, will demand rigor and consistency in future work. But it is also explicitly a motivated activity; it is not, nor does it try to be, an objective science. Equity is a value judgment; justice is a social act.

Consequently, the role of "science" can be questioned—are the social sciences and the humanities "objective"? This can be additionally converted into questions of "fairness", which translates directly into the perceived (and often affected) role of government as an unmotivated and impartial exercise. Beer (2014) noted "fairness" as an example of an inappropriate reduction of variety, one that he hoped would be overcome. A retreat to numbers and quantifiable results across a population with as little variety as possible is much simpler than a messy, chaotic procedure that requires recognition of specific groups, consideration of each group's history, and a fine-tuning of the distribution of the outcomes. That this retreat into numbers is never itself completely objective—it relies on categories, and therefore on power relations just as much as anything else—and that it generally entrenches the previous power structure and inequitable distribution of costs and benefits that preceded it is usually not outweighed by the need for simplicity bolstered by the claim of objectivity.

Suggestions that cost, benefits, debt, and financing are only one window into issues of equity and justice, and that many other routes need to be considered, are likely to be met with bafflement, resistance, or assertions that it's "not the way the world works." Proposals that alternative structures may be created to share power in new ways—even if these are more in keeping with how the specific resource should be managed, à la Ostrom (1990, 2005), or with how a specific kind of infrastructure can be operated (a rich field in a world with rapidly evolving technologies; see for example (Powell 2021))—are so far afield from the institutional and market-based thinking in which these agencies are immersed that they are unlikely to be understood, let alone implemented.

A consequence of this is that it is not simply a question of finding like-minded and well-intentioned individuals within the government whom social scientists and humanists can interact, inform, and support. Instead, what one is likely to find is that individuals within these institutions have very detailed knowledge about the way those institutions work—something that is likely to be a mystery to an outsider. Within this milieu these individuals can navigate reasonably well and can be effective within the boundaries of their roles. But it can be a challenge to ensure that the questions they may ask, and the answers that we, as advisors, may give, will map nicely to this labyrinth. We may see how the low-level questions that they are able to ask and within which they work may integrate with high-level concerns—and, on occasion, they may see this, too—but there may be little to do about it because the branches of the maze that are theirs are restricted only to answers that may not fit what we see as the real issues. This is not to say that finding like-minded and well-intentioned individuals is not critical; only that it is not sufficient.

One other side to this, then, is to ensure that policymakers are able to find what they need from us. This compels a variety of actions. Resolving theoretical confusion may be one that seems internal (and hence can be done at our own pace) but may actually be imperative: a field that is in theoretical flux (and perhaps archaeology is at such a point, if it truly is a new "dawn") is exciting, but frustrating to outsiders. If resolution is not possible, clarity can help.

Further: If we desire relevance, we must work with urgency. PR100 ended in December 2023. As this book is moving to press in 2025, Puerto Rico has been hit by two more blackouts in only a few months (A.P. News 2025). A legitimate critique, extendable to many projects (Klein 2025), is whether 24 months of modeling and discussion of justice was worth the delay. Governments must get things done. The costs of inaction are both human and political, and the contributions of social scientists must be (correctly) seen as contributing to progress, rather than inhibiting.

Among the theoretical imperatives is a clarification of our stance on objectivity. Anthropology is perhaps the social science most comfortable with the idea that it operates in a non-objective way. Anthropologists are subjective instruments incapable of objective measurement; and Anthropologists rarely assess human behavior fully objectively, but instead focus very specifically on relationships of power and their implications for our society as a whole, but especially for the powerless. This does not make us less scientific; it merely declines to believe that "objective" sciences are any more so. None of this is easy to convey to people without deep training. We must find a way to do so.

And finally, we should focus on examples when we can. If we claim that there are alternatives to top-down state power, we should be able to document them. We are at the start of this project, but works like Graeber and Wengrow, Thurston and Fernandez-Götz, and others, suggests that we have the benefit of an apparent legion of examples—when we learn to see them.

However, there is an additional dimension that must be considered. Much of the above has focused on the scenario where policymakers are interacting with social scientists and practitioners of the humanities for beneficent reasons: an attempt to manage complexity, an attempt to solve problems, a seeking of our help to create more positive outcomes. This describes large portions of the federal government in the U.S., and, it is hoped, in many other parts of the world. But the levers of control do not guarantee this outcome, and it is entirely possible for actors within these governments to deploy their strategies and exert their power for alternative ends, whether these merely be perversions of a vision of power serving one group or, possibly, their own greatness, or for some baser goal—greed and lust (including lust for power) exist. And, while most people within federal institutions have limited ability to modify the structures within which they work, real power within these structures lies in the ability to change, reorganize, or even abolish them. My comments here imply that some restructuring can be good—all three views suggest that complex institutions can become self-serving and take on forms that pervert their original benefits—but it is also true that this can be done to achieve ill ends. The long-term view of archaeology, moving as it is away from simple views of "collapse" to more nuanced views of reorganization and negotiated power, may provide a useful window on these processes, how to facilitate or even manage them, and potentially how to oppose them. Most of us in the social sciences and the humanities, both as researchers and as citizens, approach governance with the hope that it will create outcomes that lift our societies upward toward our ideals. As we approach the second quarter of the twenty-first century, we must hope that our leaders have these same goals, and we must be prepared to find whatever roles we can if they do not.

References

Adams, W. Y., and E. W. Adams. 1991. *Archaeological Typology and Practical Reality: A Dialectical Approach to Artifact Classification and Sorting*. 1st ed. Cambridge: Cambridge University Press.

AP News. 2025. *A Look at Why an Island-Wide Blackout Hit Puerto Rico and What Caused It*. 17 Apr 2025. https://apnews.com/article/puerto-rico-blackout-power-outage-causes-6b1f71e33136a3f97b8238568cd664ea. Accessed 8 May 2025.

Appadurai, A. 2011. Introduction: Commodities and the politics of value. In *The Social Life of Things: Commodities in Cultural Perspective*, ed. A. Appadurai, 3–63. Cambridge: Cambridge University Press.

Ashby, W. R. 1991. Requisite variety and its implications for the control of complex systems. In *Facets of Systems Science*, 405–417. Boston, MA: Springer.

Baggu, M., and R. Burton. 2024. *Puerto Rico Grid Resilience and Transitions to 100% Renewable Energy Study (PR100): Final Report*. https://www.osti.gov/servlets/purl/2335361/. Accessed 10 Feb 2025

Beer, S. 2014. *Designing Freedom*, The CBC Massey Lectures. Toronto, ON: House of Anansi Press.

Biden, J. R. 2024. *National Security Memo 22*. https://irp.fas.org/offdocs/nsm/nsm-22.pdf. Accessed 24 Jan 2025

Bush, G. W. 2002. The Department of Homeland Security. https://www.dhs.gov/sites/default/files/publications/book_0.pdf. Accessed 10 Feb 2025

Crumley, C. L. 1976. Toward a locational definition of state systems of settlement. *American Anthropologist* 78:59–73. https://doi.org/10.1525/aa.1976.78.1.02a00050.

Crumley, C. L. 1995. Heterarchy and the analysis of complex societies. In *Heterarchy and the Analysis of Complex Societies*, ed. R. M. Ehrenreich, C. L. Crumley, and J. E. Levy, 1–5. Washington, DC: American Anthropological Association.

Crumley, C. L. 2003. Alternative forms of social order. In: *Heterarchy, Political Economy, and the Ancient Maya: The Three Rivers Region of the East-Central Yucatán Peninsula*, ed. V.L. Scarborough, F. Valdez, and N.P. Dunning, 136–146. Society for American Archaeology. Tucson, AZ: University of Arizona Press.

Cybersecurity and Infrastructure Security Agency Act of 2018. 2018. https://www.congress.gov/115/plaws/publ278/PLAW-115publ278.pdf

Cybersecurity and Infrastructure Security Agency. 2019. *National Critical Functions Set*. https://www.cisa.gov/sites/default/files/publications/national-critical-functions-set-508.pdf. Accessed 24 Jan 2025

Cybersecurity and Infrastructure Security Agency. 2021. *National Critical Functions: Status Update to the Critical Infrastructure Community*. https://www.cisa.gov/sites/default/files/publications/2021_ncf-status_update_508.pdf. Accessed 24 Jan 2025

Cybersecurity and Infrastructure Security Agency. 2023. *NCF Decomposition Methodology Fact Sheet 508*. https://www.cisa.gov/sites/default/files/2023-04/ncf-decomposition-methodology_fact-sheet_508.pdf. Accessed 24 Jan 2025

Department of Energy. 2024. *Energy Justice | What is PR100 | PR100*. https://pr100.gov/about/energy-justice. Accessed 10 Feb 2025

Dunnell, R. C. 1971. *Systematics in Prehistory*. New York, NY: The Free Press.

Durkheim, E. 2013. *The Division of Labor in Society*, Kindle Edition. Digireads.com.

Feinman, G. M., and Joyce Marcus, eds. 1998. *Archaic States*. Santa Fe, NM: School of American Research Press.

Flannery, K. V. 1968. Archaeological systems theory and Early Mesoamerica. In *Anthropological Archaeology in the Americas*, ed. B. J. Meggers, 67–87. Washington DC: Anthropological Society of Washington.

Foucault, M. 2012. *The Archaeology of Knowledge*. Westminster: Knopf Doubleday.

Graeber, D. 2015. *The Utopia of Rules: On Technology, Stupidity, and the Secret Joys of Bureaucracy*. Brooklyn, NY: Melville House.

Graeber, D., and D. Wengrow. 2021. *The Dawn of Everything: A New History of Humanity*. New York: Farrar, Straus and Giroux.

Klein, N. 2018. *The Battle for Paradise: Puerto Rico Takes on the Disaster Capitalists*. Chicago, IL: Haymarket Books.

Klein, E. 2025. Opinion | Biden's Team Wishes They'd Moved So Much Faster. *The New York Times*, 13 Apr 2025. https://www.nytimes.com/2025/04/13/opinion/doge-abundance-government-bulding.html. Accessed 8 May 2025.

Kohler, T. A., and S. E. van der Leeuw, eds. 2007. *The Model-Based Archaeology of Socionatural Systems*. Santa Fe, NM: School for Advanced Research Press.

Latour, B. 1996. On interobjectivity. *Mind, Culture, and Activity* 3 (4): 228–245.

Menkel-Meadow, C. 2007. Restorative justice: what is it and does it work? *Annual Review of Law and Social Science* 3:161–187. https://doi.org/10.1146/annurev.lawsocsci.2.081805.110005.

Minet, C. 2019. María's death toll: on the crucial role of Puerto Rico's investigative journalists. In *Aftershocks of Disaster: Puerto Rico Before and After the Storm*, ed. Y. Bonilla and M. LoBrón. Chicago, IL: Haymarket Books.

Murphy, J. T. 2017. *Complexity Theory*. Oxford: Oxford University Press.

O'Brien, M. J., R. L. Lyman, and R. D. Leonard. 1998. Basic incompatibilities between evolutionary and behavioral archaeology. *American Antiquity* 63:485–498. https://doi.org/10.2307/2694632.

Ostrom, E. 1990. *Governing the Commons: The Evolution of Institutions for Collective Action*. Cambridge: Cambridge University Press.

Ostrom, E. 2005. *Understanding Institutional Diversity*. Princeton, NJ: Princeton University Press.

Powell, A. B. 2021. *Undoing Optimization: Civic Action in Smart Cities*. New Haven, CT: Yale University Press.

Puerto Rico Legislative Assembly. 2019. *Puerto Rico Energy Public Policy Act* (Act 17)

Sahlins, M., and E. R. Service, eds. 1960. *Evolution and Culture*. Ann Arbor, MI: University of Michigan Press.

Scott, J. C. 2009. *The Art of Not Being Governed: An Anarchist History of Upland Southeast Asia*. New Haven, CT: Yale University Press.

Scott, J. C. 2017. *Against the Grain: A Deep History of the Earliest States*. New Haven, CT: Yale University Press.

Scott, J. C. 2020. *Seeing Like a State: How Certain Schemes to Improve the Human Condition Have Failed*. New Haven, CT: Yale University Press (Veritas paperback edition).

Tackling the Climate Crisis at Home and Abroad. Federal Register 02/01/2021. 2021. https://www.federalregister.gov/documents/2021/02/01/2021-02177/tackling-the-climate-crisis-at-home-and-abroad. Accessed 24 Jan 2025

Thorn, A. 2022. *I Emailed My Doctor 133 Times: The Crisis in the British Healthcare System*. https://www.youtube.com/watch?v=v1eWIshUzr8. Accessed 11 Feb 2025

Thurston, T. L., and M. Fernandez-Götz, eds. 2021. *Power from Below in Premodern Societies: The Dynamics of Political Complexity in the Archaeological Record*. Cambridge: Cambridge University Press.

U. S. Government Accountability Office. 2022. *Critical Infrastructure Protection: CISA Should Improve Priority Setting, Stakeholder Involvement, and Threat Information Sharing*. | U.S. GAO. https://www.gao.gov/products/gao-22-104279. Accessed 24 Jan 2025

Wachtel, A., D. Melander, and O. Hart. 2022. *ReNCAT: The Resilient Node Cluster Analysis Tool*. https://www.sandia.gov/app/uploads/sites/273/2022/12/ReNCAT_The-Resilient-Node-Cluster-Analysis-Tool.pdf

Wolf, E. R. 1999. *Envisioning Power: Ideologies of Dominance and Crisis*. Berkeley, CA: University of California Press.

Bridges Between Academe and the Public Sector: Reflections on a Career and Initiatives of the National Library of Medicine

Jeffrey S. Reznick

Abstract This chapter offers perspectives on bridging academe and the public sector through 25 years of professional experience—15 in federal service and ten in higher education and the nonprofit sector. It argues that professionally trained historians can be well-suited to achieve such bridging by embracing their expertise while communicating and collaborating across disciplinary boundaries. Successful bridging depends upon being actionable, intentional, and strategic in one's career trajectory. It also depends upon self-awareness, self-empowerment, and resilience; building, maintaining, and growing a network of trusted and mutually supportive colleagues; setting priorities and goals, and being flexible and open to the fact that opportunities to bridge academe and the public sector can arise by design and by chance. When they happen by design, be prepared to fail. When they happen by chance, be comfortable being uncomfortable taking an unfamiliar path. The journey can be deeply meaningful, and the destination can be a rewarding career through which one can be an impactful envoy for historical training and the history profession.

Keywords Career development · Public service · Collaboration · Resilience

The author is grateful to the NLM/NIH for supporting the writing and editing of this chapter, as well as his presentation of earlier versions of it at the Princeton University colloquium "Resilience and Sustainability: Past Trajectories, Contemporary Directions, Policy Relevance Princeton University," June 3–5, 2024; New York Academy of Medicine conference, "The Future of Historical Medical Libraries in the Digital Age," September 25, 2024, and Georgetown University, Department of History forum "Georgetown PhDs and Jobs Beyond the Academy." He thanks the editors of this volume for their feedback and support, as well as Gregory Afinogenov, Michelle DiMeo, Jason Gart, Beth Maser, Emily Matson, Nicole Milano, Beth Mullen, Ken Koyle, Frank Vitale IV, and Amanda Wilson.

J. S. Reznick (✉)
National Library of Medicine (NLM), National Institutes of Health (NIH), Bethesda, MD, USA
e-mail: jeffrey.reznick@nih.gov

J. F. Haldon, R. Fernandes (eds.), *Bridging History and Policy*, Understanding Complex Systems, https://doi.org/10.1007/978-3-032-24379-9_13

1 Introduction

Discussion abounds regarding historians bridging academia and the public sector, involving themselves in public policy, and developing and sustaining personal and professional resilience along the way. This chapter offers perspectives on these subjects based on 25 years of professional experience, 15 in federal service and a decade in higher education and the national nonprofit sector. It argues that professionally trained historians can be well-suited to bridge academe and the public sector, and involve themselves in public policy, by embracing their expertise while communicating and collaborating across disciplinary boundaries. Successful bridging depends upon being actionable, intentional, and strategic in one's career trajectory. It also depends upon self-awareness, self-empowerment, and resilience; building, maintaining, and growing a network of trusted and mutually supportive colleagues; setting priorities and goals, and being flexible and open to the fact that opportunities to bridge academe and the public sector can arise by design and by chance. When they happen by design, be prepared to fail. When they happen by chance, be comfortable being uncomfortable taking an unfamiliar path. The journey can be deeply meaningful, and the destination can be a rewarding career through which one can be an impactful envoy for historical training and the history profession.

2 Background and Career Trajectory

The National Library of Medicine (NLM) has multiple complementary identities that consistently make it a dynamic and interesting place to be in public service. Administratively, the library is one of the 27 institutes and centers which constitute the National Institutes of Health (NIH), which itself is part of the U.S. Department of Health and Human Services (HHS) (NIH 2024a). As part of the NIH and located physically on its Bethesda, Maryland, campus, the NLM is increasingly essential to advancing the mission of the agency, especially in the areas of artificial intelligence, data science, and achieving a "whole-of-society approach" to improving human health (Bertagnolli 2024).

The NLM is also one of the five national libraries of the United States, along with the Library of Congress, National Library of Agriculture, National Library of Education, and the National Library of Transportation. Each of these institutions is a major hub for multidisciplinary collaboration and research. Each employs individuals of a variety of backgrounds who collaborate on a variety of public service-focused initiatives which support the historical research enterprise in its variety of forms—from digital humanities scholarship based on datasets to curated born-digital collections to exhibitions and peer-reviewed publications contributing to the research ecosystem.

As a national library, the NLM is authorized by Congress to collect, organize, and preserve materials pertinent to medicine, make these materials and related resources publicly available, provide reference and research assistance, and engage in such other activities as deemed appropriate and the library's resources permit (U.S. Government Publishing Office). It is a noble and important mission the library shares with its counterparts, and research libraries overall, to be storehouses of knowledge and homes of multidisciplinary expertise which combine to define boundaries of research inquiry (Carr 2000).

This identity and purpose gives meaning to yet another identity of the NLM: It is the world's largest biomedical library with origins dating from the early nineteenth century, as the Library of the Surgeon General's Office of the U.S. Army. Over time, multiple locations housed the library as it grew, changed names, and ultimately found its current home as part of the NIH (Fig. 1). Beyond representing institutional growth and change, this trajectory reflects the work of generations of civil servants in building, preserving, and making available to the public the library's patrimony: its world-renowned collection about the human condition which spans eleven centuries, originates from nearly every part of the globe, and encompasses millions of items of a variety of physical and digital formats. Throughout its modern history, the NLM has demonstrated the research, teaching, and learning value of this patrimony in a variety of ways that support its Congressional authorization: curating exhibitions, publishing catalogs and books, sponsoring public programs, supporting staff

Fig. 1 Collage depicting the locations of the US National Library of Medicine and its predecessor institutions from 1862 to the present. From left to right are, (top row) Riggs Bank Building, Washington, DC (1862–1866) and Ford's Theatre, Washington, DC (1866–1887); (bottom row) the "Old Red Brick" building on the National Mall (1887–1962) and the campus of the National Institutes of Health, Department of Health and Human Services, Bethesda, Maryland (1962–present) (Reznick and Koyle 2017). Courtesy National Library of Medicine, National Institutes of Health

in discussing collections with diverse audiences, and overseeing resources which enable researchers to identify and study the library's collections and related resources.

Climatology and meteorology feature prominently in the history and collections of the NLM. During the early days of the library, in the 1830s, "the recording of meteorological data became one of the unique tasks assigned by the Army's leadership to its medical officers at frontier posts. Such data collection had been undertaken almost since the establishment of the Army medical department, primarily to study the suspected links between climate and disease" (Reznick and Koyle 2017: 10). Familiar with studies in Europe that attempted to measure the effects of population on local climates, Joseph Lovell, the first U.S. Army surgeon general, published the first compilation of this data in 1826, covering the years 1822–1825 (Figs. 2 and 3).

The results were conflicting but fundamentally valuable. As Lovell explained, "while one contends, that as population increases and cultivation extends the climate becomes warmer, another is equally convinced that it becomes colder, and a third, that there is no change in this respect" (Lovell 1826: 3). However, Lovell understood that across the young republic of America there was still much unpopulated and uncultivated land, and many military posts were in areas that were on the verge of human development. He believed that keeping meteorological records of these areas would provide invaluable data in support of future conclusions. The consistent meteorological records he and his successors achieved through the nineteenth century are considered a substantial foundation of the nation's historical weather data (Reznick and Koyle 2017: 10).

Of a piece with this history of the NLM is its 1970 exhibition *The Darkening Day* which chronicled health aspects of environmental pollution framed by historical and contemporary concerns of scientists and scholars about "the life-threatening despoliation of his world" (*NIH Record* 1970). In 2020, my colleagues and I recognized the fiftieth anniversary of *The Darkening Day* with a new online exhibition, *Fifty Years Ago: The Darkening Day* (Fig. 4). It highlighted examples of research, programs and policies, public messaging, and action taken by the U.S. Department of Health, Education and Welfare and federal scientists from the U.S. Public Health Service, as awareness of the detrimental impacts of pollution on health grew in the years preceding 1970 (Fig. 4) (NLM 2021; Blakemore 2020). We complemented this exhibition with publication of a scholarly essay, "Darkening Day: Air Pollution Films and Environmental Awareness, 1960–1972" and an associated public program, "Peril in the Air: Pollution Activism on Film," which explored the intersection of filmmaking, government and medicine working together to drive environmental awareness and policy (NLM 2020b, NIH 2021, *NIH Record* 2021). Subsequently, on NLM's popular blog *Circulating Now*, my colleagues and I curated and launched a virtual tour of the historical collections of the library "featuring materials which speak to a key issue of our time, and of previous times: the relationship between climate and health" (NLM 2023b) (Fig. 5).

It is a privilege and pleasure working at an institution nearing two centuries of public service through its collecting, preserving, curating, and democratizing

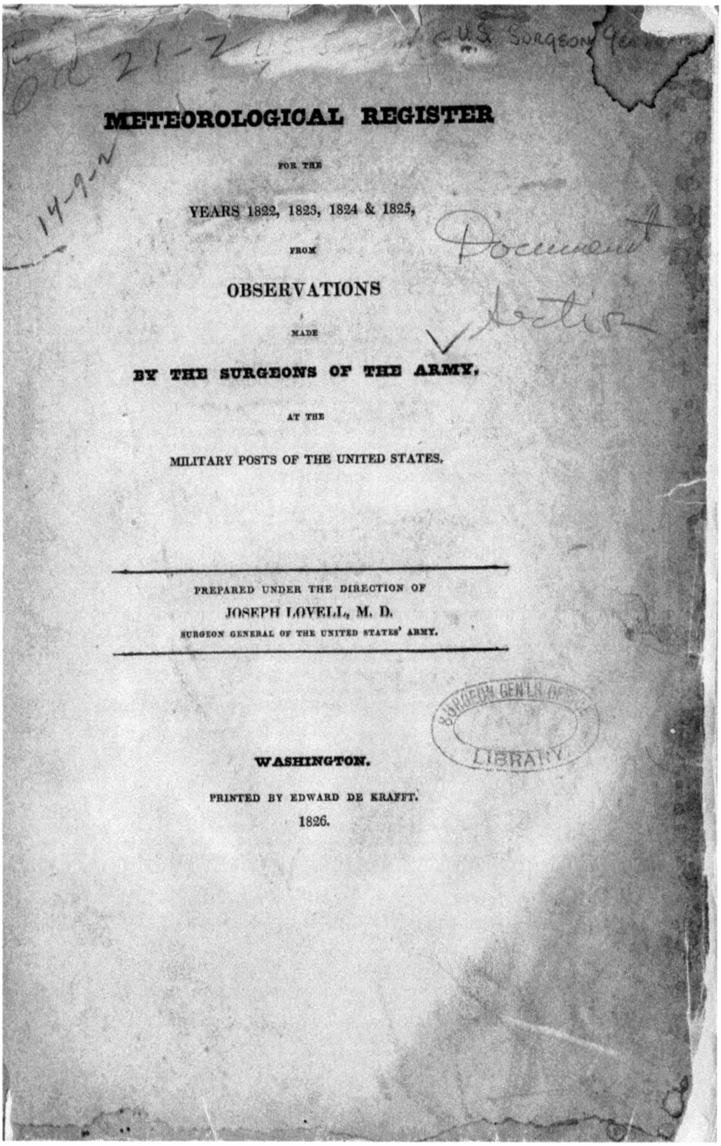

Fig. 2 Surgeon General Lovell prepared The *Meteorological Register* recognizing that there was a unique opportunity in the United States to examine and record the impact of population growth, agriculture, and deforestation on the environment, an opportunity that did not exist in Europe because the spread of civilization there had taken place over millennia rather than over the course of a few decades, as was happening in early-nineteenth-century North America. As Lovell stated, he prepared his tables "in the form that appears best calculated for reference, in order to preserve the facts thus collected." Lovell proposed that observations should be made for 8 or 10 years "in order to ascertain what changes, if any, have taken place, either in the mean temperature, the range of the thermometer, the course of the winds, or the weather" after settlement of the country (Lovell 1826; Reznick and Koyle 2017: 12). Courtesy National Library of Medicine, National Institutes of Health

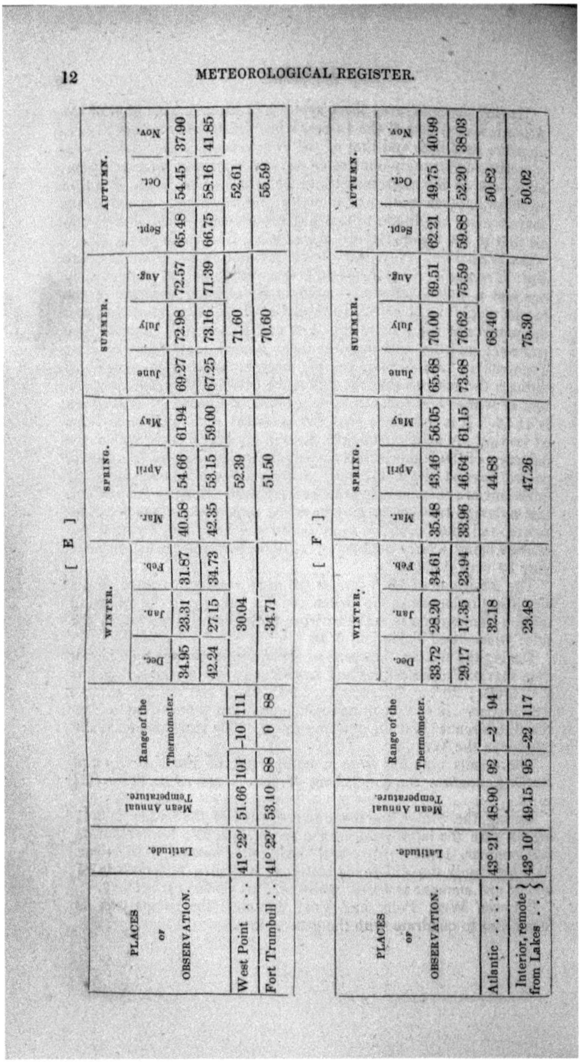

12 METEOROLOGICAL REGISTER.

[E]

PLACES of OBSERVATION.	Latitude.	Mean Annual Temperature.	Range of the Thermometer.			WINTER. Dec.	Jan.	Feb.	SPRING. Mar.	April.	May.	SUMMER. June.	July.	Aug.	AUTUMN. Sept.	Oct.	Nov.
						34.95	23.31	31.87	40.58	54.66	61.94	69.27	72.98	72.57	65.48	54.45	37.90
						42.24	27.15	34.73	42.35	53.15	59.00	67.25	73.16	71.39	66.75	58.16	41.85
West Point . . .	41° 22'	51.66	101	-10	111		30.04			52.39			71.60			52.61	
Fort Trumbull . .	41° 22'	53.10	88	0	88		34.71			51.50			70.60			55.59	

[F]

PLACES of OBSERVATION.	Latitude.	Mean Annual Temperature.	Range of the Thermometer.			WINTER. Dec.	Jan.	Feb.	SPRING. Mar.	April.	May.	SUMMER. June.	July.	Aug.	AUTUMN. Sept.	Oct.	Nov.
						33.72	28.20	34.61	35.48	43.46	56.05	65.68	70.00	69.51	62.21	49.75	40.99
						29.17	17.35	23.94	33.96	46.64	61.15	73.68	76.62	75.59	59.88	52.20	38.03
Atlantic	43° 21'	48.90	92	-2	94		32.18			44.83			68.40			50.82	
Interior, remote from Lakes . .	43° 10'	49.15	95	-22	117		23.48			47.26			75.30			50.02	

Fig. 3 Surgeon General Thomas Lawson continued Lovell's collection of meteorological observations, preparing the *Meteorological Register for the Years 1826–1830* and therein retaining his tabular format to display temperatures, prevailing winds, and sky conditions. The result was a two-volume set of meteorological registers that provided detailed climate data for the years 1822–1830 (Lawson 1840: 12; Reznick and Koyle 2017: 14). Courtesy National Library of Medicine, National Institutes of Health

knowledge about the human condition across time and place. Before I joined the NLM, I held a series of executive leadership roles in the national nonprofit sector. In each of these roles, I used my knowledge, skills, and abilities as a historian to advance the missions of my affiliated organizations. I also pursued scholarly historical research as a formal part of my work, publishing on subjects aligned with the interests and history of my organizations. For example, at the National Museum of Health and Medicine, where I served as senior curator, and at the American Occupational Therapy Foundation, where I directed its Institute for the Study of Occupation and Health, I completed the research and writing for my second book, about the humanitarianism of the novelist John Galsworthy supporting soldiers

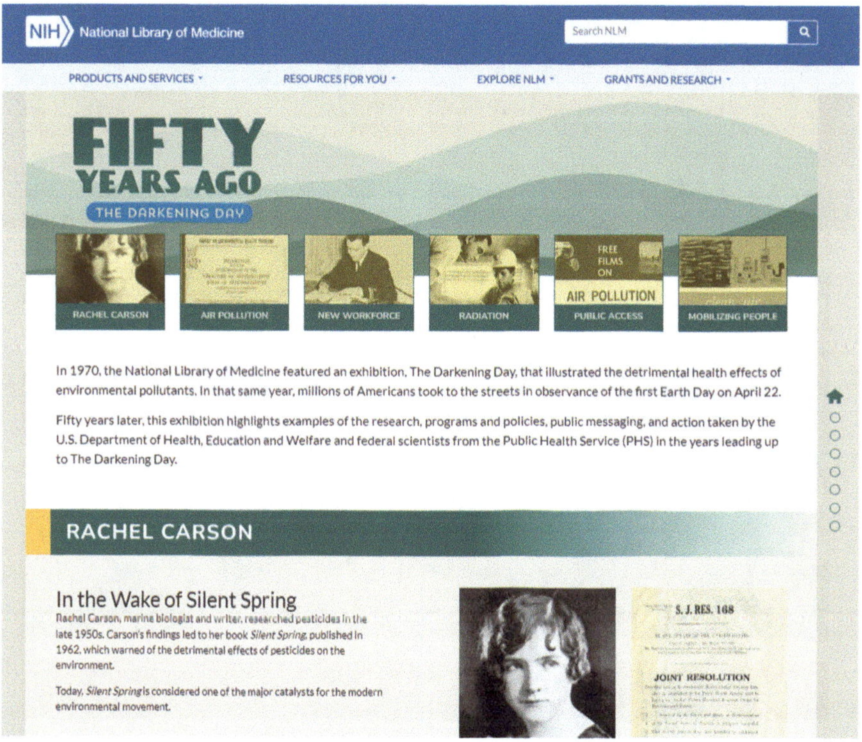

Fig. 4 Homepage of the NLM exhibition *Fifty Years Ago: The Darkening Day*, which highlights examples of the environmental health research, programs and policies, public messaging, and action taken by the U.S. Department of Health, Education and Welfare and federal scientists from the Public Health Service leading up to 1970, when the NLM exhibition *The Darkening Day* debuted. https://www.nlm.nih.gov/exhibition/fiftyyearsago/. Courtesy National Library of Medicine, National Institutes of Health

disabled in the First World War (Reznick 2009), as well as a related chapter, "Prostheses and Propaganda: Materiality and the Human Body in the Great War," in the book *Matters of Conflict: Material Culture, Memory, and the First World War* (Reznick 2004). Such bridging of my academic work and public service enabled me to connect my affiliated organizations to new stakeholders and enrich their present-day missions through connections to the past. It also broadened my own professional horizons as I discovered wider appreciation of my historical skills, new audiences for my research and writing, and new ways of thinking about the relevance of history to the present and future.

This experience points to hallmarks of my bridging academe and the public sector, a journey that was both intentional and organic as it grew from circumstances of professional opportunity and personal interest. I did not pursue this journey to arrive on "the other side" or beyond academe, but rather to reach a place *connecting* academe with the public sector where I could realize continued professional growth by

Fig. 5 *NLM Collections Tour: Climate and Health*, Circulating Now blog post. April 20, 2023. https://circulatingnow.nlm.nih.gov/2023/04/20/nlm-collections-tour-climate-and-health/. Courtesy National Library of Medicine, National Institutes of Health

applying my training in a mission-focused organization, collaborating with a variety of individuals who shared common interests, and, through both, achieving meaningful work. Underpinning this intention was my persistent desire to apply my skills as a trained historian in ways that could yield dialogue both within and beyond the field as well as applicability to address challenges, problems, and questions of our world. My later years of graduate school, partly informed by the challenging state of the academic job market, made me curious about where my training as a historian could take me and how it could help me meet new people and engage in activities involving the combination of history and public service. My cumulative leadership experience in the national nonprofit sector, together with my academic background, eventually enabled me to land in public service at the NLM, as a leader and subject-matter expert who could effectively work with people of diverse backgrounds and training, represent and engage with the collections and related programs of the library, and advance key policies which inform federal service (Downey 2021).

3 Public Service and Policy

"Policy—and its cousin, legislation—make the world go round," former NLM Director Dr. Patricia Brennan wrote. She explained further that:

> They lay out a course of action, guide decisions, and set the parameters for future choices. While policies and legislation are being crafted, it's a tug of war between details and context, minutiae and meaning, big picture and nuance, with that push and pull yielding documents that govern actions for years, often for decades if not longer (Brennan 2019).

A variety of related policies have governed my work at the NLM, as they do the work of all federal employees. Over the years, through my historical training and cumulative management and leadership experience, I have had many opportunities with colleagues to support and implement these policies as they advance the mission of the library as a global resource for health information.

Open Access

Foremost among the policies with which I engage as a federal historian is open access, meaning the provision of free access to peer reviewed, scholarly, and research information to all, "…requir[ing] that the rights holder grants worldwide irrevocable right of access to copy, use, distribute, transmit, and make derivative works in any format for any lawful activities with proper attribution to the original author" (Swann 2012). I have collaborated with many colleagues to advance this policy in a variety of ways.

Shortly after my arrival at the NLM, in support of its 175th anniversary and associated book, *Hidden Treasure*, about the history and historical collections of the library, I worked with my colleague Dr. Michael Sappol, editor of the volume, to negotiate an open access agreement with its publisher, enabling a complete digital copy to be freely and publicly available via NLM Digital Collections (2012) (Fig. 6). Subsequently, I worked with my colleague Elizabeth Mullen to serialize the book on the NLM's popular blog *Circulating Now*, bringing its rich content to an even wider audience (NLM n.d.-a).

A few years later, I worked with colleagues to craft and lead the NLM's partnership with the Wellcome Trust to digitize, and include in the library's world-renowned, open-access repository PubMed Central (PMC), the full runs of diverse journals that chart the development of medical science over the last 150 years, including two of the historical community's most sought-after journals in digital form, *The Hospital* and *The Indian Medical Gazette*. Building measurably on the 2004–2010 NLM-Wellcome Medical Journal Backfiles Digitization Project, this second chapter in the partnership resulted in millions of articles, along with their human- and computer-readable citations—a historical treasure trove spanning three centuries—becoming publicly available to anyone anywhere in the world and for

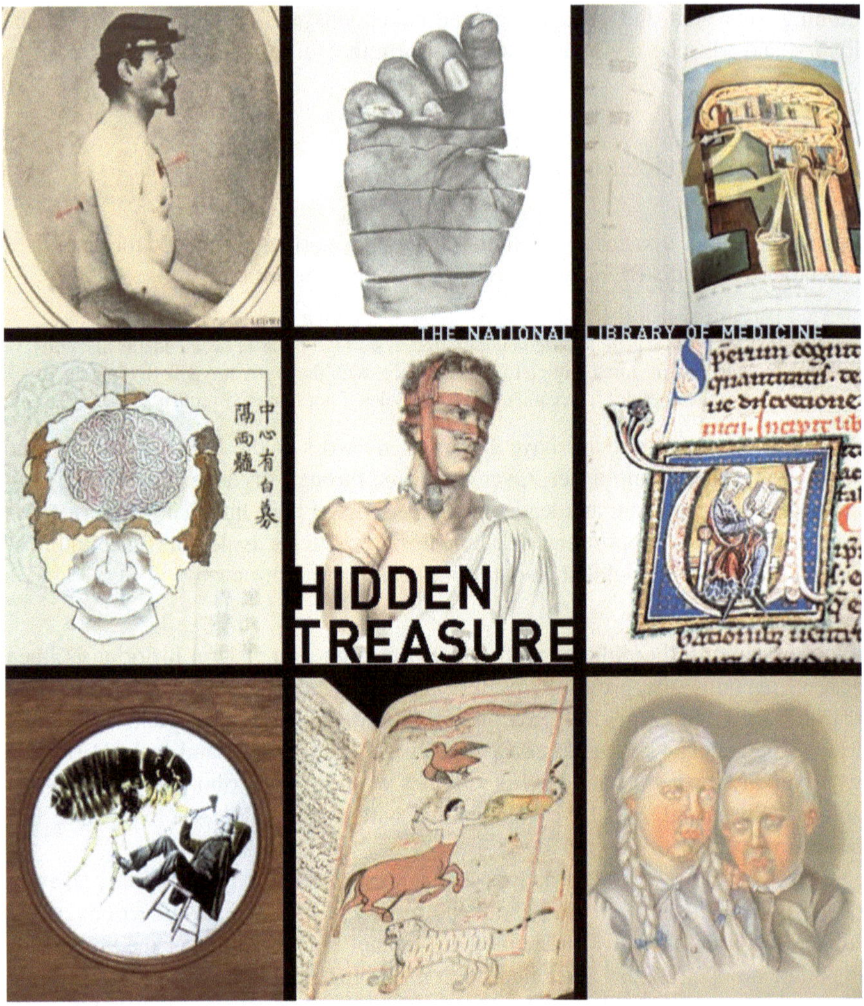

Fig. 6 *Hidden Treasure: The National Library of Medicine*. New York: Blast Books, 2012. http://resource.nlm.nih.gov/101569502. Courtesy Blast Books and National Library of Medicine, National Institutes of Health

any purpose (Reznick et al. 2019). Subsequently, I supported an outstanding multidisciplinary team of librarians and technical specialists in continuing to grow the valuable historical corpus of PMC by making available more than 55,000 individual articles from the back issues of more than a dozen journals spanning the 1820s to the 1910s and falling under the Creative Commons Public Domain Mark (Dunne et al. 2023; NLM 2019a; Reznick and Dunne 2024). As the NLM explained at the conclusion of its landmark partnership with Wellcome:

> Researchers, educators, and students will benefit from this vast corpus of historical biomedical information for generations to come…questions about past, present, and future

> epidemics will more likely have answers...advances in medicine and science during wartime can be better understood, aiding the thoughtful development of new treatments, without unnecessarily retracing steps covered in earlier research... and...the development of the medical profession, and changes in the experience of patients, can be appreciated in greater detail, to improve the delivery of healthcare for all (NLM 2019a, b).

Additionally, I worked with my colleague Kenneth M. Koyle to co-edit a new illustrated history of the NLM, intended for a general audience and to inspire learning about the development and public service of our institution during its nearly 200-year history (Reznick and Koyle 2017) (Fig. 7). I also worked with its publisher to make a complete digital copy of this book, like *Hidden Treasure*, freely available via NLM Digital Collections, and again with my colleague Elizabeth Mullen to serialize it on *Circulating Now* (NLM n.d.-b). Through these collaborations, many have come to learn about the NLM and its vast collections, not only more scholars but also many individuals who have a general interest in libraries and history, and who never knew in the first place that the United States has a national medical library.

These open access projects inspired yet another which I co-conceived and co-edited with Elizabeth Mullen during the COVID-19 pandemic, and in close cooperation with Corinne Guimont and Emily Hills at Virginia Tech Publishing: *Circulating Now, Full Circle: From the Historical Collections of the National Library of Medicine* (Fig. 8). Based on the aforementioned blog, this book marries newly written material with selected posts from the hundreds authored by dozens of individuals who contributed to the blog over the course of nearly a decade (Fig. 9). It organizes these selected posts thematically to examine, annotate, and enhance what the *Washington Post* called the "varied, lively and sometimes surprising" content of its original source (Blakemore 2018). Throughout, readers will also find a dozen reflections on selected posts written by their original authors—interludes that convey the persistent meaning in the lives of their authors of their contributions and the subjects they address. The resulting volume expands and realizes anew the original mission of *Circulating Now* while joining an increasing number and variety of scholarly and popular books born from and inspired by blogs: from historical fiction and nonfiction to web-based comics and travel guides, twitter handbooks and best practices in business to animal-welfare advocacy initiatives and advice columns. By extension, as Mary Culler and E. Thomas Ewing explain in their preface, *Circulating Now, Full Circle* contributes to evolving conversations about and guidelines informing how blogs, blogging, and collections born from blogs reflect not only the convergence of our digital age with new ways of writing and longstanding appreciation of "the book" and traditional book culture, but also the diverse and changing ways in which academics undertake research, teach, and talk with their colleagues and the public; students learn and engage with technology and contemporary events; authors and editors conceive, reconceive, and share their work; and readers and publishers receive this work and engage with it (Mullen and Reznick 2024: 2–3).

These and many other open access projects I have led, co-led, and supported have helped to democratize access to history and open the NLM and its collections and resources to the nation and the world. Such work is enormously satisfying,

Fig. 7 *Images of America: US National Library of Medicine*. Mount Pleasant, SC: Arcadia Publishing, 2017. Published open-access through a public-private partnership with Arcadia. Additionally, all 170+ images which appear in the book are archived and freely available in NLM Digital Collections. http://resource.nlm.nih.gov/101706419. Courtesy Arcadia Publishing and National Library of Medicine, National Institutes of Health

knowing that it contributes to shaping present and future research questions posed by a variety of disciplines as well as teaching and learning about the human condition across time and place as it can be understood through the collections of the world's largest biomedical library.

Fig. 8 *Circulating Now, Full Circle*. Blacksburg, VA: VT Publishing, 2024. Published open-access and freely available in NLM Digital Collections. https://doi.org/10.21061/circulating-now. http://resource.nlm.nih.gov/101706419. Courtesy VT Publishing and National Library of Medicine, National Institutes of Health

Fig. 9 Dozens of individuals of varied backgrounds have published hundreds of stories on *Circulating Now*, sharing the myriad ways NLM historical collections and programs inform research, teaching, learning, and public service. Courtesy National Library of Medicine, National Institutes of Health

Open Science and Transparency of Research

While open access increases the reach and impact of research, it does not automatically ensure transparency in how research is, or was, conducted or reported. The policy of open science helps to achieve this goal through embedding transparency in the research ecosystem wherein research products and processes are available and known to all, all parties involved in the products and processes are respected, and key ten of security and privacy are upheld fostering collaborations, reproducibility, and equity (The White House Office of Science and Technology Policy 2023).[1] As a historian, I have worked alongside my colleagues in the areas of archives and policy to advance open science and transparency retrospectively, helping to ensure that lessons of the past inform the present and future of biomedical research, health care, public health, and healthy behavior.

In the fall of 2023, my colleagues and I collaborated to host representatives of the leadership of Voices For Our Fathers Legacy Foundation and guide them in their research using the NLM's collection of reproduced documents from the U.S. Public Health Service (USPHS) "Study of Untreated Syphilis in the Negro Male at Tuskegee and Macon County, Alabama," and from the subsequent federal ad hoc committee which declared the study unethical, shut it down, and led to compensation for victims of the research and major changes in research practices and policies, above all the National Research Act of 1974 (Fig. 10). Following this visit, we worked further together, and with Fisk University, to make this collection available digitally, expressly to shine a light on the injustices perpetuated on the Black men in

[1] Equity is defined here as "the consistent and systematic fair, just, and impartial treatment of all individuals, including individuals who belong to underserved communities that have been denied such treatment, such as Black, Latino, and Indigenous and Native American persons, Asian Americans and Pacific Islanders and other persons of color; members of religious minorities; lesbian, gay, bisexual, transgender, and queer (LGBTQ+) persons; persons with disabilities; persons who live in rural areas; and persons otherwise adversely affected by persistent poverty or inequality" (The White House).

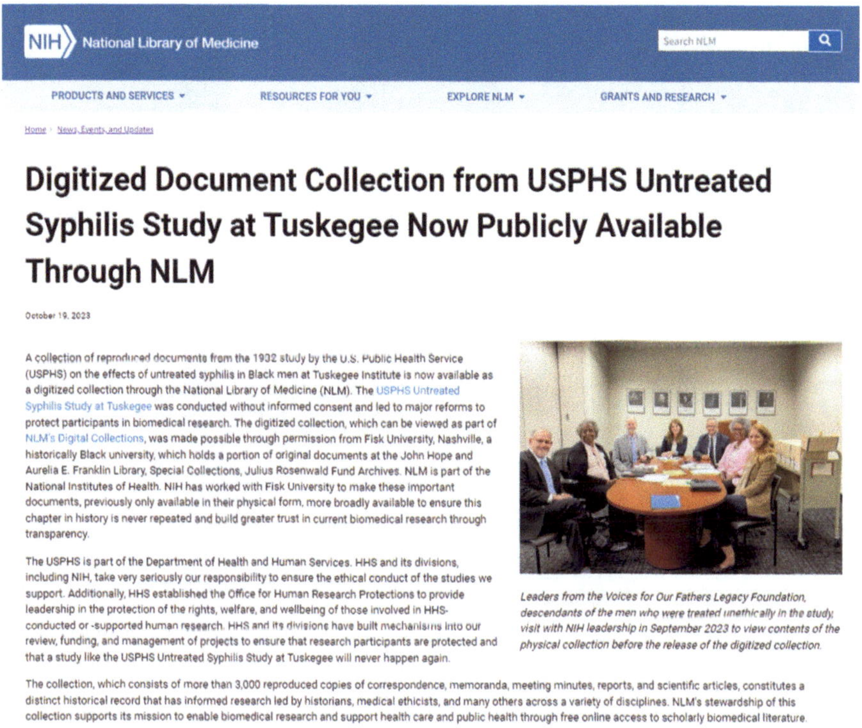

NIH National Library of Medicine

Search NLM

PRODUCTS AND SERVICES ▾ RESOURCES FOR YOU ▾ EXPLORE NLM ▾ GRANTS AND RESEARCH ▾

Home › News, Events, and Updates

Digitized Document Collection from USPHS Untreated Syphilis Study at Tuskegee Now Publicly Available Through NLM

October 19, 2023

A collection of reproduced documents from the 1932 study by the U.S. Public Health Service (USPHS) on the effects of untreated syphilis in Black men at Tuskegee Institute is now available as a digitized collection through the National Library of Medicine (NLM). The USPHS Untreated Syphilis Study at Tuskegee was conducted without informed consent and led to major reforms to protect participants in biomedical research. The digitized collection, which can be viewed as part of NLM's Digital Collections, was made possible through permission from Fisk University, Nashville, a historically Black university, which holds a portion of original documents at the John Hope and Aurelia E. Franklin Library, Special Collections, Julius Rosenwald Fund Archives. NLM is part of the National Institutes of Health. NIH has worked with Fisk University to make these important documents, previously only available in their physical form, more broadly available to ensure this chapter in history is never repeated and build greater trust in current biomedical research through transparency.

The USPHS is part of the Department of Health and Human Services. HHS and its divisions, including NIH, take very seriously our responsibility to ensure the ethical conduct of the studies we support. Additionally, HHS established the Office for Human Research Protections to provide leadership in the protection of the rights, welfare, and wellbeing of those involved in HHS-conducted or -supported human research. HHS and its divisions have built mechanisms into our review, funding, and management of projects to ensure that research participants are protected and that a study like the USPHS Untreated Syphilis Study at Tuskegee will never happen again.

Leaders from the Voices for Our Fathers Legacy Foundation, descendants of the men who were treated unethically in the study, visit with NIH leadership in September 2023 to view contents of the physical collection before the release of the digitized collection.

The collection, which consists of more than 3,000 reproduced copies of correspondence, memoranda, meeting minutes, reports, and scientific articles, constitutes a distinct historical record that has informed research led by historians, medical ethicists, and many others across a variety of disciplines. NLM's stewardship of this collection supports its mission to enable biomedical research and support health care and public health through free online access to scholarly biomedical literature.

Fig. 10 NLM announcement of the digital availability of its archival collection pertaining to the U.S. Public Health Service (USPHS) "Study of Untreated Syphilis in the Negro Male at Tuskegee and Macon County, Alabama." The NLM collects, preserves, and makes publicly available collections such as this one to advance open access, improve transparency in research, and ensure that lessons of the past inform the present and future of biomedical research, health care, public health, and healthy behavior. https://www.nlm.nih.gov/news/Collection-Untreated-Syphilis-Study-Tuskegee.html. Courtesy National Library of Medicine, National Institutes of Health

the study, ensure this chapter in history is never repeated, and build greater trust in current biomedical research through transparency. Up to this point—indeed since the executive secretary of the federal ad hoc advisory panel deposited it at the library in 1973—this collection of historical documents and other papers had only been available to study in the NLM reading room (NLM 2023a).

Several months after this collaboration, acting NLM director Dr. Stephen Sherry invited me to offer the NLM Board of Regents an overview of the history and current relevance of the aforementioned collection (NIH 2024b), as well as the teamwork which yielded its digitization and availability to the world. Moreover, nearly a year after my colleagues and I had worked together to make this collection digitally accessible, we reconvened to support leadership of HHS, NIH, and NLM in joining with VOFLF representatives to celebrate the NIH-VOFLF partnership *Advancing Trust, Transparency and Health Equity in Biomedical Research*. Together, this leadership unveiled and dedicated a memorial plaque which I had the privilege of

Fig. 11 Commemorative plaque in the NLM herb garden which is now "shining a light on the injustice of the USPHS Study of Untreated Syphilis in the Negro Male at Tuskegee and Macon County, Alabama, 1932–1972." The QR code points to the associated NLM archival collection at https://resource.nlm.nih.gov/2934097R. Photo: Chia-Chi Charlie Chang. Courtesy *NIH Record*, National Institutes of Health

co-curating with my colleagues in the NIH Office of Science Policy, NIH Office of Communications and Public Liaison, and NLM Office of Communications and Public Liaison. Located prominently in the NLM herb garden, this memorial now complements the digitized collection of associated documents, shining a light on the injustice of the unethical USPHS study, and, in so doing, calling attention to its historical significance for biomedical research. The QR code featured on the plaque connects viewers directly and freely to the permalink of the collection in NLM Digital Collections (*NIH Record* 2024) (Fig. 11).

My involvement in this series of policy-focused historical projects was a poignant bookend to historical expertise I provided more than a decade earlier when my research in the NLM collections helped to inform public information on the 1946–1948 U.S. Public Health Service STD Inoculation Study and the joint statement of HHS and State Department leadership on the study, which reaffirmed commitment to the highest standards of ethics in medical research (U.S. Department of Health and Human Services, 2010a, b; U.S. Department of State 2010).

Interagency Collaboration

As Dr. Patricia Brennan wrote further about NLM and policy, the library participates in "trans-NIH and interagency working groups and committees" and "communicates with stakeholder groups with similar missions and interests" (Brennan

2019). In this context, too, I have contributed as a historian by conceiving, initiating, and leading the library's partnership with the National Endowment for the Humanities (NEH) to bring together scholars, scientists, librarians, archivists, healthcare professionals, and others in humanities and biomedical communities to share expertise and develop new research agendas (NEH 2020; NLM 2020a, b, c). Over a decade, the initiatives of this partnership collectively reached thousands of individuals, advancing open scholarship, teaching, and learning about the present and past interplay of science and society in a variety of contexts, including epidemic disease, racism and health inequality, and medical ethics (Vitale IV and Reznick 2024). Foremost among the scholarly programs and research outputs of the partnership was *Viral Networks: Connecting Digital Humanities and Medical History*, a peer-reviewed, open access book published following the eponymous conference supported by the NEH/NLM alliance (NIH 2019; NLM 2019a, b) (Fig. 12). Including a foreword I had the privilege of authoring, this book anthologizes the research presented at that conference, spanning seven centuries, multiple continents, and highlighting emerging digital humanities methodologies including data visualization and network analysis (Ewing and Randall 2018). In the words of one reviewer, the *Viral Networks* book

> [as] an electronic publication…is more than a "book." In line with digital humanities research, the essays resemble composite works featuring narrative content and diagrams, plus links to data sets and interactive data visualizations. The publication reflects the workshop's experimental and experiential dimensions while presenting intriguing scholarly essays on diverse facets of health and human connectivity (Garwood 2020).

Notably, the open access format of the *Viral Networks* book was itself an outcome of the NEH/NLM partnership as it enabled cooperation with Virginia Tech and VT Publishing. Here again, leveraging institutional partnerships enabled the library and its partners to advocate jointly for scholarly content to be made publicly accessible, an effort which has been met with success measured by more than 12,000+ abstract views, 9700+ downloads, and 640+ reads of *Viral Networks* since its publication.

The NEH-NLM partnership I led also allowed the agencies to respond nimbly to the COVID-19 pandemic, first by supporting a virtual symposium *Reporting, Recording & Remembering the 1918 Influenza Pandemic*, convened in cooperation with Virginia Tech (NIH 2020; NLM 2020c). The symposium invited undergraduate students studying the history of data in social contexts to present their research on various medical, social, and cultural aspects of the 1918 pandemic. Moreover, the program included comments from National Institute of Allergy and Infectious Diseases Senior Scientific Advisor Dr. David Morens and historian Dr. Nancy Bristow of the University of Puget Sound. More than 500 individuals viewed the symposium in real time, and, at the time of this publication, more than 1500 had watched the archived proceedings on-demand. The *NIH Record* covered *Reporting, Recording & Remembering the 1918 Influenza Pandemic* on its front page, under the headline "History Comes Alive: Students Learn Lessons from Previous Pandemic" (*NIH Record* 2020).

Fig. 12 *Viral Networks: Connecting Digital Humanities and Medical History*. Blacksburg, VA: VT Publishing 2018. This peer reviewed, open access volume grew out of the 2018 *Viral Networks workshop*, hosted by the History of Medicine Division of the National Library of Medicine, funded by the Office of Digital Humanities of the National Endowment for the Humanities, and organized by Virginia Tech. https://doi.org/10.21061/viral-networks • http://resource.nlm.nih.gov/101738722. Courtesy VT Publishing and National Library of Medicine, National Institutes of Health

Following the success of this symposium, the NEH-NLM partnership enabled the agencies to work further with Virginia Tech to organize *Data, Health, and the Digital Humanities: Shared Horizons II*, a series of virtual programs, and another open access book (NEH 2022; NLM 2022a). Through its very character as a virtual scholarly initiative focused on studying challenging stories of human experience during the pandemic, *Shared Horizons II* reflected the hallmarks of its historic time. Each contributor brought to it not only their disciplinary perspectives but also their own experiences of lockdowns, masking, and seeing news stories in real time about pandemic-related health disparities among high-risk and underserved populations, including racial and ethnic minority groups and rural communities. Each faced social distancing combined with virtual interactions, realizing the benefits, drawbacks, and implications of both. Each witnessed the race for a vaccine, its subsequent distribution, and then the race to receive "the jab" and subsequent boosters, all while learning how to use different kinds of COVID-19 home test kits and wondering when the pandemic would become endemic (Vitale IV and Reznick 2024).

These and related subjects informed the two virtual keynote lectures of *Shared Horizons II*, the first by Kim Gallon, PhD, Associate Professor of Africana Studies at Brown University, entitled "Shutting the Digital Back Door: Creating Tech Justice with Health Data Liquidity and the Digital Humanities" (NIH 2022b), and the second by Katy Kole de Peralta, PhD, Clinical Assistant Professor of History at Arizona State University, entitled "Life after Lockdown: Pandemic Perspectives from Peru" (NIH 2022a). My colleagues and I also published interviews with these speakers on *Circulating Now*, to expand awareness of their associated talks and their scholarship as it drew on NLM collections and related resources (NLM 2022b, c).

The contributors to the envisioned book attended these virtual lectures and, following each one, met virtually with the speakers for in-depth discussion and exchange of ideas about the impact of pandemic events on their research, teaching, and public service. The groups discussed witnessing pandemic death and the disparity of public health resources in real time via media coverage. They shared their experiences of building connections with colleagues through technology while longing for renewed physical engagement and coping with isolation, even as it sometimes gave way to welcome periods of contemplation. They discussed realizing the flexibility and navigating the limits of scholarship and research in the digital space, as well as the need to be patient until circumstances could allow for renewed access to valued collections for research. Through these conversations, a distinct sense of community and camaraderie arose among *Shared Horizons II* participants. The resulting open access book *Challenging Stories: Rethinking Health in the Spaces between Data and Narrative* (Fig. 13), to which I had the privilege of coauthoring the afterword with my colleague Frank Vitale IV, is as much a mirror of their dialogue and witness to unprecedented times as it is a memorial of a once-in-a-lifetime event impacting human experience and health. Apropos of the circumstances informing its conception and production, as the editors explain in the introduction to their book, they chose to call the volume "challenging"

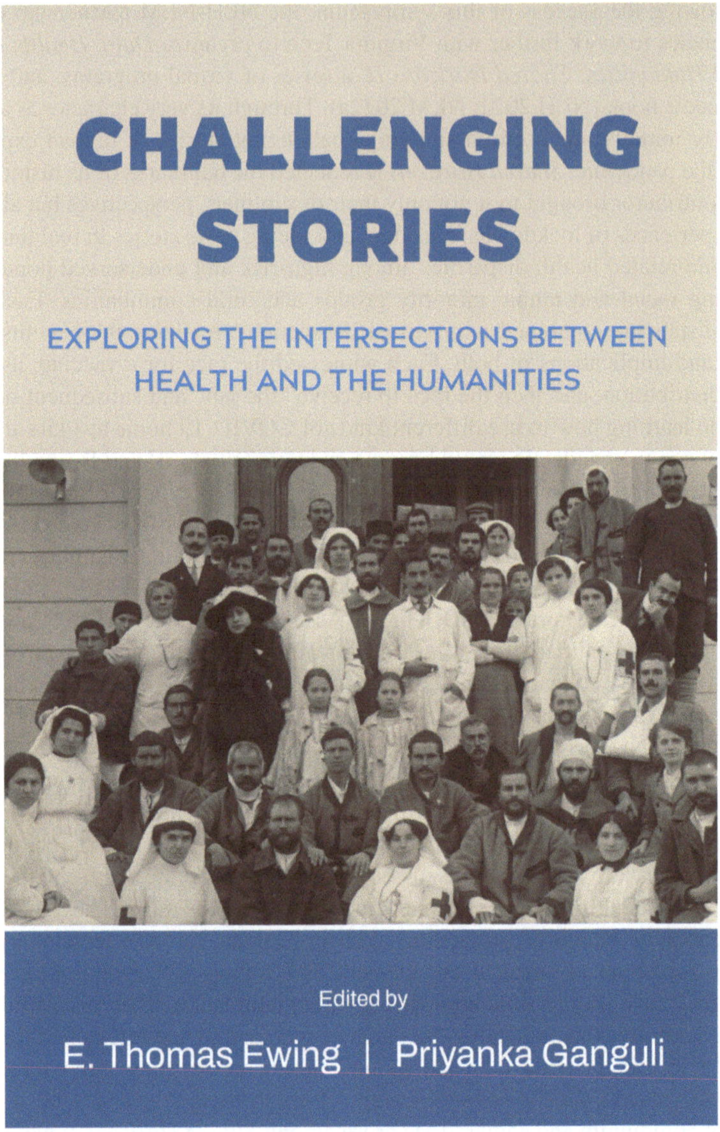

Fig. 13 Challenging stories: Rethinking health in the spaces between data and narrative. Blacksburg, VA: VT Publishing, 2024. This peer reviewed, open access volume grew out of the 2022 *Data, Health, and the Digital Humanities: Shared Horizons II* (DH^2) series of all-virtual programs hosted by the National Library of Medicine, funded by the Office of Digital Humanities of the National Endowment for the Humanities, and organized by Virginia Tech. https://doi.org/10.21061/challengingstories, https://collections.nlm.nih.gov/ChallengingStories. Courtesy VT Publishing and National Library of Medicine, National Institutes of Health

> …because of the dual meaning of the word in its most common forms: as an adjective, challenging can mean demanding, difficult, or exacting but as a verb, the word can also mean confronting, defying, or competing. Embedded in the book's title, therefore, is a tension between challenging stories, that is, stories of exacting or difficult circumstances related to diseases, medicine, and health, but also challenging stories, in the sense of questioning the narrative format as a way to explain and experience disease, medicine and health (Ewing and Ganguly 2024: 4–5).

Framed as such, this original and collaborative research output born from the COVID-19 pandemic achieves even more as it helps readers see individuals—of the past and the recent present living through challenging times "for who they are and for what they represent." As the editors explain further with reference to the historic photograph on the front of the book, and, on its back cover, a portion of the *New York Times* commemorative list of the first 100,000 deaths from the pandemic: "We may not know their names, ages, or traits, as summarized in the *New York Times*, and we do not see their faces, as in the hospital photograph, but their stories provide the illustration that we need to understand their lives and why they mattered. The challenges posed by their stories are challenges for scholars to interpret and readers to understand" (Ewing and Ganguly 2024: 7).

Leading the NLM's impactful partnership with the NEH, and contributing to its research outputs which advance the complementary missions of both agencies, stand among the most rewarding experiences of my public service career.

4 Lessons

These examples of my policy-focused historical and collaborative work at the NLM reflect a constellation of interrelated principles of thinking and action for historians who wish to bridge academe and the public sector:

1. Be open and flexible with your knowledge and skills as a historian. Deliberately share both and make them a part of conversations about policy, and initiatives which inform policy. Policy conversations can and should involve multiple perspectives. Therefore, if you wish to involve yourself in policy, you need to position yourself to do so, contributing your knowledge, skills, and abilities to policy dialogue.
2. Be empowered through your expertise as a historian, your research and writing skills, and your public speaking skills. Such self-empowerment can help you substantially on your journey to bridge academe and the public sector, enabling you to network and collaborate effectively outside your professional defined "lane" and beyond your personal comfort zone. It will also help you open new professional doors and accomplish a variety of goals.
3. Be amenable to pursuing multiple professional pathways on your journey. Do not put all your eggs in one career basket, look for opportunities to apply your expertise through collaboration, and build a work culture of mutual respect and support. Along the way, recognize that sometimes you need to educate others

about the value of what historians can bring to the table. Moreover, when you see a challenge or opportunity to apply your historical knowledge and skills, seize it. For example, when you learn about an individual or an organization appreciating or seeking a historical perspective, seize the opportunity to get to know them and potentially work with them. As you bridge academe and the public sector, embrace opportunities to bring your historical expertise to the table, connecting it with organizations you encounter, and people you meet, on your journey.

4. Build your network and be mutually supportive by offering to be a resource for people who are a resource for you. Keep in mind that some individuals in academe may have public sector career knowledge and experience to share, but many do not because they work primarily in academe. Therefore, you cannot and should not expect to bridge academe and the public sector through networking only with individuals within academe. You need to network beyond this space to build, maintain, and grow a network of trusted colleagues to whom you can turn for mutual support. Building such a supportive network of colleagues, family, and friends can be one way of building resilience in your journey from academe to the public sector.

   Most importantly: Look after yourself, both personally and professionally, and prioritize your future professional goals based on your interests and life circumstances. Pursue the work-life balance *you* wish to achieve on your journey bridging academe and the public sector.

5 Conclusion

Twenty-five years ago, there was very little open discussion within the field of history about bridging academe and the public sector. Most graduate programs offered little if any support to do so, and it was challenging to find like-minded individuals with whom you could share experiences and perspectives, and discuss career strategies. As of the writing of this chapter, such support and resources are far more prevalent and accessible, thanks to our increasingly connected world and particularly social media through which influencers in the field of history, and across the disciplines, share their own bridging experience with hallmarks of empowerment, networking, goal setting, and flexibility.

Reflecting on the arc and accomplishments of my career, I believe that historians can—and should—contribute to public policymaking and implementation, and take on a variety of roles in the public sector wherein they can make impactful contributions. I also believe that, in taking on these roles, historians can—and should—become envoys for the field history beyond the field itself, demonstrating the value of their collaboration, knowledge, and skills in addressing challenges, problems, and opportunities of our time. For myself, it has been—and remains—a meaningful and rewarding journey, lessons from which I am happy to share and pay forward.

References

Bertagnolli, Monica M. 2024. Connecting lab, clinic, and community. *Science* 384 (6700): 1049. https://www.science.org/doi/10.1126/science.adq2140.

Blakemore, Erin. 2018. The real history behind Harry Potter magic and WWI poison gas treatments. *Washington Post*. Apr 7, 2018. https://www.washingtonpost.com/national/health-science/the-real-history-behind-harry-potter-magic-and-wwi-poison-gas-treatments/2018/04/06/b7c14c6c-3824-11e8-9c0a-85d477d9a226_story.html

Blakemore, Erin. 2020. Educational films reflect evolving views in 1960s about the health dangers of air pollution, *Washington Post*. September 19, 2020 https://www.washingtonpost.com/health/air-pollution-health-risk-history/2020/09/17/5fc1965a-f854-11ea-be57-d00bb9bc632d_story.html. Accessed Nov 18, 2024.

Brennan, Patricia. 2019. NLM and public policy. *Musings from the Mezzanine: Innovations in Health Information from the National Library of Medicine*. Mar 19, 2019. https://nlmdirector.nlm.nih.gov/2019/03/19/nlm-and-public-policy/. Accessed Nov 18, 2024.

Carr, David. 2000. In the contexts of the possible: libraries and museums as incendiary cultural institutions. *RBM: A Journal of Rare Books, Manuscripts, and Cultural Heritage* 1 (2): 117–134. https://doi.org/10.5860/rbm.1.2.186.

Downey, Miranda. 2021. Lessons in practical macromanaging: Dr. Jeffrey Reznick's perspectives on leadership and public service. In *Collaboration, Empathy & Change: Perspectives on Leadership in Libraries and Archives in 2020*, ed. Trevor Owens and Angelina Wong, 113–125. SocArXiv Papers. https://doi.org/10.31235/osf.io/3gnds.

Dunne, Kristina, Kenneth M. Koyle, and Jeffrey S. Reznick. 2023. What's old is new to discover! *Musings from the Mezzanine: Innovations in Health Information from the National Library of Medicine*. Sept 20, 2023. https://nlmdirector.nlm.nih.gov/2023/09/20/whats-old-is-new-to-discover/. Accessed Nov 18, 2024.

Ewing, E. Thomas, and Priyanka Ganguly. 2024. *Challenging Stories: Rethinking Health in the Spaces between Data and Narrative*. Blacksburg, VA: VT Publishing. https://doi.org/10.21061/challengingstories.

Ewing, E. Thomas, and Katherine Randall. 2018. *Viral Networks: Connecting Digital Humanities and Medical History*. Blacksburg, VA: VT Publishing. https://doi.org/10.21061/viral-networks. https://publishing.vt.edu/site/books/e/10.21061/viral-networks/. Accessed Nov 18, 2024.

Garwood, Deborah A. 2020. Review of viral networks: connecting digital humanities and medical history. *The American Archivist* 83 (2): 475–480. https://doi.org/10.17723/0360-9081-83.2.475.

Lawson, Thomas. 1840. *Meteorological Register for the Years 1826, 1827, 1828, 1829, and 1830: From Observations Made by the Surgeons of the Army at the Military Posts of the United States*. Philadelphia, PA: Haswell, Barrington, and Haswell. http://resource.nlm.nih.gov/101144924. Accessed Nov 18, 2024.

Lovell, Joseph. 1826. *Meteorological Register for the Years 1822, 1823, 1824 & 1825: From Observations Made by the Surgeons of the Army at the Military Posts of the United States*. Washington, DC: Edward De Krafft. http://resource.nlm.nih.gov/60721380R. Accessed Nov 18, 2024.

Mullen, Elizabeth, and Jeffrey S. Reznick. 2024. *Circulating Now, Full Circle: From the Historical Collections of the National Library of Medicine*. Blacksburg, VA: VT Publishing. https://doi.org/10.21061/circulating-now.

National Endowment for the Humanities (NEH). 2020. *NEH & NLM Renew Partnership to Collaborate on Research, Education, and Career Initiatives*. https://www.neh.gov/news/neh-and-nlm-renew-partnership-collaborate-research-education-and-career-initiatives. Accessed Nov 18, 2024.

National Endowment for the Humanities (NEH). 2022. *NEH Co-Sponsors Shared Horizons II Virtual Workshop on Data, Health, and Digital Humanities*. https://www.neh.gov/news/

neh-co-sponsors-shared-horizons-ii-virtual-workshop-data-health-and-digital-humanities. Accessed Nov 18, 2024.
National Institutes of Health (NIH). 2019. *Viral Networks, Reconnected: A Digital Humanities/History of Medicine Research Forum.* https://videocast.nih.gov/watch=28992. Accessed Nov 18, 2024.
National Institutes of Health (NIH). 2020. *Reporting, Recording, and Remembering the 1918 Influenza Pandemic Research Symposium.* https://videocast.nih.gov/watch=36347. Accessed Nov 18, 2024.
National Institutes of Health (NIH). 2021. *Peril in the Air: Pollution Activism on Film.* https://videocast.nih.gov/watch=41224. Accessed Nov 18, 2024.
National Institutes of Health (NIH). 2022a. *Life after Lockdown: Pandemic Perspectives from Peru.* https://videocast.nih.gov/watch=46011. Accessed Nov 18, 2024.
National Institutes of Health (NIH). 2022b. *Shutting the Digital Back Door: Creating Tech Justice with Health Data Equity Liquidity and the Digital Humanities.* https://videocast.nih.gov/watch=46001. Accessed Nov 18, 2024.
National Institutes of Health (NIH). 2024a. *List of Institutes and Centers.* https://www.nih.gov/institutes-nih/list-institutes-centers. Accessed Nov 18, 2024.
National Institutes of Health (NIH). 2024b. *NLM Board of Regents Meeting.* https://videocast.nih.gov/watch=54494. Accessed Nov 18, 2024.
National Library of Medicine (NLM). 2019a. *NLM and Wellcome Complete Partnership to Provide Free Access to Hundreds of Years of Medical Research.* https://www.nlm.nih.gov/news/NLM_and_Wellcome_Complete_Partnership.html. Accessed Nov 18, 2024.
National Library of Medicine (NLM). 2019b. *Open-Access Book Based on 2018 Viral Networks Workshop Now Available.* https://wayback.archive-it.org/org-350/20210227202026/https://www.nlm.nih.gov/news/Open_Access_Book_Now_Available.html. Accessed Nov 18, 2024.
National Library of Medicine (NLM). 2020a. *NEH and NLM Renew Partnership to Collaborate on Research, Education, and Career Initiatives.* https://wayback.archive-it.org/org-350/20210227203045/https://www.nlm.nih.gov/news/NEH_and_NLM_Renew_Partnership_to_Collaborate_on_Research_Education_and_Career_Initiatives.html. Accessed Nov 18, 2024.
National Library of Medicine (NLM). 2020b. Darkening day: Air pollution films and environmental awareness, 1960–1972. *National Library of Medicine: Medicine on Screen.* https://medicineonscreen.nlm.nih.gov/2020/09/08/darkening-day-air-pollution-films-and-environmental-awareness-1960-1972/
National Library of Medicine (NLM). 2020c. *NLM Hosts Research Symposium: Reporting, Recording, and Remembering the 1918 Influenza Pandemic.* https://wayback.archive-it.org/org-350/20210227200532/https://www.nlm.nih.gov/news/NLM_Virtual_Research_Symposium.html. Accessed Nov 18, 2024.
National Library of Medicine (NLM). 2021. *NLM Launches a New Online Exhibition—Fifty Years Ago: The Darkening Day.* https://www.nlm.nih.gov/news/New_Online_Exhibition_DarkeningDay.html. Accessed Nov 18, 2024.
National Library of Medicine (NLM). 2022a. *NLM to Host Data, Health, and the Digital Humanities: Shared Horizons II.* https://www.nlm.nih.gov/news/NLM_to_Host_Data_Health_and_the_Digital_Humanities_Shared_Horizons_II.html. Accessed Nov 18, 2024.
National Library of Medicine (NLM). 2022b. Shutting the digital back door. *Circulating Now: From the Historical Collections of the National Library of Medicine.* https://circulatingnow.nlm.nih.gov/2022/10/03/shutting-the-digital-back-door/. Accessed Nov 18, 2024.
National Library of Medicine (NLM). 2022c. Life after lockdown: pandemic perspectives from Peru. *Circulating Now: From the Historical Collections of the National Library of Medicine.* https://circulatingnow.nlm.nih.gov/2022/11/03/life-after-lockdown-pandemic-perspectives-from-peru/. Accessed Nov 18, 2024.

National Library of Medicine (NLM). 2023a. *Digitized Document Collection from USPHS Untreated Syphilis Study at Tuskegee Now Publicly Available Through NLM*. https://www.nlm.nih.gov/news/Collection-Untreated-Syphilis-Study-Tuskegee.html. Accessed Nov 18, 2024.

National Library of Medicine (NLM). 2023b. NLM collections tour: climate and health. *Circulating Now: From the Historical Collections of the National Library of Medicine*. https://circulatingnow.nlm.nih.gov/2023/04/20/nlm-collections-tour-climate-and-health/. Accessed Nov 18, 2024.

National Library of Medicine (NLM). n.d.-a. Tag: Hidden treasure. *Circulating Now: From the Historical Collections of the National Library of Medicine*. https://circulatingnow.nlm.nih.gov/tag/hidden-treasure/. Accessed Nov 18, 2024.

National Library of Medicine (NLM). n.d.-b. Tag: Images of America. *Circulating Now: From the Historical Collections of the National Library of Medicine*. https://circulatingnow.nlm.nih.gov/tag/images-of-america/. Accessed Nov 18, 2024.

NIH Record. 1970. *NLM Exhibit Chronicles Environmental Pollution*. https://nihrecord.nih.gov/sites/recordNIH/files/pdf/1970/NIH-Record-1970-09-29.pdf. Accessed Nov 18, 2024.

NIH Record. 2020. *History Comes Alive: Students Learn Lessons from Previous Pandemic*. https://nihrecord.nih.gov/2020/06/26/students-learn-lessons-previous-pandemic. Accessed Nov 18, 2024.

NIH Record. 2021. *Scholars Study History of Pollution Activism*. https://nihrecord.nih.gov/sites/nihrecord/files/pdf/2021/NIH-Record-2021-10-15.pdf. Accessed Nov 18, 2024.

NIH Record. 2024. *Event Honors NIH Partnership with Voices for Our Fathers Legacy Foundation*. https://nihrecord.nih.gov/2024/10/11/event-honors-nih-partnership-voices-our-fathers-legacy-foundation. Accessed Nov 18, 2024.

Reznick, Jeffrey S. 2004. Prostheses and propaganda: Materiality and the human body in the Great War. In *Matters of Conflict: Material Culture, Memory, and the First World War*, ed. Nicholas J. Saunders, 51–61. London: Routledge.

Reznick, Jeffrey S. 2009. *John Galsworthy and Disabled Soldiers of the Great War*. Manchester: Manchester University Press.

Reznick, Jeffrey S., and Kristina Dunne. 2024. The medical bulletin and so much more. *Circulating Now: From the Historical Collections of the National Library of Medicine*. Feb 8, 2024. https://circulatingnow.nlm.nih.gov/2024/02/08/the-medical-bulletin-and-so-much-more/. Accessed Nov 18, 2024.

Reznick, Jeffrey S., and Kenneth M. Koyle. 2017. *U.S. National Library of Medicine*. Charleston, SC: Arcadia. http://resource.nlm.nih.gov/101706419. Accessed Nov 18, 2024.

Reznick, Jeffrey S., Christy Henshaw, Laura Randall, Rosalyn Leiderman, and Kathryn Funk. 2019. PubMed Central offers a historical treasure trove. *History News Network*. Aug 4, 2019. https://www.historynewsnetwork.org/article/pubmed-central-offers-a-historical-treasure-trove. Accessed Nov 18, 2024.

Sappol, Michael, ed. 2012. *Hidden Treasure: The National Library of Medicine*. New York: Blash Books. http://resource.nlm.nih.gov/101569502. Accessed Nov 18, 2024.

Swann, Alma. 2012. *Policy Guidelines for the Development and Promotion of Open Access, UNESCO*. https://unesdoc.unesco.org/ark:/48223/pf0000215863. Accessed Nov 18, 2024.

The White House Office of Science and Technology Policy. 2023. *Report to the U.S. Congress on Financing Mechanisms for Open Access Publishing of Federally Funded Research*. https://bidenwhitehouse.archives.gov/wp-content/uploads/2024/06/2024-Report-to-Appropriations-Committee-on-Scholarly-Publishing-and-Public-Access-Implementation.pdf. Accessed Nov 18, 2024.

U.S. Department of Health and Human Services. 2010a. *Information on the 1946–1948 United States Public Health Service STD Inoculation Study*. https://web.archive.org/web/20101005235945/https://www.hhs.gov/1946inoculationstudy/index.html. Accessed Ap 22, 2025.

U.S. Department of Health and Human Services. 2010b. *Joint statement by Secretaries Clinton and Sebelius on a 1946–1948 Study*. https://web.archive.org/web/20101004003440/http://www.hhs.gov/news/press/2010pres/10/20101001a.html. Accessed Apr 22, 2025.

U.S. Department of State. 2010. *Joint statement by Secretary of State Hillary Rodham Clinton and Secretary of Health and Human Services Kathleen Sebelius on the U.S. Public Health Service Sexually Transmitted Disease Inoculation Study of 1946-1948*. https://2009-2017.state.gov/secretary/20092013clinton/rm/2010/10/148464.htm. Accessed Nov 18, 2024.

U.S. Government Publishing Office, 42 U.S.C. https://www.govinfo.gov/content/pkg/USCODE-2011-title42/html/USCODE-2011-title42-chap6A-subchapIII-partD.htm. Accessed Nov 18, 2024.

Vitale, Frank, IV, and Jeffrey S. Reznick. 2024. From shared horizons to impactful collaboration and engagement: The interagency partnership of the National Endowment for the Humanities/National Library of Medicine, 2012–2024. *Interagency Journal* 14 (2): 17–31.

The Resilience of Cities: From the Present to the Past and Back Again

Michael E. Smith

Abstract I propose a method for linking archaeological or historical evidence with research on urban resilience today. The greatest harms from climate change—the most severe negative impacts on the greatest numbers of people—occur in cities, particularly cities in the Global South. How can archaeology and history contribute to this topic? I begin with the literature on contemporary urban adaptations to climate change, and highlight a list of twenty-one adaptation measures identified in the latest report by the IPCC (Intergovernmental Panel on Climate Change). I select four of these adaptation measures—water provisioning, food production, livelihoods, and housing—plus urban relocation, and illustrate some of the pertinent archaeological and historical research. I then describe four criteria for evaluating the long-term success of cities (persistence, resilience to shocks, growth, and prosperity), and discuss how these can be used to test or evaluate the five adaptation measures in the past. The final step in my proposed method—the coproduction of knowledge with urban sustainability scientists and policy makers to integrate these findings into broader scientific and policy realms—has yet to be carried out.

Keywords Cities · Resilience · Shocks · Relevance · Persistence

1 Introduction

Most of the contributors to this volume follow a common procedure in linking their archaeological and historical research with current concerns. They analyze their data, draw conclusions about past societies and social trends, and then cite literature on resilience or sustainability to show the relevance of the research. In short, this is an analytical movement from past to present. While this approach can yield important insights and findings—as the chapters here demonstrate—I propose a different analytical process. I begin with research and publications on adaptations to climate

M. E. Smith (✉)
Arizona State University, Tempe, AZ, USA
e-mail: mesmith9@asu.edu

J. F. Haldon, R. Fernandes (eds.), *Bridging History and Policy*, Understanding Complex Systems, https://doi.org/10.1007/978-3-032-24379-9_14

change today, select key themes that are amenable to archaeological and historical analysis, and then explore how these themes are enriched by our findings on the past.

This present-to-past approach has two implications. First, it suggests that a focus on ***urban*** climate change resilience and adaptations—as compared with general societal adaptations—may be the domain where our data on the past have the greatest potential to contribute to contemporary research and policy on resilience and sustainability. Second, it highlights some of the major disjunctions between our research and contemporary work that need to be addressed if our data are going to be made useful to contemporary concerns.

Figure 1 illustrates the analytical procedure I follow in this paper. After an introduction to the importance of cities for research on climate change adaptation, I review the climate-change adaptation measures proposed by the IPCC for cities today (step 1). I then identify several of these that leave evidence in the archaeological and historical records (step 2). I give a brief sketch of how the success of these

Fig. 1 Analytical movement between past and present

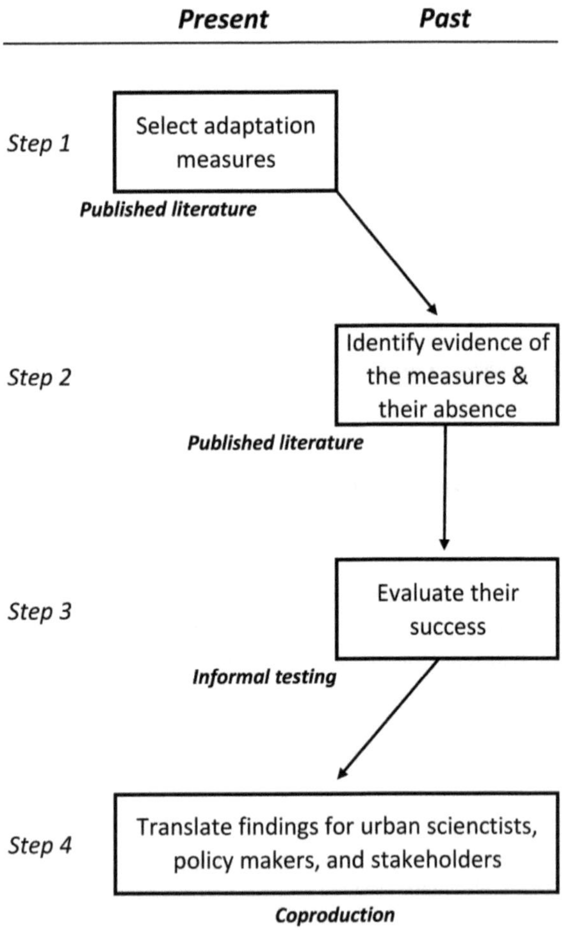

measures might be evaluated archaeologically (step 3), drawing on Smith (2023c). The final step, of translating the results to be of value to urban sustainability science today, involves coproduction—the joint production of knowledge by urban sustainability scientists, policy makers, stakeholders, and scholars of the past. This may be the most difficult part of the research process, and I leave this for development in future works.

2 Why Are Cities Important?

Cities are commonly viewed from either a negative perspective—as places of pollution, violence, crowding, and poverty—or a positive perspective—as places that generate economic growth and progress. Table 1, based on Satterthwaite (2016: 4), summarizes the most common negative and positive perspectives on cities today.

Research on sustainability and resilience is converging on the view that cities are key places for policy solutions to many problems of climate change adaptation. The concentration of people and poverty in cities—particularly in the Global South—means that the harms arising from global warming are felt most acutely in cities. But the economic benefits of cities and urbanization—including agglomeration effects and the more efficient use of resources in cities—mean that cities constitute a major part of the solution to many of the problems caused by climate change. This view now dominates both the research (Bai 2023; Dodman et al. 2022: 909; Satterthwaite 2016) and policy literatures on climate change adaptations today (Creutzig et al. 2024; United Nations 2023).

This growing appreciation for the centrality of cities and urbanization to climate change adaptation today has been expressed as follows:

> "Cities are both a hotbed of climate threats and a hotbed of climate solutions," said Jessica Troni, Head of UNEP's Climate Change Adaptation Unit. "More and more cities are developing adaptation plans, and we've seen cutting-edge innovations across the world, from rainwater harvesting systems to green infrastructure" (United Nations Environment Programme 2022).

Table 1 Negative and positive views of cities

Negative	Positive
Parasites on the economy, & on rural areas	Places of innovation, social justice, & economic success
Places that concentrate & generate pollution & carbon emissions	Places with the healthiest populations & low levels of pollution
Drivers of climate change	Places with a high quality of life
Concentrations of poverty, inequality & violence	Places for inclusive development of livelihoods, services, & government

Based on Satterthwaite (2016: 4)

This formulation provides an opening for archaeologists and historians to contribute to research and policy on climate change adaptations today. Quantitative research now shows that agglomeration effects—the processes that raise the per-capita economic productivity in cities and fuel their beneficial outcomes (Glaeser 2011; Storper 2013)—occurred in ancient urban systems. Settlement scaling research has revealed that past urban systems had the same quantitative levels of agglomeration effects as do urban systems today (Lobo et al. 2020; Ortman et al. 2020). These findings are a powerful statement that those urban dynamics based on face-to-face social interactions (Smith 2019a, 2023b) operated in both the past and the present. This finding provides a justification for looking to past urban contexts for ideas about cities today.

3 Urban Climate Change Adaptation Measures

Researchers in the climate and sustainability fields took a broad concept with a long history in the biological and social sciences—adaptation—and redefined it—as "climate change adaptation"—with a much narrower domain. In place of the former emphasis on adjustments that can be measured by their effects over time, climate change adaptation became defined as deliberate actions and policies undertaken to ameliorate the effects of climate change. This change in meaning is discussed in Oliver-Smith (2016), Orlove (2022), and Smith (2023c). In the words of Oliver--Smith, "The term adaptation has shifted from referring to a basic and omnipresent process of change in life to being a policy driven set of formal strategies and projects" (Oliver-Smith 2016: 63). See Table 2, which is based on Jones et al. (2021) and Thornton and Manasfi (2010).

In the Sixth Assessment Report Working Group II, the IPCC authors state: "Adaptation is defined, in human systems, as the process of adjustment to actual or expected climate and its effects in order to moderate harm or take advantage of beneficial opportunities" (Pörtner et al. 2022: note 10). That report's chapter on urban adaptations (Dodman et al. 2022), lists twenty-one specific "adaptation measures;" see Table 3. This list of typical of other discussions of urban climate change adaptation (e.g., Lobo et al. 2023; Magnan et al. 2020; Prieur-Richard et al. 2019; Wasley et al. 2023).

While most scholars would probably agree that the adaptation measures listed in Table 3 can likely contribute to ameliorating the effects of global warming, the

Table 2 The concept of adaptation

Climate-change adaptation	Adaptation in biology & anthropology
Anticipatory	Reactive
Outcome assessment is guesswork	Outcomes can only be judged in retrospect
Negative connotation (forced to do something)	Positive connotation (creative force for change)

Sources: Jones et al. (2021), Thornton and Manasfi (2010)

Table 3 Specific urban adaptation measures used by the IPCC (Dodman et al. 2022)

1	Water provisioning & management	Emergency management & security
2	Food production & security	Energy Infrastructure
3	Livelihoods & social protection	Flood management
4	Housing & building design	Health
		Information & communication technology
	Built form	Land-use planning
	Air quality regulation	Riverine flood impact reduction
	Coastal flood protection	Stormwater & sanitation
	Coastal management	Temperature regulation
	Cultural heritage & institutions	Transport
	Education & communication	Water & sanitation

Note: Items numbered 1–4 are examples discussed in the text

empirical question of whether they in fact work remains unanswered. Empirical measurement of adaptation success is difficult because these are complex domains, the baseline for comparison is moving, and there are limited data available to make meaningful assessments (Fisher 2022). Most works that discuss the success or effectiveness of climate change adaptations (e.g., Adger et al. 2005; Eriksen et al. 2021; Serra et al. 2022; Singh et al. 2021) employ lists of abstract principles (e.g., effectiveness, efficiency, equity, flexibility) in place of any kind of testing of actual real-world outcomes.

One reason for the difficulty in evaluating the success of adaptation measures is the short time frame available in studies of urban sustainability today. The serious consequences of global warming are recent and sudden, and it is simply too soon to know the outcomes of most adaptation measures. Examining change over longer time frames, of course, is a strength of history and archaeology, providing an opportunity to contribute to the study of adaptation measures. If we can identify such adaptations in the past, it may prove possible to evaluate their success or failure over the long haul.

4 Testing Urban Adaptations: Urban Success Measures

In a separate paper (Smith 2023c) I develop a model of urban success for past cities. I begin with the concept of successful livelihoods as defined by Osbahr et al. (2010: 2): "Taking resilience theory as a starting point, we define the process of successful adaptation as that which increases system resilience but also, giving explicit treatment to governance, as that which promotes legitimate institutions to generate and sustain collective action." Urban success in the past is a similar concept, and I propose three dimensions of measurement: persistence (the longevity of the city), population growth, and prosperity; see Fig. 2. Here, I add a fourth measure of urban success, resilience to shocks.

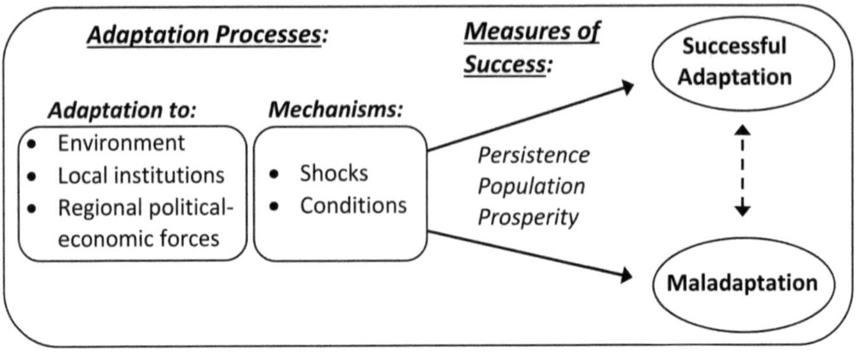

Fig. 2 Urban success conceptual model. From Smith (2023c: 4)

1. *Persistence.* Although the notion of persistence is part of many definitions of sustainability (Costanza and Patten 1995), persistence is not part of contemporary discussions of urban resilience or climate change adaptation, largely because of their limited time scales (Smith 2023a). Archaeological research on the persistence of early cities and settlements is in its infancy (Bird et al. 2024; Carballo et al. 2022; Smith et al. 2021; Lawrence et al. 2025), and it is not yet clear whether empirical findings on this topic will prove useful for understanding contemporary urban climate change adaptations. As a measure of past urban success, however, persistence seems appropriate.
2. *Population Growth* is a common measure of adaptedness and evolutionary success in biology (Peck and Waxman 2018) and economic history (Bairoch 1988; Storper 2013). While larger cities may generate more problems than smaller cities (see above), they are also more productive on a per capita basis (Lobo et al. 2020). Using city size as a measure of ancient urban success can be difficult, given the reluctance of many archaeologists to engage in population reconstruction (Smith 2023b: Chapter 3). As ancient demographic reconstructions become more common, this measure will assume greater significance.
3. *Prosperity* is a common measure of urban and societal success today (Conceição, this volume), where the term generally means “more choices, richer lives, and an improved quality of life” (Budowski et al. 2010). The application of this concept in archaeology and history is still in its infancy (Jongman et al. 2019; Munson and Scholnick 2022; Smith 2019b).
4. *Resilience to Shocks* is a topic with growing research in archaeology and history (Haldon et al. 2020; Izdebski et al. 2018; Riris et al. 2024; Smith 2026). The epistemological status of resilience is complex, since the concept can be viewed as both a cause and an effect, and usage may shift between specified and general resilience. *Specified resilience* refers to the specific response of a system to a shock; it is sometimes phrased as resistance, “for whom, what, where, when and why” (Meerow and Newell 2019). *General resilience* describes the overall ability of a system to survive unspecified shocks and persist through time (Walker and Salt 2012). Most empirical applications of the resilience concept in archae-

ology and history focus on specified resilience, whereas settlement persistence can be viewed as a measure of general resilience (Smith 2026).

A fundamental tenet of my argument that past cities are relevant to urban climate change adaptation today is that the effects of global warming are shocks that are comparable to the kinds of shocks that past cities faced. Therefore, the overall relevance argument is not limited to the ways past cities faced climate change, or even environmental changes. In other words, these contemporary shocks to cities are examples of the broader category of shocks that cities have faced throughout history (Glaeser 2022), a theme I explore more fully in Smith (2026).

5 Urban Adaptation Measures in the Past

I have selected four of the urban climate change adaptation measures from Table 3 plus an additional measure to illustrate how archaeological and historical research on past cities might contribute to an understanding of urban adaptations today (Table 4). Other adaptation measures could be used for this exercise. This is an illustrative discussion, not a full analysis; I suggest some archaeological and histori cal examples, but there is not space for full contextualization.

1. *Water provisioning and management.* Because facilities in the past for the control and delivery of water—for both agriculture and domestic consumption—were often durable infrastructural features, they not infrequently survive for archaeological documentation. Numerous urban water features were used in the cities of the Classic period Maya. Two types of reservoir have been identified: large storage facilities located in the centers of cities (Scarborough et al. 2012), and smaller domestic reservoirs located adjacent to residences (Chase and Cesaretti 2018). Many of these features were constructed early in the history of individual cities, which subsequently grew and flourished for several centuries. This suggests that such features were successful anticipatory adaptations, as evaluated by persistence and growth. These Maya cities later suffered catastrophic declines (the "Maya collapse") whose explanation continues to elude archaeologists.
2. *Food production and security.* Much of the land in the low-density cities of the Maya, Khmer, and other early tropical urban systems was devoted to agricultural

Table 4 Adaptation measures documented archaeologically

	Adaptation measure	Examples	Success measure
1	Water provisioning & management	Maya	Persistence, growth
2	Food production & security	Maya	Persistence, growth
3	Livelihoods & social protection	Byzantine	Prosperity (negative)
4	Housing & building design	Maya	Persistence, growth
5	Relocation of cities	Various	Persistence, growth

production. In many Maya cities, intensive kitchen garden cultivation has been documented archaeologically (Isendahl 2012), and cities located in hilly areas—such as Caracol—were filled with agricultural terraces within the urban landscape (Chase and Weishampel 2016). As in the case of water infrastructure, these farming systems were long-lived practices whose success is suggested by the persistence and growth of Maya cities. Barthel and Isendahl (2013) have argued that urban agriculture made early cities resilient, but this is a post-hoc explanation not based on any testing of alternatives. It would be possible to test their ideas by comparing the persistence, growth, or prosperity of two groups of Maya (or other) cities: those with prominent urban agricultural features, and those lacking such features.

3. *Livelihoods and social protection.* Izdebski et al. (2018) describe several cases where Mediterranean empires achieved resilience on the backs of the poor. Imperial relief to provincial areas after disasters often had the effect of enriching landlords and other elites, while forcing peasants into greater servitude and poverty; see also Haldon and Rosen (2018). By showing "the social burden of resilience" (Izdebski et al. 2018) in the past, these and other cases give greater impetus to efforts to achieve climate justice today (Castán Broto 2021; Henrique and Tschakert 2021).
4. *Housing and building design.* Scholars of vernacular architecture have long recognized the efficient climate-responsive design of indigenous housing in many parts of the world (Oliver 2003). These observations are now being touted as models to improve the adaptedness of urban housing in the Global South (Bahramifar et al. 2022). Erika Guttmann-Bond (2019) and other archaeologists have argued that ancient (vernacular) housing can serve a similar role in providing models for urban housing today. These early vernacular houses are superior to the shoddy and sometimes miserable mass-produced housing that is increasingly common throughout the modern world.
5. *Relocation of cities.* Urban relocation is not included in the IPCC listing of adaptation measures (Dodman et al. 2022), perhaps because it is too radical an idea to be considered by most cities trying to adapt to climate change. While not a regular occurrence, the movement of cities from one location to another was not uncommon in the distant past. Historians and archaeologists have documented a number of historical settings where city movement was quite common (Demand 1990; Musset 2002), and there are numerous isolated cases of relocated cities in other areas (Smith 2024; Smith et al. 2025).

One conclusion is that when authorities in the past felt the need to move a city, they were able to do it. This finding may or may not shed light on contemporary discussions about whether sea level rise will require cities like Miami to be moved (Glavovic et al. 2022; Pilkey et al. 2016). Cities today are far larger and more complex than early cities. Furthermore, the forms of governance today are very different, making it harder for authorities to unilaterally order something like the relocation of a city. In Michael Mann's terms, most modern rulers have far less "despotic power"—the ability of a leader to carry out his or her will without consulting civic groups or other power holders—than did the rulers of early states (Mann 1984), and this is one reason why the task of moving a city now seems like such a gargantuan undertaking.

6 Is It Relevant?

Will the trajectory between past and present outlined above produce relevant research? This is hard to judge until the fourth step—translate findings for urban scientists, policy makers, and stakeholders—is carried out. The generation of societally-relevant conclusions from data on the past is complex and difficult (See Introduction, this volume). Policy scholars agree that if research findings are to be accepted by policy makers or other users of knowledge, the research findings need to be credible, salient, and legitimate (Cash et al. 2003; Fischhoff 2020; Matson et al. 2016: Chapter 5; Tang and Dessai 2012).

1. *Credibility* refers to scientific findings based on rigorous methods applied to empirical evidence (Gamoran 2018; Roosen and Curtis 2018). The lack of quantitative data and the testing of hypotheses in much of contemporary archaeology and history greatly inhibits the credibility of our findings with respect to contemporary issues (Kohler and Rockman 2020; Smith 2023a).
2. *Saliency* describes the linkages between research results and policy concerns. This requires that the historian (or archaeologist) have deep knowledge of the relevant non-historical literature and be able to make clear bridging arguments between the two domains. Another way of phrasing this is to emphasize the importance of transdisciplinary approaches to the process of linking past and present. Transdisciplinary research describes deep integration of two or more disciplines to produce results that transcend individual disciplines (Baerwald 2010; Jacobs and Frickel 2009).
3. *Legitimacy* refers to the fairness or lack of bias of both the individual researchers and the methods and research. One avenue for achieving such legitimacy is to involve non-academics in the production and applications of research results. In environmental studies and sustainability science, the co-production of research with stakeholders and others has grown tremendously in importance in the past decade (Kirchhoff et al. 2013; Norström et al. 2020; Solecki et al. 2021). The co-production of knowledge is my fourth step (Fig. 1). It involves both scientific translation among disciplines, and interactions with stakeholders, and policy makers.

In the field of sustainability science, research results with credibility, salience, and legitimacy have been termed "actionable science" (Kirchhoff et al. 2013), or "usable knowledge" (Clark et al. 2016). It will be hard for archaeology and history to achieve the levels of credibility, salience, and legitimacy on ancient resilience and sustainability needed to contribute effectively to contemporary work (Haldon et al.

2024; Smith 2021, 2023a). If we reorient our efforts to focus more explicitly and directly on those topics of greatest importance in research on climate change adaptations today—particularly cities and urbanization—we will have greater chance of successfully translating our findings into results that are useful and relevant today.

Acknowledgements I thank John Haldon for inviting me to the conference "Resilience and sustainability: past trajectories, contemporary directions, policy relevance," and for support and discussions. I benefitted greatly from discussions with participants in the conference.

References

Adger, W. N., N. W. Arnell, and E. L. Tomkins. 2005. Successful adaptation to climate change across scales. *Global Environmental Change* 15:77–86.

Baerwald, T. J. 2010. Presidential address: Prospects for geography as an interdisciplinary discipline. *Annals of the Association of American Geographers* 100:493–401.

Bahramifar, B., E. Gharehbashloo, and A. Hosseini. 2022. Environmentally responsive design in the vernacular architecture of mountainous regions: The case of Kang village, Iran. *Journal of Housing and the Built Environment* 37:1283–1317.

Bai, X. 2023. Make the upcoming IPCC cities special report count. *Science* 382:eadl1522.

Bairoch, P. 1988. *Cities and Economic Development: From the Dawn of History to the Present.* Chicago: University of Chicago Press.

Barthel, S., and C. Isendahl. 2013. Urban gardens, agriculture, and water management: Sources of resilience for long-term food security in cities. *Ecological Economics* 86:224–234.

Bird, D., R. Kyle Bocinsky, K. M. Reese, and T. A. Kohler. 2024. Settlement persistence in the prehispanic Central Mesa Verde region: A dynamic analysis. *Journal of Archaeological Science: Reports* 56:104515.

Budowski, M., R. Tillmann, W. Keim, and M. Amacker. 2010. Conceptualizing "precarious prosperity": Empirical and theoretical elements for debate. *International Journal of Comparative Sociology* 51:268–288.

Carballo, D. M., G. M. Feinman, and A. López Corral. 2022. Mesoamerican urbanism: Indigenous institutions, infrastructure, and resilience. *Urban Studies* 62 (3): 507–524. https://doi.org/10.1177/00420980221105418.

Cash, D. W., W. C. Clark, F. Alcock, N. M. Dickson, N. Eckley, D. H. Guston, J. Jäger, and R. B. Mitchell. 2003. Knowledge systems for sustainable development. *Proceedings of the National Academy of Sciences* 100:8086–8091.

Castán Broto, V. 2021. *Just Climate Adaptation in Cities: Reflections for an Interdisciplinary Research Agenda.* London: British Academy.

Chase, A. S. Z., and R. Cesaretti. 2018. Diversity in ancient Maya water management strategies and landscapes at Caracol, Belize, and Tikal. *Guatemala. Wiley Interdisciplilnary Reviews: Water* 6:e1332.

Chase, A. S. Z., and J. F. Weishampel. 2016. Water capture and agricultural terracing at Caracol, Belize as revealed through Lidar and GIS. *Advances in Archaeological Practice* 4:357–370.

Clark, W. C., L. Van Kerkhoff, L. Lebel, and G. C. Gallopin. 2016. Crafting usable knowledge for sustainable development. *Proceedings of the National Academy of Sciences* 113:4570–4578.

Costanza, R., and B. C. Patten. 1995. Defining and predicting sustainability. *Ecological Economics* 15:193–196.

Creutzig, F., et al. 2024. Towards a public policy of cities and human settlements in the 21st century. *npj Urban Sustainability* 4:29.

Demand, N. H. 1990. *Urban Relocation in Archaic and Classical Greece: Flight and Consolidation*. Norman: University of Oklahoma Press.

Dodman, D., B. Hayward, M. Pelling, V. Castán Broto, W. Chow, E. Chu, R. Dawson, L. Khirfan, T. McPhearson, A. Prakash, Y. Zheng, and G. Ziervogel. 2022. Chapter 6: Cities, settlements and key infrastructure. In *Climate Change 2022: Impacts, Adaptation, and Vulnerability. Contribution of Working Group II to the Sixth Assessment Report of the Intergovernmental Panel on Climate Change*, ed. H.-O. Pörtner et al., 907–1040. New York: Cambridge University Press.

Eriksen, S., et al. 2021. Adaptation interventions and their effect on vulnerability in developing countries: Help, hindrance or irrelevance? *World Development* 141:105383.

Fischhoff, B. 2020. Making behavioral science integral to climate science and action. *Behavioural Public Policy* 5:439–453.

Fisher, S. 2022. *How Do We Measure The Success of Adaptation and Does It Matter?* Climate Change Series. Kings College London. https://www.kcl.ac.uk/how-do-we-measure-the-success-of-adaptation-and-does-it-matter.

Gamoran, A. 2018. Evidence-based policy in the real world: A cautionary view. *The Annals of the American Academy of Political and Social Science* 678:180–191.

Glaeser, E. L. 2011. *The Triumph of the City: How Our Greatest Invention Makes us Richer, Smarter, Greener, Healthier, and Happier*. New York: Penguin.

Glaeser, E. L. 2022. Urban resilience. *Urban Studies* 59:3–35.

Glavovic, B. C., R. Dawson, and W. T. L. Chow. 2022. Cross-chapter paper 2: Cities and settlements by the sea. In *Climate Change 2022: Impacts, Adaptation and Vulnerability: Contribution of Working Group II to the Sixth Assessment Report of the Intergovernmental Panel on Climate Change: Summary for Policymakers*, ed. H.-O. Pörtner, D. Roberts, et al., 2163–2194. IPCC.

Guttmann-Bond, E. 2019. *Reinventing Sustainability: How Archaeology Can Save the Planet*. Oxford: Oxbow.

Haldon, J., and A. Rosen. 2018. Society and environment in the East Mediterranean ca 300–1800 CE. Problems of resilience, adaptation and transformation. Introductory essay. *Human Ecology* 46:275–290.

Haldon, J., M. Eisenberg, L. Mordechai, A. Izdebski, and S. White. 2020. Lessons from the past, policies for the future: Resilience and sustainability in past crises. *Environment Systems and Decisions* 40:287–297.

Haldon, J., L. Mordechai, A. Dugmore, M. Eisenberg, G. Endfield, A. Izdebski, R. Jackson, L. Kemp, I. Labuhn, T. McGovern, S. E. Metcalfe, K. Morrison, T. Newfield, and B. Trump. 2024. Past answers to present concerns. The relevance of the premodern past for 21st century policy planners: Comments on the state of the field. *Wiley Interdisciplinary Reviews: Climate Change* e923.

Henrique, K. P., and P. Tschakert. 2021. Pathways to urban transformation: From dispossession to climate justice. *Progress in Human Geography* 45 (5): 1169–1191. https://doi.org/10.1177/0309132520962856.

Isendahl, C. 2012. Agro-urban landscapes: The example of Maya lowland cities. *Antiquity* 86:1112–1125.

Izdebski, A., L. Mordechai, and S. White. 2018. The social burden of resilience: A historical perspective. *Human Ecology* 46:291–303.

Jacobs, J. A., and S. Frickel. 2009. Interdisciplinarity: A critical assessment. *Annual Review of Sociology* 35:43–65.

Jones, J. H., E. Ready, and A. C. Pisor. 2021. Want climate-change adaptation? Evolutionary theory can help. *American Journal of Human Biology* 33:e23539.

Jongman, W. M., J. P. A. M. Jacobs, and G. M. K. Goldewijk. 2019. Health and wealth in the Roman empire. *Economics & Human Biology* 34:138–150.

Kirchhoff, C. J., M. Carmen Lemos, and S. Dessai. 2013. Actionable knowledge for environmental decision making: Broadening the usability of climate science. *Annual Review of Environment and Resources* 38:393–414.

Kohler, T. A., and M. Rockman. 2020. The IPCC: A Primer for Archaeologists. *American Antiquity* 85:627–651.

Lawrence, D., M. W. de Gruchy, I. Hinojosa-Baliño, and A. Al-Hamdani. 2025. Long-term trends in settlement persistence in southwest asia: implications for sustainable urbanism, past, present and future. *Urban Studies* 62:543–559.

Lobo, J., L. M. A. Bettencourt, M. E. Smith, and S. G. Ortman. 2020. Settlement scaling theory: Bridging the study of ancient and contemporary urban systems. *Urban Studies* 57:731–747.

Lobo, J., et al. 2023. Integration of urban science and urban climate adaptation research: Opportunities to advance climate action. *npj Urban Sustainability* 3:32.

Magnan, A. K., E. L. F. Schipper, and V. K. E. Duvat. 2020. Frontiers in climate change adaptation science: Advancing guidelines to design adaptation pathways. *Current Climate Change Reports* 6:166–177.

Mann, M. 1984. The autonomous power of the state: Its origins, mechanisms and results. *European Journal of Sociology/Archives Européennes de Sociologie* 25:185–213.

Matson, P., W. C. Clark, and K. Andersson. 2016. *Pursuing Sustainability: A Guide to the Science and Practice*. Princeton, NJ: Princeton University Press.

Meerow, S., and J. P. Newell. 2019. Urban resilience for whom, what, when, where, and why? *Urban Geography* 40:309–329.

Munson, J., and J. Scholnick. 2022. Wealth and well-being in an Ancient Maya community. *Journal of Archaeological Method and Theory* 29:1–30.

Musset, A. 2002. *Villes nomades du nouveau monde*. Paris: Editions de l'Ecole des Hautes Etudes en Sciences Sociales.

Norström, A. V., et al. 2020. Principles for knowledge co-production in sustainability research. *Nature Sustainability* 3:182–190.

Oliver, P. 2003. Coping with climate. In *Dwellings: The Vernacular House World Wide*, 128–149. London: Phaidon Press.

Oliver-Smith, A. 2016. The concepts of adaptation, vulnerability, and resilience in the anthropology of climate change: Considering the case of displacement and migration. In *Anthropology and Climate Change: From Encounters to Actions*, ed. S. A. Crate and M. Nuttall, 58–85. Walnut Creek, CA: Taylor and Francis.

Orlove, B. 2022. The concept of adaptation. *Annual Review of Environment and Resources* 47:535–581.

Ortman, S. G., J. Lobo, and M. E. Smith. 2020. Cities: Complexity, theory, and history. *PLoS One* 15:e0243621.

Osbahr, H., C. Twyman, W. N. Adger, and D. S. G. Thomas. 2010. Evaluating successful livelihood adaptation to climate variability and change in Southern Africa. *Ecology and Society* 15 (2): 27.

Peck, J. R., and D. Waxman. 2018. What is adaptation and how should it be measured? *Journal of Theoretical Biology* 447:190–198.

Pilkey, O. H., L. Pilkey-Jarvis, and K. C. Pilkey. 2016. *Retreat from a Rising Sea: Hard Choices in an Age of Climate Change*. New York: Columbia University Press.

Pörtner, H.-O., D. C. Roberts, M. M. B. Tignor, E. Poloczanska, K. Mintenbeck, A. Alegría, M. Craig, S. Langsdorf, S. Löschke, V. Möller, A. Okem, and B. Rama, eds. 2022. *Climate Change 2022: Impacts, Adaptation and Vulnerability: Contribution of Working Group II to the Sixth Assessment Report of the Intergovernmental Panel on Climate Change: Summary for Policymakers*. IPCC.

Prieur-Richard, A.-H., B. Walsh, M. Craig, M. L. Melamed, M. L. Colbert, M. Pathak, S. Connors, X. Bai, A. S. Barau, and H. Bulkeley. 2019. *Global Research and Action Agenda on Cities and Climate Change Science, Full Version*. Geneva: World Climate Research Programme.

Riris, P., F. Silva, E. Crema, A. Palmisano, E. Robinson, P. Siegel, J. French, E. K. Jørgensen, Y. Maezumi, S. Solheim, J. Bates, B. Davies, Y. Oh, and X. Ren. 2024. Frequent disturbances enhanced the resilience of past human populations. *Nature* 629:837–842.

Roosen, J., and D. R. Curtis. 2018. Dangers of noncritical use of historical plague data. *Emerging Infectious Disease journal* 24:103–110.
Satterthwaite, D. 2016. Successful, safe and sustainable cities: Towards a new urban agenda. *Commonwealth Journal of Local Governance* 19:3–18.
Scarborough, V. L., N. P. Dunning, K. B. Tankersley, C. Carr, E. Weaver, L. Grazioso, B. Lane, J. G. Jones, P. Buttles, F. Valdez, and D. L. Lentz. 2012. Water and sustainable land use at the ancient tropical city of Tikal, Guatemala. *Proceedings of the National Academy of Sciences* 109 (31): 12408–12413.
Serra, V., A. Ledda, M. G. G. Ruiu, G. Calia, V. Mereu, V. Bacciu, S. Marras, D. Spano, and A. De Montis. 2022. Adaptation to climate change across local policies: An investigation in six Italian cities. *Sustainability* 14:8318.
Singh, C., S. Iyer, M. G. New, R. Few, B. Kuchimanchi, A. C. Segnon, and D. Morchain. 2021. Interrogating "effectiveness" in climate change adaptation: 11 guiding principles for adaptation research and practice. *Climate and Development* 14 (7): 650–664.
Smith, M. E. 2019a. Energized crowding and the generative role of settlement aggregation and urbanization. In *Coming Together: Comparative Approaches to Population Aggregation and Early Urbanization*, ed. A. Gyucha, 37–58. Albany, NY: State University of New York Press.
Smith, M. E. 2019b. Quality of life and prosperity in ancient households and communities. In *The Oxford Handbook of Historical Ecology and Applied Archaeology*, ed. C. Isendahl and D. Stump, 486–505. New York: Oxford University Press.
Smith, M. E. 2021. Why archaeology's relevance to global challenges has not been recognized. *Antiquity* 95:1061–1069.
Smith, M. E. 2023a. How can research on past urban adaptations be made useful for sustainability science? *Global Sustainability* 6:e4.
Smith, M. E. 2023b. *Urban Life in the Distant Past: The Prehistory of Energized Crowding*. New York: Cambridge University Press.
Smith, M. E. 2023c. Urban success and urban adaptation over the long run. *Open Archaeology* 9:20220285.
Smith, M. E. 2024. Can we move our climate-threatened cities? Ancient examples show it's possible to transplant entire metropolises—but the costs are steep. *Zocalo/Public Square*, Nov 11, 2024. https://www.zocalopublicsquare.org/move-climate-threatened-cities-managed-retreat/
Smith, M. E. 2026. Cities, shocks, and persistence: New approaches to urban resilience in the past. *Global Sustainability,* in press.
Smith, M. E., J. Lobo, M. A. Peeples, A. York, B. Stanley, K. Crawford, N. Gauthier, and A. Huster. 2021. The persistence of ancient settlements and urban sustainability. *Proceedings of the National Academy of Sciences* 118:e201855118.
Smith, M. E., C. Carleton, C. Ebert, D. Hu, D. Lawrence, J. Lobo, S. Ortman, P. Roberts, and I. Romanowska. 2025. Urban relocation as an adaptation strategy in the ancient world. *Paper presented at the MR 2025 Conference: Mobility, Adaptation, and Wellbeing in a Changing Climate, Columbia University*.
Solecki, W., G. C. Delgado Ramos, D. Roberts, C. Rosenzweig, and B. Walsh. 2021. Accelerating climate research and action in cities through advanced science-policy-practice partnerships. *NPJ Urban Sustainability* 1:3.
Storper, M. 2013. *Keys to the City: How Economics, Institutions, Social Interactions, and Politics Shape Development*. Princeton, NJ: Princeton University Press.
Tang, S., and S. Dessai. 2012. Usable science? The UK climate projections 2009 and decision support for adaptation planning. *Weather, Climate, and Society* 4:300–313.
Thornton, T. F., and N. Manasfi. 2010. Adaptation—genuine and spurious: Demystifying adaptation processes in relation to climate change. *Environment and Society: Advances in Research* 1:132–155.
United Nations. 2023. *Synergy Solutions for a World in Crisis: Tackling Climate and SDG Action Together Report on Strengthening the Evidence Base*. New York: United Nations, Department of Economic and Social Affairs.

United Nations Environment Programme. 2022. Around the world, cities race to adapt to a changing climate. *News Stories*. https://www.unep.org/news-and-stories/story/around-world-cities-race-adapt-changing-climate#:~:text=%E2%80%9CCities%20are%20both%20a%20hotbed,harvesting%20systems%20to%20green%20infrastructure

Walker, B., and D. Salt. 2012. *Resilience Practice*. Washington, DC: Island Press.

Wasley, E., T. A. Dahl, C. F. Simpson, L. W. Fischer, J. F. Helgeson, M. A. Kenney, A. Parris, A. R. Siders, E. Tate, and N. Ulibarri. 2023. Chapt. 31: Adaptation. In *Fifth National Climate Assessment*, ed. A. R. Crimmins et al. Washington, DC: U.S. Global Change Research Program.

Policy-Relevant Environmental History in an Era of Environmental Solutionism: Problems and Prospects

Katherine C. Snow

Abstract Environmental solutionism (ES) approaches environmental policy, and any intervention in nature, solely in terms of problems and solutions. ES is arguably a deeply flawed framework. Many of the Western approaches and policies ES has spawned can be characterized as failures if we consider their enormously adverse impacts on our ecological—and thus overall survival—prospects. ES-driven policy usually leads to a self-referential endless problem-solution-problem loop (Cockerill et al. *Environmental Realism: Challenging Solutions*. Cham: Palgrave-Macmillan, 2017), drifting away from addressing the state of the environment itself. ES also entails a normatively questionable environmental ethic. All told, any search for policy-driven paths to improving our current ecological prospects undertaken within the ES framework is arguably fatally impoverished from the outset. Yet ES remains the dominant approach to the environment in twenty-first century Western and global policy discourse. ES is therefore also poised to deeply shape and distort the ways in which an increasing number of academic fields, including environmental history, engage in trying to produce environmental policy-relevant research. Environmental realism (ER) offers one potential alternative to ES. ER can potentially re-frame both environmental policy thinking itself, and which types of research questions in environmental history align most with possible policy relevance. Given ES's inertia, reaching a place where environmental policymakers stop defaulting to ES frameworks—and could instead begin to explore ER's relative advantages—will likely require much more investigation and critique of ES and its long hold over our environmental imagination. Environmental history can thus find immediate policy relevance via studies of the history of ES itself, using the environmental past to increase our understanding of ES's origins, strengths, and severe weaknesses as a human environmental strategy.

Keywords Environmental solutionism · Environmental policy · Environmental realism · Environmental history

K. C. Snow (✉)
CCHRI and HMEI, Princeton, NJ, USA
e-mail: kcsnow@princeton.edu

J. F. Haldon, R. Fernandes (eds.), *Bridging History and Policy*, Understanding Complex Systems, https://doi.org/10.1007/978-3-032-24379-9_15

1 Introduction

Drawing in part from Cockerill et al., we can initially define *environmental solutionism* (ES) as the environmental policy framework or set of assumptions according to which:

(a) Nature, natural processes, and our environment are understood and represented either as a series of problems or puzzles which humans must solve, and/or as a source of object-like goods and resources we can use in solving these problems;
(b) Each natural problem and natural resource is treated as isolatable from one another as well as from the biosphere as a whole, with the human "problem-solvers" likewise treated as coming in from outside the problems to solve them, and coming in from outside the resources to take them; and,
(c) Technological interventions, and specialized scientific and engineering expertise, are usually considered the cornerstones of the most appropriate human "solutions" to environmental "problems" (Cockerill et al. 2017: 5f.).

ES is arguably a deeply flawed approach. ES-driven policy usually slides into what Cockerill et al. call the endless problem-solution-problem cycle (Cockerill et al. 2017). When a policy is initially framed in terms of the need to solve a well-defined problem (rather than in terms of interacting with or considering some aspect of nature or the environment itself), over time the policy drifts into a self-referential project of sustaining, repairing, and expanding the initial successful "solution," rather than thinking about underlying environmental conditions and outcomes. For example, in the well-known case of the Western-led twentieth-century industrialization of agriculture, this industrialization shift was at first hailed as a "solution" to the "problem" of insufficient food output for growing populations. But the industrialization of agriculture itself soon created rafts of new problems which subsequent "environmental" policy has continually tried to solve—preserving the industrial solution, at the expense of the environment. As Schneider noted in 2011, since the post-World War II industrialization of agriculture in the US:

> … nature has reacted strongly against some of the main tenets of industrialized production. Pests attack monocultural crops with increased ferocity; insects and plant pests develop resistance to pesticides; bacteria develop resistance; and disease threatens animals raised in stress and close confinement.
>
> Rather than refine our approach and recognize that a pure industrialized model works against nature, we have reacted with increased reliance on technological fixes for the problems that arise. Chemical inputs replace depleted soil nutrients. New and more powerful pesticides are applied to combat animal and plant pests that have become resistant to the old pesticides. Antibiotics are used extensively in livestock production, not just to treat disease but as a preventative measure. There is a new and ever faster moving technological treadmill, with new chemicals and biologics constantly in need. Short-term fixes may be found, but there is much to suggest that we are losing the battle in the long run (Schneider 2011: 21–22).

Many other contemporary Western environmental policies and positions ES has generated can also be characterized as [impending] failures if we consider their enormously adverse impacts on our ecological—and thus overall survival—prospects. ES also entails using and perpetuating a normatively questionable environmental ethic. As we will expand upon briefly as well in the next section (Sect. 2), arguably any search for a policy-driven path out of our current environmental crisis which is undertaken within an ES framework is fatally impoverished from the outset. Despite this, ES remains the dominant approach to the environment in twenty-first century Western and global policy.

Even the most cursory glance at the global discourse on environmental questions reveals ES's pervasiveness.[1] In the case of climate change, for example, the text of the U.N. Paris Agreement of 2015 identifies global mean temperature rise as the primary definable problem that requires a human solution[2] (UNFCCC 2015). The increase in the parts per million (ppm) concentration of CO_2 (and other greenhouse gases) in the earth's atmosphere is framed as the secondary or supporting problem. Rising CO_2 ppm is sometimes considered on its own or with a view to its own negative impacts (such as ocean acidification); but it is more commonly considered as a problem which needs to be solved solely because it serves as the main contributing cause of the primary problem (global mean temperature rise). The ES framing of climate change has led to numerous rounds of talks among governments and corporations on how and why to pursue various "climate solutions" including the expansion of low-carbon energy production (particularly via wind, solar, and nuclear projects); the construction of carbon capture and storage (CCS) plants or development of other large-scale carbon dioxide removal (CDR) methods and projects; and solar radiation modification (SRM) and other "geoengineering" approaches (Baur et al. 2023; Lawrence et al. 2018). Arguably, the only "problem" these efforts seek to "solve" is that of global heat increase as an undesired environmental feedback potentially affecting our ability to burn enormous amounts of carbon-based fuels daily; these "climate solutions" do not refer directly to the environment itself or how we should interact with it. Many geoengineering proposals, including SRM, do not seek any greenhouse gas reductions at all, and many of the other "solutions" entail

[1] A UN climate action page offers: "Good news is that solutions do exist!" (https://www.un.org/en/climatechange/climate-solutions). A search for "solutions" on the UN Climate Change page yields over 55,000 results (https://unfccc.int/gcse?q=solutions#gsc.tab=0&gsc.q=solutions&gsc.page=1). A sample scholarly literature search for "climate solution(s)" restricted to journal article titles alone returns thousands of entries; for book titles, more than 600; when moved to keyword, over 5400 and over 4700 respectively. "Nature-based solutions" have become part of the jargon in both the Paris Agreement and the Convention on Biological Diversity, two of the major global treaties on the environment, and feature in the chapter "Options for Decision Makers" (Chapter 6) in the recent IPBES Global Report on the planetary biodiversity crisis (IPBES 2019).

[2] The actual text reads that the goal of the Agreement is "Holding the increase in the global average temperature to well below 2 °C above pre-industrial levels and pursuing efforts to limit the temperature increase to 1.5 °C above pre-industrial levels" (UNFCCC 2015). Interestingly, this comes after an elaborate preface in which many broad problems are invoked, from the stated need for sustainable development, climate justice, and indigenous and gender rights, to sustainable consumption by rich countries and the need to protect ecosystem integrity (UNFCCC 2015).

deep environmental damage of their own of various types, such as extensive minerals mining, water use, or habitat disturbance and conversion.

Talk of pursuing "solutions" to environmental "problems" of course also fits neatly into the economics-first argot of the contemporary policy world, and the West's centering of almost all its policies on a perceived imperative of ceaseless economic growth, which in turn relies upon capitalism's ability to constantly seek profits via various forms of accumulation and surplus (Snow and Kluiving 2022). This economic growth-centered strategy itself displays a form of macro-scale ES thinking. With a constantly growing population (whether growing in terms of net resource consumption or sheer numbers of individuals, cf. Snow 2024) needing their environmental and survival needs met, but in a post-agrarian society in which small-scale subsistence agriculture has been largely ended, the imagined abundance of capital steps in to solve the problem of survival, thus also launching a dominating problem-solution-problem cycle in which economic growth must be preserved at all costs as the master "solution" to end all environmental (and even societal) "problems." In place of an abundance of land and farms, people trade their time and labor to be able to partake of the abundance of capital, so as to be able to then purchase all their environmental needs on the market. In this system, whatever is needed from nature, must be purchasable. Those provisioning the market with things like food and housing materials must at the same time do so on a basis which is as cost-saving (and thus, often, as environmentally destructive) as possible, so as to still be able to profit from the provisioning. The whole ceaseless economic growth model has been challenged since at least the 1970s (Meadows et al. 1972) and is already showing many cracks, from the extraordinary environmental (and social) damage it is causing, to the need for governments to supply vast subsidies to keep the system turning. But in true ES problem-solution-problem cycle fashion, there is still no ability, within this ES approach, to question anything fundamental about it. Only problems and solutions exist. Nature appears as either the source of some problem which must be solved because it threatens to slow down growth with unwanted feedback or scarcity, or it appears as a source of natural resources and materials available for human use in solving these feedback and scarcity problems. In the case of climate change, placing "climate solutions" on the policy table as additive, purchasable, goods and services avoids curtailing or threatening economic growth, and indeed, serves as just one more box of temporary technological-fix bandages for the growth model itself. Climate scientists have overall embraced ES; only a minority of scientific researchers have published on potential risks and unintended consequences involved with massively building out renewable energy capacity (Holechek et al. 2022), pursuing CDR at a large scale (Dooley et al. 2021), or pursuing geoengineering (Baur et al. 2023; Carlson & Church 2024; NASEM 2021), though many environmental activists and some indigenous communities have voiced opposition to geoengineering in particular, and have begun to question "solutions" talk in general being applied to the environment. Those economists and other social science researchers critical of the notion of endless economic growth tend to work apart from the scientists and social scientists currently designing climate "solutions" for policymakers, and thus far, it is really only these "solutions" which have made any (small) impact on policy, mostly in the form of a raft of new wind and solar power projects.

The purpose of this chapter is to highlight what the current dominance of ES over environmental policy thinking means for the growing effort by environmental history, among other disciplines, to pursue research which is relevant to the policy domain. Environmental history—like all of environmental studies, from the environmental humanities to the biological and climate sciences—is presumably interested in producing policy-relevant research for the same reason that all parts of environmental studies currently implicitly claim normative and social relevance: their oft-articulated goal of helping the West to recognize its current trajectory of deepening environmental crisis, understand its origins and causes, and move off of it before it is too late (cf. e.g. Ripple et al. 2017). After laying out (in Sect. 2) a few more of the problems with ES, (in Sect. 3) some of the potential relative advantages of environmental realism (ER), and (in Sect. 4) some initial research questions environmental history undertaken in an ER vein might find relevant for the policy realm, I will conclude (in Sect. 5) with briefly considering some lingering problems with this above-noted assumption, broadly shared across environmental studies, that academic research, through the production of facts and their scholarly interpretation, can meaningfully help move Western society onto a new environmental trajectory.

2 Some Chief Flaws of Environmental Solutionism (ES)

As just touched upon in Sect. 1, ES comes with heavy logical and ethical baggage. It is of course erroneous to think that the real natural world we inhabit, the natural world within and from which we form all the human-nature interchanges and physical outcomes we call our "environment," solely exists or interacts with us as a linear chain of isolatable problems we can approach and solve as though from without (cf. also Cockerill et al. 2017 on this point). The earth is made up of millions of types of elements, processes, species, and dynamics, both known and mostly unknown to us, which characterize it at any given moment, and nothing can really be separated from the whole; everything on our planet [eventually] interacts with everything else (Cockerill et al. 2017; Snow 2024). We could never describe the earth completely even in principle, since our language is a process of abstracting from only the things we can (and choose to) experience and isolate. Even the most thorough "complexity science" or "earth systems" type of planetary model which strives for computer-aided depth and completeness is just adding *interconnections among* the different members of this same highly abstracted and selective set.

The ES approach takes our selectiveness and our ability to form abstractions about the natural world to an even more extreme level. To reach the point where as human beings, we could consider the full meaning or significance of a highly impactful intervention into our environment or the broader natural world to be simply that we are finding the "solution" to a "problem" is of course itself also the result of a very long and highly complex social and evolutionary story. But if we continue to apply the same simplification of the environment into a mere interface in this new era, in which our technological and other impacts have become so inordinate, we will continue to pose a perhaps unsurvivable threat to our own and many other species as well, and change the entire biosphere in ways which are normatively questionable (as well as, again, potentially un-survivable). This is because, no matter what technological powers we have been able to gain in part by thinking of the environment in this very ES way, overall, the ES way of approaching the natural world and our environment is inadequate to reality. At the macro-scale, the ES assumption that a problem-solution representation of our environment can function to adequately model the real world such that, on its own and without any additional forms of environmental thinking or cognizing, it sets us up for survival success over the long term, is simply already being physically disproven as our contemporary environmental history unfolds. The "problems" and "solutions" represented in the ES view are properly speaking only activities, often akin to experiments, undertaken *within* the hugely complex whole that exists all around us which the ES framework cannot account for, even as the feedback coming "in" to the problems and solutions "from" this larger whole grows ever more significant.

ES's de facto conflation of a chosen activity within the world, with the world itself, links with ES's significant ethical shortcomings. As just discussed, most of the world is abstracted away entirely in the ES view of the environment. This is functional: the real focus of ES only *begins* where a human solver arrives to do away with a natural problem, a process which usually now entails a high degree of technological complexity and the deployment of special skills and machines. It is simply not possible to add in other moral components or attach other moral dimensions to nature at this juncture; the only moral good within the framework is whether the defined problem is successfully solved or not—again, usually entailing whether or not some machine or system works. Global extractivism and the oil-based way of doing business are uncontestable within ES, because they are intertwined with the mega-scale commitment to growth we have already discussed as the larger-scale "solution" which must constantly be upheld and fixed. Indeed, oil-centered extractivism is the material means by which this constant growth strategy has even temporarily been able to sustain itself—it has done so only by way of the "throughput of vast quantities of … fossil fuel stocks" through our societies and economy (Nekola et al. 2013: 129). As part of the external driver of this whittled-down view of nature, and beneficiaries of its moral vacuousness in turn, neither oil-based extractivism nor any one of its numerous environmentally ethically questionable offshoot policies and practices (such as the production of massive amounts of plastic packaging), are visible within the ES frame itself in any way which makes them available for interrogation or critique on any sort of ethical grounds.

Yet even if within ES, it is impossible to consider the environment in any way other than as a collection of components either generating problems for us, and/or being available for our use in crafting anthropogenic solutions to these (and other, purely social) problems by serving as a pot of resources, the fact *that* ES is the West's way of approaching the natural world is an inherently [un]ethical stance. We might detect at most a thin trace of some form of consequentialist ethics still clinging to the deployment of ES. While there are many ways of defining consequentialism (Sinnott-Armstrong 2023), in the most basic sense, consequentialism means weighing whether a decision or action is moral or right by looking at the consequences which result from it, rather than by considering the decision or action itself or what it actually consists of doing. In the case of choosing to deploy ES as the West's way of interfacing with the natural world, thereby licensing all the environmental behaviors which have flowed from this choice, consequentialism might want to claim that embracing ES has led the West to be able to elicit benefits (for humans) from the earth unprecedented in human history. ES could conceivably potentially be morally defended (by the consequentialist) as part of what best equips us to extract these benefits, since deriving these benefits always entails carrying out environmental and other-species destruction, and beyond this also seems to require seeing and analyzing the environment in a certain way. Cauterization and hyperanalysis makes us effective environmental actors; removing any moral revulsion we might [once] have felt at carrying out the destruction of non-human life or turning our landscapes into seas of grey boxes full of moving machines, leads us to be able to sustain the economic growth model and proceed toward ever-greater benefits for ever-more humans unimpeded. But this is of course a questionable defense of the ethics of choosing the ES paradigm. Weighing environmental destruction against human benefits, always questionable on many levels, has become even more so after a century or two of accelerating ES. Our resulting outsized technological power and consumption levels have changed the cost and benefit rationales at our disposal even if we wanted to indulge in a consequentialist defense of "needing" to only think about nature in an ES mindset. The overarching (and also ES-shaped) economic growth imperative means ES only needs a single litmus test, a binary yes/no, regarding whether or not someone will *pay* for whatever we are going into the environment to take, or to make. (For all the ink spilled over the "profit motives" of exploiters of the environment such as oil companies, they are mere middlemen: the harm itself arguably is overdetermined the moment someone decides to pay for its end product.) But this level of the complete monetization of nature, and concurrent removal of any moral hesitancy which would require some other litmus test be used beyond some end user's willingness to pay for something, before changing a habitat or landscape forever, seems increasingly to be propelling us not toward net benefits, but toward net losses for humanity (and for other species) the scope of which are almost unimaginable.

The ethics of choosing ES are arguably even further weakened by the "historical" qualifier which properly speaking usually attaches to ES's consequentialist rationale.[3] A time duration element often implicitly extends out the horizon on

[3] Historical consequentialism is usually thought of as a political ethics in which the final sum utility, and net rightness or wrongness, of a political system (say, a monarchy or a democracy) can only be judged at an historical time scale, where we see how many are hurt versus helped by the system over time, how long it helped the society last, and so forth (Floyd 2009; Muller 1997). Muller presents historical consequentialism as a form of utilitarianism associated with conservative thinkers like Burke and de Maistre (cf. e.g., Muller 1997: 7f., 145), yet we might also discern

which we might presumably find the moral justification for adopting an ES mindset today. Environmental scientists also often fall into making rival, but mirror-image, claims focused on the future,[4] where they emphasize the future consequences for nature (and people) of not stepping off our current environmental trajectory (Ripple et al. 2017). They thus overlook the fact that ES is already using the long frame of the future, imagining that our environmentally utilitarian mindset of today is needed for an eventual triumphalist outcome for our species, even a kind of "final solution" for the human species in which it triumphs over the environment altogether. In ES, human technological intervention in and large-scale damage to nature, and the mindset which allows it, are all part and symbol of our species' survival project writ large. For scientists, the transformation of the earth and societies into a ruin in the future is invoked as a looming tragedy. For the ES-linked, growth-devoted, faith in humankind view, sometimes infused with notes of traditional theism and/or romanticism, even a future state of ruin and collapse might simply symbolize that the human species has fulfilled its destiny to move on to another planet, find some form of religious redemption in place of earthly life, and/or at the very least meet its fitting tragic end which is still somehow ennobling of the human—which in this case would be a species which at the very least tried its most valiantly to fulfill its greatest ambitions before it was struck down from "without." Such conflicting meanings are already arguably embedded in the existing anthropogenic ruins-or-monuments in our landscapes today (Snow and Kluiving 2022; Stewart 2020).

Overall, the deployment of ES entails quite a negative or even simply absent environmental ethic, and arguably the use of such an amoral approach to nature as our main means of interacting with it is, as a whole activity or position, actually nihilistic, in more than one sense of that term (Snow 2026).

Both the logical and the ethical flaws in ES constitute heavy baggage for the framework and raise key structural or procedural questions for any academic field, including environmental history, seeking to interface with environmental policy-making in the early twenty-first century. The patent logical flaws with ES flow from the clear artificiality of thinking of the natural world as a series of idealized and graspable problems, instead of an infinitely complex place and space. The ethical or normative dubiousness of ES has just been noted. Environmental historians may well both normatively prefer, and logically require, a different framework within which to seek policy-relevant research questions. They may even be able to make their first contribution to the environmental policy realm by using environmental history to investigate and critique ES itself, adding to the evidence base suggesting

its relevance for understanding how political systems grounded in Hegel or Marx might seek to justify their actions and policies.

[4] Likewise, some of the only meaningful national-scale environmental legislation in the United States to date has dealt with the future: the Endangered Species Act, which seeks to prevent the complete extinction of species which are nearing this final existential brink, and the creation of national monuments or protected conservation zones which are intended to not change as time passes, and so bring a glimpse of the future into the present, including in ways resembling a vision of the afterlife and/or Eden.

the need for policymakers to turn away from it entirely or at least significantly supplement it.

3 Environmental Realism (ER) as Anti-solutionism

In 2017 Cockerill et al. were the first to propose *environmental realism* (ER) as an alternative to environmental solutionism, defining ER roughly as follows:

> Environmental realism (ER) is a commitment to unpack the deep flaws in, and reject, "solutionism" as an approach to the natural world and the environments we shape for ourselves within it (Cockerill et al. 2017).

For these authors, as noted earlier, ES's way of diagnosing environmental issues as simple, linear "problems" which need discrete "solutions," with the human problem-solver as a type of *deus ex machina* with no connection with the problem beforehand (or afterward), fails on multiple levels (Cockerill et al. 2017). Though humans may tend to conceptualize themselves as problem-solving planetary engineers, they can never in fact escape their embeddedness within the earth and its multitude of interconnected energetic processes and millions of species (Snow 2024). Imagined "solutions" to discrete environmental challenges or "problems" do not in any way stay confined to that "problem;" it is impossible to address or affect only one thing at a time in the real environment (Cockerill et al. 2017).

Again, Cockerill et al. mostly define ER as a position from which to understand and critique ES, and a place-holder for future work which must identify in more detail what ER might offer by way of positive alternatives. Drawing on past scholars, including those who offered earlier criticisms of *techno-solutionism* in particular (cf. the third assumption held by ES listed in our definition of ES in Sect. 1 above), Cockerill et al. argue that human beings err when they model environmental conditions as though they can be translated into a series of convergent problems; the environment gives us only divergent, or "wicked", problems, if we must use the "problem" term at all. In this way, ER becomes the framework from within which we can confront wicked problems without oversimplifying them (Cockerill et al. 2017). These authors partly critique ES as a tendency which humans fundamentally in some way share with other species, since it derives from evolutionary pressures they call the Malthusian-Darwinian Dynamic (MDD), and which therefore we must consciously draw out and contest lest it lock us in to a doomed path long-term (cf. Fig. 1) (Cockerill et al. 2017). In contemporary environmental policy terms, ES for these authors is a type of socialized late modern form of the MDD (Cockerill et al. 2017).

ER has as its first priority working to further delineate and understand the many flaws in ES when used as a [sole] framework for decision-making about our environment. In addition to the logical and ethical drawbacks of ES touched upon in the previous section, deepening the critique of ES is also physically imperative. With each iteration of the problem-solution-problem cycle, entropy rises in the

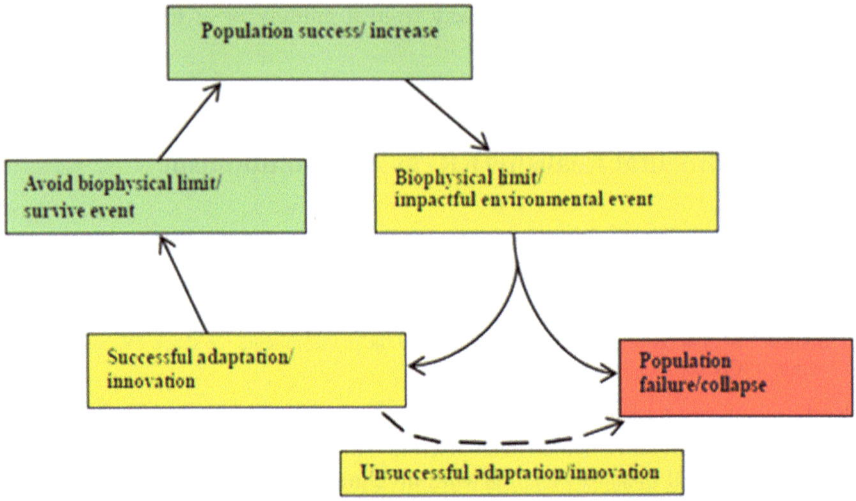

Fig. 1 An evolutionary dynamic underpinning solutionism: Constant Malthusian environmental or social pressures as "problems" requiring constant Darwinian adaptation or social innovation as "solutions." Figure adapted from Cockerill et al. (2017): 9, Figure 1.1, "The problem-solution-problem cycle." Used with permission of the authors

environment and solutions become more difficult to sustain; we are using up the earth's ecological potential energy on sustaining solutions at the expense of directing our attention to the state of the environment itself, even as we meet with less and less success in so doing (Cockerill et al. 2017). Overall, ES has led the West into a crisis state of increased immersion in, and ongoing perpetuation of, severe anthropogenic environmental degradation, contamination, and vanishing (SEDCOV) globally, with no clear way out (Snow 2024).

Beyond merely arguing against ES, ER is poised to lay many new positive directions for further research (including by this chapter's author, in work which is currently ongoing). "Realism" is of course a wide-ranging term depending on the context. In the simplest possible sense of the term, ER can first and foremost represent the need to return to focusing on the "real world" of our direct experience rather than our idealized and abstract versions of it. In policy terms, this amounts to a need to foreground and consider the immediate, local, and particular meanings and ramifications of environmental decisions. Drawing from more specific senses of the term "realism," I am also working to identify how the realist traditions in both philosophy and political science can contribute to building up the ER framework. Philosophical realism's tradition of emphasizing the external world's independence from human cognition (and human beings and ideas more generally), and the realist tradition in political science and international relations with its emphasis on thinking through how one's country and policies appear to rivals or from "without," and how to survive in a strictly speaking noncontrolled and irrational system, are both well-poised to add depth to the paradigm. Accepting the objective reality of the natural world itself apart from humans, while also considering from an external standpoint (rather than from the standpoint of which "problems" the impacts "solve" for us) what our impacts on the natural world really have been to date, can potentially also increase our acknowledgment and understanding of the key paradox pointed out by Hamilton, that we humans are currently both ultimately utterly dependent on the biosphere and helpless in terms of this dependence, and at the same time unprecedentedly capable of impacting and harming the biosphere at scale in a way which speaks to our enormous power as a species, at least in the immediate term (Hamilton 2017: 85).

ER is also poised to oppose ES's easy optimism and too-sanguine sets of assumptions (Hamilton 2017) and resist, for example, taking up terms like "adaptation" (a concept straight out of the MDD cycle, cf. Figure 1), "resilience," or "sustainability" into our environmental policies and concomitant academic research. Such terms appear to assume up front much of the outcome they are supposed to be investigating, namely, implying certainty that there must be a way in which the natural world will always offer the human species a golden plateau for indefinite survival, as long as humans figure out the right "solutions" to current environmental "problems." Concepts like "sustainability" euphemize what is simply at its core our deeply held ES, with its belief in a well-planned, effectively managed future in which the living world has been reduced to only solved problems and useful materials. From an ER perspective, we can critique these imagined plateaus in a number of ways.

4 The Policy Relevance of Histories of ES

As ER is developed further, ER can potentially re-frame not only environmental policy thinking itself, but also which types of research questions in environmental history align with possible policy relevance. In the interim, one way to begin policy relevant environmental historical research which does not simply adopt and perpetuate ES could be to interrogate and write more of the history of ES itself. Given ES's inertia, reaching a place where environmental policymakers stop automatically defaulting to ES frameworks—and could instead begin to explore ER's relative advantages as these are developed in the future—will likely require a great deal of additional investigation and critique of ES and its long hold over our environmental imagination. Using the environmental past to increase our understanding of ES's origins, strengths, and severe weaknesses as a human environmental strategy could contribute to helping policymakers recognize, and perhaps eventually begin to move away from, their own ES.

Much remains to be explored, for example, regarding the MDD dynamic's ostensible evolutionary origins. Again, Cockerill et al. (2017), also drawing from others (particularly Nekola et al. 2013), equate ES with a socialized form of the MDD, and equate the MDD with the rudimentary reproduction-maximizing survival strategy found in many complex life forms including our own, also deeming it pervasive in humans throughout time and place (cf. Section 3, including Fig. 1, above). These claims merit additional environmental historical research, which could draw from evolutionary history, natural history, Paleolithic and Neolithic history, and animal ethology. By also considering the distinct differences between our environments "then" and "now," such histories could unearth new ways of understanding ES's biological non-serviceability for twenty-first-century Western society.

Any more recent past societies, with different sorts of (i.e., textual) records to work with, and which are on the familiar list of alleged "collapse" cases—Mesopotamia, or ancient Egypt, Greece, or Rome—could also be interrogated for whether something like the MDD or ES played a role in these collapses, as for example Nekola et al. (2013: 128) somewhat loosely assert.

Tracing the history of ES into the modern era, environmental historians could also refine Cockerill et al.'s placing of part of the blame for our contemporary ES on "Enlightenment thinking," which "promoted a false barrier between humans and our biophysical surroundings" (Cockerill et al. 2017: 22). This is arguably not a full or fair representation of the environmental views coming out of the Enlightenment as a whole, and we should perhaps hesitate to present this as a key reason for our own ES in the twenty-first century. Likewise, environmental history interacting with the history of science and technology could potentially uncover new ways of conceptualizing how and in what senses we *have* now arrived at a *novel* type of semi-separation between humans and nature, and why this matters for understanding the shortcomings of ES as a framework for weighing the permissibility of drastic environmental impacts in the twenty-first century.

Seeking to use environmental history to better understand ES's role in our creation of our contemporary human environments should not entail writing the same type of accounts as the existing ones specifying some aspect of the chain of events impacting the environment since the Industrial Revolution. Much of this history has already been written; the outlines are well-known. Causal investigations into ES's role would need to operate at a higher level of analysis or abstraction, seeking to foreground the role an ES-like approach to nature played in deeming certain steps in the chain of events advisable, walling off some reactions and responses to the steps once they had been taken, etc. Simply detailing the long chain of events which has led us to today does not appear to affect policymakers or the public, perhaps not least because historical consequentialist narratives continually subsume any apparent moral response to this chain of events into thinking about a longer-term time frame which usually features humanity's technologically-fueled redemption and/or tragic yet heroic end. Emphasizing the role of the ES mindset itself in landing us with all the ecological and social consequences we face today might provide policymakers and the public a different angle on the familiar histories, an angle which identifies a causal role for a cognitive framework which is still very much with us but which might in turn be possible to change.

More environmental histories of Western religion could also potentially hold relevance for shedding light on how ES emerged and functioned as an environmental strategy or mindset across past times and places. There is much still to be uncovered regarding the role of religion in how and why past cultures either embraced, or, perhaps more interestingly, eschewed, various forms of ES. Elsewhere I lay the groundwork for thinking about the link between secularism and the loss of certain human capacities for "metarational cognition" (Sandkaulen 2023: 35), a[n impending] loss which already preoccupied the realist thinker Friedrich Jacobi in the late eighteenth century. In Jacobi's view, metarational cognition was central to understanding, and responding logically and ethically to, our world. First-order logic and the perfect world models it permitted was a kind of toy version of this broader form of reason, one unsuited for relying upon as our mainstay to guide us through real existence or use as our standard for ultimate truth. For Jacobi, those who pursued banishment of the metarational faculty in favor of reasoning only in line with imagined perfect world-systems built through logical forms of cognition alone, and consisting only of provable yes/no propositions modeled on mathematics, were not more rational as a result, but in an important way, far less rational (Snow 2026). An environmental history which intersected with the history of thought, and the history of Western religion, could consider these and other aspects of how the transition to secularism led humans to change our environment by being a transition inherently accelerative of ES. Considering whether secularism's historical rise has been intertwined with the loss of some rational capacity needed for proper environmental cognition (Snow 2026), with ES in effect taking its place, might also hold far more relevance for the policy domain than the still common environmental histories of religion which turn on some version of the disenchantment thesis.

5 Conclusion

Even if environmental history adopts an ER framework, or in the interim, writes histories of ES which help us gain critical perspectives upon it, certain structural obstacles to it ever proving policy-relevant still linger. This is because, simply put, the scholarly activity of uncovering and interpreting matters of fact is different from the exercise of power. Even if we were able to shift policy on the environment away from ES toward ER, much of intellectual study unavoidably engages in such extensive forms of abstraction that it remains functionally a kind of idealism for purposes of comparison with the policy realm, a realm which deals with power and how it is really being distributed and exercised, in real time, among groups of men (and a few women) with elections, legal actions, and even legitimized state violence as their ultimate means of arbitrating among groups and their interests.

It is also important to acknowledge the ideas of J. Benda and others who have proposed that academics and the real world of the exercise of power should actually seek to avoid deliberate overlap or convergence of any type. Writing in Europe before and after the Second World War, Benda warned that the realm of power is a fatal bed of Procrustes for the kinds of pure inquiry and art which first the church, and now the academy, should instead always actively shelter from the outside world (Benda 1969 [1928]). Benda was concerned that having the intellectual class, ostensibly engaged in the disinterested search for truth, seek to apply their findings to the realm of politics and practical questions—the domain of self-interest and power—was destructive for society as well as for the intellectual class itself, removing this class's sole *raison d'être* and value to society while also infusing political discourse with a mislaid language of ultimacy or final appeal, particularly in the era of secularism where no higher church remained to offer its alternative arbitration of even higher truths. For Benda, the very "essence of the intellectual is to confer sovereignty upon the universal" (Benda 1946: 31[5])—i.e., the scholar must judge truth (and the artist beauty) according to some type of universalized standard or idea—while the realm of power cannot escape a duty to the individual, the subjective, the anecdotal, and the national. Mixing the two would lead, in Benda's view, to dangerously virulent forms of populism and totalitarianism, including violence and war carried out at a far more wide-ranging scale than in his view it had been in ages past (Benda 1969 [1928]).

Whether we want to go as far as Benda or not, policymakers' thought-processes and decision-spaces in general, at least as they currently exist in the West, simply do not turn on the kinds of things that interest historians or anchor most intellectual inquiry. If we want to propose that scholarship can converge with policymaking, we need to at the very least explain why we think we have overcome this deep difference. Idealizations of policymakers as rational decision-makers awaiting the most rigorously tested theories the academy can provide, should likewise be discarded (this is also part of what ER can emphasize). Even the imagined neat interface between environmental studies and an idealized "environmental policy" czar, perhaps one with a scientific background, is of questionable value. In the contemporary West, it is not usually our designated "environmental" policies which affect nature the most; most SEDCOV has resulted from economic policy (as touched upon above), transportation policy, trade agreements, defense postures and alliances, housing and urban development policy, tax regulation, lobbying and political donations, and numerous other domains and dynamics in governments and geopolitics (Snow 2024). The environmental historian, or any environmental studies researcher, thus may even have basic expertise mismatch with the very policymakers most likely to have the greatest impacts on nature.

All told, concentrating on the "meta-policy" imperative of better understanding the problematic character of ES, ES's deep prevalence in Western environmental decision-making, and how ER may constitute a better alternative, may be the most fruitful domain in which the environmental historian may initially find some research questions relevant to policy. At the same time, historians can never fully escape the idealized world-construction intertwined with their discipline, nor can they avoid certain questions which dog any intellectual field's attempt to cross into the realm of decision-making on behalf of millions of people in a context in which political elections, legal procedures, and ultimately state-sanctioned violence, frame debate and action. ER does hold promise as a new framework within which policymakers, philosophers, and scientists and social scientists might meet and carry out something of a re-set in talking about the environment, one which might allow all parties to, at the very least, discuss and debate possible future courses of action and

---

[5] In French, "*l'essence de l'intellectuel est de conférer une souveraineté à l'universel*".

human impacts while referencing the actual natural world and our environments within it, not imagined "problems" or inherited "solutions."

References

Baur, S., A. Nauels, Z. Nicholls, B. M. Sanderson, and C.-F. Schleussner. 2023. The deployment length of solar radiation modification: an interplay of mitigation, net-negative emissions and climate uncertainty. *Earth Syst. Dynam.* 14:367–381. https://doi.org/10.5194/esd-14-367-2023

Benda, J. 1946. L'esprit européen. In *L'esprit européen: Rencontres internationales de Genève, Tome I.* Neuchâtel: Les Éditions de la Baconnière, 1947, 5–38. http://palimpsestes.fr/textes_philo/jaspers/rencontres.pdf

Benda, J. 1969 [1928]. *The Treason of the Intellectuals (La trahison des clercs)*, Translated by Richard Aldington. New York: Norton.

Carlson, Alana M., and Mary Church. 2024. *The Risks of Geoengineering: Accelerating Biodiversity Loss and Compounding Planetary Crises.* Washington, DC: Center for International Environmental Law (CIEL). http://www.jstor.org/stable/resrep64185.

Cockerill, K., M. Armstrong, J. Richter, and J. G. Okie. 2017. *Environmental Realism: Challenging Solutions.* Cham: Palgrave-Macmillan.

Dooley, K., E. Harrould-Kolieb, and A. Talberg. 2021. Carbon-dioxide removal and biodiversity: A threat identification framework. *Global Policy* 12:34–44. https://doi.org/10.1111/1758-5899.12828.

Floyd, J. 2009. Is political philosophy too ahistorical? *Critical Review of International Social and Political Philosophy* 12 (4): 513–533. https://doi.org/10.1080/13698230903471376.

Hamilton, C. 2017. *Defiant Earth: The Fate of Humans in the Anthropocene.* Cambridge: Polity Press.

Holechek, J. L., H. M. E. Geli, M. N. Sawalhah, and R. Valdez. 2022. A global assessment: can renewable energy replace fossil fuels by 2050? *Sustainability* 14 (8): 4792. https://doi.org/10.3390/su14084792.

IPBES Secretariat, E. S. Brondizio, J. Settele, S. Díaz, and H. T. Ngo, eds. 2019. *Global Assessment Report on Biodiversity and Ecosystem Services of the Intergovernmental Science-Policy Platform on Biodiversity and Ecosystem Services.* Bonn. https://doi.org/10.5281/zenodo.3831673.

Lawrence, M. G., S. Schäfer, H. Muri, V. Scott, A. Oschlies, N. E. Vaughan, O. Boucher, H. Schmidt, J. Haywood, and J. Scheffran. 2018. Evaluating climate geoengineering proposals in the context of the Paris Agreement temperature goals. *Nature Communications* 9:3734. https://doi.org/10.1038/s41467-018-05938-3.

Meadows, D. H., D. L. Meadows, J. Randers, and W. W. Behrens III. 1972. *The Limits to Growth.* Washington, DC: Potomac Associates.

Muller, J. Z. 1997. Frontmatter. In *Conservatism: An Anthology of Social and Political Thought from David Hume to the Present*, ed. J. Z. Muller, i–vi. Princeton: Princeton University Press. https://doi.org/10.1515/9780691213118 fm.

National Academies of Sciences, Engineering, and Medicine (NASEM). 2021. *Reflecting Sunlight: Recommendations for Solar Geoengineering Research and Research Governance.* Washington, DC: National Academies Press. https://doi.org/10.17226/25762.

Nekola, J. C., C. D. Allen, J. H. Brown, J. R. Burger, A. D. Davidson, T. S. Fristoe, et al. 2013. The Malthusian-Darwinian dynamic and the trajectory of civilization [Forum piece]. *Trends in Ecology & Evolution* 28 (3): 127–130.

Ripple, W. J., C. Wolf, T. M. Newsome, M. Galetti, M. Alamgir, E. Crist, M. I. Mahmoud, W. F. Laurance, and 15,364 scientist signatories from 184 countries. 2017. World scientists' warning to humanity: A second notice. *BioScience* 67 (12): 1026–1028. https://doi.org/10.1093/biosci/bix125.

Sandkaulen, B. 2023. Jacobi and Spinoza. In *Friedrich Heinrich Jacobi and the Ends of the Enlightenment: Religion, Philosophy, and Reason at the Crux of Modernity*, ed. A. J. B. Hampton, 38–48. Cambridge: Cambridge University Press.

Schneider, S. A. 2011. Reconsidering the industrialization of agriculture. *Journal of Environmental Law and Litigation* 26 (1): 19–28.

Sinnott-Armstrong, W. 2023. Consequentialism. *The Stanford Encyclopedia of Philosophy* (Winter 2023 Edition). ed. E. N. Zalta and U. Nodelman. https://plato.stanford.edu/archives/win2023/entries/consequentialism/

Snow, K. C. 2024. Responding to the West's environmental security paradox: organic national security and the contemporary state embrace of severe anthropogenic environmental degradation, contamination, and vanishing (SEDCOV). *Global Security: Health, Science and Policy* 9 (1): https://doi.org/10.1080/23779497.2024.2358754.

Snow, K. C. 2026. *Our Inevitable Third Spinoza Controversy: Ontologies of Necessity and Environmental Nihilism*. New York: Palgrave-Macmillan.

Snow, K. C., and S. J. Kluiving. 2022. Reading the anthropocene through landscape archeology: Historical and contemporary landscapes of accumulation in the Netherlands and Lebanon. *The International Journal of Environmental Sustainability* 18 (2): 1–22. https://doi.org/10.18848/2325-1077/CGP/v18i02/1-22.

Stewart, S. 2020. *The Ruins Lesson: Meaning and Materiality in Western Culture*. Chicago: University of Chicago Press.

UNFCCC. 2015. The Paris Agreement. https://unfccc.int/sites/default/files/english_paris_agreement.pdf

Case Studies

Visualizing Risk, Remembering Disaster, Creating Resilience: Medieval Hydrological Extremes and What They Can Teach the Twenty-First Century

Martin Bauch

Abstract Premodern hydrological extreme events in Central Europe surpassed the floods and droughts of the twentieth and twenty-first centuries in terms of their dimensions. Nevertheless, they are still largely unknown in the public debate and, unlike other disasters, are often not present in collective memories. In particular, historic floods that predate instrumental measurements have not been considered in state authorities' assessment of infrastructural risks. These floods have, however, left behind a robust source base that allows scholars to draw conclusions about the height of such extreme events. In the context of anthropogenic climate change and the ensuing expectation of more extreme heavy precipitation events in combination with higher drought risks, this paper argues that these medieval "freak" events should no longer be disregarded when developing strategies for risk prevention.

Keywords Floods · Droughts · Medieval · Risk · Mitigation · Memory

1 Introduction

When, immediately after the devastating July flood of 2021—particularly along the Ahr, a tributary of the Rhine in western Germany—those affected and politically responsible spoke out, their statements followed a long historical tradition: No one could have imagined such a thing, the water had never been this high before, it had never arrived so suddenly. Even in their wording, these remarks closely resembled what chroniclers in the Middle Ages and the early modern period recorded after similar events. In 2021, however, references to divine wrath were absent from the reports; instead, there were occasional mentions of a "backlash from nature." Hydrologists have since pointed to comparable or even larger floods of the Ahr in

M. Bauch (✉)
Leibniz Institute for the History and Culture of Eastern Europe [GWZO], Leipzig, Germany
e-mail: martin.bauch@leibniz-gwzo.de

J. F. Haldon, R. Fernandes (eds.), *Bridging History and Policy*, Understanding Complex Systems, https://doi.org/10.1007/978-3-032-24379-9_16

the years 1804 and 1910 (Roggenkamp and Herget 2015). Furthermore, the connection between the genesis and increasing frequency of extreme weather events and climate change, which attribution research has examined in the wake of the floods, deserves mention. (Tradowsky et al. 2023). The infrastructural adaptations that were already being widely debated in the aftermath of the catastrophe will take much longer—if they ever can be implemented in a reasonable and feasible manner. Indeed, public awareness lacks a long-term environmental-historical perspective, one that would identify at-risk areas even when they have remained untouched by disasters for decades or centuries (Schäfer et al. 2021). A culture of remembrance for meteorological extreme events of all kinds is barely developed in Central Europe (Bauch et al. 2021b). This lack of collective memory extends beyond floods to include droughts, which tend to be documented and recalled primarily through scientific measurements, and only for comparatively recent periods (Fig. 1). The brief window of public attention following the devastating event of the Ahr flood in 2021 made it possible to highlight this gap in national media (Bauch et al. 2021c).

This map also clearly demonstrates that drought is a *slow-onset disaster*, distinguishing it chronologically from short-term extreme events such as the previously discussed floods, storm surges, or earthquakes. Instead, it bears greater resemblance to desertification, glacier melt, soil salinization, ocean acidification, and rising sea levels—all environmental risks associated with anthropogenic climate change that often remain below the threshold of human perception for long periods.

The 2022 drought period attracted considerable media attention, not least because scientific assessments suggested it was the most severe drought in Europe since the Middle Ages, that is, in the past 500 years (Toreti et al. 2022). Unexpectedly, medieval droughts thus entered the public spotlight—an especially intriguing development given that even researchers in the emerging field of climate history, situated at the intersection of the natural and humanities disciplines (White et al. 2018), had addressed individual heat years but not the prolonged drought period in Central Europe that extended over decades in the fifteenth century (Brázdil et al. 2018). The claim was based on a publication by the Joint Research Centre of the European Commission, a research-based policy advisory body at the European level. Explicitly targeting decision-makers, the JRC maintains a *Global Drought Observatory*, a platform providing a database of global drought events based on measurements dating back to 1950.

Where, then, did the striking historical classification of drought events over the past millennium—or, in the case of the Ahr flood, the historical perspective that was ultimately overlooked—originate? The first step is to outline the possibilities that emerge for reconstructing past hydrological extremes such as droughts and floods when scholars combine historical and paleoclimatic research. Once these phenomena have been established, it becomes possible to address how these disasters affected societies in the past and to identify patterns in their contemporary responses with particular attention to premodern practices of remembrance. Finally, the question arises as to how this knowledge might apply to modern societies: How can the premodern era help to inform the twenty-first century? Or is looking into this distant and murky mirror ultimately of little use for our current discussions on mitigating the effects of climate change?

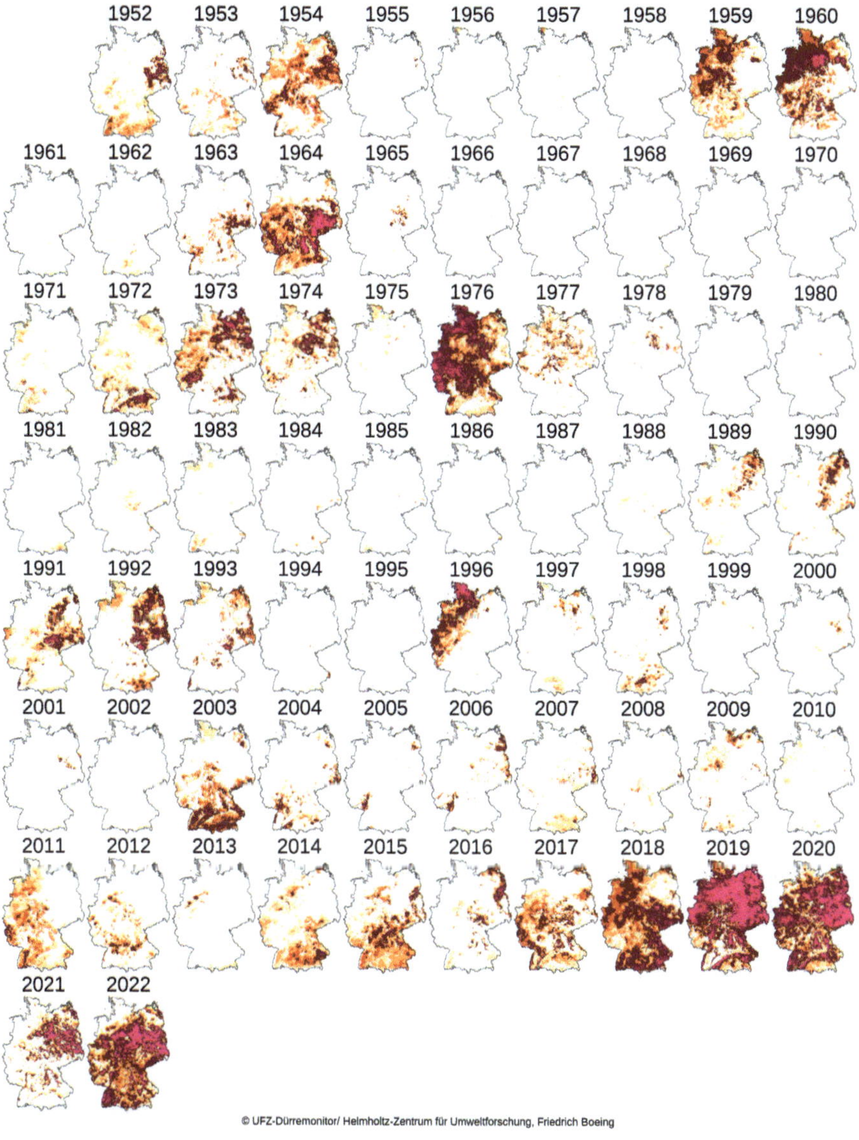

Fig. 1 Drought intensities during the vegetation period from April to October in Germany, 1942–2022. Source: UFZ-Dürremonitor/Helmholtz-Zentrum für Umweltforschung, Leipzig, Germany

2 Reconstructing Precipitation Extremes Based on Proxy Data: Tree Rings, Grape Harvests, Narrative Accounts, Inscriptions

There are essentially three ways to obtain information about droughts, extreme rainfall events, and floods for periods predating instrumental records: tree rings, grape harvest records, and narrative accounts and historical inscriptions. The most precise data on precipitation can be derived from the analysis of tree rings. While tree growth at high elevations is primarily influenced by temperature, growth in lower areas is largely determined by precipitation. Tree rings thus provide reliable proxy data, i.e., indirect indicators of wet phases and droughts—especially when multiple tree-ring chronologies from individual sites are compared and compiled to produce more generalized averages. This approach enables the reconstruction of precipitation levels with annual precision, albeit only for the growing season (typically June to August).

Reliable reconstructions on this basis are, however, not always possible because trees provide no information for the rest of the year and dendroclimatological data are not equally available across all regions of Europe. It was within this dataset that the first indications of a so-called *megadrought* in the fifteenth century were found (Cook et al. 2015), characterized by decades of significantly below-average summer precipitation (June–August) between 1437 and 1473. Within this extended period, only two isolated years exhibited a positive drought index (PDSI) in Central Europe, as evidenced in the aggregated tree-ring data of the *Old World Drought Atlas* (Fig. 2).

A second, remarkably precise method for reconstructing the meteorological characteristics of summers does not rely on traditional scientific methods such as analyzing tree rings but instead uses the dates of grape harvests as documented at viticultural sites over many centuries. The start of the harvest was collectively regulated, i.e. no one was allowed to harvest before a certain date, as in the case of

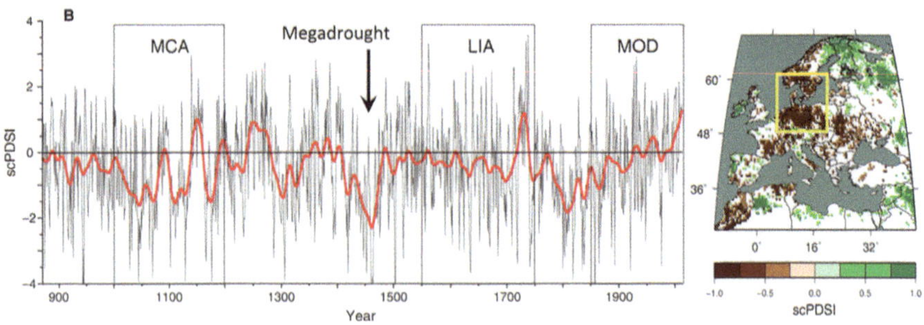

Fig. 2 Average of the OWDA reconstruction of drought indices for the past 1150 years within the yellow-marked rectangle on the map to the right, highlighting the major climatic epochs: "Medieval Climate Anomaly" (MCA), "Little Ice Age" (LIA), and the modern period. Source: Cook et al. (2015), Fig. 3B Lizenz: CC BY-NC 4.0

Beaune, France, where the documentation stretches back to 1354. Scholars of climate history have long recognized the potential of analyzing these grape harvest dates to assess the warmth and dryness of preceding summers: The less precipitation and the higher the temperatures, the earlier the harvest could begin (Labbé et al. 2019). Such conditions generally benefited the wine quality, as well. In fact, the oldest surviving European white wine, the *Steinwein* from Würzburg that dates to 1540 embodies this principle: This historically remarkable vintage—already considered extraordinary at the time and featured in the online climate-historical exhibition *Weathered History* (Bauch and Feitsch 2021)—stems from a year of particular interest in climate history (see below).

The written records of the grape harvest dates in Beaune allow for the creation of a graph (Fig. 3) illustrating the recurrence of extremely hot, dry summers in the premodern period. However, the years associated with the *megadrought* of the fifteenth century—except for its immediate onset in 1420 and its conclusion in 1473—do not appear to have been characterized by extreme heat. It should be noted, of course, that such records of grape harvests have only regional significance—in this case, for Burgundy, rather than for all of Central Europe. Nevertheless, it is striking that, from the year 2000 onward, hot summers have become increasingly frequent. In fact, the drought summer of 2018 led to the earliest opening of the grape harvest since 1354. Here, for the first time, the well-known *hockey stick* curve typical of anthropogenic climate change—previously established in scientific reconstructions—emerges solely on the basis of historical sources.

The third source for historical drought periods, as well as for times of heavy rainfall and flooding, consists of narrative historical documents—i.e., chronicles, annals, and diaries, as well as in inscriptions or letters, that include records of droughts, prolonged rainfall, and floods, along with their consequences (Pfister

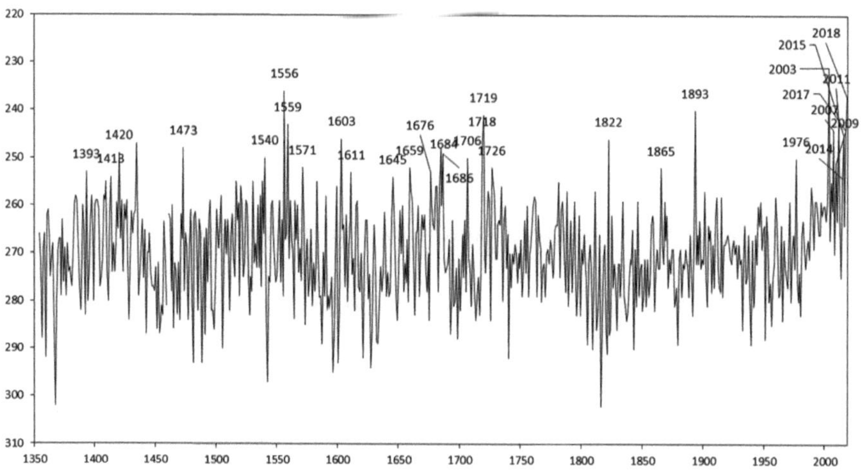

Fig. 3 Data on the start of the grape harvest as the day of the year (y-axis) in Beaune (Burgundy), based on written sources for the period 1354–2018. The 5% of years with the earliest harvest dates are marked with their respective years. Source: Labbé et al. (2019), Fig. 10 Licence: CC BY-NC 4.0

2018). These sources are particularly useful for identifying and characterizing individual extreme years; using such records, climate historians have, for instance, analyzed water shortages in the year 1473 (Camenisch et al. 2020) or, even more extensively, to study the *millennium drought* of 1540 (Wetter et al. 2014). Unlike other types of data, historical documents provide information about precipitation—or its absence—during autumn, winter, and spring. These records are, however, not without their own problems: They are often fragmentary and subjective, and it can be difficult to define precise locations. Furthermore, their geographic distributions is quite uneven.

A central challenge is that such qualitative data cannot be easily integrated into quantitative reconstructions, such as drought indices derived from tree rings. This has led to the adoption of the somewhat problematic method of *climate indices* (Nash et al. 2021), which attempts to translate qualitative descriptions of temperature and precipitation for specific periods (typically seasons) into numerical values on a scale (usually from +3 to –3). In the case of the mid-fifteenth-century *megadrought* in Central Europe, precipitation and temperature indices were compared with dendroclimatological reconstructions based on tree-ring data for entire decades (Ionita et al. 2021). Surprisingly, the findings from these decadal indices do not support the hypothesis of a prolonged megadrought—neither in terms of reduced precipitation nor elevated temperatures. Such an extreme event would almost certainly have left a more pronounced imprint on the historical record of late medieval Europe. These indices build upon pioneering work in historical climatology for Central Europe (Glaser 2008); the underlying dataset is available online (www.tambora.org). From the perspective of historical-critical methodology, many of the written sources used are of questionable reliability, which inevitably affects the robustness of the indices. Each of the data foundations presented for reconstructing historical drought periods thus has its own specific advantages and limitations. Making reliable statements that can be considered valid for entire years or decades remains extraordinarily difficult. Despite decades of foundational research, our knowledge—particularly beyond tree-ring reconstructions—remains insufficiently robust.

3 The Impact of Droughts and Societal Responses

The socioeconomic consequences of premodern droughts (Brázdil et al. 2020) reveal striking parallels to the effects of more recent water shortages like in the summer of 2022 as described above. For example, this passage from a Regensburg chronicle both vividly describes the year 1540 and draws a comparison to 1473, which was still remembered then as a year of extreme heat:

> From March until July 28 [1540], it rained little, almost not at all, so that everything that should have grown in the fields was severely scorched, especially the pastures, and the livestock nearly starved. It was so hot that the wheat was already being harvested and brought into the barns by St. Margaret's Day (June 10). There was no dew, as people said

> had been the case in the dry summer that was counted in 1473. But, however dry that summer had been, there had been no shortage of crops or fruit, and everything had grown in abundance. [...] I have heard from credible people that field mice died in the fields for lack of water. Furthermore, many forests and woods burned down, so that it would be fair to say that our descendants may rightfully call and recognize this as a dry summer. (Widmann 1878: 161.)

The author, the cleric Leonhart Widmann, was the son of vintners and may have been particularly attuned to weather phenomena and their effects for this reason. His account thus provides a paradigmatic characterization of the socioeconomic consequences of the *millennium summer* of 1540, which serves here as a representative example. Grain harvests and livestock farming could be negatively affected, though only in extreme cases; generally speaking, dry, warm summers benefited the production of staple grains (Pribyl 2017) and wine, both in terms of quantity and quality. Animals, however, suffered from water shortages, and forest fires became more frequent.

Just as more recent episodes of low water levels have threatened energy production in our modern world, premodern energy production could be threatened, as well. In the premodern case the crucial factor was not, of course, cooling towers for nuclear power, but rather watermills. Many premodern communities relied on hydropower for proto-industrial production—for example, for the textile sector—and even more essential processes like milling grain into flour. Drying rivers also disrupted transportation, today as back then, for waterways generally provided the most cost-effective means of moving bulk goods such as grain, beer, or wine during this period. In extreme cases, such as the multi-year drought in the Mediterranean region from 1302 to 1304 (Bauch et al. 2021a), prolonged lack of rainfall led to price surges and even scarcity of drinking water. Such events forced cities to respond; they expanded their water infrastructure, built new wells, extended water supply systems, and developed ports to facilitate grain imports during periods of food scarcity.

The Tuscan city of Siena's response to the drought of 1302/03 is a particularly striking example. Siena is situated atop a ridge, far from major rivers, but the city leaders pursued solutions that included locating a hidden, legendary underground river *Diana* and the acquiring and expanding the port city of Talamone in southern Tuscany to import grain. The contemporary poet Dante Alighieri mocked both endeavors in his *Divine Comedy*: "Them wilt thou see among that people vain/Who hope in Talamone, and will lose there/More hope than in discovering the Diana)" (*Purgatorio*, Canto XIII, Longfellow 1867). Pragmatic responses to a premodern drought thus found their way into a masterpiece of medieval literature.

The question of whether prolonged droughts led to an increased frequency of urban fires, as has been suggested for the millennium drought of 1540 (Pfister 2017), remains contested in research (Zwierlein 2011: 102–110). The proposed mechanism is straightforward: Medieval buildings were largely timber structures with wooden shingles or thatched roofs, and a prolonged drying of these structures would have heightened fire risk. Medieval chroniclers noted a connection here: "Many cities were consumed by house fires due to the drought and barrenness that prevailed in this year [1244]" (Wattenbach 1851: 541). A statistically significant correlation between drought phases in the thirteenth and fourteenth centuries and urban fires has indeed been observed in Italy and France. Notably, early forms of organized municipal firefighting brigades first emerged in Italy in the early thirteenth century. Likewise, it was after a surge in fire disasters across Central Europe in the spring of 1342 that authorities there took action: Emperor Louis the Bavarian issued a construction ordinance for his residence city of Munich just days after the devastating Landshut city fire; the new ordinance mandated tiled roofs and banned thatched roofs and wooden shingles within the city walls (Bauch 2019).

As one must expect, premodern responses to drought disasters were not always pragmatic in the modern sense—though some measures might be interpreted as early medieval forms of public welfare. It bears remembering that those who experienced extreme environmental changes in the Middle Ages consistently viewed these as divine punishment. Drawing on biblical examples, they understood natural events to be God's commentary on the moral quality of the society affected. It was thus not at all irrational for them to respond to these events with religious means—for instance, with penitential sermons, such as the one delivered just a week after the great city fire of Florence on June 10, 1304, when the Dominican preacher Giordano da Pisa admonished his fellow citizens that the fire had merely fulfilled God's will (Bauch et al. 2021a).

In keeping with this belief, it made sense to attempt to influence divine will—through penitential processions, for example (Brázdil et al. 2020). Such processions are well-documented for premodern Catalonia in the context of droughts. Similarly, in Florence in 1355, a Marian icon was carried through the city for the first time to end a prolonged winter drought. The processions featuring this *Madonna dell'Impruneta* continued to be performed in response to extreme events such as disasters, plagues, and wars well into the twentieth century. They serve as a prime example of social coping strategies in the face of drought. In fact, in the drought-stricken spring of 2023, such supplication processions were held in southern France and Spain for the first time in 150 years, demonstrating just how deeply rooted this response remains. It must, of course, be regarded as a fortunate coincidence that, merely hours after such a procession in Perpignan on March 18, a remarkable 36.8 l of rainfall per square meter fell—despite meteorological forecasts to the contrary (Bauch 2023). This is particularly striking given that the saint whose relics had just been ceremonially carried through the city, Gauderic of Perpignan, is traditionally venerated as a protector against excessive rainfall.

4 Reconstructing Floods and Their Impacts: The Instructive Example of 1342

The general principles for reconstructing drought periods also apply, in large part, to periods of increased precipitation. With only minor limitations, excessive rainfall—like droughts—can be traced in tree rings and, where available, grape harvest records, provided these events occurred during the respective growing seasons. In the case of extreme flooding events, however, inscriptions and narrative sources such as chronicles play an even more critical role.

Rather than examining various flood events across multiple centuries, the following discussion focuses on a single, remarkable year: 1342. This year has long fascinated researchers due to a series of extreme floods, making it a paradigmatic case for studying the reconstruction, impact, and historical memory of premodern flood disasters.

Establishing a precise chronology of events for 1342 is challenging. As early as the beginning of April, when spring-like temperatures led to the second snowmelt of the waning winter, cold conditions returned unexpectedly. The Carinthian chronicler and Cistercian monk Johann von Viktring (ca. 1270–1347) describes the phenomenon in striking detail:

> This year, at the beginning of April, as the ice melted everywhere and the grasses sprouted from the pores of the earth, an unexpected cold, with the freezing of waters, the density of winds and snow, brought a second winter, such that the force of the cold struck many people. And when the ice finally thawed and the accumulation of snow was split by the rays of the sun, it was as if the inundation of all the great rivers and the small streams flowing throughout all of Europe uprooted villages, people, trees, fields, and meadows down to their roots and carried them off to lower riverbeds. (Johann von Viktring 1909: 225–226.)

This account, an exceptionally detailed description of a large-scale flood progressing from small tributaries to major rivers, provides rare insight into the destruction of urban and agricultural landscapes as well as the profound morphological transformations caused by erosion. It is often linked to the prominent *Magdalena Flood* of July 1342. However, Johann von Viktring's report differs significantly in its contours from other accounts: It does not describe heavy rainfall but rather a cold snap, followed by an intensified thaw, which in turn triggered severe flooding and erosion. There is thus no contradiction between these flood events and the documented dry spell that contributed to a heightened frequency of urban fires in the spring and early summer of 1342 (Bauch 2019). The discrepancy in the reported timing of this second onset of winter and the related flood events—unattested in other sources for April—may be explained by the location of the Carinthian monastery on the southern side of the main Alpine ridge, where snowmelt and flooding followed different seasonal rhythms than in regions on the northern side.

Unsurprisingly, Viktring interprets these dramatic environmental events through a religious lens: "As if, in a revival of punishment for the sins of humanity, a second deluge had burst forth after the first, when the floodgates of heaven were opened for the human race" (Johann von Viktring 1909: 226). He frames the previously described catastrophic landscape of tributaries, main rivers, towns, villages, and fields in theological terms—as the setting for a *second deluge.* This interpretation is significant, not only because it reflects medieval modes of understanding natural disasters, but also because his phrasing is somewhat ambiguous: The Latin phrase *secundus exilierit cathaclismus* can be read as an allusion to a biblical-style cataclysm or as a more profane reference to a second such flood event within the same year, 1342. This dual meaning underscores the complex interplay between historical observation and religious interpretation in medieval accounts of environmental disasters.

Yet the most significant flood event was still to come. The so-called St. Mary Magdalene's Flood—or simply the Magdalena Flood—of July 1342 is widely regarded as the most extreme flooding event in Central Europe within the past millennium (Bauch 2019). Meteorological reconstructions suggest that a major Vb weather pattern, a recurrent storm track responsible for heavy precipitation across Central Europe, played a key role in triggering the disaster. Another proposed explanation is the presence of a Central European trough situation, which further intensified the rainfall (Mudelsee et al. 2004). In historical research, the flood is commonly associated with the feast day of St. Mary Magdalene (July 22), though contemporary sources rarely identify this specific date as the peak of the flooding (Weikinn 1958: 205–216). One of the best-documented examples of the event is found in reports from Frankfurt am Main, where the floodwaters of the Main River reached their highest level on the night of July 24/25. After midnight, the surging waters rose up around the stone bridge connecting Frankfurt with Sachsenhausen. The southern bridge tower collapsed, bringing down the bridge chapel with it (Brockhoff, Wissenbach 2010: 14). A contemporary account describes the destruction: "Afterwards, on St. Jacob's Eve at 1 o'clock, the water carried away the bridge and the tower towards Sachsenhausen, the pier with the pretty chapel was razed to the ground, except for six arches towards Frankfurt" (Froning 1884: 2, 5). Only six bridge piers on the northern side, facing Frankfurt, remained intact. The catastrophic flooding in Frankfurt marked the culmination of a flood wave that had moved down the Main and its tributaries in the preceding days (Fig. 4). The disaster unfolded in rapid succession: On July 19, 1342, the Pegnitz River overflowed its banks and flooded Nuremberg. One day later, Bamberg was inundated, losing its bridge to the raging waters. By July 21, the flood had reached Würzburg, destroying its stone bridge and rising up the steps of the cathedral (Weikinn 1958: 204, 208, 210–211).

It can reasonably be assumed that smaller crest waves from the western tributaries of the Main reached Frankfurt earlier than the peak flood surge, as narrative sources describe a 4-day rise in water levels before the flood's main wave ultimately caused the collapse of the city's stone bridge. Two anonymous chroniclers provide detailed, largely consistent accounts of the areas inundated between July 19 and 22: Almost all of Sachsenhausen, as well as twelve churches throughout Frankfurt, were flooded to varying degrees (Froning 1884: 5, 140). They also list specific houses and streets, noting that only one city gate remained unaffected due to its elevated position (Fig. 5) (Schwind 1984). Despite the inherent challenges of such

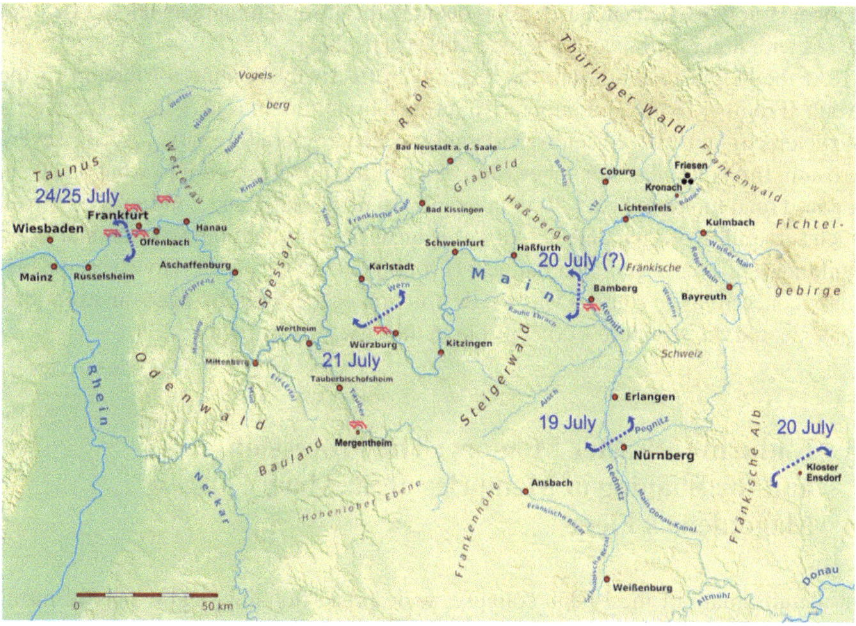

Fig. 4 Reconstruction of the moving flood peak of the July flood of 1342 in the Main River basin. Map: BerndH/Modifications by M. Bauch. Source: Wikimedia Commons, public domain

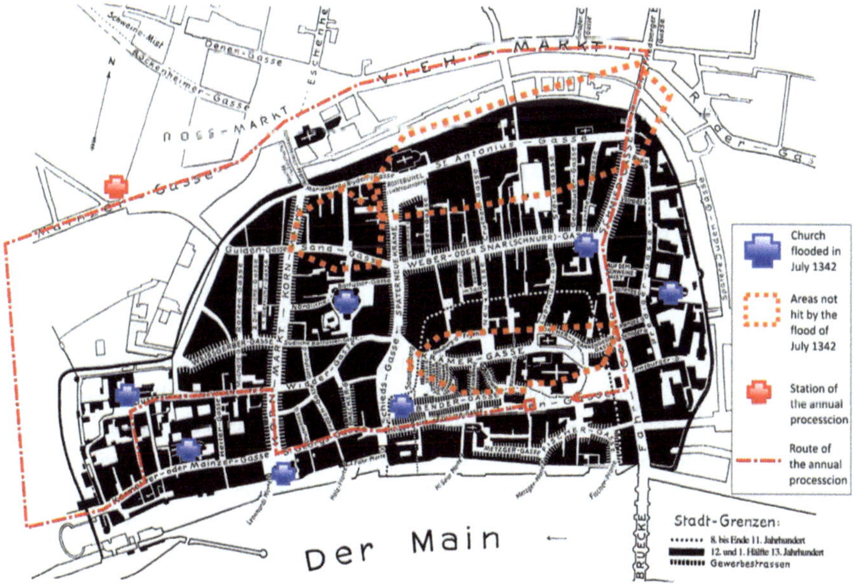

Fig. 5 Reconstructed route of the prayer procession on the eve of St. Mary Magdalene's Day in Frankfurt during the late Middle Ages. From: Nosbisch (1930) (Wikimedia Commons). Edited by M. Bauch (License: CC BY-ND 4.0)

a reconstruction, Stephanie Eifert has deemed this information plausible when compared with nineteenth-century town plans (Eifert 2024: 105).

At the height of the flood, the city moat effectively became a tributary of the Main (Froning 1884: 2), temporarily turning Frankfurt into an island. The river's flow velocity must have been considerable, as contemporary reports describe severe erosion: In Sachsenhausen, an erosion channel the flood carved into what had been a paved road measured over 30 m in length, 16 m in width, and 7 m in depth. Given such forceful hydrodynamic activity, it is unsurprising that both wooden and stone buildings suffered significant damage (Froning 1884: 2, 5, 140). However, the primary concern in the sources was the destruction of the Main Bridge—an event that underscored the structure's crucial role in the city's infrastructure.

5 Enduring Disaster Memory: The Procession and the Shaping of Memories of St. Mary Magdalene's Flood

In the aftermath of the bridge collapse, widespread flooding, and extensive infrastructure damage, it is hardly surprising that the residents of Sachsenhausen sought refuge on the Mühlberg hill towards Offenbach, where they even constructed temporary shelters. Meanwhile, the inhabitants of Frankfurt fled to villages north of the city (Froning 1884: 5). Their state of mind is described as one of deep fear (*territi*), with some believing that the complete destruction of their town (*oppida subversionem timentes*) was imminent—a reaction that seems entirely plausible given the scale of the disaster.

For three consecutive days, from July 19 to 21, the waters of the Main rose rapidly, only to recede slowly over the following days (Eifert 2024: 106). However, it was the dramatic collapse of the bridge on the night of St. James's Day (July 25) that had the greatest psychological impact on the population. The severity of the event is reflected in the response: on July 26, after a day of fasting, the city held its first recorded supplicatory procession. This extraordinary act of communal devotion involved all social groups, including the clergy, as hundreds of barefoot participants carried candles through the devastated town (Froning 1884: 5–6). At the heart of the procession was Frankfurt's principal church, St. Bartholomew's—often referred to as the "cathedral" (though not formally a bishop's seat)—which had remained largely unaffected by the floods and thus played a central role in the ritual. While the precise route of this supplicatory procession is unknown, it must have stood in stark contrast to earlier processions. Processions were not uncommon in Frankfurt; records from 1318 to 1323 document processions on Palm Sunday and Candlemas, among other occasions. More relevant to the context of the flood, however, was the *Letania maior*, the large-scale supplicatory procession held annually on April 25, St. Mark's Day. This procession crossed the Main Bridge to Oberrad, while the *letaniae minores*, smaller supplicatory processions before Ascension Day, took a different route—leading from St. Bartholomew's via St. Leonhard's to the Weißfrauenkloster. Additionally, the chapter of St. Bartholomew organized processions across the Main Bridge to Sachsenhausen, specifically to the Deutschherren church, on major Christian feasts such as Easter, Ascension, and Pentecost (Gedeon 2005: 10–11).

The July 26 procession, however, was different. Unlike the scheduled annual processions, this was a direct and spontaneous response to a traumatic event—marking a critical moment in the city's collective memory of disaster and resilience.

The spontaneous procession held on July 26, 1342 (Froning 1884: 82), marked the beginning of an annual commemorative ritual (Gedeon 2000: 21–26). Surprisingly, however, the traditional procession that ensued in subsequent years was not scheduled to coincide with the peak of the flood on July 24 or 25, when the bridge was destroyed, but rather with the feast day of St. Mary Magdalene on July 22. Participation in the procession was mandatory for all key social groups within Frankfurt's civic community (Froning 1884: 82–83).

The precise route of the procession (Fig. 5) was not recorded in detail until the early sixteenth century (Froning 1884: 82–83). It began at St. Bartholomew's, Frankfurt's principal church, and proceeded to the Weißfrauenkirche, named after the white habit of the Sisters of St. Mary Magdalene, or penitential sisters, who resided there (Gedeon 2005: 32). Until the church's destruction in 1944, an inscription on its main portal recalled the flood, though with a slightly altered chronology: "In 1342, on the eve of the Magdalene Festival, the Main flooded the city, and the council and people of Frankfurt visited me on the basis of their vow" (Froning 1884: 2, note 4; Wolff and Jung 1896: 110). After leaving the walled city through the Mainz Gate, the procession paused for a solemn service at the Rossmarkt, in front of the Maternus Chapel, before continuing along the cattle market—modern-day Zeil Street—to the Bornheimer Tor, where it re-entered the city walls and concluded at St. Bartholomew's (Froning 1884: 83). Notably, it seems likely that the route followed the same pattern established immediately after the flood, for it bypasses the areas that had been inundated in 1342—except for Sachsenhausen, which remained inaccessible via the destroyed bridge until the late 1340s (Gedeon 2005: 11). This hypothesis is further supported by the omission of the bridge, which was presumably only restored around 1346, and the exclusion of Sachsenhausen, which could only be reached once the crossing was rebuilt (Eifert 2024: 112).

A detailed account by the early modern local historiographer Latomus in Frankfurt's *Deutsche Annalen* suggests that inscriptions inside flooded churches may also have served as memorial markers for the disaster. He meticulously recorded the water levels within various churches: "The churches were all full of water as follows: Saint Nicholas's Church: 6 shoe-lengths high, Saint Jacob's Church: 3 shoe-lengths high, The Friars' Church: 4 shoe-lengths high, Saint Elisabeth's in Sachsenhausen, The Church of the Holy Spirit, Saint Anna, The Church of the Teutonic Order; Our Lady's Church of the Order of Friars Minor Capuchin; The Church of the Penitential Sisters of St. Mary Magdalene" (Froning 1884: 82). The carefully orchestrated and spatially performative nature of the procession ensured that participants not only recalled the flood of 1342 but also inscribed its memory into the urban landscape. This act of collective remembrance persisted in Frankfurt until the Reformation (Beumer 1969).

It is crucial to note, however, that the flood's peak in Frankfurt occurred on July 24/25, not on St. Mary Magdalene's Day, July 22. Yet the strong symbolic association with Mary Magdalene is unmistakable: the Church of the Penitential Sisters, with its vow inscription, the Magdalene Altar in the cathedral, and the bridge chapel—dedicated in part to Mary Magdalene—that collapsed into the river (Oven and Becker 1880). In effect, Frankfurt's civic authorities branded their disaster commemoration, deliberately associating it with St. Mary Magdalene, despite the original procession lacking this association. This was no arbitrary choice. Mary Magdalene was not only a widely venerated saint but also a fitting intercessor in a medieval worldview that interpreted disasters as divine punishment for collective sin. The immediate reaction to the flood—a spontaneous one-day fast—suggests that the citizens of Frankfurt saw the disaster as a moment of moral reckoning. In such a crisis, the city required a powerful advocate before God: Magdalene, the repentant sinner, whose intercession could secure divine mercy for the city (Gedeon 2005: 24–26).

Thus, while the actual crisis—the July 1342 flood—was over relatively quickly, the heightened awareness of sinfulness and fear of divine retribution endured (Eifert 2024: 113). The annual penitential procession on St. Mary Magdalene's Day became not merely a means of commemorating a past catastrophe but also a ritualized expression of collective crisis management (Schenk 2018). It served as a spatial reenactment of the city's vulnerability to flooding, while simultaneously functioning as a communal act of protection through penitence, performative piety, and appeals to transcendent safeguarding—ultimately to God, mediated by the intercessory power of Mary Magdalene. Perhaps the most striking illustration of the overlap between religious devotion, fear of divine punishment, and hopes for supernatural protection is found in one particular detail: By the 1460s at the latest, boys dressed as angels accompanied the procession. These children wore white robes adorned with stars and carried wooden wings, painted green and decorated with gilded mirrors and peacock feathers (Gedeon 2005: 18). In this way, the participants were not only reminded of the flood's impact—through the water levels marked in each church—but also visually reassured of the celestial protection surrounding their city, presented in the form of a *tableau vivant* of embodied angels.

The Frankfurt example deserves such a detailed look here because it offers highly instructive insights into how the course of a disaster, contemporary interpretative frameworks, and religiously connoted, performative practices facilitated both coping mechanisms and long-term remembrance. Even the largest flood of the past millennium in Central Europe has left few comparably dense traces in the historical record outside of Frankfurt, despite the occasional discovery of inscriptions or high-water marks from the events of 1342. The case of Frankfurt is paradigmatic in two key respects. On the one hand, it demonstrates how flood-prone areas within a city were effectively anchored in collective memory through performative practices—an act of remembrance that persisted for centuries. This represents the pragmatic, concrete aspect of premodern memorial practices following catastrophic floods. On the other hand, however, there is an aspect that may seem alien to modern observers: The prevailing societal response to the flood was individual and collective penitence, which was understood as the most appropriate reaction, even as technological and infrastructural measures were also undertaken (Bauch 2019). The dominant explanatory framework for extreme natural events was divine wrath—correspondingly, the notion of *innocent victims* was virtually nonexistent before the sixteenth century (Labbé 2019).

In this context, societal resilience was not primarily focused on material reconstruction but rather on securing the souls of the deceased—whether through collective remembrance and intercessory prayer in public processions or through individual acts of devotion. A striking example of this is a reliquary cross commissioned in Göttingen (Lower Saxony) in the mid-1350s to commemorate a goldsmith who drowned in the summer floods of 1342 (Fig. 6). The inscription on the cross is the only known historical record that names a victim of the greatest flood disaster in Central Europe over the past thousand years (Arnold 1980: no. 5).

Fig. 6 Inscription on a mid fourteenth-c. reliquary cross from St. Alban's parish in Göttingen: "In the year 1342 the goldsmith Hermann drowned in the flood of St Margret's Day"). Obviously, local disaster memory already a decade later mixed up the feast days and associated the flooding with Margret instead of Mary Magdalene. Image: Martin Bauch

6 Lessons from a Distant Mirror: Contextualization—Adaptation—Memory—Applicable Knowledge

Even though scholars generally regard the premodern concept of divine retribution and the coping strategies associated with it as only relevant to our modern context in a metaphorical sense—one might think here of the discourse which personifies nature and speaks of *revenge* for human exploitation or the eschatological interpretations found among some climate activists—prayer processions, despite certain performative similarities to climate protests in public spaces, are likely not the key lesson that climate history offers in the context of contemporary anthropogenic climate change. Instead, three key aspects should be emphasized in conclusion:

First, there is a strong need to place present-day experiences of extreme droughts, heavy rainfall, and catastrophic flooding in a historical framework. However, this can lead—incorrectly—to trivialization and relativization. Without question, there have been years of severe drought in the past, some of which may have caused even longer regional dry spells than those we have experienced so far. Likewise, flood events such as that of 1342 have not yet been matched in the twenty-first century. An example of such misuse is the attempt to refer to historical events like the millennium drought of 1540 or catastrophic historical floods to downplay modern-day events like the Ahr valley flood in 2021. What both grape harvest records and tree-ring data unequivocally demonstrate is that it is not the isolated extreme years that should alarm us now, but rather the increasing frequency of such extremes since around 2003. In the case of flooding, it is not merely the meteorological event itself but the rising damage potential due to urbanization and structural interventions in floodplains—factors that did not exist to the same extent in pre-industrial contexts. Climate history, therefore, cannot be used to argue against the observations and projections of contemporary and future-oriented climate science. References to individual extreme events in historical comparisons are not incorrect, yet they remain misleading: Rather than offering reassurance, they should serve as a warning. Even though claims such as the worst drought since the Middle Ages are difficult to verify, historical climate research provides valuable insights into the range of meteorological extremes that have occurred within the bounds of natural variability. In doing so, it helps delineate the range of possibility for future extreme events.

Second, climate history demonstrates that past societies repeatedly found ways to adapt to meteorological extremes and shifting climatic conditions (Degroot et al. 2021)—this applies to both droughts (Bauch et al. 2021a) and floods (Bauch 2019). While this historical adaptability can offer a certain degree of encouragement, it should not lead to complacency. Premodern societies functioned under entirely different technological, social, and demographic conditions. Moreover, we are no longer willing—nor should we be—to accept the sacrifices in life expectancy and living standards, or the social inequalities in terms of the impacts of meteorological extremes, that our ancestors tolerated in premodern times.

Third, and perhaps most crucially, we can learn from the premodern period how to effectively commemorate climatic extremes (Bauch et al. 2021b, c), how to visualize them, and how to use this memory to raise awareness of environmental hazards. The commemorative function of processions and inscriptions has been systematically examined in the case of Frankfurt, where the Reformation severed the chain of remembrance that had been sustained through penitential processions for two centuries. Numerous other examples, nevertheless, demonstrate how premodern events were kept alive in collective memory through religious performances well into the twentieth century (Erthel 2009; Bauch 2015).

Of course, such historical practices find only indirect continuity in contemporary narratives that frame anthropogenic climate change as *nature's revenge*. The most significant conveyer of memory—a widely accepted religious interpretation of extreme events and the associated rituals—no longer plays a comparable role in the largely secular twenty-first century. In this context, flood markers in public spaces harbor greater potential as warning signs of flood risks. Their historical predecessors, dating back to the late Middle Ages (Fig. 7), have, in some cases, even yielded practical knowledge applicable to the present: Until the destruction of World War II, flood level markings from the so-called *Magdalena Flood* of July 1342 were still visible in Frankfurt's urban churches. These inscriptions enabled a retrospective calculation of water levels and discharge volumes for this historic flood event (Mudelsee et al. 2004; Herget et al. 2015). A similar approach has been taken to analyze the Ahr valley flood of July 2021 (Roggenkamp and Herget 2022) and, more generally, to reconstruct flooding events along the Rhine between Germany and Switzerland (Wetter et al. 2011).

Fig. 7 Floodmarks on the so called "Red Building" of the Old Town Hall in Würzburg, with references, among others, to the "St. Mary Magdalene's Flood" of 1342 and the "Ice Flood" of 1784. The older floodmarks are certainly not contemporary but have been plausibly reconstructed from older sources. Image: Martin Bauch

Comparisons between modern flood risk maps and historical evidence from 1342 reveal striking discrepancies. In Würzburg, for example, historical inscriptions indicate that the 1342 floodwaters reached the stone steps of the cathedral (Borchardt 1988, No. 61). Modern flood risk maps produced by the relevant authorities (Fig. 8) do not, however, predict that floodwaters would reach this point—even under the HQ_{extrem} scenario, i.e., the most extreme flood event conceivable using today's models. These inconsistencies underscore the importance of integrating historical data into contemporary flood risk assessments to both challenge assumptions about the severity of past events and the adequacy of current protective measures.

That this is not an isolated case becomes evident when examining Hannoversch Münden, a small town in Lower Saxony located where the Werra and Fulda rivers merge to form the Weser. At the local parish church of St. Blasius, an in situ medieval floodmark inscription referring to 1342 has been preserved (Wehers 2006, No. 61). This marker only partially corresponds with the extreme flood scenario modeled for the Fulda and does not align at all with the maximum projected flood levels for the Werra (Fig. 9).

In both cases, historical flood inscriptions and descriptions in historical texts provide clear evidence of the maximum water levels reached in the premodern period. Nevertheless, because these data predate the use of modern instruments, officials charged with designing public flood protection systems in the twentieth and twenty-first centuries have not granted them adequate consideration. The dangers of relying exclusively on instrumental measurements in such calculations became tragically evident during the Ahr valley flood of 2021 (Roggenkamp and Herget 2022).

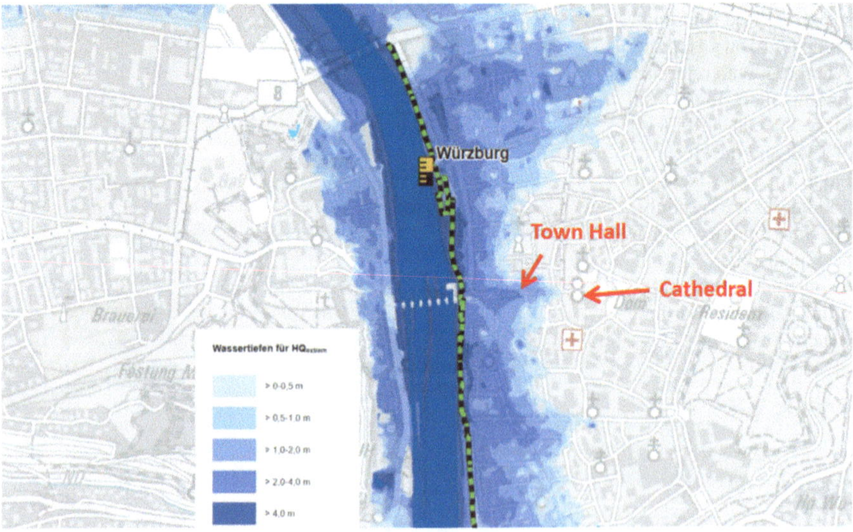

Fig. 8 Worst-case flood scenario HQ_{extrem} for flooding of the Main River with places mentioned in historical sources as flooded marked. Image: Martin Bauch. Source: Bayerisches Landesamt für Umweltschutz

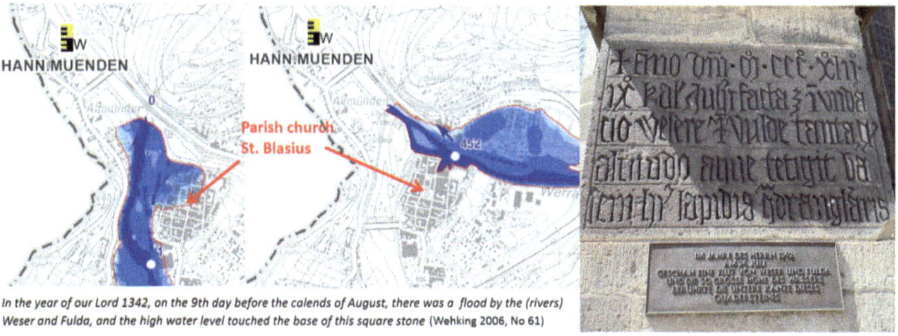

Fig. 9 Worst-case flood scenario HQ_{extrem} for flooding of the Werra and Fulda rivers with the parish church St. Blasius marked. Memorial inscription on this church indicating the height of water. Image (right): Martin Bauch. Maps of HQ_{extrem} flood scenarios (left): Niedersächsischer Landesbetrieb für Wasserwirtschaft, Küsten- und Naturschutz., modified by M. Bauch

In the context of the droughts discussed earlier, two additional forms of disaster memory deserve attention. The first is chronosticha or chronograms—mnemonic verses that were particularly popular in the early modern period. These inscriptions, often placed on public buildings or incorporated into historical works, encoded both the year and the event itself using Latin phrases in which Roman numerals were embedded. The millennium drought of 1540, for example, was commemorated through a carefully crafted verse referencing the extreme low water levels of European rivers: *eXICCata LeVIs CVr fLVMIna CerVi reqVIrIs* ("Why do you seek the stag, when the sun has dried up the rivers?"). When the uppercase letters are interpreted as Roman numerals and added together (*M+CCCC+LL+VVVV+X+IIIII*), they yield the drought year: 1540. While such mnemonic textual forms (Schupp 2003) are unlikely to resonate with contemporary audiences, another premodern memorial technique remains highly relevant: the so-called hunger stones found in Central European rivers.

Hunger stones are markers and inscriptions carved into riverbed rocks, visible only during periods of extreme low water. They are particularly dense along the Elbe River, both on the Czech and German sides (Elleder et al. 2020). One of the most striking examples is found in Děčín, northern Bohemia, where the hunger stone bears engraved years of past low water events (Fig. 10). A powerful inscription succinctly conveys the socioeconomic consequences of such droughts: "If you see me, weep." In August 2018, climate activists from Greenpeace echoed this historical warning when they placed a modern hunger stone in the riverbed of the Elbe in Magdeburg. Their inscription—"If you see me, the climate crisis is here."—was intended as a protest against the use of coal-fired power plants in Germany.

To summarize: A wealth of records illuminates the full range of hydrological extremes that have occurred in Central European history. These records also reveal traditional and historically tested methods of disaster memory, which could be refined and adapted for the present. Even though historical flood and drought records were often shaped by the religious worldview of their time and preserved within

Fig. 10 Low-water mark along the Elbe River (so-called "Hunger Stone") with year inscriptions since 1616 and inscriptions with warnings ("If you see me, weep") at Tetschen-Bodenbach in 1911, now Děčín, Czech Republic. Source: Wikimedia Commons, public domain

theological frameworks, they nevertheless hold tangible value for the twenty-first century. They can contribute to social resilience against flood events in an era of anthropogenic climate change. The memorial techniques of the premodern period, moreover, did not merely set standards for visualization but also ensured that extreme events remained embedded in collective memory for centuries. In the face of mounting pressure to adapt to human-induced climate change, modern society would do well not to overlook this historical perspective—however distant it may seem.

References

Arnold, W. 1980. *Die Inschriften der Stadt Göttingen*. München: Reichert (Die deutschen Inschriften Göttinger Reihe, 19).

Bauch, M. 2015. Der Regen, das Korn und das Salz: die Madonna di San Luca und das Wettermirakel von 1433. *Quellen und Forschungen aus italienischen Archiven und Bibliotheken* 95 (1): 183–212. https://doi.org/10.1515/qfiab-2015-0008.

Bauch, M. 2019. Die Magdalenenflut 1342 am Schnittpunkt von Umwelt- und Infrastrukturgeschichte: Ein compound event als Taktgeber für mittelalterliche Infrastrukturentwicklung und Daseinsvorsorge. *NTM. Zeitschrift für Geschichte der Wissenschaften, Technik und Medizin* 27 (3): 273–309. https://doi.org/10.1007/s00048-019-00221-y.

Bauch, M. 2023. "Wenn Du mich siehst, dann weine": Dürren in der Vormoderne. *Aus Politik und Zeitgeschichte* 28–29:45–53.

Bauch, M., and D. L. Feitsch, eds. 2021. *Die Wetterseiten der Geschichte/Weathered History*. Online exhibition. https://artsandculture.google.com/exhibit/weathered-history/hwJiMeBlg6zDLg

Bauch, M., et al. 2021a. A Prequel to the Dantean Anomaly: the precipitation seesaw and droughts of 1302-1307 in Europe. *Climate of the Past* 16 (12): 2343–2358.

Bauch, M., H.-R. Bork, and A. Izdebski. 2021b. Vergessenes Extremwetter: Umwelthistorische Wegweiser auf dem Pfad der Resilienz. *Aus Politik und Zeitgeschichte* 40–41:50–54.

Bauch, M., H. -R. Bork, and A. Izdebski. 2021c. Vergessenes Extremwetter. Uns fehlt eine Erinnerungskultur für meteorologische Katastrophen: Ein Plädoyer für umweltgeschichtliche Warnhinweise, Frankfurter Allgemeine Zeitung, 20. Juli 2021: 11.

Beumer, J. 1969. Die Prozessionen im katholischen Frankfurt während der Reformationszeit. *Archiv für Mittelrheinische Kirchengeschichte* 21: 105–118.

Borchardt, K. 1988. *Die Würzburger Inschriften bis 1525, auf der Grundlage des Nachlasses von Theodor Kramer unter Mitarbeit von Franz Xaver Herrmann*. Wiesbaden: Reichert (Die Deutschen Inschriften, 27).

Brázdil, R., et al. 2018. Documentary data and the study of past droughts: a global state of the art. *Climate of the Past* 14 (12): 1915–1960. https://doi.org/10.5194/cp-14-1915-2018.

Brázdil, R., et al. 2020. Droughts in historical times in Europe, as derived from documentary evidence. In *Palaeohydrology: Traces, Tracks and Trails of Extreme Events*, ed. J. Herget and A. Fontana, 65–96. Cham: Springer.

Brockhoff, E., and B. Wissenbach, eds. 2010. *Frankfurts Alte Brücke: Gestern, heute, morgen*. Frankfurt am Main: Societäts-Verlag.

Camenisch, C., et al. 2020. Extreme heat and drought in 1473 and their impacts in Europe in the context of the early 1470s. *Regional Environmental Change* 20 (1): L02202. https://doi.org/10.1007/s10113-020-01601-0.

Cook, E. R., et al. 2015. Old World megadroughts and pluvials during the Common Era. *Science Advances* 1 (10): 1–9. https://doi.org/10.1126/sciadv.1500561.

Degroot, D., et al. 2021. Towards a rigorous understanding of societal responses to climate change. *Nature* 591 (7851): 539–550. https://doi.org/10.1038/s41586-021-03190-2.

Eifert, S. 2024. *Kritische Infrastrukturen und Knoten in Netzen als Grundlage einer Infrastruktur-Geschichte der Vormoderne: Betrachtungen zu Frankfurt am Main und Mainz im Spätmittelalter*. Dissertation. Darmstadt: Technische Universität Darmstadt. https://tuprints.ulb.tu-darmstadt.de/27711/

Elleder, L., L. Kašpárek, J. Šírová, and T. Kabelka. 2020. Low water stage marks on hunger stones: verification for the Elbe from 1616 to 2015. *Climate of the Past* 16 (5): 1821–1846. https://doi.org/10.5194/cp-16-1821-2020.

Erthel, T. 2009. Der Schmidtstedter Gedenkstein von 1316: Ein seltenes Kleindenkmal der spätmittelalterlichen Klima- und Kulturgeschichte Erfurts. *Mitt(h)eilungen des Vereins für Geschichte und Altert(h)umskunde von Erfurt* 70:8–16.

Froning, R., ed. 1884. *Frankfurter Chroniken und annalistische Aufzeichnungen des Mittelalters*. Frankfurt: Carl Jügel (Quellen zur Frankfurter Geschichte, 1.

Gedeon, L. 2000. Prozessionen in Frankfurt am Main. *Archiv für Mittelrheinische Kirchengeschichte* 52:11–54.

Gedeon, L. 2005. *Zur Geschichte der Prozessionen in Frankfurt am Main*. 2nd ed. Marburg: Gedeon.

Glaser, R. 2008. *Klimageschichte Mitteleuropas: 1200 Jahre Wetter, Klima, Katastrophen*, 2nd updated edn. Darmstadt: Wissenschaftliche Buchgesellschaft.

Herget, J., A. Kapala, M. Krell, et al. 2015. The Millennium Flood of July 1342 revisited. *Catena* 130:82–94.

Ionita, M., et al. 2021. Past megadroughts in central Europe were longer, more severe and less warm than modern droughts. *Nature Communications Earth & Environment* 2 (1): 61. https://doi.org/10.1038/s43247-021-00130-w.

Johann von Viktring. 1909. *Johannis Abbatis Victoriensis Liber certarum historiarum.* 2 vols., ed. F. Schneider. *MGH Scriptores rer. Germ.* N.S. Hannover, Leipzig: Hahnsche Buchhandlung.

Labbé, T. 2019. Aux origines des politiques compassionnelles: émergence de la sensibilité envers les victimes de catastrophes à la fin du Moyen Âge. *Annales. Histoire, Sciences Sociales* 74 (1): 45–71. https://doi.org/10.1017/ahss.2019.139.

Labbé, T., et al. 2019. The longest homogeneous series of grape harvest dates, Beaune 1354-2018, and its significance for the understanding of past and present climate. *Climate of the Past* 15 (4): 1485–1501. https://doi.org/10.5194/cp-15-1485-2019.

Longfellow, H. W., ed. 1867. *The Divine Comedy of Dante Alighieri*. Boston: Ticknor & Fields.

Mudelsee, M., M. Börngen, G. Tetzlaff, and U. Grünewald. 2004. Extreme floods in central Europe over the past 500 years: role of cyclone pathway 'Zugstrasse Vb'. *Journal of Geophysical Research: Atmospheres* 109 (D23101): 224–245.

Nash, D. J., et al. 2021. Climate indices in historical climate reconstructions: a global state of the art. *Climate of the Past* 17 (3): 1273–1314. https://doi.org/10.5194/cp-17-1273-2021.

Nosbisch, W. 1930. *Das Wohnungswesen der Stadt Frankfurt am Main*. Frankfurt am Main: Hochbauamt und Wirtschaftsamt der Stadt Frankfurt am Main.

Oven, A. H. E., and J. Becker. 1880. *Die Kapelle der H. Katharina auf der Mainbrücke zu Frankfurt mit gleichartigen Stiftungen des christlichen Mittelalters*. Frankfurt am Main: Verein für Geschichte und Altertumskunde.

Pfister, C. 2017. When Europe was burning: the multi-season mega-drought of 1540 and arsonist paranoia. In *Historical Disaster Experiences: Towards a Comparative and Transcultural History of Disasters Across Asia and Europe*, ed. G. J. Schenk, 155–188. Heidelberg: Springer.

Pfister, C. 2018. Evidence from the archives of societies: documentary evidence—overview. In *The Palgrave Handbook of Climate History*, ed. S. White, C. Pfister, and F. Mauelshagen, 37–48. London: Palgrave Macmillan.

Pribyl, K. 2017. *Farming, Famine and Plague: The Impact of Climate in Late Medieval England.* Cham: Springer.

Roggenkamp, T., and J. Herget. 2015. Historische Hochwasser der Ahr: Die Rekonstruktion von Scheitelabflüssen ausgewählter Ahr-Hochwasser. *Heimatjahrbuch Kreis Ahrweiler* 47:150–154.

Roggenkamp, T., and J. Herget. 2022. Hochwasser der Ahr im Juli 2021—Abflussabschätzung und Einordnung. *Hydrologie und Wasserwirtschaft* 66 (4): 40–49.

Schäfer, A., et al. 2021. Hochwasser Mitteleuropa, Juli 2021 (Deutschland). *CEDIM FDA-Report Nr. 1—Nordrhein-Westfalen & Rheinland-Pfalz.* 21 July 2021. https://doi.org/10.5445/IR/1000135730

Schenk, G. J. 2018. Krisenrituale: Vom Nutzen und Nachteil kommunaler Selbstinszenierungen angesichts drohender Gefahren am Beispiel von Straßburg im Elsass. In *Kommunale Selbstinszenierungen: Städtische Konstellationen zwischen Mittelalter und Neuzeit*, ed. M. Stercken and C. Hesse, 123–154. Zürich: Chronos.

Schupp, W. 2003. Das Chronogramm als kulturgeschichtliches Phänomen: Dokumentarischer Überblick. *Herold-Jahrbuch NF* 8:127–188.

Schwind, F. 1984. Karte 34A: Frankfurt vom frühen Mittelalter bis zur Mitte des 17. Jahrhunderts. In *Geschichtlicher Atlas von Hessen: Text- und Erläuterungsband*, ed. F. Schwind, E. E. Stengel, and F. Uhlhorn, 232–241. Marburg: Hessisches Institut für Landesgeschichte.

Toreti, A., et al. 2022. *Drought in Europe July 2022*. EUR 31147 EN. Luxembourg: Publications Office of the European Union. https://doi.org/10.2760/014884

Tradowsky, J. S., et al. 2023. Attribution of the heavy rainfall events leading to severe flooding in Western Europe during July 2021. *Climatic Change* 176:90. https://doi.org/10.1007/s10584-023-03502-7.

Wattenbach, W. 1851. Continuatio Sancrucensis Secunda. In *Monumenta Germaniae Historica, Scriptores (in folio)*, ed. G. H. Pertz, vol. 9, 637–646. Hannover: Hahnsche Buchhandlung.

Wehking, S. 2006. *Die Inschriften des Landkreises Göttingen*. Wiesbaden: Reichert (Die deutschen Inschriften Göttinger Reihe, 12.

Weikinn, C. 1958. *Quellen zur Witterungsgeschichte Europas von der Zeitwende bis zum Jahre 1850: Zeitwende - 1500*. Berlin: Akademie Verlag (Quellensammlung zur Hydrographie und Meteorologie, 1.

Wetter, O., C. Pfister, R. Weingartner, et al. 2011. The largest floods in the High Rhine Basin since 1268 assessed from documentary and instrumental evidence. *Hydrological Sciences Journal* 56 (5): 733–758.

Wetter, O., et al. 2014. The year-long unprecedented European heat and drought of 1540: a worst case. *Climatic Change* 125:349–363.

White, S., C. Pfister, and F. Mauelshagen, eds. 2018. *The Palgrave Handbook of Climate History*. London: Palgrave Macmillan.

Widmann. 1878. Leonhart Widmann's Chronik von Regensburg (1511–43, 1552–55). In *Die Chroniken der baierischen Städte Regensburg, Landshut, Muhldorf, München*, ed. K. Hegel, 3–244. Leipzig: S. Hirzel (Die Chroniken der deutschen Städte, 15).

Wolff, C., and R. Jung. 1896. *Die Baudenkmäler in Frankfurt am Main: Kirchenbauten*. Frankfurt am Main: Th. Völcker.

Zwierlein, C. 2011. *Der gezähmte Prometheus: Feuer und Sicherheit zwischen Früher Neuzeit und Moderne*. Göttingen: Vandenhoeck & Ruprecht.

Climate-Sensitive Infectious Diseases, an Ancient Problem with Present-Day Public Health Importance

Gina E. C. Charnley

Abstract Infectious disease outbreaks have been an ever-present threat to human society throughout history, from the Black Death, potentially causing a decrease in Europe's fourteenth century population of 50%, to the 2019 COVID-19 pandemic, leading to public health and economic turmoil. Since the establishment of modern epidemiology in the 1800s, scientists and physicians have continually worked to gain a greater understanding of disease transmission and distribution. A key factor which has driven epidemics and pandemics, is climate, weather and the environment, from cholera epidemics dating back to the fifth century, to vector-borne diseases and control in Ancient Egypt. However, the scale and speed of anthropogenic climate change, land use change and increasing travel and trade are threats to infectious disease control not previously seen in the Earth's natural history. There has been an erosion of traditional transmission barriers and an expansion of the ecological niche for many pathogens, thereby increasing the risk of introductions and establishment in new areas. There are many lessons to be learnt throughout history related to changing infectious risks, including past successes and shortcomings. We must integrate these insights into modern policy to effectively control future threats, to protect human health, the environment and the global economy.

Keywords Climate-sensitive infectious diseases · Climate change · One health · Zoonoses

1 Brief History of Infectious Diseases and Epidemiology

Infectious diseases have always been a major threat not just to human society, but to the natural world, for example, the Dutch Elm Disease epidemic in the 1970s in the UK led to the death of 30 million trees (Potter et al. 2011), while the spread of the fungal disease chytridiomycosis has caused the decline or extinction of nearly 200

G. E. C. Charnley (✉)
Imperial College London, London, UK
e-mail: georgina.charnley@imperial.ac.uk

J. F. Haldon, R. Fernandes (eds.), *Bridging History and Policy*, Understanding Complex Systems, https://doi.org/10.1007/978-3-032-24379-9_17

species of frog (Skerratt et al. 2007). Many infectious diseases possess the ability to jump species barriers and cause significant human mortality and morbidity, for example, *Yersinia pestis,* the causative agent of the Black Death which claimed around 50% of the European population between 1347 and 1358, is spread via the bites of fleas, and maintained via rodent infections (Spyrou et al. 2016). More recently, the HIV/AIDS pandemic was caused by a mutation of the Simian immunodeficiency virus and spread to humans via non-human primates (Heeney et al. 2006), while the COVID-19 pandemic which caused public health and economic turmoil was very likely due to zoonotic spillover (Bloom et al. 2021).

Due to the threat that infectious disease causes to health and society, humans have continually strived to gain a greater understanding of disease transmission and control. The field of epidemiology can be traced back to the 1800s, with the seminal work of John Snow, considered one of the founders of epidemiology. During a cholera epidemic in 1848 in London, Snow hypothesised that the disease was spread via contaminated water, and traced back the source of the contamination to a pump on Broad Street, the removal of the pump handle led to the epidemic subsiding (Newsom 2006). Since Snow's pioneering work, there have been significant advances in travel, laboratory techniques, mathematics, education and computing, which have had a profound impact on how the field of modern epidemiology has been shaped and evolved. Our ability to store and process a significant amount of information digitally, has meant that a large part of epidemiology has now moved towards computer-based modelling, processing large and geographically diverse datasets and identifying patterns and trends with speed and precision like never before (Massad and Ortega 2008).

Computer-based epidemiology including statistical modelling, mathematical modelling and machine learning techniques have allowed us to explore what drives disease transmission and outbreaks with incredible flexibility. By continually incorporating new data and knowledge into models we are able to create a predictive system which continually improves in specificity and sensitivity with time. The high predictive performance of some modelling techniques in particular have led to a growing field of outbreak and disease predictions and scenario-based projections including early warning systems and long-term projections. This has been a highly useful output of epidemiological modelling for policy, and has led to the co-creation of many models to allow for better resource allocation and preparedness. A field which has particularly made use of predictions and projections is climate-related epidemiology, due to our ability to provide both short and longer term weather and climate forecasts. However, the drive to look forward has potentially reduced our need or willingness to look back, leaving historical lessons and knowledge to be forgotten. Here, we explore a brief history of climate-sensitive infectious diseases (CSIDs), how these risks and threats have been controlled in the past, potential difficulties in exploiting these techniques today and what we could learn to reduce transmission and save lives.

2 Brief History of Climate Change

Our planet is designed to change and has done throughout history, due to shifts in the tectonic plates and the Earth's tilt and solar cycles. These changes alter the distribution and composition of water, rocks and the atmosphere and have continually altered life on Earth, bringing at times dramatic changes to the biosphere. We have documented these changes in geological time scales, such as periods (of which we are in the Quaternary Period, see Fig. 1) and smaller geochronologic units known as epochs, with our current epoch being the Holocene (Stern and Kaufmann 2014). Climate change is a natural phenomenon within these units, which are measured using paleoclimatological records such as rocks, ice cores, ocean and lake sediment and tree rings, and are used to define these distinct geological periods. The planet naturally moves through cycles of warmer periods (interglacials) and ice ages (glacials), through alterations in the Sun and the Earth's orbit, emissions from volcanoes and changes to atmospheric greenhouse gas (GHG) levels (e.g., carbon dioxide, methane, nitrogen oxides, water vapour) (Fordham et al. 2020).

Although climate change may not be new, nor are the ways in which the planet is changing (e.g., changing atmospheric GHG composition, increasing temperatures), anthropogenic climate change is a new phenomenon in the Earth's history. Since the onset of the Industrial Revolution (late eighteenth century), humans have been using one of the Earth's natural cooling mechanisms, the depositing of carbon out of the atmosphere and underground via the decay of organic matter and rocks, and burning these carbon stores. The release of this carbon back into the atmosphere releases energy, which has been quintessential to the advancement of humans, but is

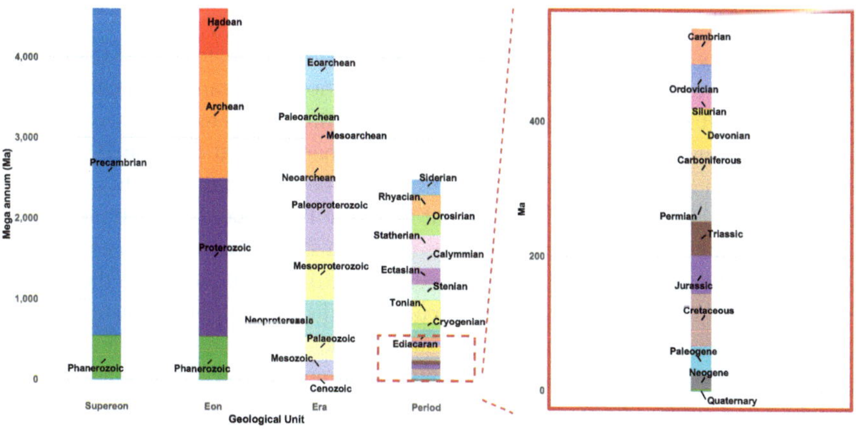

Fig. 1 Geological time periods from the beginning of Earth (~4 billion years ago) to now measured in mega annum (millions of years since present). The top panel shows the full history and the bottom panel shows from the end of the Precambrian Supereon (~541 Ma). The geological units are in ascending order of size from left to right, smaller units (e.g., epoch and age) are not included. Source: Adapted from the Geological Society of America 2022

causing global temperatures to rise. A greater concentration of GHGs in the atmosphere enhances the greenhouse effect, trapping a larger amount of the Sun's radiation and heat in the Earth (Abram et al. 2016). The burning of this carbon, known as fossil fuels, coupled with land use alterations, has caused changes to the Earth's atmosphere and its teleconnections between land and water. Natural changes to atmospheric composition typically take place over long time scales, often millions of years, whereas, with anthropogenic climate change, these changes are occurring at rates not documented in the Earth's natural history, putting huge pressure on the biosphere, cryosphere, hydrosphere and atmosphere (Stern and Kaufmann 2014).

Atmospheric composition is a key driver for changes in the climate and weather. Weather is defined by the state of the atmosphere, and more specifically its pressure, causing changes to cloudiness, wind, temperature and precipitation, and fluctuating on hourly to weekly time scales. Regional weather can also be partially governed by local factors such as topography, the presence of large water bodies and proximity to coasts and cities. The climate is defined by long-term patterns in the weather, occurring on timescales of 30 years or longer. Changes to the climate, both natural and anthropogenic, are identified as changes in the mean and/or variability of climate properties, such as seasonal variability or long-term alterations to rainfall or temperature (Met Office 2024). The human influenced warming of the Earth has a catalytic effect on precipitation, sea level and natural hazards. For example, increasing temperatures, alters ocean circulation and the evaporation of water along with the water holding capacity of the atmosphere, leading to longer and more intense tropical storms and monsoons (Wasko et al. 2016).

3 Exploring Climate-Sensitive Infectious Diseases

The complexity of the Earth's climate makes attributing climate change to changes in society very challenging, in terms of food, migration and health (Van Oldenborgh et al. 2021). Attribution needs caution, due to what this means to blame weather and climate on events we can do something about (Charnley and Kelman 2024). Our inaccuracies in attribution are relatively high and the interest of climate change by the media, politicians and the general public has at times led to sensationalization and over-attribution e.g., climate refugees (Kelman 2019). How CSIDs are defined is still an evolving field and what constitutes as a CSID is contentious, as the climate is very rarely the only variable that impacts the distribution and transmission of infectious diseases. Furthermore, there are human behavioural changes that are linked to climate change that are also playing an important role in pathogen dynamics including urbanisation, land use and agricultural changes and globalisation. Despite difficulties in defining CSIDs, there are a number of water-borne, vector-borne, rodent-borne and air-borne pathogens which we largely consider to be partially driven by climate and weather, including cholera, arboviruses, leptospirosis and meningitis (Omazic et al. 2019).

Weather and climate can impact infectious disease both directly and indirectly. An example of a direct relationship between the climate and infectious diseases would be via changes to how the pathogen behaves in the environment in terms of survival and growth. Bacteria and fungi require a set range of variables for survival (e.g., temperature, humidity and light), and therefore extreme hot or cold temperatures, outside of these optimal growth ranges can alter pathogen growth, limiting the opportunities for an infective dose (Charnley et al. 2021). For example, food-borne pathogens such as typhoid, proliferate in warmer environments (Gao et al. 2022). It is not solely air temperatures which can alter pathogens, changes to sea-surface temperatures and subsequently salinity, can impact the proliferation of non-*cholerae Vibrio* spp. in coastal regions, leading to an increasing ear, skin and gastrointestinal disease (Johnson 2015). Increasing rainfall can result in increased vector breeding sites and elevated humidity can facilitate vector survival, however, too much rainfall, in combination with high winds, can lead to destruction of breeding sites and increased vector mortality (de Souza and Weaver 2024). Water is important for pathogen dispersal for water- and rodent-borne diseases, however the quantity of water can affect the concentration of pathogens, increasing them during droughts and diluting them during flooding (Charnley et al. 2022). Finally, changes to wind and desertification can impact pathogens, particularly air-borne pathogens that can move via droplets and aerosolization (Vergadi et al. 2022). For example, meningitis transmission in the Meningitis Belt (largely the Sahel region at 11.7°-15.1° latitude), is thought to be driven by desertification in the region allowing the pathogen to be transported longer distances via wind (Sultan et al. 2005).

An important indirect relationship between climate and infectious disease is how changes to the weather impact human behaviour. Natural hazards for example alter how we behave, and result in an exacerbation of pre-existing vulnerability, leading to an increase in pathogen exposure. Natural hazards often lead to a breakdown in services, including water, sanitation and hygiene (WaSH), which can lead to a proliferation of water-borne diseases, as people are forced to drink contaminated water due to a lack of alternatives (Charnley et al. 2022). It isn't solely drinking contaminated water which can cause disease, assisting in post-disaster clean up is a known risk factor for a number of rodent-borne diseases including leptospirosis. Furthermore, the movement of people into camp or shelter settings following natural hazards can lead to unsanitary and poorly ventilated environments leading to an increase in air-borne pathogens such as influenza (Charnley et al. 2021).

Our movement into large settlements and urban environments has been a significant demographic shift of the last century, as people move in search of better services, jobs and improved quality of life. However, urban environments come with their own risks for infectious diseases due to generally higher population densities, the effects of pollution on respiratory fitness, the urban heat island effect, poor urban planning and the development of informal settlements and high throughput of people and goods (Alirol et al. 2011). Vectors and pathogens are quickly adapting to urban environments, due to the large number of susceptible people and some are thriving in this ecological niche. For example, cities offer a warmer climate, abundant impermeable services where water can collect, artificial light, increased municipal waste and higher numbers of susceptible people, leading to many vectors becoming highly adaptive to the urban environment, including *Aedes albopictus* (the primary dengue vector) and *Culex pipiens* (the primary West Nile virus vector) (Montalvo et al. 2022). Furthermore, more densely populated areas give a favourable selection to anthropophilic mosquitoes, which has shown to cause adaptations to *Anopheles* mosquitoes (Hing et al. 2016).

With advancements to road, rail, sea and air travel, the movements of goods and people which may have historically taken months, can now be achieved in a matter of hours. This incredible feat of engineering has greatly advanced human society, however, this comes with its own threats. Infectious diseases were historically constrained geographically to the location of a relatively fixed pool of susceptible people, with epidemics starting and ending quickly, as the number of recovered and immune individuals increased. However, with fast transport options, the pool of susceptible individuals is ever expanding, and is no longer geographically confined leading to a far greater threat of pandemics than previously seen in human history (Carmona-González and Sánchez-Martín 2021), with SARS, MERS (Khan et al. 2013), COVID-19 (Christidis and Christodoulou 2020) and mpox (Kinoshita et al. 2023) being concerning recent examples.

Since the evolution of early humans around 2 million years ago, there is evidence of anthropogenic changes to our environment and exploitation of resources. In the past century, anthropogenic influence on the landscape and environment has increased most rapidly via deforestation, expansions of agriculture, pollution, depletion of fisheries and changes to the nitrogen cycle. These changes are very important for infectious diseases, particularly zoonotic diseases, as these changes to the environment impact all plants and animals in the ecosystem. Some hypotheses for how changes to the land are driving infectious disease include changes to cross-species transmission rates via perturbation to multi-host disease systems and via exposure of novel hosts to new diverse pathogen pools (Murray and Daszak 2013). Changes to land influences how animals and vectors behave, where they find food, water and safety, where and when they breed and the formation of colonies, which can impact pathogen transmission and dynamics by new and changing selection pressures (Lambin et al. 2010).

One of the largest advances to agriculture is the invention of irrigation, dating back to the Middle East and North Africa in 6000 BCE. Irrigation allowed humans to grow crops in previously inhospitable environments. However, with irrigation came contamination, and the creation of vector breeding sites often close to human settlements, greatly increasing infectious disease risk (Katzenelson et al. 1976). Moving forward, World War II resulted in a huge collapse to European agriculture and the economy and Europe saw an urgent need to increase food production to prevent widespread starvation. However, 80 years on, these policies are still in place, largely because they are economically beneficial to large corporations. The availability of agricultural innovation and the expansion of intensive agriculture are largely seen in parts of the world with comparatively little food poverty, with huge amounts of food wasted (Lang and Barling 2012). In many low- and middle-income countries, a large proportion of agriculture is still carried out using small-scale and relatively simple techniques, driven and made financially possible due to cheap, child and slave labour (Odijie 2020), which is exploited in other regions (e.g., Europe) via seasonal agricultural workers (Oxfam International 2024). The poor working and living conditions of migrant workers can result in a number of risk factors for infectious diseases related to WaSH, housing and access to healthcare.

It is not just arable agriculture that has seen shifts in recent decades, intensive animal agriculture has also significantly increased, and seen a range of issues, namely the treatment of the animals in life and death, and the risks this causes to infectious diseases. The stresses that these animals face, both physically and psychologically, has led to the mutation of new strains of pathogens (e.g., *Escherichia coli* O157 in intensive cattle production (Juska et al. 2003)), and the increased transmission of both animal (e.g., avian influenza H1N1 transmission in foie gras production ducks (Guinat et al. 2019)) and human (e.g., the spread of methicillin-resistant *Staphylococcus aureus* in intensive Danish pig production (Agersø et al. 2012)) pathogens. Even with the expansion of animal agriculture there is still a market for bush meat and game hunting, with these practices sometimes seen as delicacies and luxuries, along with a more healthy option to industrial meats (van Vliet and Mbazza 2011). A reduction in this practice would be very important for reducing zoonotic disease risk, for example, Ebola and HIV are thought to have crossed the species barrier via consumption of fruit bats and chimpanzees, respectively (Kurpiers et al. 2016). Human/wildlife contact is increasing by mixing different agricultural systems with wildlife habitats. For example, the 1998–1999 Malaysia Nipah outbreak was thought to have originated via the expansion of pig and mango co-production into fruit bat habitat, leading to a spillover event (Daszak et al. 2013). Furthermore, habitat destruction leads to higher stress and cortisol levels within wildlife populations, which has been suggested as a driving mechanism for pathogen mutation and evolution (Hing et al. 2016).

The changes that temperature, rainfall, wind and natural hazards pose to pathogens directly and indirectly, along with large scales changes to human society including urbanisation, land use and agriculture changes and globalisation has dramatically altered the way disease and pathogens behave and spread, likely leading to much of the contention around defining CSIDs. However, like climate change, CSIDs are not new. We have historical documentation of how we have controlled and managed these changing risks for centuries, with both successes and failures, which may help shine a light on how to control CSIDs in the future.

4 Historical CSID Control

The science of ecology, the study of the relationships between living organisms, including humans, and their physical environment, is fundamental to CSID control, recognising the connection between humans and the natural world. Ecological approaches to CSID have become increasingly popular, as many CSIDs are zoonotic and have animal reservoirs and hosts. The gradual shift in the biological

Fig. 2 Shows a summary of some of the mechanisms in which climate and weather can directly and indirectly play a role in driving infectious disease outbreaks. The schematic shows ways in which climate, land use and human behaviour may increase CSIDs and decrease CSIDs

sciences towards multi-causal and systematic understandings of infectious diseases, should not be forgotten when considering what is driving transmission (Scheiner 2009). Here, a number of historical strategies (either intentionally or otherwise) are proposed to control CSIDs via changes to the environment, hosts and vectors or the human population.

One of the most well-studied and documented vector-borne diseases (VBD) is malaria, as this is a disease of ancient origin and the first VBD of humans to be identified in the late 1800s. Long before the *Plasmodium* parasites were identified as the causative agent of malaria and *Anopheles* mosquitoes as the vector, there was an understanding that mosquitoes, or residing in places where mosquitoes were abundant e.g., marshes, could lead to fever and malaise (Bruce-Chwatt and de Zulueta 1980). Therefore, household-level vector control strategies to reduce the nuisance of mosquitoes and illness have been documented as far back as ~3000 BC. A number of Ancient societies including Rome, Egypt and Greece recorded measures to reduce contact between mosquitoes and people. Many of these ancient strategies relied on mechanical control and included sleeping in high buildings to increase wind and reduce the vector's ability to fly and the use of bed nets in both Egypt and Greece. Furthermore, Marco Polo's documentation of his travels to India in the thirteenth century noted the use of bed curtains (Wilson et al. 2020).

Warming out of the last glacial period, ~10,000 years ago, resulted in an expansion of humans, parasites and vectors. However, it was not just the climate that drove changes to vector distributions and their associated diseases. For example, malaria was common in Britain during the Medieval Warm Period (900–1300) but did not decrease during the Little Ice Age (1650–1840). Declines in malaria and eventual eradication in Europe was largely driven by anthropogenic land use changes which disrupted vector populations and broke parasitic cycles

(Bruce-Chwatt and de Zulueta 1980). Changes included the drainage and clearing of wetlands and marshes to allow for agricultural expansion. After the realisation of the effectiveness of drainage, the practice flourished globally during the late 1800s and early 1900s (Wilson et al. 2020).

Draining has been achieved and used in more sophisticated and targeted techniques to reduce standing water, including large drainage systems developed by the Greeks and Romans. In the late 1700s, there were significant investments in sewer cleaning to reduce standing water in the US in response to a yellow fever outbreak. Sewage water is nutrient rich and removing such water sources can be particularly important, due to the preference of some vectors for polluted water. Furthermore, reducing polluted water removes the opportunity of exposure to the population and therefore potential pathogens, as seen with the Broad Street pump in 1848 in London (Newsom 2006). Another source of polluted water found important for vector breeding in the 1700s was bilge water, which collects in the bottom of boats. It was identified that *Aedes aegypti* was brought to Philadelphia, US via Haiti, and resulted in the yellow fever outbreak. In response, policy was put in place to enforce bilge water being pumped out of ships before anchoring in their destination (Middleton 1928; Lamborn 1890).

Vector control saw huge changes after World War II with the invention of DDT, where it was used effectively to control lice-borne typhus amongst European populations. The subsequent liberal (and over) use of DDT and future insecticides began, starting with smaller scale indoor spraying and expanding to large scale outdoor and aerial spraying in the 1950s onwards (Nosten et al. 2022). The widespread use of DDT has been very successful in the eradication of malaria and yellow fever in North America and Europe and the control of leishmaniasis and tsetse populations in Africa and Asia (Nosten et al. 2022; Lun et al. 2015; de Raadt 2005). However, chemical supply is determined by markets which are turbulent in nature and therefore supply is not always guaranteed. For example, typhus increased during World War II due to shortages of effective rodenticides. Global and regional economic crises and collapses can result in inflated prices, reducing the cost-effectiveness of chemical control (Anstead 2020).

Access to healthcare ensures prompt diagnosis and therefore control of transmission, but healthcare has not historically, nor is it still, available to all. For example, identifying the importance of swift identification of plague cases and appropriate quarantines were considered highly successful in stopping epidemics (Zietz and Dunkelberg 2004). Furthermore, the admission to healthcare centres and access to professionals often means appropriate treatment, reducing transmission. The invention of intravenous hydration therapy in the early 1900s has been a significant step forward in reducing mortality due to the water- and food-borne diseases such as *Vibrio cholerae*. However, it wasn't until the late 1950s that hydration therapy really began to reduce mortality, and this was largely due to the realisation that if fluid intake and output was measured accurately, the correct amount of fluid supplementation could be given. These calculations were not possible without the Watten cot, a simple sheet with a hole in it, so water intake and outtake can be easily measured via a bucket placed underneath (Sack 2013). This invention meant that the excrement of those infected could be disposed of in a safe manner, avoiding onward transmission.

The key to reducing the transmission of any disease is to reduce the exposure to the population, and for water- and food-borne diseases, the source of contamination. Isolating these sources are key in preventing and stopping outbreaks. However, in times when widespread outbreaks are not occurring, it can be very difficult to ensure that food and water is safe, even today. To control this threat, humans have continually developed new methods to ensure food and water safety, particularly for vulnerable groups such as children and older groups. The shift from eating raw to cooked food was a significant turning point in the evolution of humans, with evidence of humans deliberately starting fires and cooking food at least 780,000 years ago. Even today, this is still possibly the most widespread method of controlling food-borne diseases globally, and is used in many parts of the world to ensure water safety (Newell et al. 2010). Further historical methods to ensure food safety include acidification of food to reduce pathogen concentration, such as the addition of curdled goats milk, lemon and tamarind. Acidification is still used by a large proportion of the global population, whereas in higher income countries, food safety legislation through the food supply chain and national water treatment infrastructure reduces a large part of the risk for diseases such as cholera, shigella and typhoid (Charnley et al. 2022).

A number of the historical strategies discussed here were not solely effective in reducing disease transmission, and improvements to quality of life were needed to end outbreaks. Typhus, is a parasitic disease caused by *Rickettsia typhi and Rickettsia felis,* which is often self limiting, but does have severe manifestations in about 25–30% of cases. There was a dramatic increase in the number of cases from 1930 to 1944 in the US, due to the diversification of Southern agriculture away from cotton and the displacement of the smaller black rat by the larger brown rat in many areas. However, attempts to control the disease by fumigation and rat eradication were unsuccessful. A large proportion of the population at the time lived in poor housing due to the Great Depression and a reduction in cases only came after a push to improve living conditions and hygiene (Anstead 2020). Additionally, improving living conditions was seen as important in the 1800s to ensure the profitability of the mining industry, as many workforces were greatly depleted by infectious diseases due to overcrowded and unhygienic mining camps (Shanks 2022). The possible first reported epidemic of plague was the first century, however, it wasn't until the third pandemic in the 1800s when the causative agent (*Yersinia pestis*), intermediate host (rats) and vector (fleas) were identified. These discoveries resulted in better treatment and vaccination options, however, it wasn't solely therapeutics that resulted in the end of the pandemic. Significant progress to improve sanitation and handwashing, improving the living conditions of many Europeans and reducing poverty was largely responsible for curbing the epidemic (Newell et al. 2010).

5 Challenges for Modern Application

The strides which humans have made in the formation of society are truly incredible and possibly unique to the species. With the formation of tribes, settlements, societies and culture, we have continually questioned how to improve our quality of life and how we should morally behave towards each other and the wider world. We have to consider present values and beliefs when considering previous infectious disease control measures and how these may challenge modern day application. Extreme and aggressive forms of disease control, which were highly effective, may not be ethically and environmentally sound according to current standards. For example, vector control has historically been achieved through widespread insecticide spraying and drainage of wetlands (Wilson et al. 2020). However, wetlands provide important ecosystem services and widespread insecticide resistance means that these interventions would no longer be acceptable or effective.

A method of reducing zoonotic disease transmission risk and the risk of disease to the livestock industry through history has been the widespread culling of wildlife. However, culling animals to prevent zoonotic disease risk is often a futile exercise, as the zoonotic potential of animals changes through time, and removing one, can create an environment for another species to act as carriers. Very rarely are all animals killed, and therefore simply the distribution of the pathogen changes, for example, after years of badger culling in the United Kingdom, there has been limited impacts on the rate of bovine tuberculosis reactors (Langton et al. 2022). Morally as a species we see the issues of killing animals and damaging the planet and ecosystems in which we live, understanding that species do not live in isolation, filling an important niche to both predators and prey within the system, and removing one can create ecosystem collapse (Miguel et al. 2020). Perhaps a more realistic approach going forward is to understand how we can better live alongside wildlife populations, and where possible to not encroach further into their habitats with housing and agriculture.

It is not just our treatment of the environment and wildlife, but also of other humans that creates issues in implementing past control measures. For example, mandatory quarantines have long been used to contain the spread of infectious disease. However, in modern society, these can be very difficult to enforce and be very poorly accepted, as was witnessed during the COVID-19 pandemic. In modern democratic political systems, free from dictatorships and monarchic rule, imposing such restrictions on those in a population can have challenges. Quarantines have been used historically to prevent importation events, but with the sheer expanse of the global shipping industry and density of air traffic, this will remain a challenge to monitoring disease importation in modern society (Tatem et al. 2006). Furthermore, the enforcement of quarantine can reduce healthcare-seeking behaviours, which can be counterintuitive to disease control and monitoring (Bigo et al. 2021). This is particularly concerning as many infectious diseases are under-reported and under funded, making it difficult to track and trace outbreaks. For example, differences in strain genetics has been suggested as a reason for the relentlessness of the seventh cholera pandemic, however, we still do not have a consensus (Rodó et al. 2024).

Many infectious disease risk factors have been linked to urban environments, such as overcrowding and higher temperatures, and shifts into settlements created new risks for infectious diseases relating to humans. Previously, some of these issues, such as a contaminated water source, could be solved by simply moving away from the risk factor (Connolly et al. 2021). However, countries and individuals have invested significant human and economic resources not just into cities but also smaller human settlements, and these cannot simply be abandoned due to pathogen risk. It is important that we continually work on improving living conditions and ensure a healthy environment, resilient to higher temperatures and more extreme and erratic rainfall and storms.

Making the living environment more resilient to climate change and wellbeing in some instances can be counterintuitive to infectious disease control. As we aim to build cities with enhanced greening and blueing, which has many positive impacts on the urban environment and population health and wellbeing, this can create an ideal environment for new vector and zoonotic risk factors (Chirebvu et al. 2021). Furthermore, we have moved to restore many ecosystems, such as wetlands and wildlife populations, which is very important to ensure healthy environments, however, this can increase the risk for CSIDs (Gibb et al. 2020). Projects which involve tree planting are a simple method of carbon capture and storage and provide shade to reduce temperatures. However, many countries which are enforcing and encouraging these projects, do not have a sufficient number of young trees to meet these targets, leading to the importation of non-native species, further damaging ecosystems and potentially importing new infectious diseases to plants and animals and new pests and vectors (Environmental Audit Committee 2023). It is important that we strike the correct balance in these projects and understand the new risk factors that we may be creating in them, so these can be effectively managed.

As the global population grows, so does the number of people living in poverty. The larger the population which lives in poverty, the more difficult it is, in terms of financial and human resources, to improve living standards as a method of disease control. Exacerbating this issue is the fact that many higher income countries are actually seeing population declines and with the majority of population growth seen in lower-income countries. With an expansion of gender equality, often comes a decline in birth rates (up to a certain point), but until we can ensure this for a larger proportion of women, the large population living in extreme poverty is likely to remain (Kramer 2013). To achieve the level of poverty alleviation needed to reduce the global burden of infectious diseases and CSIDs, scaling up of resources and coordination is needed. It may be more realistic and effective to employ bottom-up, rather than top-down techniques, to reduce the risk of corruption and make effective coordination of projects easier. With so many people still living in poverty, this will reduce our ability to implement even the most basic and cost-effective CSID control strategies, for example, food and water treatment through heat and acidification, relies on the provisions of certain resources, fuel, fruits and livestock, which many people do not have access to (Middlemiss and Gillard 2015).

6 Ways Forward

We cannot discuss the burden of infectious disease and the effects of climate change and not discuss poverty and inequity. As shown through the historic examples here, many of the most damaging infectious diseases to historical societies, such as cholera, malaria, plague and typhus, have been largely controlled by improving people's quality of life. Those most vulnerable both within communities and globally are those most impacted by infectious disease and the impacts of climate change, largely due to a lack of options to adapt to and ensure health and safety. This connection perhaps highlights the most tangible link between infectious diseases and climate change.

There is a glaring need to address the number of people living in poverty, with 648 million people still living in extreme poverty (<2.15USD/day) and despite significant gains in poverty reduction in recent decades, there has been a plateau in progress since 2010 (WorldBank 2024). With poverty comes cascading risk factors, including inadequate living conditions, such as overcrowding, poor hygiene and poor ventilation, and poor access to WaSH and healthcare, significantly increasing opportunity for exposure to the pathogen. Two billion people are without safe drinking water, 3.6 billion are without safely managed sanitation and 2.3 billion lack adequate hand washing facilities at home, all of which are considered a basic human right (World Health Organization 2019). Marginalisation adds to these issues as it not only drives people into poverty but also keeps people in cycles of poverty, moreover, conflicts around the world are exacerbating poverty and marginalisation and are linked to large numbers of infectious disease outbreaks.

We should not ignore the lessons of the past around poverty and marginalisation, which have historically been the main drivers of infectious disease outbreaks, with climate playing a lesser role. We have more control and resources than ever before to support vulnerable groups and ensure a healthy planet. Lifting people out of poverty fundamentally gives them options and opportunities to make choices, particularly around their health and safety. Many people consume food and water from sources where safety cannot be guaranteed, or live in areas where housing is insufficient to reduce contact with vectors and wildlife, largely due to a lack of alternatives. By giving people the ability to adapt with appropriate resources, along with education to make informed choices, people can act to prevent their exposure to these pathogens. No area of the planet will escape the effects of climate change, however, the discussion of widespread water-borne disease outbreaks such as cholera and rotavirus is not occurring around high-income countries, and this is solely due to the options these populations have to avoid contaminated food and water, not due to the changes in the climate.

Climate change will no doubt have an effect on many aspects of human life, including infectious diseases and associated outbreaks, either through its direct effect on the pathogen or reservoirs, or via climate driven changes to vulnerability. However, epidemiology is a discipline which requires a holistic approach to understanding pathogen and outbreak dynamics, and weighting the importance of climate change on infectious diseases too highly, may result in an oversight of other, very important factors. We have major gaps in our understanding of the transmission of many diseases and without answers to such key questions, it makes it challenging to quantify the role that the climate is playing in the transmission and exacerbation of these pathogens.

I hope here, by presenting a brief history of CSIDs and their control, I have helped to highlight the complex history of control of many of these pathogens. In looking forward to understanding how we adapt to the threats that climate change poses, we must not lose sight of the past and what we can learn from that. Earth has been here long before humans, and it provides a rich history we can use to improve the health of people and the planet.

References

Abram, N. J., H. V. McGregor, J. E. Tierney, M. N. Evans, N. McKay, and D. S. Kaufman. 2016. Early onset of industrial-era warming across the oceans and continents. *Nature* 536 (7617): 411–418. https://doi.org/10.1038/nature19082.

Agersø, Y., H. Hasman, L. M. Cavaco, K. Pedersen, and F. M. Aarestrup. 2012. Study of methicillin-resistant Staphylococcus aureus (MRSA) in Danish pigs at slaughter and in imported retail meat reveals a novel MRSA type in slaughter pigs. *Veterinary Microbiology* 157 (1–2): 246–250. https://doi.org/10.1016/j.vetmic.2011.12.002.

Alirol, E., L. Getaz, B. Stoll, F. Chappuis, and L. Loutan. 2011. Urbanisation and infectious diseases in a globalised world. *The Lancet Infectious Diseases* 11 (2): 131–141. https://doi.org/10.1016/S1473-3099(10)70223-1.

Anstead, G. M. 2020. History, rats, fleas, and opossums: The ascendency of flea-borne typhus in the United States, 1910–1944. *Tropical Medicine and Infectious Disease* 5 (1): 37. https://doi.org/10.3390/tropicalmed5010037.

Bigo, D., E. Guild, and E. M. Kuskonmaz. 2021. Obedience in times of COVID-19 pandemics: A renewed governmentality of unease? *Global Discourse* 11 (3): 471–489. https://doi.org/10.1332/204378921X16131219322821.

Bloom, J. D., Y. A. Chan, R. S. Baric, P. J. Bjorkman, S. Cobey, B. E. Deverman, and R. Medzhitov. 2021. Investigate the origins of COVID-19. *Science* 372 (6543): 694. https://doi.org/10.1126/science.abf1739.

Bruce-Chwatt, L. J., and J. De Zulueta. 1980. *The Rise and Fall of Malaria in Europe: A historico-epidemiological study*. Oxford: Oxford University Press.

Carmona-González, N., and M. P. Sánchez-Martín. 2021. Pandemics and globalisation: Parallel paths throughout history. *Revista de Economía Mundial* 58:233–250.

Charnley, G. E. C., I. Kelman, K. A. Gaythorpe, and K. A. Murray. 2021. Traits and risk factors of post-disaster infectious disease outbreaks: A systematic review. *Scientific Reports* 11 (1): 5616. https://doi.org/10.1038/s41598-021-85044-0.

Charnley, G. E. C., I. Kelman, and K. A. Murray. 2022. Drought-related cholera outbreaks in Africa and the implications for climate change: A narrative review. *Pathogens and Global Health* 116 (1): 3–12. https://doi.org/10.1080/20477724.2021.2003795.

Charnley, G. E. C., and I. Kelman. 2024. Perspectives on climate change and infectious disease outbreaks: Is the evidence there? *npj Climate Action* 3 (1): 61. https://doi.org/10.1038/s44168-024-00073-2.

Chirebvu, E., M. J. Chimbari, and B. N. Ngwenya. 2021. Assessment of mosquito breeding sites in urban areas: A case study of Gaborone. *Botswana. African Health Sciences* 21 (2): 783–792. https://doi.org/10.4314/ahs.v21i2.38.

Christidis, P., and A. Christodoulou. 2020. The predictive capacity of air travel patterns during the global spread of the COVID-19 pandemic: Risk, uncertainty and randomness. *International Journal of Environmental Research and Public Health* 17 (10): 3356. https://doi.org/10.3390/ijerph17103356.

Connolly, C., R. Keil, and S. H. Ali. 2021. Extended urbanisation and the spatialities of infectious disease: Demographic change, infrastructure and governance. *Urban Studies* 58 (2): 245–263. https://doi.org/10.1177/0042098019897398.

Daszak, P., C. Zambrana-Torrelio, T. L. Bogich, M. Fernandez, J. H. Epstein, K. A. Murray, and H. Hamilton. 2013. Interdisciplinary approaches to understanding disease emergence: The past, present, and future drivers of Nipah virus emergence. *Proceedings of the National Academy of Sciences* 110 (Supplement 1): 3681–3688. https://doi.org/10.1073/pnas.1201243109.

Environmental Audit Committee. 2023. *Seeing the wood for the trees: The contribution of the forestry and timber sectors to biodiversity and net zero goals*. London: UK Parliament. Available at: https://publications.parliament.uk/pa/cm5803/cmselect/cmenvaud/529/report.html.

Fordham, D. A., S. T. Jackson, S. C. Brown, B. Huntley, B. W. Brook, D. Dahl-Jensen, et al. 2020. Using paleo-archives to safeguard biodiversity under climate change. *Science* 369 (6507): eabc5654. https://doi.org/10.1126/science.abc5654.

Gao, Q., Z. Liu, J. Xiang, Y. Zhang, M. X. Tong, S. Wang, et al. 2022. Impact of temperature and rainfall on typhoid/paratyphoid fever in Taizhou, China: Effect estimation and vulnerable group identification. *The American Journal of Tropical Medicine and Hygiene* 106 (2): 532. https://doi.org/10.4269/ajtmh.21-0815.

The Geological Society of America. 2022. *GSA Geological Time Scale Version 6.0*. Available from: https://www.geosociety.org/GSA/gsa/timescale/home.aspx

Gibb, R., L. H. Franklinos, D. W. Redding, and K. E. Jones. 2020. Ecosystem perspectives are needed to manage zoonotic risks in a changing climate. *British Medical Journal* 371:m3389. https://doi.org/10.1136/bmj.m3389.

Guinat, C., J. Artois, A. Bronner, J. L. Guérin, M. Gilbert, and M. C. Paul. 2019. Duck production systems and highly pathogenic avian influenza H5N8 in France, 2016–2017. *Scientific Reports* 9 (1): 6177. https://doi.org/10.1038/s41598-019-42205-1.

Heeney, J. L., A. G. Dalgleish, and R. A. Weiss. 2006. Origins of HIV and the evolution of resistance to AIDS. *Science* 313 (5786): 462–466. https://doi.org/10.1126/science.1123016.

Hing, S., E. J. Narayan, R. A. Thompson, and S. S. Godfrey. 2016. The relationship between physiological stress and wildlife disease: Consequences for health and conservation. *Wildlife Research* 43 (1): 51–60.

Johnson, C. N. 2015. Influence of environmental factors on Vibrio spp. in coastal ecosystems. *Microbiology spectrum* 3 (3): 10–128.

Juska, A., L. Gouveia, J. Gabriel, and K. P. Stanley. 2003. Manufacturing bacteriological contamination outbreaks in industrialized meat production systems: The case of *E. coli* O157:H7. *Agriculture and Human Values* 20:3–19.

Katzenelson, E., I. Buium, and H. I. Shuval. 1976. Risk of communicable disease infection associated with wastewater irrigation in agricultural settlements. *Science* 194 (4268): 944–946.

Kelman, I. 2019. Imaginary numbers of climate change migrants? *Social Sciences* 8 (5): 131.

Khan, K., J. Sears, V.W. Hu, J.S. Brownstein, S. Hay, D. Kossowsky, R. Eckhardt, T. Chim, I. Berry, I. Bogoch, and M. Cetron. 2013. Potential for the international spread of Middle East respiratory syndrome in association with mass gatherings in Saudi Arabia. *PLoS Currents* 5.

Kinoshita, R., M. Sassa, S. Otake, F. Yoshimatsu, S. Shi, R. Ueno, M. Suzuki, and D. Yoneoka. 2023. Impact of airline network on the global importation risk of mpox, 2022. *Epidemiology & Infection* 151:e60.

Kramer, S. P. 2013. *The other population crisis: What governments can do about falling birth rates*. Washington D.C./Baltimore: Woodrow Wilson Center Press/Johns Hopkins University Press.

Kurpiers, L. A., B. Schulte-Herbrüggen, I. Ejotre, and D. M. Reeder. 2016. Bushmeat and emerging infectious diseases: Lessons from Africa. In *Problematic Wildlife: A Cross-Disciplinary Approach*, ed. F. M. Angelici, 507–551. Cham: Springer.

Lambin, E. F., A. Tran, S. O. Vanwambeke, C. Linard, and V. Soti. 2010. Pathogenic landscapes: Interactions between land, people, disease vectors, and their animal hosts. *International Journal of Health Geographics* 9:1–3.

Lamborn, R. H. 1890. *Dragon Flies vs Mosquitoes. Can the Mosquito Pest be Mitigated? Studies on the life history of irritating insects, their natural enemies and artificial checks*. New York: D. Appleton & Co.

Lang, T., and D. Barling. 2012. Food security and food sustainability: Reformulating the debate. *The Geographical Journal* 178 (4): 313–326.

Langton, T. E., M. W. Jones, and I. McGill. 2022. Analysis of the impact of badger culling on bovine tuberculosis in cattle in the high-risk area of England, 2009–2020. *Veterinary Record* 190 (6): e1384.

Lun, Z. R., M. S. Wu, Y. F. Chen, J. Y. Wang, X. N. Zhou, L. F. Liao, et al. 2015. Visceral leishmaniasis in China: An endemic disease under control. *Clinical Microbiology Reviews* 28:987–1004. https://doi.org/10.1128/CMR.00080-14.

Massad, E. N. R., L. Ortega, C. de Barros, and C. J. Struchiner. 2008. Modern epidemiology. In *Fuzzy Logic in Action: Applications in Epidemiology and Beyond*, ed. E. Massad, L. C. De Barros, and C. J. Struchiner, 41–57. Cham: Springer. (Studies in Fuzziness and Soft Computing, 232).

Met Office. 2024. What is climate? [Online]. Available from: https://www.metoffice.gov.uk/weather/climate/climate-explained/what-is-climate

Middlemiss, L., and R. Gillard. 2015. Fuel poverty from the bottom-up: Characterising household energy vulnerability through the lived experience of the fuel poor. *Energy Research & Social Science* 6:146–154.

Middleton, W. S. 1928. The yellow fever epidemic of 1793 in Philadelphia. *Annals of Medical History* 10:434.

Miguel, E., V. Grosbois, A. Caron, D. Pople, B. Roche, and C. A. Donnelly. 2020. A systemic approach to assess the potential and risks of wildlife culling for infectious disease control. *Communications Biology* 3 (1): 353. https://doi.org/10.1038/s42003-020-01160-1.

Montalvo, T., A. Higueros, A. Valsecchi, E. Realp, C. Vila, A. Ortiz, V. Peracho, and J. Figuerola. 2022. Effectiveness of the modification of sewers to reduce the reproduction of *Culex pipiens* and *Aedes albopictus* in Barcelona. *Spain. Pathogens* 11 (4): 423. https://doi.org/10.3390/pathogens11040423.

Murray, K. A., and P. Daszak. 2013. Human ecology in pathogenic landscapes: Two hypotheses on how land use change drives viral emergence. *Current Opinion in Virology* 3 (1): 79–83. https://doi.org/10.1016/j.coviro.2013.01.006.

Newell, D. G., M. Koopmans, L. Verhoef, E. Duizer, A. Aidara-Kane, H. Sprong, M. Opsteegh, M. Langelaar, J. Threlfall, F. Scheutz, and J. van der Giessen. 2010. Food-borne diseases—the challenges of 20 years ago still persist while new ones continue to emerge. *International Journal of Food Microbiology* 139:S3–S15. https://doi.org/10.1016/j.ijfoodmicro.2010.01.021.

Newsom, S. W. 2006. Pioneers in infection control: John Snow, Henry Whitehead, the Broad Street pump, and the beginnings of geographical epidemiology. *Journal of Hospital Infection* 64 (3): 210–216. https://doi.org/10.1016/j.jhin.2006.06.020.

Nosten, F., D. Richard-Lenoble, and M. Danis. 2022. A brief history of malaria. *La Presse Médicale* 51 (3): 104130. https://doi.org/10.1016/j.lpm.2022.104130.

Odijie, M. 2020. Cocoa and child slavery in West Africa. In *Oxford Research Encyclopedia of African History*, ed. T. Spear. Oxford: Oxford University Press. https://doi.org/10.1093/acrefore/9780190277734.013.432.

Omazic, A., H. Bylund, S. Boqvist, A. Högberg, C. Björkman, M. Tryland, B. Evengård, A. Koch, C. Berggren, A. Malogolovkin, and D. Kolbasov. 2019. Identifying climate-sensitive infectious diseases in animals and humans in Northern regions. *Acta Veterinaria Scandinavica* 61:1–2. https://doi.org/10.1186/s13028-019-0474-0.

Oxfam International. 2024. Millions of migrant farm workers exploited in Europe's fields, says Oxfam. [Online]. Available from: https://www.oxfam.org/en/press-releases/millions-migrant-farm-workers-exploited-europes-fields-says-oxfam.

Potter, C., T. Harwood, J. Knight, and I. Tomlinson. 2011. Learning from history, predicting the future: The UK Dutch elm disease outbreak in relation to contemporary tree disease threats. *Philosophical Transactions of the Royal Society B: Biological Sciences* 366 (1573): 1966–1974. https://doi.org/10.1098/rstb.2010.0398.

de Raadt, P. (2005). The history of sleeping sickness. [Online]. Available from: http://www.who.int/trypanosomiasis_african/country/history/en/. Geneva: World Health Organization.

Rodó, X., M. J. Bouma, M. À. Rodríguez-Arias, M. Roy, P. De Yebra, D. Petrova, M. García-Díez, and M. Pascual. 2024. Strain variation and anomalous climate synergistically influence cholera pandemics. *PLOS Neglected Tropical Diseases* 18 (8): e0012275. https://doi.org/10.1371/journal.pntd.0012275.

Sack, D. A. 2013. A new era in the history of cholera: The road to elimination. *International Journal of Epidemiology* 42 (6): 1537–1540. https://doi.org/10.1093/ije/dyt198.

Scheiner, S. M. 2009. The intersection of the sciences of biogeography and infectious disease ecology. *EcoHealth* 6:483–488. https://doi.org/10.1007/s10393-009-0274-z.

Shanks, G. D. 2022. Historical gold mining infectious disease epidemics. *Internal Medicine Journal* 52 (8): 1441–1445. https://doi.org/10.1111/imj.15595.

Skerratt, L. F., L. Berger, R. Speare, S. Cashins, K. R. McDonald, A. D. Phillott, H. B. Hines, and N. Kenyon. 2007. Spread of chytridiomycosis has caused the rapid global decline and extinction of frogs. *EcoHealth* 4 (2): 125–134. https://doi.org/10.1007/s10393-007-0093-5.

de Souza, W. M., and S. C. Weaver. 2024. Effects of climate change and human activities on vector-borne diseases. *Nature Reviews Microbiology* 1–6. https://doi.org/10.1038/s41579-024-00913-7.

Spyrou, M. A., R. I. Tukhbatova, M. Feldman, J. Drath, S. Kacki, J. B. de Heredia, S. Arnold, A. G. Sitdikov, D. Castex, J. Wahl, and I. R. Gazimzyanov. 2016. Historical *Y. pestis* genomes reveal the European Black Death as the source of ancient and modern plague pandemics. *Cell Host & Microbe* 19 (6): 874–881. https://doi.org/10.1016/j.chom.2016.05.012.

Stern, D. I., and R. K. Kaufmann. 2014. Anthropogenic and natural causes of climate change. *Climatic Change* 122:257–269. https://doi.org/10.1007/s10584-013-1007-x.

Sultan, B., K. Labadi, J. F. Guégan, and S. Janicot. 2005. Climate drives the meningitis epidemics onset in West Africa. *PLOS Medicine* 2 (1): e6. https://doi.org/10.1371/journal.pmed.0020006.

Tatem, A. J., D. J. Rogers, and S. I. Hay. 2006. Global transport networks and infectious disease spread. *Advances in Parasitology* 62:293–343. https://doi.org/10.1016/S0065-308X(05)62009-X.

Van Oldenborgh, G. J., K. van Der Wiel, S. Kew, S. Philip, F. Otto, R. Vautard, A. King, F. Lott, J. Arrighi, R. Singhand, and M. van Aalst. 2021. Pathways and pitfalls in extreme event attribution. *Climatic Change* 166 (1): 13. https://doi.org/10.1007/s10584-021-03071-7.

van Vliet, N., and P. Mbazza. 2011. Recognizing the multiple reasons for bushmeat consumption in urban areas: A necessary step toward the sustainable use of wildlife for food in Central Africa. *Human Dimensions of Wildlife* 16 (1): 45–54. https://doi.org/10.1080/10871209.2011.535240.

Vergadi, E., G. Rouva, M. Angeli, and E. Galanakis. 2022. Infectious diseases associated with desert dust outbreaks: A systematic review. *International Journal of Environmental Research and Public Health* 19 (11): 6907. https://doi.org/10.3390/ijerph19116907.

Wasko, C., A. Sharma, and S. Westra. 2016. Reduced spatial extent of extreme storms at higher temperatures. *Geophysical Research Letters* 43 (8): 4026–4032. https://doi.org/10.1002/2016GL068509.

Wilson, A. L., O. Courtenay, L. A. Kelly-Hope, T. W. Scott, W. Takken, S. J. Torr, and S. W. Lindsay. 2020. The importance of vector control for the control and elimination of vector-borne diseases. *PLoS Neglected Tropical Diseases* 14 (1): e0007831. https://doi.org/10.1371/journal.pntd.0007831.

World Bank. 2024. *Poverty, prosperity, and the planet: Building a sustainable and inclusive future*. Washington, DC: World Bank. Retrieved November 16, 2024, from https://www.worldbank.org/en/publication/poverty-prosperity-and-planet.

World Health Organization. 2019. 1 in 3 people globally do not have access to safe drinking water—UNICEF, WHO. Retrieved from https://www.who.int/news/item/18-06-2019-1-in-3-people-globally-do-not-have-access-to-safe-drinking-water-unicef-who

Zietz, B. P., and H. Dunkelberg. 2004. The history of the plague and the research on the causative agent *Yersinia pestis*. *International Journal of Hygiene and Environmental Health* 207 (2): 165–178. https://doi.org/10.1078/1438-4639-00259.

History as a Barrier to Climate Change Adaptation and Conservation at the World Heritage Site, Tipasa, Algeria

Joanne Clarke

Abstract The World Heritage Site, Tipasa, is located on the Mediterranean coast 70 km east of Algiers. It was inscribed on the World Heritage List in 1982 by the Algerian State Party to UNESCO. This Punic/Roman/Byzantine city is situated in the centre of the modern town of Tipaza and as such is at risk from multiple anthropogenic threats to its integrity, leading to it being placed on the UNESCO List of Heritage Sites in Danger from 2002 to 2006. In addition, the site is highly exposed to coastal erosion, which will be exacerbated by more frequent and severe storms in the future. Despite these multiple threats to Tipasa's integrity, including climate change driven sea-level rise and coastal erosion, numerous requests by UNESCO for an adequate conservation and management plan, and for its experts to be consulted on local planning and development activities, have been largely ignored; the site continues to suffer from misuse by visitors, while the State Party makes decisions about the site *contra* to the advice of the World Heritage Committee. In this paper reasons for the protracted and ongoing difficulties in managing Tipasa are explored. It is argued that Tipasa suffers from multiple interconnected historical colonial barriers to successful adaptation which place the site at greater risk of losses and damages than other Algerian World Heritage Sites, the most detrimental being a lack of engagement with, or valuation of, the site by residents of the modern town of Tipaza.

Keywords Climate change losses and damages · Adaptation barriers · Dissonant heritage · Colonialism · Value

J. Clarke (✉)
Durham University, Durham, UK
e-mail: joanne.t.clarke@durham.ac.uk

J. F. Haldon, R. Fernandes (eds.), *Bridging History and Policy*, Understanding Complex Systems, https://doi.org/10.1007/978-3-032-24379-9_18

1 Introduction

Tipasa was a Punic/Roman/Christian town situated on three small hills overlooking the sea on the north coast of Algeria and surrounded by the modern city of Tipaza (Fig. 1). The site today includes three entities: two archaeological parks, separated by a commercial port, and the Royal Mauritanian Mausoleum. The extant remains are impressive, comprising (among other important structures) a Punic necropolis on the eastern side of the harbour; a *Cardo Maximus,* a Christian basilica and numerous civic buildings laid with intricate mosaics, located on the western side of the harbour. Slightly inland is the Numidian Royal Mausoleum of Mauretania (Benali Aoudia and Belkacemi Zebda 2020; Izza-Guiri 2011).

Algeria's coastal zone is at significant risk from both natural and anthropogenic hazards which will be exacerbated in the future by more frequent and severe storms (Amarni et al. 2021; Boughedir 2015; Chaib et al. 2020; Djili et al. 2024). Coastal erosion has been recently identified as a particular threat to heritage sites along the Mediterranean littoral (Reimann et al. 2018). Parts of Tipasa have already been claimed by the sea (Fig. 2) with The United Nations Educational, Scientific and Cultural Organization (UNESCO) recommending repair to an eroding cliff face, a survey of underwater heritage, and an extension of the buffer zone to include elements of Tipasa that are underwater (ICOMOS 2017). Large parts of the site are

Fig. 1 Tipasa looking southwest (courtesy of Jane Chick)

Fig. 2 Aerial closeup of the Cardo Maximus and the Villa of the Frescoes showing the eroding front and the loss of structures (@algeria_gems)

situated immediately on the sea front with no sea defences, although sea defences are common along other parts of the Algerian shoreline (Rabehi et al. 2022). Even though historic shoreline retreat is not caused by climate change, sea-level rise combined with more frequent and extreme seas will speed up the process leading to an existential threat to the site in the coming decades.

A recent analysis of future impacts of extreme seas on coastal heritage sites in Africa by Vousdoukas et al. (2022) found that at baseline (2010), 2.6% of Tipasa is currently exposed to a 100-year flood event. By 2100 under moderate CO_2 emissions this will increase to 6.7% and under high emissions to 9.5%. It is now understood that global warming will increase the frequency of the so-called one-in-100-year event (Vousdoukas et al. 2022) to something like a one-in-ten-year event, meaning that return periods are becoming much shorter increasing the likelihood loss of heritage assets will occur. Crucially, some of Tipasa's most iconic buildings are at the

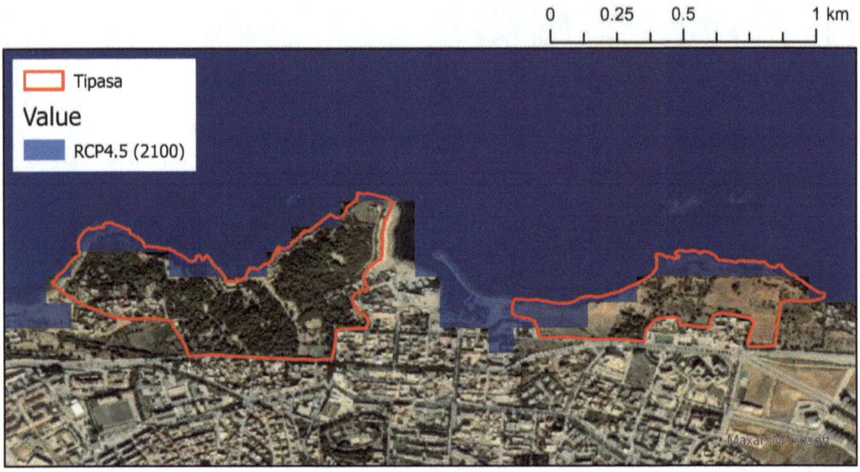

Fig. 3 Modelling of Tipasa flooding at 2100 under a 'business as usual' warming pathway (courtesy of Lena Reimann)

coast and are among those most at threat (Fig. 3). Extreme sea levels at 2100 under a moderate carbon emission pathway will threaten almost all of the Great Basilica and associated structures, much of the *Cardo* and the Villa of the Frescoes, with the Punic necropolis predicted to be the most severely impacted of all heritage assets with a possible 100% of the area flooded during extreme seas caused by storm surges. Storm surges are becoming stronger and more frequent on the Algerian coast (Amarouche et al. 2020) therefore measures are required to protect heritage exposed at the coast. Moreover, Vousdoukas et al. (2022) only considered flooding caused by storm surges, they did not take into account existing vulnerabilities due to subduction and coastal erosion, a specific threat to Tipasa.

2 Tipasa, a World Heritage Site

Tipasa was inscribed as a World Heritage Site in 1982 on the basis of Criteria III and IV, stating that the site "bears exceptional testimony to the Punic and Roman civilizations now disappeared" and "[t]he architectural and archaeological vestiges … reflect in a significant manner the contacts between the indigenous civilizations and the Punic and Roman waves of colonization between the 6th century B.C. and the 6th century A.D" (UNESCO World Heritage List n.d. https://whc.unesco.org/en/list/193/).

The site was founded by the Carthaginians in the 6th century BC (Stillwell et al. 2017) as a small Punic trading port and a Phoenician commercial outpost and trading centre (Benali Aoudia and Chennaoui 2017, 173; Stillwell et al. 2017). As part of western Numidia, its local kings assisted Rome in the second Punic War (Czapski 2019; Stillwell et al. 2017) but later incurred Rome's hostility, eventually becoming a Roman province as part of the Romanization of North Africa (Czapski 2019; Quevedo et al. 2023). In the third century AD, Tipasa was Christianized, with the Great Basilica, Basilica Alexander and the Basilica of St Salsa bearing testimony (Czapski 2019). Tipasa was later conquered by the Vandals in the fifth century AD and was briefly under Byzantium rule in the sixth century AD before being conquered by the Arabs, after which the city went into decline (Stillwell et al. 2017).

Characteristic of Tipasa is the co-mingling of Indigenous traits with successive colonizing elements that can be observed in the architecture and material remains. Yet, despite its perfect location between the mountains and the sea, its rich history, its ancient multiculturalism, and its unique mixing of Indigenous and colonial traits, the State Party has paid little attention to facilitating national and international interest in the site as a tourist destination, nor to its potential as a site of national pride and cultural value. Instead, in 2002 Tipasa was placed on the List of World Heritage in Danger because of a complete deficit of management and conservation plans first requested by UNESCO in 2001 and supported by a grant of $35,000 from the World Heritage Fund for the *Elaboration d'un plan d'urgence et mise en oeuvre de mesures correctrices pour le Site Archéologique de Tipasa* (Izza-Guiri 2011, 25; UNESCO 2002 List of Heritage Sites in Danger https://whc.unesco.org/en/decisions/939). As Algeria had just emerged from a brutal civil war in 2002 it is not surprising that the site fell into disrepair over the previous decade, nevertheless, repairs commissioned by UNESCO and funded by a grant from the World Heritage Fund were never forthcoming (UNESCO 2002 under factors affecting the property identified in previous reports https://whc.unesco.org/en/soc/2604).

By 2006, when Tipasa was removed from the List of Heritage Sites in Danger, some threats identified in previous reports had been addressed but slow natural deterioration due to shore-line change, wind erosion, and sea salt continued to impact the remains, along with pollution and waste, encroachment of urban constructions and inadequate conservation of the archaeological vestiges (https://whc.unesco.org/en/soc/1112). By 2007, "[d]eliberate destruction of heritage: Deterioration of the remains due to vandalism, theft and uncontrolled visitation causing accumulation of rubbish" (https://whc.unesco.org/en/soc/4603) had become the most concerning impacts on the property. In 2017 a team of experts from the International Council on Monuments and Sites (ICOMOS) visited Tipasa and made 13 recommendations with a number of parts to each, suggesting that solutions could be found to "[a]ll of these recommendations…through the organization of meetings on the site of national and international experts specialized in the relevant areas of expertise in order to formulate proposals for solutions to be submitted to the World Heritage Centre…in particular ICOMOS and ICCROM before their adoption and implementation" (ICOMOS 2017). This and other recommendations were ignored by the State Party despite the presence of a report commissioned in 2006 by the Ministère de l'Aménagement du Territoire et de l'Environnement, which recommended "Protection et valorisation de sites historiques et culturels de la région PAC dans une approche d'intégration aux milieux naturel et socioéconomique" (*Programme d'aménagement côtier* 2006).

In 2021 The World Heritage Committee reported that the State Party had submitted a State of Conservation Report (2020) which described progress on a number of conservation issues to do with monitoring and maintenance of the site. However, a comprehensive Management Plan had still not been submitted. UNESCO, concerned with the urgent situation of the eroded cliff supporting the West Archaeological Park, which required an expert mission to plan long-term solutions, urged the State Party to arrange such a visit. Instead, in its 2023 State of Conservation report (https://whc.unesco.org/en/list/193/documents/), the State Party said "En conclusion, considérant que les travaux de renforcement de la falaise support des vestiges du parc ouest, ont été réalisés et achevés, la mission consultative conjointe Centre du patrimoine mondial/Icomos sur le bien, afin d'obtenir des conseils sur les solutions à long term pour renforcer la falaise sous le parc et sur les questions connexes dans le cadre du projet d'aménagement portuaire proposé n'est plus à l'ordre du jour, étant donné que la falaise a été sécurisée, et les travaux de consortement achevés."

This statement was in effect a direct rebuttal of UNESCO's request to send an expert team to help advise on remedial measures to underpin the eroded cliff supporting the archaeological remains and to monitor and report on the port development. In the minutes of the World Heritage Convention 2024 (whc-24-46com-17-en_2024) UNESCO expressed considerable concern that the multiple infrastructure projects being undertaken around the site, including the construction of a breakwater, the stabilization of the cliff beneath the East Archaeological Park and the development of the port and harbour were all being undertaken without input from World Heritage experts and that these projects "*will* have a cumulative negative impact on the site's Outstanding Universal Value". By 2024, without having seen the condition of the site, the minutes of the World Heritage Committee (whc24-46com-7B-en_2024) recorded the following threats:

1. Deliberate destruction of heritage: Deterioration of the remains due to vandalism, theft and uncontrolled visitation causing accumulation of rubbish
2. Erosion and siltation/deposition: Natural degradation caused by littoral erosion, marine salt, rainwater runoff and vegetation covering part of the inscribed sector
3. Housing
4. Human resources: Lack of capacities for site conservation
5. Illegal activities: Urbanisation on the outskirts of the property
6. Illegal construction provoking land disputes
7. Impacts of tourism/visitor/recreation
8. Management activities
9. Marine transport infrastructure: Proposed port development
10. Unsuitable restoration techniques, and poor conservation conditions for the archaeological remains

The failure of the State Party to comply with the terms of the World Heritage Convention's Mission Statement (https://whc.unesco.org/en/about/) raises questions over the long-term viability of the site, but perhaps of greater concern—at least in the short term— is the complete lack of regard for the site and for its deteriorating condition by the residents of Tipaza. For Izza-Guiri (2011, 114) this is because the local population remain indifferent to the archaeology, allowing illegal activities to take place; in Chennaoui's (2013, 482) opinion the local population have become detached from the site as the archaeological vestiges have deteriorated. Whichever the case, this apparent absence of connection and identification with the city's archaeological remains is not typical of how Algerians view their World Heritage Sites—Tipasa appears to be the exception. Algeria has six other sites inscribed on the World Heritage List, including two further Roman cities, Djémila and Timgad, both of which are reported as being in generally good condition. It must be concluded therefore that for some reason, whether consciously or unconsciously, the archaeological remains of Tipasa have either lost their cultural value or never had it in the first place.

3 Valued Places

That this conclusion has some basis in fact is glimpsed through a recent study by Kettab and Chabbi-Chemrouk (2017) which explored local perceptions of 'significant places' for a cross section of Tipazan society. Through a combination of semi-structured interviews, mental maps and questionnaires, Khettab and Chabbi-Chemrouk were able to show that the inhabitants of Tipaza have a well developed and culturally specific hierarchy of locally significant places. Their objectives were to explore socio-cognitive representations and how these influence the socio-cultural meanings associated with favourite local urban places (Kettab and Chabbi-Chemrouk 2017, 544). What was clear from their results was that physical features were recognized as favourite places but that these were entirely composed of natural landscapes especially those related to the sea (Kettab and Chabbi-Chemrouk 2017, 551). In contrast historic places were not mentioned at all by the residents of Tipaza, although the archaeological parks were mentioned by non-local Algerian students studying at a regional university in the area, but even in this case it was almost entirely in association with the sea. Instead, the archaeological ruins were negatively perceived by the local community, producing feelings of insecurity and lack of respect. It was noted that local people avoided visiting the site with family and friends (Kettab and Chabbi-Chemrouk 2017; 552).

Unfortunately, Khettab and Chabbi-Chemrouk's study didn't explore reasons for these negative socio-cultural feelings towards Tipasa, leaving open the question of individual and social valuation—why some heritage is valued when other heritage is not. It is interesting to note that the modern town of Tipaza and its surroundings are home to the largest Tamazight-speaking group of western Algerian (Chenouis) people, an Amazigh ethnic group native to the Chenoua Mountains, which dominate the town. Amazigh people see themselves as Indigenous North Africans, descended from nomadic (Numidian) tribespeople who inhabited the African continent before the arrival of successive waves of colonists, including Phoenician/Punic traders to North Africa in the first millennium BC (Broodbank and Lucarini 2019) and who are associated with the Carthaginians. As such Amazigh people have a highly developed sense of their Indigenous African identity. It is perhaps unsurprising therefore, that the Chenouis idea of homeland embodies landscapes and mountains, which are indelibly connected to intangible heritage such as language and poetry. As Habiba Djahnine relays in her films about Chenoua and its people (Petty 2025), the land does not simply refer to a geographical location but rather to an entire Kabyle and Algerian culture existing in the mountains (Petty 2025, 55). The fact that Mount Chenoua overshadows Tipaza perhaps explains why the (majority Chenouis) townspeople have such a deep sense of connection with their culturalized-but-natural surroundings. Even so, given that the archaeological ruins of Tipasa comprise a complex palimpsest of Indigenous and non-Indigenous architectural elements of exquisite virtuosity still begs the question; why is there both local and national ambivalence toward it?

Heritage does not have value in and of itself beyond innate properties which may set it apart from other places, things and behaviours (Labadi 2013). Heritage is ascribed value in culturally mediated contexts. Value is therefore culturally specific and mutable. Amongst the same population value is ascribed to places, things and behaviours unequally. Azzopardi et al. (2023, 370) suggest that there is a lack of clarity over the term value, listing four value 'types'; transcendental value, which is shared across cultures and could be thought of as similar to UNESCO's concept of Outstanding Universal Value, instrumental value, which refers to value in relation to something else (a Stradivarius violin in relation to another make of violin, for example); intrinsic value, which is value based on innate properties (as mentioned above) and relational value, which is contextual and mediated by relationships. Relational value is socially constructed and is often the type of value ascribed to local heritage. Alfred Gell (1992, 43) in his seminal paper on the technology of enchantment, argued that some 'things' have the capacity to cast a spell over us so that we see the world in an enchanted form, but things can only enchant us when we acquiesce to being enchanted through 'networks of intentionality'. This is the basis of relational value from which the logical extension must be that networks of intentionality can work negatively upon us, leading to feelings of ambivalence, disassociation and alienation.

4 Dissonant Heritage

For reasons of history and identity, Algeria has had a difficult relationship with its heritage. Before French colonization, sites of significance were 'stewarded' by local 'custodians'. These were places imbued with individual and social identity linked to remembered traditions, rituals, ways of life and people. Without these connections heritage sites were conceived of as disconnected, alien, belonging to others. In pre-colonial Algerian houses it was not unusual to see re-used Roman capitals and other architectural features from long-forgotten ruins incorporated into the structural fabric of homes (Gueliane and Bouchemal 2021, 258). This was not an act of disrespect but rather because they were simply found to be aesthetically pleasing. By the arrival of the French colonists in 1830 the status of the colony and the organization of Algeria into provinces gave rise to new legislation and a new interest in Classical—essentially European—heritage (Gueliane and Bouchemal 2021, 258). During the first years of colonial rule archaeological excavations were authorized with little concern for more than the fortunes to be made from the collection of antiquities sent to France and indelibly knitted into the construction of a new French identity and a new way of life imagined on its ‘north-facing southern shores’ (Gueliane and Bouchemal 2021, 264). This changed with the establishment of the General Inspectorate of Historic Monuments and Archaeological Museums of Algeria, at which point the idea of heritage became integrated into the French ‘settler’ psyche, who wished to build an ‘Algerian identity’ in French Algeria (Gueliane and Bouchemal 2021, 264).

By the 1930s heritage had become a symbol of the greatness of Algeria’s Latin roots supporting the developing ideological discourse around French Latin Algeria (Gueliane and Bouchemal 2021, 265). The aim was to legitimize French colonial rule. The Historical Monuments Act of 1930 on the protection of monuments and objects of historical and artistic interest, allowed for the appropriation by the Algerian Government of any private property deemed to be of national interest without the consent of the owner (Oulebsir 2004, 223). This effectively enshrined in law a policy of ‘land grab’ by the French colonial administrators, which included heritage sites previously stewarded by Indigenous Algerians.

After the country’s independence in 1962 supporters of the socialist Government rubbed up hard against a new Arab/Islamic identity (Hill 2006). Heritage sites were lost in this debate, Classical sites being seen as the remnants of a colonial past, while Indigenous heritage sites had little to do with the new political and social realities on the ground. Colonial legislation for the protection of monuments and objects of historical and artistic interest, as in so many other instances around the world following the liberation of countries from colonial rule, remained in place, largely because it was easier to do so than try to decolonize antiquities law. Thus from 1962 until its inscription on the World Heritage List in 1982, Tipasa’s legacy was one of colonial French Algerian appropriation and alienation, leaving the site little chance of being incorporated into local Chenouis identity.

Shockley (2023) says that ‘place making’ is a particular form of value ascribed to locations that hold special meaning for people (see also Tuan 1977, 1991; Tschakert et al. 2017; Herrick 2018). Often the meaningful connections that make a location a place involve a specific history, one that contributes to the identity of an individual or people. “Particular places matter to individuals in virtue of embodying their history and cultural identities and this is why their loss is felt so acutely” (Shockley 2023; also O'neill 2008, 66). Significant places are bound up with identity, history, psychological wellbeing, and flourishing. Flourishing requires authentic choice (Shockley 2023) and often it is historical links that create meaningful connections to places, making a location part of individual or group identity (Adger et al. 2011). Despite it being inscribed on the World Heritage List, all of the threads required for identity creation and place making by Indigenous Chenouis were, by 1982, missing at Tipasa.

5 Albert Camus

Albert Camus, the French Algerian philosopher and poet, loved Tipasa (Fig. 4), so much so that the site is the focus of one of his essays, *Noces à Tipasa* written around 1936–7—and also mentioned in at least one other *L'Été* published in 1954, (Camus 1939, 1954) in which Camus reminisces at the beginning of the War of Independence on the changes to Tipasa, now closed and surrounded by barbed wire, still full of the flowers of Spring—changed but unchanged (Todd 2015). Yet despite Camus' fame and deep attachment to his native land, Algeria never reciprocated that love. Camus is not part of the school curriculum; his books cannot be found in libraries or bookshops (Hammer 2013). He and his works have been erased from the collective memory of Algeria.

Despite this, a monument erected to the memory of Camus in 1961 (Figs. 5 and 6) still stands at Tipasa. Erected at a particularly fraught period during the Algerian

Fig. 4 Albert Camus at Tipasa (Wikipedia)

Fig. 5 Stele to Albert Camus, Tipasa (Wikipedia)

Fig. 6 A close up of the Camus stele (Wikipedia)

War of Independence, its inscription is a quotation from his essay *Noces à Tipas*a that says (English translation): "I understand here what is called glory: the right to love beyond measure". Had the protagonists (his friends) had any concern for the condition of the site, or for the lack of engagement by the residents of the town of Tipaza, they may have questioned whether the stele was either timely or well considered. The quote on the stele is taken out of context, the full quote from *Noces à Tipasa* reads "I understand here what is called glory: the right to love without measure. There is only one love in this world. To hold a woman's body is also to hold against yourself this strange joy that descends from the sky to the sea. Later, when I throw myself into the absinths to bring their perfume into my body, I will be aware, against all prejudices, to accomplish a truth that is that of the sun and will also be that of my death" (Camus 1936–7). Instead, the quote is truncated on the stele and as such hints at the 'glory' (of war?) and the 'right' to love (a country?) beyond measure. Was this deliberate? We will never know but interpreted in the context of the backdrop of war the stele stands as a battle cry for French Algeria. That it was also placed along the sight line of the Chenoua Mountains signals more than simply the love of Tipasa by Camus, or even the glory of French Algeria, but perhaps more portentously, it is a reference to the significance of the landscape and mountains that define Indigenous (Chenouis) culture.

It is not surprising therefore, that the residents of Tipaza feel dissonance toward their archaeological heritage. The appropriation of the site now apparently complete; its association with French Algeria inalienable. What is surprising however, is that unlike other examples of conflicted African heritage there has been no attempt to re-appropriate or re-present the site as Amazigh heritage, particularly given the very strong Numidian elements (including the Mausoleum). De Jong (2022, 3–12) tells the story of the toppling of the statue in 2017 of Louis Faidherbe (Governor of West Africa, 1854–61 and 1863–5) in Dakar, Senegal. The event is known as 'Faidherbe Must Fall', with the toppling being part of the reappropriation of Senegal for the Senegalese. A sustainable Tipasa will not be possible without the reappropriation of the site by the residents of Tipaza into Chenouis culture, if that means that Camus' stele must fall, then that may be the only route to salvaging the site.

6 Conclusion

But what of the State Party? Why do barriers to successful conservation of Tipasa continue to frustrate the World Heritage Committee. On a national scale Algeria has never fostered an international tourist sector; it has not needed to because of its wealth of natural gas (Ouki 2019). Heritage is often of national importance when it is valued for its economic returns through tourism—cultural capital as it is prosaically termed. Although Algeria can be forgiven for Tipasa being on the UNESCO List of Heritage Sites in Danger at the end of its 'dark decade' during the Civil War it still has a duty of care to its World Heritage as set out in the World Heritage Convention. Algeria might argue that it is doing this, but it breaks the Convention by not involving World Heritage experts in decisions around major infrastructure changes to the site. There appears to be a tension between Algeria's desire to be a State Party to the World Heritage Convention but not to have to abide by its legal obligations. It is also unclear whether heritage officials working at a national level are aware of the ambivalence of Tipaza's local population toward the archaeological remains, or to the complexities of the reasons for this ambivalence. Khettab and Chabbi-Chemrouk, the Algerian scholars whose inspirational study on 'favourite urban places in Tipaza', highlight this ambivalence, have probably not had their work picked up by heritage officials at a national level. This is despite having presented their study at the 14th International Conference on Urban Health in Portugal in 2017 (Khettab et al. 2017). Drawing attention to the socio-cultural barriers that exist amongst the local population will be key to unlocking a sustainable future for Tipasa. Ultimately it comes down to decolonizing Tipasa for future generations; when Algeria throws off the yoke of the history of French rule, only then will Tipasa be fully valued.

Acknowledgements The inspiration for this paper arose from a collaborative project with climate scientists published in 2022 modelling the impacts of extreme seas on heritage sites in Africa. Tipasa was amongst the sites most impacted, which highlighted the need for immediate adaptive conservation measures at the site. This led to my interest in why UNESCO had reported barriers to such adaptive measures and ultimately to my researching this paper. I would therefore like to thank my colleagues without whom I would not have embarked on this exercise; Nick Simpson, whose dedication to climate change-heritage adaptation has been an inspiration; Salma Sabour and Nadia Khalaf, who understand North African Indigenous cultures better than any of us; our modellers, Michalis Vousdoukas and Rosh Ranasinghe, who introduced me to this threatened site; and our other team members, Lena Reinman, Carley Isles and Birgitte Ouweneel. May there be many more papers arising from our 2022 work.

References

Adger, W. N., J. Barnett, F. S. Chapin III, and H. Ellemor. 2011. This must be the place: underrepresentation of identity and meaning in climate change decision-making. *Global Environmental Politics* 11 (2): 1–25.

Amarouche, K., A. Akpınar, R. E. Çakmak, F. Houma, and N. E. I. Bachari. 2020. Assessment of storm events along the Algiers coast and their potential impacts. *Ocean Engineering* 210:107432.

Amarni, N., L. Fernane, and R. Belkessa. 2021. Évaluation de la vulnérabilité côtière du littoral centre ouest algérien (cherchell), sous l'angle de la géomatique. *Geo-Eco-Marina* 27:55–82.

Azzopardi, E., J. O. Kenter, J. Young, C. Leakey, S. O'Connor, S. Martino, et al. 2023. What are heritage values? Integrating natural and cultural heritage into environmental valuation. *People and Nature* 5 (2): 368–383.

Benali Aoudia, L., and D. Belkacemi Zebda. 2020. How to manage and enhance archaeology and landscape at the Royal Mausoleum of Mauretania (Tipasa, Algeria). *The International Archives of the Photogrammetry, Remote Sensing and Spatial Information Sciences* 44:513–520.

Benali Aoudia, L., and Y. Chennaoui. 2017. The archaeological site of Tipasa, Algeria: What kind of management plan? *Conservation and Management of Archaeological Sites* 19 (3): 173–196.

Boughedir, S. 2015. Case study: disaster risk management and climate change adaptation in Greater Algiers: overview on a study assessing urban vulnerabilities to disaster risk and proposing measures for adaptation. *Current Opinion in Environmental Sustainability* 13:103–108.

Broodbank, C., and G. Lucarini. 2019. The dynamics of Mediterranean Africa, ca. 9600–1000 BC: An interpretative synthesis of knowns and unknowns. *Journal of Mediterranean archaeology* 32 (2): 195–267.

Camus, A. 1939. *Noces à Tipasa*. Paris: Gallimard.

Camus, A. 1954. *L'Été*. Paris: Gallimard.

Chaib, W., M. Guerfi, and Y. Hemdane. 2020. Evaluation of coastal vulnerability and exposure to erosion and submersion risks in Bou Ismail Bay (Algeria) using the coastal risk index (CRI). *Arabian Journal of Geosciences* 13:1–18.

Chennaoui, Y. 2013. The protective and enhancement plan of the archaeological sites of Tipasa: A first of its kind in Algeria. In *Arqueología: Actas del Primer Congreso Internacional de Buenas Prácticas en Patrimonio Mundial*, ed. Alicia Castillo, 481–496. Madrid: Universidad Complutense de Madrid.

Czapski, M. 2019. Three ancient cities of North Africa and their Roman baths: Tiddis, Timgad, Tipasa. Actual state of preservation. In *Greco-Roman Cities at the Crossroads of Cultures: The 20th Anniversary of Polish-Egyptian Conservation Mission Marina el-Alamein*, ed. Rafał Czerner and Grażyna Bąkowska-Czerner, 81–95. Oxford: Archaeopress.

De Jong, F. 2022. *Decolonizing Heritage: Time to Repair in Senegal*. Cambridge: Cambridge University Press.

Djili, M., K. Mezouar, and N. Benaissa. 2024. Wave climate, sediment transport and shoreline evolution in the West Littoral of Algeria. *Ocean Science Journal* 59 (3): 39.

Gell, A. 1992. The technology of enchantment and the enchantment of technology. In *Anthropology, Art, and Aesthetics*, ed. Jeremy Coote, 40–63. Oxford: Clarendon Press.

Gueliane, N., and K. Bouchemal. 2021. Algeria and its heritage: Inventory of the various heritage policies, from the pre-colonial to colonial and post-colonial times. In *Transcultural Diplomacy and International Law in Heritage Conservation: A Dialogue between Ethics, Law, and Culture*, ed. Olimpia Niglio and Eric Yong Joong Lee, 257–272. Singapore: Springer.

Hammer, J. 2013. Why is Albert Camus Still a Stranger in His Native Algeria? *Smithsonian Magazine*. https://www.smithsonianmag.com/innovation/why-is-albert-camus-still-a-stranger-in-his-native-algeria-13063/.

Herrick, C. N. 2018. Self-identity and sense of place: Some thoughts regarding climate change adaptation policy formulation. *Environmental Values* 27 (1): 81–102.

Hill, J. N. 2006. Identity and instability in postcolonial Algeria. *The Journal of North African Studies* 11 (1): 1–16.

ICOMOS. 2017. *Rapport de la Mission Conjointe de Conseil Centre du Patrimoine Mondial/ ICOMOS, Tipasa (Algére) (C 193) 8–11 Avril 2017*. International Council on Monuments and Sites: UNESCO.

Izza-Guiri, F. 2011. *Les nouveaux modèles de la muséologie active appliqués à la présentation des sites archéologiques: cas du site archéologique de Tipasa (Algérie)*. PhD thesis:. Université Mouloud Mammeri Tizi Ouzou.

Kettab, S., and N. Chabbi-Chemrouk. 2017. Sense of place in the coastal town of Tipaza in Algeria: Local-community's socio-cognitive representations. *International Journal of Sustainable Built Environment* 6:544–554.

Khettab, S., N. Chabbi-Chemrouk, and S. Kentache. 2017. Integrating socio-cognitive dimension in urban management tools: Perceived access to favorite urban places in Tipaza, Algeria. In *Conference: 14th International Conference on Urban Health: Health Equity-New Urban Agenda and Sustainable Development Goals. Coimbra, Portugal.*

Labadi, S. U. N. E. S. C. O. 2013. *Cultural Heritage, and Outstanding Universal Value: Value-Based Analyses of the World Heritage and Intangible Cultural Heritage Conventions*. Lanham, Md: Rowman & Littlefield.

Programme d'aménagement côtier (PAC) "Zone côtière algéroise". Rapport final intégré. 2006. Programme d'actions prioritaires. Centre d'activités regionals, février 2006. Alger: République Algerienne Democratique et Populaire, Ministère de l'aménagement du territoire et de l'environment.

O'neill, J., A. Holland, and A. Light. 2008. *Environmental Values*. London: Routledge.

Ouki, M. 2019. *Algerian Gas in Transition: Domestic Transformation and Changing Gas Export Potential*. OIES paper, NG 151. Oxford: The Oxford Institute for Energy Studies.

Oulebsir, N. 2004. *Les usages du patrimoine: Monuments, musées et politique coloniale en Algérie (1830–1930)*. Paris: La maison des sciences de l'homme.

Petty, Sheila. 2025. Environment, sustainable development and cultural heritage. Returns to the Mountain (*Retours à la montagne*, 2010). In *Habiba Djahnine: Memory Bearer*, ed. Sheila Petty, 55–70. Edinburgh: Edinburgh University Press.

Quevedo, A., J. García-Sánchez, R. Khellaf, and Y. Bensaidani. 2023. The territory of ancient Tipasa, Algeria: Archaeological survey, material culture, and connectivity in Central Maghreb. *African Archaeological Review* 40 (4): 673–709.

Rabehi, W., H. O. Housseyn, M. A. Bouhlala, S. Kreri, O. Benabbou, M. El Amin Larabi, and H. Dellani. 2022. Spatial monitoring of coastal protection dikes. Case study of the touristic Beach "Palm Beach, West Algiers, Algeria". In *European Spatial Data for Coastal and Marine Remote Sensing: Proceedings of International Conference EUCOMARE 2022-Saint Malo, France*, ed. S. Niculescu, 149–169. Cham: Springer International Publishing.

Reimann, L., A. T. Vafeidis, S. Brown, J. Hinkel, and R. S. Tol. 2018. Mediterranean UNESCO World Heritage at risk from coastal flooding and erosion due to sea-level rise. *Nature communications* 9 (1): 4161.

Shockley, K. 2023. Adaptation, flourishing, and the importance of place. *Regional Environmental Change* 23 (3): 99.

Stillwell, R., W. L. MacDonald, and M. Holland McAllister. 2017. *The Princeton Encyclopedia of Classical Sites*. Princeton: Princeton University Press.

Todd, O. 2015. *Albert Camus: a life*. London: Random House.

Tschakert, P., J. Barnett, N. Ellis, C. Lawrence, N. Tuana, M. New, C. Elrick-Barr, R. Pandit, and D. Pannell. 2017. Climate change and loss, as if people mattered: values, places, and experiences. *Wiley Interdisciplinary Reviews: Climate Change* 8 (5): e476.

Tuan, Y. F., 1991. A view of geography. Geographical review, 99–107.

Tuan, Y. F. 1977. *Space and Place: The Perspective of Experience*. Minneapolis: University of Minnesota Press.

UNESCO World Heritage List. https://whc.unesco.org/en/list/193/

Vousdoukas, M. I., J. Clarke, R. Ranasinghe, L. Reimann, N. Khalaf, T. M. Duong, et al. 2022. African heritage sites threatened as sea-level rise accelerates. *Nature Climate Change* 12 (3): 256–262.

Impactful Engagement of Scientific Organisations in Parliamentary Policy-Making: The European Geoscience Union Biodiversity Task Force of 2022–2024

Chloe Hill, Felicia O. Akinyemi, Viktor J. Bruckman, A. Rita Carrasco, Bikem Ekberzade, Adam Izdebski, Annegret Larsen, and Adriano Sofo

Abstract This chapter discusses broader implications of the activities of the European Geoscience Union Biodiversity Task Force. Created in 2022 from volunteer members of the EGU as a science-for-policy initiative, the Task Force focused its efforts on advising different members and groups within the European Parliament in the context of the legislative process on the EU Nature Restoration Law. The chapter deals with the limitations, potential and challenges in scientists' involvement in the legislative process in environmental and historical context.

Keywords Evidence-based policymaking · Science for policy · Climate change · Biodiversity · Science advice

C. Hill
European Geosciences Union, Munich, Germany

F. O. Akinyemi
Karlstad University, Karlstad, Sweden

V. J. Bruckman
Austrian Academy of Sciences, Vienna, Austria

A. R. Carrasco
University of Algarve, Faro, Portugal

B. Ekberzade
Istanbul Technical University, Istanbul, Türkiye

A. Izdebski (✉)
Nicolaus Copernicus University, Torun, Poland

A. Larsen
Wageningen University and Research, Wageningen, Netherlands

A. Sofo
Università degli Studi della Basilicata, Potenza, Italy

J. F. Haldon, R. Fernandes (eds.), *Bridging History and Policy*, Understanding Complex Systems, https://doi.org/10.1007/978-3-032-24379-9_19

1 Introduction

To enhance the use of evidence in policy and practice, numerous organizations aim to foster research-policy engagement initiatives. In the current timeframe with the effects of climate change imminent and biodiversity loss a recognized threat, the collaboration of science and policymaking has become a necessity (Evans and Cvitanovic 2018; Gluckman et al. 2021; Ekberzade et al. 2024).

Despite the extensive science for policy frameworks established by many governments and international organizations—such as the US, the UK, the UN, and the EU—ensuring that scientific information reaches every relevant policy or political process remains a distant goal. Therefore, rather than waiting for governments and other public bodies to reach out to them, scientists and scientific institutions should intensify their bottom-up efforts to engage in public policymaking. This, however, is not an easy task, not due to the lack of goodwill among policymakers, but primarily because of a perceived incompatibility of the worlds of science and policy. Policymakers prioritize fast decision-making and more immediate effects, whereas scientists generally need to invest a longer amount of time into collecting all the relevant evidence and account for both short-term and long-term consequences of specific actions.

Thus, without a realistic understanding of how policy works and without a workable plan in place, bottom-up efforts of scientists to engage in policymaking can easily result in frustration that discourages the involved academic experts and organisations from any further activity. For success in engaging with policy, scientists also need to address the "information usability gap" (Lemos et al. 2012) from the onset of the intention to engage. The gap arises because researchers often assume that the information they produce is useful, without fully understanding the needs of decision-making or policymaking processes. At the same time, end-users may have unrealistic expectations or misunderstand how existing information applies to their decisions.

In this chapter, we present a success story of a grassroots, bottom-up approach to policy engagement by a scientific organization. We explore how members of a Task Force created by the European Geosciences Union (EGU), the leading organisation for Earth, planetary and space science research in Europe, successfully provided advice to the European Parliament on the Nature Restoration Law, a landmark nature conservation regulation. The Task Force provided relevant, contextualized, and useful scientific evidence on key aspects of the Nature Restoration Law until the final text was adopted by the EU in July 2024.

As a bottom-up organization that is driven by its members, the EGU is interdisciplinary and inclusive by its very nature. With 22 different scientific divisions, it represents a vast spectrum of disciplines that deal with the study of the planet Earth and the outer space of which it is part. In recent years, apart from drawing primarily on experts from geology and geography, it opened up to life- as well as social sciences, e.g. by setting up an Inter-and Transdisciplinary Session program (ITS), expanding its expertise base even more. Its seven members who engaged with the European

Parliament—the authors of this paper, together with Chloe Hill, the Policy Manager of the EGU—came together through an internal selection process within the organization. They formed a task force with the aim to provide relevant and timely scientific evidence to European-level policymakers, and thus support evidence-informed decisions and legislation related to biodiversity. This Task Force decided to focus on the Nature Restoration Law due to its binding nature and far-reaching aims to set conservation and restoration targets for the EU countries that together should not only stop, but reverse the direct threats towards biodiversity loss in Europe.

2 Creating the Necessary Science for Policy Infrastructure within a Scientific Organization

The EGU is the leading organization for Earth, planetary, and space science research in Europe. With almost 21,000 members, it aims to foster both fundamental and applied geoscience research that addresses key societal and environmental challenges. While the EGU's most recognized initiatives are its annual General Assembly which welcomes over 20,000 participants in Vienna each year and its 19 open-access journals, its Policy Programme has been gaining traction in recent years with both Europe's scientific and policy communities wanting to support evidence-informed decision-making.

Established in 2016, the EGU's Policy Programme aims to both empower researchers to engage in the policymaking process by providing resources on how to effectively engage and prepare accurate, relevant, timely, and actionable scientific information for European policymakers. In addition to this, the EGU's Policy Programme supports Europe's science for policy mechanisms and would like to help strengthen the science-policy ecosystems and support the integration of research into policy. The EGU has a number of initiatives to achieve these goals including the EGU's Science for Policy Pairing Scheme, Science for Policy events in Brussels, Science for Policy Webinars, EGU General Assembly sessions and Hangouts, support for policy officers volunteering within their EGU scientific division, and resources such as the EGU Science for Policy Newsletter and GeoPolicy Blog post. However, the EGU Biodiversity Task Force was the first EGU initiative that aimed to provide policymakers with science advice directly.

The Biodiversity Task Force was created by the EGU in early 2022 to support the translation and dissemination of relevant geo-scientific information related to biodiversity. The final work program was followed by a thorough internal discussion with EGU's elected Council of representatives and joint agreement. It was decided that the primary aim was to provide European policymakers with the most relevant and timely scientific evidence available to ensure that new biodiversity-related legislation was underpinned by research, for the sake of more effective implementation and successful outcomes.

The Task Force was not only a new concept for the EGU but also a relatively new one for scientific organizations. It is often challenging for membership-based organizations to take initiative and provide scientific evidence and advice to policymakers given the wide range of disciplines and perspectives that they represent. Ensuring that the science advice provided is approved by all members or even a council of representatives can be time-consuming and often results in the advice being either softened or expanded to include more insights and information that is then not relevant or useful for those who need to use it. One of the first hurdles for the EGU was establishing the concept of a Policy Priority Area, a primary topic that the Union would focus its science for policy efforts and activities for at least 3 years. Having this concept approved by the Council of elected EGU representatives in October 2020, enabled the EGU Policy Programme to find a topic that would be relevant for both European policymakers and the geoscience community. In 2021, Biodiversity was selected as the EGU's 2022–2024 Policy Priority Area after an investigation into Europe's policy landscape to understand the policy areas that were likely to be at the forefront of discussion and a stakeholder mapping to identify who was already working on these policy areas and who would be likely to need scientific evidence. Both of these exercises were essential to select a Policy Priority Area that would be useful for policymakers and to help the selected Task Force members in selecting specific tasks.

The EGU Biodiversity Task Force's success was highly dependent on its members and it was therefore vital that members were chosen through a structured selection process despite the work being undertaken voluntarily. Experts working on biodiversity from all relevant disciplines, and independently of an existing or future EGU membership, were invited to apply to join the Task Force. Shortlisted members were subsequently interviewed by EGU's Policy Manager and EGU Science for Policy Working Group. The selection process aimed to identify individuals who had a range of biodiversity-relevant expertise as well as various policy and communication skills. It was essential that all members selected were willing to work with researchers who were outside of their own discipline and that they were comfortable working on broader topics that went beyond their specific area of expertise. Not only did this selection process ensure a well-rounded team of experts was selected for the Task Force but also enabled the EGU to build a dynamic group that was motivated to work together. From the outset till the end, the work of the Task Force was led and coordinated by the EGU's Policy Manager. Although the initial steps of establishing a Policy Priority Area, selecting a relevant topic, and building a Task Force with members who complemented each other required time and resources, it was also essential to ensure that the Task Force had policy impact.

3 Identifying the Ongoing Policy Process: The EU'S Nature Restoration Law

The Nature Restoration Law (NRL) is a binding piece of legislation that sets standards and thresholds to restore, rewild, and protect natural habitats (European Commission, 2020). As a planned component of the Green Deal, its proposed ambitious targets were expected and initially welcomed, but in a few years resulted as well in political polarization as the legislative discussions progressed. The Green Deal was introduced in 2019 as a roadmap to help the EU transition to a sustainable, climate-neutral economy by 2050. Although ambitious, much of the political polarization around the targets only began once specific legislation to meet these targets was proposed. The Green Deal was also introduced during a time when the imperative was seen to take action and play a participatory role in the passing of this legislation. Effects of climate change were more tangible than ever, and the loss of biodiversity due to anthropogenic interference was clear (Ordonez et al. 2024; Svenning et al. 2024; Hering et al. 2023).

During this time, the role of biodiversity loss in exacerbating compound hazards was not only a priority for the EU, but also for the research community with studies highlighting the threat of ecosystem collapse and the need to preserve biodiversity and ecosystem integrity at all costs (Ameca et al. 2024; Brown et al. 2021; Li et al. 2022; Walz et al. 2021). When the NRL was initially proposed by the European Commission, there was hope that the ambitious targets would help to curb the negative anthropogenic effect on ecosystems, not only giving them room to recuperate, but also the human communities a chance to find means to co-exist with nature. However, as the legislation progressed and was debated by the European Parliament and the Council of the European Union (the EU's two political institutions that are jointly responsible for amending and adopting, and rejecting legislation), it became clear that the ambitious targets proposed by the Commission were unlikely to pass.

The Parliament's right-wing and centre-right parties, Identity and Democracy European Conservatives and Reformists, and the European People's Party were against the legislation, stating that the additional regulatory measures would increase the burden on farmers, disrupt supply chains, and impact European food production (EPP Group 2023; Ruissen 2023, 2024). They also claimed that it would require excessive land to be reserved and subsequently unavailable for other uses such as food and energy production and housing. Despite internal and external groups, including the European Commission's own food security assessment (European Commission 2023), negating these claims, it was clear that the NRL would be more politicized and politically controversial than the EGU Biodiversity Task Force had initially expected.

In May 2023, the legislation's two associated Committees (the Committee on Agriculture and Rural Development and the Committee on Fisheries) recommended that the NRL be rejected. In June 2023, the primary Parliamentary Committee overseeing the legislation, the Committee on Environment, Public Health and Food Safety, held a final vote on the legislation that resulted in 44 votes in favor and 44 votes against the amended legislation with no abstentions. Without a majority in the committee supporting the amended NRL proposal, it was sent to the plenary (a formal session with all Members of the Parliament present) with a proposal to reject the text. The proposal for rejection did not pass in plenary (312 votes to 324 and 12 abstentions) and on 12 July, the final Parliamentary vote adopted the Nature Restoration Law with 336 votes in favor, 300 against, and 13 abstentions. However, this was not without compromise and diluted targets, including the removal of the legislation's entire section on peatland restoration.

Following this, the European Parliament and the Council came together to negotiate the final text as part of the Trilogue negotiations, during which the restoration of peatland ecosystems was reintroduced. This standard procedure is overseen by the European Commission (hence it is known as the Trilogue) and ensures that all institutions approve of the final version of the legislation. It was highly unusual for Europe's political institutions to continue to debate legislation following this process, but the Nature Restoration Law's final hurdle—having the Trilogue's approved text adopted by both the Parliament and the Council remained uncertain. It was finally adopted on 29 July 2024 after the Council pushed back its vote for several months and narrowly adopted the agreed-upon text by one vote after the Austrian Minister went against the instructions of her coalition partner to support the legislation.

So why did this piece of legislation, which seemed so hopeful when initially proposed both during the roadmap of the Green Deal and in its original legislative form as proposed by the Commission, become so controversial? And how can scientific groups effectively engage with politicized issues that require scientific evidence?

4 Providing Scientific Evidence in a Polarized Political Environment

When the Task Force began to engage with the Nature Restoration Law, the primary aim was to improve the legislative text, to help ensure it was comprehensive enough, and that it would be able to be implemented and monitored effectively. However, as the Task Force's work progressed, pushback from some Parliamentary groups and external stakeholders became louder and it became increasingly clear that the legislation may not make it past the initial plenary vote. This was surprising to the Task Force members who saw the initial evidence-based proposal and, from a geoscience perspective, understood the environmental, social, and potential economic benefits of the legislation's targets.

However, some industry representatives in the parliament saw the legislation as a direct threat to their interests and campaigned against its implementation. The Task Force was deeply concerned as its members witnessed some of these campaigns using mis- and disinformation within their key talking points. This ranged from misleading statements about food security to overstated administrative burdens, to falsely claiming that the impact assessment did not consider certain aspects. This misinformation contradicted research, was unfounded, and was dangerous in that, if accepted by the general public, would nullify sound science.

As the NRL became more polarized with misinformation seeping into the wider discourse, it also garnered more media attention, resulting in an increasing number of researchers and civil society groups becoming activated. This resulted in another excellent example of researcher engagement with 6000 scientists signing an open letter that debunked the misinformation that was being spread about both the NRL and the Sustainable Use Regulation (Pe'er et al. 2023). While this was outside of the scope of the EGU Biodiversity Task Force, it was an excellent tool to highlight the important role that evidence and the research community needed to play when talking with policymakers.

Not only was the increasing polarization of the NRL resulting in the spread of misinformation, it also made it increasingly challenging for the EGU Biodiversity Task Force to distance itself from the politics while providing necessary scientific evidence. Many of the Taskforce members had little to no prior political engagement. But there was a strong will and the realization of, from a scientific perspective, the imminence of the matter at hand. The consensus within the group was to put science first despite the odds. This set a standard and specific perspective to approach an extremely political matter, and helped the members to stay objective throughout.

The biggest challenge for the group was to get in direct contact with the MEPs who were involved in the legislation process. The EGU's Policy Manager set up parliamentary contacts through her network. The group agreed to communicate the scientific message to everyone, not just to a specific audience, but also to MEPs from different political camps—including those who strongly opposed the NRL. Members of the Task Force also volunteered to reach out to specific members in their native language where possible, increasing the likelihood of the information being used. It was imperative not to leave anyone behind, and bring everyone on the same page to take imminent measures to restore nature.

5 Step One: Making ourselves Known

The European Commission's first consultation for the EU Nature Restoration Law was opened between 11 January 2021 and 05 April 2021, and involved gathering input from stakeholders, including scientists, environmental organizations, industry representatives, and the public. The Task Force was not formed in time for the first consultation, but was ready to respond to the second open consultation for the EU Nature Restoration Law which took place between June 24th and August 22nd, 2022. This consultation also invited scientists, environmental organisations, and other representatives of different social and interest groups, to contribute by any means to technically strengthen the nature restoration agenda. The Task Force responded to this request by providing timely and relevant scientific feedback and publishing a longer document, the *EGU Biodiversity Task Force Response to the EU Nature Restoration Law* (Hill et al. 2022), that provided more details and scientific evidence on each of the points outlined in the direct response.

This document was disseminated to key policymakers in the European Parliament and Commission along with other stakeholders who were engaging with the Nature

Restoration Law. It was made public on the EGU website and distributed to other researchers via the EGU's GeoPolicy Blog and Science for Policy Newsletter. The document provided specific suggestions to improve practices, and engage community and other stakeholders more efficiently.

The Task Force emphasized the importance of enhancing future environmental preparedness by accounting for the impacts of climate change and human activities on natural resources. Additionally, they advocated for the incorporation of remediation strategies within the Nature Restoration Law to address biodiversity degradation resulting from past actions. The Task Force also recommended recognizing soil health as a crucial target for restoration due to its direct relationship with biodiversity. The members called for clearer and more robust ecosystem targets to prioritize restoration efforts based on quantifiable milestones and implementation costs. Moreover, they highlighted the need for research on ecosystem feedback mechanisms and socio-ecological systems to strengthen connectivity between ecosystems. Facilitating knowledge transfer among Member States was crucial to accelerate action, avoid duplication, and create universal guides and indicators to support effective application and monitoring of the Nature Restoration Law. Finally, the Task Force highlighted the need for increased community engagement, through evidence-informed initiatives that incorporate local (indigenous) knowledge to enhance the implementation of restoration measures.

6 Step Two: Direct Engagement with the European Parliament

To further disseminate the evidence and recommendations provided in the Task Force's response to the European Commission consultation and supplementary report, the Task Force hosted the event "Supporting EU's biodiversity targets by bridging the science-policy divide" (European Bureau for Conservation and Development 2022) in collaboration with the European Parliament Intergroup on Climate Change, Biodiversity and Sustainable Development. This event was hosted inside the European Parliament on November 15th, 2022 and was chaired by Helen Glaves (EGU President, 2021 to 2023; EGU News 2022). Highlighting the recommendations provided in the EGU response to the Nature Restoration Law, the Task Force members present in the Parliament emphasized the need for scientific information to support the achievement of the EU biodiversity targets' by creating synergies between different ecosystems restoration plans, and maintaining the habitats' conservation status. They argued that provision should be made to collect science-based indicators on a long-term basis to evaluate the benefits that monitoring, restoring and maintaining different ecosystems will bring. The message of the Task Force, acting as an honest broker (Pielke and Roger 2007), was shaped in a way that aimed to support policymakers in achieving biodiversity targets in Europe through providing timely and contextualised scientific information.

Not only did this event highlight the key messages from the panelists below but also directly involved the Rapporteur and two shadow Rapporteurs of the NRL file, the Members of the European Parliament who were directly responsible for handling the legislation. This ensured that the Task Force was able to engage the three Members who were most involved and interested in the NRL, providing them with insights and building trust. Event report and further details are available as "Supporting EU's biodiversity targets by bridging the science-policy divide" (European Bureau for Conservation and Development 2022).

7 Step Three: Engaging with Other Stakeholders

The Task Force's efforts to focus on a pressing issue were rewarded. After the Task Force responded to the European Commission's consultation on the NRL, disseminated the outputs more widely, and hosted an event inside the European Parliament, they were invited to give a brief presentation on their perspective on the NRL, and join the follow-up discussion, during an online event of the European Parliament's Intergroup on Biodiversity, Hunting, Countryside. During this event, the Task Force members detailed that biodiversity and resilience of ecosystems are related, and that current restoration practices are limited in fighting biodiversity loss and mitigating the effects of climate change. The NRL provided a chance to improve restoration, move towards more functional restoration techniques, and include nature-based solutions. A strong point was being made that to counteract biodiversity loss, local communities had to be included into restoration practices. After several short statements from members of the Intergroup, follow-up discussions evolved mainly around drought resilience of forests and the NRL.

8 Step Four: Intensifying the Task Force's Activity during the Key Phases of the Parliamentary Process

The European Parliament's work to amend and adopt or reject legislation is far more than a single vote. As outlined in the above section, negotiations of the legislative text are influenced by at least three Parliamentary Committees (the primary committee and two associate committees) as well as all of the Members of the European Parliament who vote during the plenary. Thus, the discussion and voting period for the Nature Restoration Law lasted 18 months. This enabled the EGU Biodiversity Task Force to synthesize available scientific knowledge around the specific topics or themes that were being discussed, thereby providing policymakers with clear and scientifically-sound messages that were most useful to them.

8.1 Suggesting Amendments to the Nature Restoration Law Legislation

After engaging directly with the European Parliament via the EGU-Intergroup event, the Task Force was contacted by an assistant of a Member of the European Parliament with a request to provide some suggested amendments to the legislation. While the evidence and general recommendations to improve the NRL was appreciated, the assistant requested that more specific direction was given in terms of the changes we would like to see in the legislative text.

While providing specific suggestions to legislative text is a process that is relatively common within certain interest groups, industry representatives and NGOs, it is more unusual for scientific organisations and research institutions. This is because science advice generally aims to provide relevant, contextualised, and useful scientific information to policymakers without encouraging them to select one policy option over another. Science advice aims to enable policymakers to use scientific evidence in policy making but to allow them to make the decision also considering factors outside of the scientific information provided. Although providing specific suggestions for amendments that would edit the legislative text goes beyond this, the Task Force decided that it was an important step to participate in.

The decision to provide specific amendment suggestions was driven by the desire to ensure the evidence that the group had previously outlined was included in the legislation. Once drafted, the suggested amendments were shared to specific Members of the European Parliament who were the most engaged with the NRL. Many of the suggestions were taken on and subsequently proposed by various Members of the Parliament. Providing direct amendments to legislation is not a step that can or should be taken by every scientific group, however in this case it was an effective method of integrating evidence and encouraging greater scientific engagement.

8.2 Restoring Peatlands: Evidence-Based Insights for Policymakers

Despite peatland restoration having a wide range of scientifically proven benefits, including climate change mitigation, improved soil health, increased the resilience of ecosystems to extreme weather events, and increased agricultural productivity, it was still one of the most contentious parts of the NRL due to the potential impact that restoring these areas could potentially have on farmers.

Through discussions with those working in the Parliament, it became clear to the Task Force that Article 9, the one that specifically addressed peatland restoration, was likely to be weakened or eliminated completely. To ensure that Members of the Parliament had access to the relevant information, the Task Force put together a policy brief that not only highlighted the potential benefits of restoring these areas but also the considerations (Ekberzade et al., 2023). The group hoped that outlining the evidence behind these two aspects would provide an impartial, comprehensive overview that provided policymakers with the key aspects within a short document. This policy brief was also translated into Polish, a native language of one of the Task Force members. As peatlands was also an upcoming issue for national discussion in Poland, in the context of the upcoming national elections, it was hoped that this translated version would resonate with both Polish Members of the European Parliament and policymakers working on a national level. Although this additional translation step took time, it soon proved worthy as a major Polish opinion newspaper picked up the topic (Danielewicz 2023).

In addition to translating the policy brief in Polish, Task Force members also personally sent it to Members of the Parliament who were from their home country. While the working language in the Parliament is English, many Members of the Parliament and their assistants still prefer to communicate in their native language and also appreciate receiving information from the constituents whom they represent. It was therefore theorized that this would increase the likelihood of the email and attached documents (which were in English) being read.

8.3 Restoring Forest Ecosystems: Evidence-Based Insights for Policymakers

Article 12, Restoration of forest ecosystems, was one of the critical and heavily debated parts of the NRL. During the Compromise Amendments (CA) stage this section was revised, detailed, and in the end was quite comprehensive. However many of the scientifically sound and logical CAs were voted down later on, and the Article risked being killed altogether. It was imperative that something had to be done to keep forests in the NRL, so the Task Force penned what would later be known as their "Forest document".

Almost 39% of the entire area of EU-27 is covered by forests, ranging from 1.5% (Malta) to 66.2% (Finland) across its member countries (Milicevic 2023), making the area of forest ecosystems roughly as large as agricultural land with a total share of 38% (EUROSTAT 2022). Forest ecosystems play a key role in climate change mitigation and biodiversity conservation as they hold the largest share of terrestrial carbon and at the same time provide a multitude of niches for species, thus preserving biodiversity. Moreover, the use of forest biomass has the potential to abate CO2 emissions if it is used as construction material and replacing traditional construction materials, such as steel and concrete, or when used as a feedstock material for energy generation. As such, it is one of the few options that provide renewable energy while not being intermittent. At the same time, services provided by forests are threatened by the changing climate, including the devastating wildfires of recent years, as well as large-scale forest dieback due to droughts and associated bark beetle infestations which bring back memories of the great forest dieback discussions in the 80s.

The key challenge is that forest ecosystems are very diverse. They extend within a wide horizontal and vertical spread, from warm and dry lowland mediterranean to alpine and boreal forests. Consequently, there is no silver bullet solution, and measures taken will have different implications in member countries, leading to an ambivalent discussion. Yet the Task Force believed that the inclusion of forests in the NRL was of utmost importance, and the members therefore suggested the implementation of a series of key indicators that describe the state of a given forested area. Essential for tracking changes is a monitoring system that would provide constant information and updates of key indicators. They therefore emphasized that the use of existing monitoring systems and national assessments should provide the basis for the consistent monitoring approach.

The resulting document, "Restoring Forest Ecosystems: Evidence-based insights for policymakers" (Hill et al. 2023) emphasized the need of including forests in the NRL; highlighted the benefits of forest ecosystem restoration, in particular for addressing climate change and the biodiversity crisis (and its interconnection); suggested pathways on how to approach and monitor a successful forest ecosystem restoration while acknowledging the entire range of ecosystem services provided by forests.

9 Challenges and Lessons Learned: Working in an Interdisciplinary Team

One of the defining characteristics of the EGU Biodiversity Task Force was the broad range of expertise and skills of its individual members. As policy challenges become more complex, it is becoming increasingly important to provide science advice that considers a range of scientific perspectives. This provides policymakers with a broader range of relevant information and helps to ensure that key aspects are not overlooked. However, working within an interdisciplinary team requires flexibility, active listening, greater project management and a longer amount of time.

While working in an interdisciplinary team had some challenges, the Task Force members found it incredibly rewarding and were able to produce more relevant, contextualised, and useful information for policymakers than they would have been able to otherwise. Therefore, we hereby recommend that any group or task force established with the intent to provide science advice should first consider the range of expertise that is likely to be useful, and then aim to integrate a wide range of scientific disciplines.

9.1 Understanding the Political Landscape

Each political region (whether it be local, national or international) has its own political landscape that researchers should aim to understand before or at least while engaging with it. Understanding the political landscape enables scientific groups to better understand the current and upcoming legislation and what the information needs of policymakers are likely to be. Without this understanding, it is more likely that the information synthesized and disseminated to the policy community will not be relevant to their work and therefore will not be used. The stakeholder mapping that was undertaken prior to the establishment of the Biodiversity Task Force ensured that a relevant, albeit broad range of topics was selected. Scoping out the landscape and understanding what the policy community needed took another 3 months once the Task Force was established. While time consuming, the brainstorming sessions and the stakeholder mapping ensured that the scientific evidence provided by the group in the following years was used in an efficient and relevant manner. Ongoing landscape mapping and discussions with those working on the Nature Restoration Law throughout the 3 years of the Biodiversity Task Force's work guaranteed that the documents produced directly addressed the policy needs and were therefore compact, relevant and useful.

Both the policy and research community have a very limited amount of time and it is therefore vital that all scientific advice and policy engagement is strategic. Understanding the policy landscape that you are aiming to engage with before creating a Task Force can help to ensure that the topic selected is relevant and timely. Furthermore, it is essential to continue to build upon this knowledge as the political landscape and policy needs change.

9.2 *Maintaining the Role of Honest Broker*

Pielke and Roger (2007), describes the honest broker as a scientist or groups of researchers who aim to provide policymakers with relevant, synthesized, and contextualised information without narrowing the scope of the choices that the policymaker has. Rather than advocating for a specific outcome or policy option, they aim to support the policymaker in making an evidence-informed decision given the best available scientific evidence.

At the onset, neither the EGU nor the members of the Task Force expected that they would get involved in a policy process that would turn into a heated political debate. This means that while initially the Task Force expected to fulfill a safe and comfortable honest broker expert role, they instead had to carefully navigate between political hurdles to ensure that relevant and contextualised impartial evidence could be provided. In this regard, the Task Force made clear that their support for the legislation was due to the scientific evidence that showed the value and benefits that the NRL would provide. The Task Force also avoided diving into the political discussions on the social impact that the NRL would have on stakeholder groups such as farmers. Instead, the members decided to stick with providing evidence that was related to their own expertise—primarily aspects relating to geo-biodiversity and the environment. In not negating the social or political arguments being made for or against certain stakeholder groups and focusing on their broad but still limited area of expertise, the Task Force was able to maintain greater impartiality. Therefore, while policy is close to politics, it is important for scientific groups aiming to provide information to avoid unnecessarily engaging in advocacy or activism as this can detract from their expertise and evidence that they are providing.

In our case, we as the Biodiversity Task Force, entered the policy process with the intention of being honest brokers and our consultation report, as well as EU Parliament events (Steps 1–2), were designed as such. However, as the debate over the NRL and its coverage became highly politicised, and scientific evidence was either ignored or manipulated by lobby groups, we found ourselves moving into the advocate role. By doing so we were in fact advocating for sound science, and we ensured that we kept our advocacy for the NRL within the boundaries of scientific evidence. However, while aiming solely for maintaining the honest broker's role seemed more aligned with the goals of the EGU and our own values, we were concerned that due to our stance and advice we could be perceived as issue advocates. For instance, in Step 4, could preparing the peatland document at the point when peatland protection was removed from the NRL, and sending this document to MEPs and the media, still be considered just brokering of scientific evidence, or were we in fact advocating for an issue?

9.3 *Keeping up with the Policymaking Pace*

Another challenge, a more practical one, was the rhythm and pace of the policymaking process. Policymaking, when taking place, operates very quickly, and deadlines or windows of opportunity to engage are short and imminent. It requires a group whose members are eager to rearrange their other commitments to engage in such a process that is much unlike anything taking place in the science world. What is more, there is no way one could prepare or easily plan: bouts of intensive engagement are separated by long periods of silence. Managing that for a single scientist can be extremely difficult, but for a well-coordinated group of scientists, with different levels of engagement and timelines, relatively easy to do.

It is therefore recommended that Task Forces engaging with policy processes have someone who is in a paid position with a dedicated schedule, and therefore able to spend a significant amount of time supporting the group and providing instructions and clarification when needed. A growing number of knowledge brokers, who work on the science-policy interface and have an inbuilt understanding of the policy landscape in which the scientific group is aiming to engage with are now being hired by research institutions and organisations for this purpose.

9.4 *Direct Engagement with Legal Text*

One more challenge—again, rather unexpected that the Task Force came across was the need to propose legal texts for amendments at certain stages of the legislative process. Science organisations aim for impartiality and distance themselves from politics, and hence do not consider themselves as potentially involved in drafting a legislation text. The Task Force members did not plan to participate in this either, and were not prepared to do it. However, this is what most policymakers, especially at the parliament level ultimately aim for, and due to our success, we were invited to participate in this process. As the members of the Task Force, we felt unprepared, we had to reach out, and create an *ad hoc* external network of legal support.

The main lesson here is that the policy world, and in particular politics, is not familiar with the idea of the honest broker who should step back in the very final moment, before the actual legal text or concrete solutions for real problems are being constructed. Conversely, this is something that the lobbyists do: their goal is to influence legal text or and its implementation. In our opinion, if scientists or science organisations decide to engage in the policymaking process, they should be ready to also take this step and not fear for their credibility. They owe this to the society who funds their research and their existence, and whether they engage in this final step or not, it does not affect their stance as participants of the policy or political process. It just leaves them less influential and successful.

10 Conclusions: What Worked and Why

In the end, the Biodiversity Task Force was successful, their level of success measured by the passing of the Nature Restoration Law and the concrete solutions it adopted, in particular, the peatland and forest articles. Obviously, this was not our work alone on the science side, but that of dozens of other scientists and organisations who had been conducting research and contributing to a vast array of scientific evidence. We merely tapped into that pool of knowledge, from our individual scientific disciplines, and where necessary we reached out to our colleagues and peers to support our mission to uphold science in an era of misinformation. In the end, from our own perspective, we succeeded in engaging in a policymaking process that had a positive outcome for society and nature. But this, of course, is never a given and scientists should be prepared for negative outcomes too, including complete failures, and should think of policymaking and politics as a long-term process, which a scientist can get in and out of depending on their career stage, availability, and personal values and goals.

Our success would not have been possible without a facilitator/coordinator—the Policy Manager of the EGU—whose existing networks and time needed to maintain and expand them, were crucial for our engagement in the policy process. This person also monitored the entire policymaking process and "activated" our group whenever needed or relevant. Consequently, we recommend that universities and science organisations who want to get involved in science for policy hire officers or managers who could fulfill this role, as it is not possible for scientists to do it on their own. Scientists maintain their own networks in other realms, i.e. in science, and it is not possible for them to follow both their own research, the developments in their field, and the policy making process which can be complicated. Both are needed for successful activities in the realm of science for policy. Importantly, even if such manager or officer roles exist at some universities, such persons are often not easily accessible to scientists, and our suggestion would be to appoint topical officers. In our case, it worked out because our policy officer focused on the Nature Restoration Law and during the lifetime of the Task Force, was always available for us and vigilant. Thus, in a university setting, a policy officer should be assigned a specific law or topic, at least for a period of 2–3 years, and communicate this to scientists at the university, and then work with them together in a broker or advocate role. Scientists involved in policy, in turn, should accept that their role is to be generalists for their field and discipline, to collect and critically evaluate and synthesise the evidence, from publications and from expert colleagues—rather than to promote their own ideas and research results, which will almost always be too narrow to meet the needs of a policy process.

References

Ameca, E., Y. Nie, R. Wu, R. Mittermeier, W. Foden, and F. Wei. 2024. Identifying protected areas in biodiversity hotspots at risk from climate and human-induced compound events for conserving threatened species. *The Science of the Total Environment* 938:173192. https://doi.org/10.1016/j.scitotenv.2024.173192.

Brown, Ch. J., et al. 2021. Opportunities for improving recognition of coastal wetlands in global ecosystem assessment frameworks. *Ecological Indicators* 126:107694. https://doi.org/10.1016/j.ecolind.2021.107694.

Danielewicz, M. 2023. Gdy słyszycie "torf", wzruszacie ramionami. A to coś, bez czego sobie nie poradzimy. *Gazeta Wyborcza*, 12.07.2023 https://poznan.wyborcza.pl/poznan/7,36001,29962777,gdy-slyszycie-torf-wzruszacie-ramionami-a-to-cos-bez-czego.html

Evans, M. C., and C. Cvitanovic. 2018. An introduction to achieving policy impact for early career researchers. *Palgrave Communications* 4:88. https://doi.org/10.1057/s41599-018-0144-2.

EGU News. 2022. *Supporting EU's biodiversity targets by bridging the science-policy divide: An EGU-Intergroup event!* Accessed Feb 14, 2025, from https://www.egu.eu/news/927/

European Bureau for Conservation and Development. 2022. *Hybrid Event: Supporting EU's biodiversity targets by bridging the science-policy divide*. Accessed Feb 14, 2025, from https://ebcd.org/events/hybrid-event-supporting-eus-biodiversity-targets-by-bridging-the-science-policy-divide/

European Commission. 2023. *Commission acts for global food security and for supporting EU farmers and consumers*. Accessed Feb 14, 2025, from https://ec.europa.eu/commission/presscorner/detail/en/ip_22_1963

European Commission. 2020. *EU Biodiversity Strategy for 2030*. Accessed Feb 14, 2025, from https://eur-lex.europa.eu/legal-content/EN/TXT/?uri=celex%3A52020DC0380

Ekberzade, B., A. R. Carrasco, A. Izdebski, A. Sofo, A. Larsen, F. O. Akinyemi, V. J. Bruckman, N. Baker, S. Clark, and C. Hill. 2024. Fostering transformative change for biodiversity restoration through transdisciplinary research. *Geosciences Communication* 7:57–61. https://doi.org/10.5194/gc-7-57-2024.

Ekberzade, B., A.R. Carrasco, M.J. Polo, V.J. Bruckman, A. Sofo, A. Izdebski, F.O. Akinyemi, A. Larsen, N. Baker, and S. Clark. 2023. *Restoring peatlands: Evidence-based insights for policymakers: EU Nature Restoration Law. The Biodiversity Task Force, European Geosciences Union.* https://www.egu.eu/media/filer_public/42/49/4249ec49-3987-4e38-b4cf-716fcae7e82f/egu_-_restoring_peatlands_-_evidence_based_insights_for_policymakers.pdf

EPP Group. 2023. *EPP Group withdraws from negotiations on nature restoration law*. Accessed Feb 14, 2025, from https://www.eppgroup.eu/newsroom/epp-group-withdraws-from-negotiations-on-nature-restoration

EUROSTAT 2022. *Farms and farmland in the European Union—statistics*. Accessed Feb 3, 2025, from https://ec.europa.eu/eurostat/statistics-explained/index.php?title=Farms_and_farmland_in_the_European_Union_-_statistics

Hering, D., et al. 2023. Securing success for the Nature Restoration Law. *Science* 382 (6676): 1248–1250. https://doi.org/10.1126/science.adk1658.

Hill,C.,F.O.Akinyemi,V.Bruckman,R.Carrasco,B.Ekberzade,…andA.Sofo.2023.*Restoringforest ecosystems: Evidence-based insights for policymakers*. https://www.egu.eu/media/filer_public/a3/0e/a30e2d50-e653-4702-94b6-cf0af80a120f/restoring_forests_doc_formatted_v2.pdf

Hill, C., F.O. Akinyemi, V. Bruckman, R. Carrasco, B. Ekberzade, … and A. Sofo. 2022. *EU Nature Restoration Law, EGU Response. The EGU Biodiversity Task Force*. https://www.egu.eu/static/fe2c2d9d/policy/biodiversity/Nature_Restoration_Law_EGU_response.pdf

Gluckman, P. D., A. Bardsley, and M. Kaiser. 2021. Brokerage at the science–policy interface: from conceptual framework to practical guidance. *Humanities and Social Sciences Communications* 8:84. https://doi.org/10.1057/s41599-021-00756-3.

Li, B. V., C. N. Jenkins, and W. Xu. 2022. Strategic protection of landslide vulnerable mountains for biodiversity conservation under land-cover and climate change impacts. *Proceedings of the National Academy of Sciences* 119 (2): e2113416118. https://doi.org/10.1073/pnas.2113416118.

Lemos, M. C., C. J. Kirchhoff, and V. Ramprasad. 2012. Narrowing the climate information usability gap. *Nature Climate Change* 2:789.

Milicevic, V. 2023. The European Union and Forests. *Factsheets on the European Union—2025*. Accessed Feb 3, 2025, from https://www.europarl.europa.eu/erpl-app-public/factsheets/pdf/en/FTU_3.2.10.pdf

Ordonez, A., F. Riede, S. Normand, and J. C. Svenning. 2024. Towards a novel biosphere in 2300: rapid and extensive global and biome-wide climatic novelty in the Anthropocene. *Philosophical Transactions of the Royal Society B. Biological Sciences* 379:20230022. https://doi.org/10.1098/rstb.2023.0022.

Pe'er G. et al. 2023. *Scientists support the EU's Green Deal and reject the unjustified argumentation against the Sustainable Use Regulation and the Nature Restoration Law*. Accessed Feb 14, 2025, from https://zenodo.org/records/8128624

Pielke, J., and A. Roger. 2007. *The Honest Broker: Making Sense of Science in Policy and Politics*. Cambridge: Cambridge University Press.

Ruissen B.-J. 2023. *European Parliament puts nature before demands of society and economy*. Accessed Feb 14, 2025, from https://ecrgroup.eu/article/european_parliament_puts_nature_before_demands_of_society_and_economy

Ruissen B.-J. 2024. *Adoption of nature restoration law unwise*. Accessed Feb 14, 2025, from https://ecrgroup.eu/article/ruissen_ecr_group_adoption_of_nature_restoration_law_unwise

Svenning, J. C., M. A. McGeoch, S. Normand, A. Ordonez, and F. Riede. 2024. Navigating ecological novelty towards planetary stewardship: challenges and opportunities in biodiversity dynamics in a transforming biosphere. *Philosophical Transactions of the Royal Society B. Biological Sciences* 379:20230008. https://doi.org/10.1098/rstb.2023.0008.

Walz, Y., S. Janzen, L. Narvaez, A. Ortiz-Vargas, J. Woelki, N. Doswald, and Z. Sebesvari. 2021. Disaster-related losses of ecosystems and their services. Why and how do losses matter for disaster risk reduction? *International Journal of Disaster Risk Reduction* 63:102425. https://doi.org/10.1016/j.ijdrr.2021.102425.

Information Flow, Legacies of Learning and Climate Change Adaptation in Norse Greenland

Rowan C. Jackson and Andrew J. Dugmore

Abstract Information availability, how it is perceived, understood and utilised can play a key role in determining resilience and sustainability. We explore two aspects of this: firstly, how information flows across lived and utilised environments; and secondly, how it passes between generations. Different information behaviours, information access and information limits can shape societal responses to environmental challenges, successful or not. In the study of information literacy and information practice, a key idea is that of *information landscapes*—where tangible landscapes are used as an analogy or metaphor. People navigate a metaphysical information landscape each time they interact with an actual landscape, and thus the tangible analogy or metaphor can itself be viewed in those terms- for example, tangible landscapes viewed scientifically will have areas rich or poor in potential proxy environmental records, some of which may have be investigated and other not; the same landscapes may have rich cultural associations related to collective memory, personal experiences, placenames, stories and texts—or not. We explore spatial and temporal aspects of information through a case study of Norse Greenland which existed from the late tenth to mid-15th centuries AD. Insights drawn from the contrasting information flows and outcomes for Norse and Inuit society in the past have implications for our understanding of twenty-first century approaches to childhood learning, sustainable practices and the unfolding climate crisis. We could learn from past experiences, and whilst not immediate and easily quantifiable, innovative approaches to education could promote, societal resilience and sustainability.

Keywords Cultural transmission · Childhood · Toys · Landscape learning

---

R. C. Jackson (✉) · A. J. Dugmore
Edinburgh University, Edinburgh, UK
e-mail: Rowan.Jackson@ed.ac.uk; Andrew.Dugmore@ed.ac.uk

J. F. Haldon, R. Fernandes (eds.), *Bridging History and Policy*, Understanding Complex Systems, https://doi.org/10.1007/978-3-032-24379-9_20

1 Introduction

In this chapter we consider the underpinnings of resilience and sustainability by examining the relationship between landscape learning, the construction of cultural landscapes, and information across the lived environment over multiple generations in the medieval North Atlantic. Using environmental, archaeological and historical evidence from the medieval Norse settlement areas in Greenland and the wider Scandinavian North Atlantic region, we explore three interrelated factors through the lens of information. First, we consider how Norse settlers in Greenland imported and adapted a cultural niche from existing environments in their homelands in West Norway and as they established land holdings in the British Isles and North Atlantic islands. Secondly, we explore the basis of societal continuity and persistence over multigenerational timescales by assessing how information was passed between generations and knowledge gained (particularly in the childhood years). Thirdly, we consider how information flowed across cultural and wild landscapes over the longue durée of the Norse occupation in Greenland to better understand its persistence for more than 450 years in a hostile environment, and its ultimate fate. This is with the broader objective of understanding adaptive strategies and capacities over the long durée and the potential relevance of this and other historical and archaeological case studies for policy.

2 Navigating Information Landscapes

Information availability, how it is perceived, and how it is utilised can play a significant role in the efficacy of decision-making in the long-term. In the contemporary world, information is abundant and plays a fundamental role in day-to-day decision-making through news media, weather forecasts, geospatial mapping, fitness tracking, and a plethora of platforms that support work, travel, education, healthcare systems, environmental monitoring, and social media (e.g., Harari 2024). How information is networked throughout society has a bearing on what information is collected, processed and acted upon (Lloyd et al. 2013). Beyond the networked nature of the spatial flows of information is the specific cultural behaviour associated with information gathering, processing and actioning—how information is perceived within a cognitive landscape, including the decision-making biases that drive the ideational limits and timing of components of that landscape (Ingold 1993; Henrich et al. 2010; Henrich 2020).

Several different spatially-related terms have been used to conceptualise the factors that influence information behaviours (Savolainen 2021). These include an *information environment* (Lievrouw 2001), *information grounds* (Pettigrew 1999), *information fields* (Johnson 2003), *information space* (Cisek and Krakowska 2019), and *information worlds* (Jaeger and Burnett 2010). In this chapter, we choose to focus on the idea of an *information landscape* as developed by Lloyd (2006). Her model provides a conceptual geography of the information world people navigate in many different aspects of daily life. The information sources available to a college student, for example, can include a variety of written material, lectures, peer discussion, personal observations and experiences (Cisek and Krakowska 2019). Lloyd (2012) developed the idea of an *information landscape*, using tangible landscapes as an analogy for every day information spaces. Whilst the explanatory power of the landscape analogy or metaphor for lay users may have both benefits and shortcomings (Fabrikant et al. 2010; Savolainen 2021), a tangible landscape can itself be viewed in terms of information concentrations, gaps and flows; it may, for example, include areas rich in cultural associations related to personal experiences, place-names, stories and texts. Spatial and temporal variations in the familiarity of information landscapes have the potential to make sustainable practise elusive (Crabtree et al. 2023). This variability of information flow from the landscape and how this is translated into human activities behaviours can be explored through historical and archaeological case studies with multi-century evidence of human interaction with changing environments.

2.1 Information Flow: Recognising the Drivers for Different Behaviours

The EnIFPe model of information flow identifies filters, barriers and distortions that allow users to examine environmental information utilised by different cultures and groups within a specified geographical range and timescale (Crabtree et al. 2023). Contrary to Optimum Foraging Theory (OFT), the EnIFPe model does not assume that practices of resource-use are optimised to local resource availability. This is because cultural practices influence the way environmental information is collected and interpreted (Zeder 2015). By drawing attention to the way environments are *perceived*, the EnIFPe model does not assume objective observations of a changing biotic and abiotic environment, but draws upon memories of previous environments, and social and cultural values attached to different resources (Riede 2012).

EnIFPe quantifies the disjuncture between the perfect and imperfect flow of information between a human community and a resource landscape comprising both a constructed niche and wild foraging areas. To address this, a consilience of palaeoenvironmental, archaeological, historical, and environmental information is needed. *Total Information* (*Int*) refers to information about all possible environmental variability over a defined timescale. *Available Information* (*Ina*) refers to information that humans have available to them at each chosen time interval. *Usable Information* (*Inu*) recognised that not all available information is usable in each defined cultural group and may also be subject to significant processing costs. Finally, *Wielded Information* (*Inw*) is the information implemented to utilise environmental resources for human benefit (Crabtree et al. 2023). The EnIFPe model also incorporates the term (λ) for information limited or degraded by perception. Information may be lost in intergenerational transmission, spatial limitations across the landscape, migration to new environments, losses in sharing, cognitive losses such as memory, and other social and cultural factors limiting the fidelity, quality, or identification of environmental information (Laland et al. 2016; Laland and O'Brien 2010; Mesoudi 2016).

Accounting for perceptual limitations, Crabtree et al. (2023) formalise this model in the following equation:

$$In_w = \left(\left(\left(In_t\left(\lambda\right)\right)\eta_p\right)\eta_a\right)$$

Or:

$$In_t\left(\lambda\right) = In_a$$

$$\left(In_a\right)\eta_p = In_{u.}$$

$$\left(In_u\right)\eta_a = In_w$$

Where:

In_t = total information
In_a = available information
In_u = usable information
In_w = wielded information
λ = losses of information due to perceptual limitations ($\lambda_{1...n}$)
η_p = cost of processing *available information* to become *usable information*
η_a = cost of actioning *usable information* to become *wielded information*

Each aspect of information flow captured in the model's equation is quantified using a four- point scale—no loss (1.0), partial loss (0.75), substantial loss (0.25) and near total loss (0.1)— of information. Whilst this model bears similarities with OFT models it holds a closer continuity with ideas of niche construction (Zeder 2015). We agree with Marston's (2021) view that optimum foraging models allow the exploration of trade-offs of decision-making in agricultural societies, not as a theory of behaviour but as an example of an optimal use of information (see also Jackson et al. 2018). As environments are dynamic, the variable flows of information and the utilisation of this information will change through time, which raises the question how knowledge is passed between generations and how this intergenerational transmission may facilitate or inhibit adaptation to changing circumstances.

2.2 Information Flow Through Time

The temporal flow of information or the intergenerational transmission of knowledge has become a popular focus in historical sciences and heritage studies for the ability to follow the co-evolution of environmental change and transmitted cultural information including knowledge, beliefs, skills and symbolic associations with local environments (Ingold 2007a; Mesoudi 2016). Significant debate has also alternated around the processing of environmental information, including the mechanisms of cultural transmission between generations. For example, Pinker (2010) argues that human cognitive capacity is responsible for greater adaptability to a range of environments than most other species, whereas Boyd et al. (2011) contest that an interplay of learning and copying behaviours slowly accumulate over multiple generations of social information and technological transfer. Such debates centre on the difference between the individualist 'cognitive niche' and a collective 'cultural niche' (Boyd et al. 2011). The latter focus on the basis for the macroevolutionary study of cumulative cultural evolution when viewed over multiple generations of transmitted information and practice.

Beyond this, anthropologists also debate the vectors of intergenerational transmission: notably whether information is passed culturally or socially. Mesoudi et al. (2006, Boyd and Richardson 1988, 1996, see also Mesoudi 2011, 2016) view culture as a Darwinian evolutionary process that can be understood through the conceptual and methodological toolkit of evolutionary biology. According to evolutionary theories of culture, social learning should be selective about copying behaviours (Laland 2004; Laland and Brown 2011), demography and population densities will influence the complexity of transmitted information (Shennan 2001; Boyd et al. 2011), and the evolution of techno-complexes in material culture and language evolution can also be followed along phylogenetic and phylogeographic maps (Riede 2011; Riede et al. 2016). For Ingold (2007a), this model is too reductive to incorporate the complexity of the human experience, including the processes of 'enculturation' and 'enskilment'. Rather than cultural transmission as analogous to gene flows, culture is aggregated as a social process of learning of how to operate in a complex socio-cultural system (Ingold 2007a). For social anthropologists like Ingold, the transmission and learning of cultural information cannot be reduced to a standard model of transmission, but rather a complex entanglement built out of apprenticeship and experience of the human and non-human world (Ingold 2000; see for example Walls 2016). However, Ingold does not suggest an incompatibility between cultural evolution and social anthropological fields. Augustin Fuentes has, more recently, expanded this call for synthesis—in what he terms the Extended Evolutionary Synthesis (EES)—into a model of the cultural niche that satisfies both neo-Darwinian models of fitness and reproduction and ethnographic models that recognise the non-reductive nature of each social and cultural context (Fuentes 2009, 2016). Synthesising these models rejects the 'linear causality' of biological models of cultural evolution but retains the importance of both human culture and human biology. In essence, this synthesis recognised Ingold's call for an overlapping inquiry into the complex entanglement between human perception of the environment and co-evolutionary models of human-environment adaptation (see Laland and Brown 2011).

This call for an EES diverts attention from reductive models about improving information quality and transmission, and instead focuses on the complex interplay of spatial, temporal and cultural perceptions of environmental information.

Landscape learning (Rockman 2003), an approach developed at the interface between archaeology and macroevolutionary theory, provides a useful framework for identifying how information is gathered about resource availability when humans encounter new or unfamiliar environments, and considers how information flows between generations (Rockman 2003, 2009).

Adding a further strand to this integrative approach, Fuentes (2009, 2016) utilises Bourdieu's (1977) *habitus* concept that recognised how complex 'histories, patterns and trajectories of human behaviour' (Fuentes 2009: 15) form 'structuring structures' (Bourdieu 1990: 53). We can think of these structuring structures in parallels with the continuity of complex and interwoven genetic, ecological and cultural inheritance—a so-called triple inheritance aligned with niche construction theory (NCT) (Odling-Smee et al. 2013). This conceives of the changes made by previous generations as having a structured influence on practices in the present and future.

For farming societies, the increased predictability of domesticated plants and animals within the farming niche can be understood through the triple inheritance model (Fig. 1) where humans and other organisms within the niche pass on genetic, ecological, and cultural information between generations to provide enhanced and more predictable returns (Zeder 2015). Critically, cultural inheritance is the accumulation of social and environmental information from previous generations through observation and experimentation with responses to ecological change over

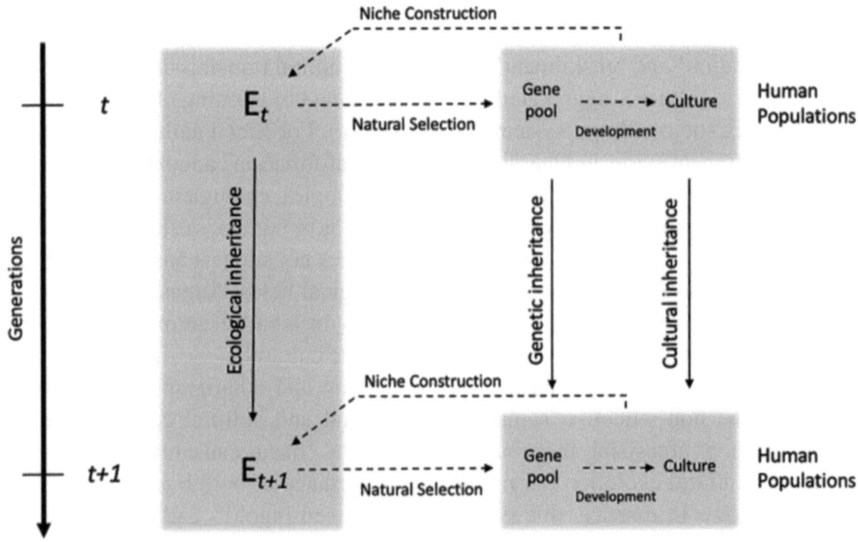

Fig. 1 A diagrammatic representation of the flows of inheritances between generations that are all elements of an information landscape; people shape ecological inheritances through niche construction, which also influences genetic inheritances through its effects on human populations; biological inheritances are be in turn influenced by those of culture which encompasses the intergeneration flow of information

multiple generations accumulating knowledge of how systems changework (Odling-Smee et al. 2013).

Combining the triple inheritance model from NCT with our EnIFPe model provides a way to exploring disruptions caused by a combination of incomplete knowledge, flawed perception, limited cognition and an unwillingness or inability to act on information that is available and understood- aspects of potential interest to modern policy makers (Crabtree et al. 2023). To avoid reductive models of decision-making in Norse Greenlandic society, recognition of the structure norms and practices that ground what decisions were made, when and why, and within the whereabouts of the perceived landscape is important if we are to perceive the landscape at the time and scale of Norse decision-making—rather than through the hindsight of our own perception of the past (see Lucas 2010, 2019; Hicks 2015).

3 Settlement Scales and Patterns of Activity: Habitus and Taskscapes

By focusing on household and landscape scales in tandem, evidence of everyday, seasonal, and interannual human activities can be understood in the context of environmental, political, and economic changes that take place across regional and continental scales.

The concepts of *habitus* (Bourdieu 1977) and *taskscapes* (Ingold 1993) have significant application in sociology and anthropology but have played a limited role in archaeological interpretation (Last 1995; Hicks 2015). Some social and historical archaeologists have described the utility of habitus, and particularly its usefulness in understanding how material differences condition social norms and structures within past societies, but this literature has remained highly theoretical and speculative (Last 1995). Because habitus explores the situated context of social norms and practices in society, it deals with the materials and conditions in which social space is structured (Bourdieu 1998). For archaeology, as John Barrett (1988: 9) explains, the material residues of the past provide evidence of social practices: "archaeology is the empirical examination of material evidence to discover how such practices were maintained within particular material conditions." The material objects within the household and the evidence of human impacts on the landscape provide an accumulation of evidence of social practices that were conditioned by world views, values, gender, age, class, external markets, political power, and access to natural resources. Connecting this framework with taskscapes adds temporal context to these material conditions and allow us to consider how space is used given the existing knowledge, technocomplex and material constraints of the surrounding environment (Ingold 2000; Hicks 2015).

Taskscapes is a concept first outlined in Tim Ingold's (1993) paper *The Temporality of the Landscape*, which expands archaeological knowledge of past landscapes from static traces of the past to a recognition of ongoing practices within a changing landscape—the activities that have shaped and been shaped by the environment. Ingold invites the reader to avoid clinical division of nature and culture to recognise less tangible but normative categories such as landscape, temporality and dwelling to connect rhythms and social practices of the past that constitute the human experience (see also Hartman et al. 2017; Hegmon 2016) In an article revisiting Ingold's influence on the archaeological discipline, Hicks (2015) argues that the focus of archaeology is revisiting of the temporality of the landscape. In other words, archaeology is an emergent discipline studying 'residues' of the past through cycles of accumulated knowledge and interpretation of the past as new theory and method emerges (Lucas 2001, 2019; Latour 1987; Chapman and Wylie 2016).

The material past may be reinterpreted at multiple scales to unlock new ideas of everyday, seasonal and interannual change in Greenland, and those of the Scandinavian North Atlantic more broadly. Focus on the household scale upwards aims to invert the perspective of the researcher from a downward, expansive perspective—a Euclidian view—of the past to a bottom-up, interpretive, and phenomenological perspective that examines capacities, social life, daily activities, and socio-cultural practices at different times of year and historical moments in the last 1200 years of settlement in the North Atlantic islands. This bottom-up view is the product of understanding our Euclidian view of the past, but also a recognition of the interwovenness of the material objects and landscapes that shaped Norse day-to-day life. This corresponds with the 'new materialist' focus on the relationship between people and the objects and landscapes that structure their experience, and, in turn, are experienced differently over time (Hicks 2015; Ingold 2007b).

4 Norse Greenland: Adaptation with Limits

Medieval Greenland provides a 'completed experiment' of c. 450-year occupation by Norse farmer/hunters in discrete settlement areas, whose provisioning strategies we can compare to a later Inuit settlement from the fourteenth century CE that continues to this day (Jackson et al. 2022). Having successfully established two major settlements in southwest Greenland—the Eastern and Western Settlements—and a third—Middle Settlement—in the late tenth century CE (Fig. 2), the Norse Greenlanders were confronted by two episodes of unprecedented climate change, the first in the thirteenth century CE and the second in the fifteenth century CE (Nelson et al. 2016). The latter coincides with major political-economic changes in Europe (Nedkvitne 2018) and the arrival of the Inuit in the Western and Eastern Settlement area (Gulløv 2008; Golding et al. 2011). We can explore initial provisioning choices, adaptation of the provisioning system in response to changes in the local resource system, and the different resource strategies selected by the High to Late Medieval Norse and Late Medieval and Early Modern Inuit (see Jackson et al. 2018). Using the EnIFPe model we evaluate the contrasting information flow and culture- specific strategies for provisioning and adapting the cultural niche.

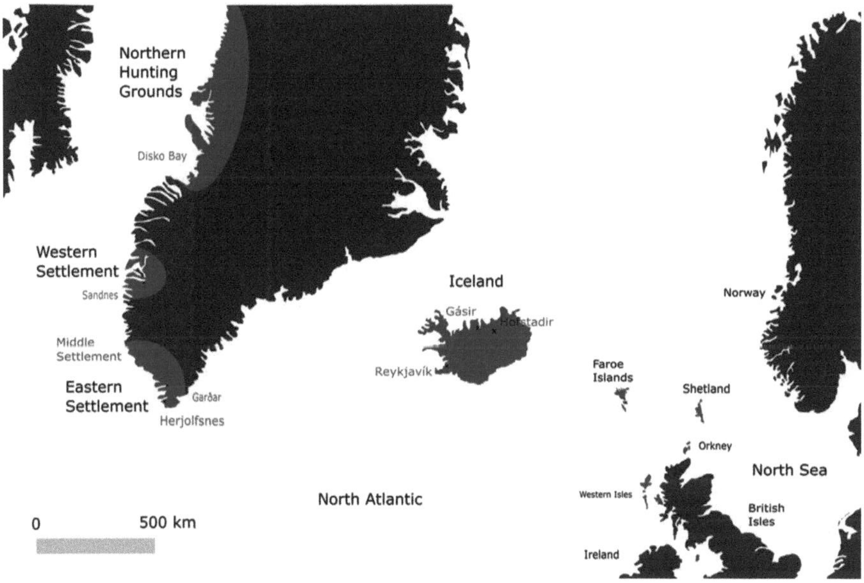

Fig. 2 Iceland was the key North Atlantic 'stepping stone' that enable the Norse to reach Greenland. The Eastern, Middle and Western Settlements in southern Greenland enabled the Norse to exploit the Northern Hunting Grounds for walrus and Arctic exotica; Ivory traded into Europe came from the west coast as far as northern Greenland. Trade routes from Greenland passed south of Iceland and the Faroe Islands, and north of Shetland to make landfall in western Norway

The Norse settlement of Greenland in 985 CE introduced am animal husbandry subsistence system supplemented by the hunting and gathering of wild resources—a balanced subsistence system developed in the Scandinavian homelands and refined across the North Altantic islands (Dugmore et al. 2005, 2006). In Greenland, animal husbandry required the introduction of both domestic animals and the construction of a suitable farming niche (Jackson et al. 2018; Riede 2011). Despite the sub-Arctic location at the fringes of viable farming, domestic animals ranging from dogs, sheep and goats, to pigs, cattle and horses were successfully introduced (McGovern 1985; McGovern et al. 1996; McGovern et al. 2009). In the marginal environments of the North Atlantic, the Norse could not subsist by animal husbandry alone– wild terrestrial and marine resources were required to support the early settlements as cultural landscapes and domestic assemblages were refined to environmental constraints (Ogilvie et al. 2009; Brewington et al. 2015). Farming was made possible by substantial ecological engineering- the construction of field systems and a range of agricultural buildings from barns and byres to herding structures (Madsen 2014, 2019). Within each island context, including Greenland, resilient subsistence systems were organised through a balance of both imported domesticated livestock, wild plants, and terrestrial and marine animals (Dugmore et al. 2007, 2012; Jackson et al. 2018). In the Faroe Islands, Iceland and Greenland, hunting and foraging remained an essential component of the economy and the subsistence system that included both heavily and lightly managed cultural landscapes (Madsen, 2014; Jackson et al., 2018).

The accumulation of knowledge about the location and timing of resources would have formed a mental model of the seasonal limits and constraints of the environment. This is effectively visualised in Thomas McGovern's (1980) model of the Norse 'seasonal round' in the Western Settlement of Greenland. Jackson et al. (2018) further refined this model to highlight the spatial distribution of Norse hunters and farmers throughout the economic year—an associated year with a long inactive winter and a short but highly active summer. As the seasonal round illustrates, the Norse economic activity is most intense but also spatially distributed throughout 3 months in the summer (McGovern, 1985). This likely created a task-labour balancing act that maximised energetic output relative to resource returns, with limited margins for error (Jackson et al., 2018).

The resource system was centred around the farm as an economic unit and embedded within a *hreppr* socio-political grouping of 21 farms around which economic tasks and legal disputes would have been organised (Vesteinsson, 2009; Vesteinsson et al., 2019). This organisational and cultural centring on the farm created a sunk cost within the encultured landscapes of the fjord systems and pastures of southwest Greenland, despite key economic resources being spatially mobile and abundant on the outer fjords or upland environments (McGovern, 1980). Indeed, the best explanation for the Norse establishing settlements in Greenland was their need for a base to exploit wild resources that were not available in Iceland in the late tenth century including walrus ivory and hides, furs and arctic exotica -such as narwhal tusks and birds of prey (Frei et al. 2015). Despite the focus on hunting as a *raison d'être*, a farming identity was maintained- even though the settlement had to contend with poor soils, and a restricted biota, and productivity limited by short, cool growing seasons and winter sea ice (Adderley and Simpson 2006). The result was farming close to fundamental ecological limits. The emphasis on a farming identity is evidenced by the effort put into landscape modification and niche construction. Archetypical Icelandic farms, with turf and stone buildings, home fields and herding structures were established, and the post twelfth century contraction of occupied areas focused settlement on the inner fjord areas of southwestern Greenland, and the parts most suitable for farming, but detached the population from crucial marine resources essential for survival (Madsen 2014).

5 From Optimised to Perceptive Models of the Norse Landscape

Central to the question of why the Norse Greenland settlements disappeared in the mid-fifteenth century CE is why the Norse failed to optimise their energetic returns from hunting and gathering, as did the Inuit, as the ecology changed in the late-13th and 15th centuries respectively? An optimised strategy that provide highly adaptive for the Inuit between the 14th and 20th centuries in Greenland was a mobile, diversified economic strategy that makes use of a highly refined techno-complex and local traditional knowledge of artic-subarctic ecosystems (Gullov 1997, 2004; Hastrup et al. 2018; Ford et al. 2015, 2018). Making use of locally and seasonally abundant resources, the Inuit adaptive strategy is more mobile and attuned location, timing and the transmission of information about how to efficiently utilise marine and terrestrial wild resources (Hillemann 2023). If this is an optimised foraging strategy, why did the Norse not adopt a rational response to environmental pressures?

We know that deviations from 'optimal' farming strategies can be driven by social factors: social status in Norse societies was dependent on the capacity of households to maintain cattle, which both provided dairy products and secured independence and reproductive rights for farmers (Vasey 1996). Archaeofaunal assemblages of domestic animals from the initial settlement period reflect mix associated with farms in West Norway. Whilst these assemblages were refined to reflect the harsh conditions of West Greenland, cattle were maintained to the very end of settlement, a persistence that may be viewed as the triumph of cultural values over the most efficient methods of provisioning in the sub-arctic (Perdikaris and McGovern 2008; McGovern et al. 1996). Cultural concerns probably made the maintenance of mixed herding an imperative even for low status farms with limited resources. Thus, pragmatic stocking decisions (such as switching from cattle to hardier collections of goats during periods of colder conditions) may have been tempered by social considerations. Poor weather, such as late spring thaws, cold summers and early winters would have hard-hit medium and low-ranking farms with small home fields, restricted fodder supplies and limited numbers of livestock. Farms unable to maintain biological replacement of their livestock would become beholden to larger farms that could cover significant losses with their larger livestock holding and richer resource base facilities (see Nelson et al. 2016 SI). A necessary strategy for small and medium-sized farms would have been to transition from high to lower proportions of cattle and increase the relative proportion of sheep and particularly goat species (McGovern et al. 2014; Madsen 2014) but also increase the harvesting of wild resources—such as marine mammals, caribou and birds.

Foraging for wild resources beyond the farm was a major component of the Norse subsistence economy. Dietary records suggest that initially 20–40% of Norse subsistence was from marine resources (Arneborg et al. 1999, 2012) and early archaeofauna assemblages from the 11th–13th centuries show high proportions of common, harp and hooded seal species (Ogilvie et al. 2009; Smiarowski et al. 2017). As the climate cooled further in the mid-thirteenth century, the proportion of ice-riding harp seals in the archaeofauna increased (Ogilvie et al. 2009), and in a consistent, related change isotopic data from exhumed human remains indicates an increasing dependence on marine mammals (Arneborg et al. 2012). The marine isotope signature of human remains increase from 20–40% in the 11th–13th centuries to 60–80% in the 14th–15th centuries (Arneborg et al. 2012). This correlates with evidence of increased sea-ice build-up in the Eastern Settlement in the late spring (Jensen et al. 2004).

This transition in Norse Greenland from farmers who hunted, to hunters who farmed has been interpreted as evidence of high adaptive capacity and resilience that did, however, have limits, and the settlement came to an end in the fifteenth century for reasons that remain enigmatic (Borreggine et al. 2023; Dugmore et al. 2007, 2012, 2013; Zhao et al. 2022). Was this conclusion inevitable, or was it due in part to 'sub optimal' provisioning strategies? In the late 20th and early 21st centuries, the disappearance of the Norse has been explained through environmental determinism, resilience theory, historical ecology, normative climate change adaptation theory (Jackson et al. 2018).

Various authors have speculated whether the end of Norse settlement was a function of choices they made (e.g. Diamond 2005; Dugmore et al. 2013). This brings us back to the limitations of medieval Scandinavian niche construction and optimal foraging theory. The Norse left a lasting imprint of the ecological niches of SW Greenland. Field systems they created are still ecologically distinct 500 years later, but there were distinct limits in the niche modifications that could be achieved with the technology and labour available to the Norse. Soils were enhanced, and fields drained or irrigated but fundamental constraints to the growing season and labour availability imposed by climate and the demands of the seasonal round could not be overcome. In buffering these shortcomings, Norse foraging and the wider extension of the human niche was effective from the late tenth century and into the fourteenth century and underwent major changes of emphasis after the climatic shocks of the mid- thirteenth century- but was it 'optimal'- were other foraging strategies possible but not followed, and if not why not?

Evidence from isotopic and zooarchaeological investigations indicate that the Norse managed cool and unpredictable climates by adjusting the proportion of cattle-to-sheep/goat and sheep- to-goat across domestic assemblages reared within the most heavily managed parts of the constructed niche, and by increasing energy intake from marine proteins gathered by hunting over wider areas (McGovern et al. 2014; Arneborg et al. 2012). Both the non-migratory Harbour seals and caribou living around the farming areas were exploited sustainably, and while this did ensure the animals were not wiped out, it did limit the total harvest possible. The Norse worked around those limitations by harvesting the migrating populations of ice-riding Harp and Hooded seals. Their populations were so large, that a limited number of Norse hunters, operating in the narrow time window available in the spring whilst the seals were within reach, could not significantly deplete their numbers and the potential for large-scale ecological engineering by the Norse was limited.

Assessment of this provisioning strategy in terms of information flow reveals some significant characteristics and crucial lacunae.

- Firstly, the Norse Greenlander's harvest of migrating seals probably drew on communal hunting strategies for pilot whales developed in their homelands in the eastern North Atlantic. This was characterised by a short-term communal effort to hunt a periodic abundance of marine mammals, utilising technology (e.g. boats) and techniques (e.g. netting, stabbing and clubbing) that were familiar.

- Secondly, *available, usable* and *wielded* information on the bonanza of marine mammals were likely limited because the location and timing of the springtime migration was shaped by sea ice conditions that were variable. Unprecedented climate change could dramatically alter both time timing and offshore location of the migration—with potentially dire consequences if the spring migration was late—or driven further out to sea because of ice conditions. As the annual spring seal migration became increasingly important for provisioning in Norse Greenland 'unknowable unknowns' were also embedded as critical points of failure. Unlike other staple components of the provisioning system (such as farmed products or the harvest of caribou and non- migratory populations of seals), information flow crucial to the successful harvest of migrating seals was subject to key limitations.
- Thirdly, a comparison of the archaeofaunas from Norse middens with modern records of seal catches by Inuit hunters operating in same areas draws out key differences (Ogilvie et al. 2009). Ringed seals are targeted by modern Inuit hunters - whereas these animals rarely occur the Norse archaeofaunas. Medieval written sources reveal that the Norse Greenlanders were aware that Ringed seals lived under sea ice and fashioned breathing holes - even though they did not hunt them (Schiøt et al. 2022). Considering information flow this suggests that there was awareness but knowledge of how to hunt these seals was lacking. The Inuit could hunt Ringed seals through the breathing holes in the ice because of their mastery of sophisticated harpoon hunting techniques, but the Norse Greenlanders lacked both the necessary technology and hunting knowledge- in terms of EnIFPc that means *perceived, usable* and *wielded* information were all severely compromised (Table 1).

The Western Settlement of Norse Greenland had access to reliable sources of caribou, which would have provided a highly energy efficient resource to utilise even if handling time to catch and process the resource was extensive. During the Norse settlement there, archaeofaunal evidence shows that catches of non-migratory Common seals were maintained at similar substantial levels before and after the climate downturns of the thirteenth century. Despite the cooler conditions post ca. 1250 AD, summer drift ice conditions in that part of Greenland were probably rare, which would have favoured the seals and the Norse harvest of them. In contrast, the Eastern Settlement areas, despite lying farther to the south, would have been affected by increased drift ice moving around the southern tip of Greenland from the east coast. The impact of this ice on the shore-based colonies of Common seals probably accounts for their declining abundance in archaeo faunas from the south after ca. 1250 AD (Dugmore et al. 2009). The depopulation of the Western Settlement in c. 1350 AD, would have meant the loss of both opportunities to hunt Caribou and Common Seals. Meanwhile in the southern major area of settlement, the Norse pulled away from the coastal areas retreating to the heavily managed constructed

Table 1 Energetic returns from hunting wild species that are found in Norse middens in Greenland, compared to the sum of losses of information losses due to perceptual limitations, the cost of processing available information to become usable information and the cost of actioning usable information to become wielded information. The highest fidelity of information flow probably related to Caribou, non-migratory seals, seabirds and mollusca. The lowest fidelity of information flow probably related to the Bearded and Ringed Seals

Diet Breadth Crude Rank						
Rank	Species	Catch Frequency (zooarch. data)	Mean Catch	Mean Kg Recoverable Per Catch	Information flow rank	References
1	Caribou	High frequency	102	48.1	2	Smith (1991); Kinloch et al. (1992)
2	Harp Seal	Medium frequency	135	36	4	Kinloch et al. (1992)
2	Common Seal	Medium frequency	N/A	26.5	1	Smith (1991); Kinloch et al. (1992)
3	Seabirds (unspecified)	High frequency	2.6	1.1	3	Smith (1991)
4	Mollusca	High frequency	0.2	0.2	1	Smith (1991)
5	Bearded Seal	Low Frequency	273	68	5	Kinloch et al. (1992)
5	Ringed Seal	Low frequency	45	18	5	Kinloch et al. (1992)

niche spaces of the inner fiords they would have both increased the costs of harvesting migrating marine mammals from the wild and further eroded information flows about them.

6 Perceptual Limits and Learning Where, What and when

If we are to consider why the Norse failed to optimise their adaptive strategies as the climate and ecology of southwest Greenland changed, it is important to consider the learning environment and the material evidence of structured practice—or material culture that structured the living environment—and the continuity of learning practices that influenced how children would have interacted with familiar and unfamiliar environments. To assess this, we focus on the material evidence of 'structuring structures' that conditions how the Norse learned within and responded to the changing environmental, social and political-economic context of Greenland and the wider Medieval North Atlantic.

6.1 *Learning Where?: Learning Environment*

The learning practices of the Norse would have been heavily influenced by the cultural environments in which children developed. In a series of papers by Riede and colleagues (2018; Nowell et al. 2020), the developmental setting and its influence on innovation and adaptability has been explored a series of prehistoric settings. These articles have drawn specific attention to the ability of cultures to transmit environmental knowledge between generations and to produce the optimum conditions for innovation. In particular, the characteristics of the developmental setting have been highlighted (Riede et al. 2018). The Norse learning environment would have had a significant influence on their capacity to observe environmental change and adjust behaviours and technologies to suit the demands of such changes.

The Norse were confined indoors through the long winter months and key activities were games, object play and the teaching of law and the church. What seems lacking was unsupervised time to explore the surrounding environment and experiment with miniature technologies. 'Unstructured time' has been recognised as key for the development of problem- solving capabilities and creative skills (Russ and Fiorelli 2010; Riede et al. 2018). Table 2 shows key characteristics of the pre-adolescent development setting, types of social learning (pedagogy), and socialisation for the Norse. Much of the Norse learning experience would have been structured within the household and prescribed to legal and moral guidance of the social and ecclesiastical elite (Nedkvitne 2009; Vesteinsson 2009).

Norse miniatures and objects of conform closely to central characteristics of their culture. The conformity of these objects delivers important information on how each child fits within the adult world and delivers important environmental knowledge in the process. As we will see, the conformity of Norse objects of play is suited to sedentism and cultural environments, but could have been found wanting in terms of preparation for hunting and adaptation to climate change.

Table 2 Learning environments and learning modes in Norse Greenland; these shaped key constraints on the flow of information, childhood development, and the ability of the Norse to navigate changing information landscapes

	Norse
Development setting	Household, cultural environment
Pedagogy	Prescriptive
	Dialogue, questions, reading, writing, situated learning, observation
Socialisation	Development, knowledge obtained

6.2 Learning What? Childhood Objects from Norse Contexts

Evidence of Norse social and environmental learning is more limited but can be examined in part through Medieval literature and the archaeological record. Norse learning appears, limited and conformed to the cultural landscapes and dwellings of the farm. Evidence of children's games and objects of play have been located within communal living spaces, which suggests that play took place indoors, especially in the cold, harsh winter months. This said, evidence of outdoor play—such as that with animal bones—is unlikely to either survive outdoors or be located within archaeological contexts.

Norse children's toys and miniatures may be divided into four categories identified from major sites reports in Greenland. Table 3 presents object descriptions, the number of finds matching this description and notes from site reports and publications about the object characteristics. The majority of these finds were identified in early twentieth century excavation reports in Meddelelser om Grønland, with a significant number of artefacts being identified in Roussell's (1936) *Sandnes and Neighbouring farms*. This site and excavation report describes the largest selection of wooden artefacts from any site in Greenland: Sandnes (V51). Significant finds from this site include a full model ship, two stem-posts from model boats and a whalebone battle axe. Other toys and miniatures were identified in the surrounding farms of Austmannadal 4 (V52), a steatite doll, and Austmannadal 5 (V53d), a toy trencher and a weaving sword or toy bearing a figurative drawing. These finds were all recorded within the household.

Other significant finds include two children's frocks (boy and girl) from *Herjolfsnes* (Ø111) graveyard excavations (Nørlund 1936) bearing a close resemblance with styles distinctive to Norse Greenland but bearing similar characteristics to those of other Norse frocks in the Viking Age and Medieval periods (Østergård 2004; Hayeur-Smith et al. 2015). At Nipáitsoq (V54), six astragal bones have been interpreted as a children's game. The smooth polished surfaces of these objects indicate repeated handling (Buckland et al., 1983). A more recent report on the investigation of Ø34, by Georg Nyegaard (2018), identified four well-preserved wooden horse figurines.

6.3 Boats and Sailing

In Poul Nørlund's 1930 excavation of Sandnes (W51), in the Western Settlement, one complete toy boats and two stem-posts from a model boat(s) were identified (see Table 3). Aage Roussell subsequently analysed the object finds from W51, drawing particular attention to the toy (Fig. 3), which was identified as a *Kvalsund*-type ship—a 4-oared boat—bearing similarities with boats dating to the 6th–seventh century from Norway (Roussell, 1936). The clinker-built design marked by characteristic lines from stem to stern, a sharp incurved stem and stern, and a hole

Table 3 Miniatures and toys recovered from archaeological excavations in Norse Greenland

Typology	Object	No.	Note	Site	References
Weapons	Battle axe of whalebone	1	Roussell notes the conformity with similar battle axes in Norway	Sandnes (V51)	Roussell (1936)
	Weaving sword or toy	1	"oblong weaving sword of whalebone with a slim shaft... could be a toy sword." "This interpretation would fit better with the figurative drawing representing a sword fight."	Austmannadal 5 (V53d)	Roussell (1936)
	Weaving sword or toy	1	"Could also be a toy sword"	Brattahlid (Ø28a)	Roussell (1936)
	Handle fragment of toy sword	1	"toy sword or weaver's stick"	Ø17a	Roussell (1936)
Household Miniatures	Toy cooking pots of soapstone	2		Ø34	Roussell (1936)
	Toy bowl of wood	2		Ø34	Roussell (1936)
	Small Vessels	3	Object not identified as a toy, but it bears the characteristics of a miniature	Ø71	Roussell (1936)
	Toy trencher	1	"Toy trencher (?)" Question mark on account of size	Austmannadal 5 (V53d)	Roussell (1936: 276); Imer (2017: 159)
	Small lamp	1	Object not identified as a toy, but it bears the characteristics of a miniature	Ø71	Buckland et al. 1983: 90
	Soapstone vessel	1	"Perhaps a toy" on account of its size	Herjolfsnes (Ø111)	Nørlund and Stenberger (1934)
Domestic Livestock Toys	Small carved horses	4	"Several small carved wooden toy horses were found in the mire. One of these showed an unmistakable resemblance to the Icelandic breed"	Ø34	Nørlund and Stenberger (1934)
Ships/Boats	Keel-shaped piece of wood	1	"Perhaps a toy boat"	Brattahlid (Ø28a)	Nørlund (1924)

(continued)

Table 3 (continued)

Typology	Object	No.	Note	Site	References
	Stem-post models	2	Two small pieces of wood identified as models—same rounded line as a boat	Sandnes (V51)	Nørlund (1924)
	Model Ship	1	Roussell notes similarities with the Kvalsund ship—a 4- oared boat—from Scandinavia	Sandnes (V51)	Væbek (1992)
Child Domestic Games/ Play	Steatite doll representing man	1	4cm in height	Austmannadal 4 (V52)	Væbek (1992)
	Polished astragal bones	6	"six polished astragali, polished by repeated handling, which may represent a child's game."	Nipáitsoq (V54)	Væbek (1992)
Clothing	Children's frocks	2		Herjolfsnes (Ø111	Nyegaard (2018: 31)
Total		**31**			

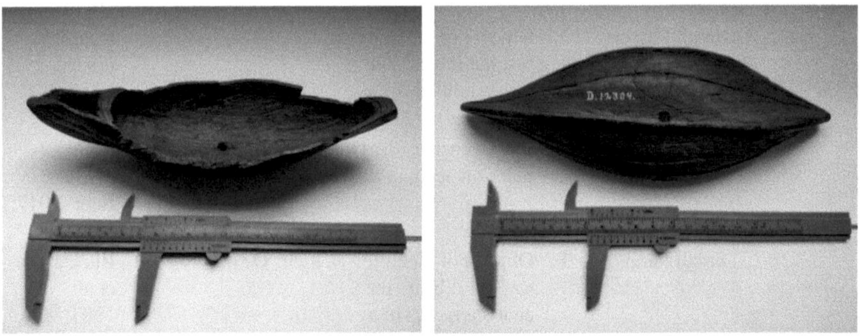

Fig. 3 Upper (LHS) and lower (RHS) views of the model ship recovered from Sandnes (V51) (Væbek 1992). Detailing on the underside of the model shows this is a representation of a wooden clinker-built boat. As noted in Table 3, Roussell notes similarities between this model and the Kvalsund ship, a 4- oared boat from Scandinavia. (Photograph: R. Jackson)

in the bow where the mainsail would have attached. The size and marking on the boat closely resemble the small boats used for movement within or between settlement areas (and hunting grounds) and the 6-oared boat used to travel to Northern Hunting Grounds (*Nordurseta*). *Grœnlandiae vetus chorographia* described the use of six-oared boats in the late-summer hunting voyages to the northern hunting grounds, where walrus and other arctic exotica would be hunted for trade on European markets (McGovern 1979; Ljungqvist 2021; Frei et al. 2015). So, it is feasible that this boat played a symbolic role in teaching children about adult activities associated with the Greenland walrus hunt (Nordurseta), as well as travel in the Viking world.

Several similar finds have been documented in Norse settlements in the Faroe Islands, the British Isles and Norway (Gardela 2012; Roach 2007). Roach (2007) records nine Viking Age toy boat finds in the Faroe Islands and fifteen model/toy boats have been identified in Norway (Roach 2007). All these boats conform with the characteristic shape of fishing boats, carrier vessels, or longboats, and in certain cases the clinker design and keel are pronounced details. However, the differences in the length and size of these boats suggests an emphasis on different boat types.

Viking boats can be understood as cultural archetypes, as vehicles of the Norse expansion and hegemony over northwest Europe and the North Atlantic. As Roussell (1936: 100) writes, "there is nothing surprising in a hunting vessel being carved out as a plaything." because objects of play deliver essential information about the adult world. Ben Raffield (2019) has argued that the co-occurrence of boats, horses and other domestic species play objects may have spoken to the martial nature of Norse society. However, the boats and boat toys would have also had a broader significance to expansion, settlement and trade in the North Atlantic (Jesch 2001, 2015) and to the emergence of a regional identity in Scandinavia (Price 2019, 2015; Crumlin-Pedersen & Thye 1995). The earliest representation of longboats is located in the bronze-age rock carvings from Sweden and the Ansarve Stone Ship, Sweden (Price 2015). These artistic expressions draw attention to the importance of boats for both movement and the development of identity.

Viking shipbuilding was highly adapted to the demands of local trade and fishing. However, the physical and ecological characteristics of southwest Greenland would have presented significant challenges to Scandinavian-style boatbuilding from the eleventh century onwards, their maintenance, and use. In Greenland, the climate is not suitable for the growth of standing timber and these settlements would have been reliant on external trade boats for movement and local driftwood and imported timber for repair and maintenance (Nedkvitne 2018).

The model boat could be interpreted as a qualifier toy, with which children could prepare themselves for seafaring or apprenticeships in the craft of shipbuilding. In Kroka-Rafn Saga this process of familiarisation with ship design is captured in an account of children playing with a toy vessel.

> It was widely told that Rafn Steinsson had built a sea-going cargo vessel, and this was regarded as strange news, when so many called him a fool. It had happened, however, that a Norseman with his son had visited Rafn's father over the winter. The boys were of the same age, the Norseman's son and Rafn. The Norseman's son had as a toy brought with him a little ship of the kind which in Norway comes closest to our sea- going cargo vessels. Before the Norse boy left, he gave his ship to Rafn, who had played with it when he was lying in the warm- house, and it was after this that he built his ship. (Edgren 1988:157)

The significance of this account, as Roach (2007) explains, is the relationship between the object of play and the construction of Rafn's ocean-going vessel. Though it is unlikely that the events described in this account are accurate, the account does reflect processes of cultural transmission and social learning. Play would have allowed familiarisation with the design characteristics of the boat and most likely prepared Rafn for an apprenticeship in his adolescent years where he could acquire shipbuilding skills.

6.4 Weapons and Militarism

Toy weapons are common among miniatures and play objects across settlements throughout Scandinavia and the North Atlantic, and feature prominently in written records (Raffield 2019; Gardela 2012; Callow 2006; Lillehammer 1989). Miniature swords, axes, knives, spears and bow-and-arrow sets have all been recorded in Norway, Sweden, Iceland, the Faroe Islands and the British Isles. Norse were a warrior culture and feuding may have been common to Greenlandic society (Lynnerup 2000). Accounts of children's play with weapons, violent games and behaviour, emulation of warrior culture, and demonstrations of masculinity feature in across the saga genre, including the accounts of *Njáls saga* and *Egil's saga skallagríms-sonar* (Raffield 2019; Miller et al., 2014). Excavations in Greenland have produced at least four toy weapons- an axe and three swords.

One of the most significant object finds from Sandnes (W51)—in addition to the complete model boat—was a small axe head of whalebone (L. 13.9, W. 5.1), classified as a weapon (Fig. 4). This axe head bears the characteristic shape of a tenth century Wheeler H axe head, though the shape is also likely to have been dictated by the brittleness of the whalebone. An iron axe head recovered from Tunuarmiut, bears a similar shape and size (Roesdahl and Wilson 1992; Kopár 2009). Roussell (1936) classifies this as a battle axe on account of the grain of the bone being worked at right-angles to the edge, which would prevent its flaking when in use. He acknowledges that whalebone would be difficult to sharpen and use as a work tool for cutting wood but does reason that such an implement could be used in warfare. Roussell (1936) does not, however, fully dismiss the possibility of this object being a toy.

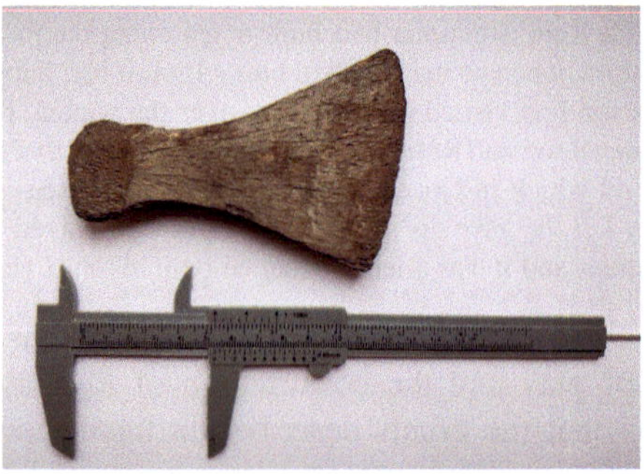

Fig. 4 A small axe head of whalebone (L. 13.9, W. 5.1) from Sandnes

> The unusual material does not directly justify our dismissing the specimen as a toy. In size it is moderate, 13.9cm from but to edge, but if we compare it with a number of iron axes… it does not seem to be so small after all (Roussell 1936: 105).

It is true that the axe is not the smallest axe-head recovered in a Norse context, but this is not sufficient evidence to infer that the axe is not an object of play. There are multiple examples of Norse artefacts that are made using whalebone. This is suggested to have been an adaptation to the scarcity of iron. Belt buckles, trenchers, a spade, arrow tips, and even an object resembling a padlock have been fabricated using whalebone (Væbek 1992; McGovern 1980). Roussell (1936) goes on to explain that the axe would have been strong enough to make "an impression upon even the thickest of skulls" (105–106). This is seen as justification to classify the object along with other weapons, and to interpret its design as an adaptation of weapon design to the scarcity of iron.

Three toy swords have been identified in Norse contexts in Greenland—two wooden weaving swords from Ø28a and Ø17a, and a whalebone sword from V53d. Across sites these site reports each of the finds is recorded as either a "weaver's sword" or a "toy sword". Weaving would have been practiced in each household across Greenland, and it is therefore difficult to differentiate these important production tools from children's play objects. The sword from V53d in contrast to the other two objects, bears a distinctive engraving of two warriors engaged in a sword fight (see Imer, 2017: 159).

Miniature weapon finds—including axes and swords—recovered from child graves in Iceland suggest that this was a normative gendered behaviour for boys of 7 to 12 years (Callow 2006). Excavated child graves at Stranmur and Laufahvamur show evidence of miniature axes and other weapons (i.e., knives, spears). Excavations in the Faroe Islands and Dublin have also recovered miniature weapons, including wooden swords that bear similarities with the swords recovered from Greenland Evidence of multiple similar finds of this type supports Ben Raffield's argument that toys associated with violence and conflict reinforced and perpetuated the cultural norm in Norse society. Such toys can be viewed as objects of enculturation in the Viking way of life—of societies characterised by feuding, disputes and organised warfare.

6.5 *Horses and Transportation*

Four toy horse figurines have been identified at Norse sites in the Eastern Settlement of Greenland (Nyegaard 2018). These are the only figurines from Greenland to be identified as toys. However, other horse figurines have been identified from other sites across Greenland, including loom weights and metal figurines. Nyegaard (2018) notes that one of the toys horses bears a distinct resemblance to the Icelandic breed. These horses also share characteristics with other toy horses from Norway (Christophersen 1987), Iceland (Callow 2006), the Faroe Islands (Dahl 1979) and the British Isles (Lang 1988).

Horses were an essential part of the Norse domestic assemblage for transportation and would have also held a symbolic importance in Norse culture, in horsemanship and for skirmishes in feuding and conflict (Hedenstierna-Jonson 2009). According to Raffield (2019), animal sacrifice together with warrior assemblages is traditionally viewed as the archetypal burial of Viking warriors. Grave excavations in Sweden and Norway show the ritual importance of horses and their symbolic association with warrior culture and status. In Birka (Sweden), two horses were sacrificed together with a wide assemblage of weaponry in a burial chamber (Price 2019). Horses were associated with pagan burial customs and masculinity, but the significance of horses persists into the Christian era and its symbolic importance is noted across Scandinavia and the North Atlantic islands (Nyegaard 2018; Raffield 2019). Horses were clearly a status symbol but would have been costly to own and maintain in subarctic conditions.

Horse bones make up a small percentage of the Norse archaeofauna assemblages in Greenland (Degerbøl 1934, 1936; McGovern 1985). Only two horse bones were recovered from Sandnes (V51), whereas GUS recovered 62 fragments (McGovern et al. 1996; Enghoff 2003). On Ø34, where the four toy horses were recovered, horses made up only 0.2% of mammal bones (Nyegaard 2018).

6.6 *Bones as Toys*

Objects of play do not only have to be pre-formed objects or miniatures. Ethnographic and archaeological evidence from Icelandic farm culture provides a record of children playing with animal bones in games and improvising bone shapes as toys (Callow 2006; Lillehammer 1989). In the twentieth century, children are recorded making use of sheep jawbones as pistols in games of cowboys and Indians, whilst in the mid-eighteenth century, bones were used to imitate farm animals (Eldjárn 1965; Callow 2006). Without evidence of object shaping or wear, it is impossible to know whether the Greenland Norse used animal bones as toys. There are recorded cases, however, where archaeofauna remains in Greenland do resemble games that have been recorded in ethnographic accounts in Iceland. Six polished astragalus bones from room III at Nipáitsoq (V54) in the Western Settlement have been interpreted as objects of play (Buckland et al. 1983). Polishing by repeated handling indicated that the bones were used in a children's game called astragals, or knucklebones, which derives its name from the astragalus bone—most often from a lamb (Lovett 1901). Similarly, ethnohistorical evidence of children using such bones to cast fortunes and play 'farms' has been recorded in nineteenth century Iceland (Árnason and Davídsson 1887). The correspondence between ethnohistorical evidence and archaeological evidence for object wear led the Buckland et al. (1983) to interpret room III as the main living area of the house where play activities could be conducted in a relatively safe environment.

The use of animal bones as objects of play presents a challenge for archaeologists looking to uncover evidence of cultural knowledge transmission and social learning practices in pre- historic societies. However, as Buckland et al.' (1983) research illustrates, analysis of archaeofauna specimens can show evidence of childhood play activities through a comparative ethnographic lens with Iceland. Evidence of children's play and particularly games such as 'farms' provides partial evidence of social learning associated with the spatial organisation of farming, and ingrains an identity rooted in sedentism and animal husbandry. This is further recalled in the oral history of Icelanders in the twentieth century, where children were remembered as having imagined the bones as sheep, cattle and other domesticated animals (Callow 2006). Bone play objects will be largely missing or poorly preserved in the archaeological record, but they are also likely to represent the most common play object in Norse society (Callow 2006).

7 Discussion

In this study so far, we have highlighted the efficacy of the EnIFP model as a bridge between reductive models of human behaviour, such as OFT, and models of behaviour that recognise cultural decisions in context and with consideration of perception of the environment and agency to choose beyond optimised energy balance. Such debates as OFT-NCT have been common across the anthropology discipline, whether they concern the neothic revolution and the transition from hunter-gathering to farming and animal domestication (Zeder, 2015, 2016), the basis for the primacy of *Homo Sapiens* as the most successful users of information on their environments (Pinker 2010; Boyd et al. 2011), or the local, irreducible complexity of human cultural practices, beliefs and skills to adaptive decision-making (Ingold 2007a, 2007b; Mesoudi 2016). Beyond but not out with these debates are important lessons for the present day and information that is important in decision-making about how we characterise human adaptation to the environment.

7.1 Utility of the EnIFPe Model?

The EnIFPe model offers a conceptual bridge between optimised and so-called EES models of human behaviour. It does so by avoiding assumptions of human behaviour to explain human decision-making. Instead, the model asks what potential there is for ecological information to be used by a given group. Costs of processing and actioning information are a product of perceptual limitations and the cultural choices and characteristics of a given society (Crabtree et al. 2023). Norse Greenland can be understood through four socio-ecological characteristics that shape the efficiency of information flow: scale, temporality (or seasonality), cultural preferences, and investment. Using these themes, we can explain how environment and culture interact to influence the utilisation of a resource system and its fate over different time scales.

7.2 Scales of Interaction: Processing Information Over Space

The scale of information flow, namely how large it is and how readily individuals or a community may follow this information within a given geographical area will have a significant influence on the intensity of information processing and the number of complex interactions. For the Greenlandic Norse, the spatial area covered to exploit resources for subsistence and market economies was vast and transcended both terrestrial and marine food webs (Smiarowski et al. 2017; Madsen 2019). In the immediate spatial range was the farm and wider cultural landscape. Land was cleared, adapted and augmented to produce predictable returns from hay cultivation and grazing for animal husbandry. This environment comprised infield, outfield and common grazing land, networked across the landscape from farm dwelling to irrigation systems and specialised shielings to support seasonal livestock grazing (transhumance) and milking (Ledger et al. 2017; Madsen 2014). Such environments hold evidence of high information flow, with sustained human activity throughout the active seasons on upland and outfield pastures, and the near farm environment in the winter months (McGovern 1980). Beyond the cultural environments were the known but highly dynamic wild environments of the outer fjord sea cliffs, inner fjord uplands close to the ice cap, and the marine environments stretching from Cape Farewell to Baffin Bay that were utilised for seabirds, caribou, and seal and walrus respectively. Such environments were foraged in the active season but were changeable and included significant numbers of migratory species covering a vast spatial range. The critical challenge for the Norse in Greenland, was therefore one of scaled interaction with a changing ecology. As conditions changed over time, the knowledge of how the local ecology would change were therefore limited by the capacity to cover such large distances in a short active window away from the settlement areas of southwest Greenland.

7.3 Timing in a Resource Catchment: Anticipating Environmental Change

Such interactions also change over time and can have unexpected impacts at the scale of catchment that users operate within. Archaeofauna from farm middens across the Eastern and Western Settlements, together with species migration data and historical records, the Norse organised their subsistence system within an intense active summer winter. As Jackson et al. (2018) explain, this intense window of activity made what was a highly refined and seemingly adapted subsistence system brittle to changes in timing of resource and labour resources throughout the landscape. Changes to the predictability of species within a shorter active season would have had catastrophic consequences for Norse provisioning.

7.4 *Knowledge Transfer and Childhood Learning*

This increasingly narrow window in the active season and changing predictability, particularly of distant wild resources on the outer fjord and northwest of Greenland, would have made existing knowledge difficult to apply (Jackson et al. 2024). Social learning and the selective process of copying is essential to the fidelity of information and skill that support adaptation to local environmental conditions. Cultural evolutionary models suggest that optimised transfer of adaptive behaviour will be based on selective copying behaviours, but the cultural norms and beliefs of Norse society provide no evidence that they adopted more effective Inuit hunting technologies and the skills required to use them.

In addition to information flows across land and seascapes, heavily and lightly managed areas, close and distant, it flows between generation, crucially shaping knowledge, world view, values and the ability to adapt to both survive and adapt to changing conditions. Analysis of Norse toys and miniatures, provides a vivid insight into how children would have familiarised themselves with adult activities (Jackson et al. 2024). The archaeological evidence tells us that Norse children played with objects that would have familiarised them with farming, household activities, sailing and conflict, but there is no evidence of play connected with hunting marine mammals. Whilst this may not have been an issue through the first centuries of settlement when a majority of the Norse Greenlanders' diet came from terrestrial sources, it could have become key omission after the climate shocks of the mid-thirteenth century when the harvest of wild resources became key to survival (Jackson et al. 2024). The restricted range of Norse children's toys combined with an instructional didactic style of teaching evidenced from written sources suggests both restricted information flow and a high degree of path dependence that constrained adaptation to climatic change. In contrast, study of Inuit toys, miniatures, childhood play, and learning shows they learn highly adapted behaviours locally tuned technologies and hunting skills (Boas 1888; Jenness 1922; Guemple 1988; Park 1998). Ethnographic studies have revealed Inuit approaches that prioritise unstructured learning aid the development of creative skills and problem-solving capabilities (Park 2005). In contrast to the Norse, the Inuit successfully navigated the climatic changes of both the 13th and 15th centuries in Greenland.

7.5 *Priorities: How Do you Make Decisions?*

In Jared Diamond's *Collapse,* a significant lesson he draws from the extensive global review of 'societies that failed' was 'decreased support from friendly neighbours' undermining vital strategic, political and economic ties. This is undoubtedly a factor in the decline of the Norse settlement areas, whether through outward migration or mass starvation. From the fourteenth century, the Norse not only experienced increased climate variability and cooling, with the onset of the Little Ice Age, but also political and economic changes in Europe that devalued walrus ivory in favour of bulk commodities (Dugmore et al. 2007; Nedkvitne 2014). Decisions about how to respond to external changes were ultimately cultural and about how information was perceived and processed (Crabtree et al. 2023). Imer's (2017) runic data from prayer sticks and other marked material culture suggests a strong devotion to European Christianity and the conformity of architecture and artefacts (Høegsborg 2014) highlight a socio-cultural connection to norms of life across with broader Norse diaspora of the North Atlantic.

7.6 *Investment: Where Do you Place your Priorities?*

Investment, not only in economic ties as covered in the previous section, but also the cultural attachment to place, ways of seeing the landscape, and the continuity of what is of social value to a group sits has an important bearing on the decisions that are available as viable options. Differences between the Norse and Inuit in their perception of the landscape were most likely substantial even if cultural contact for trade and even the potential for some level of learning was possible. The Norse were a Christian, farming culture with a calendar and religious feasts that correspond with churchgoing, land and livestock management, and the utilisation of a wood and iron age material culture. The material significance of each object within Norse assemblages speaks to the substantial cultural, social and economic investment in materials that correspond with a Scandinavian-European way of seeing the household, landscape and activities therein. The cultural filters upon which the material properties of the land, household and objects correspond with a social world cannot be reduced to rational decision-making about investment, but rather a cultural investment and perception of the taskscape—what action is done within the landscape and how cumulative cultural information and significance filters priorities and responses to external change.

8 Conclusions: Adapting Lessons from Information Flow

To contextualise information flow with contemporary climate change adaptation research, we adapt Adger and Barnett's (2009) *Four Reasons for Concern about Climate Change* to highlight four lessons from the past. This editorial highlighted concerns about how adaptation is translated into action, whether information is acted upon, and how different socio-cultural contexts respond to and perceive future impacts and risks differently. Our argument is not that information is directly relevant or analogous to the challenge of context-specific or 'place- based' adaptation to climate change, but rather that historical information has an important role to play for making 'humble inquiry' with policy-makers (Schein 2013) and citizen scenario- development (Davidson and Kemp 2024) about the mutli-faceted challenges of medium and long- term adaptation to climate change (Haldon et al. 2025).

Scale of information flow may offer a limited opportunity for action, leading to disequilibrium.

Adger and Barnett caution that 'the scale of change and interconnectedness of impact may… [limit] the window of opportunity for adaptation' (2009: 2800). In the contemporary world, greenhouse gas emission is contributing to 'dangerous interference' such as sea-level rise, flooding, extreme heat, and forest fires (*IPCC*, 2023). Culture can be conceived as both a capacity and limit in responding to environmental change (Adger et al. 2013). Limits and barriers may be encountered when planning adaptive responses to climate change, but while barriers may be overcome over a short to long duration through individual adjustments through to system-wide change, limits to adaptation cannot be overcome without major transformation (Moser and Ekstrom 2010). The completed experiments of the past explored in this paper provide spatial and temporal evidence of the perceptual limits and barriers to adaptation in the medium and long term. Local ecological changes can challenge the sustainability of adaptive strategies when they reach their limits if the scale of change is not identified, or the strategy becomes increasingly inefficient (Dugmore et al. 2012; Jackson et al. 2018).

High adaptive capacity does not mean information is obtained and acted on.

Countries and communities may have the capacity to adapt to environmental changes, but this does not guarantee that action will be taken (Adger and Barnett 2009). This is observed across span of the Norse occupation in Greenland and is directly relevant to information flow. The Norse Greenlander's had a high adaptive capacity, but the settlement disappeared in the fifteenth century. As Jackson et al. (2018) explain, the Norse experiences cultural limits to adaptation that created sub-optimal adaptive strategies as combined farming-hunting strategies became increasingly inefficient. This is because the Norse culture itself had co-evolved in temperate environments of Scandinavia and expanded cultural landscapes into the subarctic during the Medieval Climate Anomaly to take advantage of abundant, high-value walrus ivory and suitable lands for settlement (Frei et al. 2015). Cultural path dependency is an important consideration in contemporary societies and communities experiencing climate change impacts, as adaptive strategies will be constrained by cultural barriers and limits including food choice, attachment to place, and perceptions of the environment and ecology (Adger et al. 2013).

Existing culture-specific adaptive strategies may become maladaptive.

Concerns that existing adaptive strategies could provide maladaptive has been a subject of significant debate in adaptation literatures. For example, the characteristics of transformation adaptation and how this will avoid poor contextualisation of adaptive strategies (Pelling 2011), lags in adaptive planning (Kates et al. 2012; Wise et al. 2014), or the development of system-wide changes across society (O'Brien 2011, 2012). More general climate change adaptation literatures focus on barriers and limits (Moser and Ekstrom 2010; Dow et al. 2013; Berkhout and Dow 2022; Adger et al. 2013) and the sustainability of adaptation strategies (Eriksen et al. 2011). Such literatures focus on the challenges of sustaining social, cultural, and economic capacities to respond to environmental change (Folke et al. 2010). But how we make sense of such concepts is often limited to highly theoretical debate and without sufficiently long temporal horizons (Ford et al. 2018). Archaeology and history therefore hold impetus to explore factors underpinning to limits to adaptation, including unsustainable practices. As this paper has shown, information flow can be inhibited by a lack of accurate information about changes across entire resource systems and perceptual limits (see Crabtree and Dunne 2022). This has important implications for environmental management and governance because understanding how local resources, and particularly common-pool resources, requires a longer view of impacts by humans to determine accurate baselines and environmental health.

Local adaptations require intergenerational transmission of knowledge to understand interactions between multiple spatial and temporal scales of information flow.

Building upon the previous point that no one size fits all, assessing whether adaptations are successful requires information about social context and metrics to identify outcomes (Adger and Barnett 2009). Information flow utilises historical information to identify how local resource systems have responded to environmental change and what strategies are appropriate in response to environmental change. The Norse adaptive strategies were generalist and flexible to local ecological conditions in the stable climates of the medieval climate anomaly (c. 900–1250 CE) throughout the North Atlantic, but it was not until subsequent changes to climate, economic, political and social interactions changed that subsistence and market systems became stressed (Nelson et al. 2016). Without an understanding of long-term variations to local resource systems could the Norse identify the sustainability of their model of subsistence (Jackson et al. 2018). The Inuit, by contrast, were capable of applying specialised adaptive strategies that suited the local ecology and climate.

In contemporary societies, identifying renewable and sustainable practices that can share a regenerative future—bridging the health of ecosystems, society, economies and indigenous worldviews—will be essential to navigating the multiple uncertainties identified in international reports, including the Human Development Reports (UNDP 2022, 2024), IPCC Assessment Reports (IPCC 2021, 2022), and annual Sustainable Development Goals reports (Sachs et al. 2024). Taking a long view could inform some sense of the future we want and need.

References

Adderley, P. W., and I. A. Simpson. 2006. Soils and palaeo-climate based evidence for irrigation requirements in Norse Greenland. *Journal of Archaeological Science* 33:1666–1679.

Adger, N., J. Barnett, K. Brown, N. Marshall, and K. O'Brien. 2013. Cultural dimensions of climate change impacts and adaptation. *Nature Climate Change* 3 (2): 112–117.

Adger, N. W., and J. Barnett. 2009. Four reasons for concern about adaptation to climate change. *Environment and Planning A* 41 (12): 2800–2805.

Arneborg, J., J. Heinemeier, N. Lynnerup, H. L. Nielsen, N. Rud, and Á. E. Sveinbjörnsdóttir. 1999. Change of diet of the Greenland Vikings determined from stable carbon isotope analysis and 14C dating of their bones. *Radiocarbon 41* (2): 157–168.

Arneborg, J., N. Lynnerup, J. Heinmeier, J. Møhl, N. Rud, and Á. E. Sveinbjörnsdóttir. 2012. Norse Greenland Dietary Economy ca. 980-ca. AD 1450: Introduction. *Journal of the North Atlantic* 3:1–39.

Árnason, J., and Ó. Davídsson. 1887. *Íslenskar gátur, skemmtanir, víkivakar og bular, I*. Copenhagen: Hid íslenzka bókmenntafélag.

Barrett, J. C. 1988. Fields of discourse: Reconstituting a social archaeology. *Critique of Anthropology* 7 (3): 5–16.

Berkhout, F., and K. Dow. 2022. Limits to adaptation: Building an integrated research agenda. *WIREs Climate Change* 14 (3): e817.

Boas, F. 1888. The Central Eskimo. In *Sixth Annual Report of the Bureau of Ethnology to the Secretary of the Smithsonian Institution, 1884-1885*. Washington D.C.: Government Printing Office.

Borreggine, M., K. Latychev, S. Coulson, E. M. Powell, J. X. Mitrovica, G. A. Milne, and R. B. Alley. 2023. Sea-level rise in Southwest Greenland as a contributor to Viking abandonment. *Proceedings of the National Academy of Sciences* 120 (17): e2209615120.

Bourdieu, P. 1977. *Outline of a Theory of Practice*. Cambridge: Cambridge University Press.

Bourdieu, P. 1990. *Logic Out of Practice. Translated by Richard Nice*. Stanford, CA: Stanford University Press.

Bourdieu, P. 1998. *Practical Reason: On the Theory of Action*. Stanford, CA: Stanford University Press.

Boyd, R., and P. J. Richerson. 1988. *Culture and the evolutionary process*. Chicago: University of Chicago press.

Boyd, R., and P. J. Richerson. 1996. Why culture is common, but cultural evolution is rare. *Proceedings of the British Academy* 88:77–94.

Boyd, R., P. J. Richerson, and J. Henrich. 2011. The cultural niche: Why social learning is essential for human adaptation. *Proceedings of the National Academy of Sciences* 108 (2): 10918–10925.

Brewington, S., M. Hicks, A. Edwald, A. Einarsson, K. Anamthawat-Jonsson, G. Cook, P. Ascough, K. L. Sayle, S. V. Arge, M. Church, and J. Bond. 2015. Islands of change vs. islands of disaster: Managing pigs and birds in the Anthropocene of the North Atlantic. *The Holocene* 25 (10): 1676–1684.

Buckland, P. C., G. Sveinbjarnardóttir, D. Savory, T. H. McGoven, P. Skidmore, and C. Andreasen. 1983. Norsemen at Nipaitsoq, Greenland: A paleoecological investigation. *Norwegian Archaeological Review* 16 (2): 86–98.

Callow, C. 2006. First steps towards an archaeology of children in Iceland. *Archaeologia Islandica* 5:55–96.

Chapman, R., and A. Wylie. 2016. *Evidential Reasoning in Archaeology*. London: Bloomsbury Academic.
Christophersen, A. 1987. *Trondheim–en by i middelalderen*. Trondheim: Strindheim trykkeris forlag.
Crabtree, S. A., and J. A., Dunne. 2022. Towards a science of archaeoecology. *Trends in Ecology & Evolution* 37 (11): 976–984.
Crabtree, S. A., J. G. Kahn, R. Jackson, S. A. Wood, I. McKechnie, et al. 2023. Why are sustainable practices often elusive? The role of information flow in the management of networked human-environment interactions. *Global Environmental Change* 78:102597.
Crumlin-Pedersen, O.C., and M.B. Thye, eds. 1995. The Ship as a Symbol in Prehistoric and Medieval Scandinavia. Copenhagen: National Museum of Denmark (Studies in Archaeology and History 1).
Cisek, S., and M. Krakowska. 2019. The diary method and analysis of student's mental representations of information spaces as the research approach in information behaviour research. *Information Research* 24 (4):
Dahl, S. 1979. *Forn barnaleiku i Foroyum. Mondul* 3:3–13.
Davidson, J. P., and L. Kemp. 2024. Climate catastrophe: The value of envisioning the worst-case scenarios of climate change. *Wiley Interdisciplinary Reviews: Climate Change* 15 (2): e871.
Degerbøl, M. 1934. Animal remains from the West Settlement in Greenland. *Meddlelelser on Grønland* 88 (3):
Degerbøl, M. 1936. Animal bones from Norse ruins at Brattahlid. *Meddelelser on Grønland* 88 (5):
Diamond, J. 2005. *Collapse: How societies choose to fail or survive*. London: Penguin.
Dow, K., F. Berkhout, B. L. Preston, R. J. T. Klein, G. Midgley, and M. R. Shaw. 2013. Limits to adaptation. *Nature Climate Change* 3 (4): 305–307.
Dugmore, A. J., M. J. Church, P. C. Buckland, K. J. Edwards, I. Lawson, et al. 2005. The Norse landnám on the North Atlantic islands: An environmental impact assessment. *Polar Record* 41 (216): 21–37.
Dugmore, A. J., M. J. Church, K. A. Mairs, T. H. McGovern, A. J. Newton, and G. Sveinbjarnardóttir. 2006. An over-optimistic pioneer fringe? Environmental perspective on medieval settlement abandonment in Þórsmörk, Southern Iceland. In *The dynamics of Northern Societies*, ed. B. Grønnow, J. Arneborg, and H. C. Gulløv, 333–344. Copenhagen: National Museum of Denmark. (Studies in Archaeology and History 10).
Dugmore, A. J., C. Keller, and T. H. McGovern. 2007. The Norse Greenland settlement: Reflections on climate change, trade and the contrasting fates of human settlements in the Atlantic islands. *Arctic Anthropology* 44 (1): 12–37.
Dugmore, A. J., C. Keller, T. H. McGovern, A. F. Casely, and K. Smiarowski. 2009. Norse Greenland settlement and limits to adaptation. In *Adapting to Climate Change: Thresholds, Values, Governance*, ed. N. W. Adger, I. Lorenzoni, and K. L. O'Brien, 96–113. Cambridge: Cambridge University Press.
Dugmore, A. J., T. H. McGovern, O. Vésteinsson, J. Arneborg, R. Streeter, and C. Keller. 2012. Cultural adaptation, compounding vulnerabilities and conjunctures in Norse Greenland. *Proceedings of the National Academy of Sciences* 109 (10): 3658–3663.
Dugmore, A. J., T. H. McGovern, R. Streeter, C. K. Madsen, K. Smiarowski, and C. Keller. 2013. "Clumsy Solutions" and "Elegant Failures": Lessons on climate change adaptation from the settlement of the North Atlantic. In *A Changing Environment for Human Security: Transformative Approaches to Research, Policy and Action*, ed. L. Sygna, K. O'Brien, and J. Wolf. London: Routledge.
Edgren, T., 1988, Om leksaksbåtar från vigingatid och tidig medeltid. In *Festskrift til Olaf Olsen*, ed. O. Olsen, 157–64.Copenhagen
Eriksen, S., P. Aldunce, C. S. Bahinipati, R. D. A. Martins, J. I. Molefe, C. Nhemachena, et al. 2011. When not every response to climate change is a good one: Identifying principles for sustainable adaptation. *Climate and Development* 3 (1): 7–20.
Eldjárn, K. 1965. Leketøy. In *Kulturhistorisk leksikon for nordisk middelalder*, ed. I. Andersson and J. Granlund, vol. 10, 489–495. Copenhagen: Rosenkilde and Bagger.

Enghoff, I. B. 2003. *Hunting, fishing and animal husbandry at "The Farm Beneath the Sand", western Greenland: An archaezoological analysis of a Norse farm in the Western Settlement*. Copenhagen: Danish Polar Center. (Meddelelser om Grønland, Man & Society 28).

Fabrikant, S. I., D. R. Montello, and D. M. Mark. 2010. The natural landscape metaphor in information visualization: The role of commonsense geomorphology. *Journal of the American Society for Information Science and Technology* 61 (2): 253–270.

Folke, C., S. R. Carpenter, B. Walker, M. Scheffer, T. Chapin, and J. Rockström. 2010. Resilience thinking: Integrating resilience, adaptation and transformability. *Ecology and Society* 15:20.

Ford, J. D., G. McDowell, and T. Pearce. 2015. The adaptation challenge in the Arctic. *Nature Climate Change* 5:1046–1053.

Ford, J. D., T. Pearce, G. McDowell, L. Berrang-Ford, J. S. Sayles, and E. Belfer. 2018. Vulnerability and its discontents: The past, present, and future of climate change vulnerability research. *Climatic change* 151:189–203.

Frei, K. M., A. N. Coutu, K. Smiarowski, R. Harrison, C. K. Madsen, J. Arneborg, et al. 2015. Was it for walrus? Viking age settlement and medieval walrus ivory trade in Iceland and Greenland. *World Archaeology* 47 (3): 439–466.

Fuentes, A. 2009. A new synthesis: Resituating approaches to the evolution of human behaviour. *Anthropology Today 25* (3): 12–17.

Fuentes, A. 2016. The extended evolutionary synthesis, ethnography, and the human niche: Toward an integrated anthropology. *Current Anthropology* 57 (S13): S13–S26.

Gardela, L. 2012. What the Vikings did for fun? Sports and pastimes in medieval northern Europe. *World Archaeology* 44 (2): 234–247.

Golding, K. A., L. A. Simpson, J. E. Schofield, and K. J. Edwards. 2011. Norse-Inuit interaction and landscape change in southern Greenland. A geochronological, pedological and palynological investigation. *Geoarchaeology* 26 (3): 315–345.

Hastrup, K., A. Mosbech, and B. Grønnow. 2018. Introducing the North Water: Histories of exploration, ice dynamics, living resources, and human settlement in the Thule Region. *Ambio* 47:162–174.

Guemple, L. 1988. Teaching social relations to Inuit children. In *Hunter Gatherers 1—Property, Power and Ideology*, ed. T. Ingold, D. Riches, and J. Woodburn. Oxford: Berg.

Gulløv, H. C. 1997. From Middle Age to Colonial Times. *Meddelelser om Grønland* 23 (199):

Gulløv, H. C. 2004. *Gronlands Forhistorie*. Copenhagen: Gyldendal.

Gulløv, H. C. 2008. Booths from early Norse Greenland–or tjaldat búðir from landnáma Greenland. In *Símunarbók*, ed. C. Paulsen and H. D. Michelsen, 90–105. Tórshavn: Faroe University Press.

Haldon, J., L. Mordechai, A. Dugmore, M. Eisenberg, G. Endfield, et al. 2025. Past answers to present Concerns. The relevance of the premodern past for 21st century policy planners: Comments on the state of the field. *Wiley Interdisciplinary Reviews: Climate Change* 16:e923.

Harari, Y. N. 2024. *Nexus: A brief history of information networks from the stone age to AI*. New York: Random House.

Hartman, S., A. E. J. Ogilvie, J. H. Ingimundarson, A. J. Dugmore, G. Hambrecht, and T. H. McGovern. 2017. Medieval Iceland, Greenland and the New Human Condition: A case study in integrated environmental humanities. *Global and Planetary Change* 156:123–139.

Hayeur Smith, M., J. Arneborg, and K. P. Smith. 2015. The "Burgundian" hat from Herjolfsnes, Greenland: new discoveries, new dates. *Danish Journal of Archaeology* 4 (1): 21–32.

Hedenstierna-Jonson, C. 2009. A brotherhood of feasting and campaigning: The success of the northern warrior. In *From Ephesos to Dalecarlia. Reflections on Body, Space and Time in Medieval and Early Modern Europe*, ed. E. Regner, C. von Heijne, L. Kitzler Åhfeldt, and A. Kjellström, 43-56. Stockholm: Museum of National Antiquities (Studies 11. Stockholm Studies in Archaeology 48).

Hegmon, M. 2016. Archaeology of the human experience: An introduction. *Archeological Papers of the American Anthropological Association* 27 (1): 7–21.

Henrich, J. 2020. *The WEIRDest people in the world: How the West became psychologically peculiar and particularly prosperous*. London: Penguin.

Henrich, J., S. J. Heine, and A. Norenzayan. 2010. The weirdest people in the world? *Behavioral and Brain Sciences* 33 (2-3): 61–83.

Hicks, M., Á. Einarsson, K. Anamthawat-Jónsson, Á. Edwald, Æ. T. Thórsson, and T. H. McGovern. 2015. Community and conservation: Documenting millennial scale sustainable resource use at Lake Mývatn, Iceland. In *The Oxford Handbook of Historical Ecology and Applied Archaeology*, ed. C. Isendahl and D. Stump, 226–245. Oxford: Oxford University Press. https://doi.org/10.1093/oxfordhb/9780199672691.013.36.

Hillemann, F., B. A. Beheim, and E. Ready. 2023. Socio-economic predictors of Inuit hunting choices and their implications for climate change adaptation. *Philosophical Transactions of the Royal Society B 378* (1889): 20220395.

Høegsborg, 2014. 'Houses and households in Viking Age Scandinavia: some case studies' In Kristiansen, M.S. and Giles, K. (eds). *Dwellings, identities and homes: European housing culture from the Viking Age to the Renaissance*. Jutland Archaeological Society Publications.

Imer, L. M. 2017. *Peasants and Prayers: The inscriptions of Norse Greenland.* Copenhagen: University Press of South Denmark.

Ingold, T. 1993. The temporality of the landscape. *World Archaeology* 25 (2): 152–174.

Ingold, T. 2000. *The Perception of the Environment: Essays in livelihood, dwelling and skill.* London: Routledge.

Ingold, T. 2007a. The trouble with "evolutionary anthropology". *Anthropology Today* 23 (2): 13–17.

Ingold, T. 2007b. *Materials against materiality. Archaeological dialogues* 14 (1): 1–16.

IPCC, 2021: Climate Change 2021: The Physical Science Basis. Contribution of Working Group I to the Sixth Assessment Report of the Intergovernmental Panel on Climate Change [Masson-Delmotte, V., P. Zhai, A. Pirani, S.L. Connors, C. Péan, S. Berger, N. Caud, Y. Chen, L. Goldfarb, M.I. Gomis, M. Huang, K. Leitzell, E. Lonnoy, J.B.R. Matthews, T.K. Maycock, T. Waterfield, O. Yelekçi, R. Yu, and B. Zhou (eds.)]. Cambridge University Press, Cambridge, United Kingdom and New York, NY, USA, 2391 pp. https://doi.org/10.1017/9781009157896.

IPCC, 2022: Climate Change 2022: Impacts, Adaptation, and Vulnerability.Contribution of Working Group II to the Sixth Assessment Report of the Intergovernmental Panel on Climate Change [H.-O. Pörtner, D.C. Roberts, M. Tignor, E.S. Poloczanska, K. Mintenbeck, A. Alegría, M. Craig, S. Langsdorf, S. Löschke, V. Möller, A. Okem, B. Rama (eds.)]. Cambridge University Press. Cambridge University Press, Cambridge, UK and New York, NY, USA, 3056 pp., https://doi.org/10.1017/9781009325844.

IPCC. 2023. Summary for policymakers. In *Climate Change 2023: Synthesis Report. Contribution of Working Groups I, II and III to the Sixth Assessment Report of the Intergovernmental Panel on Climate Change*, ed. H. Lee and J. Romero, 1–34. Geneva, Switzerland: IPCC. https://10.59327/IPCC/AR6-9789291691647.001.

Jackson, R., J. Arneborg, A. Dugmore, C. Madsen, T. McGovern, K. Smiarowski, and R. Streeter. 2018. Disequilibrium, adaptation, and the Norse settlement of Greenland. *Human Ecology* 46:665–684.

Jackson, R., J. Arneborg, A. Dugmore, R. Harrison, S. Hartman, et al. 2022. Success and failure in the Norse North Atlantic: origins, pathway divergence, extinction and survival. In *Perspectives on Public Policy in Societal–Environmental Crises: What the Future Needs from History*, ed. A. Izdebski, J. Haldon, and P. Filipkowski, 247–272. Cham: Springer International Publishing.

Jackson, R., A. Dugmore, and F. Riede. 2024. Legacies of childhood learning for climate change adaptation. *Global Environmental Change* 87:102878.

Jaeger, P. T., and G. Burnett. 2010. *Information Worlds: Social Context, Technology and Information Behavior in the Age of the Internet*. New York: Routledge.

Jenness, D. 1922. The life of the Copper Eskimos. In *Report of the Canadian Arctic Expedition, XII*. Ottawa: F.A. Acland.

Jensen, K. G., A. Kuijpers, N. Koç, and J. Heinemeier. 2004. Diatom evidence of hydrographic changes and ice conditions in Igaliku Fjord, South Greenland, during the past 1500 years. *The Holocene* 14 (2): 152–164.

Jesch, J. 2015. *The Viking diaspora*. London: Routledge.

Jesch, J. 2001. *Ships and Men in the Late Viking Age: The Vocabulary of Runic Inscriptions and Skaldic Verse (NED-New edition)*. Rochester NY-Melton UK: Boydell & Brewer. https://www.jstor.org/stable/10.7722/j.ctt163tb4f.

Johnson, J. D. 2003. On contexts of information seeking. *Information Processing & Management* 39 (5): 735–760.

Kates, R. W., W. R. Travis, and T. J. Wilbanks. 2012. Transformational adaptation when incremental adaptations to climate change are insufficient. *Proceedings of the National Academy of Sciences* 109 (19): 7156–7161.

Kinloch, D., H. Kuhnlein, and D. C. G. Muir. 1992. Inuit foods and diet: A preliminary assessment of benefits and risks. *Science of the Total Environment* 122:247–278.

Kopár, L. 2009. The Use of Artistic Media in Norse Greenland. *Journal of the North Atlantic* 2:102–113.

Laland, K. N. 2004. Social learning strategies. *Learning and Behavior* 32 (1): 4–14.

Laland, K. N., and G. R. Brown. 2011. *Sense and Nonsense*. 2nd ed. Oxford: Oxford University Press.

Laland, K. N., and M. J. O'Brien. 2010. Niche construction theory and archaeology. *Journal of Archaeological Method and Theory* 17:303–322.

Laland, K., B. Matthews, and M. W. Feldman. 2016. An introduction to niche construction theory. *Evolutionary ecology* 30:191–202.

Lang, J. T. 1988. *Viking Age Decorated Wood*. Dublin: Royal Irish Academy.

Last, J. 1995. The Nature of History. In *Interpreting Archaeology: Finding meaning in the past*, ed. I. Hodder, M. Shanks, A. Alexandri, V. Buchli, J. Carman, J. Last, and G. Lucas. London: Routledge.

Latour, B. 1987. *Science in Action: How to follow scientists and engineers through society*. Cambridge MA: Harvard University Press.

Ledger, P. M., K. J. Edwards, and J. E. Schofield. 2017. Competing hypotheses, ordination and pollen preservation: landscape impacts of Norse landnám in southern Greenland. *Review of Palaeobotany and Palynology*, 236, pp.1–11.

Lievrouw, L. A. 2001. New media and the "pluralization of life-worlds": A role for information in social differentiation. *New Media & Society* 3 (1): 7–28.

Lillehammer, G. 1989. A child is born. The child's world in an archaeological perspective. *Norwegian Archaeological Review* 22 (2): 89–105.

Ljungqvist, F. C., A. Seim, and H. Huhtamaa. 2021. Climate and society in European history. *WIREs Climate Change* 12 (2): e691.

Lloyd, A. 2006. Information literacy landscapes: An emerging picture. *Journal of Documentation* 62 (5): 570–583.

Lloyd, A. 2012. Information literacy as a socially enacted practice: Sensitising themes for an emerging perspective of people-in-practice. *Journal of Documentation* 68 (6): 772–783.

Lloyd, A., M. Anne Kennan, K. M. Thompson, and A. Qayyum. 2013. Connecting with new information landscapes: information literacy practices of refugees. *Journal of Documentation* 69 (1): 121–144.

Lovett, E. 1901. The ancient and modern game of Astragals. *Folklore* 12:280–293.

Lucas, G. 2001. *Critical Approaches to Fieldwork*. London: Routledge.

Lucas, G. 2010. Triangulating absence: exploring the fault lines between archaeology and anthropology. In *Archaeology and Anthropology: Understanding Similarity, Exploring Difference*, ed. D. Garrow and T. Yarrow, 28–39. London: Oxbow Books.

Lucas, G. 2019. *Writing the Past: Knowledge Production and Literary Production in Archaeology*. London: Routledge.

Lynnerup, N. 2000. Life and death in Norse Greenland. In *Vikings: The North Atlantic Saga*, ed. W. W. Fitzhugh and E. Ward, 285–294. London: Smithsonian Institution Press.

Madsen, C. K. 2014. *Pastoral Settlement, Farming, and Hierarchy in Norse Vatnahverfi, South Greenland*. PhD. University of Copenhagen.

Madsen, C. K. 2019. Marine shielings in medieval Norse Greenland. *Arctic Anthropology* 56 (1): 119–159.

Marston, J. M. 2021. Archaeological approaches to agricultural economies. *Journal of Archaeological Research* 29:327–385.

McGovern, T. H. 1979. *The paleoeconomy of Norse Greenland: Adaptation and extinction in a tightly bounded ecosystem*. PhD: Columbia University.

McGovern, T. H. 1980. Cows, harp seals, and churchbells: Adaptation and extinction in Norse Greenland. *Human Ecology* 8 (3): 245–275.

McGovern, T. H. 1985. Contributions to the paleoeconomy of Norse Greenland. *Acta Archaeologica* 54:73–122.
McGovern, T. H., T. Amorosi, S. P. Perdikaris, and J. W. Woollett. 1996. Zooarchaeology of Sandnes V51: Economic change at a chieftain's farm in West Greenland. *Arctic Anthropology* 33 (2): 94–122.
McGovern, T.H., S. Perdikaris, I. Mainland, P. Ascough, V. Ewens, … and R. Harrison. 2009. The archaeofauna. In *Hofstadir: Excavations of a Viking Age Feasting Hall in North-Eastern Iceland*, ed. G. Lucas, 168–252. Reykjavík: Inst. of Archaeology (Monograph Series 1).
McGovern, T. H., R. Harrison, and K. Smiarowski. 2014. Sorting sheep and goats in medieval Iceland and Greenland: Local subsistence or world system. In *Long-term human Ecodynamics in the North Atlantic: An archaeological study*, ed. R. Harrison and R. A. Maher, 153–176. Lanham: Lexington Publishers.
Mesoudi, A., A. Whiten, and K. N. Laland. 2006. Towards a unified science of cultural evolution. *Behavioral and brain sciences* 29 (4): 329–347.
Mesoudi, A. 2011. *Cultural Evolution: How Darwinian theory can explain human culture and synthesize the social sciences*. Chicago: University of Chicago Press.
Mesoudi, A. 2016. Cultural evolution: a review of theory, findings and controversies. *Evolutionary Biology* 43:481–497.
Moser, S. C., and J. A. Ekstrom. 2010. A framework to diagnose barriers to climate change adaptation. *Proceedings of the National Academy of Sciences* 107 (51): 22026–22031.
Miller, R. L., P. Knippertz, C. Pérez García-Pando, J. P. Perlwitz, and I. Tegen. 2014. Impact of dust radiative forcing upon climate. In *Mineral dust: A key player in the Earth system*, ed. P. Knippertz and J.-B. W. Stuut, 327–357. Dordrecht: Springer.
Nedkvitne, A. 2009. *The Social Consequences of Literacy in Medieval Scandinavia*. Turnhout: Brepols.
Nedkvitne, A. 2014. *The German Hansa and Bergen 1100-1600*. Köln: Böhlau.
Nedkvitne, A. 2018. *Norse Greenland: Viking Peasants in the Arctic*. London: Routledge.
Nelson, M. C., S. E. Ingram, A. J. Dugmore, R. Streeter, M. A. Peeples, T. H. McGovern, et al. 2016. Climate changes, vulnerabilities, and food security. *Proceedings of the National Academy of Sciences* 113 (2): 298–303.
Nørlund, P. 1924. Buried Norsemen at Herjolfsnes. Meddelelser om Grønland 67 (1): 1–270.
Nørlund, P. 1930. Norse ruins at Gardar. *Meddelelser om Grønland* 76:1–170.
Nørlund, P. 1936. Viking Settlers in Greenland. Copenhagen: Munksgaard.
Nørlund, P., and M. Stenberger. 1934. *Brattahlid. Meddelelser om Grønland* 88 (1): 1–161.
Nowell, A., M. C. Langley, and F. Riede. 2020. Children and innovation: A Wenner-Gren Workshop. *Evolutionary Anthropology* 29 (1): 6–8.
Nyegaard, G. 2018. Dairy farmers and seal hunters: subsistence on a Norse farm in the Eastern Settlement, Greenland. *Journal of the North Atlantic* 37:1–80.
O'Brien, K. 2011. Responding to environmental change: A new age for human geography? *Progress in Human Geography* 35:542–549.
O'Brien, K. 2012. Global Environmental Change II. From Adaptation to Deliberate Transformation. *Progress in Human Geography* 36 (5): 667–676.
Odling-Smee, J., D. H. Erwin, E. P. Palkovacs, M. W. Feldman, and K. N. Laland. 2013. Niche construction theory: A practical guide for ecologists. *The Quarterly Review of Biology* 88 (1): 3–28.
Ogilvie, A. E. J., J. M. Woollett, K. Smiarowski, J. Arneborg, et al. 2009. Seals and sea ice in medieval Greenland. *Journal of the North Atlantic* 2:60–80.
Østergård, E. 2004. *Woven into the earth: Textiles from Norse Greenland*. Aarhus: Aarhus University Press.
Park, R. W. 1998. Size counts: The miniature archaeology of childhood in the Thule and Dorset cultures of Arctic Canada. *Archaeological Papers of the American Anthropological Association* 15 (1): 53–64.
Park, R. W. 2005. Growing up north: Exploring the archaeology of childhood in Thule and Dorset cultures of Arctic Canada. *Archaeological Papers of the American Anthropological Association* 15:53–64.

Pelling, M. 2011. *Adaptation to Climate Change: From Resilience to Transformation*. London: Routledge.

Perdikaris, S., and T. H. McGovern. 2008. Codfish and kings, seals and subsistence: Norse marine resource use in the North Atlantic. In *Viking Voyagers*, ed. T. R. Rick and J. M. Erlandson, 187–214. Oakland: UCLA Press.

Pettigrew, K. E. 1999. Waiting for chiropody: Contextual results from an ethnographic study of the information behaviour among attendees at community clinics. *Information Processing & Management* 35 (6): 801–817.

Pinker, S. 2010. The cognitive niche: Coevolution of intelligence, sociality, and language'. *Proceedings of the National Academy of Sciences* 107 (2): 8993–8999.

Price, N. 2019. *The Viking Way: Magic and Mind in Late Iron Age Scandinavia*. Oxford: Oxbow Books.

Price, T. D. 2015. *Ancient Scandinavia: An Archaeological History from the First Humans to the Vikings*. Oxford: Oxford University Press.

Raffield, B. 2019. Playing Vikings: Militarism, hegemonic masculinities, and childhood enculturation in Viking Age Scandinavia. *Current Anthropology* 60 (6): 813–835.

Riede, F. 2011. Adaptation and niche construction in human prehistory: A case study from the southern Scandinavian late glacial. *Philosophical Transactions of the Royal Society B* 366:793–808.

Riede, F. 2012. Theory for the A-theoretical: niche construction theory and its implications for environmental archaeology. In *N-TAG TEN. Proceedings of the 10th Nordic TAG conference at Stiklestad, Norway 2009*, ed. R. Berge, M.E. Jasinski and K. Sognnes, 87-98. Oxford: Archaeopress. (BAR International Series 2399).

Riede, F., A. H. Sørensen, J. Dietrich, M. Skaaning Høegsberg, M. V. Nordvig, and E. B. Nielsen. 2016. Learning from the past–teaching past climate change and catastrophes as windows onto vulnerability and resilience. In *Teaching Climate Change in the Humanities*, ed. S. Siperstein, S. Lemenager, and S. Hall, 126–135. New York: Routledge.

Riede, F., N. N. Johannsen, A. Högberg, A. Nowell, and M. Lombard. 2018. The role of play objects and object play in human cognition and innovation. *Evolutionary Anthropology* 27 (1): 46–59. https://onlinelibrary.wiley.com/doi/10.1002/evan.21555/full.

Roach, A. 2007. Model boats in the context of maritime history and archaeology. *The International Journal of Nautical Archaeology* 37 (2): 313–334.

Rockman, M. 2003. Knowledge and learning in the archaeology of colonization. In *Colonization of Unfamiliar Landscapes: The archaeology of adaptation*, ed. M. Rockman and J. Steele, 3–24. London: Routledge.

Rockman, M. 2009. New World with a New Sky: Climatic variability, environmental expectations, and the historical period colonization of eastern North America. *Historical Archaeology* 44:4–20.

Roesdahl, E., and D. M. Wilson. 1992. *From Viking to Crusader: The Scandinavian Europe, 800-1200*. New York: Rizzoli.

Roussell, A. 1936. Sandnes and the Neighbouring Farms. *Meddelelser om Grønland* 88:2.

Russ, S. W., and J. A. Fiorelli. 2010. Developmental approaches to creativity. In *The Cambridge handbook of creativity*, ed. J. C. Kaufman and J. R. Sternberg, 233–249. Cambridge: Cambridge University Press.

Sachs, J., D. Lafortune, and G. Fuller. 2024. The SDGs and the UN Summit of the Future. Sustainable Development Report 2024. Paris: SDSN, Dublin: Dublin University Press. https://doi.org/10.25546/108572

Savolainen, R. 2021. Information landscapes as contexts of information practices. *Journal of Librarianship and Information Science* 53 (4): 655–667.

Schein, E. 2013. *Humble Inquiry: The Gentle Art of Asking Instead of Telling*. San Fancisco: Berrett-Koehler Publishers.

Schiøtt, S., Tejsner, P. & Rysgaard, S. (2022). Inuit and Local Knowledge on the Marine Ecosystem in Ilulissat Icefjord, Greenland. *Hum Ecol* 50, 167–181.

Shennan, S. 2001. Demography and cultural innovation: a model and its implications for the emergence of modern human culture. *Cambridge Archaeological Journal* 11 (1): 5–16.

Smiarowski, K., R. Harrison, S. Brewington, M. Hicks, F. J. Hérbert, et al. 2017. Zooarchaeology of the Scandinavian settlements in Iceland and Greenland: Divergent pathways. In *Oxford Handbook of Zooarchaeology*, ed. U. Albarella, M. Rizzetto, H. Russ, K. Vickers, and S. Viner-Daniels, 147–163. Oxford: Oxford University Press.

Smith, E. A. 1991. *Inujjamiut Foraging Strategies: Evolution of an Arctic Hunting Economy*. New York: A. de Gruyter.

UNDP (United Nations Development Programme). (2022). *Human Development Report 2021-22: Uncertain Times, Unsettled Lives: Shaping our Future in a Transforming World.* New York.

UNDP (United Nations Development Programme). (2024). *Human development report 2023-24: Breaking the gridlock: Reimagining cooperation in a polarized world.* New York.

Vasey, D. E. 1996. Population regulation, ecology, and political economy in preindustrial Iceland. *American Ethnologist* 23 (2): 366–392.

Væbek, C. L. 1992. Vatnahverfi–An inland district of the Eastern Settlement in Greenland. Meddelelser om Gronland. *Man and Society* 17:1–132.

Vésteinsson, O. 2009. Parishes and communities in Norse Greenland. *Journal of the North Atlantic* 2 (sp2): 138–150.

Vésteinsson, O., Hegmon, M., Arneborg, J., Rice, G. and Russell, W. G., 2019. Dimensions of inequality. Comparing the North Atlantic and the US Southwest. *Journal of Anthropological Archaeology* 54:172–191.

Walls, M. 2016. Making as a didactic process: situated cognition and the chaine operatoire. *Quaternary International* 405:21–30.

Wise, R. M., I. Fazey, M. S. Smith, S. E. Park, H. C. Eakin, E. R. M. A. Van Garderen, and B. Campbell. 2014. Reconceptualising adaptation to climate change as part of pathways of change and response. *Global Environmental Change* 28:325–336.

Zeder, M. 2015. Core questions in domestication research. *Proceedings of the National Academy of Sciences* 122 (11): 3191–3198.

Zeder, M.A., 2016. Domestication as a model system for niche construction theory. *Evolutionary Ecology* 30 (2): 325–348.

Zhao, B., I. S. Castañeda, J. M. Salacup, E. K. Thomas, W. C. Daniels, et al. 2022. Prolonged drying trend coincident with the demise of Norse settlement in southern Greenland. *Science. Advances* 8 (12): eabm4346.

Communal Organization of Labor, Water Management, and the Intensification of Agriculture in the Greater Angkor Region, Ninth–Fifteenth Centuries CE

Sarah Klassen

Abstract Archaeology offers a deep-time perspective on how societies have responded to environmental stress, revealing adaptive strategies and resilient systems that allowed urban centers to persist for centuries. This chapter explores Angkor, the capital of the Khmer Empire, as a compelling case study in long-term urban resilience and adaptation. At its height in the twelfth and thirteenth centuries CE, Angkor supported a population of almost one million, sustained by an elaborate water management system that redistributed rivers through vast channels and reservoirs. This infrastructure supported rice agriculture and protected the city against seasonal flooding and drought. While Angkor eventually experienced political and economic decline, paleoenvironmental and archaeological research reveals that the city survived several severe droughts. These findings suggest that earlier phases of adaptation were successful and that it was only during later environmental stressors, combined with political and social shifts, that Angkor's systems were no longer sustainable. This chapter highlights how Angkor's history serves as a natural experiment in urban resilience, offering valuable insights into the dynamics of societal persistence and transformation in the face of environmental uncertainty.

Keywords Water management · Drought · Resilience · Angkor · Cambodia

1 Introduction

Archaeology has a long and rich tradition of studying the complex interactions between societies and their environments. By analyzing material remains, settlement patterns, and environmental data, archaeologists can identify the characteristics of

S. Klassen (✉)
University of Toronto, Toronto, ON, Canada

University of Colorado, Boulder, CO, USA

J. F. Haldon, R. Fernandes (eds.), *Bridging History and Policy*, Understanding Complex Systems, https://doi.org/10.1007/978-3-032-24379-9_21

resilient systems and specific adaptive strategies that have allowed societies to adapt and persist over centuries, even in the face of environmental challenges, resource scarcity, and social upheaval (Redman 2013). In many cases, the findings may not be revelatory, but archaeological case studies can provide important reminders of fundamental principles, concepts that are often overlooked but remain valuable when considering the design of more sustainable and resilient cities today.

Angkor, located in present-day Cambodia, was the center of the Angkorian world, also referred to as the Khmer Empire (Hendrickson et al. 2023) (Fig. 1). Khmer inscriptions suggest that Jayavarman II established the kingdom in 802 CE, unifying fragmented polities into a single sociopolitical system that persisted until 1431 CE, marked by the supposed sacking of Angkor by the Ayutthaya Kingdom (Briggs 1951; Cœdès 1968). Unification triggered a period of rapid urbanization and territorial expansion. By the twelfth century CE, the Angkorian world had become the dominant power in mainland Southeast Asia, with Angkor at its political, religious, and economic heart (Hendrickson et al. 2023). The city flourished for centuries and amassed a population of 700,000–900,000, supported by a vast and intricately engineered water management system that sustained its growing population and agricultural base (Klassen et al. 2021b, 2022). Angkor's infrastructure managed water resources by rerouting rivers into massive channels and holding basins that protected the urban landscape from flooding and enabled rice agriculture (Fletcher et al. 2008). As the city expanded, state-sponsored and local temple communities became increasingly centralized, organizing labor at a supra-household

Fig. 1 Satellite imagery of Angkor in relation to Cambodia. The large rectangle visible in the satellite imagery on the left is the West Baray, Angkor Thom is the large square in the middle of the image, and Angkor Wat is the square to the south of Angkor Thom. Bing Maps (QGIS Basemap). Scale 1:6548. Microsoft Corporation. (3/28/2025)

level to generate a surplus that sustained the urban population, especially during the classic Angkor period (Klassen et al. 2022; Klassen and Evans 2020).

The period of agricultural intensification in the twelfth and thirteenth centuries coincided with a time of rapid urban growth, but it also marked the beginning of a gradual political and economic decline. Scholars have proposed that, among other factors, climate stressors, including prolonged, multidecade droughts, may have played a key role in this decline (Buckley et al. 2010, 2014; Day et al. 2012; Evans et al. 2023b; Hua et al. 2017; Penny et al. 2019). However, that research also indicated that Angkor did not face just one period of devastating droughts—it endured and adapted to at least two earlier major drought events (Buckley et al. 2010). Remarkably, the city's water infrastructure and societal systems successfully weathered these two earlier periods of drought, demonstrating significant resilience and adaptability to environmental stress. These droughts make Angkor a natural experiment in urban resilience, offering a rare opportunity to study how complex societies confront ecological challenges. By analyzing how Angkor's infrastructure, governance, and social organization responded differently during the final period of drought, we can better understand the interplay of the environmental, political, and social factors that ultimately contributed to the city's decline.

2 Mapping the Development of the Greater Angkor Region

Decades of mapping efforts, including the influential 2007 map of Angkor created by Pottier and Evans, revealed that Angkor was a sprawling low-density urban complex consisting of hundreds of temples, occupation mounds, and residential areas intricately connected through an extensive network of hydraulic infrastructure (Evans 2007; Pottier 1999). This sophisticated water management system, which includes channels, reservoirs (barays), and embankments, was crucial in managing flows of water across the landscape and ultimately sustaining the city's population and agricultural base over centuries (Fletcher et al. 2008).

These early maps of Angkor show large empty spaces in the city's center, not because these areas were uninhabited but because aerial and satellite imagery cannot be used to detect archaeological features beneath dense forest cover (Evans 2007). The central area, home to major temples such as Angkor Wat and the Bayon, is heavily shrouded by thick vegetation, which obscures ground-level features and makes them difficult to see in satellite and aerial imagery (Evans 2007; Pottier 1993, 1999). As a result, the early maps of central Angkor are less detailed than those of less vegetated areas.

The introduction of light detection and ranging (Lidar) technology has revolutionized the archaeology of Angkor by revealing previously hidden features in these so-called "empty" areas (Evans et al. 2013). By penetrating the forest canopy and producing high-resolution topographic data, Lidar data clearly reveal a highly organized and intricately structured urban landscape, including residential neighborhoods, road networks, and additional hydraulic infrastructure (Fig. 1) (Evans et al.

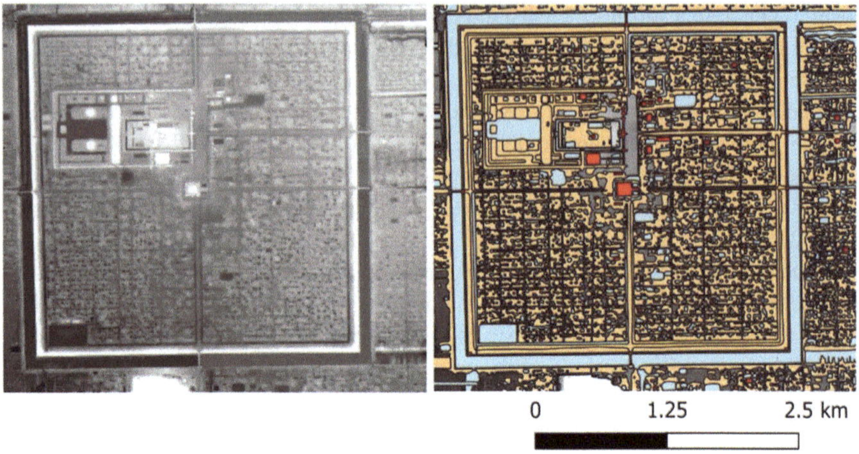

Fig. 2 Left: Lidar imagery of Angkor Thom from the Khmer Archaeological Lidar Consortium (KALC), the Greater Angkor Project (GAP), and the Authority for the Protection of the Site and Management of the Region of Angkor (APSARA). Right: Mapping of Angkor Thom. This mapping work is the culmination of many years of work by an international group of collaborators from the Khmer Archaeological Lidar Consortium (KALC), the Greater Angkor Project (GAP), and the Authority for the Protection of the Site and Management of the Region of Angkor (APSARA)

2013). As such, the Lidar data allowed us to "fill in" these gaps with remarkable precision. Archaeologists have now been able to document an astonishing array of previously unmapped features, including residential complexes, roads, channels, embankments, and small temples, all of which are parts of a carefully planned and interconnected urban system. With the Lidar data, we have now mapped over 27,000 archaeological features across the Greater Angkor Region, adding more than 20,000 new features to the existing map (Fig. 2). These new maps have transformed our understanding of Angkor's urban footprint. In addition to a loosely connected series of temple complexes, Lidar has shown that Angkor has a densely occupied urban core that is connected to the hinterlands via a sophisticated and highly engineered hydraulic network that manages water flow and distribution across the entire region (Evans et al. 2013; Klassen et al. 2021b).

3 The Rise of Urbanism at Angkor

By integrating decades of archaeological research at Angkor, including radiocarbon dates, ceramic typologies, architectural sequences, and historical records with analytical methods, including semisupervised machine learning algorithms and Bayesian modeling, archaeologists have been able to establish a detailed chronology of Angkor's urban development (Carleton et al. 2023; Klassen et al. 2018,

2021b). This analysis revealed a clear trajectory of urban development at Angkor, which archaeologists have divided into several periods on the basis of archaeological, inscriptional, and architectural evidence (Carter et al. 2021).

At its foundation in 802 CE, Angkor was not a single unified city but a network of three separate urban centers distributed across the Greater Angkor Region. Important temple complexes anchored these early centers, serving as focal points for religious, political, and economic activity. The urban footprint during this period was relatively dispersed, with smaller residential and agricultural communities spreading out from these centers and across the landscape.

Over time, major temple construction projects signaled a shift toward greater centralization at Angkor. The once-separate centers began to consolidate, forming a more cohesive urban core at the heart of Angkor. This period resulted in a dramatic increase in urban density, which was supported by the construction of large-scale hydraulic infrastructure. The increased population density and expanding infrastructure during this period suggest a period of political strength and economic prosperity. By 1113 CE, the landscape had begun to take its final form. The central area of Angkor became densely occupied, with residential neighborhoods, road networks, and religious complexes forming a highly organized and interconnected urban system (Evans et al. 2023a). This urban density continued to grow into the final period of Angkor, which we define as extending to the beginning of the fourteenth century. Research suggests that Angkor may have supported a population of up to 900,000 at its height, with over 150,000 nonagricultural producers living within the civic-ceremonial centers, making it one of the largest cities in the preindustrial world (Klassen et al. 2021b). This extraordinary population size reflects not only Angkor's political and economic power but also the sophisticated infrastructure and resource management strategies that support such a large and complex urban society.

4 An Elaborately Engineered Agricultural Landscape

The economy of Angkor was based on rice agriculture, which supported its large population and complex urban infrastructure for hundreds of years. At the heart of this agricultural system was a vast, intricately engineered landscape that transformed a natural floodplain spanning more than 3000 km^2 into one of the world's most sophisticated preindustrial water management networks (Fletcher et al. 2008; Goloubew 1941; Groslier 1979). Centralized, state-sponsored hydraulic infrastructure underpins this system, regulating water flow, controlling flooding, and potentially supporting multiple seasons of rice cultivation across the landscape (Klassen and Evans 2020).

Much of the early scholarship on Angkor's agricultural system focused on these large-scale, state-sponsored hydraulic features, primarily because of their monumental size and association with royal authority and state power (Van Liere 1982). Khmer political ideology deeply intertwined kingship and water management, reinforcing the idea that the rulers of Angkor wielded divine authority through their ability to symbolically and productively manage water (Bourdonneau 2010).

One of the most iconic examples of this state-level infrastructure is the West Baray, a massive artificial reservoir covering more than 17 km^2 (over 6.5 square miles). Built in the eleventh century, this above-ground reservoir remains one of the world's largest man-made reservoirs; remarkably, it is still in use nearly a millennium after its construction. Its sheer scale reflects not only the Khmer Empire's engineering prowess but also the central role that water management played in maintaining political and economic stability and its ability to manage water resources on a monumental scale (Fletcher et al. 2008).

Angkor's agricultural system, however, was not solely dependent on these state-sponsored mega-projects. In addition to the large reservoirs and channels commissioned by the kings, a decentralized network of local temple communities also played a crucial role in water management and rice production. Temple communities likely served multiple functions beyond religious worship. At the local level, they acted as hubs for social organization, economic coordination, and facilitated social networking among neighboring communities, enabling collective decision-making and cooperation that regulated labor and allocated resources at a local scale (Hawken and Klassen 2023; Klassen and Evans 2020). They also formed a hierarchical system that collected and redistributed agricultural surplus to larger state temples in the civic-ceremonial core of Angkor (Lustig and Lustig 2019; Sedov 1963). This hierarchical flow of goods and resources helped sustain the political and religious authority of the Khmer elite and reinforced the centralized power structure of the empire.

Archaeologists have identified over 1000 temple communities across the Greater Angkor Region, each centered around a primary temple and supported by an average of three reservoirs. Recent research, aided by deep learning, suggests that these temple communities extend well beyond the boundaries traditionally considered "the Greater Angkor Region" (Klassen et al. 2023; Landauer et al. 2025); however, for this study, we consider only the temples within the traditional 3000 km^2 boundary. These temple communities are linked by more than 1000 km^2 of connected ancient rice fields (Hawken 2011). Coordinating water movement across such a complex landscape would have required large-scale organization and cooperation, likely facilitated by temple-based authorities. Successful rice cultivation depends on equitable water distribution through shared channels and reservoirs and among rice fields. If one community hoards too much water or diverts it for individual use, there could be cascading ramifications. When fields are left fallow due to a lack of water, pests can rapidly spread across the landscape, devastating neighboring crops and threatening the broader food supply. This interdependence meant that water management was not just an agricultural issue but also a critical social and political concern.

While Angkor was clearly a highly engineered and meticulously organized urban landscape, a large question remains: how was this complex infrastructure utilized to provide food and resources for a population that may have reached up to

700,000–900,000 people at its peak while simultaneously generating sufficient surplus to support monumental construction projects such as Angkor Wat?

5 Development of a Landscape for Agriculture Through Top-down and Bottom-up Methods

To understand how Angkor generated so much surplus, it is essential to examine the interplay between two distinct yet interconnected types of infrastructure. The first is the state-sponsored centralized infrastructure, which includes large reservoirs (barays), channels, and embankments constructed and maintained under the authority of the Khmer kings. The second is the localized, decentralized systems managed by temple communities at the village level, which regulate water flow and rice cultivation through smaller reservoirs and local channels.

Social institutions that regulate access to water play crucial roles in water management systems. These systems are often traditionally categorized as either top-down (centralized, state-controlled) or bottom-up (localized, community-driven). However, analyses of Angkor's water management over time suggest a hybrid system that integrates both approaches. While identifying these systems archaeologically is valuable, diachronic maps have further advanced these analyses (Klassen et al. 2021b). These maps enable us to trace changes in the urban and agricultural landscape over time, allowing for a more detailed understanding of whether individual temple communities had access to the state-sponsored hydraulic network.

A nearest-neighbor analysis indicates that temples cluster statistically around newly constructed and preexisting state-sponsored infrastructure as they are built. This clustering suggests that local systems were not developing in isolation but were instead being established and expanded in coordination with the state-sponsored network. In other words, local temple communities adapted to and built upon the broader hydraulic system created by the Angkorian elite (Klassen 2018; Klassen and Evans 2020).

Angkor's builders laid the foundations for its monumental landscape in the early Angkorian period. During this period, temple units expanded dramatically across the landscape. The bottom-up temple communities began occupying previously undeveloped land, rapidly developing agricultural systems and increasing the geographic extent of the Greater Angkor Region. During this time, the first extensive state-sponsored hydraulic infrastructure began to take shape, with significant investments in water management systems, including reservoirs and channels. These temple communities played a significant role in expanding the agricultural frontier, converting untapped lands into productive rice fields. This period marked the beginning of the long-term interaction between religious structures and agricultural production at Angkor, with temples emerging as central hubs for spiritual and practical activities (Klassen and Evans 2020).

In the tenth century CE, temple nucleation around the East Baray coincided with the construction of the massive reservoir. This pattern continued in the following centuries, shifting toward the West Baray and other state-sponsored hydraulic projects and newly established civic-ceremonial centers. These networks expanded into a massive low-density urban system, where temple communities used state-built infrastructure while likely maintaining some degree of autonomy over land ownership and agricultural practices (Klassen and Evans 2020). By the eleventh and twelfth centuries, the footprint of Angkor had taken its final form, with state and local systems forming a highly integrated and interdependent network. From this period on, the urban and agricultural fabric became increasingly "infilled" as new temple communities and agricultural fields emerged to take advantage of the existing infrastructure (Klassen 2018; Klassen and Evans 2020).

By the Classic Angkor period, the dynamics of the landscape shifted dramatically as the pace of new temple foundations slowed. An analysis of Angkorian inscriptions by Lustig and Lustig (2019) suggested that this may be related to increasing competition over land. The authors identified a trend in the land sales records of higher-ranked individuals (identified as high rank because of their caste titles) gradually acquiring land from lower-ranked individuals and communities. This trend intensified over time until the final period of Angkor's history, when there were no more inscriptions referencing landownership by any lower-caste individuals. It is important to consider whether the meaning of caste titles evolved over time, as this could affect how we interpret these patterns of land acquisition. However, the landscape data do appear to reflect this same interpretation as the land becomes increasingly infilled, and larger temple complexes appear to subsume the land of smaller ones.

When the landscape and inscriptional data are combined, it seems that as virgin land grew increasingly scarce during this period, the elites or the state purchased land from previously founded agricultural communities. This shift suggests growing economic inequality and increasing centralization of landownership, which may have had significant social and political consequences (Lustig and Lustig 2019). During this time, the city's urban core saw a rise in nonproducers living in the civic-ceremonial center, including elites, priests, and artisans. Major construction projects, such as Angkor Wat (built around 1140 CE) and the massive temples constructed by Jayavarman VII at the end of the twelfth century, reflect this increasing focus on grandiose religious and political structures. These monumental temples symbolized the king's power and helped consolidate state control over the agricultural and social systems. The elite and state likely consolidated land ownership to exert more direct control over the agricultural system, presumably ensuring that it generated surpluses for the urban population, including those in the newly founded civic-ceremonial centers. The strategic control of land and water resources would likely have been essential for supporting the growing population in Angkor's core, particularly in light of the increasing demands placed on the empire by monumental building projects and a rising elite class.

6 Land Dynamics and Generating an Agricultural Surplus for the Urban Core

The analysis of Angkor's urban and agricultural landscape reveals distinct development phases, each marked by changing land use patterns, water management, and social complexity. Changes in land ownership and agricultural administration during later periods of Angkor had significant implications for the agricultural system, leading to increased competition for land and the gradual concentration of ownership among elites. Inscriptional evidence shows a decline in references to free landowners by the mid-eleventh century CE, suggesting that land previously owned by lower-class individuals was being absorbed by elites. This shift coincided with intensified urbanization and a growing reliance on agricultural surplus.

On the basis of this idea, archaeologists have analyzed urban land use patterns at Angkor, focusing on the relationships among temple output, population density, and distance from the urban core (Klassen et al. 2022). They also assessed which temples have preferential access to state-sponsored water management infrastructure. An analysis of the percentage of temples with direct access to the state-sponsored hydraulic network over time indicates fluctuations between 50% and 80% for most of Angkor's history, suggesting that a substantial portion of temple communities were integrated into the state-controlled water system. However, access to this infrastructure declined in the final periods of Angkor, possibly reflecting broader political and environmental challenges (Klassen 2018; Klassen and Evans 2020). For example, the temple on the left in Fig. 3 is directly adjacent to a state-sponsored channel, meaning that it has direct access to state-managed water resources. In

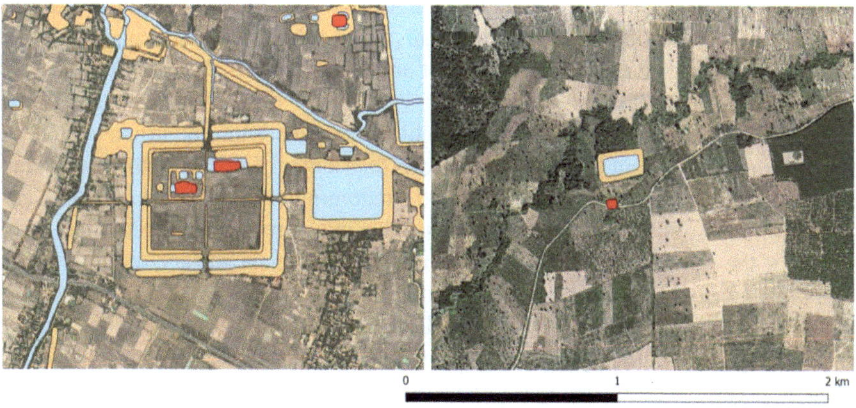

Fig. 3 Left: Large temple with direct access to state water management infrastructure. Right: Small temple without access to state water management infrastructure. Bing Maps [QGIS Basemap]. Scale [1:6548]. Microsoft Corporation. [3/28/2025]. The mapped features are the culmination of many years of work by an international group of collaborators from the Khmer Archaeological Lidar Consortium (KALC), the Greater Angkor Project (GAP), and the Authority for the Protection of the Site and Management of the Region of Angkor (APSARA)

contrast, the temple on the right sits upstream of all major infrastructure, suggesting that it relied on localized water management systems rather than state-sponsored channels.

A 2022 analysis revealed a clear pattern of declining productivity with increasing distance from the city center. Temple communities closer to the political and religious heart of the city had access to better infrastructure and greater social and economic opportunities, which would have driven up both land value and population density. Moreover, declining productivity further from the city center likely reflects the effects of decreasing land values due to higher transportation costs—an economic principle that remains relevant in modern urban systems. In contemporary cities, land values tend to be greater in areas with better infrastructure and closer proximity to economic and political hubs, and we see a similar dynamic playing out at Angkor (Klassen et al. 2022).

However, areas with direct access to state-sponsored irrigation infrastructure partially mitigated this decline. In other words, temple communities located along major channels and reservoirs could sustain higher levels of agricultural productivity, even if they are relatively far from the urban core, owing to their ability to access more stable and managed water supply and transportation networks at the core.

This analysis also revealed that communities closer to the core produced larger surpluses per laborer even though they had less land per laborer than the more distant areas did. Interestingly, despite having more land available per farmer, these outer areas produced less rice per laborer. This is likely due to the greater proximity to water management infrastructure and the intensification of farming practices closer to the urban core. The more centrally located lands benefitted from a more efficient and well-maintained irrigation system, which increased their productivity, even if the land was in a more limited supply (Klassen et al. 2022).

These surpluses could be utilized by the Angkor state to feed nonfood producers in the urban core, especially during the final period, which was associated with large populations in the civic-ceremonial center and the monumental building projects of the twelfth and thirteenth centuries.

While we expect that agricultural surpluses helped sustain the urban center, we are still uncertain about how the surplus was distributed. The rise of inequality during the final period of Angkor, with land predominantly controlled by elites and state temples, suggests that much of the surplus may have been concentrated in the hands of the ruling elite. Angkor was a highly hierarchical society, and it is likely that the majority of the population, including farmers, did not receive an equal share of the surpluses they produced. Nonetheless, there are indications that the average farmer may have indirectly benefited from the state's role in providing public goods, such as defense against external threats and access to free healthcare, which may have provided a safety net for some (Klassen et al. 2022).

This pattern of declining productivity and increasing land area per person with distance provides further evidence that Angkor functioned as a highly structured and economically stratified urban system. The combination of centralized state control over significant infrastructure and increasing concentration of land among the elite likely reinforced these patterns over time. As land ownership became increasingly consolidated under the upper elite and state-affiliated temples, rural temple communities may have become more economically dependent on the state, contributing to shifts in social and political dynamics in the final centuries of the empire (Klassen et al. 2022). Similarly, it seems plausible that the greater numbers of nonproducers living in the civic-ceremonial centers were highly dependent on surplus and that there may have been little room for variability in harvest especially as Angkor experienced the third period of droughts.

7 Reduced Redundancy

Redundancy refers to the diversity of functionally analogous components that allow for multiple means of accomplishing similar ends within a system. Redundancy reduces the vulnerability of the system during periods of rapid change and can help prevent disasters by allowing other aspects of the system to compensate for specific failures. A 2018 study compared redundancies in the infrastructure of the systems at Angkor used to store water between state hydraulic infrastructure and local reservoirs (Klassen 2018).

To calculate redundancy at Angkor, this analysis used harnessed water calculations from the natural capital section of this paper to determine how water was distributed between features. This method compared the redundancy between the state hydraulic infrastructure and local reservoirs. In every period, the four large reservoirs (East Baray, West Baray, Jayatataka, and Indratataka) held the majority of the water in the system, never less than 96%. On the basis of this definition of redundancy, the periods with the lowest percentage of water stored in state infrastructure (800–850 CE, 950–1000 CE, and 1200–1300 CE) had the highest redundancy. However, the variation among periods remained minimal, suggesting that the system lacked significant redundancy in any era (Fig. 4).

One key difference is that the West Baray was no longer functioning during the period of droughts and monsoons in the thirteenth century. The West Baray was constructed shortly before the first period of drought and continued to function during the second period of drought. Paleobotanical evidence suggests that the West Baray no longer retained water by the end of the twelfth century CE, which coincides with the beginning of the third drought and had minimal levels of water until the late sixteenth century CE (Penny et al. 2018). Penny et al. (2018) suggested that the drying of the West Baray is unlikely to be related to reduced rainfall. Instead, the authors suggest that the water may have been redirected into features associated with Angkor Wat or, following Dumarçay, this period may mark a shift in the hydraulic system from storing water to a greater reliance on channels. These interpretations are consistent with Buckley et al.'s (2010) hydroclimatic reconstructions that the end of the twelfth century CE was characterized by a period of high-magnitude monsoons. It is possible that the West Baray was drained to remove excess water from the system or to help mitigate the damage caused by high flows during high-magnitude monsoons. Regardless of the cause, the timing of the drying

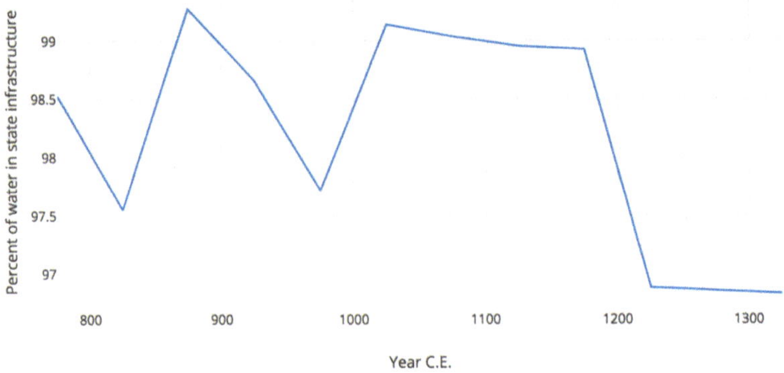

Fig. 4 Redundancy of water management resources stored in state-sponsored water management infrastructure, from Klassen (2018)

of the West Baray meant that the water management system during the third drought could store only half as much water as that during the first two droughts. This finding supports expectations that large amounts of stored water allowed the system to function successfully during the first and second droughts but that it was more vulnerable during the third drought.

8 Assessing Vulnerabilities to the System

By the post-Angkorian period, temple construction had largely ceased, and Angkor entered a phase of gradual decline. The once-thriving urban infrastructure fell into disrepair, and the intricate network of agricultural and water management systems that had sustained the empire began to unravel (Brotherson 2019). External threats and internal sociopolitical shifts further weakened the centralized state's ability to maintain control over its vast urban and agricultural landscape. The deterioration of water management infrastructure and declining agricultural productivity were likely among the key factors in Angkor's collapse as a political and cultural center (Penny et al. 2019).

This decline underscores the sophisticated yet fragile nature of Angkor's water management system. State-sponsored infrastructure enabled large-scale agricultural production and political stability, and locally managed systems played a crucial role in resource distribution. The integration of centralized and decentralized approaches allowed Angkor to sustain a vast population for centuries, but this balance eventually faltered, coinciding with political and economic challenges that set the stage for decline.

A crucial distinction emerges when examining the final major drought: by this time, Angkor's agricultural system had become highly centralized and concentrated.

While efficient, increasing elite control over land and resources may have inadvertently heightened the city's vulnerability to environmental shocks. With fewer entities managing most of the land and water infrastructure, Angkor's ability to adapt to fluctuations in water availability diminished. Moreover, a growing percentage of nonproducers in the urban core were dependent on surpluses. The combination of land consolidation, rising urban demand, and environmental pressures may have ultimately strained the system to a breaking point.

In addition to elite land control, other factors contributed to Angkor's declining adaptive capacity. Despite its vast reservoirs and channels, the city lacked redundancy in its water management system and failures in one part of the network could have cascading effects (Penny et al. 2018). Crucially, the West Baray, a key piece of infrastructure and a major source of water and an absorber of excess flows from monsoons, was no longer operational (Penny et al. 2005). Additionally, path dependencies in land use and infrastructure investments made it difficult to implement alternative strategies as conditions changed. For example, a 2021 analysis investigated how one feature that was built to expand the defensible area of Angkor was constrained by path dependencies of the water management system (Klassen et al. 2021a). These structural rigidities may have limited Angkor's ability to respond flexibly to shifting environmental and sociopolitical challenges.

In summary, Angkor's rise and fall were influenced by shifts in land use, hydraulic management, and social organization. Early periods saw decentralized temples and agricultural systems facilitating expansion, but increasing centralization and elite control led to greater inequality and rigidity. By the thirteenth century, the interplay of intensifying urbanization, agricultural centralization, and climate challenges created a highly vulnerable system. While state investments in water management and food production allowed Angkor to flourish for centuries, these same systems ultimately constrained the city's adaptability.

These insights highlight the potential risks of over centralization and the importance of flexibility, redundancy, and equitable resource distribution in sustaining complex societies, although the individual variables are difficult to isolate. Angkor's case serves as a valuable reminder for contemporary cities grappling with climate instability by underscoring the potential benefit of adaptable infrastructure, adaptive governance, and balanced resource management.

Acknowledgments I extend heartfelt gratitude to the institutions, organizations, and individuals whose support and collaboration have contributed to decades of research that have made this chapter possible. I would especially like to acknowledge the contributions of the Authority for the Protection and Management of Angkor and the Region of Siem Reap (APSARA), the National Authority of Preah Vihear (NAPV), the Khmer Archaeological Lidar Consortium (KALC), the École française d'Extrême-Orient (EFEO), and the Greater Angkor Project for their assistance and resources, which have greatly enriched our study of this historical and cultural landscape.

Parts of this research have been funded by the Rust Family Foundation, the Social Sciences and Humanities Research Council of Canada Postdoctoral Fellowship, the National Science Foundation Doctoral Dissertation Research Improvement Awards (no. 1638137), the European Research Council Marie Skłodowska-Curie Individual Fellowship (no. 896092), the Archaeology Centre at the University of Toronto, and the Center for Collaborative Synthesis in Archaeology at CU Boulder.

Large language models (Grammarly, Curie, Rubriq and OpenAI) have been used as support tools for proofreading and editing assistance. The AI-assisted interactions served as supplementary support, whereas the critical evaluation, analysis, and originality of arguments and final editorial decisions remain entirely those of the author.

Finally, I would like to thank the Climate Change and History Research Initiative at Princeton University for a delightful conference at Princeton, NJ, which inspired this volume. And the Coalition for Archaeological Synthesis and the Urban Adaptation to Climate Change workshop funded by the Amerind Foundation where I was able to further explore some of these ideas.

References

Bourdonneau, É. 2010. Pour en finir avec la « cité hydraulique » ? *Bulletin de l'École Française d'Extrême-Orient* 97–98:409–437.

Briggs, L. P. 1951. *The Ancient Khmer Empire*. Bangkok: White Lotus Press.

Brotherson, D. J. 2019. *Commerce, the Capital, and Community: Trade ceramics, settlement patterns and continuity throughout the demise of Angkor*. PhD Thesis. University of Sydney.

Buckley, B. M., K. J. Anchukaitis, D. Penny, R. Fletcher, E. R. Cook, M. Sano, C. Nam Le, A. Wichienkeeo, T. T. Minh, and T. M. Hong. 2010. Climate as a contributing factor in the demise of Angkor, Cambodia. *Proceedings of the National Academy of Sciences* 107:6748–6752.

Buckley, B. M., R. Fletcher, S.-Y. S. Wang, B. Zottoli, and C. Pottier. 2014. Monsoon extremes and society over the past millennium on mainland Southeast Asia. *Quaternary Science Reviews* 95:1–19.

Carleton, W. C., S. Klassen, J. Niles-Weed, D. Evans, P. Roberts, and H. S. Groucutt. 2023. Bayesian regression versus machine learning for rapid age estimation of archaeological features identified with Lidar at Angkor. *Scientific Reports* 13 (1): Article 1. https://doi.org/10.1038/s41598-023-44875-0.

Carter, A. K., S. Klassen, M. T. Stark, M. Polkinghorne, P. Heng, D. Evans, and R. Chhay. 2021. The evolution of agro-urbanism: A case study from Angkor, Cambodia. *Journal of Anthropological Archaeology* 63:101323. https://doi.org/10.1016/j.jaa.2021.101323.

Cœdès, G. 1968. *The Indianized States of Southeast Asia*. Canberra: Australian National University Press.

Day, M. B., D. A. Hodell, M. Brenner, H. J. Chapman, J. H. Curtis, W. F. Kenney, A. L. Kolata, and L. C. Peterson. 2012. Paleoenvironmental history of the West Baray, Angkor (Cambodia). *Proceedings of the National Academy of Sciences* 109 (4): 1046–1051.

Evans, D. 2007. *Putting Angkor on the Map: A New Survey of a Khmer "Hydraulic City" in Historical and Theoretical Context*. PhD Thesis. University of Sydney.

Evans, D., R. Fletcher, C. Pottier, J. B. Chevance, D. Soutif, B. S. Tan, et al. 2013. Uncovering archaeological landscapes at Angkor using Lidar. *Proceedings of the National Academy of Sciences* 110 (31): 12595–12600. https://doi.org/10.1073/pnas.1306539110.

Evans, D., R. Fletcher, S. Klassen, C. Pottier, and P. Wijker. 2023a. Trajectories of urbanism in the Angkorian world. In *The Angkorian World*, ed. Mitch Hendrickson, Miriam T. Stark, and Damian Evans, 173–194. London: Routledge.

Evans, D., M. Polkinghorne, R. Fletcher, D. Brotherson, T. Hall, S. Klassen, and P. Wijker. 2023b. Perspectives on the "Collapse" of Angkor and the Khmer Empire. In *The Angkorian World*, ed. Mitch Hendrickson, Miriam T. Stark, and Damian Evans, 541–553. London: Routledge. https://library.oapen.org/handle/20.500.12657/75014.

Fletcher, R., D. Penny, D. Evans, C. Pottier, M. Barbetti, M. Kummu, T. Lustig., and Authority for the Protection and Management of Angkor and the Region of Siem Reap (APSARA) Department of Monuments and Archaeology Team. 2008. The water management network of Angkor, Cambodia. *Antiquity* 82 (317): 658–670.

Goloubew, V. 1941. L'hydraulique urbaine et agricole à l'époque des rois d'Angkor. *Bulletin Économique de l'Indochine* 1:9–18.

Groslier, B.-P. 1979. La cité hydraulique angkorienne: Exploitation ou surexploitation du sol? *Bulletin de l'École Française d'Extrême-Orient* 66:161–202.

Hawken, S. 2011. *Metropolis of Ricefields: A Topographical Classification of a Dispersed Urban Complex*. Sydney: The University of Sydney.

Hawken, S., and S. Klassen. 2023. Angkor's local temple communities: Towards an algorithmic approach to understanding Angkorian suburban settlement patterns. In *The Angkorian World*, ed. Mitch Hendrickson, Miriam T. Stark, and Damian Evans, 195–215. London: Routledge.

Hendrickson, M., M. T. Stark, and D. Evans, eds. 2023. *The Angkorian World*. Routledge. https://doi.org/10.4324/9781351128940.

Hua, Q., D. Cook, J. Fohlmeister, D. Penny, P. Bishop, and S. Buckman. 2017. Radiocarbon dating of a speleothem record of paleoclimate for Angkor, Cambodia. *Radiocarbon* 59 (6): 1873–1890.

Klassen, S. 2018. *Adaptive Capacity of the Water Management Systems of Two Medieval Khmer Cities, Angkor and Koh Ker*. PhD Thesis. Arizona State University.

Klassen, S., and D. Evans. 2020. Top-down and bottom-up water management: A diachronic model of changing water management strategies at Angkor, Cambodia. *Journal of Anthropological Archaeology* 58:101166. https://doi.org/10.1016/j.jaa.2020.101166.

Klassen, S., J. Weed, and D. Evans. 2018. Semi-supervised machine learning approaches for predicting the chronology of archaeological sites: A case study of temples from medieval Angkor, Cambodia. *PLoS One* 13 (11): e0205649. https://doi.org/10.1371/journal.pone.0205649.

Klassen, S., T. Attorre, D. Brotherson, R. Chhay, W. Johnson, I. Moffat, and R. Fletcher. 2021a. Deciphering a timeline of demise at medieval Angkor, Cambodia using remote sensing. *Remote Sensing* 13 (11): 2094.

Klassen, S., A. K. Carter, D. H. Evans, S. Ortman, M. T. Stark, A. A. Loyless, et al. 2021b. Diachronic modeling of the population within the medieval Greater Angkor Region settlement complex. *Science Advances* 7 (19): eabf8441. https://doi.org/10.1126/sciadv.abf8441.

Klassen, S., S. G. Ortman, J. Lobo, and D. Evans. 2022. Provisioning an early city: Spatial equilibrium in the agricultural economy at Angkor, Cambodia. *Journal of Archaeological Method and Theory* 29 (3): 763–794. https://doi.org/10.1007/s10816-021-09535-5.

Klassen, S., T. Pappagallo, and D. Evans. 2023. From the jungle to the lab: Using remote-sensing and deep learning to map archaeological features in lab-based settings. In *Digital Archaeology. Promises and Impasses*, ed. Tuna Kalaycı, Karsten Lambers, and Victor Klinkenberg, 76–94. Leiden: Sidestone Press. (*Analecta Praehistorica Leidensia* 51). https://doi.org/10.59641/f48820ir.

Landauer, J., S. Klassen, A. O. Wijker, J. van der Kroon, A. Jaszkowski, and W. B. V. der Vaart. 2025. Beyond the Greater Angkor Region: Automatic large-scale mapping of Angkorian-period reservoirs in satellite imagery using deep learning. *PLoS One* 20 (3): e0320452. https://doi.org/10.1371/journal.pone.0320452.

Lustig, E., and T. Lustig. 2019. Losing ground: Decline of Angkor's middle-level officials. *Journal of Southeast Asian Studies* 50 (3): 409–430. https://doi.org/10.1017/S0022463419000365.

Penny, D., C. Pottier, M. Kummu, R. Fletcher, U. Zoppi, M. Barbetti, and S. Tous. 2005. Hydrological history of the West Baray, Angkor, revealed through palynological analysis of sediments from the West Mebon. *Bulletin de l'Ecole Française d'Extrême-Orient* 92 (3): 497–521.

Penny, D., C. Zachreson, R. Fletcher, D. Lau, J. T. Lizier, N. Fischer, D. Evans, C. Pottier, and M. Prokopenko. 2018. The demise of Angkor: Systemic vulnerability of urban infrastructure to climatic variations. *Science Advances* 4 (10): eaau4029. https://doi.org/10.1126/sciadv.aau4029.

Penny, D., T. Hall, D. Evans, and M. Polkinghorne. 2019. Geoarchaeological evidence from Angkor, Cambodia, reveals a gradual decline rather than a catastrophic 15th-century collapse. *Proceedings of the National Academy of Sciences* 116 (11): 4871–4876.

Pottier, C. 1993. *Préparation d'une carte archéologique de la région d'Angkor*. Mémoire de DEA.
Pottier, C. 1999. *Carte Archéologique de la Région d'Angkor. Zone SudI*. PhD Thesis. Université Paris III - Sorbonne Nouvelle.
Redman, C. L. 2013. Resilience theory in archaeology. *American Anthropologist* 107 (1): 70–77.
Sedov, L. A. 1963. On the problem of the economic system in Angkor Cambodia in the IX XII centuries. Translated by Antonia Glasse. *Narody Asii i Afriki, Istoria, Ekonomika, Kul'tura* 6:73–81.
Van Liere, W. J. 1982. Was Angkor a hydraulic society? *Ruam Botkhwam Prawat Sat* 4:36–48.

What Price Success? Environmental and Human Costs of South Indian Agricultural Histories

Kathleen D. Morrison

Abstract Despite its widespread use, the concept of sustainability is highly ambiguous, with multiple interpretations of its meaning. Among these, the 'needs' of the present and future remain largely undefined, a significant omission given highly unequal levels of consumption, past and present. Food systems and land use currently have a large environmental footprint; reducing the damage inherent in the current agro-industrial model can be informed by insights from the thousands of years of agrarian history studied by historians and archaeologists. Indeed, many past and present agricultural regimes have been held up as examples of sustainability. Too often, however, such claims are based primarily on temporal longevity without consideration of past power relations. Using data from multiple trajectories of agricultural change in southern India, I argue that even longstanding historical systems have tradeoffs and may be built on foundations of social inequality, suggesting that historical scholars pay close attention to diverse social and environmental effects of past lifeways.

Keywords South India · Sustainability · Agriculture · Archaeology · Irrigation · Rainfed farming

1 Sustainability and Ambiguity

The concept of sustainability, which first came to prominence in the late 1980s, has by now become thoroughly institutionalized, both in global governance and in business. In the latter, both cost-cutting efforts and public relations have led to an entirely new 'sustainability industry,' with its own defined positions and career tracks. Kick-started by the 1987 publication of the World Commission on

K. D. Morrison (✉)
University of Pennsylvania, Philadelphia, PA, USA
e-mail: kathy.morrison@sas.upenn.edu

J. F. Haldon, R. Fernandes (eds.), *Bridging History and Policy*, Understanding Complex Systems, https://doi.org/10.1007/978-3-032-24379-9_22

Environment and Development (WCED) report, *Our Common Future*, commonly referred to as the Brundtland commission, the term sustainability was rapidly adopted. Based on a request by the United Nations general assembly to develop "a global agenda for change" (1987:5), the Brundtland commission report famously championed the concept of 'sustainable development.' Defining sustainability as "meeting the needs of the present without compromising the ability of future generations to meet their own needs," the WCED report spawned numerous additional studies. As Holmberg (1994, cited in Mebratu 1998:502) noted just 7 years later, there were already more than 80 different definitions of the term, most related in some way to the Brundtland phrasing. Sustainability has remained central to global development and is now enshrined in the United Nation's current 17 official sustainable development goals (SDGs).

Despite its popularity, the concept of sustainability has also come under considerable critique, in part for its essential ambiguity (Mebratu 1998). Salas-Zapata and Ortiz-Muñoz (2018) show that scholars use the term variously—referring to sustainability as a set of criteria, a vision or goal, an object, or an approach—and sometimes more than one of these meanings in the same sentence. In this schema (Fig. 1), the Brundtland definition is primarily a vision or goal (Fig. 1b), defining an aspirational future. Since then, sustainability has arguably become more of an object (Fig. 1c), tracked and quantified by dedicated sustainability professionals. In order to realize the Brundtland vision, however, those deploying sustainability as an approach (Fig. 1d) surely require some set of criteria (Fig. 1a) to evaluate diverse strategies proposed as 'sustainable' (closest to Fig. 1c). It seems evident from all this that a more precise and varied vocabulary is needed.

Definitional debate has often rightly centered around the question of 'needs,' especially the implication that currently unmet needs (i.e. among the poor) also must be considered in any plan for the future. In this sense, sustainability has often been seen as necessarily centering equality or as progressive (e.g. Coulthard et al. 2011). One can also, however, see the concept as (perhaps inadvertently) status quo oriented, today's 'needs' in many cases being yesterday's luxuries. Needs are culturally rather than biologically defined, and beyond the level of base subsistence can be highly variable. One might further argue that contemporary 'needs,' even though

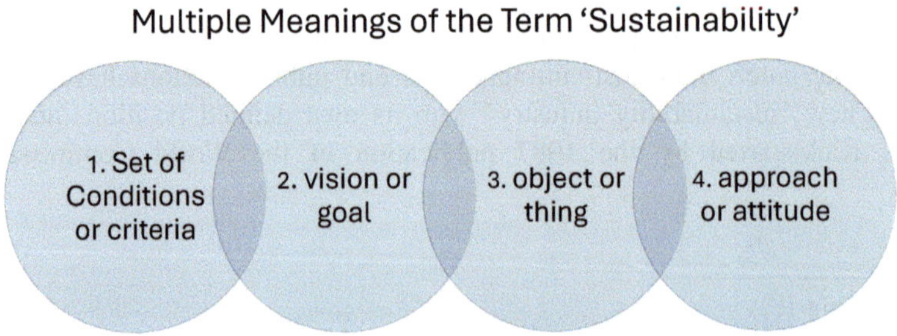

Fig. 1 The multiple uses and meanings of the term sustainability. Redrawn from Salas-Zapata and Ortiz-Muñoz (2019), text in © has been slightly edited for clarity

these are not being fully met on a global scale, have *already* damaged our planet to a significant degree. Maintaining the status quo, even in its current inequitable form, is a recipe for ecological disaster. Even without clarity on what the 'needs of the future' might be, the 'needs' of the present are already too much for planetary boundaries to bear (Williams et al. 2025; Brown 2017). What we need, then, is not to sustain our world as it is, but to transform it. While the term sustainability has indeed been used to express this very sentiment, it seems oddly unsuited to the task, especially in light of its institutionalization as an adjunct to programs of 'development.'

The idea of sustainability is intrinsically historical. While the Brundtland definition links present and future, many scholars have noted that examples of 'sustainable' practices—on which more below—are often ones with long histories that have continued into the present (forms of 'traditional' agriculture, for example), or which have died out but might be revived (e.g. Guttmann-Bond 2010; Zagata et al. 2020). In this sense, the past presents a significant repertoire of experience and a valuable resource for the future. If, however, we consider that this very same past also led to our current (unsustainable) planetary boundary-breaking moment, then it seems critical to also focus on the more problematic historical processes leading up the present. In a world where, for example, the wealthiest 1% emit as much greenhouse gas emissions as two-thirds of humanity (Oxfam 2023), understanding the development of institutionalized inequality seems like a critical environmental as well as social research goal. Mining history for models of 'sustainability' thus requires us to ask 'sustainable for whom?' The subjects of this concern include ecosystems, species, societies, and individuals with, however, little agreement on how to balance conflicting demands on the planet. If people, domesticates, and soils all prosper, does a reduction in forest cover make a particular land use regime unsustainable? The Brundtland definition is not very helpful here. It seems to prioritize humans over the plants and animals perhaps lost with the forest, a clear statement of values, but taking it to its logical extreme seems to require that we have to wait and see—or somehow predict—if this forest loss eventually leads to people unable to meet present and future needs. In some sense, then, we can never really assess sustainability with full confidence, an intrinsic ambiguity that calls for a level of humility.

2 Agriculture and Food

Currently, agriculture is a significant contributor to global greenhouse gas emissions, with paddy rice contributing about 13% to global methane emissions (Ritchie et al. 2020). Although current levels of food production are more than enough to feed the global population, a huge proportion of food is wasted and this, along with high levels of inequality and unrest has resulted, by UN estimates, between 713 and 757 million people facing hunger in 2023 (FAO 2024). The environmental footprint of industrial agriculture is, further, very large, contributing, for example, to coastal dead zones and accelerating biodiversity loss. It is therefore important to promote farming and food systems that reduce or eliminate the damage inherent in the current agro-industrial model.

The agrarian crisis in India can be indexed by an appalling number of farmer suicides over the last 30 years or so, following the opening up of the national economy to world markets in 1990s, a process known as economic liberalization (Deshpande and Arora 2010; Vasavi 2008). Understandings of the crisis vary, but there is a documented link (Kennedy and King 2014:1) between "…the percentage of marginal farmers, cash crop production, and indebted farmers, and suicide rates." The causes of farmer suicides are complex. The specificity of agrarian suicide, which is not concentrated among the poorest members of rural society such as landless laborers, suggests that they are more than a simple response to scarcity. As Shah (2012:1159–60) argues:

> A wide range of scholarly literature … shows that the suicides are a result of social and structural transformation, especially the way in which these transformations contribute to the hegemonic reproduction of rural–urban and agriculture–industry inequality. Ignoring this sizeable literature on structural reasons for suicide, liberal developmental approaches commonly reduce suicides to a variety of shortfalls, such as reduction in prices, and to various forms of water and resource scarcities.

She goes on to argue (Shah 2012:1160), "Suicides are thus incorporated in the metanarrative of scarcity that has shaped half a century of agrarian development entirely focused on techno-institutional changes." Government and development actors thus tend to focus on technological 'fixes,' the same logic behind the disastrous Green Revolution policies of the mid-twentieth century and more recent 'solutions' such as large dam projects, a 'New Green Revolution' and a proposal to interlink India's rivers (Friedmann 1990; Mehta and Mehta 2013). Shah's ethnographic work among elderly residents of Devangere District, Karnataka, (where water is much more abundant than in our study area discussed below) shows strikingly different historical experiences of food scarcity, underlining the need to consider agricultural systems and their potential 'sustainability' in light of specific gender, caste, and class-based experiences. She (2012;1170) writes:

> Those who projected the image of India as a dying and hungry nation in order to justify the introduction of the green revolution were referring to the hunger and food shortage faced by dispossessed people, such as both of the lower caste women I interviewed. These people experienced food shortage for much of their lives not because the food was in short supply. The higher caste men I interviewed in the same age group living in the same region had sufficient access to food, even during famine. To reiterate the point already made by several historians, the socio-economic dispossession created famine and hunger, not the shortage of food.

Long-lived traditional agricultural systems, thus, have had diverse effects on communities as well as natural environments, effects which may continue to structure expectation and affect (Shah 2012). As we move back in time, it often becomes difficult to recover the multiplicity of historical experiences such as those revealed by oral histories, but this does not make them irrelevant to the 'lessons from the past' offered by historical scholars (Morrison 2026).

2.1 Food Sovereignty

Among the most aspirational formulations of what farming and food systems could be is that of food sovereignty (Wittman 2009). As defined by Via Campesina (https://viacampesina.org/en/what-is-food-sovereignty/):

> Food sovereignty is the right of peoples to healthy and culturally appropriate food produced through ecologically sound and sustainable methods, and their right to define their own food and agriculture systems. It puts the aspirations and needs of those who produce, distribute and consume food at the heart of food systems and policies rather than the demands of markets and corporations. It defends the interests and inclusion of the next generation. It offers a strategy to resist and dismantle the current corporate trade and food regime, and directions for food, farming, pastoral and fisheries systems determined by local producers and users.

While sustainability is invoked in this definition, it does go further in specifying what this might mean via its combined focus on (human) rights and aspirations and on "ecologically sound methods," presumably referring to the natural world. While the Brundtland definition refers simply to 'needs,' Via Campesina's statement more carefully contextualizes consumption ("healthy and culturally appropriate food," the latter something that might be expected to vary in time and place), while centering agency and choice. People are cast not only as consumers, but also as producers and distributors, broadening the focus significantly to larger socio-economic structures. Via Campesina obviously takes a position on which structures are the problem, something advocates of technological 'fixes,' discussed below, may disagree with, but I argue that the broader definitional framework provided by the food sovereignty literature represents an improvement over the problematic and ambiguous notion of sustainability. When we ask: 'sustainable for whom,' we raise similar questions of value, not only balancing human needs against those of other species, but also attending to social, cultural, and historical contexts.

3 Archaeology and History

Historians and archaeologists who argue that past practices were 'sustainable,' are using the concept as an object, as a system or set of strategies and practices with particular characteristics. Evaluating such arguments can be challenging. Environmental measures such as soil health, hydrological stability, or features of local ecosystems over time would seem critical, but these required targeted research, and such measures are rarely available. As discussed above, the social and cultural impacts of specific systems would also seem critical, though again, these may be difficult to uncover, requiring extensive research. Despite these challenges, historical evidence can provide a rich source of inspiration. As Stump (2010: 1251) notes:

> … any appeal to the twin concepts of sustainability and conservation invites comparisons between the contemporary and historical situations on the grounds that both refer to the

> need to balance short-term gains with long term resource maintenance. Since the future is unknown, the sustainability of a system must be predicted either through experimentation or by reference to the behavior of similar systems in the past. The histories of specific economies or environments may therefore be employed as potential sources of positive or negative precedents on the grounds that if sustainability can be demonstrated in the past, then this at least suggests the possibility of future sustainability. Conversely, if a mode of resource use can be shown to have caused environmental depletion in the past, or can be likened to a past community that collapsed or suffered as a result of similar practices, then this would seem to indicate that the system in question is unsustainable.

Too often, however, scholars have taken sheer longevity of a system as *a priori* evidence for sustainability. Stump (2010) discusses the example of the East African site of Engariku, an irrigated and terraced site with a 400-year history of supporting intensive cultivation. Engariku's relic field system has been variously characterized as *both*, in Stump's (2010) phrasing, "ancient and backward," and "long lived and sustainable." The simple inversion of colonial narratives of degradation and lack of progress into post-colonial sustainability narratives, as well as their remixing into competing development agendas, is a familiar story from South Asia as well as East Africa (Morrison 2014; cf. Fairhead and Leach 1996). Stump (2010: 1253) makes the critical point that all of these opposing narratives of Engariku are built on shaky empirical ground: "… the point to be emphasized here is not simply that these competing narratives produce opposing conclusions, but rather that they do so by reference to unsubstantiated perceptions of the past."

Just as Stump makes the case that what he calls "unresolved historical questions" of "indigenous conservation" (2010:1259, and see Lang and Stump 2017; Fisher 2020) can be evaluated archaeologically, so I also argue that we can understand past agricultural systems in southern India in both social and agroecological terms, skipping the problematic language of 'sustainability' to focus on the causes, courses, and consequences of agricultural change; consequences including both social and environmental outcomes. In the final sections of this paper, I discuss two main forms of agricultural production in southern India, both with long historical records continuing to the present. Both have been held up as solutions to the present agrarian crisis though usually, as Stump points out for Engariku, without much supporting evidence.

4 South Indian Agrarian Trajectories

In southern India, many crops and animal breeds, agricultural features and technologies, and methods of production have continued in use for as much as 5000 years, testament to their historical endurance and viability. But can we say they are sustainable? The Brundtland definition is noticeably silent on just whose needs are met in such systems, but if agrarian histories are to be used as examples of sustainable agriculture, it's worth asking just whose needs—humans and nonhumans—were being sustained. As Stump argues, the mere persistence of a system is not sufficient grounds to argue for or against sustainability. Context matters.

The Deccan plateau of southern India lies in the rainshadow of the Western Ghat mountain chain. Tilting gently down from west to east, the northern Karnataka tableland is broken by chains and outcrops of high granitic hills, dramatic landscape features that have helped shape rural livelihoods for millennia. In this semi-arid landscape, rainfall is low and highly variable, falling almost exclusively during the summer monsoon. Using a combination of archaeology, text-based history, and paleoecology, we have studied the last 5000 years of land use in this region, identifying at least four major strategies: hunting and gathering; pastoralism; rainfed (dry) farming of millets and pulses combined with herding; and intensive perennial (wet) agriculture. These are not fully exclusive categories and indeed, the very diversity and flexibility of land use practices seems to be an important way people have thrived in this challenging environment.

This long land use history is also associated with social and political change and modifications of vegetation, soils, and biodiversity. As outlined below, both dry and wet farming have extended histories in this region, but calling either 'sustainable' on that basis alone seems insufficient. To the extent that the present always differs from the past in some ways, wholesale recommendations of one approach or another can have little value. This does not, however, mean that there is nothing to be learned from historical analysis. Understanding the limits and possibilities of past land use practices requires more contextual and targeted analyses. For whom are these systems sustainable? Who benefits and who pays? An agrarian system can "meet the needs" of a group of people, while still being extremely unequal. If "needs" refer to a baseline of subsistence or mere survival, that is a low bar. On the human side of the equation, we might also ask if and how the system allows for a standard of human flourishing, not only if bellies are filled. More broadly, practices such as burning, grazing, plowing, irrigation, planting, hunting—the suite of activities associated with diverse land use practices—shape plant and animal habitat and distributions, impact soils and hydrology, and of course, over the very long term, affect global climate. Some forms of environmental damage certainly 'compromise the ability of future (human) generations' to meet their needs. Others might not, but may still entail significant damage to non-human life—extinction, extirpation, biodiversity loss—that if they have unknown impacts on humanity, certainly also raise the question: sustainable for whom?

4.1 Dry Farming in Southern India

The development of agriculture in South Asia was a mosaic process, with multiple non-synchronous centers of early farming and a combination of local domestication of plants and animals alongside continued borrowing and experimentation attested to by the movement of domesticates across long distances. Farming of millets and pulses began around 3000 BCE in southern India, with several locally domesticated small grains later supplemented by African millets, and by non-local grains such as wheat, barley, and rice (Fuller 2006, 2011; Winchell et al. 2018). The latter were, however, grown only in very small quantities and the transformative development of large-scale rice agriculture in South India appears to have begun only around 2000 years ago in the wetter regions of the far south, with more arid regions adopting rice more slowly, alongside the expansion of irrigation infrastructure. Millets require very little water and can be grown with or without supplemental watering, but rice is a thirsty crop, here only grown as paddy, or flooded field cropping.

South Indian dry farming has always integrated domestic animals, including caprids and cattle, with secondary products such as manure, traction, and milk at least as important as meat. Overall, the 5000-year history of dry farming is characterized by extensive use of fallows, intercropping, diverse crop repertoires and ongoing experimentation with new crops and landraces. In the low and variable rainfall areas of northern Karnataka, settled villages were often linked to significant levels of mobility, with movement common in bad years, whether caused by poor monsoons, political unrest, or high levels of taxation. The capacity of millet-pulse farming to support very large populations is not entirely clear (cf. Petrie et al. 2016) and is certainly dependent on technologies of transport. Certainly, the labor investment (human and animal) in dry farming is less than that of irrigated rice, and both historians and ethnographers have commented on the relatively flatter social hierarchy associated with dry farmed regions (Morrison 2015, 2016). Millets are known to be nutrient rich, especially in comparison with rice, so their relatively lower productivity is also balanced by well-studied health implications.

By the first few centuries BCE, in our study region, dry farming was increasingly supported by a range of soil and water control features, from gravel-mulched fields to terraces, to complex systems of runoff-fed reservoirs (often known as tanks). Reservoirs were built as early as the first few centuries CE (Bauer and Morrison 2014), but in our study area became important only after the first millennium CE, with the expansion of cities (Morrison 2000, 2009). Reservoirs, many of them centuries old and still in use, continue to be important features across southern India and Sri Lanka, with 'The Cascaded Tank-Village System in the Dry Zone of Sri Lanka" officially designated as one of the Globally Important Agricultural Heritage Systems (GIAHS) by the Food and Agriculture Organization (FAO) of the UN. Advertised on the GIAHS home page as "Traditional knowledge and sustainable practices for global solutions," this dry-zone reservoir system is explicitly marked as an example of sustainability.

With 5000 years of millet and pulse farming and 1000 years of reservoir-assisted farming all going strong today, traditional South Indian dry farming systems are often seen as sustainable. Depending on the degree of landscape modification and population density, the environmental impacts of dry farming are moderate in comparison with irrigated systems. However, despite the pervasive myth of harmonious community-managed resources (Morrison 2009, 2015, 2016), dry farmers have long been vulnerable to state and elite action.

Between the fourteenth and sixteenth centuries, the imperial city of Vijayanagara, capital of the eponymous empire that claimed large parts of southern India, was sustained in part by canal-irrigated rice and other wet crops. Reservoir building also followed urban population growth, with the more extensive tracts not suitable for canal building used for dry farming and grazing. While these strategies predated the establishment of the city, many new reservoirs were added to the existing network, with a particular construction boom in the early sixteenth century (Morrison 2009). Notable for their lofty sluice gates and evocation of temple architecture, reservoirs of this period tend to be significantly more elaborate in scale and ornamentation than earlier facilities. Contemporaneous inscriptions reveal a moral and political economy of prestation, with public donations serving both spiritual, political, and economic purposes. Among the most prestigious forms of donation was (financing) the construction of reservoirs, a route to power and prestige followed by many aspirational elites (Morrison 2009, 2012). Following the abandonment of the city of Vijayanagara at the end of the sixteenth century, many of the reservoir systems around the city were abandoned, leaving a record of silted-in, breached, and otherwise unsuccessful facilities. While the pattern is not absolute, it seems that many of these grandiose gestures instantiated both in texts and material remains were more successful as vehicles for elite display than as support for dry farming. These particular reservoirs are not so much testament to ancient wisdom as ancient politics, though other reservoirs have had more consistent histories of use, highlighting the need for contextual analysis.

Esha Shah's (2008:663) historical analysis, which included oral histories of lower caste tank diggers whose perspectives never emerge in the inscriptional record, also reveals the power dynamics involved in these celebrated systems, from non-payment of wages to low-caste tank builders to human sacrifice. She explains:

> Folk literature on tanks—stories, legends, and songs—originates from three sources. The first set of stories and myths I found were narrated to me by members of the artisan caste of Voddas, who are rarely mentioned in the inscriptional source or in south Indian historiography but who figure prominently in folk accounts as tank builders.... The myths and stories remembered by Voddas are markers of their identity and thus are usually not associated with any particular tank. A second set of stories narrated by higher-caste farmers and temple priests, in which Voddas also figure significantly, are usually associated with specific tanks. The third type of folk literature consists of songs about the sacrifice of women in tanks, and these are usually sung during times of drought and water scarcity by Dalit women—formerly an untouchable, lower caste. Almost every tank in the semiarid region of south Karnataka has a story or a sacrifice song attached to it.

Thus, while dry farming regions have been characterized by less social hierarchy than irrigated ones, making a living as a dry farmer in this region has always been somewhat precarious, risks posed both by the erratic monsoons and by always-changing contexts of power.

4.2 *Irrigated Farming in Southern India*

The expansive range of reservoirs across southern India and Sri Lanka means that they occur in different rainfall zones and in regions with varied topography and geology, making their agrarian potential highly variable. Where canals or other perennial water sources are linked to reservoirs, as they often are where topography allows, entirely different crops can be supported, including high-status wet rice. In the dry zone of Sri Lanka, both canal- and runoff-fed reservoirs were vital to the support of early cities (Myrdal-Runebjer 1996; Gilliland et al. 2013), suggesting that they, too, were enmeshed in local power relations. This does not, in itself, mean that reservoir systems are 'unsustainable,' any more than their historical persistence means the opposite. In every case, the assessment is contextual. The 'needs' of low caste people sacrificed for tanks were clearly not being met; in the present, that same reservoir might provide critical support to a local family.

Rice, originally domesticated outside southern India, came to be central to the region, with words for food and for rice lexically identical in several South Indian languages. Grown in a small way during the Iron Age (Kingwell-Banham 2019; Morrison et al. 2015), large-scale rice production seems to have become important only around the Early Historic period (300 BCE- CE 300), also the time of initial urbanization in the south. As I have described elsewhere (Morrison 2016, and see Gutiérrez 2018), by CE 1000, elite cuisines built around rice were well-established in southern India, with a marked distinction between the primarily dry-farmed ingredients used in the foods of the poor and the water- and labor-intensive components of elite and temple cuisines. In more arid regions, wet agriculture required substantial investments in infrastructure such as canals and anicuts, the large diversion weirs that redirected river water into the hundreds of kilometers of ancient canals that we have documented around the city of Vijayanagara. All of these canals have continued in use, an impressive 600-plus year record of continuous cultivation.

In this region, irrigated farming was (and is) highly productive, supporting one of the largest cities in Asia during the sixteenth century. Because paddy rice receives a significant proportion of nutrients from water-borne sources rather than soil, it can maintain fertility for a long time. In our study area, the construction of a hydroelectric dam across the Tungabhadra River in the 1940s and 50 s inundated some of the ancient canal headworks, blocking the silt-rich water that once flowed to local fields. These days, farmers use chemical fertilizers on rice fields. Where this newer technology has replaced anicuts, there is clearly a loss, seen in both water quality and challenges associated with more centralized government control over water distribution versus the canals that still use traditional headworks (Mollinga 2014; Morrison 2000).

Even discounting the very substantial investment in the construction and maintenance of irrigation works, paddy rice is highly labor intensive, often associated with deep structural hierarchies and often unfree labor. Weeding, transplanting, harvesting, and other work can occur throughout the year, often conflicting with the labor demands of more seasonal rainfed fields. If the question 'sustainable for whom?' is asked of wet rice, the answer must certainly leave out more of the population than it does for reservoir irrigation, and many more than for other forms of land use like rainfed farming, pastoralism, or foraging. High productivity has a cost, one not always reconcilable with the 'everyone wins' ethos of some sustainability boosters.

The ecological impacts of irrigated agriculture are more thoroughgoing than that of dry farming, involving significant changes in hydrology and soils. Land continuously under wet rice forms what are called paddy soils, a kind of hardpan that makes alternative land uses difficult. In our study area, the Iron Age (1200–300 BCE) levels at the site of Kadebakele are rich in the remains of grassland animals (Wilcox Black 2022; Morrison et al. 2022), diversity that drops in subsequent periods, likely both a consequence of changes in wild animal use and decline in grassland species. Nineteenth century and later accounts of the region document other environmental changes such as the presence and more recent decline of grassland ungulates and large predators such as tigers across the area, where dry farming and grazing cover considerably more land than the canal-irrigated zone near the city of Vijayanagara (circa 1300–1600). The water birds now associated with rice-growing areas, however, may have benefitted from the extension of paddy fields. Finally, in terms of future generations, it should be noted that rice paddies, like other wetlands, produce methane, a potent greenhouse gas.

5 Discussion

Many South Indian agricultural systems have proven to be exceptionally long lived. While not unchanging, rainfed farming of millets and pulses has sustained local residents for nearly 5000 years. Runoff-fed reservoirs, many organized into long interconnected chains, harvest annual rainfall from hills and hill ranges, making ingenious use of drainage and topography. In our study area in northern Karnataka, some reservoirs are nearly a thousand years old, but in other areas they appear even earlier. Anicuts, long and low diversion dams, divert water from the braided course of the Tungabhadra River, feeding canals that have supported irrigated crops for more than 600 years without a break. If sheer longevity were a measure of sustainability, then any of these might qualify. There is no doubt that the embodied knowledge and experience of generations of South Indian farmers, herders, and others have left us with a wealth of information valuable for both present and future. The highly diverse repertoires of plants and animals, domestic and wild, present a stark comparison to industrial monocropping, traditional agrobiodiversity reflected in healthier diets and habitats. Practices such as intercropping, fallowing, and manuring make rainfed farming feasible in this semi-arid landscape. In rice-growing areas, careful preparation of nursery paddies, the transplanting of seedlings, and minute control over the flow of water produce abundant yields. Bullock-drawn plows are still the norm here, with traction, dairy, and manure critical elements of an agrarian system that does not rely on fossil fuels. Other traditional technologies—terraces, gravel-mulched fields, reservoirs, canals, anicuts, wells, and more—are also outcomes of long experience with this landscape, artifacts of past efforts and aspirations for secure and culturally appropriate food (Morrison 2016). As we seek to meet the needs of the future, this history is rich with possibility. As Stump (2010) argued for Engariku, however, to simplify these complex experiences as either "ancient and backward" or "long lived and sustainable" is to mischaracterize their diverse social and environmental effects.

Dry farming in this region has had less dramatic environmental impacts than irrigation, but the uncertain rains make producer mobility and flexibility critical, with fallows always a necessary strategy for the regeneration of soil fertility. Both green and animal manures require access to woodland and animals; bullocks and cows are precious resources. Access to land for both farming and for grazing and wood collection is of course foundational. In the Medieval period, farmers often responded to taxation or unrest by running away (Stein 2005); to be successful, this strategy requires opportunities elsewhere. Millets and pulses, well-adapted to local conditions, are also notably healthful, a property accounting for the current millet revival among urban elites (Meek 2022). Often supported by a range of small soil and water control features, the success of rainfed farming still depends on external factors such as the timing and amount of rain. Historically, dry farming has been associated with more modest levels of social inequality, perhaps in part because it can support lower population densities.

The famed reservoir or tank systems of southern India and Sri Lanka represent a kind of middle ground between dry farming and intensive irrigated agriculture. Where they are filled year-round (by abundant rainfall, canals, or permanent streams), reservoirs can support highly valued crops such as rice, that consume both water and labor in significant quantities. Many reservoirs are, however, only seasonally filled and in the semi-arid regions of north Karnataka, most cannot support wet crops such as rice. Reservoirs also vary significantly in size, connectivity, and—critically- in social and political arrangements for maintenance and water distribution. In our survey area around the city of Vijayanagara, the attractiveness of reservoirs as vehicles for elite display (Morrison 2012) in the sixteenth century led to the construction of a large number of failed facilities, breached, silted in, and abandoned alongside the capital city. This record does not mean that reservoirs are 'unsustainable' as a whole, but points rather to the importance of context, especially as tank restoration projects gain traction (e.g. Deivalatha and Ambujam 2011). Romantic notions of community management are also laid bare by the work of Esha Shah (2008, 2012) documenting inbuilt caste and gender-based violence within communities.

Irrigated rice is exceptionally productive, with irrigation making it possible to produce several crops per year. In southern India, rice was transformed from an imported crop grown only in small quantities into a major cultural and economic focus. Millet and pulse-based diets, once universal, became the food of the poor during the Medieval period as political and ritual elites adopted water and labor-intensive wet crops. In the area around the city of Vijayanagara, a network of canals taken off from the Tungabhadra River have continuously watered an area of wet crops for more than 600 years. Unlike dry farming, perennially irrigated fields can support larger and denser populations. The development of paddy soils and the wholesale transformation of vegetation and hydrology represents a major environmental change. Even without the use of fossil fuels in production, flooded fields contribute to the production of greenhouse gases via methane generation, though dam construction has made chemical fertilizers necessary, blocking the flow of nutrient-rich silt downstream. In this and other areas under wet rice, deeply unequal regimes of land and labor have emerged, a juxtaposition of wealth and poverty. The price of success here is therefore very high, and the question 'sustainable for whom?' has clear winners and losers.

Both the promise and limits of traditional agricultural systems demand more contextual and empirical analysis; they are too important to be blithely labeled sustainable or unsustainable. We require more precise conceptual structures that reckon with both the human and non-human consequences of specific practices. No land use system is without limits and consequences, and even past land use was always political (cf. Fisher 2024) but the vast archive of the past remains a critical resource for meeting the needs—and aspirations—of the future.

References

Bauer, A. M., and K. D. Morrison. 2014. Water management and reservoirs in India and Sri Lanka. In *The Encyclopedia of the History of Science, Technology, and Medicine in Non-Western Cultures*, ed. H. Selin, 3rd ed., 2207–2214. Amherst: Springer Verlag.

Brown, Katrina. 2017. Global environmental change II: Planetary boundaries – a safe operating space for human geographers? *Progress in Human Geography* 41 (1): 118–130.

Coulthard, Sarah, Derek Johnson, and J. A. McGregor. 2011. Poverty, sustainability and human wellbeing: A social wellbeing approach to the global fisheries crisis. *Global Environmental Change* 21 (2): 453–463.

Deivalatha, A., and N. K. Ambujam. 2011. Sustainable agriculture productivity through restoration of tank irrigation system with stakeholder decision - case study in rural tank eco system. *International Journal of Biodiversity and Conservation* 3 (11): 527–539.

Deshpande, R. S., and Saroj Arora. 2010. *Agrarian Crisis and Farmers' Suicide*. New Delhi; Thousand Oaks, CA: Sage.

Fairhead, James, and Melissa Leach. 1996. *Misreading the African Landscape: Society and Ecology in a Forest-Savanna Mosaic* (African Studies, Series Number 90). Cambridge: Cambridge University Press.

FAO 2024 The State of Food Security and Nutrition in the World https://openknowledge.fao.org/server/api/core/bitstreams/39dbc6d1-58eb-4aac bd8a-47a8a2c07c67/content/cd1254en.html#gsc.tab=0

FAO. Globally Important Agricultural Heritage Systems (GIAHS), The Cascaded Tank-Village System in the Dry Zone of Sri Lanka, Sri Lanka, https://www.fao.org/giahs/giahs-around-the-world/sri-lanka-cascaded-tank-village-system/en

Fisher, Chelsea. 2020. Archaeology for sustainable agriculture. *Journal of Archaeological Research* 28 (3): 393–441.

Fisher, Chelsea. 2024. What ancient farmers can really teach us about adapting to climate change - and how political power influences success or failure. *Down to Earth*, February 27, 2024.

Gale General OneFile (accessed May 22, 2025). https://link-gale-com.proxy.library.upenn.edu/apps/doc/A784185271/ITOF?u=upenn_main&sid=summon&xid=bfff5dd5.
Friedmann, H. 1990. The origins of Third World food dependence. In *The Food Question: Profit Versus People?* ed. H. Bernstein, 13–31. London: Earthscan Publications.
Fuller, Dorian Q. 2006. Agricultural origins and frontiers in South Asia: A working synthesis. *Journal of World Prehistory* 20 (1): 1–86.
Fuller, Dorian Q. 2011. Finding plant domestication in the Indian subcontinent. *Current Anthropology* 52 (S4): S347–S362.
Gilliland, K., et al. 2013. The dry tank: Development and disuse of water management infrastructure in the Anuradhapura hinterland, Sri Lanka. *Journal of Archaeological Science* 40 (2): 1012–1028.
Gutiérrez, Andrea. 2018. Jewels set in stone: Hindu temple recipes in medieval Cōḻa epigraphy. *Religions* 9 (9): https://doi.org/10.3390/rel9090270.
Guttmann-Bonn, Erika. 2010. Sustainability out of the past: How archaeology can save the planet. *World Archaeology* 42 (3): 355–366.
Kennedy, Jonathan, and Lawrence King. 2014. The political economy of farmers' suicides in India: indebted cash-crop farmers with marginal landholdings explain state-level variation in suicide rates. *Globalization and Health* 10:16. http://www.globalizationandhealth.com/content/10/1/16.
Kingwell-Banham, Eleanor. 2019. Dry, rainfed or irrigated? Reevaluating the role and development of rice agriculture in Iron Age-Early Historic South India using archaeobotanical approaches. *Archaeological and Anthropological Sciences* 11 (12): 6485–6500.
Lang, Carol, and Daryl Stump. 2017. Geoarchaeological evidence for the construction, irrigation, cultivation, and resilience of 15th–18th century AD terraced landscape at Engariku, Tanzania. *Quaternary Research* 88 (3): 382–399.
Mebratu, Desta. 1998. Sustainability and sustainable development: Historical and conceptual review. *Environmental Impact Assessment Review* 18 (6): 493–520.
Meek, David. 2022. From marginalized to miracle: Critical bioregionalism, jungle farming and the move to millets in Karnataka, India. *Agriculture and Human Values* 39 (3): 871–883.
Mehta, Dharmendra, and Naveen K. Mehta. 2013. Interlinking of rivers in India: Issues and challenges. *Geo-Eco-Marina* 19:137–143.
Mollinga, Peter P. 2014. Canal irrigation and the hydrosocial cycle. The morphogenesis of contested water control in the Tungabhadra Left Bank Canal, South India. *Geoforum* 57:192–204.
Morrison, K. D. 2000. *Fields of Victory: Vijayanagara and the Course of Intensification*. New Delhi: Munshiram Manoharlal.
Morrison, K.D. 2009. *Daroji Valley: Landscape History, Place, and the Making of a Dryland Reservoir System* (Vijayanagara Research Project Monograph Series 18). Delhi: Manohar Press.
Morrison, K. D. 2012. Doorways to the divine: Vijayanagara reservoirs and rural devotional landscapes. *South Asian Studies* 28 (2): 157–169.
Morrison, K. D. 2014. Conceiving ecology and stopping the clock: Narratives of balance, loss, and degradation. In *Shifting Ground: People, Animals, and Mobility in India's Environmental History*, ed. M. Rangarajan and K. Sivaramakrishnan, 39–64. Oxford: Oxford University Press.
Morrison, K. D. 2015. Archaeologies of flow: Water and the landscapes of Southern India past, present, and future. *Journal of Field Archaeology* 40 (5): 560–580.
Morrison, K. D. 2016. From millets to rice (and back again?): Cuisine, cultivation and health in early South India. In *A Companion to South Asia in the Past*, ed. Gwen Robbins Schug and S. Walimbe, 358–373. New York: Wiley Blackwell.
Morrison, K.D. (2025), Beyond "Lessons From the Past": Archaeology and Environmental Crisis. Am. Anthropol., 127: 887–889. https://doi.org/10.1111/aman.70005
Morrison, K. D. 2026. Beyond 'Lessons from the past:' Archaeology and environmental crisis, vital topics forum: Archaeology, politics, and environmental crisis. *American Anthropologist*.

Morrison, K. D., Seetha N. Reddy, and Arunima Kashyap. 2015. Agrarian transitions in Iron Age Southern India: Social and environmental implications. In *South Asian archaeology 2012*, ed. V. Lefèvre, A. Didier, and B. Mutin, 185–196. Paris: Agence France-Muséums.

Morrison, K. D., C. M. Sinopoli, K. Wilcox Black, M. Trivedi, A. Bauer, M. Lycett, S. Haricharan, J. Bates, and S. Reddy. 2022. From the Southern Neolithic to the Iron Age: A view from Kadebakele. In *Beyond Stones and More Stones*, ed. Ravi Korisettar, vol. 3, 146–213. Bengaluru: The Mythic Society.

Myrdal-Runebjer, E. 1996. *Rice and Millet: An Archaeological Case Study of a Sri Lankan Transbasin Irrigation System*. Stockholm: University of Gothenburg Department of Archaeology. Oxfam, November 20, 2023. Richest 1% emit as much planet-heating pollution as two-thirds of humanity. https://www.oxfam.org/en/press-releases/richest-1-emit-much-planet-heating-pollution-two-thirds-humanity

Petrie, C. A., et al. 2016. Feeding ancient cities in South Asia: Dating the adoption of rice, millet and tropical pulses in the Indus Civilisation. *Antiquity* 90 (354): 1489–1504.

Ritchie, H., Rosado, P., & Roser, M. 2020. Breakdown of carbon dioxide, methane and nitrous oxide emissions by sector. Published online at OurWorldinData.org. Retrieved from: https://ourworldindata.org/emissions-by-sector [Online Resource].

Sala-Zapata, Walter A., and Sara M. Ortiz-Muñoz. 2019. Analysis of meanings of the concept of sustainability. *Sustainable Development* 27:153–161.

Salas-Zapata WA, Ortiz-Muñoz SM. 2019. Analysis of meanings of the concept of sustainability. Sustainable Development. 27:153–161. https://doi.org/10.1002/sd.1885

Shah, Esha. 2008. Telling otherwise: A historical anthropology of tank irrigation technology in South India. *Technology and Culture* 49 (3): 652–674. https://doi.org/10.1353/tech.0.0054.

Shah, Esha. 2012. "A life wasted making dust": Affective histories of dearth, death, debt and farmers' suicides in India. *The Journal of Peasant Studies* 39 (5): 1159–1179.

Stein, Burton. 2005. *The New Cambridge History of India: Vijayanagara*. Cambridge: Cambridge University Press.

Stump, Daryl. 2010. "Ancient and backward or long-lived and sustainable?" The role of the past in debates concerning rural livelihoods and resource conservation in Eastern Africa. *World Development* 38 (9): 1251–1262.

United Nations. 1987. *Our Common Future. Report of the World Commission on Environment and Development (WCED)*. Oxford: Oxford University Press.

Vasavi, A. R. 2008. *Suicides and the Making of India's Agrarian Crisis*. Bangalore: National Institute of Advanced Studies.

Wilcox Black, Kelly. 2022. *Excavating the Deep History of Degradation: Animal Husbandry and the Environmental Impacts of Livestock Grazing in Pre and Early Historic South India*. PhD dissertation, department of Anthropology. Chicago: University of Chicago.

Williams, Amanda, Paolo Perego, and Gail Whiteman. 2025. Boundary conditions for organizations in the Anthropocene: A review of the Planetary Boundaries framework 10 years on. *Journal of Management Studies* 62 (4): 1811–1846.

Winchell, Frank, et al. 2018. On the origins and dissemination of domesticated sorghum and pearl millet across Africa and into India: A view from the Butana group of the far eastern Sahel. *The African Archaeological Review* 35 (4): 483–505.

Wittman, Hannah. 2009. Reworking the metabolic rift: La Vía Campesina, agrarian citizenship, and food sovereignty. *Journal of Peasant Studies* 36 (4): 805–826.

Zagata, Lukas, Lee-Ann Sutherland, Jiří Hrabák, and Michal Lostak. 2020. Mobilising the past: Towards a conceptualisation of retro-innovation. *Sociologia Ruralis* 60 (3): 639–660.

Resilience and Vulnerability of Tokugawa Japan to Climate Changes

Takeshi Nakatsuka

Abstract In central Japan, past summer climate has been precisely reconstructed using tree-ring cellulose oxygen isotope ratios (δ^{18}Ocel) for the last 2600 years (Nakatsuka et al., Clim Past 16:2153–2172, 2020). Given that there are positive relationships between the δ^{18}Ocel and annual rice yields in the Tokugawa period (seventeenth to nineteenth centuries), the influence of climate changes can be discussed in the context of the rice productivity. The multi-decadal variations in rice productivity always caused numerous famines, probably because people could not survive long-lasting crop failures. Although famines did not result in peasant uprisings during the early part of the Tokugawa period until the 1730s, crop failures always induced numerous peasant uprisings after 1750s. The difference in societal response to climate change between the early and later parts of the Tokugawa period can be explained by various factors including the decline in the financial situation of the Tokugawa shogunate and the rapid development of a market economy from the early eighteenth century. The historical change in the relationship between famine and peasant uprisings during the Tokugawa era in Japan is an example of adaptations to climate change. Similar research can be conducted at various periods and regions by using high time-resolution climate and/or crop yield records. The results of such work can then be compared with results from other periods and areas to generate common lessons for climate adaptability in human societies.

Keywords Climate change · Famine · peasant uprising · Tokugawa Japan

T. Nakatsuka (✉)
Nagoya University, Nagoya, Japan
e-mail: nakatsuka.takeshi.m0@f.mail.nagoya-u.ac.jp

J. F. Haldon, R. Fernandes (eds.), *Bridging History and Policy*, Understanding Complex Systems, https://doi.org/10.1007/978-3-032-24379-9_23

1 Introduction: Advances in Historical Climate Adaptation Studies in Japan

In recent years, the frequency of severe meteorological disasters such as heat waves, droughts, and floods associated with global warming has increased. The fact that this warming is caused by the increase in anthropogenic greenhouse gases since the Industrial Revolution has been made clear beyond doubt by the research of many scientists gathered at the IPCC (IPCC Working Group 1 2021). Among the various IPCC-related studies, paleoclimatology has contributed to clarifying how climate change after the Industrial Revolution differs from that before it by reconstructing temperature variations around the world on an annual basis over the past two millennia (PAGES 2 k consortium 2013, 2019; Neukom et al. 2019; Esper et al. 2024). While such data on past climate variations reconstructed with high temporal resolution is used to clarify the causes of global warming, it has stimulated research on the historical climate adaptation, which clarifies how past human societies responded to climate changes that occurred in various regions at various times in the past by comparing them with historical and archaeological materials, and the subject of this research has expanded to more detailed phenomena from older times (Di Cosmo et al. 2021; Manning et al. 2023).

In order to advance research on historical climate adaptation, high-temporal resolution paleoclimatic data and abundant historical materials on past human activities are necessary. These two elements are most abundant in Europe, and traditionally, research on historical climate adaptation has been most advanced in Europe (Pfister and Wanner 2021). On the other hand, in Japan, although there was a wealth of historical and archaeological materials, there were few high-temporal resolution paleoclimatic data, so until recently, little research on historical climate adaptation had been conducted. The situation in Japan has been changing dramatically in recent years due to the development of paleoclimatology, as described below. In particular, the Historical Climate Adaptation Project (https://www.chikyu.ac.jp/nenrin/index_e.html) at the Research Institute for Humanity and Nature in Kyoto, Japan, which was conducted from 2014 to 2019, involved detailed reconstruction of past climate variations mainly using tree rings and verification by comparing them with historical materials, leading to rapid progress in both paleoclimatology and historical climate adaptation studies over several thousand years from prehistoric to early modern Japan (Nakatsuka et al. 2020–2021). In this paper, I will draw on these findings and focus on the early modern period (Tokugawa period: 1603–1868 CE), for which historical data is the most abundant and the historical relationship between climate and society can be understood in the most detail, to offer an insight into how human society was (or was not) able to adapt to climate change and what the reasons for this were.

Early modern Japan, or Tokugawa Japan (seventeenth to nineteenth centuries), has several characteristics (Hirano 2021). First, Japan was essentially closed to the outside world at that time, and due to its geographical location as an island nation, it imported almost no food, and had to deal with poor harvests caused by bad climate on its own. Second, Japan at that time had a highly developed market economy, including a futures market for staple products such as rice, and a logistics network was formed for the entire country using coastal ships through the seas surrounding the Japanese archipelago. Third, Japan at that time had the shogunate system, with about 300 feudal domains ruled by samurai lords in various parts of Japan under the Tokugawa shogunate, and various policies were implemented in each region, which led to various successes and failures in climate adaptation in each region. Fourth, Japan at that time had a huge amount of written historical materials related to various livelihoods such as agriculture and commerce, written by people belonging to various classes, from government officials to ordinary citizens, which makes it possible to conduct various research on historical climate adaptation. These characteristics of the Tokugawa period can also be seen as making Japan a "miniature analogy" of the modern, globalized world, and Tokugawa Japan also has a lot of potential in the study of the historical climate adaptation.

However, research on historical climate adaptation in early modern Japan only began in earnest a few years ago, when paleoclimatic data became more abundant, and we are not yet at the stage where we can thoroughly examine the whole picture with sufficient historical material to back it up. Therefore, in this limited essay, I would like to focus on one aspect of research in the historical climate adaptation, using early modern Japan as an example, namely, the time scale of variations, particularly societal response to climate change over several decades, and propose a new research axis for comparative history across time and region to evaluate social resilience against climatic and environmental changes.

2 Development of High-temporal Resolution Paleoclimate Data: Tree-ring Data

In paleoclimatology, various proxies are used to reconstruct climate, among which tree-ring width is the proxy most commonly used around the world. The United States and Europe were the first to use tree-ring width to reconstruct paleoclimate, whereas in Japan, little research has been done until recently to reconstruct climate using tree-ring width, especially summer climate, which has a major impact on the growth of rice, the main grain in Japan. The reason for this is that climate in Japan is warm and humid, which is very suitable for tree growth, so firstly, slight changes in summer climate do not affect tree-ring width at all, but rather changes in winter climate determine tree-ring width through changes in the photosynthetic period, and secondly, most Japanese forests are densely populated, as in tropical and subtropical forests, so that the ecological disturbance from neighboring trees on tree-ring width is very large, and the signal of climate variations contained in tree-ring width is masked. However, recently in Japan along with many other countries in the Asian monsoon region, it has become possible to accurately reconstruct summer climates using oxygen isotope ratios ($\delta^{18}O$) of cellulose contained in tree rings, and conditions for historical climate adaptation studies are rapidly being established.

Tree-ring cellulose $\delta^{18}O$ changes depending on two meteorological factors: the precipitation isotope ratio and relative humidity in summer season when photosynthesis occurs (McCarroll and Loader 2004). Therefore, in Japan, any wooden materials made of any tree species can be dated accurately by the dendrochronological method using the tree-ring cellulose $\delta^{18}O$. Therefore, a mutually beneficial relationship has developed between architectural historians, archaeologists, and dendrochronologists in which they exchange wood samples, such as pillars and boards from old buildings and materials excavated from ruins, and their dating results. It has rapidly led the establishment of annually resolved continuous time-series on the tree-ring cellulose $\delta^{18}O$ for the past several thousand years in Japan (Sano et al. 2022, 2023).

The tree-ring cellulose $\delta^{18}O$ has a linear relationship, that is positively correlated with the precipitation isotope ratio and inversely correlated with the relative humidity. Furthermore, since the precipitation isotope ratio is negatively correlated with the precipitation amount in Japan, and the relative humidity is in general positively correlated with the precipitation amount, the tree-ring cellulose $\delta^{18}O$ can be used to reconstruct the past variations in summer precipitation in Japan at annual time resolution. In addition, since there is a clear inverse correlation between summer precipitation and temperature in Japan, the tree-ring cellulose $\delta^{18}O$ can also estimate the variation in temperature through precipitation. Figure 1a shows continuous time-series of tree-ring cellulose $\delta^{18}O$ for the past 2600 years in central Japan, constructed by combining data obtained from a total of 67 long-aged coniferous trees, including living trees, architectural materials, archaeologically excavated woods, and naturally buried logs (Nakatsuka et al. 2020).

The summer climate variations in central Japan estimated from this data match well with the annual reconstruction of summer precipitation from weather records in diaries in Japan since the seventeenth century (Mizukoshi 1993), decadal to centennial variations in summer wet/dry conditions estimated from document records of meteorological disasters from the tenth to seventeenth centuries (Fujiki 2007), and centennial to millennial variations in summer temperature based on pollen analysis of peat deposits (Sakaguchi 1983). It was proven that the data accurately reproduces past summer climate variations on all time scales, from years to millennia.

Figure 1b shows the tree-ring cellulose $\delta^{18}O$ compared to the data on average land temperatures in the Northern Hemisphere (Mann et al., 2008). It suggests that the Tokugawa period from the seventeenth to the nineteenth century was the wettest and coldest period in Japan, as well as in the rest of the world, and that various climatic crises due to floods and cold damages may have occurred. In fact, unlike many other countries in the world that experienced many crises due to cooling in the seventeenth century (Parker 2013), nationwide development of rice paddies and an increase in population occurred in Japan during the same seventeenth century. In the following, I will consider how Japanese people adapted to the climate at that time by comparing the tree ring cellulose $\delta^{18}O$ with various socio-economic data of early modern Japan at a high time resolution.

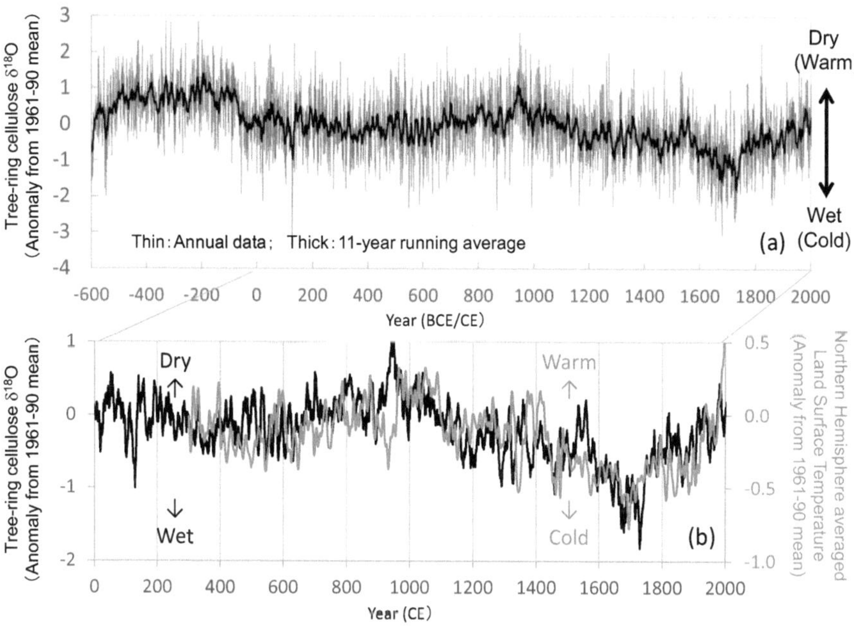

Fig. 1 (**a**) Multi-millennial variations in tree-ring cellulose $\delta^{18}O$ in central Japan (Black: Nakatsuka et al. 2020) and (**b**) its long-term variation (11 year running mean) in comparison with northern hemisphere land surface temperature (Gray: Mann et al. 2008)

3 Comparison with Socio-economic Data: Discovery of Multi-decadal Cycles

Kamatani et al. (2016) collected time-series data on taxable production, mainly rice, from three villages around Lake Biwa, the largest lake in Japan, in present Shiga prefecture near the ancient capital of Kyoto, recorded on annual tax invoices from local lords during the Tokugawa period, and compared the standardized average values across the three villages with the tree-ring cellulose $\delta^{18}O$ in central Japan (Fig. 2a). There were clear positive correlations both on annual and decadal basis, and it became clear that the increase in summer precipitation, indicated by the decrease in tree-ring cellulose $\delta^{18}O$, led to a decrease in rice production due to flooding caused by the rise in the water level of Lake Biwa. Nakatsuka (2022) compared the average data on rice yield per area of paddy fields recorded from the eighteenth centuries among villages on the highlands in present Yamanashi Prefecture, central Japan (Sato 1987) with the tree-ring cellulose $\delta^{18}O$ in central Japan, and again, showed a clear positive correlation between rice yield and tree-ring cellulose $\delta^{18}O$ (Fig. 2b). Here, it can be interpreted that the decrease in summer temperature corresponding to the decrease in tree-ring cellulose $\delta^{18}O$ caused cold damage and reduced rice production.

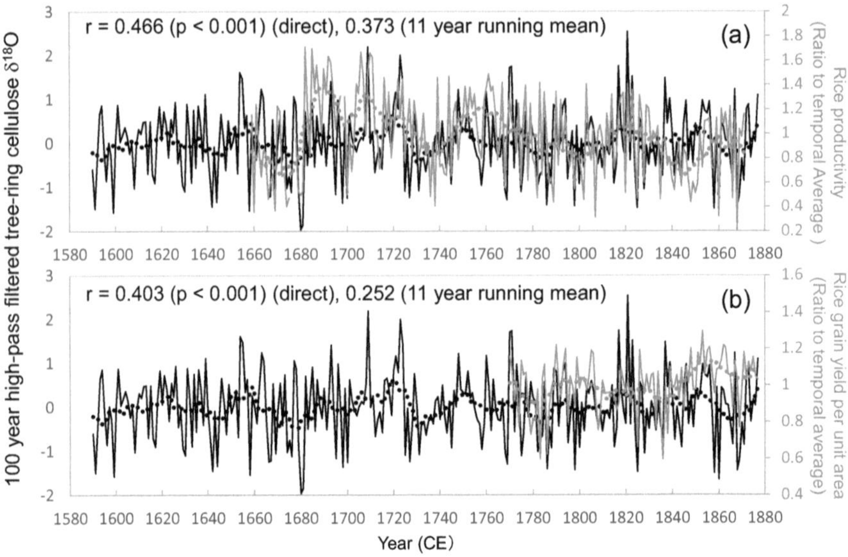

Fig. 2 (**a**) Variations in tree-ring cellulose δ^{18}O in central Japan (Grey: Nakatsuka et al. 2020) during Tokugawa period in comparison with variations in the rice productivity averaged among three villages around Lake Biwa in present Shiga prefecture (Black: Kamatani et al. 2016) and (**b**) rice grain yield per unit area among many villages on highlands in present Yamanashi prefecture (Black: Sato 1987). Solid and dotted lines indicate yearly and 11 year running mean values, respectively

These results imply that by using the variations in tree-ring cellulose δ^{18}O in central Japan in Fig. 1a, we can reproduce, with a certain degree of accuracy, the annual and decadal variations in rice production, the most important grain in Japan, over the past 2000 years or more. In fact, Fig. 2 only shows the components of the data in Fig. 1a that have periodicities of less than 100 years, and do not take into account long-term variations of more than 100 years. Over the time scale of more than 100 years, the regional rice production may change due to the factors other than climate, such as changes in farmland area and innovations in agricultural technology, and Fig. 2 merely shows the strong relationship between climate and agricultural production in the time scale of several decades or less.

By comparing this data with the total number of yearly famines recorded in a timeline describing the history of feudal domains throughout Japan during the Tokugawa period (Kimura et al. 2015), I found a clear characteristic in Fig. 3a (Nakatsuka 2022). As shown in Fig. 2, rice productivity was thought to have varied large both in annual and decadal time scales in response to climate variations, but major famines across the country only occurred during the periods when the climate became the wettest and coldest in the multi-decadal climate cycles. The three major famines during the Tokugawa period, the Kyoho, Tenmei, and Tenpo famines, all occurred at that time, and the other famines with significant peaks in the number of famines also occurred when the tree-ring δ^{18}O hit the bottom of their multi-decadal cycle.

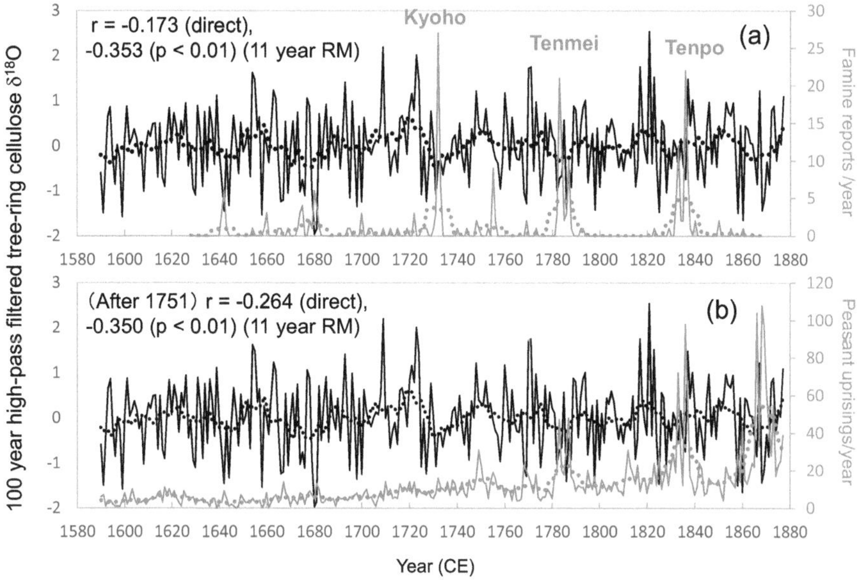

Fig. 3 (**a**) Variations in tree-ring cellulose $\delta^{18}O$ (Gray: Nakatsuka et al. 2020) in central Japan during Tokugawa period in comparison with yearly numbers of famine reports over Japan (Black: Kimura et al. 2015) and (**b**) peasant uprisings over Japan (Black: Aoki 1971) (**b**). Solid and dotted lines indicate yearly and 11 year running mean values, respectively

So how did society at that time respond to the occurrence of such a great famine? Nakatsuka (2022) compared the tree-ring cellulose $\delta^{18}O$ with time-series of the yearly number of peasant uprisings during the Tokugawa period (Aoki 1971) (Fig. 3b). In the first half of the Tokugawa period, peasant uprisings did not increase even when famines increased, meaning there was no relationship, but in the second half of the Tokugawa period, that is after 1732 CE, the Kyoho famine, countless peasant uprisings always occurred during a great famine. In the 1860s, during the years of poor harvests indicated by the decrease in tree-ring cellulose $\delta^{18}O$, famines themselves no longer occurred very often because the isolationist policy ended and food imports began. However, large-scale uprisings occurred throughout Japan, which can be inferred to have been an indirect cause of the downfall of the Tokugawa Shogunate. As such, there were significant differences in the way societies respond to multi-decadal major climate cycles between the periods. What is the background to this?

4 Why Is Human Society Vulnerable to Multi-decadal Cycles?

First, let us consider the underlying mechanism of the reason why famines occur when the climate changes over multi-decadal cycles, rather than inter-annual cycles. As shown in Fig. 4, the population and living standard in a human society must be

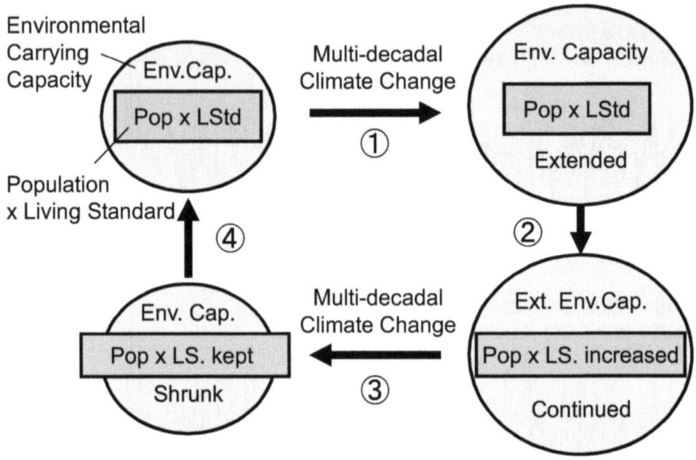

Fig. 4 A conceptual model to explain why human societies are vulnerable to enhanced multi-decadal climate cycle. (1) Enhancement of environmental carrying capacity for local residents by increased agrarian productivity, (2) Expansion of human population and/or living standards in response to enhanced environmental capacity, (3) Reduction of environmental capacity by decreased agrarian productivity, (4) Emergence of famines, wars and refugees and enforced reduction of human population and/or living standards due to failure to adapt to reduced environmental carrying capacity

within the environmental carrying capacity, which is determined by factors such as agricultural productivity. In other words, there is a natural limit to the population and living standard that can be supported with limited food. The size of the circle in Fig. 4 must correspond to the entire Earth in the contemporary world, reflecting the global economy, but in prehistoric Japan it would have corresponded to a single settlement, and in Tokugawa Japan it may have corresponded to a single feudal domain.

Suppose that at some point a major climate variation with a multi-decadal cycle occurs, causing an increase in agricultural production. If the increased productivity returns to normal within a few years (in case of an inter-annual cycle), people might simply thank God for the brief period of good harvest and start stockpiling grain, but a multi-decadal cycle would see a period of good harvest lasting for 10 to 20 years, during which people would increase their population and/or improve their living standard. However, since this is a multi-decadal cycle, the carrying capacity will eventually return to normal. At that time, there will be many young people who were born in a time of good harvest and want to continue living a rich life, but the reduced carrying capacity will mercilessly attack people, and the excess population will be forcibly reduced by famines and the emergence of refugees. If this is an inter-annual cycle, it can be dealt with by stockpiling grain, and the population will not suddenly expand in a year of good harvest. On the other hand, if this is a multi-centennial cycle, there will be time to take proactive measures such as expanding the area of farmland and innovating agricultural technology, or to take passive measures such as suppressing the birth rate. However, in the case of multi-decadal cycle, corresponding to the lifespan of human being, a serious time lag will occur between the population, living standards, and the environmental carrying capacity (such as agricultural productivity), making it difficult to respond.

Such a simple mechanism may lie behind the relationship between multi-decadal climate variations and the occurrence of famines, as shown in Fig. 4. Of course, societal responses to it are diverse, as shown in Fig. 3b, so an important subject in studies of the historical climate adaptation should be to search for historical examples in which the universal crises created by the mechanism in Fig. 4 were avoided and to understand the factors behind them.

5 What Determined Success or Failure of Adapting to Crises in Tokugawa Japan?

The time lag between changes in agricultural productivity and changes in population and living standards caused by multi-decadal climate cycle, as shown in Fig. 4, could have had a significant impact on human societies throughout the world history. However, as shown in Fig. 3b, even during the same Tokugawa period in Japan, the ability of society to respond to the multi-decadal cycles in productivity varied greatly from era to era (and actually from region to region). There are thought to be two main reasons for this.

First, the resources of the many mines that supported the finances of the Tokugawa Shogunate in the seventeenth century were almost depleted by the first half of the eighteenth century (Ohno 1996), causing the Shogunate's finances to deteriorate and making it unable to provide relief to the starving people even in the event of a great famine. In fact, during the Kyoho famine that occurred over a wide area of western Japan in 1732 CE, Shogun Tokugawa Yoshimune directly sent stockpiled rice from Edo (present-day Tokyo), where the Shogunate was located, to the various domains in western Japan to provide direct relief for the famine, so the famine did not lead to peasant uprisings at that time. However, after that, the Shogunate lost its financial power and was no longer able to provide relief for famines, and during the periods of poor harvests in multi-decadal climate cycles, numerous peasant uprisings broke out all over Japan, demanding tax reductions and exemptions. As long as the government's finances were abundant, famines would occur but uprisings would not occur, but as the government's finances became poor, famines would lead directly to uprisings. This is a common knowledge that is still relevant today, but this is what actually happened.

Second, the rapid development of the market economy from the first half of the eighteenth century onwards made speculative trading of rice and other commodities expanded. In 1730 CE, Shogun Tokugawa Yoshimune authorized the opening of a market for futures trading of rice and other commodities in Osaka, the commercial center of Japan near Kyoto (Takatsuki 2018). Rice futures trading not only provided a new means of fundraising for feudal lords who secured financial resources for local politics by selling rice, but also had the economic effect of stabilizing rice prices in normal times. However, in times of emergency such as major famines, rice futures trading, combined with merchants' hoarding and withholding of rice, induced speculative trading, leading to abnormal price hikes and causing numerous riots. In fact, people in Japan at that time, not only local government (feudal) officials and merchants, but even ordinary rural farmers, were researching rice prices on a daily basis and were concerned with how to sell rice at a high price to make a profit. As a result, during the Tenmei famine of 1783 CE, in the Sendai domain of the northeast region of Japan, officials sold off all of their stockpiled rice in the face of soaring rice prices, resulting in 150,000 people starving to death (Kikuchi 2003). The market economy, both in the Tokugawa period and in the present day, has both the ability to avoid crises and the tendency to exacerbate them.

These two factors are based on theories that have been universally discussed in researches on early modern Japanese history, but they are merely hypotheses, and there may be other reasons. For example, there is a possible hypothesis that is closer to the perspective of environmental history. The rapid development of new rice paddies in the seventeenth century led to a rapid expansion of agricultural productivity, and population in Japan nearly doubled in the 100 years (Hayami 2012). The excessive development of rice paddies led to the devastation of mountains as forests were cut down and turned into grassland in search of grass fertilizer, which led to the frequent occurrence of floods and other disasters (Takei 2015). The expansion of such disasters, combined with the increase in population itself, may have reduced people's ability to adapt to changes in environmental carrying capacity due to the multi-decadal climate cycles. What determined the success or failure of Japanese climate adaptation during the Tokugawa period is an issue that should be discussed from various angles in the future.

6 Conclusion: Multi-decadal Cycles as a Test of Crisis Response Capabilities in Societies

Owing to the recent progress in climate reconstructions with high time resolution, the actual climate variations that occurred in historical times are becoming clearer all over the world. Climate variations had influenced the carrying capacity of premodern societies around the world through agricultural production and other factors. In particular, multi-decadal climate cycle brings about an essential time lag between changes in population and living standards and changes in carrying capacity, so it is conceivable that it caused famines and social unrest associated with them. Cases like those in Fig. 4 must have existed not only in Japan during the Tokugawa period, but also all over the world since the beginning of agriculture. What is important here is to understand the resilience of society, how people were able to adapt to the social crises brought about by the multi-decadal climate cycle.

The multi-decadal climate cycle may be able to serve as a kind of touchstone to measure the crisis response capabilities of historical societies.

Tree rings can mainly reveal summer climate, so the strong relationship between tree-ring cellulose $\delta^{18}O$ and rice yields shown in Fig. 2 can be found in monsoon Asian regions like Japan, where there is a lot of summer rain and the crop of rice grows in the summer. A similar relationship between tree-ring data and grain yields may not be easily found in regions like the area around the Mediterranean, where there is a lot of winter rainfall and the crop of wheat grows from winter to spring. However, because the multi-decadal cycle in agricultural productivity itself can be reconstructed from historical documents, the relationship in Fig. 4 should be able to be confirmed even in Europe from ancient times onwards, where historical documents arc abundant.

The multi-decadal cycles in carrying capacity shown in Fig. 4 are caused by a variety of factors, not just climate change. These include, of course, artificial variations in carrying capacity caused by the introduction of new technologies and institutions. New technologies and institutions often rapidly expand productivity, and accordingly, population and living standards also expand rapidly. However, excessive use of new technologies and institutions often produces serious side effects, making it difficult to maintain a population and living standards that have expanded once. Behind the various ongoing crises in the world, including environmental problems such as global warming and ecosystem degradation, and political instability caused by growing poverty and inequality, there are the difficulties in the livelihoods of people around the world who are at the mercy of these cycles of expansion and contraction of carrying capacity that occur over a multi-decadal time scale.

How can people adapt to such large fluctuations in carrying capacity that occur at multi-decadal time scales? This is a universal question in human history that transcends time and place and is still relevant today. I believe that advancing research into the comparative history of adaptation to multi-decadal climate cycles, or more generally, the comparative history of adaptation to multi-decadal changes in carrying capacity around the world, will be one of the common challenges in the research of climate and environmental history.

References

Aoki, K. 1971. *Comprehensive Chronology of Peasant Uprisings*. Tokyo: San-ichi Shobo. (in Japanese).

Di Cosmo, N., S. Wagner, and U. Büntgen. 2021. Climate and environmental context of the Mongol invasion of Syria and defeat at 'Ayn Jālūt (1258–1260 CE). *Erdkunde* 75:87–104.

Esper, J., M. Torbenson, and U. Büntgen. 2024. 2023 summer warmth unparalleled over the past 2,000 years. *Nature* 631:94–97.

Fujiki, H., ed. 2007. *Chronological Table of Medieval Meteorological Disasters in Japan*. Tokyo: Koshi-Shoin. (in Japanese).

Hayami, A. 2012. *The World of Historical Demography*. Tokyo: Iwanami-Shoten. (in Japanese).

Hirano, T. 2021. How will the perspective of early modern history change (or not)? - Overview of the entire era. In *A new view of climate and new possibilities for Japanese history (Rereading Japanese history from the perspective of climate change)*, ed. T. Nakatsuka, K. Kamatani, M. Sano, K. Ito, and A. Tsushima, vol. I, 161–171. Kyoto: Rinsen-Shoten. (in Japanese).

Historical Climate Adaptation Project. *Societal Adaptation to Climate Change: Integrating Palaeoclimatological Data with Historical and Archaeological Evidences*. Research Institute for Humanity and Nature. https://www.chikyu.ac.jp/nenrin/index_e.html.

IPCC Working Group 1. 2021. *Climate Change 2021: The Physical Science Basis* (IPCC Sixth Assessment Report), IPCC.

Kamatani, K., M. Sano, and T. Nakatsuka. 2016. Payment of the land tax and the change of climate in the Early Modern ages. *Journal of Japanese History* 646:36–56. (in Japanese).

Kikuchi, I. 2003. *Reading Early Modern Society from Famines*. Tokyo: Azekura-Shobo. (in Japanese).

Kimura, M., T. Fujino, and S. Murakami, eds. 2015. *Encyclopaedia of Feudal Domain History*. Vol. I-VII. Tokyo: Yuzan-Kaku. (in Japanese).

Mann, M. E., Z. Zhang, M. K. Hughes, R. S. Bradley, S. K. Miller, S. Rutherford, and F. Ni. 2008. Proxy-based reconstructions of hemispheric and global surface temperature variations over the past two millennia. *Proceedings of the National Academy of Sciences* 105:13252–13257.

Manning, S. W., C. Kocik, B. Lorentzen, and J. P. Sparks. 2023. Severe multi-year drought coincident with Hittite collapse around 1198–1196 BC. *Nature* 614:719–724.

McCarroll, D., and N. J. Loader. 2004. Stable isotopes in tree rings. *Quaternary Science Reviews* 23:771–801.

Mizukoshi, M. 1993. Climatic reconstruction in central Japan during the Little Ice Age based on documentary sources. *Journal of Geography* 102:152–166. (in Japanese).

Nakatsuka, T. 2022. *History of Climate Adaptation in Japan*. Tokyo: Yoshikawa-Kobunkan. (in Japanese).

Nakatsuka, T., M. Sano, A. Li, C. Xu, A. Tsushima, Y. Shigeoka, et al. 2020. A 2600-year summer climate reconstruction in central Japan by integrating tree-ring stable oxygen and hydrogen isotopes. *Climate of the Past* 16:2153–2172.

Nakatsuka, T. et al., eds., 2020–2021. *Rereading Japanese History from the Perspective of Climate Change, Volumes I–VI*. Kyoto: Rinsen-Shoten. (in Japanese).

Neukom, R., N. Steiger, J. J. Gómez-Navarro, J.-H. Wang, and J. P. Werner. 2019. No evidence for globally-coherent warm and cold periods over the preindustrial Common Era. *Nature* 571:550–554.

Ohno, M. 1996. *The Financial History of the Edo Shogunate*. Tokyo: Yoshikawa-Kobunkan. (in Japanese).

PAGES 2k consortium. 2013. Continental-scale temperature variability during the last two millennia. *Nature Geoscience* 6:339–346.

PAGES 2k Consortium. 2019. Consistent multidecadal variability in global temperature reconstructions and simulations over the Common Era. *Nature Geoscience* 12:643–649.

Parker, G. 2013. *Global Crisis: War, Climate Change and Catastrophe in the Seventeenth Century*. New Haven: Yale University Press.

Pfister, C., and H. Wanner. 2021. *Climate and Society in Europe: The Last Thousand Years*. Bern: Haupt.

Sakaguchi, Y. 1983. Warm and cold stages in the past 7600 years in Japan and their global correlation. *Bulletin of Department of Geography, University of Tokyo* 15:1–31.

Sano, M., Z. Li, Y. Murakami, M. Jinno, Y. Ura, A. Kaneda, and T. Nakatsuka. 2022. Tree ring oxygen isotope dating of wood recovered from a canal in the ancient capital of Japan. *Journal of Archaeological Science: Reports* 45:103626.

Sano, M., K. Kimura, F. Miyake, F. Tokanai, and T. Nakatsuka. 2023. Two new millennium-long tree-ring oxygen isotope chronologies (2349–1009 BCE and 1412–466 BCE) from Japan. *Radiocarbon* 65:721–732.

Sato, T. 1987. *Development and Structure of Rice Cultivation in Japan - Historical Analyses of Tsubokari-Cho*. Tokyo: Yoshikawa-Kobunkan. (in Japanese).

Takatsuki, Y. 2018. *Osaka Dojima Rice Market: The Edo Shogunate vs the Market Economy*. Tokyo: Kodansha. (in Japanese).

Takei, K. 2015. *A Turning Point for Edo Japan: What Did the Rapid Increase in Rice Paddies Bring?* Tokyo: NHK Books. (in Japanese).

Heritage of Fire in the American Southwest: Ancient Landscape Management, Traditional Ecological Knowledge, and Contemporary Challenges

Arlene Miller Rosen, Alison Damick, and Samantha Krause

Abstract In recent decades, residents and land managers in the American Southwest have been plagued by persistent wildfires causing devastation to natural resources, property, and loss of life in this region which is already stressed by long periods of recurring droughts. Many of these fires accelerate due to an abundance of undergrowth related to nearly 150 years of fire suppression policies. In recent decades, some Western scholars have drawn attention to the fact that Native Americans have accumulated traditional knowledge about these landscapes and the importance of fire cycles for maintaining ecozones, biodiversity, as well as economically important plants. This has influenced some policy makers to suggest that fire cycles play an important role in the maintenance and sustainability of ecozones across this region.

Our recent work in the upper Rio Grande Valley of New Mexico suggests that humans have played a role in igniting beneficial fires throughout deep time in the Southwest. Our geoarchaeological and phytolith evidence from three drainages (Dixon, Tesuque Creek, Arroyo de los Chamisos) shows that natural fires appear to have occurred very infrequently from ca. 40,000 BP, until the terminal Pleistocene and early Holocene when fire frequency accelerated and intensified with time throughout the past 19,000 years. This suggests that naturally ignited fires were infrequent before humans arrived in the Southwest, and that most fires were ignited on a regular basis after their arrival, accelerating during the middle to late Holocene Archaic Period. This study suggests that traditional knowledge of sustainable landscape management is rooted in deep time, and there is much to learn from this traditional heritage of controlling 'firescapes' across the American Southwest.

A. M. Rosen (✉)
University of Texas at Austin, Austin, TX, USA
e-mail: amrosen@austin.utexas.edu

A. Damick
University of Tennessee, Knoxville, TN, USA

S. Krause
Texas State University, San Marcos, TX, USA

J. F. Haldon, R. Fernandes (eds.), *Bridging History and Policy*, Understanding Complex Systems, https://doi.org/10.1007/978-3-032-24379-9_24

Keywords American Southwest • Fire histories • Traditional ecological knowledge • Geoarchaeology

1 Introduction

In recent decades, the American Southwest has been plagued by persistent wildfires that have caused devastation to natural resources, property, and loss of life. These fires also have had destructive effects on wildlife and biodiversity in this region, which is already stressed by long periods of recurring droughts. Destructive fires are increasing in both the number and severity of individual occurrences (Singleton et al. 2019; Parks et al. 2023). Climate change leading to our steadily warming planet has played an important role in fire regime changes, due to droughts leading to greater amounts of flammable fuel building up in fire-prone regions. The extent of fire destruction is exacerbated due to expanded arid areas that lack the moisture content to slow burning, or robust root systems to hold hillslope and stream bank sediments in place after fires sweep through. Much of this destruction also is enhanced by current land-use practices and heightened by ignition due to human error or vandalism. Today, human ignition plays a very significant role in the initiation of fire starts, contributing to around 77% of all fires across the Western United States (Fusco et al. 2016; Cattau et al. 2020). Furthermore, many of these fires accelerate due to an abundance of undergrowth which has thickened across the Southwest as a result of nearly 150 years of fire suppression policies. In recent decades, however, there has been increasing understanding that fire cycles play an important role in the maintenance and sustainability of ecozones across this region (Roos 2020).

Over the last ca. 40 years, in an effort to develop more sustainable land management practices, Western scholars have drawn attention to the fact that there is much we can learn from the traditional ecological knowledge of Indigenous peoples in the Americas and elsewhere. In North America, known to Native peoples as "Turtle Island", Native Americans have accumulated traditional knowledge about managing landscapes of the Southwest over the course of thousands of years, and throughout major cycles of climatic changes (Damick et al. 2022; Roos et al. 2022). A key tool for the management of these landscapes has been the regular use of fire for maintaining consistency in vegetation communities, wildlife, and biodiversity, as well as encouraging the growth of economically important plants over the course of generations. These traditions, memories and experiences of fire-generated landscape management practices are important for us to understand for maintaining modern ecozones and biodiversity (Maclean et al. 2023).

We can gain much information about Indigenous traditional ecological knowledge (TEK) for maintaining modern landscapes through collaboration between Indigenous stakeholders, academics, and government agencies. It is a sad truth that much of the TEK has been lost after hundreds of years of genocide and repression of Native traditions and ways of knowing. This unfortunate loss of past ecological knowledge highlights the fact that historical and archaeological research can be used to reach into the distant past and help assemble evidence for lost lifeways and relationships between human ecological traditions and behaviors.

The discipline of Environmental Archaeology has many tools for reconstructing past lifeways and ecological interactions from investigations of data taken during excavations at archaeological sites (on-site data) as well as the landscapes between archaeological sites (off-site data). Some of the on-site methods include analyses of faunal remains and macro- and micro-botanical materials which help us understand how past societies interacted with the biological spheres of their home ranges. Off-site methods include reconstruction of ancient landscapes and hydrology using geo-archaeology of sediment profiles, lake cores, pollen and phytolith analyses. These techniques help us reconstruct ancient landscapes, ecozones, and the ways they changed through time because of shifts in climate and human land use. By using these methods, we can reconstruct and recover some of the lost Traditional Ecological Knowledge of past peoples who lived on these landscapes and managed them over the course of generations throughout many thousands of years of deep time. Additionally, the techniques of environmental archaeology are far less invasive than traditional full-scale excavation, allowing for better preservation of intact sacred landscapes and places while still recovering significant information about the past.

To better understand and reconstruct fire histories and land use over thousands of years in the American Southwest, we used geoarchaeological and phytolith techniques to investigate sediment deposits from arroyo exposures in northern New Mexico. Our work in the upper Rio Grande Valley of New Mexico has shown that prominent charcoal lenses within sediment sections represented these beneficial fires that were likely the result of Indigenous land management over the course of nearly 20,000 years. Our geoarchaeological and phytolith evidence from three drainages (Arroyo de los Chamisos in Santa Fe, Cañada de Ojo Sarco in Dixon, and Tesuque Creek) (Fig. 1) show that natural fires appear to have occurred very infrequently throughout the Pleistocene from ca. 40,000 BP, until the terminal Pleistocene/early Holocene when fire frequency accelerated and intensified with time throughout the past 19,000 years.

2 Modern Fire Regimes in the Southwest

The relationship between fire histories and European ideals of landscape productivity and aesthetics goes back hundreds of years to the first Anglo-European colonization of the forests of the Northeastern US. The Anglo-European settler colonists were interested in establishing both subsistence and later cash-crop plantation farming. As such they perceived the forest as antithetical to these goals, and landscape fires to be a threat to established farms and villages. Europeans also failed to understand the forests as cultural landscapes and used the excuse of "terra nullius" (unused land, or wilderness) to justify their continued expansion into Native

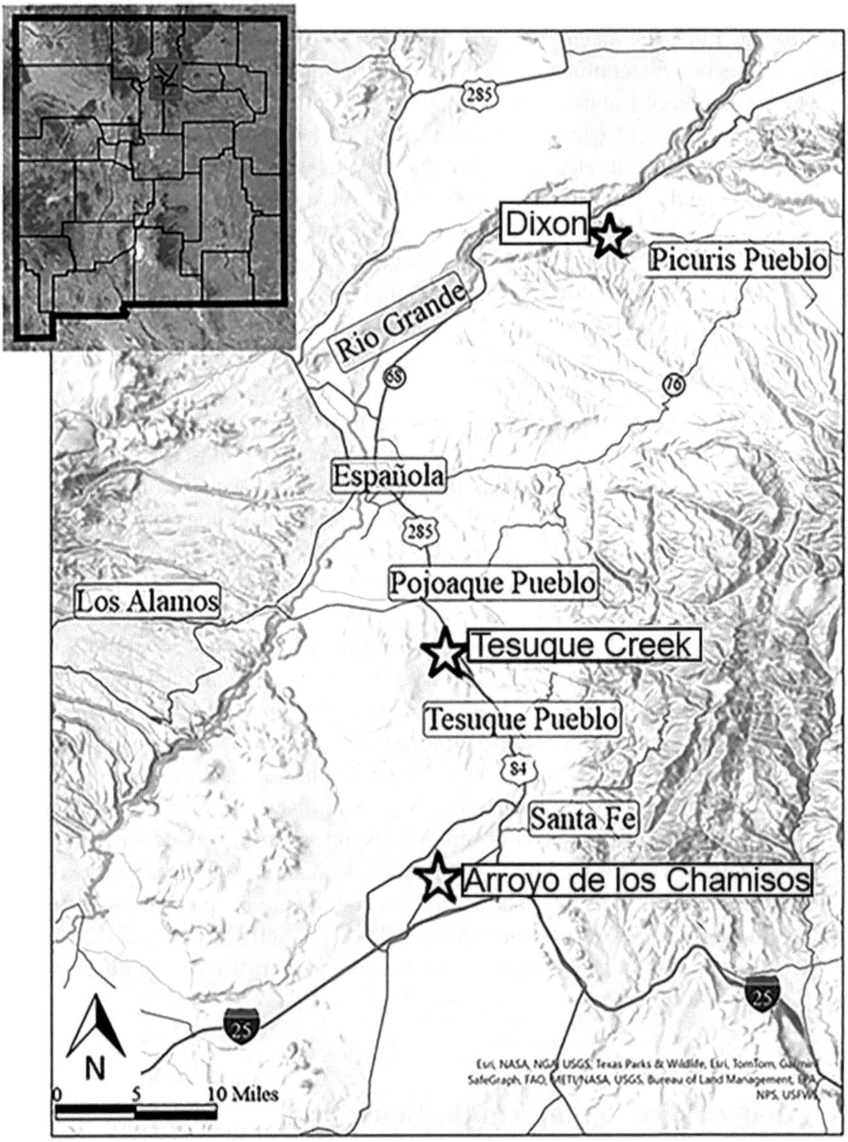

Fig. 1 Map showing locations of geoarchaeological alluvial sections mentioned in this study

territories, a process known as the Doctrine of Discovery (Miller 2019). To further their goals, both economic and territorial, they actively repressed the Natives and their systems of land management. By doing so, they halted the patterns of regular human-induced ignition cycles within the areas of their reach (Vinyeta 2022).

These European perceptions of landscapes and the dichotomy of "Wilderness" versus "Domesticated" landscapes heavily influenced American perceptions of terrains and policies for managing diverse environments as European colonists made their way west across North America (Denevan 1992, 2011; Sáenz-Ceja and Mendoza 2024; Guiterman et al. 2019). The concept of a "Pristine Wilderness" as "God's Garden", informed creation and maintenance of the country's Forest Service (established in 1905) and National Park Service (founded in 1916) for over 100 years (Mckim 2017; Fletcher et al. 2021). It also helped to formulate the US attitudes to the Indigenous populations who lived on these landscapes on one hand as the child-like "noble savage" who exerted a light ecological footprint and under-used economically useful regions, and on the other, as peoples who were not maintaining the protected "wild" areas in a way that would preserve the pristine "natural" succession of a non-human "wilderness" (Vinyeta and Bacon 2024).

A clear example of these concepts comes from the history of the founding of Yosemite National Park in 1864. At that time, the founding of National Parks in themselves was considered a way to use what was considered to be useless land. Figueiredo quotes an article by Alfred Runte, an environmental historian, entitled "Yellowstone: It's Useless, So Why Not a Park?" to demonstrate this attitude to the foundation of the first National Parks—Yellowstone and Yosemite (Figueiredo 2007: 14). Later, the park Commissioners defined one of their missions as the preservation of Yosemite Valley's "pristine beauty". They perceived that the Native "gardening" was contrary to that particular goal, and the Native use of fire to maintain the landscape was "… as unwelcome in the newly founded park as the Indians themselves …". This contributed to the rationale for removing the Natives from the area of park (Figueiredo 2007: 29). To illustrate this, Figueiredo presents photographs from 1867 and 2007 respectively. The earlier photograph shows a valley bottom with broad open meadows (Fig. 2), and the more recent photograph shows very dense stands of conifers (Fig. 3, replicated here in a more recent photograph). Although since the 1960s in the US, new perspectives on the importance of Indigenous land management have begun to acknowledge the use of fire as an essential tool for maintaining the stability of landscapes in the American Southwest, some federal agencies still maintain a goal of preserving an "untrammeled character within wilderness areas" (Aycrigg et al. 2022: 1).

However, with all the supposed best intentions to preserve a kind of "natural" wildlife environment, wildfires still run rampant in the Southwestern United States. Much of the literature written about these recent fire events rightfully raises the alarm about the impact of rising temperatures and global warming implicated as contributing factors to severe droughts which leave behind abundant desiccated vegetation, and hence a powder keg of fuel waiting to explode in uncontrollable wildfires. This sadly has played out many times over the past few decades, with notable examples in New Mexico, Arizona, and especially California (Mueller et al. 2020b). The most recent of these was the devastation of the Los Angeles area fires in December 2024–January 2025. These fires leave profound devastation to human life, property, and wildlife, and are the cause of major episodes of soil erosion when the rainy season takes hold.

Although recent climate change has led to a major increase in fuel load, human ignitions are the most prevalent contributor to wildfire starts around the American West in the present (Keeley and Syphard 2018; Nagy et al. 2018; Hantson et al.

Fig. 2 Photograph of Yosemite Valley by Carleton Watkins, 1867

Fig. 3 Photo of Yosemite Valley in the twenty-first century (Photo by David Iliff. License: CC BY-SA 3.0) (https://en.wikipedia.org/wiki/File:Tunnel_View,_Yosemite_Valley,_Yosemite_NP_-_Diliff.jpg)

2022). Fusco and others (2016) show that out of a total of 116,680 ignitions in all of the ecoregions of the American West (including Great Plains, Marine West Coast Forest, Mediterranean California, the North American Desert, the Northwestern Forested Mountains, Southern Semiarid Highlands, and the Temperate Sierras), the lightning-ignited fires constitute only 23% whereas anthropogenic ignitions are 77% of total wildfire starts.

As alarming as this may sound, and the teachings of "Smokey Bear" notwithstanding, the human contribution to fire ignitions is not a recent phenomenon. Indigenous populations were avid landscape managers, at the time of contact with colonial Europeans, and have traditional knowledge of complex ecological relationships between biological entities that stretches back for generations (Roos et al., 2020). The Southwestern landscape was traditionally managed for the benefit of sustainable human use of resources, the stability of plant and animal populations, and as a buffer against out-of-control wildfires. Within this context, the Native use of fire has been integral to traditional systems of land-use and management (Damick et al. 2022; Kimmerer 2018; Kimmerer and Lake 2001; Knight et al. 2022; Lightfoot et al. 2013; Long et al. 2021; Roos 2020; Roos et al. 2018, 2021).

This understanding of land-management practices of Indigenous peoples of the Americas has challenged the concept of a light ecological footprint on the part of hunter-gathering societies which infused the European consciousness since the time of the first contacts and underwrote so much of their territorial expansion (Denevan 1992, 2011; Graeber and Wengrow 2023). Although this ever-increasing awareness that Native communities had a significant knowledge of and impact on North American plants, animals, and landscapes, there are only a handful of studies which demonstrate the time depth of these human management systems. There is little hard evidence for the earliest environmental management that stretches back more than about 6000 years (Roos et al. 2018, 2021; Mueller et al. 2020a). However, we now know that Indigenous populations were present in the American Southwest from at least 23,000 years ago, based on the footprint evidence at White Sands, New Mexico (Pigati et al. 2023). This tells us we may only be seeing a picture of human land management in the Americas through a very short lens. In order to understand the relationships between fire histories and resilient and/or sustainable landscapes, vegetation, and humans, we must examine them from a deep-time perspective, using a suite of paleoecological proxies.

While interest in and research surrounding these issues is increasing, important questions remain open. Some of the most pressing include: (1) When can we say that landscapes in the SW have been altered by fire and transformed away from the concept of a pre-human "pristine landscape" recognizable in the paleoecological archives, and (2) once we establish a proverbial line in the sand to divide the pre-human from the human environments, should we aim to achieve landscape sustainability by attempting to recreate this pre-human environment? We will begin by attempting to answer the first question.

3 Ancient Fire Regimes in the American West

North America is an important laboratory for examining fire histories in the pre- and extant human world. This is because we have a general "beginning point" for the first human footfalls in the American West, and a fairly clear idea of when there was a pre-human landscape. For now, we can place that pre-human landscape throughout most of the Pleistocene up to the Last Glacial Maximum at 23,000 BP (Pigati et al. 2023). There is no archaeological evidence for human sites before the LGM, and only occasional evidence for Paleoindian occupation after that time, until the great Clovis expansion around 13,500 years ago.

Human impact on a landscape is often first identified through the presence of charcoal records in sediment archives (D'Andrea et al. 2023; Roos et al. 2018; Thompson et al. 2021). To understand the nature of evidence for human management of landscapes in the American Southwest, we examined charcoal data recording landscape fires in sediment records including lake cores and alluvial sections dating from well before the peopling of the Americas. This investigation was based on geological, geomorphological, and other paleoecological reports of studies across New Mexico and northwestern Mexico, as well as our own geoarchaeological studies of three alluvial sections in our study area of northern New Mexico. These latter included Arroyo de los Chamisos, Santa Fe, NM, dated to the Pleistocene at 39,500 BP, the Arroyo Cañada de Ojo Sarco, Dixon, NM dated between ca. 12,000 – 8200 cal BP, and Tesuque Creek, NM dated from 3700–2700 cal. BP.

In our literature review of a total of 34 publications we identified 78 charcoal dates from 17 separate study areas in New Mexico and 14 study areas in northwestern Mexico. Figure 4 shows the range of occurrences of charcoal within sediment

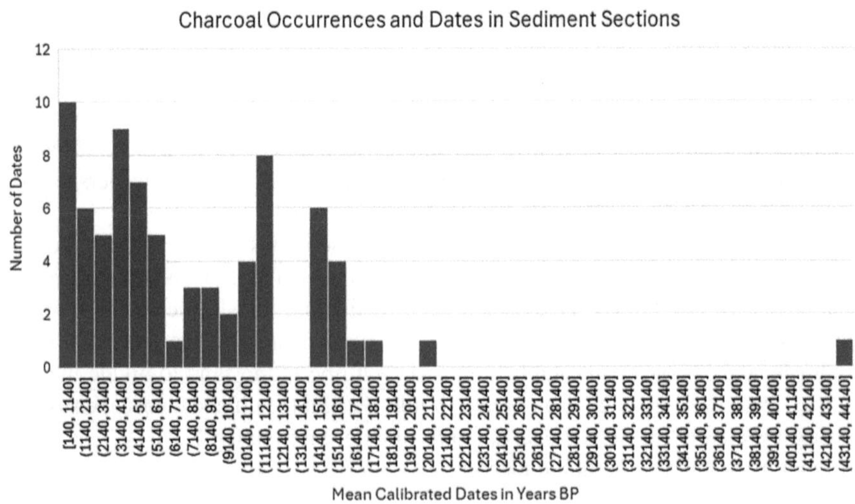

Fig. 4 Graph of charcoal frequencies and dates throughout New Mexico and northern Mexico from the Pleistocene (ca. 40,000 BP) through the late Holocene

sections dating back to 43,000 years BP. It is clear from this graph that the single pre-LGM occurrence of charcoal is dated to 43,000 years BP, close to the limit of radiocarbon dating. Importantly, between the dates of 43,000 and ca. 21,000 years ago, there is strikingly no reported charcoal from sediment deposits. However, around 21,000 years ago, charcoal begins to appear, and the numbers of occurrences progressively increase from the terminal Pleistocene through to recent times.

Although a number of studies relate wildfire histories primarily to climate change, and specifically to warm-dry episodes (Fitch and Meyer 2016; Mueller et al. 2020b), the charcoal records identified in this study do not align with the many significant climatic changes in the American Southwest during late Pleistocene through the late Holocene. On the contrary, with a few exceptions, these trends track growing human populations in this region. The exception is the dearth of landscape charcoal in New Mexican sediment archives during the Younger Dryas (12,900–11,700 cal BP), although the period coincides with the Clovis Paleoindian expansion of sites across the American West. The YD was indeed a cool/moist climatic episode in the Southwest. Without addressing the debate over the Impact Hypothesis for the start of the YD globally, and its potential relationship to fire histories, it is clear that the dark organic sediment horizons of this period across the American SW known as "Black Mats", are not a result of fires, and contain little charcoal within them (Haynes et al. 2010; Holliday et al. 2020). This is consistent with the other sediment records reported here for this time period. Although, cool-moist climates might lead to fewer lightning ignitions, other cool-moist episodes during the very Early and Late Holocene had evidence for many more landscape fires. If most charcoal deposits during the late Pleistocene were a result of human ignitions, then perhaps Clovis traditions did not include this kind of landscape management or did so only sporadically and it is not recorded as a significant signature in the late Quaternary sediment record.

Although some researchers suggest that fire ignitions mostly correlate to the abrupt onset of dry conditions (Holliday et al. 2020: 90), we posit the evidence instead indicates that the majority of ignitions from the LGM onwards were due to human ignitions. For example, our database of charcoal occurrences in New Mexico and northwest Mexico, indicates a decline in charcoal during the middle Holocene Altithermal period (ca. 9000–6000 cal BP), a marked warm/dry climatic period corresponding to the Early Archaic archaeological period. This reduction in evidence for landscape fires might be related to a decline in human occupation of the New Mexico lowlands, during this very warm, drought-ridden climatic episode, and a withdrawal to the uplands where temperatures were cooler and resources were more abundant during this time (Vierra and Post 2023). When the climate became moister and cooler in the late Holocene, the number of charcoal occurrences jumped to much higher levels. This is a period with increased human occupation, and documented evidence of more intensive use of plant resources in the prelude to cultivation of wild and then domestic plants. A number of researchers have pointed to the evidence for more intensive landscape management in the home ranges of the Late Archaic peoples, and subsequently the agricultural societies (Vierra and Vint 2022).

4 Reforestation and "Rewilding" the American Landscapes

In the above discussion, we addressed the issue of the American perceptions of "natural wilderness" spaces, mostly referring to the National Forests and National Parks. These concepts aim to return to some kind of non-human environmental regime of plants and animals without the impact of humans on these landscapes. These ideas disregard the fact that humans are a keystone species who most likely have been managing landscapes of the American West since the first human entry into North America. This means that the plants and animals we see in the West were altered by the human ecological touch for millennia. They were adapted to both recurring fire cycles, and to the introduction of non-native plants and animals even in pre-colonial times.

Our work in northern New Mexico demonstrates that in the Late Archaic period Native American foragers were low-level cultivators of wild plants, including endogenous agaves, but also some which were never found as endogenous species in the area. This includes our phytolith evidence for the *Sabal* sp. palmetto, which was cultivated on the floodplains of Tesuque Creek, in northern New Mexico during the Late Archaic Period (Damick et al. 2021), as well as phytolith remains of this same palmetto within Early Archaic ovens in southwest Texas (Rosen and Hart, in preparation). This is an exogenous plant with no natural history within New Mexico or southwest Texas, and no recorded natural stands in these regions. The stalk of the plant was roasted and eaten as a starchy-type of bread by historic-period Native communities of southeast Texas and Louisiana (Damick et al. 2021). Our findings at Tesuque Creek, show that the quantities of *Sabal* palmetto phytoliths increase at a time when agave phytoliths decrease in density. It is likely that this is a result of the cooler/moister climatic conditions of the period between 3000–2000 cal. BP (Hall 2023). The palmetto is especially well-adapted to thrive in these cooler conditions, whereas the agaves would be less tolerant of the cold and damp floodplain environments. Our evidence suggests that the Late Archaic foragers introduced the *Sabal* palmetto to maintain the input of starch-rich plants in their diet. These findings add a new perspective to the Indigenous management of endogenous and exogenous plants in their home ranges.

In the present-day world residents of the American Southwest are facing intensified Global Warming, recurrent long-lasting episodes of drought, and ever-increasing fire ignitions—both human and climate-related. Given these environmental challenges, perhaps we should not be aiming to re-forest and "re-wild" with plants that we feel represent past "pristine" plant communities, but rather, to find new types of plants, endogenous or "invasive" exogenous species which thrive under the very real environments created by global warming, greater occurrences of droughts, and the impact of the inevitable episodes of wildfires. In addition to climate and environmental change leading to more fire vulnerability, human-ignitions are increasingly exacerbated by expanding populations into more rural areas of the American West. We suggest that the goal of reforestation shouldn't be to create and maintain a "natural" "God's Garden", but rather, our attention should focus on managing these landscapes to preserve fire resistance, sustainable regenerative vegetation communities, and increase biodiversity to our forests and national parks. This can be achieved best by increasing our tolerance for the more beneficial "invasive" species of plants and animals which have found a home in the American West, and not try to maintain endogenous species which are no longer well-adapted to the realities of our new climate and large human populations.

5 Conclusions

Fire frequency and intensity continues to increase in the American Southwest. The challenges described above affect all aspects of local livelihoods throughout the region at many levels, including resilience of local populations, the ways in which we conserve National Parks and other federal lands, as well as agriculture and livestock management. Increased fires have seriously impacted the biodiversity of this region which degrades ecosystem services and impacts economic and recreational land use. As our planet experiences a more rapid rate of change linked to human activities, a deeper understanding of the long-term human-environment interactions on the landscape is crucial for future decision making. This is ever truer as we confront the challenges of past land management strategies like widespread fire suppression and forest clearing. Native communities have been recounting the violence these strategies do the environment for centuries, but their voices have only recently begun to be recognized widely in conservation, policy, and public media circles (Christianson et al. 2022; Maclean et al. 2023).

Environmental archaeology and the use of proxy datasets from a variety of sources and records provide a wealth of information focused on the deep historical relationships humans have had with fire in the American Southwest. These records can support the revitalization of traditional land management strategies. This growing body of research underscores the fact that early human populations practiced land management in diverse ways throughout history and interacted with local environments with unique approaches as required by the changing circumstances and needs of those communities and landscapes. Our ongoing research of geoarchaeological and phytolith evidence from drainages across northern New Mexico shows that natural fires were rare until the terminal Pleistocene/early Holocene when fire frequency accelerated and intensified with time, demonstrating the human cultural connection with fire as a tool for managing the landscape. However, the absence of widespread burning during the Clovis expansion may indicate that cultural burning strategies were not universal across hunter-gatherer-forager communities in the Southwest and changed over time and place. Our work on the alluvial sediments of the Late Archaic period drainage at Tesuque Creek shows that in that context, communities were burning alongside other land management practices such as the introduction of the exogenous palmetto, to sustainably manage floodplain vegetation for its foraging potential, and perhaps to supplement the decline of succulents in a wetter, cooler environment.

Our research suggests that naturally ignited fires were infrequent before humans arrived in the Southwest, and that most fires were ignited on a regular basis by Archaic foragers throughout much of the Holocene and by agricultural societies in the late Holocene. This is supported by the presence of exogenous wild plants brought in by foragers, within some of the burn levels from our alluvial profiles. This indicates that traditional knowledge of sustainable landscape management is rooted in deep time extending back to the terminal Pleistocene and early Holocene, and that there is much to learn from this traditional heritage of controlling "firescapes" across the American Southwest. The Native traditions of introducing exogenous plants for their resilience and sustainability might serve as an example to us as a way forward in our own management of these landscapes for resilience.

References

Aycrigg, J. L., T. R. McCarley, R. T. Belote, et al. 2022. Wilderness areas in a changing landscape: changes in land use, land cover, and climate. *Ecological Applications* 32:1–20.

Cattau, M. E., C. Wessman, A. Mahood, et al. 2020. Anthropogenic and lightning-started fires are becoming larger and more frequent over a longer season length in the U.S.A. *Global Ecology and Biogeography* 29:668–681.

Christianson, A. C., C. R. Sutherland, F. Moola, et al. 2022. Centering Indigenous voices: The role of fire in the Boreal Forest of North America. *Current Forestry Reports* 8:257–276.

D'Andrea, R. M., R. S. Anderson, K. L. Cole, et al. 2023. Climate and human impact on vegetation and fire in an arid Colorado Plateau ecosystem in Western North America. *Quaternary Science Reviews* 321 (3): 108374. https://doi.org/10.1016/j.quascirev.2023.108374.

Damick, Alison, Arlene Rosen, and S. Ortman. 2021. Palm springs on the Rio Grande: Insight into Archaic forager plant use from phytoliths recovered from a Late Holocene alluvial section in northern New Mexico. *PLoS One* 16 (10): e0258231.

Damick, Alison, S. Krause, and Arlene Rosen. 2022. Building resilient landscapes in a semi-arid watershed: Anthropogenic and natural burning histories in Late Holocene Tesuque Creek, northern New Mexico. *The Holocene* 32:1437–1449.

Denevan, W. M. 1992. The pristine myth: the landscape of the Americas in 1492. *Annals of the Association of American Geographers* 82:369–385.

Denevan, W. M. 2011. The "pristine myth" revisited. *Geographical Review* 101:576–591.

Figueiredo, Y. 2007. Inventing Yosemite Valley: national parks and the language of preservation. *Historical Geography* 35:12–37.

Fitch, E. P., and G. A. Meyer. 2016. Temporal and spatial climatic controls on Holocene fire-related erosion and sedimentation, Jemez Mountains, New Mexico. *Quaternary Research* 85:75–86.

Fletcher, M. S., R. Hamilton, W. Dressler, et al. 2021. Indigenous knowledge and the shackles of wilderness. *Proceedings of the National Academy of Sciences* 118 (40): e2022218118.

Fusco, E. J., J. T. Abatzoglou, J. K. Balch, et al. 2016. Quantifying the human influence on fire ignition across the western USA. *Ecological Applications* 26:2388–2399.

Graeber, D., and D. Wengrow. 2023. *The Dawn of Everything: A New History of Humanity*. New York: Picador.

Guiterman, C. H., E. Q. Margolis, C. H. Baisan, et al. 2019. Spatiotemporal variability of human–fire interactions on the Navajo Nation. *Ecosphere* 10:e02932.

Hall, S. A. 2023. Late Quaternary fluvial environments at Abo Arroyo, New Mexico, U.S.A.: response to millennial-scale climate change. *Journal of Sedimentary Research* 93:413–429.

Hantson, S., N. Andela, M. L. Goulden, et al. 2022. Human-ignited fires result in more extreme fire behavior and ecosystem impacts. *Nature Communications* 13:2717.

Haynes, C. V., J. Boerner, K. Domanik, et al. 2010. The Murray Springs Clovis site, Pleistocene extinction, and the question of extraterrestrial impact. *Proceedings of the National Academy of Sciences* 107:4010–4015.

Holliday, V. T., P. J. Bartlein, A. C. Scott, et al. 2020. Extraordinary biomass-burning episode and impact winter triggered by the Younger Dryas cosmic impact 12,800 years ago, parts 1 and 2: a discussion. *The Journal of Geology* 128:69–94.

Keeley, J. E., and A. D. Syphard. 2018. Historical patterns of wildfire ignition sources in California ecosystems. *International Journal of Wildland Fire* 27:781–799.

Kimmerer, R. W. 2018. Mishkos kenomagwen, the lessons of grass: Restoring reciprocity with the good green earth. In *Traditional Ecological Knowledge: Learning from Indigenous Practices for Environmental Sustainability*, ed. M. K. Nelson and D. Shilling, 27–56. Cambridge: Cambridge University Press.

Kimmerer, R. W., and F. K. Lake. 2001. The role of indigenous burning in land management. *Journal of Forestry* 36–41.

Knight, C. A., L. Anderson, M. J. Bunting, et al. 2022. Land management explains major trends in forest structure and composition over the last millennium in California's Klamath Mountains. *Proceedings of the National Academy of Sciences* 119:e2116264119.

Lightfoot, K. G., R. Q. Cuthrell, C. J. Striplen, et al. 2013. Rethinking the study of landscape management practices amoung hunter-gatherers in North America. *American Antiquity* 78:285–301.

Long, J. W., F. K. Lake, and R. W. Goode. 2021. The importance of Indigenous cultural burning in forested regions of the Pacific West, USA. *Forest Ecology and Management* 500:119597.

Maclean, K., D. L. Hankins, A. C. Christianson, et al. 2023. Revitalising indigenous cultural fire practice: benefits and partnerships. *Trends in Ecology and Evolution* 38:899–902.

Mckim, D. 2017. God's Garden: Nature, order, and the Presbyterian conception of the British North American "wilderness". *Journal of Canadian Studies/Revue d'études canadiennes* 51:398–433.

Miller, R. J. 2019. The doctrine of discovery: The international law of colonialism. *Indigenous Peoples' Journal of Law, Culture and Resistance* 5:35.

Mueller, N. G., R. N. Spengler, A. Glenn, et al. 2020a. Bison, anthropogenic fire, and the origins of agriculture in eastern North America. *The Anthropocene Review* 8:141–158.

Mueller, S. E., A. E. Thode, E. Q. Margolis, et al. 2020b. Climate relationships with increasing wildfire in the southwestern US from 1984 to 2015. *Forest Ecology and Management* 460:117861.

Nagy, R. C., E. Fusco, B. Bradley, et al. 2018. Human-related ignitions increase the number of large wildfires across US ecoregions. *Fire* 1:4.

Parks, S. A., L. M. Holsinger, K. Blankenship, et al. 2023. Contemporary wildfires are more severe compared to the historical reference period in western US dry conifer forests. *Forest Ecology and Management* 544:121232.

Pigati, J. S., K. B. Springer, J. S. Honke, et al. 2023. Independent age estimates resolve the controversy of ancient human footprints at White Sands. *Science* 382:73–75.

Roos, C. I. 2020. Scale in the study of Indigenous burning. *Nature Sustainability* 3:898–899.

Roos, C. I., M. N. Zedeño, K. L. Hollenback, et al. 2018. Indigenous impacts on North American Great Plains fire regimes of the past millennium. *Proceedings of the National Academy of Sciences* 115:8143–8148.

Roos, C. I., T. M. Rittenour, T. W. Swetnam, et al. 2020. Fire suppression impacts on fuels and fire intensity in the western US: Insights from archaeological luminescence dating in northern New Mexico. *Fire* 3:32.

Roos, C. I., T. W. Swetnam, T. J. Ferguson, et al. 2021. Native American fire management at an ancient wildland–urban interface in the Southwest United States. *Proceedings of the National Academy of Sciences* 118:e2018733118.

Roos, C. I., C. H. Guiterman, E. Q. Margolis, et al. 2022. Indigenous fire management and cross-scale fire-climate relationships in the Southwest United States from 1500 to 1900 CE. *Science. Advances* 8:eabq3221.

Sáenz-Ceja, J. E., and M. E. Mendoza. 2024. Temporal and spatial patterns of fire regime disruption in conifer forests of western North America. *Physical Geography* 45:439–471.

Singleton, M. P., A. E. Thode, A. J. S. Meador, et al. 2019. Increasing trends in high-severity fire in the southwestern USA from 1984 to 2015. *Forest Ecology and Management* 433:709–719.

Thompson, J. C., D. K. Wright, S. J. Ivory, et al. 2021. Early human impacts and ecosystem reorganization in southern-central Africa. *Science Advances* 7:eabf9776.

Vierra, B. J., and S. S. Post. 2023. Foragers in transition: The Middle Archaic in the Northern Rio Grande Valley. *KIVA Journal of Southwestern Anthropology and History* 89:139–166.

Vierra, B. J., and J. M. Vint. 2022. Climate change and the Neolithic in the American Southwest. *Journal of Anthropological Research* 78:59–83.

Vinyeta, K. 2022. Under the guise of science: how the US Forest Service deployed settler colonial and racist logics to advance an unsubstantiated fire suppression agenda. *Environmental Sociology* 8:134–148.

Vinyeta, K., and J. Bacon. 2024. Backfire: the settler-colonial logic and legacy of Smokey Bear. *Environmental Politics* 1–26.

Planetary Health and ONE Paleopathology: Climate Adaptation, Risk, and Resilience in the Holocene

Gwen Robbins Schug and Jane E. Buikstra

Abstract Climate change poses significant challenges to human health and security through both direct impacts from extreme weather events and indirect effects mediated through changing ecosystems. This paper introduces ONE Paleopathology (OPP) as a deep-time perspective within the Planetary Health (PH) framework, examining how past human-environment interactions inform our understanding of present and future health challenges. Through case studies of malaria and historical syndemics, we demonstrate how OPP contributes to understanding the complex relationships between environmental change, social inequality, and human health. We first examine how climate change is altering malaria transmission patterns globally, while highlighting the value of Indigenous and Local Knowledge (ILK) systems in disease management. We then analyze two historical syndemic case studies: the pellagra epidemic in nineteenth-century Italy and the 1918 influenza pandemic at the Mississippi State Asylum. These examples illustrate how environmental changes, socioeconomic inequality, and institutional practices intersect to create health disparities, particularly among marginalized populations. The Italian case reveals how mono-cropping and capitalism contributed to a syndemic of malnutrition, mental illness, and tuberculosis, while the Mississippi case demonstrates how racial segregation and institutionalization exacerbated pandemic outcomes. These historical perspectives provide crucial insights for addressing contemporary health challenges in the context of climate change. We argue that incorporating OPP into PH frameworks enables better understanding of long-term human adaptations to environmental change and more effective, equitable responses to current health crises.

Keywords ONE Paleopathology · Climate change · Environmental health · Syndemics

---

G. R. Schug (✉) · J. E. Buikstra
UNC, Greensboro, Greensboro, NC, USA
e-mail: gmrobbin@uncg.edu

J. F. Haldon, R. Fernandes (eds.), *Bridging History and Policy*, Understanding Complex Systems, https://doi.org/10.1007/978-3-032-24379-9_25

1 Introduction

Climate change is already having a significant impact on human health and security. Direct impacts from extreme weather events and rising temperatures, as well as those mediated through changing ecosystems, interact with human social institutions to create inequities in health around the globe. Some of the major challenges posed by disturbance of the biosphere include: respiratory disease, antimicrobial resistance, toxin exposures, malnutrition, heat stroke, cardiovascular disease, changing patterns of infectious disease transmission, civil strife and interpersonal violence, and mental health impacts.

In the face of accelerating climate change, the contemporary world faces a suite of challenges that resonate deeply across the planetary spectrum, affecting not only human populations but all life forms (Kemp et al. 2022; Solomon 2007; Woodward et al. 2014). The unprecedented pace and scale of anthropogenic global warming surpasses that of any recorded Rapid Climate Change (RCC) events, yet the archaeological and paleoclimatic record provides our most valuable predictive framework for understanding how such rapid shifts impact human societies, fauna, and ecosystems (Burke et al. 2018; Ceballos et al. 2015; Robbins Schug 2020; Robbins Schug et al. 2023; Rockman and Hritz 2020; Solomon 2007; Stephens et al. 2019).

Recognizing this, the Intergovernmental Panel on Climate Change (IPCC) has emphasized that strategic responses to an increasingly warm future must be rooted in foundational research that models physical, social, and biological vulnerabilities, alongside pathways for resilience (Doherty et al. 2009). Within this effort, anthropology holds a pivotal role, integrating humanistic, social, and scientific approaches to illuminate our species' evolutionary trajectory and contextualize the current environmental crisis. Such deep-time perspectives underscore the complex interrelations between cultural, historical, and ecological dynamics, providing critical insights for developing equitable, sustainable strategies (Larsen 2023; Lewis et al. 2023; Robbins Schug et al. 2023).

The ONE Health (OH) framework has gained significant traction as a global strategy for interdisciplinary research, focusing on the intersections between environmental, animal, and human health (Adisasmito et al. 2022). Originally stemming from the ONE Medicine concept (Cassidy 2018), OH has long been promoted by the World Health Organization as essential for addressing zoonotic infection risks (Bidaisee and Macpherson 2014; Bird and Mazet 2018; Cunningham et al. 2017; Day 2010; Webster et al. 2016). More recently, OH has broadened to encompass health risks posed by global climate change, integrating concerns like zoonotic spillover, food security, pollution, and syndemics (Zinsstag et al. 2018).

From this convergence of ideas, the Planetary Health (PH) movement emerged as an extension of OH, driven by the need for urgent action on climate change. Planetary Health is defined as a solutions-oriented, transdisciplinary field, which seeks to address human impacts on Earth's ecosystems and how these disrupt global health systems (Whitmee et al. 2015). In response to the gravity of these challenges, the PH Alliance was established in 2015, quickly evolving into a global movement advocating for equitable, sustainable solutions to climate-induced health crises. This holistic framework emphasizes ethical, scientific, and profound societal transformations to the emerging new uncertainty complex—a period marked by planetary-scale environmental shifts, increasing political polarization, and the need for profound societal transformations (UNDP 2022). The movement acknowledges that contemporary human demographic and epidemiological patterns are shaped by policies that undermine a sustainable future. Thus, a core research goal is understanding the boundaries within which human societies can continue to thrive.

While both OH and PH share overlapping research interests, PH aims to address failures in governance and knowledge that prevent meaningful policy changes for human survival. The explicit mission of PH is to achieve the highest attainable standard of health, well-being, and equity worldwide by critically examining the political, economic, and social systems that shape the future of humanity (Whitmee et al. 2015). Building on both of these concepts, we are advocating for ONE Paleopathology (OPP). OPP was developed by paleopathologist Jane Buikstra and veterinary pathologist Elizabeth Uhl. OPP adds a deep-time perspective to OH and PH. Methodologically, OPP is distinguished by its integration of comparative veterinary pathology, ancient genomics, and osteological analysis of human remains, enabling a fuller reconstruction of host-pathogen co-evolution and ecological disease context than any one of these fields can produce independently. It also confronts persistent challenges to the relevance of paleopathology to contemporary issues such as disciplinary silos, underutilization of genomic techniques, limited research scope, and missed opportunities to use the past as natural experiments for addressing current and future planetary health challenges.

Adding Robbins Schug's expertise in climate-related issues, the three researchers recently led a 2-day ONE Paleopathology Workshop at Durham University August 4–6, 2024, preceding the International Society of Evolutionary Medicine and Public Health meeting. The workshop's central themes—Disease Spread, Environmental Health and Toxicity, and Climate Change—were explored through the lens of deep time and paleopathology (Stamer et al. 2026).

Key outcomes of this initiative included identifying critical areas for expanding the OPP knowledge base and fostering communication with non-specialist audiences, particularly the public and policymakers, to bridge the gap between scientific research and broader societal understanding. This chapter defines the application of OPP as part of the global PH initiative. We focus here on endemic and epidemic zoonotic transmission of Malaria and the syndemic of social inequality, malnutrition, mental health challenges, interpersonal violence, and tuberculosis. Read together, the cases that follow are methodological exemplars of an OPP approach: a shared workflow that triangulates environmental change, nutritional stress, and institutional practice against embodied evidence of disease. By placing malaria ecology alongside historic syndemics of pellagra–tuberculosis and institutional influenza, we show how ecological perturbations and inequitable institutions co-produce vulnerability in different ways across time and sociocultural contexts. The comparative logic yields a replicable template for interpreting past health and generating testable hypotheses for future research.

2 Malaria in Our Changing Environment

The impacts of anthropogenic climate change on malaria are already becoming apparent. Global warming is expanding the geographic range of Anopheles mosquitoes, the primary vectors of malaria, into new regions, particularly in higher altitudes and temperate zones that were once inhospitable to the disease (Ryan et al. 2020; Caminade et al. 2019). Recent studies estimate that by 2080, an additional 76 million people in sub-Saharan Africa could be at risk of malaria infection due to climate-induced changes in temperature and rainfall patterns (Ryan et al. 2019). These projections are particularly concerning for highland regions in sub-Saharan Africa, Asia, and South America, where rising temperatures will create favorable conditions for mosquito populations (Karypidou et al. 2020).

However, the expansion of malaria is not limited to tropical and subtropical regions. As temperatures rise, mosquito vector populations are likely to reestablish themselves in areas of the Global North, including parts of Europe, North America, and northern Asia (Fletcher 2022; Kulkarni et al. 2022). This shift has already been observed in countries like the United States, where recent outbreaks of malaria have been linked to extreme weather events, such as flooding and hurricanes, which create ideal breeding grounds for mosquitoes (Samarasekera 2023).

In addition to direct temperature and precipitation effects, extreme weather events linked to climate change, such as the El Niño-Southern Oscillation (ENSO), are predicted to exacerbate malaria epidemics. ENSO events have already been linked to malaria outbreaks in regions such as Mozambique, Pakistan, and Ethiopia, and are expected to increase in frequency and intensity as global warming progresses (Mabaso and Ndlovu 2012; Kulkarni et al. 2022). These events create conditions—such as excessive rainfall and flooding—that lead to an increase in stagnant water, providing more breeding habitats for mosquitoes.

Nevertheless, focusing solely on environmental factors ignores the broader social determinants of health that play a crucial role in malaria transmission. Vulnerable populations, particularly those in poverty-stricken areas with limited access to healthcare and inadequate infrastructure, are disproportionately affected by malaria (Onyango et al. 2016). Climate change compounds these vulnerabilities, as rising temperatures and changing rainfall patterns further strain public health systems in regions already struggling to control malaria. Effective responses to malaria in the context of climate change must therefore be multifaceted, addressing not only the environmental drivers of the disease but also the socio-economic and political factors that shape its transmission.

3 Planetary Health and Malaria: Interdisciplinary and Indigenous Knowledge for Addressing Climate-Driven Disease

Planetary Health, as an interdisciplinary field, focuses on the connections between human health, environmental change, and the sustainability of Earth's systems. When it comes to malaria, PH emphasizes how environmental degradation, climate change, and social factors intersect to influence the transmission and spread of this disease. The PH framework highlights the deep connections between human health, environmental change, and sustainability. As climate change continues to accelerate, many long-standing health challenges, such as malaria, are re-emerging in new forms and expanding into regions where they were previously absent. In this framework, malaria is not seen as a standalone issue but rather as part of a broader suite of health concerns that arise from human disruptions to natural systems. Several pressing concerns that emerge from the PH perspective on malaria include:

3.1 *Climate Change and Mosquito Ecology*

Climate change is a central concern in the PH perspective on malaria. Rising global temperatures, changes in precipitation patterns, and extreme weather events are all driving changes in the geographical distribution and intensity of malaria transmission. Warmer temperatures expand the range of *Anopheles* mosquitoes, allowing them to thrive in areas previously too cold for them, such as highland regions in Africa, South America, and Asia (Ryan et al. 2020; Ryan et al. 2019; Caminade et al. 2014). Similarly, changes in rainfall can lead to more standing water, creating additional mosquito breeding sites. As temperatures rise and ecosystems change, millions of people in previously malaria-free regions may become vulnerable to the disease. This includes parts of the Global North, such as Europe and North America, which have historically been free of endemic malaria but could soon see mosquito populations capable of transmitting *Plasmodium* parasites (Fletcher 2022). This expansion into new areas is one of the most pressing concerns that PH seeks to address, highlighting the need for robust public health and environmental management strategies.

3.2 *Extreme Weather Events and Epidemics*

PH perspectives also emphasize the role of extreme weather events, which are becoming more frequent and severe due to climate change. Events such as flooding, hurricanes, and El Niño-Southern Oscillation ENSO cycles can significantly increase the risk of malaria epidemics. These events often lead to displacement of populations, breakdowns in sanitation, and increases in stagnant water, which are ideal breeding conditions for mosquitoes (Mabaso and Ndlovu 2012). Populations displaced by extreme weather events, such as those affected by flooding or cyclones, face heightened vulnerability to malaria. Recent examples include malaria outbreaks in Mozambique and Pakistan following floods, where displaced populations and damaged infrastructure worsened transmission rates (Samarasekera 2023). Addressing this concern requires improving climate resilience in public health planning, particularly in vulnerable regions.

3.3 Ecosystem Degradation and Biodiversity Loss

From a PH perspective, environmental degradation, such as deforestation, agricultural expansion, and habitat fragmentation, plays a significant role in malaria transmission. Deforestation and land-use changes reduce biodiversity, often leading to environments dominated by specific mosquito species that are more efficient vectors of malaria (Ellwanger et al. 2022). Forest loss can also push wildlife, which may harbor other mosquito-borne diseases, closer to human populations, increasing the risk of zoonotic spillover. The destruction of ecosystems increases the risk of malaria and other vector-borne diseases. Deforestation in the Amazon, for example, has been linked to rising malaria cases as mosquito habitats expand into areas cleared for agriculture (Burkett-Cadena and Vittor 2018). Protecting biodiversity and maintaining healthy ecosystems are thus key strategies in reducing the transmission of malaria within the PH framework.

3.4 Socio-Economic Inequalities and Health Disparities

PH highlights the intersection of environmental change and socio-economic factors in exacerbating health disparities. Malaria disproportionately affects low-income populations who often have limited access to healthcare, sanitation, and preventive measures such as bed nets and insecticides (Onyango et al. 2016). These populations are more vulnerable to the impacts of climate change, including increased malaria transmission, because they have fewer resources to adapt to changing environmental conditions. Socio-economic inequalities amplify the impacts of malaria, particularly in regions where public health infrastructure is weak. In sub-Saharan Africa, for example, rural and impoverished communities bear the greatest malaria burden (Ricci 2012). PH calls for equitable access to healthcare and disease prevention strategies to mitigate the disproportionate impacts of malaria on vulnerable populations.

3.5 Zoonotic Spillover and Emerging Diseases

PH perspectives on malaria also consider the risk of zoonotic spillover—the transmission of diseases from animals to humans. As ecosystems are disrupted by climate change and human encroachment, wildlife that carry *Plasmodium* parasites capable of infecting humans such as *P. knowlesi*, a monkey malaria parasite are more likely to encounter human populations. These zoonotic malaria strains pose a growing threat in regions like Southeast Asia (Naserrudin et al. 2022). The potential for zoonotic spillover of malaria parasites, particularly in regions experiencing deforestation and biodiversity loss, is a pressing concern that PH seeks to address. Protecting natural habitats and reducing human-wildlife contact can help mitigate the risk of zoonotic malaria and other emerging infectious diseases.

4 Managing Malaria: Indigenous and Local Knowledge (ILK) Systems

In many Indigenous societies, knowledge of local ecosystems, weather patterns, and disease vectors has been passed down through generations, providing a rich source of information for disease prevention and control. For example, traditional healers in sub-Saharan Africa and South America have long used medicinal plants to treat malaria and its symptoms. Artemisia annua, from which the modern anti-malarial drug artemisinin is derived, has been used in traditional Chinese medicine for centuries (Tu 2017). Similarly, Indigenous communities in the Amazon have developed a wide range of plant-based remedies for malaria, many of which have yet to be scientifically studied (Frausin et al. 2015).

ILK also provides insights into the relationship between environmental change and disease transmission. In Zimbabwe, for example, local knowledge about the connections between weather patterns and malaria outbreaks has been integrated into early warning systems that help predict and prevent epidemics (Macherera et al. 2017). These systems draw on observations of rainfall, temperature, and plant and animal behaviors to forecast the conditions that favor mosquito breeding and malaria transmission.

Moreover, ILK emphasizes the importance of maintaining biodiversity and protecting ecosystems as a means of disease prevention. In the Amazon, Indigenous communities have long practiced sustainable land management, which has helped maintain the ecological balance necessary to control mosquito populations (Garnett et al. 2018). Studies have shown that lands managed by Indigenous peoples tend to have lower rates of deforestation and higher biodiversity, both of which are critical for reducing the spread of vector-borne diseases like malaria (Dawson et al. 2021). By incorporating ILK into public health strategies, we can develop more effective and culturally appropriate interventions for malaria prevention.

However, the integration of ILK into malaria control efforts must be done in a way that respects the rights and autonomy of Indigenous peoples. Too often, ILK is treated as a resource to be extracted by researchers, without consideration for the social, political, and cultural contexts in which this knowledge is embedded (Bijoy 2022). True collaboration with Indigenous communities requires recognizing their authority and ensuring that their knowledge is used to benefit their own health and well-being, rather than being appropriated for external purposes.

4.1 ONE Paleopathology Is Deep-time ILK About Malaria

ONE Paleopathology, the study of diseases in ancient human remains, plays an essential role in addressing concerns about malaria by providing a deep-time perspective on the co-evolution of humans and malarial parasites. This field of study allows researchers to understand how malaria has shaped human biology, migration, and social structures over millennia. While OPP differs from ILK in that it is generated through formal scientific inquiry rather than transmitted within living communities, both systems offer place- and population-specific, longitudinal knowledge about human-environment-disease relationships that is otherwise inaccessible to biomedical or climate science alone. Paleopathology addresses several pressing concerns related to malaria:

4.1.1 Understanding the Evolution of Malaria

Paleopathology helps trace the evolutionary history of malaria, revealing how different *Plasmodium* species have co-evolved with human populations over time. Studies of ancient human remains have identified genetic markers of malaria resistance, such as the sickle cell trait and thalassemia, which have developed as adaptations to malaria (Kariuki and Williams 2020). These genetic adaptations offer critical insights into how malaria has shaped human evolution and provide a basis for developing strategies to manage malaria in the future. Understanding the long-term evolutionary relationship between humans and malaria is crucial for predicting how the disease might continue to evolve under the pressures of climate change. Paleopathological studies provide valuable data on how human populations have historically adapted to malaria, which can inform current public health strategies and genetic research.

4.1.2 Environmental and Social Contexts of Malaria in the Past

Paleopathology examines how environmental and social factors influenced the spread of malaria in ancient civilizations. For instance, evidence of malaria in ancient Egypt and the Roman Empire highlights how urbanization, irrigation, and environmental modification created conditions conducive to malaria transmission (Bianucci et al. 2008; Nerlich et al. 2008). These insights are relevant today, as similar processes—such as deforestation, urban sprawl, and agricultural expansion—are driving malaria transmission in modern contexts. The paleopathological record shows how human-environment interactions have historically facilitated the spread of malaria. This understanding can help policymakers and public health officials design interventions that mitigate the environmental and social drivers of malaria transmission, particularly in regions undergoing rapid development and ecological change.

4.1.3 Zoonotic Origins and the Future of Malaria

Paleopathology also addresses the zoonotic origins of malaria, shedding light on how Plasmodium parasites originally spread from animals to humans. This is especially important as we face new threats from zoonotic malaria species, such as *P. knowlesi* in Southeast Asia (Singh et al. 2004). Paleopathological evidence can help researchers understand the conditions under which zoonotic spillover occurs and how to prevent future outbreaks. The increasing risk of zoonotic malaria, driven by habitat destruction and biodiversity loss, is a pressing concern that paleopathology helps to address by providing insights into the historical and evolutionary origins of zoonotic transmission. This knowledge can inform strategies to reduce human-wildlife contact and prevent the emergence of new zoonotic diseases.

4.1.4 Disease Syndemics and Co-Morbidities

Paleopathology also explores how malaria interacts with other diseases in syndemic contexts. Syndemics occur when two or more diseases exacerbate each other's effects, often in populations facing socio-economic disadvantages. For example, paleopathological evidence from ancient human remains has shown that malaria often co-occurred with tuberculosis, particularly in regions where poverty and poor sanitation were prevalent (Roberts and Buikstra 2003). The study of past disease syndemics, such as the co-occurrence of malaria and tuberculosis, offers insights into how modern populations might experience overlapping health crises, particularly in regions where climate change, poverty, and conflict intersect. Paleopathology highlights the need for integrated public health responses that address multiple health threats simultaneously.

5 Interdisciplinary Approaches to Malaria in the Context of Planetary Health

Malaria presents a growing threat to global health in the context of climate change, but addressing this challenge requires more than biomedical solutions. It demands an interdisciplinary approach that integrates lessons from the past, insights from climate science and public health, and the invaluable knowledge of Indigenous and local communities. By bringing together these diverse perspectives, we can develop more effective strategies for managing malaria and ensuring the health and well-being of future generations.

Planetary Health must draw on insights from biology, anthropology, public health, and climate science. Each of these disciplines provides unique contributions to understanding the complex interactions between malaria, climate change, and human societies. Biological anthropology offers critical perspectives on the long-term co-evolution of humans and malaria, highlighting how genetic adaptations to malaria have shaped human populations over millennia. Paleopathological studies of ancient human remains provide direct evidence of malaria's impact on past populations, revealing how the disease has influenced human health and migration patterns (Bianucci et al. 2008; Larsen 2023). These studies also underscore the role of environmental changes—both natural and anthropogenic—in shaping the spread of malaria throughout history.

Climate science, meanwhile, provides crucial insights into how global warming and shifting weather patterns will affect the future distribution of malaria. By modeling the impacts of rising temperatures and changing precipitation patterns on mosquito habitats, climate scientists can help public health officials anticipate where malaria outbreaks are likely to occur and develop targeted interventions (Caminade et al. 2014; Ryan et al. 2020). These models must be integrated with social science research to account for the socio-economic and political factors that influence disease transmission and public health responses.

Finally, public health initiatives must be culturally informed and inclusive of ILK. In many regions where malaria is endemic, traditional medicine plays an important role in disease management, and local healers may have valuable knowledge about plant-based treatments or environmental control measures (Tu 2017; Frausin et al. 2015). Collaborating with Indigenous communities to develop culturally appropriate interventions can enhance the effectiveness of malaria prevention programs, ensuring that they are both scientifically rigorous and socially responsive.

The history of malaria demonstrates the critical role that environmental and social factors play in shaping the transmission of infectious diseases. As climate change accelerates, these same factors will continue to drive the spread of malaria, making it essential to address the root causes of disease transmission through integrated, interdisciplinary efforts. By leveraging the insights of biological anthropology, climate science, and ILK, we can develop sustainable solutions that not only control malaria but also promote broader ecological and social resilience. The following section provides OPP perspective on historic period case studies of non-infectious syndemics, illustrating the broad scope of this field of inquiry.

6 Environmental Change and Historical Syndemics

The dialectical relationship between social inequality, environmental changes, and the embodied experiences of marginalized populations is a critical focus of PH, particularly when examining how mono-cropping, socio-economic inequality, nutritional deficiency, mental health, and infectious diseases intersect. This section revisits the nineteenth- to twentieth-century experience of people living in northeastern Italy (Miller et al. 2020) and the southeastern United States (Zuckerman et al. 2022), where the introduction of *Zea mays* corn as a staple crop created significant health disparities, exacerbating malnutrition and creating an epidemic of pellagrous mania. In both places, the epidemic led to the development of asylums to house the mentally ill.

Our case study from northeastern Italy emphasizes the role of capitalism and mono-cropping in mental illness. The rise of asylums to deal with the epidemic which, in turn, facilitated the spread of infectious diseases, particularly tuberculosis (TB). Our case study from Mississippi demonstrates how people with disabilities came to live in these asylums, which made this population particularly susceptible to the 1918 Influenza pandemic. These examples from paleopathology provide a clear lens for understanding the syndemic relationships between socio-economic inequality, mental health, and infectious diseases within a framework of climate-induced environmental change.

6.1 *ONE Paleopathology in Modern Italy: Pellagra, Interpersonal Violence, and TB*

The adoption of corn as a primary food source in northern Italy during the sixteenth century followed the transatlantic introduction of crops like potatoes, tomatoes, peppers, beans, and corn into European agriculture (Mariani-Constantini and Mariani-Constantini 2007). Corn's high yield, resilience, and ability to thrive in varying conditions made it an attractive option, particularly in the Po River Valley, where agricultural communities engaged in crop rotations to manage seasonal variability (Warman 2003). As reliance on corn deepened in the nineteenth century, during the period of the *Risorgimento* Italian Unification, northern Italy transitioned to a capitalist economy, disrupting traditional agrarian life and increasing socio-economic inequality (Patriarca and Riall 2011).

The over-reliance on corn in the diet of northern Italy's lower-working-class and *braccianti* landless laborers had profound implications for public health. These workers, who lived in poverty and had limited access to a diverse diet, consumed corn *Z. mays* as their primary food source, resulting in widespread malnutrition. Corn, while calorically sufficient, is deficient in essential nutrients like niacin and tryptophan, which are necessary for preventing pellagra (Cohen and Armelagos 1984; Steckel and Rose 2002).

Pellagra was first described in the 1770s by Francesco Frapolli (Mariani-Constantini and Mariani-Constantini 2007). The rise of pellagra in Italy can be traced to reliance on a diet centered around corn which lacked essential nutrients like niacin vitamin B3 and tryptophan, leading to widespread malnutrition and mental health disorders, including pellagrous mania (Goldberger 1914). These symptoms were most common among impoverished populations, particularly in northeastern Italy, where the disease reached epidemic levels during the nineteenth and early twentieth centuries (Messedaglia 1927).

In northeastern Italy, the pellagra epidemic was not solely a result of dietary deficiency; it was also shaped by larger social and political forces. Giovanni Marzari (1810) was among the first to suggest that pellagra was linked to a diet over-reliant on corn. However, for much of the nineteenth century, competing theories about the disease's origins dominated medical discourse. Some believed that spoiled corn was to blame, while others proposed that pellagra was an infectious disease caused by a protozoan parasite, spread by the *Simulium* fly (Lombroso 1872; Goldberger 1914). These competing theories reflected deeper conflicts about the causes of illness in general in a society where food scarcity and poverty were rampant.

Louis Sambon's infectious disease theory gained traction in the early twentieth century because it aligned with prevailing views that diseases afflicting the poor were caused by personal failings or unsanitary conditions, rather than systemic issues like poverty or malnutrition (Ginnaio and Jacobs-Colas 2011). The Italian bourgeoisie and the Catholic Church were reluctant to acknowledge the links between pellagra and poverty because doing so would have implicated them in the structural inequalities that perpetuated the disease (Mariani-Constantini and Mariani-Constantini 2007). As a result, efforts to address pellagra focused on curbing its symptoms, rather than its root causes. It was not until the 1930s, when the relationship between niacin deficiency and pellagra was definitively proven through scientific studies, that effective public health measures were taken to prevent the disease (Elvehjem et al. 1937).

The Italian case of pellagra underscores the Planetary Health principle that environmental and social determinants of health must be considered in tandem. In this instance, the environmental conditions favorable for growing corn combined with the socio-economic structures that forced large populations into poverty created a perfect storm for pellagra to flourish. The failure to address the social inequalities that underpinned the epidemic prolonged its devastating effects.

The mental health effects of pellagra—characterized by confusion, memory loss, and, in extreme cases, madness—compounded the existing social challenges faced by these populations. Pellagrous mania became an endemic issue, linked not only to poor nutrition but to the broader socio-economic conditions that forced people into subsistence farming and precarious labor (Cohen and Crane-Kramer 1998). In PH perspective, this reflects a pressing concern about how food systems and climate change intersect with social inequalities to drive both malnutrition and mental health crises.

The asylums of northeastern Italy were also places where residents sometimes suffered from other issues, including vitamin D deficiency and interpersonal violence (Miller et al. 2020). Poverty and micronutrient deficiencies from a corn-based diet also weakened immune systems, making the working classes more susceptible to infectious diseases like tuberculosis TB. Malnutrition and poor living conditions created an environment where infectious diseases could flourish, particularly in overcrowded rural and urban areas. Northern Italy's shift toward industrialization and urbanization during the *Risorgimento*, combined with the impoverished conditions of *braccianti* laborers, facilitated the spread of TB in an already vulnerable population (Riall 1994; Mariani-Constantini and Mariani-Constantini 2007).

Infectious diseases like TB thrive in conditions of poverty, malnutrition, and overcrowding, forming a syndemic with other health challenges. In this case, pellagra's immunosuppressive effects increased susceptibility to TB, creating a vicious cycle of nutritional and infectious disease crises that disproportionately affected lower-class populations (Cohen and Armelagos 1984). The rise of TB in conjunction with malnutrition-driven pellagra provides a historical parallel to modern concerns about how climate change and food insecurity will exacerbate syndemics in the twenty-first century.

The pellagra epidemic in the Veneto Region illustrates how environmental and dietary changes intersect with social inequality to produce a syndemic—where multiple health challenges, such as malnutrition, mental illness, and infectious disease, exacerbate each other (Singer 2009). The reliance on corn, coupled with systemic poverty and limited access to healthcare, created a perfect storm for the spread of not just pellagra, but also violence and infectious disease.

6.2 ONE Paleopathology in Modern America: Race, Disability, and Influenza

The 1918 influenza pandemic exposed and increased the stark social vulnerabilities faced by institutionalized populations, particularly those living with disabilities. As evidenced in the study of individuals at the Mississippi State Asylum (MSA), the pandemic's impacts were not only biological but also deeply intertwined with socio-economic, racial, and environmental factors (Zuckerman et al. 2022). At the MSA, a state facility that housed individuals with acute and chronic conditions, Black patients disproportionately suffered from respiratory diseases such as influenza and tuberculosis. These health disparities were worsened by the institution's poor infrastructure, overcrowding, and segregation, which placed Black patients at a higher risk of illness and mortality (Franklin and Wilson 2020; Mitchell 1919). This case underscores how systemic inequalities—such as those created by segregation, poverty, and lack of access to healthcare—worsened health outcomes for marginalized communities, resonating with the principles of PH, which emphasize the interaction between environmental, social, and health systems.

Institutionalization created ideal conditions for the spread of infectious disease. The MSA, which housed approximately 30,000 patients between 1855 and 1935, faced persistent overcrowding and lacked adequate infrastructure, especially for its Black patients (Franklin and Wilson 2020). By the early twentieth century, most of the institutional population was Black, reflecting broader racial inequalities in access to care. Segregated living quarters, poor sanitation, and a heavy reliance on corn-based diets that contributed to pellagra compounded the risks of infectious diseases such as tuberculosis TB and influenza. During the 1918 pandemic, this overcrowding, along with inadequate healthcare and sanitation, contributed to high mortality rates among Black patients. At the MSA, the pandemic resulted in 617 infections and 67 deaths, a figure that reflected the broader racial disparities in pandemic mortality across the state (Mitchell 1919).

Pellagra disproportionately affected impoverished populations dependent on corn-based diets, creating a syndemic. The MSA's annual reports during this period noted that many Black patients arrived in poor health due to malnutrition, pellagra, and other pre-existing conditions that made them more susceptible to respiratory infections like influenza and tuberculosis (Mitchell 1919, 1926). These conditions, along with the systemic racism embedded in the healthcare system, compounded the vulnerabilities of Black patients. The pandemic's impact on this institutionalized population highlights how social determinants of health—such as race, class, and institutionalization—intersected to shape vulnerability to infectious diseases (Crenshaw 1989; Mamelund and Dimka 2021).

The increased mortality among Black patients at the MSA mirrored patterns seen throughout the United States during the pandemic. Nationally, Black communities faced higher case fatality ratios from influenza, in part due to higher rates of malnutrition and comorbidities, such as tuberculosis, that were prevalent in impoverished communities (Økland and Mamelund 2019). These disparities were further exacerbated by systemic racism, which limited access to healthcare and subjected Black patients to poorer quality medical care compared to their white counterparts (Franklin and Wilson 2020; Northington Gamble 2010). In the MSA, this racial disparity in healthcare was compounded by the institution's limited resources and overburdened staff, which struggled to provide adequate care during the pandemic (Mitchell 1919).

Male patients at the MSA were more severely affected by influenza than female patients, with higher mortality rates from respiratory causes, including influenza (Zuckerman et al. 2022). This disparity may have been due to gendered differences in labor roles within the institution. Male patients often worked in more public-facing roles, such as farming or carpentry, which increased their exposure to infection. In contrast, female patients were more likely to be engaged in domestic labor within the institution, which may have reduced their exposure to outside contacts (Zuckerman et al. 2022).

Overcrowding, insufficient care, and reliance on a limited number of caregivers exacerbated the conditions that allowed the pandemic to spread rapidly within institutions like the MSA. Black patients, already marginalized by racial and economic hierarchies, were especially vulnerable to the compounded effects of malnutrition, infectious disease, and poor institutional care (Zuckerman et al. 2022). The MSA superintendents often attributed the poor health outcomes of Black patients to biological racial differences, further entrenching systemic inequalities in care and treatment.

Additionally, the pandemic's impact on the MSA's staff—many of whom also fell ill—reduced the quality of care that could be provided to patients, further exacerbating the vulnerabilities of the institution's population (Mitchell 1919). This reduction in staff, combined with the overcrowding and poor sanitation, created an environment where infectious diseases like influenza spread rapidly.

This case study of the MSA highlights the critical importance of considering social determinants of health—such as race, class, and institutionalization—in understanding pandemic outcomes. The intersection of social identity and health risk factors in institutionalized populations reveals a deeper understanding of how systemic inequities shape health vulnerabilities during times of crisis (Robbins Schug and Halcrow 2022). The lessons from the 1918 pandemic remain relevant today, as marginalized populations continue to experience disproportionate harm during pandemics like COVID-19, where social and economic inequalities remain key drivers of disease vulnerability (Robbins Schug and Halcrow 2022).

In conclusion, the 1918 pandemic at the MSA illustrates how the intersections of race, disability, and institutionalization within a segregated healthcare system exacerbated health disparities. The higher mortality rates among Black patients and those institutionalized for disabilities reflect a broader societal failure to address the structural determinants of health. This historical case provides a framework for understanding how syndemics—where multiple health challenges exacerbate each other—play out in vulnerable populations, reinforcing the need for inclusive and equitable public health strategies in future pandemics.

6.3 Climate Change, Syndemics, and Health Inequality in a Modern Context

The Italian and American experiences with corn-based malnutrition and its syndemic effects raise concerns about how climate change will impact food systems and public health in the modern era. As rising temperatures and shifting precipitation patterns disrupt global agriculture, many regions may become dependent on a limited number of crops that can withstand these changes. This could exacerbate existing inequalities in access to nutritious food, particularly in regions where agricultural diversity is already under threat from environmental degradation (Burke et al. 2018).

The reliance on staple crops that do not meet the full nutritional needs of populations can create nutrition-related syndemics, where malnutrition, mental health disorders, and infectious diseases interact to worsen health outcomes, especially among the poorest populations. In the nineteenth-century Italian context, pellagra emerged as the result of systemic failures to provide adequate nutrition to the working class. In the twenty-first century, Planetary Health concerns focus on how climate change might reproduce similar conditions in regions facing food insecurity and economic inequality (Whitmee et al. 2015). Mental health is an often-overlooked component of climate-driven syndemics. As populations face increased stress from extreme weather events, displacement, food insecurity, and environmental degradation, the mental health impacts of malnutrition may become more pronounced. The historical example of pellagrous mania, in which nutritional deficiencies led to widespread mental illness, is a stark reminder of how intertwined diet, social inequality, and mental health can be.

The story of pellagra in Italy is a cautionary tale about the dangers of ignoring the social and environmental determinants of health. The epidemic emerged because of the intersection between dietary deficiencies, social inequality, and public health failures. From a PH perspective, pellagra represents a syndemic, where multiple health crises—malnutrition, mental illness, and infectious disease—interact and exacerbate one another, particularly in marginalized communities. As climate change threatens to disrupt food systems and exacerbate social inequalities, we must learn from the lessons of the past to prevent similar syndemics from emerging. By addressing the root causes of inequality and ensuring access to diverse, nutrient-rich foods, we can mitigate the health impacts of climate change on vulnerable populations. In doing so, we can build more resilient health systems that are better equipped to handle the complex challenges of the twenty-first century.

From this perspective too, the study of the 1918 influenza pandemic at the Mississippi State Asylum MSA underscores the importance of intersectionality as a framework for understanding environmental, social, and health systems that shape vulnerability to infectious diseases. Planetary Health highlights how the health of human populations is deeply connected to environmental conditions and social determinants—racial and gender inequality, poverty, institutionalization—that exacerbate health risks. In the case of the MSA, structural racism, overcrowding, and malnutrition—rooted in broader socio-economic and environmental conditions—created a perfect storm for the spread of infectious diseases like influenza and tuberculosis.

The segregation policies that marginalized Black patients, combined with poor sanitation and insufficient resources, mirror contemporary concerns about how environmental degradation and socio-economic inequality drive syndemics, where multiple health crises, such as malnutrition and infectious disease, compound one another. This case demonstrates the importance of addressing systemic inequalities and ensuring equitable access to healthcare and nutrition to build resilience against future pandemics, particularly for marginalized and institutionalized populations, a key tenet of PH's focus on sustainability and justice in global health systems.

7 Conclusion

The PH perspective on malaria and historical syndemics emphasizes the intricate connections between human health, dietary diversity, environmental degradation, socio-economic inequalities, and infectious disease. Climate change is accelerating the spread of malaria, expanding its range into new regions and increasing the frequency of malaria epidemics linked to extreme weather events in regions where it has not been endemic for a century or more. The lessons from OPP, including historical experiences with corn-based malnutrition are more relevant than ever as the world faces new challenges posed by environmental degradation, food insecurity, and global health disparities. In the face of climate change, modern agricultural systems must prioritize diversity, sustainability, and equitable access to nutrition to prevent the emergence of new syndemics driven by malnutrition and infectious diseases. From a PH perspective, the rise of pellagra may also create public health issues related to bias, discrimination and inequities based on race and ability, placing marginalized groups at greatest risk for pandemics.

ONE Paleopathology is an interdisciplinary approach to environmental health science in the past, providing critical historical and evolutionary context for understanding human health today. Concretely, we need to integrate paleopathological datasets into climate vulnerability assessments, embed OPP expertise in WHO and IPCC working groups alongside climate scientists and epidemiologists, and use deep-time evidence of syndemic risk to prioritize food system diversification and institutional reform in regions already identified as high-risk for climate-driven health crises. The case studies presented here provide insights for paleopathologists interested in addressing contemporary concerns from the PH and OH policy community. For the policy makers trying to work in the face of the new uncertainty complex (UNDP 2022), these case studies demonstrate the need for holistic approaches to public health that use historical sciences to address the root causes of health disparity in deep-time perspective.

References

Adisasmito, W. B., Almuhairi, S.,Behravesh, C. B., Bilivogui, P., Bukachi, S. A., Casas, N., ... & Zhou, L. (2022). One Health: A new definition for a sustainable and healthy future. *PLoS Pathogens, 18*(6), e1010537.

Bianucci, R., Mattutino, G., Lallo, R., Charlier, P., Jouin-Spriet, H., Peluso, A., Higham, T., Torre, C. and Massa, E.R., 2008. Immunological evidence of Plasmodium falciparum infection in an Egyptian child mummy from the Early Dynastic Period. *Journal of Archaeological Science 35*(7), 1880–1885.

Bidaisee, S., and C. N. L. Macpherson. 2014. Zoonoses and One Health: A review of the literature. *Journal of Parasitology Research* 2014:874345. https://doi.org/10.1155/2014/874345.

C.R. Bijoy, A., 2022. Indigenous Peoples' Rights in Asian NDCs: A Regional Assessment, Asia Indigenous Peoples Pact. Thailand. Retrieved from https://coilink.org/20.500.12592/142bbm on 15 Apr 2026. COI: 20.500.12592/142bbm.

Bird, B. H., and J. A. K. Mazet. 2018. Detection of emerging zoonotic pathogens: An integrated One Health approach. *Annual Review of Animal Biosciences* 6:121–139.

Burkett-Cadena, N. D., and A. Y. Vittor (2018). Deforestation and vector-borne disease: Forest conversion favors important mosquito vectors of human pathogens. Basic Appl Ecol. 2018 Feb;26:101–110. https://doi.org/10.1016/j.baae.2017.09.012. Epub 2017 Sep 23. PMID: 34290566; PMCID: PMC8290921.

Burke, K. D., J. W. Williams, M. A. Chandler, A. M. Haywood, D. J. Lunt, and B. L. Otto-Bliesner. 2018. Pliocene and Eocene provide best analogs for near-future climates. *Proceedings of the National Academy of Sciences* 115 (52): 13288–13293. https://doi.org/10.1073/pnas.1809600115.

Caminade, C., K. M. McIntyre, and A. E. Jones. (2019). Impact of recent and future climate change on vector-borne diseases. *Annals of the New York Academy of Sciences, 1436*(1), 157–173. https://doi.org/10.1111/nyas.13950.

Caminade, C., S. Kovats, J. Rocklov, A. M. Tompkins, A. P. Morse, et al. 2014. Impact of climate change on global malaria distribution. *Proceedings of the National Academy of Sciences* 111 (9): 3286–3291. https://doi.org/10.1073/pnas.1302089111.

Cassidy, A. 2018. Humans, other animals, and 'One Health' in the early twenty-first century. In *Animals and the Shaping of Modern Medicine: One Health and Its Histories*, ed. A. Woods, M. Bresalier, A. Cassidy, and R. M. Dentinger, 193–236. London: Palgrave Macmillan.

Ceballos, G., P. R. Ehrlich, A. D. Barnosky, A. García, R. M. Pringle, and T. M. Palmer. 2015. Accelerated modern human–induced species losses: Entering the sixth mass extinction. *Science Advances* 15:e1400253. https://doi.org/10.1126/sciadv.1400253.

Cohen, M. N., and G. J. Armelagos. 1984. *Paleopathology at the Origins of Agriculture*. New York: Academic.

Cohen, M. N., and G. M. M. Crane-Kramer, eds. 1998. *Ancient Health: Skeletal Indicators of Agricultural and Economic Intensification*. Gainesville: University Press of Florida.

Crenshaw, K. W. 1989. Demarginalizing the intersection of race and sex: A black feminist critique of antidiscrimination doctrine, feminist theory and antiracist politics. *Chicago: University of Chicago Legal Forum* 1989:139–167.

Cunningham, A. A., P. Daszak, and J. L. N. Wood. 2017. One Health, emerging infectious diseases and wildlife: Two decades of progress? *Philosophical Transactions of the Royal Society B: Biological Sciences* 372:20160167. https://doi.org/10.1098/rstb.2016.0167.

Dawson, N. M., B. Coolsaet, E. J. Sterling, R. Loveridge, N. D. Gross-Camp, S. et al. 2021. The role of Indigenous peoples and local communities in effective and equitable conservation. *Ecology and Society 26* (3):19. https://doi.org/10.5751/ES-12625-260319.

Day, M. J. 2010. One Health: The small animal dimension. *Veterinary Record* 167 (22): 847–849. https://doi.org/10.1136/vr.c6492.

Doherty, S. J., S. Bojinski, A. Henderson-Sellers, K. Noone, D. Goodrich, et al. 2009. Lessons learned from IPCC AR4: Scientific developments needed to understand, predict, and respond to climate change. *Bulletin of the American Meteorological Society* 904:497–514. https://doi.org/10.1175/2008BAMS2643.1.

Ellwanger, J. H., P. M. Fearnside, M. Ziliotto, J. M. Valverde-Villegas, E. B. G. da Veiga, et al. 2022. Synthesizing the connections between environmental disturbances and zoonotic spillover. *Anais da Academia Brasileira de Ciências* 94 (suppl 3): e20211530. https://doi.org/10.1590/0001-3765202220211530.

Elvehjem, C. A., R. Madden, F. Strong, and D. Wooley. 1937. Relation of nicotinic acid and nicotinic acid amide to canine black tongue. *Journal of the American Chemical Society* 59:1767–1768.

Fletcher, I. K. 2022. *Assessing the Impact of Global Environmental Change on Mosquito-Borne Disease: A Planetary Health Approach*. PhD thesis. London School of Hygiene & Tropical Medicine. https://doi.org/10.17037/PUBS.04668987.

Franklin, M., and S. M. Wilson. 2020. A bioarchaeological study of African American health and mortality in the post-emancipation US South. *American Antiquity* 85 (4): 652–675. https://doi.org/10.1017/aaq/2020.58.
Frausin, G., A. F. Hidalgo, R. B. S. L. Souza, V. F. Kinupp, L. C. Ming, A. et al. 2015. An ethnobotanical study of anti-malarial plants among Indigenous people on the Upper Negro River in the Brazilian Amazon. *Journal of Ethnopharmacology* 174:238–252. https://doi.org/10.1016/j.jep.2015.07.033.
Garnett, S. T., N. D. Burgess, J. E. Fa, Á. Fernández-Llamazares, Z. Molnár, C. J. Robinson, et al. 2018. A spatial overview of the global importance of Indigenous lands for conservation. *Nature Sustainability* 17:369–374. https://doi.org/10.1038/s41893-018-0100-6.
Ginnaio, M., and A. Jacobs-Colas. 2011. Pellagra in late nineteenth century Italy: Effects of a deficiency disease. *Population* 66 (3): 583–609.
Goldberger, J. 1914. The etiology of pellagra: The significance of certain epidemiological observations with respect thereto. *Public Health Reports* (1896–1970), 1683–1686.
Kariuki, S., and T. Williams. 2020. Human genetics and malaria resistance. *Human Genetics* 139 (6-7): 801–811. https://doi.org/10.1007/s00439-020-02142-6.
Karypidou, M. C., V. Almpanidou, A. M. Tompkins, A. D. Mazaris, S. Gewehr, S., et al. 2020. Projected shifts in the distribution of malaria vectors due to climate change. *Climatic Change* 163:2117–2133. https://doi.org/10.1007/s10584-020-02926-9.
Kemp, L., C. Xu, J. Depledge, K. L. Ebi, G. Gibbins, T. Kohler, et al. 2022. Climate endgame: Exploring catastrophic climate change scenarios. *Proceedings of the National Academy of Sciences* 119 (34): e2108146119. https://doi.org/10.1073/pnas.2108146119.
Kulkarni, M. A., M. Duguay, and K. Ost. 2022. Charting the evidence for climate change impacts on the global spread of malaria and dengue and adaptive responses: A scoping review of reviews. *Globalization and Health* 18:1. https://doi.org/10.1186/s12992-021-00793-2.
Larsen, C. S. 2023. The past 12,000 years of behavior, adaptation, population, and evolution shaped who we are today. *Proceedings of the National Academy of Sciences* 120 (4): e2209613120. https://doi.org/10.1073/pnas.2209613120.
Lewis, C. M., M. Y. Akinyi, S. N. DeWitte, and A. C. Stone. 2023. Ancient pathogens provide a window into health and well-being. *Proceedings of the National Academy of Sciences* 120 (4): e2209476119. https://doi.org/10.1073/pnas.2209476119.
Lombroso, C. 1872. On Pellagra. *The British and Foreign Medico-Chirurgical Review* 49 (97): 113–116.
Mabaso, M. L. H., and N. C. Ndlovu. 2012. Critical review of research literature on climate-driven malaria epidemics in sub-Saharan Africa. *Public Health* 126 (11): 909–919.
Macherera, M., M. J. Chimbari, and S. Mukaratirwa. 2017. Indigenous environmental indicators for malaria: A district study in Zimbabwe. *Acta Tropica* 175:50–59. https://doi.org/10.1016/j.actatropica.2016.08.021.
Mamelund, S. E., and J. Dimka. 2021. Not the great equalizers: Covid-19, 1918–20 influenza, and the need for a paradigm shift in pandemic preparedness. *Population Studies* 75 (sup1): 179–199.
Mariani-Constantini, R., and A. Mariani-Constantini. 2007. An outline of the history of pellagra in Italy. *Journal of Anthropological Sciences* 85:163–171.
Messedaglia, L. 1927. *Il mais e la vita rurale italiana*. Piacenza: Federazione Italiana dei Consorzi Agrari.
Miller, M., G. Robbins Schug, L. Pagani, and N. Carrara. 2020. A bioarchaeology of madness: Modernity, pellagra, and the rise of the manicomio system in the Veneto Region of Italy. In *The Routledge Handbook of the Bioarchaeology of Climate and Environmental Change*, ed. G. Robbins Schug, 255–276. London: Routledge.
Mitchell, M. D. 1919. The impact of the influenza epidemic on Mississippi institutions. *Mississippi State Medical Journal* 2:43–50.
Mitchell, C. D. 1926. *Thirty-fifth Biennial Report of the Mississippi State Insane Hospital, Jackson, Mississippi, from July 1, 1923 to June 30, 1925*. Report of the Secretary of State to the

Legislature of Mississippi: University of Mississippi. https://egrove.olemiss.edu/sta_sosrpt/9/. Accessed October 27, 2024.

Naserrudin, N. A., A. Monroe, R. Culleton, R. Hod, M. S. Jeffree, K. Ahmed, and M. R. Hassan. 2022. Reimagining zoonotic malaria control in communities exposed to Plasmodium knowlesi infection. *Journal of Physiology and Anthropology* 411:14. https://doi.org/10.1186/s40101-022-00288-y.

Nerlich, A. G., C. J. Haas, A. R. Zink, U. Szeimies, and H. G. Hagedorn. 2008. *Plasmodium falciparum* in ancient Egypt. *Emerging Infectious Diseases* 14 (8): 1317–1319. https://doi.org/10.3201/eid1408.080235.

Northington Gamble, V. 2010. "There wasn't a lot of comforts in those days": African Americans, public health, and the 1918 influenza epidemic. *Public Health Reports* 125 ((3) Suppl): 113–122. https://doi.org/10.1177/00333549101250S314.

Økland, H., and S. E. Mamelund. 2019. Race and 1918 Influenza pandemic in the United States: A review of the literature. *International Journal of Environmental Research and Public Health* 16 (14): 2487. https://doi.org/10.3390/ijerph16142487.

Onyango, E. A., O. Sahin, A. Awiti, C. Chu, and B. Mackey. 2016. An integrated risk and vulnerability assessment framework for climate change and malaria transmission in East Africa. *Malaria Journal* 15 (1): 551. https://doi.org/10.1186/s12936-016-1600-3.

Patriarca, G., and L. Riall. 2011. *The Risorgimento Revisited: Nationalism and Culture in Nineteenth-Century Italy*. Berlin: Springer.

Riall, L. 1994. *The Italian Risorgimento: State, Society, and National Unification*. Berlin: Springer.

Ricci, F. 2012. Social implications of malaria and their relationships with poverty. *Mediterranean Journal of Hematology and Infectious Diseases* 41:e2012048. https://doi.org/10.4084/MJHID.2012.048.

Robbins Schug, G., ed. 2020. *The Routledge Handbook of the Bioarchaeology of Climate and Environmental Change*. London: Routledge.

Robbins Schug, G., and S. Halcrow. 2022. Building a bioarchaeology of pandemic, epidemic, and syndemic diseases: Lessons for understanding COVID-19. *Bioarchaeology International* 61 (2): 1–22.

Robbins Schug, G., J. E. Buikstra, S. N. DeWitte, B. J. Baker, E. Berger, et al. 2023. Climate change, human health, and resilience in the Holocene. *Proceedings of the National Academy of Sciences* 120 (4): e2209472120.

Roberts, C. A., and J. E. Buikstra. 2003. *The Bioarchaeology of Tuberculosis: A Global View on a Re-emerging Disease*. Gainesville: University Press of Florida.

Rockman, M., and C. Hritz. 2020. Expanding use of archaeology in climate change response by changing its social environment. *Proceedings of the National Academy of Sciences* 117 (15): 8295–8302. https://doi.org/10.1073/pnas.1914213117.

Ryan, S. J., C. J. Carlson, E. A. Mordecai, and L. R. Johnson. 2019. Global expansion and redistribution of Aedes-borne virus transmission risk with climate change. *PLoS Neglected Tropical Diseases* 13 (3): e0007213. https://doi.org/10.1371/journal.pntd.0007213.

Ryan, S. J., C. A. Lippi, and M. F. Zermoglio. 2020. Shifting transmission risk for malaria in Africa with climate change: A framework for planning and intervention. *Malaria Journal* 19 (1): 170. https://doi.org/10.1186/s12936-020-03224-6.

Samarasekera, U. 2023. Climate change and malaria: Predictions becoming reality. *The Lancet* 402 (10399): 361–362. https://doi.org/10.1016/S0140-67362301569-6.

Singh, B., L. K. Sung, A. Matusop, A. Radhakrishnan, S. S. G. Shamsul, J. Cox-Singh, A. Thomas, and D. J. Conway, 2004. A large focus of naturally acquired Plasmodium knowlesi infections in human beings. *The Lancet, 363*(9414), 1017–1024. https://doi.org/10.1016/S0140-6736(04)15836-4.

Singer, M. 2009. *Introduction to Syndemics: A Critical Systems Approach to Public and Community Health*. Hoboken: Wiley.

Solomon, S. 2007. *Climate Change 2007: The Physical Science Basis*. Geneva: Intergovernmental Panel on Climate Change.

Stamer, J. R., Apata Mamani, M., Arriaza, B., Bendrey, R., Blevins, K., Campbell, T., ... & Buikstra, J. E. (2026). Assessing the effectiveness of the one paleopathology workshop. *Evolution, Medicine, and Public Health, 14*(1), 1–10.

Steckel, R. H., and J. C. Rose. 2002. *The Backbone of History: Health and Nutrition in the Western Hemisphere*. Cambridge: Cambridge University Press.

Stephens, L., D. Fuller, N. Boivin, T. Rick, N. Gauthier, A., et al. 2019. Archaeological assessment reveals Earth's early transformation through land use. *Science* 365 (6456): 897–902. https://doi.org/10.1126/science.aax1192.

Tu, Y. 2017. *From Artemisia Annua L. to Artemisinins: The Discovery and Development of Antimalarial Agents*. London: Academic.

UNDP. 2022. *Human Development Report 2022: Uncertain Times, Unsettled Lives: Shaping Our Future in a Transforming World*. New York: United Nations Development Programme.

Warman, A. 2003. *Corn and Capitalism: How a Botanical Bastard Grew to Global Dominance*. Chapel Hill: University of North Carolina Press.

Webster, J. P., A. Borlase, and W. J. Rudge. 2016. Who acquires infection from whom and how? Disentangling multi-host parasite transmission dynamics in the 'One Health' era. *Philosophical Transactions of the Royal Society B: Biological Sciences* 372:20160091. https://doi.org/10.1098/rstb.2016.0091.

Whitmee, S., A. Haines, C. Beyrer, F. Boltz, A.G. Capon, B.F. de Souza Dias, A. Ezeh, ... and D. Yach. 2015. Safeguarding human health in the Anthropocene epoch: Report of The Rockefeller Foundation–Lancet Commission on planetary health. The Lancet 386 (10007): 1973–2028. https://doi.org/10.1016/S0140-67361560901-1.

Woodward, A., S. Hales, N. Litidamu, D. Phillips, and J. Martin. 2014. Protecting human health in a changing world: The role of social and economic development. *Bulletin of the World Health Organization* 78 (9): 1148–1155. https://doi.org/10.1590/S0042-96862000000900010.

Zinsstag, J., L. Crump, E. Schelling, J. Hattendorf, Y. O. Maidane, K. O. Ali, et al. 2018. Climate change and one health. *FEMS Microbiology Letters* 365 (11): fny085. https://doi.org/10.1093/femsle/fny085.

Zuckerman, M. K., E. Taylor, C. M. DeGaglia, and L. B. Gibson. 2022. Institutionalization within the context of pandemic infectious disease: Examining social vulnerability to the 1918 influenza pandemic among individuals institutionalized in the Mississippi State Asylum. *Bioarchaeology International* 6 (1-2): 41. https://doi.org/10.5744/bai.2021.0006.

MIX
Papier aus verantwortungsvollen Quellen
Paper from responsible sources
FSC® C105338

If you have any concerns about our products,
you can contact us on
ProductSafety@springernature.com

In case Publisher is established outside the EU,
the EU authorized representative is:
Springer Nature Customer Service Center GmbH
Europaplatz 3, 69115 Heidelberg, Germany

Printed by Libri Plureos GmbH
in Hamburg, Germany